The Ways of Religion

Edited by

Roger Eastman

Reedley College

Harper & Row, Publishers
New York   Hagerstown   Philadelphia   San Francisco   London

⌐or my parents

Herbert Henry Eastman
Ella Coghlan Eastman

Editorial consultant: Jacob Needleman

Cover and interior illustrations: Nancy Barnes

The Ways of Religion

Library of Congress Cataloging in Publication Data

Eastman, Roger, comp.
    The ways of religion.

    Includes bibliographies and indexes.
    1. Religions—Collected works. I. Title.
BL74.E18   200′.1   74-30211
ISBN 0-06-382595-3

contents

preface

The Ways of Religion is a collection of introductory readings for the course in the world's religions. It is an attempt to combine in a single volume the various types of materials most appropriate for students. Hence the reading selections had to meet two major criteria: first that they be clear and to the point, in order that students might readily comprehend and enjoy them; and second that the readings present as fairly and forcefully as possible the unique claims, visions, and wisdom of the religions themselves.

WHY AN ANTHOLOGY?

A religion, needless to say, cannot be adequately portrayed by a cold compilation of facts, figures, and historical data, though such information is not to be neglected. But the danger, as A. C. Bouquet has warned, is that the study of the religions "may sink to the level of collecting dead insects or pressed flowers, which in the process lose all their colour and reality." The vital aspect of any religion is that it is experienced by its followers with conviction and feeling; it lives by faith, argument, and commitment.

Consequently, the religions are represented in this volume by some of their most dedicated spokesmen, by selections from sacred writings, by eminent scholars, and occasionally by more informal statements by "believers" or others with a first-hand experience of the religions about which they have written.

The Hinduism chapter, for example, begins with an introductory essay by the distinguished Sarvepalli Radhakrishnan and is followed by excerpts from the *Rig Veda* and the *Upanishads*. Selections from the *Bhagavad Gita* are prefaced by a helpful essay from Sri Krishna Prem. Yoga is described by Swami Prabhavananda, and in "What Vedanta Means to Me" Christopher Isherwood writes in very personal terms of his discovery of that important system of Hindu philosophy.

Elsewhere in the text, Mahayana Buddhism is defined by Ananda Coomaraswamy, and the materials on Confucianism include portions of the *Analects*. Abraham Heschel and Martin Buber are among those who speak for Judaism; Søren Kierkegaard and Jacques Maritain are represented in the chapter on Christianity. The poetry of the *Tao Te Ching* is presented in the brilliant translation by Gia-fu Feng and Jane English, and Muhammad is described by Philip K. Hitti.

Throughout *The Ways of Religion,* therefore, students are introduced not only to the ideas and backgrounds of the religious traditions, but also to a number of exceptional authors and primary sources which convey something of the essential *spirit* of the religions. The *variety* of authors and of types of materials should itself add interest and value to the course.

AN EMPHASIS ON THE CONTEMPORARY

Of the sixty-three reading selections in *The Ways of Religion,* forty-one were written in this century. (The principal exceptions are the readings from ancient sacred writings.) The language and thought forms of these essays, consequently, are such that they do not present unusual reading difficulties for students, and due attention is paid to recent interpretations and developments in the religions. Several of the readings, in fact, have been composed since 1970, among them Alan Watts' "Flowing with the Tao," Shunryu Suzuki's "Zen Mind, Beginner's Mind," and other materials by Herbert Fingarette, Billy Graham, Jacob Needleman, Jiddu Krishnamurti, S. H. Nasr, and Paul Kurtz.

Most of the text is of course given over to those major religions which traditionally have formed the subject matter of the world's religions course— Hinduism, Buddhism, Confucianism, Taoism, Judaism, Christianity, and Islam. Additional chapters reflect the religious searching, discoveries, and concerns of these middle decades of the twentieth century: Zen Buddhism, the *I Ching,* the Dead Sea Scrolls, African Traditional Religions, and Humanism. The final chapter samples some of the amazing diversity of religious thought in the modern world.

ACKNOWLEDGMENTS

In addition to his duties as General Editor of the Penguin Metaphysical Library and as Professor of Philosophy at San Francisco State University, and besides his own writing, Jacob Needleman followed the growth of this volume from beginning to end and offered invaluable suggestions at every step of the way. Moire Charters and Richard Paulson, my colleagues at Reedley College, contributed much appreciated assistance on particular reading selections. At Canfield Press, Ann Ludwig graciously did everything an editor can do to help the author and to improve the book. The special care exercised by Production Editor Pearl C. Vapnek is evident on every page.

> True religion is first of all
> the search for religion.
>
> Tolstoy, *Last Diaries*

Whatever else it may be, religion is also an intensely experienced and personal quest for a "way." The established institutions of religion—with their creeds, official rituals, and the weight of tradition—often overshadow the individual seeker. But on the level of that individual, religion is a vital search for that which might summon and warrant one's "ultimate concern."

Few men could illustrate the point more vividly than Miguel de Unamuno.

Wrestling with God

Born in Spain of Basque ancestry, Unamuno (1864–1936) was a poet, novelist, essayist, philosopher, professor, and university president. He was uncompromising and controversial: a pamphlet once termed him the "Greatest Heretic and Teacher of Heresy," a title that must have delighted him. Some of his books were banned; he was twice removed from the presidency of the University of Salamanca and once exiled from Spain. "If someone should organize an Unamuno party," he said, "I would be the first 'antiunamunista.' "

Unamuno's many books include *The Tragic Sense of Life* and *The Agony of Christianity*. An especially notable short story is the unsettling "Saint Emmanuel the Good, Martyr," a tale in which the distinction between faith and doubt fades into questions. "Lord, I believe; Help thou mine unbelief" was a statement from the Gospel of St. Mark that Unamuno often quoted. In his own words, "Uncertainty, allied with despair, forms the basis of faith."*

Unamuno's frame of reference was the Judaic-Christian tradition, but his thought has an existential ground that knows no boundaries. "The man we have to do with," he wrote, "is the man of flesh and bone—I, you, reader of mine, the other man yonder, all of us who walk solidly on the earth."†

Peoples as well as individuals who are spiritually lazy—and spiritual laziness is wedded to extreme economic activity—whether they know it or not, desire it or not, seek it or not, lean toward dogmatism. Spiritual laziness flees from a critical or skeptical attitude.

I say skeptical, but taking the term skepticism in its etymological and philosophical sense, because skeptic means not one who doubts but one who investigates or searches carefully, as contrasted with one who affirms and believes that he has found out. There are those who scrutinize a problem, and there are those who give us a formula, whether it's the right one or not, as its solution.

. . .

And I shall be asked, "What is your religion?" and I shall answer that my religion is to seek truth in life and life in truth; conscious that I shall not find them while I live; my religion is to struggle tirelessly and incessantly with the unknown; my religion is to struggle with God as they say Jacob did from

The Tragic Sense of Life (New York: Dover, 1954), p. 121.
†*Ibid.*, p. 1.

earliest dawn until nightfall. I shall not admit the Unknowable and the Unrecognizable of which pedants write, nor any, "beyond this thou shalt not pass." I reject any eternal *ignorabimus*. In any event I wish to reach the inaccessible.

. . . I want to fight my battle without preoccupying myself about the victory. Are there not armies and even peoples headed for sure defeat? Do we not praise those who die fighting rather than surrender? Well, this is my religion.

Those who ask me this question are seeking a dogma, a restful solution for their lazy spirits. And they are not satisfied with this alone. They want to be able to place me in one of the pigeonholes where they keep their spiritual retinue, saying of me: he is a Lutheran, Calvinist, Catholic, atheist, rationalist, mystic, or any other of these labels of whose real meaning they are ignorant but which excuse them from further thinking. I do not wish to be pigeonholed because I, Miguel de Unamuno, like any other man who claims a free conscience, am unique. "There aren't illnesses, but sick people," some doctors say, and I say there aren't opinions, but opinionated people.

. . .

If we were dealing with something which did not concern the peace of my conscience and my consolation for having been born, I would pay scant attention to the problem; but since it involves all my inner life and motivates all my actions, I cannot satisfy myself by saying, "I do not know nor can I know." I do not know, and that is certain. Perhaps I can never know, but I *want* to. I want to, and that's enough.

I shall spend my life struggling with the mystery, even without any hope of penetrating it, because this struggle is my hope and my consolation. Yes, my consolation. I have become accustomed to finding hope in desperation itself. Let me not hear the superficial and crack-brained shouting, "Paradox."

I cannot imagine a cultured person without this preoccupation, and I expect very little from a realm of culture—and culture and civilization are not the same—that is, from those who are not interested in the metaphysical aspect of the religious problem, studying only its social or political aspect. I can hope for very little contribution to the spiritual treasure of mankind from those men or those peoples who, because of mental laziness, superficiality, scionism, or whatever it may be, ignore the great eternal problems of the heart. I expect nothing from those who say, "One shouldn't think about that." I expect even less from those who believe in a heaven and a hell like those we believed in as children, and still less from those who declare with a fool's conviction, "This is all nothing but fables and myths; those who die are buried and that's the end of it." I have hope only for those who do not know, but who are not resigned to being ignorant, for those who restlessly struggle to learn the truth and who are more concerned with the struggle than with the victory.

Most of my endeavor has always been to unsettle my neighbors, to rouse their hearts, to afflict them when I can. . . . Let them seek as I seek, struggle as I struggle, and between us all we shall extract one particle of the secret from God, and this struggle will at least increase our spiritual stature.

To further this work—religious work . . . I have found it necessary to appear at times impudent and indecorous, at others harsh and aggressive, and not rarely paradoxical and nonsensical. In our benighted literature one can scarcely be heard even if he forgets himself, screams and shouts from the depths of his heart. For a time the shout was almost unknown. Writers were afraid to appear ridiculous. It was and is with them as it is with many, who allow themselves to be insulted in mid-street, fearing the ridicule of being seen with their hats on the ground and in the custody of a policeman. Not I; whenever I have felt like shouting, I have shouted. Decorum has never checked me. And this is one of the things for which I have been most blamed by my fellow writers who are so correct and so polite even when they are espousing impropriety and inobedience. The literary anarchists are concerned, above all, about matters of style and syntax. When they raise protesting voices, they do it harmoniously; their discords tend to be harmonious.

Whenever I have felt a pain I have shouted and I have done it publicly. The psalms that appear in my volume of *Poems* are but cries from my heart, in which I have sought to start the grieving chords of others' hearts playing. If they have no such chords or if, having them, they are too rigid to vibrate, my cry will not make them resound, and they will affirm that is not poetry, beginning to examine it acoustically. One can also examine acoustically the cry of a man who suddenly sees his child fall dead, and he who lacks both a heart and children will never go beyond that.

. . .

As from the plague I flee from being classified, hoping that I shall die hearing the spiritually lazy, who occasionally stop to listen to me still asking, "What is that man?" The foolish liberals and progressives will consider me a reactionary and perhaps a mystic, without knowing, of course, what this means, and the foolish reactionaries and conservatives will consider me a kind of spiritual anarchist, and all of them a miserable, scatterbrained publicity-seeker. But nobody should care about what fools think of him, be they conservative or progressive, liberal or reactionary.

Since man is stubborn, however, and hates to learn, and usually returns to his former ways even after being lectured for hours, the busybodies, if they read this, will again ask me, "Fine, but what is your solution?" And to rid myself of them I will tell them if they are seeking solutions to go to the store across the street, because mine sells no such article. My intent has been, is, and will continue to be, that those who read my works shall think and meditate upon fundamental problems, and has never been to hand them completed thoughts. I have always sought to agitate and, even better, to stimulate, rather than to instruct. Neither do I sell bread, nor is it bread, but yeast or ferment.

I have friends, and very good friends too, who advise me to abandon this work and bend my efforts toward producing some objective work, something which, as they say, is definite, with something to it, lasting. They mean something dogmatic. I declare myself incapable of it, and demand my liberty, my holy liberty, even to contradict myself if it becomes necessary. I do not know whether anything that I have done or may do will endure for years, for centuries, after my death, but I do know that if one drops a stone in the shoreless sea the surrounding waves, although diminishing, will go on ceaselessly. To agitate is something, and if, due to this agitation, somebody else follows who does something which endures, my work will be perpetuated in that.

To awaken the sleeping and rouse the loitering is a work of supreme mercy, and to seek the truth in everything and everywhere reveal fraud, foolishness and ineptitude is a work of supreme religious piety.

further reading _____

Each of the other chapters in the present volume closes with a list of suggested readings that pertain to the topic of that chapter. Here are some books of a more general nature.

Charles J. Adams (ed.), *A Reader's Guide to the Great Religions* (1965). A valuable survey of the literature of and about the major religions. Each chapter is by an authority in his field.

Donald Capps and Walter H. Capps (eds.), *The Religious Personality* (1970). Fascinating autobiographical material by Cotton Mather, Elie Wiesel, Gandhi, Gide, and others.

James W. Dye and William Forthman (eds.), *Religions of the World* (1967). An outstanding collection of readings with thorough introductory essays by the editors.

Evelyn Underhill's *Mysticism* (1910; 12th ed., 1930) and William James's *The Varieties of Religious Experience* (1902) are modern classics on the ways of the mystic.

S. G. F. Brandon, *Man and His Destiny in the Great Religions* (1962). The topic is immortality, as variously conceived by religions around the world.

Among the best of the more recent textbooks are John B. Noss, *Man's Religions* (5th ed., 1974); John A. Hutchison, *Paths of Faith* (1969); S. Vernon McCasland *et al., Religions of the World* (1969); Ninian Smart, *The Religious Experience of Mankind* (1969); and W. Richard Comstock *et al., Religion and Man* (1972). Frederick J. Streng is the editor of *The Religious Life of Man* series, which features separate volumes by different scholars on the various religious traditions.

Huston Smith's *The Religions of Man* (1958) remains an immensely popular and readable description of seven religions.

Hinduism

liberation and the yogi

introduction _____

Lead me from the unreal to the real.
Lead me from darkness to light.
Lead me from death to immortality.

Brihadaranyaka Upanishad

Its origins are obscured by the shadows of antiquity; its sacred literature is enormous. Its sects and forms of worship are innumerable. One stream of its thought stresses that there is ultimately *one* Absolute, an unseen *Brahman*, and yet there are those thousands upon thousands of gods. Such is Hinduism. R. C. Zaehner aptly called it "the proliferating jungle,"* a phrase that suggests both the continuous growth and the staggering complexity of the religion.

"There has been no such thing as a uniform stationary unalterable Hinduism whether in point of belief or practice," Sarvepalli Radhakrishnan has written. "Hinduism is a movement, not a position; a process, not a result; a growing tradition, not a fixed revelation."† Radhakrishnan summarizes, nevertheless, in the pages that follow, certain themes that have characterized much of Hindu thought. He notes especially India's overpowering emphasis upon the "spiritual," and this is evident in his discussion of "The Four Ends of Life" (the end that really matters is the spiritual) and in "The Four Stages of Life" (the final and culminating stage is that of the *sannyasin,* India's "saint"). In these idealized outlines of life, and also in the caste system, there is the recurrent theme of a spiritual progression. The movement is always toward release from the turmoil and confusion of this world and its endless cycles of time. The Hindu seeks *moksha*—liberation—and the bliss of the Eternal.

The earliest period of Hindu thought is the Vedic—the Age of the *Vedas*. The date for the beginning of the period is disputed; most estimates range from 2500 B.C. to 1500 B.C. It has been held that portions of the Vedic literature are the most ancient religious writings of the world, but the uncertainty about the date renders such claims open to question. The period closes somewhere around 600 B.C. and is followed by the Age of the Epics, which extends perhaps as late as A.D. 200.

The literature of the Vedic period is known collectively as the *Vedas,* and it comprises the most sacred scriptures of Hinduism. It is termed *śruti* (that which was "heard"). The *Vedas* are divided into four groups: *Rig Veda, Sama Veda, Yajur Veda,* and *Atharva Veda.* These, in turn, are each made up of three parts, which are historical strata. There are, first, the early hymns,

Hinduism (New York: Oxford University Press, 1966), p. 3.
†*The Hindu View of Life* (New York: Macmillan, 1927), p. 91.

CHAPTER ONE / *Hinduism*

prayers, and rites of the *Samhitas*.‡ Then there are the *Brahmanas*, which are later commentary and explanatory material attached to the *Samhitas*, and finally there are the *Aranyakas*, the "Forest Treatises." These books culminate in the *Vedanta* (literally, the "end of the *Vedas*"), which is also called the *Upanishads*, and these date from the last centuries of the Vedic period. Of all the Vedic literature, the most original and significant are the hymns of the *Rig Veda* and the very philosophical *Upanishads*, both of which are represented by selections in this chapter.

The literature of the Age of Epics is *smrti* (that which has been "remembered" and transmitted by tradition), and it includes the immense *Mahabharata*, one segment of which is the *Bhagavad Gita*. While this literature is technically considered less authoritative that the Vedic literature, the influence of some of it, particularly the *Bhagavad Gita*, upon the life of India has been incalculable. Often termed "the Bible of India," the *Bhagavad Gita* draws together most of the strands of Hindu religious thought. Some key chapters of the *Gita* are in the pages that follow, introduced by Sri Krishna Prem.

Yoga is the term for those various methods of self-discipline, meditation, and concentration that are designed to lead one to a realization of the Truth (and a state called *samadhi*). There are many forms of yoga, but the classic form is *raja-yoga* and was systematized by a great teacher, Patanjali, in the second century A.D. This is the "Yoga of Meditation" described by Swami Prabhavananda. The practice of yoga§—which permeates Hinduism —underscores the point that in Hinduism religion is meant to be not merely a "theory" or even a "faith," but an *experience* of the Divine.

In the final essay of the chapter, Christopher Isherwood recounts the experiences and thinking that led him to adopt the religious system known as Vedanta. Grounded in the philosophy of the *Upanishads*, Vedanta emphasizes that the impersonal and absolute divinity, Brahman, is the only reality. This is nondualism (*advaita*), an important corollary of which is the doctrine of *maya*, which holds that the world of our experience, while not quite unreal, not exactly an "illusion," is not, on the other hand, a reality distinct from Brahman. The individual has hidden in himself that eternal essence or spirit termed the *Atman*, and the *Atman* is *Brahman*. The task is to discover and to understand with one's entire being the true nature of that hidden Self, which is in fact the Ultimate. When that is understood, or rather *experienced*, one knows all there is to know; one realizes his oneness with the Truth.

---

‡The *Samhitas* are also called (confusingly enough) the *Vedas*, in a narrower but commonplace use of that term.

§A *yogi* (sometimes *yogin*) is one who practices yoga.

The Nature of Hinduism

Sarvepalli Radhakrishnan (1888–   ) is a man of astounding accomplishments. Born and educated in India, he was a professor of philosophy at various Indian colleges and Spaulding Professor of Eastern Religion and Ethics at Oxford University. He served as Vice Chancellor of Andhra University, held the same position at Benares Hindu University, and was Chancellor of Delhi University. Apart from his academic posts, he worked for years as the head of the Indian Delegation to UNESCO and was Chairman of the Executive Board and President of that organization. He was appointed Indian Ambassador to the Soviet Union and was Vice President and then President of India. Knighted in 1931, he holds honorary degrees from well over fifty universities.

He is the author or translator of *Indian Philosophy* (2 vols.), *The Hindu View of Life, Eastern Religions and Western Thought, The Bhagavadgita, The Dhammapada, The Principal Upanishads, An Idealist View of Life, The Philosophy of the Upanishads, East and West in Religion, The Brahma Sutra,* and many other books.

THE SPIRIT OF INDIAN PHILOSOPHY

At the very outset, it should be emphasized that Indian philosophy has had an extremely long and complex development, much more complex than is usually realized, and probably a longer history of continuous development than any other philosophical tradition.

. . .

. . . Accordingly, it is very difficult to cite any specific doctrines or methods as characteristic of Indian philosophy as a whole and applicable to all the multitudinous systems and subsystems developed through nearly four millenniums of Indian philosophical speculation.

Nevertheless, in certain respects there is what might be called a distinct spirit of Indian philosophy. This is exemplified by certain attitudes which are

Sarvepalli Radhakrishnan, "The Nature of Hinduism." Editor's title. Some notes have been omitted and the remainder renumbered.

"The Spirit of Indian Philosophy" is reprinted from Sarvepalli Radhakrishnan and Charles A. Moore (eds.), *A Sourcebook in Indian Philosophy.* Copyright 1957 by Princeton University Press; Princeton Paperback, 1967. Reprinted by permission of Princeton University Press.

"The Four Ends of Life," "The Four States of Life," and the concluding paragraph of "The Caste System" are reprinted from Sarvepalli Radhakrishnan, *Eastern Religions* and *Western Thought* (2d ed., 1940). By permission of The Clarendon Press, Oxford.

"The Caste System" (with the exception of the concluding paragraph) is reprinted from Sarvepalli Radhakrishnan, *The Hindu View of Life* (1927). Reprinted by permission of the publishers, George Allen & Unwin, Ltd.

fairly characteristic of the Indian philosophical mind or which stand as points of view that have been emphasized characteristically by Indians in their philosophies.

(1) The chief mark of Indian philosophy in general is its concentration upon the spiritual. Both in life and in philosophy the spiritual motive is predominant in India. Except for the relatively minor materialistic school of the Cārvāka and related doctrines, philosophy in India conceives man to be spiritual in nature, is interested primarily in his spiritual destiny, and relates him in one way or another to a universe which is also spiritual in essential character. Neither man nor the universe is looked upon as physical in essence, and material welfare is never recognized as the goal of human life, except by the Cārvāka. . . .

(2) Another characteristic view of Indian philosophy is the belief in the intimate relationship of philosophy and life. This attitude of the practical application of philosophy to life is found in every school of Indian philosophy. While natural abundance and material prosperity paved the way for the rise of philosophical speculation, philosophy has never been considered a mere intellectual exercise. The close relationship between theory and practice, doctrine and life, has always been outstanding in Indian thought. Every Indian system seeks the truth, not as academic "knowledge for its own sake," but to learn the truth which shall make men free. This is not, as it has been called, the modern pragmatic attitude. It is much larger and much deeper than that. It is not the view that truth is measured in terms of the practical, but rather that the truth is the only sound guide for practice, that truth alone has efficacy as a guide for man in his search for salvation. Every major system of Indian philosophy takes its beginning from the practical and tragic problems of life and searches for the truth in order to solve the problem of man's distress in the world in which he finds himself. There has been no teaching which remained a mere word of mouth or dogma of schools. Every doctrine has been turned into a passionate conviction, stirring the heart of man and quickening his breath, and completely transforming his personal nature. In India, philosophy is for life; it is to be lived. It is not enough to *know* the truth; the truth must be *lived*. The goal of the Indian is not to know the ultimate truth but to *realize* it, to become one with it.

Another aspect of the intimate inseparability of theory and practice, philosophy and life, in Indian philosophy is to be found in the universally prevalent demand for moral purification as an imperative preliminary for the would-be student of philosophy or searcher after truth. Śaṁkara's classic statement of this demand calls for a knowledge of the distinction between the eternal and the noneternal, that is, a questioning tendency in the inquirer; the subjugation of all desire for the fruits of action either in this life or in a hereafter, a renunciation of all petty desire, personal motive, and practical interest; tranquillity, self-control, renunciation, patience, peace of mind, and faith; and a desire for release (*mokṣa*) as the supreme goal of life.

(3) Indian philosophy is characterized by the introspective attitude and the introspective approach to reality. Philosophy is thought of as *ātmavidyā*, knowledge of the self. Philosophy can start either with the external world or with the internal world of man's inner nature, the self of man. In its pursuit of the truth, Indian philosophy has always been strongly dominated by concern with the inner life and self of man rather than the external world of physical nature. Physical science, though developed extensively in the Golden Age of Indian culture, was never considered the road to ultimate truth; truth is to be sought and found within. The subjective, then, rather than the objective, becomes the focus of interest in Indian philosophy, and, therefore, psychology and ethics are considered more important as aspects of branches of philosophy than the sciences which study physical nature. This is not to say that the Indian mind has not studied the physical world; in fact, on the contrary, India's achievements in the realm of positive science were at one time truly outstanding, especially in the mathematical sciences such as algebra, astronomy, and geometry, and in the applications of these basic sciences to numerous phases of human activity. Zoology, botany, medicine, and related sciences have also been extremely prominent in Indian thought. Be this as it may, the Indian, from time immemorial, has felt that the inner spirit of man is the most significant clue to his reality and to that of the universe, more significant by far than the physical or the external.

(4) This introspective interest is highly conducive to idealism, of course, and consequently most Indian philosophy is idealistic in one form or another. The tendency of Indian philosophy, especially Hinduism, has been in the direction of monistic idealism. Almost all Indian philosophy believes that reality is *ultimately* one and *ultimately* spiritual. Some systems have seemed to espouse dualism or pluralism, but even these have been deeply permeated by a strong monistic character. If we concentrate our attention upon the underlying spirit of Indian philosophy rather than its variety of opinions, we shall find that this spirit is embodied in the tendency to interpret life and reality in the way of monistic idealism. This rather unusual attitude is attributable to the nonrigidity of the Indian mind and to the fact that the attitude of monistic idealism is so plastic and dynamic that it takes many forms and expresses itself even in seemingly conflicting doctrines. These are not conflicting doctrines in fact, however, but merely different expressions of an underlying conviction which provides basic unity to Indian philosophy as a whole.

. . .

(5) Indian philosophy makes unquestioned and extensive use of reason, but intuition is accepted as the only method through which the ultimate can be known. Reason, intellectual knowledge, is not enough. Reason is not useless or fallacious, but it is insufficient. To know reality one must have an actual experience of it. One does not merely *know* the truth in Indian philosophy; one *realizes* it. The word which most aptly describes philosophy in India is

darśana, which comes from the verbal root *dṛś*, meaning "to see." "To see" is to have a direct intuitive experience of the object, or, rather, to realize it in the sense of becoming one with it. No complete knowledge is possible as long as there is the relationship of the subject on one hand and the object on the other. Later developments in Indian philosophy, from the time of the beginning of the systems, have all depended in large part upon reason for the systematic formulation of doctrines and systems, for rational demonstration or justification, and in polemical conflicts of system against system. Nevertheless, all the systems, except the Cārvāka, agree that there is a higher way of knowing reality, beyond the reach of reason, namely, the direct perception or experience of the ultimate reality, which cannot be known by reason in any of its forms. Reason can demonstrate the truth, but reason cannot discover or reach the truth. While reason may be the method of philosophy in its more intellectualistic sense, intuition is the only method of comprehending the ultimate. Indian philosophy is thus characterized by an ultimate dependence upon intuition, along with the recognition of the efficacy of reason and intellect when applied in their limited capacity and with their proper function.

(6) Another characteristic of Indian philosophy, one which is closely related to the preceding one, is its so-called acceptance of authority. Although the systems of Indian philosophy vary in the degree to which they are specifically related to the ancient *śruti,* not one of the systems—orthodox or unorthodox, except the Cārvāka—openly stands in violation of the accepted intuitive insights of its ancient seers, whether it be the Hindu seers of the Upaniṣads, the intuitive experience of the Buddha, or the similarly intuitive wisdom of Mahāvīra, the founder of Jainism, as we have it today. Indian philosophers have always been conscious of tradition and, as has been indicated before, the great system-builders of later periods claimed to be merely commentators, explaining the traditional wisdom of the past. While the specific doctrines of the past may be changed by interpretation, the general spirit and frequently the basic concepts are retained from age to age. Reverence for authority does not militate against progress, but it does lend a unity of spirit by providing a continuity of thought which has rendered philosophy especially significant in Indian life and solidly unified against any philosophical attitude contradicting its basic characteristics of spirituality, inwardness, intuition, and the strong belief that the truth is to be lived, not merely known.

. . .

(7) Finally, there is the over-all synthetic tradition which is essential to the spirit and method of Indian philosophy. This is as old as the *Ṛg Veda,* where the seers realized that true religion comprehends all religions, so that "God is one but men call him by many names." Indian philosophy is clearly characterized by the synthetic approach to the various aspects of experience and reality. Religion and philosophy, knowledge and conduct, intuition and

reason, man and nature, God and man, noumenon and phenomena, are all brought into harmony by the synthesizing tendency of the Indian mind.

THE FOUR ENDS OF LIFE

1. *Mokṣa*. The chief end of man is the development of the individual. The Upaniṣad tells us that there is nothing higher than the person. But man is not an assemblage of body, life, and mind born of and subject to physical nature. The natural half-animal being with which he confuses himself is not his whole or real being. It is but an instrument for the use of spirit which is the truth of his being. To find the real self, to exceed his apparent, outward self, is the greatness of which man alone of all beings is capable.[1] 'Verily, O Gārgī, he who departs from this world without knowing this Imperishable one is a vile and wretched creature.'[2] To inquire into his true self, to live in and from it, to determine by its own energy what it shall be inwardly and what it shall make of its outward circumstances, to found the whole life on the power and truth of spirit, is *mokṣa* or spiritual freedom. To be shut up in one's own ego, to rest in the apparent self and mistake it for the real, is the root of all unrest to which man is exposed by reason of his mentality. To aspire to a universality (*sarvātmabhāva*) through his mind and reason, through his heart and love, through his will and power, is the high sense of his humanity.

2. *Kāma*. Is this perfection consistent with normal living? There is a prevalent idea that the Hindu view concedes no reality to life, that it despises vital aims and satisfactions, that it gives no inspiring motive to human effort. If spirit and life were unrelated, spiritual freedom would become an unattainable ideal, a remote passion of a few visionaries. There is little in Hindu thought to support the view that one has to attain spiritual freedom by means of a violent rupture with ordinary life. On the other hand, it lays down that we must pass through the normal life conscientiously and with knowledge, work out its values, and accept its enjoyments. Spiritual life is an integration of man's being, in its depth and breadth, in its capacity for deep meditation as well as reckless transport. *Kāma* refers to the emotional being of man, his feelings and desires.[3] If man is denied his emotional life, he becomes a prey to repressive introspection and lives under a continual strain of moral torture. When the reaction sets in, he will give way to a wildness of ecstasy which is ruinous to his sanity and health.

3. *Artha*. The third end relates to wealth and material well-being. Though it is not its own end, it helps to sustain and enrich life. There was never in India a national ideal of poverty or squalor. Spiritual life finds full scope only in

---

[1]The *Bhāgavata says,* 'The chief end of life here is not the attainment of heaven popularly known to be the result of pious duties. It is the desire to enquire into truth' (i. 2. 10).

[2]*Bṛhadāraṇyaka Up.* iii. 8. 10.

[3]*Bhāgavata*, i. 2. 10.

communities of a certain degree of freedom from sordidness. Lives that are strained and starved cannot be religious except in a rudimentary way. Economic insecurity and individual freedom do not go together.

4. *Dharma.* While the spontaneous activities of interest and desire are to be accepted, their full values cannot be realized if their action is unrestrained. There must be a rule, a guidance, a restraint. *Dharma* gives coherence and direction to the different activities of life. It is not a religious creed or cult imposing an ethical or social rule. It is the complete rule of life, the harmony of the whole man who finds a right and just law of his living. Each man and group, each activity of soul, mind, life, and body, has its *dharma.* While man is justified in satisfying his desires, which is essential for the expression of life, to conform to the dictates of his desires is not the law of his being. He will not get the best out of them if he does not conform to the *dharma,* or the rule of right practice. A famous verse of the *Mahābhārata* says: 'I cry with arm uplifted, yet none heedeth. From righteousness (*dharma*) flow forth pleasure and profit. Why then do ye not follow righteousness?' *Dharma* tells us that while our life is in the first instance for our own satisfaction, it is more essentially for the community and most of all for that universal self which is in each of us and all beings. Ethical life is the means to spiritual freedom, as well as its expression on earth.

The *dharma* and its observance are neither the beginning nor the end of human life, for beyond the law is spiritual freedom, not merely a noble manhood but universality, the aim which ennobles the whole life of the individual and the whole order of society. Man's whole life is to be passed in the implicit consciousness of this mysterious background.

The four ends of life point to the different sides of human nature, the instinctive and the emotional, the economic, the intellectual and the ethical, and the spiritual. There is implanted in man's fundamental being a spiritual capacity. He becomes completely human only when his sensibility to spirit is awakened. So long as man's life is limited to science and art, technical invention, and social programmes, he is incomplete and not truly human. If we are insolent and base, unfair and unkind to one another, unhappy in personal relationships, and lacking in mutual understanding, it is because we remain too much on the surface of life and have lost contact with the depths. When the fountains of spirit from which the creative life of the individual and society is fed dry up, diseases of every description, intellectual, moral, and social, break out. The everlasting vagrancy of thought, the contemporary muddle of conflicting philosophies, the rival ideologies which cut through national frontiers and geographical divisions, are a sign of spiritual homelessness. The unrest is in a sense sacred, for it is the confession of the failure of a self-sufficient humanism with no outlook beyond the world. We cannot find peace on earth through economic planning or political arrangement. Only the pure in heart by fostering the mystical accord of minds can establish justice and love. Man's true and essential greatness is individual. The scriptures could point out the road but each man must travel it for himself. The law of *karma* affirms the responsibility of each individual for his life. 'The sins ye do by two and two, ye shall pay for one by one,' as Kipling called Beelzebub to remark. There is no salvation by proxy or in herds. In primitive societies there is collective responsibility, but on the hypothesis of rebirth, the guilt of an action attaches to its author. The punishment must fall on the individual, if not in this life, then in the next or perhaps in a later. The dignity and responsibility of the individual soul are recognized.

THE FOUR STAGES OF LIFE

The Hindu scheme does not leave the growth of the individual entirely to his unaided initiative but gives him a framework for guidance. Human life is represented as consisting of four consecutive stages, of which the first three fall within the jurisdiction of class or caste.[4]

1. *The Student.* Human offspring are the most helpless of all living creatures. In the absence of parental care, their chances of survival are little. The tending will have to be continued for a long period, till the child reaches the status of man. The higher the cultural level the longer is the period required for education.

The aim of education is not to pour knowledge into the resisting brain and impose a stereotyped rule of conduct on his struggling impulses: it is to help the child to develop his nature, to change him from within rather than crush him from without. The education imparted not only fits man for his role in life but gives him a general idea of the conditions of spiritual life.

2. *The Householder.* By filling his place in social life, by helping its maintenance and continuity, the individual not only fulfils the law of his own being but makes his contribution to society. Man attains his full being only by living in harmonious social relationships. Sex is a normal human function concerned with the perpetuation of the race. Marriage, love, and motherhood are glorified. The wife has an equal position with the husband in all domestic and religious concerns. Every woman has a right to marry and have a home. Celibacy is the rarest of sexual aberrations. Any preoccupation with the flesh is in itself an evil even though it may be for purposes of crucifying it. Soul and body, however different, are yet closely bound together. The things of spirit are in part dependent on the satisfaction of the body. The physical and the economic, though they may not be important in themselves, are important as means to the life of spirit.

One must learn the social and spiritual lessons of the earlier stages before one can pass on to the later. One must learn to be sober before striving to become a saint. He who does not know what it is to love as a child or a

[4]*Brhadāranyaka Up.* iv. 4. 22; *Chāndogya Up.* ii. 23. 1; *Jābāla Up.* 4.

husband or a parent cannot pretend to the love which contains them all. To withdraw the noblest elements of humanity from the married state to monk-hood is biologically and socially unhealthy. The state of the householder is the mainstay of social life. It is said that the householder shall have his life established in the supreme reality, shall be devoted to the pursuit of truth, and shall dedicate to the Eternal Being whatever activities he undertakes. Hinduism does not demand withdrawal from life into mountain tops or gloomy caves as an essential condition for spiritual life. The way to a higher life is normally through the world.

3. *The Forest Dweller*. To be, for man, is not merely to be born, to grow up, marry, earn his livelihood, found a family, and support it and pass away. That would be a human edition of the animal life. It is rather to grow upward exceeding his animal beginnings. By fulfilling his function in society, the individual begins to feel the greatness of the soul which is behind the veils of nature and longs to reach his true universality. When the children get settled and no more want his attention, he retires probably with his wife to a quiet place in the country to lead a life of inquiry and meditation and work out within himself the truth of his being, in an atmosphere of freedom from the strife of social bonds. The mystery of life, as of death, each one has to discover for himself. We can sing and taste with no tongues but our own. Though each one has to attain his purpose by his separate encounter, the result is of universal significance.

4. *The Monk*. A *saññyāsin* renounces all possessions, distinctions of caste, and practices of religion. As he has perfected himself, he is able to give his soul the largest scope, throw all his powers into the free movement of the world and compel its transfiguration. He does not merely formulate the conception of high living but lives it, adhering to the famous rule, 'The world is my country; to do good my religion'. 'Regarding all with an equal eye he must be friendly to all living beings. And being devoted, he must not injure any living creature, human or animal, either in act, word, or thought, and renounce all attachments.'[5] A freedom and fearlessness of spirit, an immensity of courage, which no defeat or obstacle can touch, a faith in the power that works in the universe, a love that lavishes itself without demand of return and makes life a free servitude to the universal spirit, are the signs of the perfected man. The *saññyāsin* is a supersocial man, a *parivrājaka*, a wandering teacher who influences spiritual standards though he may live apart from society. The difference between a Brāhmin and a *saññyāsin* is that while the former is a full member of society, living with wife and children in a well-regulated but simple home, and performing religious rites, the latter is a celibate, homeless and wandering, if he does not live in a monastery, who has renounced all rites and ceremonies. He belongs neither to his language nor to his race but only to himself and therefore to the whole world. This order is recruited from mem-

[5]*Viṣṇu Purāṇa,* iii. 9.

bers of all castes and both sexes. As the life of the *saññyāsin* is the goal of man, those who live it obtain the allegiance of society. Kālidāsa, the great Indian poet, describes this supreme ideal of life as 'owning the whole world while disowning oneself.'[6]

Hinduism has given us in the form of the *saññyāsin* its picture of the ideal man. He carries within himself the dynamism of spirit, its flame-like mobility. He has no fixed abode and is bound to no stable form of living. He is released from every form of selfishness: individual, social, and national. He does not make compromises for the sake of power, individual or collective. His behaviour is unpredictable, for he does not act in obedience to the laws of the social group or the State. He is master of his own conduct. He is not subject to rules, for he has realized in himself the life which is the source of all rules and which is not itself subject to rules. The quietude of his soul is strange, for though he is tranquil within, everything about him is restless and dynamic. His element is fire, his mark is movement.

The ideal man of India is not the magnanimous man of Greece or the valiant knight of medieval Europe, but the free man of spirit who has attained insight into the universal source by rigid discipline and practice of disinterested virtues, who has freed himself from the prejudices of his time and place. It is India's pride that she has clung fast to this ideal and produced in every generation and in every part of the country from the time of the Rṣis of the Upaniṣads and Buddha to Rāmakṛṣna and Gandhi, men who strove successfully to realize this ideal.

The ideal of the *saññyāsin* has still an appeal to the Indian mind. When Gandhi wants the political leaders to break all the ties that hold them to the world, to be ascetics owning nothing and vowed to celibacy, when he tells them that the prison should be their monastery, the coarse jail dress their religious habit, fetters and handcuffs their hair shirt and scourge, he is applying the ideal of renunciation in the political sphere.

The scheme of classes and stages is helpful but not indispensable. Mandana tells us that it is like a saddle horse which helps a man to reach his goal easily and quickly, but even without it man can arrive there. Life is a progress through stages. The race is a long one, and society should not lay on any one a burden too heavy to bear. The higher flights are not to be attempted until we train ourselves on the lower ones. We should not, however, be content to remain for all time on the lower stages. That would not be to live up to the ideal demanded of us. The goal is the vision of God and it is open to all. The world and its activities are no barriers to it but constitute the training ground.

THE CASTE SYSTEM

The institution of caste illustrates the spirit of comprehensive synthesis characteristic of the Hindu mind with its faith in the collaboration of races and

---

[6]*Mālavikāgnimitra*, i. 1.

CHAPTER ONE / *Hinduism*

the co-operation of cultures. Paradoxical as it may seem, the system of caste is the outcome of tolerance and trust. Though it has now degenerated into an instrument of oppression and intolerance, though it tends to perpetuate inequality and develop the spirit of exclusiveness, these unfortunate effects are not the central motives of the system. If the progressive thinkers of India had the power, as they undoubtedly have the authority, they would transform the institution out of recognition. It is not the evils of the system that I am here concerned with so much as the underlying principles.

Any survey of the castes of the present day will reveal the complex origin of the institution. Castes are of many kinds, tribal, racial, sectarian, occupational. Some are due to migration. When members of an old caste migrate to a different part of the country, they become a new caste.

As it is clear from the Sanskrit word *varna,* caste had originally reference to colour. If we look into the past history of India, we see how the country has been subjected to one race invasion after another. Even at the beginning of her history India was peopled by various racial groups, the dark aboriginal tribes, the sturdy Dravidians, the yellow-skinned Mongols and the blithe, forceful Aryans. Very soon she developed intimate intercourse with the Persians, the Greeks and the Scythians, and some of these settled down in India. No other country in the world has had such racial problems as India.

· · ·

In dealing with the problem of the conflict of the different racial groups, Hinduism adopted the only safe course of democracy, viz. that each racial group should be allowed to develop the best in it without impeding the progress of others. Every historical group is unique and specific and has an ultimate value, and the highest morality requires that we should respect its individuality. Caste, on its racial side, is the affirmation of the infinite diversity of human groups . . . .

· · ·

Caste was the answer of Hinduism to the forces pressing on it from outside. It was the instrument by which Hinduism civilized the different tribes it took in. Any group of people appearing exclusive in any sense is a caste. Whenever a group represents a type a caste arises. If a heresy is born in the bosom of the mother faith and if it spreads and produces a new type, a new caste arises. The Hindu society has differentiated as many types as can be reasonably differentiated, and is prepared to accept new ones as they arise. It stands for the ordered complexity, the harmonized multiplicity, the many in one which is the clue to the structure of the universe.

· · ·

Very early in the history of Hinduism, the caste distinctions came to mean the various stratifications into which the Hindu society settled. The confusion between the tribal and the occupational is the cause of the perpetuation of the old exclusiveness of the tribal customs in the still stringent rules which govern the constitution of each caste. Caste on its social side is a product of human organization and not a mystery of divine appointment. It is an attempt to regulate society with a view to actual differences and ideal unity. The first reference to it is in the Puruṣa Sūkta, where the different sections of society are regarded as the limbs of the great self. Human society is an organic whole, the parts of which are naturally dependent in such a way that each part in fulfilling its distinctive function conditions the fulfilment of function by the rest, and is in turn conditioned by the fulfilment of its function by the rest. In this sense the whole is present in each part, while each part is indispensable to the whole. Every society consists of groups working for the fulfilment of the wants of the society. As the different groups work for a common end they are bound by a sense of unity and social brotherhood. The cultural and the spiritual, the military and the political, the economic classes and the unskilled workers constitute the four-fold caste organization. The different functions of the human life were clearly separated and their specific and complementary character was recognized. Each caste has its social purpose and function, its own code and tradition. It is a closed corporation equipped with a certain traditional and independent organization, observing certain usages regarding food and marriage. Each group is free to pursue its own aims free from interference by others. The functions of the different castes were regarded as equally important to the well-being of the whole. The serenity of the teacher, the heroism of the warrior, the honesty of the business man, and the patience and energy of the worker all contribute to the social growth. Each has its own perfection.

The rules of caste bring about an adjustment of the different groups in society. The Brahmins were allowed freedom and leisure to develop the spiritual ideals and broadcast them. They were freed from the cares of existence, as gifts to them by others were encouraged and even enjoined. They are said to be above class interests and prejudices, and to possess a wide and impartial vision. They are not in bondage to the State, though they are consulted by the State. The State, as one of the groups in society, was essentially military in its organization. Its specific function was to preserve peace and order, and see to it that the different groups worked in harmony and no confusion of functions arose. The Government was an executive organization expected to carry out the best interests of the people. The Brahmins, as the advisors of the Government, point out the true interests of society.

· · ·

In spite of its attachment to the principle of non-violence, Hindu society made room for a group dedicated to the use of force, the Kṣatriyas. As long as human nature is what it is, as long as society has not reached its highest level, we require the use of force. So long as society has individuals who are hostile to all order and peace, it has to develop controls to check the anti-social elements. These anti-social forces gather together for revolt when the structure of society is shaken by war or internal dissensions. . . .

The economic group of the Vaiśyas were required to suppress greed and realize the moral responsibilities of wealth. Property is looked upon as an instrument of service. In the great days of Hinduism, the possessor of property regarded it as a social trust and undertook the education, the medical relief, the water supply and the amusements of the community. Unfortunately at the present day in almost all parts of the world the strain of money-making has been so great that many people are breaking down under it. Love of wealth is disrupting social life and is tending to the suppression of the spiritual. Wealth has become a means of self-indulgence, and universal greed is the cause of much of the meanness and cruelty which we find in the world. Hinduism has no sympathy with the view that 'to mix religion and business is to spoil two good things'. We ought not to banish spiritual values from life.

The unskilled workers and the peasants form the proletariat, the Śūdras. These castes are the actual living members of the social body each centred in itself and working alongside one another in co-operation. When a new group is taken into the fold of Hinduism, it is affiliated with one of the four castes. . . .

The system of caste insists that the law of social life should not be cold and cruel competition, but harmony and co-operation. Society is not a field of rivalry among individuals. The castes are not allowed to compete with one another. A man born in a particular group is trained to its manner, and will find it extremely hard to adjust himself to a new way. Each man is said to have his own specific nature (svabhāva) fitting him for his own specific function (svadharma), and changes of dharma or function are not encouraged. A sudden change of function when the nature is against its proper fulfilment may simply destroy the individuality of the being. We may wish to change or modify our particular mode of being, but we have not the power to effect it. Nature cannot be hurried by our desires. The four castes represent men of thought, men of action, men of feeling, and others in whom none of these is highly developed. Of course, these are the dominant and not the exclusive characters, and there are all sorts of permutations and combinations of them . . . .

The scheme of the ends of life, classes, and stages has for its aim the development of the individual. It helps him to order and organize his life instead of leaving it as a bundle of incompatible desires. It looks upon him not as a mere specimen of a zoological species but as a member of a social group which reflects in its organization the scheme of values for the realization of which the group exists. By education and social discipline the individual is helped to develop the inner conviction essential for social stability. But throughout there is insistence on the fact that the highest values are supernational and truly universal. The activities and achievements of art and science, of morality and religion, are the highest manifestations of the human spirit assimilable and communicable across barriers of blood and race. This is not to deny or underrate the importance of the group life, but the highest values of art and literature, science and philosophy, have, in principle, a universal appeal. The higher the individual the more free is he of the social order. The highest is the most universal, having transcended the need for discipline by the social scheme (*ativarṇāśrami*). He is a king among men, being a king over himself, *svayam eva rājā*. He is a citizen of the world and speaks a language that can be understood by all who call themselves men. Of the four ends the highest is spiritual freedom; of the four classes, the Brāhmin engaged in spiritual pursuits is the highest; of the four stages, that of *saññyāsa* is the most exalted. The meaning of human existence is in a larger consciousness which man does not enter so long as he remains confined in his individuality.

ralph t. h. griffith (translator) ————————————————————

HYMNS FROM THE *Rig Veda*

The *Rig Veda* is the earliest of the *Vedas* and contains slightly more than a thousand hymns divided into ten books. Composed over a long period of time by unknown authors, the hymns accordingly represent quite diverse moods and thoughts. The lovely "To Dawn" expresses awe at both the beauty and harmony of nature. There is in this hymn, as in many others, a sense of cosmic order and of man's place in nature.

The second hymn is addressed to Varuna, one of the most important of the gods. He is that "imperial ruler" who maintains order in nature and in human affairs: he causes the rain to fall, and he may forgive the sins of men.

The "Hymn of Man" tells of Purusha, the primal man, from whose sacrifice by the gods all things came into existence. Throughout "To Prajapati" there is the questioning refrain "What god shall we adore with our oblation?" Prajapati is finally named, but scholars believe that the last verse is a later addition to the hymn.

The "Hymn of Creation" may be the best-known of the hymns of the *Rig Veda*. Its questions probe past the gods (who came "later") to ask about creation and to speculate about an original chaos when "All that existed then was void and formless."

———————————————————————————————————————

TO DAWN

This light is come, amid all lights the fairest; born is the brilliant, far-extending
   brightness.
Night, sent away for Savitar's uprising, hath yielded up a birthplace for the
   morning.

The fair, the bright is come with her white offspring; to her the dark one hath
   resigned her dwelling.
Akin, immortal, following each other, changing their colours, both the
   heavens move onward.

Common, unending is the sisters' pathway; taught by the gods, alternately
   they travel.
Fair-formed, of different hues and yet one-minded, Night and Dawn clash
   not, neither do they tarry.

Bright leader of glad sounds, our eyes behold her: splendid in hue she hath
   unclosed the portals.
She, stirring up the world, hath shown us riches: Dawn hath awakened every
   living creature.

Ralph T. H. Griffith., trans., "Hymns from the *Rig Veda.*" Reprinted from Lin Yutang, ed., *The Wisdom of China and India* (New York: Random House, 1942). Notes have been omitted.

Rich Dawn, she sets afoot the coiled-up sleeper, one for enjoyment, one for wealth or worship,
Those who saw little for extended vision: all living creatures hath the Dawn awakened.

One to high sway, one to exalted glory, one to pursue his gain and one his labour;
All to regard their different vocations, all moving creatures hath the Dawn awakened.

We see her there, the child of heaven, apparent, the young maid, flushing in her shining raiment.
Thou sovran lady of all earthly treasure, flush on us here, auspicious Dawn, this morning. *(from Book I, 113)*

TO VARUNA

Sing forth a hymn sublime and solemn, grateful to glorious Varuna, imperial ruler,
Who hath struck out, like one who slays the victim, earth as a skin to spread in front of Sūrya.

In the tree-tops the air he hath extended, put milk in kine and vigorous speed in horses,
Set intellect in hearts, fire in the waters, Sūrya in heaven and Soma on the mountain.

Varuna lets the big cask, opening downward, flow through the heaven and earth and air's mid-region.
Therewith the universe's sovran waters earth as the shower of rain bedews the barley.

When Varuna is fain for milk, he moistens the sky, the land, and earth to her foundation.
Then straight the mountains clothe them in the raincloud: the heroes, putting forth their vigour, loose them.

I will declare this mighty deed of magic, of glorious Varuna, the lord immortal,
Who, standing in the firmament, hath meted the earth out with the sun as with a measure

None, verily, hath ever let or hindered this the most wise god's mighty deed of magic,
Whereby with all their flood, the lucid rivers fill not one sea wherein they pour their waters.

If we have sinned against the man who loves us, have ever wronged a brother, friend, or comrade,
The neighbour ever with us, or a stranger, O Varuna, remove from us the trespass.

If we, as gamesters cheat at play, have cheated, done wrong unwittingly or sinned of purpose,
Cast all these sins away like loosened fetters, and, Varuna, let us be thine own beloved. *(Book V, 85)*

HYMN OF MAN

A thousand heads hath Purusha, a thousand eyes, a thousand feet.
On every side pervading earth he fills a space ten fingers wide.

This Purusha is all that yet hath been and all that is to be,
The lord of immortality which waxes greater still by food.

So mighty is his greatness; yea, greater than this is Purusha.
All creatures are one-fourth of him, three-fourths eternal life in heaven.

With three-fourths Purusha went up: one-fourth of him again was here.
Thence he strode out to every side over what eats not and what eats.

From him Virāj was born; again Purusha from Virāj was born.
As soon as he was born he spread eastward and westward o'er the earth.

When gods prepared the sacrifice with Purusha as their offering,
Its oil was spring; the holy gift was autumn; summer was the wood.

They balmed as victim on the grass Purusha born in earliest time.
With him the deities and all Sādhyas and Rishis sacrificed.

From that great general sacrifice the dripping fat was gathered up.
He formed the creatures of the air, and animals both wild and tame.

From that great general sacrifice Richas and Sāma-hymns were born:
Therefrom were spells and charms produced; the Yajus had its birth from it.

From it were horses born, from it all cattle with two rows of teeth:
From it were generated kine, from it the goats and sheep were born.

When they divided Purusha, how many portions did they make?
What do they call his mouth, his arms? What do they call his thighs and feet?

The Brāhman was his mouth, of both his arms was the Rājanya made.
His thighs became the Vaisya, from his feet the Sudra was produced.

The moon was gendered from his mind, and from his eye the sun had birth;

Indra and Agni from his mouth were born, and Vāyu from his breath.

Forth from his navel came mid-air; the sky was fashioned from his head;
Earth from his feet, and from his ear the regions. Thus they formed the
   worlds.

Seven fencing-sticks had he, thrice seven layers of fuel were prepared
When the gods, offering sacrifice, bound, as their victim, Purusha.

Gods, sacrificing, sacrificed the victim: these were the earliest holy ordinances.
The mighty ones attained the height of heaven, there where the Sādhyas, gods
   of old, are dwelling. *(Book X, 90)*

TO PRAJĀPATI

In the beginning rose Hiranyagarbha, born only lord of all created beings.
He fixed and holdeth up this earth and heaven. What god shall we adore with
   our oblation?

Giver of vital breath, of power and vigour, he whose commandments all the
   gods acknowledge:
The lord of death, whose shade is life immortal. What god shall we adore with
   our oblation?

Who by his grandeur hath become sole ruler of all the moving world that
   breathes and slumbers:
He who is lord of men and lord of cattle. What god shall we adore with our
   oblation?

His, through his might, are these snow-covered mountains, and men call sea
   and Rasā his possession:
His arms are these, his are these heavenly regions. What god shall we adore
   with our oblation?

By him the heavens are strong and earth is stedfast, by him light's realm and
   sky-vault are supported:
By him the regions in mid-air were measured. What god shall we adore with
   our oblation?

To him, supported by his help, two armies embattled look with trembling in
   their spirit,
When over them the risen sun is shining. What god shall we adore with our
   oblation?

What time the mighty waters came, containing the universal germ, producing
   Agni,
Thence sprang the god's one spirit into being. What god shall we adore with
   our oblation?

He in his might surveyed the floods containing productive force and generating worship.
He is the god of gods, and none beside him. What god shall we adore with our oblation?

Ne'er may he harm us who is earth's begetter, nor he whose laws are sure, the heavens' creator,
He who brought forth the great and lucid waters. What god shall we adore with our oblation?

Prajāpati! thou only comprehendest all these created things, and none beside thee.
Grant us our hearts' desire when we invoke thee: may we have store of riches in possession. *(Book X, 121)*

HYMN OF CREATION

Then was not non-existent nor existent: there was no realm of air, no sky beyond it.
What covered in, and where? and what gave shelter? Was water there, unfathomed depth of water?

Death was not then, nor was there aught immortal: no sign was there, the day's and night's divider.
That one thing, breathless, breathed by its own nature: apart from it was nothing whatsoever.

Darkness there was: at first concealed in darkness, this All was indiscriminated chaos.
All that existed then was void and formless: by the great power of warmth was born that unit.

Thereafter rose desire in the beginning, Desire, the primal seed and germ of spirit.
Sages who searched with their heart's thought discovered the existent's kinship in the non-existent.

Transversely was their severing line extended: what was above it then, and what below it?
There were begetters, there were mighty forces, free action here and energy up yonder.

Who verily knows and who can here declare it, whence it was born and whence comes this creation?
The gods are later than this world's production. Who knows, then, whence it first came into being?

He, the first origin of this creation, whether he formed it all or did not form it,
Whose eye controls this world in highest heaven, he verily knows it, or perhaps he knows not. *(Book X, 129)*

swami prabhavananda and
frederick manchester (translators) _____

FROM THE *Upanishads*

Although they often draw their themes from earlier Vedic literature, the *Upanishads* are usually said to be the first philosophical treatises of India. They date from the eighth through the sixth centuries B.C. In all there are well over a hundred *Upanishads*, but some thirteen or so receive the most attention. Like the *Vedas*, the *Upanishads* do not express an entirely consistent point of view, but one bold thesis does predominate: the identification of Brahman and Atman—the Absolute with the essence of the individual. It is the idea so succinctly summarized by the classic line from the *Chandogya Upanishad,* "THAT ART THOU." Hence the quest for Truth in the *Upanishads* turns *inward*: the Ground of Being itself is to be found within oneself.

There follow excerpts from three *Upanishads*. The *Chandogya Upanishad* shares with the *Brihadaranyaka Upanishad* the distinction of being the most renowned of all the *Upanishads*; the *Brihadaranyaka Upanishad* is the longest and perhaps the oldest. The nature of death is discussed in the *Katha Upanishad.*

FROM THE *CHANDOGYA UPANISHAD*

One day the boy Satyakama came to his mother and said: "Mother, I want to be a religious student. What is my family name?"

"My son," replied his mother, "I do not know. In my youth I was a servant and worked in many places. I do not know who was your father. I am Jabala, and you are Satyakama. Call yourself Satyakama Jabala."

Thereupon the boy went to Gautama and asked to be accepted as a student. "Of what family are you, my lad?" inquired the sage.

Satyakama replied: "I asked my mother what my family name was, and she answered: 'I do not know. In my youth I was a servant and worked in many places. I do not know who was your father. I am Jabala, and you are Satyakama. Call yourself Satyakama Jabala!' I am therefore Satyakama Jabala, sir."

Then said the sage: "None but a true Brahmin would have spoken thus. Go and fetch fuel, for I will teach you. You have not swerved from the truth."

....

When Svetaketu was twelve years old, his father Uddalaka said to him, "Svetaketu, you must now go to school and study. None of our family, my child, is ignorant of Brahman."

Thereupon Svetaketu went to a teacher and studied for twelve years. After committing to memory all the Vedas, he returned home full of pride in his learning.

His father, noticing the young man's conceit, said to him: "Svetaketu, have you asked for that knowledge by which we hear the unhearable, by which we perceive the unperceivable, by which we know the unknowable?"

"What is that knowledge, sir?" asked Svetaketu.

"My child, as by knowing one lump of clay, all things made of clay are known, the difference being only in name and arising from speech, and the truth being that all are clay; as by knowing a nugget of gold, all things made of gold are known, the difference being only in name and arising from speech, and the truth being that all are gold—exactly so is that knowledge, knowing which we know all."

"But surely those venerable teachers of mine are ignorant of this knowledge; for if they had possessed it, they would have taught it to me. Do you therefore, sir, give me that knowledge."

"Be it so," said Uddalaka, and continued thus:

.   .   .

"As the bees make honey by gathering juices from many flowering plants and trees, and as these juices reduced to one honey do not know from what flowers they severally come, similarly, my son, all creatures, when they are merged in that one Existence, whether in dreamless sleep or in death, know nothing of their past or present state, because of the ignorance enveloping them—know not that they are merged in him and that from him they came.

"Whatever these creatures are, whether a lion, or a tiger, or a boar, or a worm, or a gnat, or a mosquito, that they remain after they come back from dreamless sleep.

"All these have their self in him alone. He is the truth. He is the subtle essence of all. He is the Self. And that, Svetaketu, THAT ART THOU."

"Please, sir, tell me more about this Self."

"Be it so, my son:

"The rivers in the east flow eastward, the rivers in the west flow westward, and all enter into the sea. From sea to sea they pass, the clouds lifting them to the sky as vapor and sending them down as rain. And as these rivers, when they are united with the sea, do not know whether they are this or that river, likewise all those creatures that I have named, when they have come back from Brahman, know not whence they came.

"All those beings have their self in him alone. He is the truth. He is the subtle essence of all. He is the Self. And that, Svetaketu, THAT ART THOU."

"Please, sir, tell me more about this Self."

"Be it so, my child:

.   .   .

". . . Bring a fruit of that Nyagrodha tree."

"Here it is, sir."

"Break it."

"It is broken, sir."

"What do you see?"

"Some seeds, extremely small, sir."

"Break one of them."

"It is broken, sir."

"What do you see?"

"Nothing, sir."

"The subtle essence you do not see, and in that is the whole of the Nyagrodha tree. Believe, my son, that that which is the subtle essence—in that have all things their existence. That is the truth. That is the Self. And that, Svetaketu, THAT ART THOU."

"Please, sir, tell me more about this Self."

"Be it so. Put this salt in water, and come to me tomorrow morning."

Svetaketu did as he was bidden. The next morning his father asked him to bring the salt which he had put in the water. But he could not, for it had dissolved. Then said Uddalaka:

"Sip the water, and tell me how it tastes."

"It is salty, sir."

"In the same way," continued Uddalaka, "though you do not see Brahman in this body, he is indeed here. That which is the subtle essence—in that have all things their existence. That is the truth. That is the Self. And that, Svetaketu, THAT ART THOU."

FROM THE *BRIHADARANYAKA UPANISHAD*

YAGNAVALKYA *(to his wife)*   Maitreyi, I am resolved to give up the world and begin the life of renunciation. I wish therefore to divide my property between you and my other wife, Katyayani.

MAITREYI   My lord, if this whole earth belonged to me, with all its wealth, should I through its possession attain immortality?

YAGNAVALKYA   No. Your life would be like that of the rich. None can possibly hope to attain immortality through wealth.

MAITREYI   Then what need have I of wealth? Please, my lord, tell me what you know about the way to immortality.

YAGNAVALKYA   Dear to me have you always been, Maitreyi, and now you ask to learn of that truth which is nearest my heart. Come, sit by me. I will explain it to you. Meditate on what I say.

It is not for the sake of the husband, my beloved, that the husband is dear, but for the sake of the Self.

It is not for the sake of the wife, my beloved, that the wife is dear, but for the sake of the Self.

It is not for the sake of the children, my beloved, that the children are dear, but for the sake of the Self.

It is not for the sake of wealth, my beloved, that wealth is dear, but for the sake of the Self.

It is not for the sake of the Brahmins, my beloved, that the Brahmins are held in reverence, but for the sake of the Self.

It is not for the sake of the Kshatriyas, my beloved, that the Kshatriyas are held in honor, but for the sake of the Self.

It is not for the sake of the higher worlds, my beloved, that the higher worlds are desired, but for the sake of the Self.

It is not for the sake of the gods, my beloved, that the gods are worshiped, but for the sake of the Self.

It is not for the sake of the creatures, my beloved, that the creatures are prized, but for the sake of the Self.

It is not for the sake of itself, my beloved, that anything whatever is esteemed, but for the sake of the Self.

The Self, Maitreyi, is to be known. Hear about it, reflect upon it, meditate upon it. By knowing the Self, my beloved, through hearing, reflection, and meditation, one comes to know all things.

Let the Brahmin ignore him who thinks that the Brahmin is different from the Self.

Let the Kshatriya ignore him who thinks that the Kshatriya is different from the Self.

Let the higher worlds ignore him who thinks that the higher worlds are different from the Self.

Let the gods ignore him who thinks that the gods are different from the Self.

Let all creatures ignore him who thinks that the creatures are different from the Self.

Let all ignore him who thinks that anything whatever is different from the Self.

The priest, the warrior, the higher worlds, the gods, the creatures, what-soever things there be—these are the Self.

As, when the drum is beaten, its various particular notes are not heard apart from the whole, but in the total sound all its notes are heard; as, when the conch-shell is blown, its various particular notes are not heard apart from the whole, but in the total sound all its notes are heard; as, when the vina is played, its various particular notes are not heard apart from the whole, but in the total sound all its notes are heard—so, through the knowledge of the Self, Pure Intelligence, all things and beings are known. There is no existence apart from the Self.

As smoke and sparks arise from a lighted fire kindled with damp fuel, even so, Maitreyi, have been breathed forth from the Eternal all knowledge and all wisdom—what we know as the Rig Veda, the Yajur Veda, and the rest. They are the breath of the Eternal.

As for water the one center is the ocean, as for touch the one center is the skin, as for smell the one center is the nose, as for taste the one center is the tongue, as for form the one center is the eyes, as for sound the one center is the ears, as for thought the one center is the mind, as for divine wisdom the one center is the heart—so for all beings the one center is the Self.

As a lump of salt when thrown into water melts away and the lump cannot be taken out, but wherever we taste the water it is salty, even so, O Maitreyi, the individual self, dissolved, is the Eternal—pure consciousness, infinite and transcendent. Individuality arises by identification of the Self, through ignorance, with the elements; and with the disappearance of consciousness of the many, in divine illumination, it disappears. Where there is consciousness of the Self, individuality is no more.

This it is, O my beloved, that I wanted to tell you.

MAITREYI "Where there is consciousness of the Self, individuality is no more": this that you say, my lord, confuses me.

YAGNAVALKYA My beloved, let nothing I have said confuse you. But meditate well the truth that I have spoken.

As long as there is duality, one sees *the other,* one hears *the other,* one smells *the other,* one speaks to *the other,* one thinks of *the other,* one knows *the other;* but when for the illumined soul the all is dissolved in the Self, who is there to be seen by whom, who is there to be smelt by whom, who is there to be heard by whom, who is there to be spoken to by whom, who is there to be thought of by whom, who is there to be known by whom? Ah, Maitreyi, my beloved, the Intelligence which reveals all—by what shall it be revealed? By whom shall the Knower be known? The Self is described as *not this, not that.* It is incomprehensible, for it cannot be comprehended; undecaying, for it never decays; unattached, for it never attaches itself; unbound, for it is never bound. By whom, O my beloved, shall the Knower be known?

This it is that I teach you, O Maitreyi. This is the truth of immortality.

FROM THE *KATHA UPANISHAD*

[*Granted three wishes, or "boons," by* DEATH, *the young* NACHIKETA *as his third wish asks of* DEATH *the secret of what happens to a man after he dies.*]

And then Nachiketa considered within himself, and said:

"When a man dies, there is this doubt: Some say, he is; others say, he is not. Taught by thee, I would know the truth. This is my third wish."

"Nay," replied Death, "even the gods were once puzzled by this mystery. Subtle indeed is the truth regarding it, not easy to understand. Choose thou some other boon, O Nachiketa."

But Nachiketa would not be denied.

"Thou sayest, O Death, that even the gods were once puzzled by this mystery, and that it is not easy to understand. Surely there is no teacher better able to explain it than thou—and there is no other boon equal to this."

To which, trying Nachiketa again, the god replied:

"Ask for sons and grandsons who shall live a hundred years. Ask for cattle, elephants, horses, gold. Choose for thyself a mighty kingdom. Or if thou canst imagine aught better, ask for that—not for sweet pleasures only but for the power, beyond all thought, to taste their sweetness. Yea, verily, the supreme enjoyer will I make thee of every good thing. Celestial maidens, beautiful to behold, such indeed as were not meant for mortals—even these, together with their bright chariots and their musical instruments, will I give unto thee, to serve thee. But for the secret of death, O Nachiketa, do not ask!"

But Nachiketa stood fast, and said: "These things endure only till the morrow, O Destroyer of Life, and the pleasures they give wear out the senses. Keep thou therefore horses and chariots, keep dance and song, for thyself! How shall he desire wealth, O Death, who once has seen thy face? Nay, only the boon that I have chosen—that only do I ask. Having found out the society of the imperishable and the immortal, as in knowing thee I have done, how shall I, subject to decay and death, and knowing well the vanity of the flesh—how shall I wish for long life?

"Tell me, O King, the supreme secret regarding which men doubt. No other boon will I ask."

Whereupon the King of Death, well pleased at heart, began to teach Nachiketa the secret of immortality.

KING OF DEATH   The good is one thing; the pleasant is another. These two, differing in their ends, both prompt to action. Blessed are they that choose the good; they that choose the pleasant miss the goal.

Both the good and the pleasant present themselves to men. The wise, having examined both, distinguish the one from the other. The wise prefer the good to the pleasant; the foolish, driven by fleshly desires, prefer the pleasant to the good.

Thou, O Nachiketa, having looked upon fleshly desires, delightful to the senses, hast renounced them all. Thou hast turned from the miry way wherein many a man wallows.

Far from each other, and leading to different ends, are ignorance and knowledge. Thee, O Nachiketa, I regard as one who aspires after knowledge, for a multitude of pleasant objects were unable to tempt thee.

Living in the abyss of ignorance yet wise in their own conceit, deluded fools go round and round, the blind led by the blind.

To the thoughtless youth, deceived by the vanity of earthly possessions, the path that leads to the eternal abode is not revealed. *This world alone is real; there is no hereafter*—thinking thus, he falls again and again, birth after birth, into my jaws.

To many it is not given to hear of the Self. Many, though they hear of it, do not understand it. Wonderful is he who speaks of it. Intelligent is he who learns of it. Blessed is he who, taught by a good teacher, is able to understand it.

The truth of the Self cannot be fully understood when taught by an ignorant man, for opinions regarding it, not founded in knowledge, vary one from another. Subtler than the subtlest is this Self, and beyond all logic. Taught by a teacher who knows the Self and Brahman as one, a man leaves vain theory behind and attains to truth.

The awakening which thou hast known does not come through the intellect, but rather, in fullest measure, from the lips of the wise. Beloved Nachiketa, blessed, blessed art thou, because thou seekest the Eternal. Would that I had more pupils like thee!

Well I know that earthly treasure lasts but till the morrow. For did not I myself, wishing to be King of Death, make sacrifice with fire? But the sacrifice was a fleeting thing, performed with fleeting objects, and small is my reward, seeing that only for a moment will my reign endure.

The goal of worldly desire, the glittering objects for which all men long, the celestial pleasures they hope to gain by religious rites, the most sought-after of miraculous powers—all these were within thy grasp. But all these, with firm resolve, thou has renounced.

The ancient, effulgent being, the indwelling Spirit, subtle, deep-hidden in the lotus of the heart, is hard to know. But the wise man, following the path of meditation, knows him, and is freed alike from pleasure and from pain.

The man who has learned that the Self is separate from the body, the senses, and the mind, and has fully known him, the soul of truth, the subtle principle—such a man verily attains to him, and is exceeding glad, because he has found the source and dwelling place of all felicity. Truly do I believe, O Nachiketa, that for thee the gates of joy stand open.

NACHIKETA Teach me, O King, I beseech thee, whatsoever thou knowest to be beyond right and wrong, beyond cause and effect, beyond past, present, and future.

KING OF DEATH Of that goal which all the Vedas declare, which is implicit in all penances, and in pursuit of which men lead lives of continence and service, of that will I briefly speak.

It is—OM.

This syllable is Brahman. This syllable is indeed supreme. He who knows it obtains his desire.

It is the strongest support. It is the highest symbol. He who knows it is reverenced as a knower of Brahman.

The Self, whose symbol is OM, is the omniscient Lord. He is not born. He does not die. He is neither cause nor effect. This Ancient One is unborn, imperishable, eternal: though the body be destroyed, he is not killed.

If the slayer think that he slays, if the slain think that he is slain, neither of them knows the truth. The Self slays not, nor is he slain.

Smaller than the smallest, greater than the greatest, this Self forever dwells within the hearts of all. When a man is free from desire, his mind and senses purified, he beholds the glory of the Self and is without sorrow.

Though seated, he travels far; though at rest, he moves all things. Who but the purest of the pure can realize this Effulgent Being, who is joy and who is beyond joy.

Formless is he, though inhabiting form. In the midst of the fleeting he abides forever. All-pervading and supreme is the Self. The wise man, knowing him in his true nature, transcends all grief.

The Self is not known through study of the scriptures, nor through subtlety of the intellect, nor through much learning; but by him who longs for him is he known.[1] Verily unto him does the Self reveal his true being.

By learning, a man cannot know him, if he desist not from evil, if he control not his senses, if he quiet not his mind, and practice not meditation.

To him Brahmins and Kshatriyas are but food, and death itself a condiment.

Both the individual self and the Universal Self have entered the cave of the heart, the abode of the Most High, but the knowers of Brahman and the householders who perform the fire sacrifices see a difference between them as between sunshine and shadow.

May we perform the Nachiketa Sacrifice, which bridges the world of suffering. May we know the imperishable Brahman, who is fearless, and who is the end and refuge of those who seek liberation.

Know that the Self is the rider, and the body the chariot; that the intellect is the charioteer, and the mind the reins.[2]

The senses, say the wise, are the horses; the roads they travel are the mazes of desire. The wise call the Self the enjoyer when he is united with the body, the senses, and the mind.

When a man lacks discrimination and his mind is uncontrolled, his senses are unmanageable, like the restive horses of a charioteer. But when a man has discrimination and his mind is controlled, his senses, like the well-broken horses of a charioteer, lightly obey the rein.

He who lacks discrimination, whose mind is unsteady and whose heart is impure, never reaches the goal, but is born again and again. But he who has discrimination, whose mind is steady and whose heart is pure, reaches the goal, and having reached it is born no more.

[1] There is another interpretation of this sentence, involving the mystery of grace: "Whom the Self chooses, by him is he attained."

[2] In Hindu psychology the mind is the organ of perception.

The man who has a sound understanding for charioteer, a controlled mind for reins—he it is that reaches the end of the journey, the supreme abode of Vishnu, the all-pervading.[3]

The senses derive from physical objects, physical objects from mind, mind from intellect, intellect from ego, ego from the unmanifested seed, and the unmanifested seed from Brahman—the Uncaused Cause.

Brahman is the end of the journey. Brahman is the supreme goal.

This Brahman, this Self, deep-hidden in all beings, is not revealed to all; but to the seers, pure in heart, concentrated in mind—to them is he revealed.

The senses of the wise man obey his mind, his mind obeys his intellect, his intellect obeys his ego, and his ego obeys the Self.

Arise! Awake! Approach the feet of the master and know THAT. Like the sharp edge of a razor, the sages say, is the path. Narrow it is, and difficult to tread!

Soundless, formless, intangible, undying, tasteless, odorless, without beginning, without end, eternal, immutable, beyond nature, is the Self. Knowing him as such, one is freed from death.

THE NARRATOR The wise man, having heard and taught the eternal truth revealed by the King of Death to Nachiketa, is glorified in the heaven of Brahma.

He who sings with devotion this supreme secret in the assembly of the Brahmins, or at the rites in memory of his fathers, is rewarded with rewards immeasurable!

KING OF DEATH The Self-Existent made the senses turn outward. Accordingly, man looks toward what is without, and sees not what is within. Rare is he who, longing for immortality, shuts his eyes to what is without and beholds the Self.

Fools follow the desires of the flesh and fall into the snare of all-encompassing death; but the wise, knowing the Self as eternal, seek not the things that pass away.

He through whom man sees, tastes, smells, hears, feels, and enjoys, is the omniscient Lord.

He, verily, is the immortal Self. Knowing him, one knows all things.

He through whom man experiences the sleeping or waking states is the all-pervading Self. Knowing him, one grieves no more.

He who knows that the individual soul, enjoyer of the fruits of action, is the Self—ever present within, lord of time, past and future—casts out all fear. For this Self is the immortal Self.

He who sees the First-Born—born of the mind of Brahma, born before the creation of waters—and sees him inhabiting the lotus of the heart, living

[3]Vishnu is here equivalent to Brahman.

among physical elements, sees Brahman indeed. For this First-Born is the immortal Self.[4]

That being who is the power of all powers, and is born as such, who embodies himself in the elements and in them exists, and who has entered the lotus of the heart, is the immortal Self.

Agni, the all-seeing, who lies hidden in fire sticks, like a child well guarded in the womb, who is worshiped day by day by awakened souls, and by those who offer oblations in sacrificial fire—he is the immortal Self.[5]

That in which the sun rises and in which it sets, that which is the source of all the powers of nature and of the senses, that which nothing can transcend—that is the immortal Self.

What is within us is also without. What is without is also within. He who sees difference between what is within and what is without goes evermore from death to death.

By the purified mind alone is the indivisible Brahman to be attained. Brahman alone is—nothing else is. He who sees the manifold universe, and not the one reality, goes evermore from death to death.

That being, of the size of a thumb, dwells deep within the heart.[6] He is the lord of time, past and future. Having attained him, one fears no more. He, verily, is the immortal Self.

That being, of the size of a thumb, is like a flame without smoke. He is the lord of time, past and future, the same today and tomorrow. He, verily, is the immortal Self.

As rain, fallen on a hill, streams down its side, so runs he after many births who sees manifoldness in the Self.

As pure water poured into pure water remains pure, so does the Self remain pure, O Nachiketa, uniting with Brahman.

To the Birthless, the light of whose consciousness forever shines, belongs the city of eleven gates.[7] He who meditates on the ruler of that city knows no more sorrow. He attains liberation, and for him there can no longer be birth or death. For the ruler of that city is the immortal Self.

The immortal Self is the sun shining in the sky, he is the breeze blowing in space, he is the fire burning on the altar, he is the guest dwelling in the house; he is in all men, he is in the gods, he is in the ether, he is wherever there is

---

[4]Brahman, the absolute, impersonal existence, when associated with the power called Maya—the power to evolve as the empirical universe—is known as Hiranyagarbha, the First-Born.

[5]The reference is to the Vedic sacrifice. Agni, whose name means fire, is said to be all-seeing, the fire symbolizing Brahman, the Revealer; the two fire sticks, which being rubbed together produce the fire, represent the heart and the mind of man.

[6]The sages ascribe a definite, minute size to the Self in order to assist the disciple in meditation.

[7]The Birthless is the Self; the city of eleven gates is the body with its apertures—eyes, ears, etc.

truth; he is the fish that is born in water, he is the plant that grows in the soil, he is the river that gushes from the mountain—he, the changeless reality, the illimitable!

He, the adorable one, seated in the heart, is the power that gives breath. Unto him all the senses do homage.

What can remain when the dweller in this body leaves the outgrown shell, since he is, verily, the immortal Self?

Man does not live by breath alone, but by him in whom is the power of breath.

And now, O Nachiketa, will I tell thee of the unseen, the eternal Brahman, and of what befalls the Self after death.

Of those ignorant of the Self, some enter into beings possessed of wombs, others enter into plants—according to their deeds and the growth of their intelligence.

That which is awake in us even while we sleep, shaping in dream the objects of our desire—that indeed is pure, that is Brahman, and that verily is called the Immortal. All the worlds have their being in that, and no one can transcend it. That is the Self.

As fire, though one, takes the shape of every object which it consumes, so the Self, though one, takes the shape of every object in which it dwells.

As air, though one, takes the shape of every object which it enters, so the Self, though one, takes the shape of every object in which it dwells.

As the sun, revealer of all objects to the seer, is not harmed by the sinful eye, nor by the impurities of the objects it gazes on, so the one Self, dwelling in all, is not touched by the evils of the world. For he transcends all.

He is one, the lord and innermost Self of all; of one form, he makes of himself many forms. To him who sees the Self revealed in his own heart belongs eternal bliss—to none else, to none else!

Intelligence of the intelligent, eternal among the transient, he, though one, makes possible the desires of many. To him who sees the Self revealed in his own heart belongs eternal peace—to none else, to none else!

NACHIKETA   How, O King, shall I find that blissful Self, supreme, ineffable, who is attained by the wise? Does he shine by himself, or does he reflect another's light?

KING OF DEATH   Him the sun does not illumine, nor the moon, nor the stars, nor the lightning—nor, verily, fires kindled upon the earth. He is the one light that gives light to all. He shining, everything shines.

This universe is a tree eternally existing, its root aloft, its branches spread below. The pure root of the tree is Brahman, the immortal, in whom the three worlds have their being, whom none can transcend, who is verily the Self.[8]

[8]The "three worlds" are the sky, the earth, and the nether world.

The whole universe came forth from Brahman and moves in Brahman. Mighty and awful is he, like to a thunderbolt crashing loud through the heavens. For those who attain him death has no terror.

In fear of him fire burns, the sun shines, the rains fall, the winds blow, and death kills.

If a man fail to attain Brahman before he casts off his body, he must again put on a body in the world of created things.

In one's own soul Brahman is realized clearly, as if seen in a mirror. In the heaven of Brahma also is Brahman realized clearly, as one distinguishes light from darkness. In the world of the fathers he is beheld as in a dream.[9] In the world of angels he appears as if reflected in water.

The senses have separate origin in their several objects. They may be active, as in the waking state, or they may be inactive, as in sleep. He who knows them to be distinct from the changeless Self grieves no more.

Above the senses is the mind. Above the mind is the intellect. Above the intellect is the ego. Above the ego is the unmanifested seed, the Primal Cause.

And verily beyond the unmanifested seed is Brahman, the all-pervading spirit, the unconditioned, knowing whom one attains to freedom and achieves immortality.

None beholds him with the eyes, for he is without visible form. Yet in the heart is he revealed, through self-control and meditation. Those who know him become immortal.

When all the senses are stilled, when the mind is at rest, when the intellect wavers not—then, say the wise, is reached the highest state.

This calm of the senses and the mind has been defined as yoga. He who attains it is freed from delusion.

In one not freed from delusion this calm is uncertain, unreal: it comes and goes. Brahman words cannot reveal, mind cannot reach, eyes cannot see. How then, save through those who know him, can he be known?

There are two selves, the apparent self and the real Self. Of these it is the real Self, and he alone, who must be felt as truly existing. To the man who has felt him as truly existing he reveals his innermost nature.

The mortal in whose heart desire is dead becomes immortal. The mortal in whose heart the knots of ignorance are untied becomes immortal. These are the highest truths taught in the scriptures.

Radiating from the lotus of the heart there are a hundred and one nerves. One of these ascends toward the thousand-petaled lotus in the brain. If, when a man comes to die, his vital force passes upward and out through this nerve, he attains immortality; but if his vital force passes out through another nerve, he goes to one or another plane of mortal existence and remains subject to birth and death.

[9]The fathers are the spirits of the meritorious dead, who dwell in another world, reaping the fruits of their good deeds, but subject to rebirth.

The Supreme Person, of the size of a thumb, the innermost Self, dwells forever in the heart of all beings. As one draws the pith from a reed, so must the aspirant after truth, with great perseverance, separate the Self from the body. Know the Self to be pure and immortal—yea, pure and immortal!

THE NARRATOR   Nachiketa, having learned from the god this knowledge and the whole process of yoga, was freed from impurities and from death, and was united with Brahman. Thus will it be with another also if he know the innermost Self.

OM . . . Peace—peace—peace.

sri krishna prem ———————————————————————

FROM *The Yoga of the Bhagavat Gita*

The *Bhagavad Gita* falls outside the Vedic "canon," but it is the best-loved of all the texts of Hinduism. Its date is uncertain: Radhakrishnan assigns it to the fifth century B.C., but most other scholars place it between that century and the second century B.C. The *Gita* is a part of the epic *Mahabharata,* which is an account of a great war between two families of cousins. The *Gita* itself opens on the eve of the war with Arjuna, the hero of one of the families, revolted by the prospect of the bloodshed to come. The god Krishna, appearing as Arjuna's charioteer, speaks to Arjuna of his responsibilities, but the dialogue (actually more a monologue by Krishna) proceeds to the purpose of life and the nature of reality. The entire dialogue is presented as a report to the old King Dhritarashtra by his charioteer, Sanjaya.

The introductory essay which follows is by Sri Krishna Prem, whose name was Ronald Henry Nixon before he took his vows as a monk of the Hindu Vaishnava sect. Born in 1898, he served in the Royal Flying Corps and held an M.A. from Cambridge, but his religious quest led him to India and a guru in an ashram* near the Himalayas. He is the author of *The Yoga of the Kathopanishad* and *The Yoga of the Bhagavat†Gita,* from which the present selection is taken. He died in 1965.

INTRODUCTION

The Bhagavat Gita needs little introduction nowadays even in the West. Many have come to value it as one of the world's great spiritual classics and not a few take it as their guide to the inner life. Of its popularity in India there is no need to speak. Though its author is unknown (for we can scarcely adopt the orthodox view that it was, as we have it, spoken by the historical Krishna on the battlefield of *Kurukshetra*) it is revered by Hindus of all schools of thought, and is one foot of the triple base on which the *Vedānta* is founded, the other two feet being the *Upanishads* and the *Brahma-Sūtras*. Every teacher who wished to claim *Vedāntic* authority for his teachings was obliged to write a commentary on it showing that it supported his views.

In consequence of this we have commentaries written from many diverse points of view, monist and dualist, pantheist and theist. Enthusiasts for action, for knowledge (*jñāna* or gnosis), or for devotion to a personal God, all find their special tenets in the Gita . . . .

· · · ·

*A secluded dwelling of a Hindu sage (guru) or the group of disciples he instructs there.
†A variant spelling of *Bhagavad*.

Sri Krishna Prem, From *"The Yoga of the Bhagavat Gita."* Reprinted by permission of Watkins (Robinson & Watkins Books Ltd). Verse numbers have been omitted, and notes have been renumbered.

Let me say at once that I care nothing at all for these learned pronouncements. To anyone who has eyes to see, the Gita is based on direct knowledge of Reality, and of the Path that leads to that Reality, and it is of little moment who wrote it or to what school he was outwardly affiliated. Those who know Reality belong to a Race apart, the Race that never dies, as Hermes Trismegistus puts it, and neither they nor those who seek to be born into the Race concern themselves with the flummeries of sects and schools.

. . . the Gita is a textbook of Yoga, a guide to the treading of the Path. By Yoga is here meant not any special system called by that name, not *jñāna yoga,* nor *karma yoga,* nor *bhakti yoga,* nor the eightfold *yoga* of Patañjali, but just the Path by which man unites his finite self with Infinite Being. It is the inner Path of which all these separate yogas are so many one-sided aspects. It is not so much a synthesis of these separate teachings as that prior and undivided whole of which they represent partial formulations.

As such, it deals with the whole Path from the beginning to the end, from what Buddhists term "Entry in the stream" to the goal of Nirvāna. It follows that the sequence of the chapters is of great importance, and that it is a mistake to do as some expositors have done and expound the teachings with no reference to the place at which they occur in the general scheme. For instance, stress has often been laid on Gita xviii, 66: "Abandoning all *dharmas,* take refuge in Me alone. Fear not, I will liberate thee from all sins," as though this teaching, which comes at the very end of the Gita, were capable of being practised in the early stages of the Path. All that results from such misplacing is emotional pietism. There is no short-cut to the Goal. The whole course has to be run by each disciple, and though, through having practised in previous lives, the early stages may for some be but a rapid recapitulation, each chapter has to be lived through in its proper sequence.

The Path is not the special property of Hinduism, nor indeed of any religion. It is something which is to be found, more or less deeply buried, in all religions, and which can exist apart from any formal religion at all. That is why the Gita, though a definitely Hindu book, the very crest-jewel of Hindu teachings, is capable of being a guide to seekers all over the world.

. . . .

THE YOGA OF THE DEJECTION OF ARJUNA

Too many readers pass by the first chapter of the Gita hurriedly as of no great importance, considering it a mere introduction to which no special significance need be attached. This, however, is a mistake. It is no doubt true that it is an introductory chapter, but introductory to what? Not merely to an historical situation or to a body of philosophic teachings that have been embedded in the epic poem, but to the Yoga itself, and, if properly understood, it has a great significance for us.[1] Like all the other chapters, it is termed a yoga, and is entitled *"Arjuna Vishāda Yoga"*—the Yoga of the Dejection of Arjuna.

. . . the Gita commences at the point where the Soul, like one awakening from sleep, has emerged from the obscurity in which it lay buried. Arjuna, as the individual Soul, finds himself on the battlefield of Kurukshetra faced by the necessity of a terrible conflict in which all his friends, relatives and former teachers are ranged against him, "eager for battle." On this field, significantly enough termed *"dharmakshetra,"* the field of *dharma* or duty, the opposing forces of *pravṛitti* and *nivṛitti* stand face to face and, from a position to which it has been guided by the Divine Krishna, the Soul, stationed between the rival armies, surveys the situation.

As long as the Soul remains hidden in the inner worlds, so long the conflict does not come to a head, and the individual passes from one experience to another in an apparently unordered fashion, as described in the introductory section. But this cannot last for ever, and after the intoxication of the awakening, symbolised by the triumphant battle fought on behalf of King Virāta, has passed off, the Soul finds itself in a situation which may well inspire dejection.

It was easy to sound the war conches in defiance and to feel the thrill of anticipated battle with the Ásurik forces of *pravṛitti*. But, suddenly, in a flash of insight which comes while the Soul is poised inactive between the two opposing tendencies, Arjuna realises for the first time all that is involved in the struggle. Relations, friends of his childhood and revered teachers are also entangled amongst his enemies, and he realises that his own heart's blood is, as it were, arrayed against him. During the long ages of slumber the Soul has contracted all sorts of relationships and has submitted to the guidance of various ideals and traditions, and only now is it realised that all these relationships must be destroyed and all these ideals, ideals that have often seemed the very goal of life, must be ruthlessly sacrificed on the battlefield, since now they are seen to be leagued with the outgoing forces of *pravṛitti* and to be opposing the destined triumph of the Soul.

Up till now the individual has been content to live within the narrow circle of race and family, and bounded by the ties of kinship he has felt that it was enough if he fulfilled the duties that he owed to his society and nation, if he attempted to live according to the ideals of his *gurus,* the religious and ethical systems in which, by birth, he found himself. But societies and races are all temporary, while the Soul is eternal and, in the end, can rest on no support but Itself. The simple creed of "my country, right or wrong" lies in ruins, destroyed by conflicting loyalties, and the ideals which had uplifted him in

[1] It is by no means intended to suggest that all the kings and warriors mentioned in this chapter have symbolic significance as individuals. Attempts to interpret them have been made, but such as I have seen bear an artificial stamp.

earlier days are powerless to guide him any longer, as they are seen to be mere mental constructions, inadequate to the needs of the Soul.

Nor is the conflict to which the Soul is called merely one with outer ties, established institutions and recognised standards of conduct and belief. In the inner world, too, he is faced with the same situation. Arrayed against him he finds the army of his desires. Not merely those desires that are conventionally considered "evil" but many others too, the desire for "harmless" enjoyment, the desire to shine in society surrounded by friends, and the desire to lead a secure and comfortable life. All these and many more have taken the field against the Soul under the leadership of the various ideals that have been harnessed to their service. The call of the blood, the prestige of habit and established custom, the ideologies which had sufficed in the past are all arrayed against him, and perhaps the most bitter fact of all is the knowledge that the glittering ideals of patriotism, of family affection and of devotion to his religion have also "eaten the food of the Kauravas,"[2] and, though they served as guides and teachers in the past, are, like Bhishma and Droṇa, in arms against the Soul and must be slain.

This is the situation with which every aspirant is faced and through which, sooner or later, all have to pass. Small wonder is it that Arjuna is overcome with utter dejection and that his bow slips from his nerveless hand as he sinks down overcome by an intolerable sadness, a sadness that is the inevitable experience of those who seek the Path. What will be the worth of victory if "those for whose sake we desire kingdom, enjoyments and pleasures" must first lie dead on the field? If all desire is renounced, will not the whole of life become an empty waste, a vast desert in the midst of which the victorious Soul will sit enthroned in desolation, exercising a vain and empty rule? For what purpose are we called to such a sacrifice and, in the end, how shall we benefit by it? "Better to eat beggars' crusts in the world than to partake of such blood-besprinkled feasts."[3] Better, that is, to enjoy what simple enjoyments can be had than to set out on this perilous path, a path to an as yet quite inconceivable Goal, and of which the only certain thing is that it leads over the dead bodies of all that we hold dear in life.

Moreover, a further doubt arises in the heart. "In the destruction of the family the immemorial traditions perish and in the perishing of traditions lawlessness overcomes the whole community." Will not the destruction of all these desires—and, above all, of these ideals—cause great confusion in the world? Society depends on the existence of the normal desires of its members and is bound up with the one-sidednesses of current ideologies. Can it be right

[2] Bhishma explained his blind acquiescence in the injustice done to Draupadi in the Kaurava Court to his having for long eaten the Kaurava food. In other words, the power of faith had long been harnessed to ancient traditions now degenerated into superstition and so become forces of Darkness.

[3] Gita, ii, 5.

to disturb in the name of the Soul's progress to an unknown Goal an equilibrium which has at least stood the test of time? Will not the aspirant, by his renunciation of desire, unfit himself to participate in the everyday life of the world, to share in the joys and sorrows of his fellow-beings, and by his shattering of the ideals enshrined in ancient traditions will he not bring chaos into the world?

> ". . . Wilt thou dare
> Put by our sacred books, dethrone our Gods,
> Unpeople all the temples, shaking down
> That law which feeds the priests and props the realms?"[4]

Such, at least, are the doubts which present themselves in the heart, some of them well founded, others ill, but all alike having their real though unacknowledged source in the feeling of gloom which invades the heart at the prospect of a life in which all desire for self will have to be renounced and utterly slain.

Nor, at this stage, is the darkness lit by any ray of light, and although the Divine Teacher is standing beside the Soul not yet has His Voice been heard. Brought by its past evolution to the field of conflict, poised, as it were, upon the very edge of battle, the Soul loses heart and sinks back terrified at the desolate outlook, an outlook in which victory seems as cheerless as defeat.

The real source of this desolation is, as has been said, the prospect of a life in which all desire and ambition will be dead. We are so used to a life in which all action has its roots in desire that we can conceive no other, and sadly ask what would be the value of such existence. Not yet has the Soul learnt that, having Krishna, it has all; that it is not for their own sakes that parents, wives and children are dear, "but for the sake of the Átman."[5]

Nevertheless, this experience of the "*vishāda,*" or sorrow, is a very necessary one, as we may see from the fact that the Buddha, too, as the first of His four Áryan Truths, set forth in eloquent words the essential sorrow of life.

The Voice of Krishna can be heard only in silence, and as long as the heart is filled with the clamour of desire the silver tones of the Voice cannot be heard. It is only when the outer world becomes utterly dark that the Ray of the Divine Star can be seen by us, for, although It shines eternally, yet it is only when the glaring sunlight of so-called life is eclipsed that we can at first perceive It.

Later, that Star will shine with such a Light that "if the splendour of a thousand suns were to blaze out together in the sky, that might resemble the glory of that Mahātma,"[6] and not all earth's tumult will be able to deafen us to the majestic rhythm of that Voice, that Voice that reverberates throughout

[4]*Light of Asia,* iv.
[5]*Brihadāranyaka Upanishad,* ii, 4.
[6]Gita, xi, 12.

the Eternities as the tides of Being thunder upon the beaches of the worlds.

But the time for those glories is not yet. At first the Light is but a dim Star twinkling faintly within and the Voice is but the sound of a nightingale "chanting a song of parting to its mate."[7] Therefore it is that, before the bright Path of the Sun can be trodden, the aspirant must enter the valley of gloom, must close his eyes and ears to the light and laughter of life, and must realise in sorrow that all that he is and all that he has is nothing, before he can see and know in joy that within his heart is the All.

"Casting away his bow and arrows, Arjuna sank down on the chariot, his mind overborne by grief," and thus, in dejection and sorrow, closes the first chapter of the Gita and the first stage of the Path.

[7]*Voice of the Silence.*

william quan judge (translator) _____

FROM THE *Bhagavad Gita*

As has been mentioned, the principal speaker in the *Bhagavad Gita* is Krishna, who is an incarnation of the Blessed One, the God of gods. In the original Sanskrit the entire *Gita* is in verse; hence the title: "The Song (*Gita*) of God (*Bhagavad*)."

CHAPTER 1

OM!

DHRITARASHTRA   Tell me, O Sañjaya, what the people of my own party and those of Pāndu, who are assembled at Kurukshetra resolved upon war, have been doing.

SAÑJAYA   King Duryodhana, having just beheld the army of the Pāndus drawn up in battle array, went to his preceptor and spoke these words:

"Behold! O Master, the mighty army of the sons of Pāndu drawn up by thy pupil, the clever son of Drupada. In it are warriors with great bows, equal to Bhīmَ and Arjuna in battle, namely, Yuyudhāna, and Virāta, and Durpada on his great car; Dhrishtaketu, Chekitāna, and the valiant king of Kāśi, and Purujit, and Kuntibhoja, with Śaibya, chief of men; Yadhāmanyu the strong, and Uttamauja the brave; the son of Subhadrā, and all the sons of Draupadī, too, in their huge chariots. Be acquainted also with the names of those of our party who are the most distinguished. I will mention a few of those who are amongst my generals, by way of example. There is thyself, my Preceptor, and Bhīshma, Karna, and Kripa, the conqueror in battle, and Aśvatthāma, and Vikarna, and the son of Somadatta, with others in vast numbers, who for my service risk their life. They are all of them practiced in the use of arms, armed with divers weapons, and experienced in every mode of fight. This army of ours, which is commanded by Bhīshma, is not sufficient, while their forces, led by Bhīma, are sufficient. Let all the generals, according to their respective divisions, stand at their posts, and one and all resolve Bhīshma to support."

The ancient chief, brother of the grandsire of the Kurus, then, to raise the spirits of the Kuru chief, blew his shell, sounding like the lion's roar; and instantly innumerable shells and other warlike instruments were sounded on all sides, so that the clangor was excessive. At this time Krishna and Arjuna, standing in a splendid chariot drawn by white horses, also sounded their shells, which were of celestial form: the name of the one which Krishna blew was Pañchajanya, and that of Arjuna was called Devadatta — "the gift of the Gods." Bhīma, of terrific power, blew his capacious shell, Paundra; and Yudhishthira, the royal son of Kuntī, sounded Ananta-Vijaya; Nakula and Sahadeva blew their shells also, the one called Sughosha, the other Manipushpaka. The prince of Kāśi, of the mighty bow; Śikhandī, Dhrishtadyumna, Virāta, Sātyaki, of invincible arm; Drupada and the sons of his royal daughter; Krishna, with the son of Subhadrā, and all the other chiefs and nobles, blew also their respective shells, so that their shrill-sounding voices pierced the hearts of the Kurus and re-echoed with a dreadful noise from heaven to earth.

Then Arjuna, whose crest was Hanumān, perceiving that the sons of Dhritarāshtra stood ready to begin the fight, and that the flying of arrows had commenced, having raised his bow, addressed these words to Krishna:

ARJUNA "I pray thee, Krishna, cause my chariot to be placed between the two armies, that I may behold who are the men that stand ready, anxious to commence the battle; with whom it is I am to fight in this ready field; and who they are that are here assembled to support the evil-minded son of Dhritarāshtra in the battle."

SAÑJAYA Krishna being thus addressed by Arjuna, drove the chariot, and, having caused it to halt in the space between the two armies, bade Arjuna cast his eyes towards the ranks of the Kurus, and behold where stood the aged Bhīshma, and Drona, with all the chief nobles of their party. Standing there Arjuna surveyed both the armies, and beheld, on either side, grandsires, uncles, cousins, tutors, sons, and brothers, near relations, or bosom friends; and when he had gazed for awhile and beheld all his kith and kin drawn up in battle array, he was moved by extreme pity, and, filled with despondency, he thus in sadness spoke:

ARJUNA "Now, O Krishna, that I have beheld my kindred thus standing anxious for the fight, my members fail me, my countenance withereth, the hair standeth on end upon my body, and all my frame trembleth with horror! Even Gāndīva, my bow, slips from my hand, and my skin is parched and dried up. I am not able to stand; for my mind, as it were, whirleth round, and I behold on all sides adverse omens. When I shall have destroyed my kindred, shall I longer look for happiness? I wish not for victory, Krishna; I want not pleasure; for what are dominion and the enjoyments of life, or even life itself, when those for whom dominion, pleasure, and enjoyment were to be coveted have abandoned life and fortune, and stand here in the field ready for the battle? Tutors, sons and fathers, grandsires and grandsons, uncles and nephews, cousins, kindred, and friends! Although they would kill me, I wish not to fight them: no, not even for the dominion of the three regions of the universe, much less for this little earth! Having killed the sons of Dhritarāshtra, what pleasure, O thou who art prayed to by mortals, can we enjoy? Should we destroy them, tyrants though they are, sin would take refuge with us. It therefore behooveth us not to kill such near relations as these. How, O Krishna, can we be happy hereafter, when we have been the murderers of our race? What if they, whose minds are depraved by the lust of power, see no sin in the extirpation of their race, no crime in the murder of their friends, is that a reason why we should not resolve to turn away from such a crime—we who abhor the sin of extirpating our own kindred? On the destruction of a tribe the ancient virtue of the tribe and family is lost; with the loss of virtue, vice and impiety overwhelm the whole of a race. From the influence of impiety the females of a family grow vicious; and from women that are become vicious are born the spurious caste called Varna-Sankara. Corruption of caste is a gate of hell, both for these destroyers of a tribe and for those who survive; and their forefathers, being deprived of the ceremonies of cakes and water offered to their manes, sink into the infernal regions. By the crimes of the destroyers of a tribe and by those who cause confusion of caste, the family virtue and the virtue of a whole tribe are forever done away with; and we have read in sacred writ, O Krishna, that a sojourn in hell awaits those mortals whose generation hath lost its virtue. Woe is me! What a great crime are we prepared to commit! Alas! that from the desire for sovereignty and pleasure we stand here ready to slay our own kin! I would rather patiently suffer that the sons of Dhritarāshtra, with their weapons in their hands, should come upon me, and, unopposed, kill me unresisting in the field.''

SANJAYA   When Arjuna had ceased to speak, he sat down in the chariot between the two armies; and, having put away his bow and arrows, his heart was overwhelmed with despondency.

CHAPTER 2

SANJAYA   Krishna, beholding him thus influenced by compunction, his eyes overflowing with a flood of tears, and his heart oppressed with deep affliction, addressed him in the following words:

KRISHNA   "Whence, O Arjuna, cometh upon thee this dejection in matters of difficulty, so unworthy of the honorable, and leading neither to heaven nor to glory? It is disgraceful, contrary to duty, and the foundation of dishonor. Yield not thus to unmanliness, for it ill-becometh one like thee. Abandon, O tormenter of thy foes, this despicable weakness of thy heart, and stand up.''

ARJUNA   "How, O slayer of Madhu, shall I with my shafts contend in battle against such as Bhīshma and Drona, who of all men are most worthy of my respect? For it were better to beg my bread about the world than be the murderer of my preceptors, to whom such awful reverence is due. Were I to destroy such friends as these, I should partake of possessions, wealth, and pleasures polluted with their blood. Nor can we tell whether it would be better that we should defeat them, or they us. For those drawn up, angrily confronting us—and after whose death, should they perish by my hand, I would not wish to live—are the sons and people of Dhritarāshtra. As I am of a disposition which is affected by compassion and the fear of doing wrong, I ask thee which is it better to do. Tell me that distinctly! I am thy disciple; wherefore instruct in my duty me who am under thy tuition; for my understanding is confounded by the dictates of my duty, and I see nothing that may assuage the grief which drieth up my faculties, although I were to obtain a kingdom without a rival upon earth, or dominion over the hosts of heaven.''

SAÑJAYA Arjuna having thus spoken to Krishna, became silent, saying: ''I shall not fight, O Govinda.'' Krishna, tenderly smiling, addressed these words to the prince thus standing downcast between the two armies:

KRISHNA ''Thou grievest for those that may not be lamented, whilst thy sentiments are those of the expounders of the letter of the law. Those who are wise in spiritual things grieve neither for the dead nor for the living. I myself never was not, nor thou, nor all the princes of the earth; nor shall we ever hereafter cease to be. As the lord of this mortal frame experienceth therein infancy, youth, and old age, so in future incarnations will it meet the same. One who is confirmed in this belief is not disturbed by anything that may come to pass. The senses, moving toward their appropriate objects, are producers of heat and cold, pleasure and pain, which come and go and are brief and changeable; these do thou endure, O son of Bharata! For the wise man, whom these disturb not and to whom pain and pleasure are the same, is fitted for immortality. There is no existence for that which does not exist, nor is there any non-existence for what exists. By those who see the truth and look into the principles of things, the ultimate characteristic of these both is seen. Learn that He by whom all things were formed is incorruptible, and that no one is able to effect the destruction of IT which is inexhaustible. These finite bodies, which envelop the souls inhabiting them, are said to belong to Him, the eternal, the indestructible, unprovable Spirit, who is in the body: wherefore, O Arjuna, resolve to fight. The man who believeth that it is this Spirit which killeth, and he who thinketh that it may be destroyed, are both alike deceived; for it neither killeth nor is it killed. It is not a thing of which a man may say, 'It hath been, it is about to be, or is to be hereafter'; for it is without birth and meeteth not death; it is ancient, constant, and eternal, and is not slain when this its mortal frame is destroyed. How can the man who believeth that it is incorruptible, eternal, inexhaustible, and without birth, think that it can either kill or cause to be killed? As a man throweth away old garments and putteth on new, even so the dweller in the body, having quitted its old mortal frames, entereth into others which are new. The weapon divideth it not, the fire burneth it not, the water corrupteth it not, the wind drieth it not away; for it is indivisible, inconsumable, incorruptible, and is not to be dried away: it is eternal, universal, permanent, immovable; it is invisible, inconceivable, and unalterable; therefore, knowing it to be thus, thou shouldst not grieve. But whether thou believest it to be of eternal birth and duration, or that it dieth with the body, still thou hast no cause to lament it. Death is certain to all things which are born, and rebirth to all mortals; wherefore it doth not behoove thee to grieve about the inevitable. The antenatal state of beings is unknown; the middle state is evident; and their state after death is not to be discovered. What in this is there to lament? Some regard the indwelling spirit as a wonder, whilst some speak and others hear of it with astonishment; but no one realizes it, although he may have heard it described. This spirit can never be destroyed in the mortal frame which it inhabiteth, hence it is unworthy for thee to be troubled for all these mortals. Cast but thine eyes towards the duties of thy particular tribe, and it will ill become thee to tremble. A soldier of the Kshatriya[1] tribe hath no duty superior to lawful war, and just to thy wish the door of heaven is found open before thee, through this glorious unsought fight which only fortune's favored soldiers may obtain. But if thou wilt not perform the duty of thy calling and fight out the field, thou wilt abandon thy natural duty and thy honor, and be guilty of a crime. Mankind will speak of thy ill fame as infinite, and for one who hath been respected in the world ill fame is worse than death. The generals of the armies will think that thy retirement from the field arose from fear, and even amongst those by whom thou wert wont to be thought great of soul thou shalt become despicable. Thine enemies will speak of thee in words which are unworthy to be spoken, depreciating thy courage and abilities; what can be more dreadful than this! If thou art slain thou shalt attain heaven; if victorious, the world shall be thy reward; wherefore, son of Kuntī, arise with determination fixed for the battle. Make pleasure and pain, gain and loss, victory and defeat, the same to thee, and then prepare for battle, for thus and thus alone shalt thou in action still be free from sin.

"Thus before thee has been set the opinion in accordance with the Sānkhya doctrine, speculatively; now hear what it is in the practical, devotional one, by means of which, if fully imbued therewith, thou shalt forever burst the bonds of Karma and rise above them. In this system of Yoga no effort is wasted, nor are there any evil consequences, and even a little of this practice delivereth a man from great risk. In this path there is only one single object, and this of a steady, constant nature; but widely-branched is the faith and infinite are the objects of those who follow not this system.

"The unwise, delighting in the controversies of the Vedas, tainted with worldly lusts, and preferring a transient enjoyment of heaven to eternal absorption, whilst they declare there is no other reward, pronounce, for the attainment of worldly riches and enjoyments, flowery sentences which prom-

---

[1] Kshatriya is the second or military caste of India.

ise rewards in future births for present action, ordaining also many special ceremonies the fruit of which is merit leading to power and objects of enjoyment. But those who thus desire riches and enjoyment have no certainty of soul and least hold on meditation. The subject of the Vedas is the assemblage of the three qualities. Be thou free from these qualities, O Arjuna! Be free from the 'pairs of opposites' and constant in the quality of Sattva, free from worldly anxiety and the desire to preserve present possessions, self-centered and uncontrolled by objects of mind or sense. As many benefits as there are in a tank stretching free on all sides, so many are there for a truth-realizing Brahman in all the Vedic rites.

"Let, then, the motive for action be in the action itself, and not in the event. Do not be incited to actions by the hope of their reward, nor let thy life be spent in inaction. Firmly persisting in Yoga, perform thy duty, O Dhananjaya,[2] and laying aside all desire for any benefit to thyself from action, make the event equal to thee, whether it be success or failure. Equal-mindedness is called Yoga.

"Yet the performance of works is by far inferior to mental devotion, O despiser of wealth. Seek an asylum, then, in this mental devotion, which is knowledge; for the miserable and unhappy are those whose impulse to action is found in its reward. But he who by means of Yoga is mentally devoted dismisses alike successful and unsuccessful results, being beyond them; Yoga is skill in the performance of actions: therefore do thou aspire to this devotion. For those who are thus united to knowledge and devoted, who have renounced all reward for their actions, meet no rebirth in this life, and go to that eternal blissful abode which is free from all disease and untouched by troubles.

"When thy heart shall have worked through the snares of delusion, then thou wilt attain to high indifference as to those doctrines which are already taught or which are yet to be taught. When thy mind once liberated from the Vedas shall be fixed immovably in contemplation, then shalt thou attain to devotion."

ARJUNA   "What, O Keśava,[3] is the description of that wise and devoted man who is fixed in contemplation and confirmed in spiritual knowledge? What may such a sage declare? Where may he dwell? Does he move and act like other men?"

KRISHNA   "A man is said to be confirmed in spiritual knowledge when he forsaketh every desire which entereth into his heart, and of himself is happy and content in the Self through the Self. His mind is undisturbed in adversity; he is happy and contented in prosperity, and he is a stranger to anxiety, fear,

---

[2]Dhananjaya—despiser of wealth.
[3]Keśava—he whose rays manifest themselves as omniscience—a name of Krishna.

CHAPTER ONE / *Hinduism*

and anger. Such a man is called a Muni.[4] When in every condition he receives each event, whether favorable or unfavorable, with an equal mind which neither likes nor dislikes, his wisdom is established, and, having met good or evil, neither rejoiceth at the one nor is cast down by the other. He is confirmed in spiritual knowledge, when, like the tortoise, he can draw in all his senses and restrain them from their wonted purposes. The hungry man loseth sight of every other object but the gratification of his appetite, and when he is become acquainted with the Supreme, he loseth all taste for objects of whatever kind. The tumultuous senses and organs hurry away by force the heart even of the wise man who striveth after perfection. Let a man, restraining all these, remain in devotion at rest in me, his true self; for he who hath his senses and organs in control possesses spiritual knowledge.

"He who attendeth to the inclinations of the senses, in them hath a concern; from this concern is created passion, from passion anger, from anger is produced delusion, from delusion a loss of the memory, from the loss of memory loss of discrimination, and from loss of discrimination loss of all! But he who, free from attachment or repulsion for objects, experienceth them through the senses and organs, with his heart obedient to his will, attains to tranquillity of thought. And this tranquil state attained, therefrom shall soon result a separation from all troubles; and his mind being thus at ease, fixed upon one object, it embraceth wisdom from all sides. The man whose heart and mind are not at rest is without wisdom or the power of contemplation; who doth not practice reflection, hath no calm; and how can a man without calm obtain happiness? The uncontrolled heart, following the dictates of the moving passions, snatcheth away his spiritual knowledge, as the storm the bark upon the raging ocean. Therefore, O great-armed one, he is possessed of spiritual knowledge whose senses are withheld from objects of sense. What is night to those who are unenlightened is as day to his gaze; what seems as day is known to him as night, the night of ignorance. Such is the self-governed Sage!

"The man whose desires enter his heart, as waters run into the unswelling passive ocean, which, though ever full, yet does not quit its bed, obtaineth happiness; not he who lusteth in his lusts.

"The man who, having abandoned all desires, acts without covetousness, selfishness, or pride, deeming himself neither actor nor possessor, attains to rest. This, O son of Priathā, is dependence upon the Supreme Spirit, and he who possesseth it goeth no more astray; having obtained it, if therein established at the hour of death, he passeth on to Nirvāna in the Supreme."

CHAPTER 3

ARJUNA   "If according to thy opinion, O giver of all that men ask, knowledge

[4]Muni—a wise man.

is superior to the practice of deeds, why then dost thou urge me to engage in an undertaking so dreadful as this? Thou, as it were with doubtful speech, confusest my reason; wherefore choose one method amongst them by which I may obtain happiness and explain it unto me.''

KRISHNA   "It hath before been declared by me, O sinless one, that in this world there are two modes of devotion: that of those who follow the Sānkhya, or speculative science, which is the exercise of reason in contemplation; and that of the followers of the Yoga school, which is devotion in the performance of action.

"A man enjoyeth not freedom from action from the non-commencement of that which he hath to do; nor doth he obtain happiness from a total abandonment of action. No one ever resteth a moment inactive. Every man is involuntarily urged to act by the qualities which spring from nature. He who remains inert, restraining the senses and organs, yet pondering with his heart upon objects of sense, is called a false pietist of bewildered soul. But he who having subdued all his passions performeth with his active faculties all the duties of life, unconcerned as to their result, is to be esteemed. Do thou perform the proper actions: action is superior to inaction. The journey of thy mortal frame cannot be accomplished by inaction. All actions performed other than as sacrifice unto God make the actor bound by action. Abandon, then, O son of Kuntī, all selfish motives, and in action perform thy duty for him alone. When in ancient times the lord of creatures had formed mankind, and at the same time appointed his worship, he spoke and said: 'With this worship, pray for increase, and let it be for you Kāmadhuk, the cow of plenty, on which ye shall depend for the accomplishment of all your wishes. With this nourish the Gods, that the Gods may nourish you; thus mutually nourishing ye shall obtain the highest felicity. The Gods being nourished by worship with sacrifice, will grant you the enjoyment of your wishes. He who enjoyeth what hath been given unto him by them, and offereth not a portion unto them, is even as a thief.' But those who eat not but what is left of the offerings shall be purified of all their transgressions. Those who dress their meat but for themselves eat the bread of sin, being themselves sin incarnate. Beings are nourished by food, food is produced by rain, rain comes from sacrifice, and sacrifice is performed by action. Know that action comes from the Supreme Spirit who is one; wherefore the all-pervading Spirit is at all times present in the sacrifice.

"He who, sinfully delighting in the gratification of his passions, doth not cause this wheel thus already set in motion to continue revolving, liveth in vain, O son of Prithā.

"But the man who only taketh delight in the Self within, is satisfied with that and content with that alone, hath no selfish interest in action. He hath no interest either in that which is done or that which is not done; and there is not, in all things which have been created, any object on which he may place dependence. Therefore perform thou that which thou hast to do, at all times unmindful of the event; for the man who doeth that which he hath to do, without attachment to the result, obtaineth the Supreme. Even by action Janaka and others attained perfection. Even if the good of mankind only is considered by thee, the performance of thy duty will be plain; for whatever is practiced by the most excellent men, that is also practiced by others. The world follows whatever example they set. There is nothing, O son of Pritha, in the three regions of the universe which it is necessary for me to perform, nor anything possible to obtain which I have not obtained; and yet I am constantly in action. If I were not indefatigable in action, all men would presently follow my example, O son of Pritha. If I did not perform actions these creatures would perish; I should be the cause of confusion of castes, and should have slain all these creatures. O son of Bharata, as the ignorant perform the duties of life from the hope of reward, so the wise man, from the wish to bring the world to duty and benefit mankind, should perform his actions without motives of interest. He should not create confusion in the understandings of the ignorant, who are inclined to outward works, but by being himself engaged in action should cause them to act also. All actions are effected by the qualities of nature. The man deluded by ignorance thinks, 'I am the actor.' But he, O strong-armed one! who is acquainted with the nature of the two distinctions of cause and effect, knowing that the qualities act only in the qualities, and that the Self is distinct from them, is not attached in action.

"Those who have not this knowledge are interested in the actions thus brought about by the qualities; and he who is perfectly enlightened should not unsettle those whose discrimination is weak and knowledge incomplete, nor cause them to relax from their duty.

"Throwing every deed on me, and with thy meditation fixed upon the Higher Self, resolve to fight, without expectation, devoid of egotism and free from anguish.

"Those men who constantly follow this my doctrine without reviling it, and with a firm faith, shall be emancipated even by actions; but they who revile it and do not follow it are bewildered in regard to all knowledge, and perish, being devoid of discrimination.

"But the wise man also seeketh for that which is homogeneous with his own nature. All creatures act according to their natures; what, then, will restraint effect? In every purpose of the senses are fixed affection and dislike. A wise man should not fall in the power of these two passions, for they are the enemies of man. It is better to do one's own duty, even though it be devoid of excellence, than to perform another's duty well. It is better to perish in the performance of one's own duty; the duty of another is full of danger."

ARJUNA "By what, O descendant of Vrishni, is man propelled to commit offenses; seemingly against his will and as if constrained by some secret force?"

KRISHNA   "It is lust which instigates him. It is passion, sprung from the quality of *rajas*,[5] insatiable, and full of sin. Know this to be the enemy of man on earth. As the flame is surrounded by smoke, and a mirror by rust,[6] and as the womb envelops the foetus, so is the universe surrounded by this passion. By this—the constant enemy of the wise man, formed from desire which rageth like fire and is never to be appeased—is discriminative knowledge surrounded. Its empire is over the senses and organs, the thinking principle and the discriminating faculty also; by means of these it cloudeth discrimination and deludeth the Lord of the body. Therefore, O best of the descendants of Bharata, at the very outset restraining thy senses, thou shouldst conquer this sin which is the destroyer of knowledge and of spiritual discernment.

"The senses and organs are esteemed great, but the thinking self is greater than they. The discriminating principle[7] is greater than the thinking self, and that which is greater than the discriminating principle is He.[8] Thus knowing what is greater than the discriminating principle and strengthening the lower by the Higher Self, do thou of mighty arms slay this foe which is formed from desire and is difficult to seize."

CHAPTER 11

ARJUNA   "My delusion has been dispersed by the words which thou for my soul's peace hast spoken concerning the mystery of the Adhyātma—the spirit. For I have heard at full length from thee, O thou whose eyes are like lotus leaves, the origin and dissolution of existing things, and also thy inexhaustible majesty. It is even as thou hast described thyself. O mighty Lord; I now desire to see thy divine form, O sovereign Lord. Wherefore, O Lord, if thou thinkest it may be beheld by me, show me, O Master of devotion, thine inexhaustible Self."

KRISHNA   "Behold, O son of Prithā, my forms by hundreds and by thousands, of diverse kinds divine, of many shapes and fashions. Behold the Ādityas, Vasus, Rudras, Aśvins, and the Maruts, see things wonderful never seen before, O son of Bharata. Here in my body now behold, O Gudākeśa, the whole universe animate and inanimate gathered here in one, and all things else thou hast a wish to see. But as with thy natural eyes thou are not able to see me, I will give thee the divine eye. Behold my sovereign power and might!"

SAÑJAYA   O king, having thus spoken, Hari,[9] the mighty Lord of mysteri-

---

[5]*Rajas* is one of the three great qualities; the driving power of nature; active and bad.
[6]The burnished metal mirrors are here referred to.
[7]The discriminating principle is *Buddhi.*
[8]"He," the Supreme Spirit, the true Ego.
[9]*Hari,* an epithet of Krishna, meaning that he has the power to remove all difficulty.

ous power, showed to the son of Prithā his supreme form; with many mouths and eyes and many wonderful appearances, with many divine ornaments, many celestial weapons upraised; adorned with celestial garlands and robes, anointed with celestial ointments and perfumes, full of every marvelous thing, the eternal God whose face is turned in all directions. The glory and amazing splendor of this mighty Being may be likened to the radiance shed by a thousand suns rising together into the heavens. The son of Pāndu then beheld within the body of the God of gods the whole universe in all its vast variety. Overwhelmed with wonder, Dhananjaya,[10] the possessor of wealth, with hair standing on end, bowed down his head before the Deity, and thus with joined palms[11] addressed him:

ARJUNA "I behold, O God of gods, within thy frame all beings and things of every kind; the Lord Brahmā on his lotus throne, all the Rishis and the heavenly Serpents.[12] I see thee on all sides, of infinite forms, having many arms, stomachs, mouths, and eyes. But I can discover neither thy beginning, thy middle, nor thy end, O universal Lord, form of the universe. I see thee crowned with a diadem and armed with mace and chakra,[13] a mass of splendor, darting light on all sides; difficult to behold, shining in every direction with light immeasurable, like the burning fire or glowing sun. Thou art the supreme inexhaustible Being, the end of effort, changeless, the Supreme Spirit of this universe, the never-failing guardian of eternal law: I esteem thee Purusha,[14] I see thee without beginning, middle, or end, of infinite power with arms innumerable, the sun and moon thy eyes, thy mouth a flaming fire, overmastering the whole universe with thy majesty. Space and heaven, and earth and every point around the three regions of the universe are filled with thee alone. The triple world is full of fear, O thou mighty Spirit, seeing this thy marvelous form of terror. Of the assemblage of the gods some I see fly to thee for refuge, while some in fear with joined hands sing forth thy praise; the hosts of the Maharshis and Siddhas, great sages and saints, hail thee, saying "svasti,"[15] and glorify thee with most excellent hymns. The Rudras, Ādityas, the Vasus, and all those beings—the Sādhyas, Viśvas, the Aśvins, Maruts, and Ushmapas, the hosts of Gandharvas, Yakshas, and Siddhas—all stand gazing on thee and are amazed. All the worlds alike with me are terrified to behold thy wondrous form gigantic, O thou of mighty arms, with many mouths and eyes, with many arms, thighs and feet, with many stomachs and

[10] Arjuna.

[11] This is the Hindu mode of salutation.

[12] These are the Uragās, said to be serpents. But it must refer to the great Masters of Wisdom, who were often called Serpents.

[13] Among human weapons this would be known as the discus, but here it means the whirling wheel of spiritual will and power.

[14] Purusha, the Eternal Person. The same name is also given to man by the Hindus.

[15] This cry is supposed to be for the benefit of the world, and has that meaning.

projecting tusks. For seeing thee thus touching the heavens, shining with such glory, with widely-opened mouths and bright expanded eyes, my inmost soul is troubled and I lose both firmness and tranquillity, O Vishnu. Beholding thy dreadful teeth and thy face like the burning of death, I can see neither heaven nor earth; I find no peace; have mercy, O Lord of gods, thou Spirit of the universe! The sons of Dhritarāshtra with all these rulers of men, Bhīshma, Drona and also Karna and our principal warriors, seem to be impetuously precipitating themselves into thy mouths terrible with tusks; some are seen caught between thy teeth, their heads ground down. As the rapid streams of full-flowing rivers roll on to meet the ocean, even so these heroes of the human race rush into thy flaming mouths. As troops of insects carried away by strong impulse find death in the fire, even so do these beings with swelling force pour into thy mouths for their own destruction. Thou involvest and swallowest all these creatures from every side, licking them in thy flaming lips; filling the universe with thy splendor, thy sharp beams burn, O Vishnu. Reverence be unto thee, O best of Gods! Be favorable! I seek to know thee, the Primeval One, for I know not thy work.''

KRISHNA "I am Time matured, come hither for the destruction of these creatures; except thyself, not one of all these warriors here drawn up in serried ranks shall live. Wherefore, arise! seize fame! Defeat the foe and enjoy the full-grown kingdom! They have been already slain by me; be thou only the immediate agent, O thou both-armed one.[16] Be not disturbed. Slay Drona, Bhīshma, Jayadratha, Karna, and all the other heroes of the war who are really slain by me. Fight, thou wilt conquer all thine enemies.''

SAÑJAYA When he of the resplendent diadem[17] heard these words from the mouth of Keśava,[18] he saluted Krishna with joined palms and trembling with fear, addressed him in broken accents, and bowed down terrified before him.

ARJUNA "The universe, O Hrishīkeśa,[19] is justly delighted with thy glory and is filled with zeal for thy service; the evil spirits are affrighted and flee on all sides, while all the hosts of saints bow down in adoration before thee. And wherefore should they not adore thee, O mighty Being, thou who art greater than Brahmā, who art the first Maker? O eternal God of gods! O habitation of the universe! Thou art the one indivisible Being, and Non-Being, that which is supreme. Thou art the first of Gods, the most ancient Spirit; thou art the final supreme receptacle[20] of this universe; thou art the Knower and that which is

---

[16]Arjuna was a famous archer who could use the celestial bow, Gāndīva, with either hand equally well.

[17]Arjuna wore a brilliant tiara.

[18]Krishna, by another name.

[19]Krishna.

[20]That is, that into which the universe is resolved on the final dissolution.

to be known, and the supreme mansion; and by thee, O thou of infinite form, is this universe caused to emanate. Thou art Vāyu, God of wind, **Agni, God of** fire, Yama, God of death, Varuna, God of waters; thou art the moon; Prajāpati, the progenitor and grandfather, art thou. Hail! hail to thee! Hail to thee a thousand times repeated! Again and again hail to thee! Hail to thee! Hail to thee from before! Hail to thee from behind! Hail to thee on all sides, O thou All! Infinite is thy power and might; thou includest all things, therefore thou art all things!

"Having been ignorant of thy majesty, I took thee for a friend, and have called thee 'O Krishna, O son of Yadu, O friend,' and blinded by my affection and presumption, I have at times treated thee without respect in sport, in recreation, in repose, in thy chair, and at thy meals, in private and in public; all this I beseech thee, O inconceivable Being, to forgive.

"Thou art the father of all things animate and inanimate; thou art to be honored as above the guru himself, and worthy to be adored; there is none equal to thee, and how in the triple worlds could there be thy superior, O thou of unrivaled power? Therefore I bow down and with my body prostrate, I implore thee, O Lord, for mercy. Forgive, O Lord, as the friend forgives the friend, as the father pardons his son, as the lover the beloved. I am well pleased with having beheld what was never before seen, and yet my heart is overwhelmed with awe; have mercy then, O God; show me that other form, O thou who art the dwelling-place of the universe; I desire to see thee as before with thy diadem on thy head, thy hands armed with mace and chakra; assume again, O thou of a thousand arms and universal form, thy four-armed shape!"[21]

KRISHNA "Out of kindness to thee, O Arjuna, by my divine power I have shown thee my supreme form, the universe, resplendent, infinite, primeval, and which has never been beheld by any other than thee. Neither by studying the *Vedas,* nor by alms-giving, nor by sacrificial rites, nor by deeds, nor by the severest mortification of the flesh can I be seen in this form by any other than thee, O best of Kurus. Having beheld my form thus awful, be not disturbed nor let thy faculties be confounded, but with fears allayed and happiness of heart look upon this other form of mine again."

SAÑJAYA Vāsudeva[22] having so spoken reassumed his natural form; and thus in milder shape the Great One presently assuaged the fears of the terrified Arjuna.

ARJUNA "Now that I see again thy placid human shape, O Janārdana,

[21] Arjuna had been accustomed to see Krishna in his four-armed form, not only in the images shown in youth, but also when Krishna came into incarnation, and could therefore look on the four-armed form without fear.

[22] A name of Krishna.

who art prayed to by mortals, my mind is no more disturbed and I am self-possessed.''

KRISHNA ''Thou hast seen this form of mine which is difficult to be perceived and which even the gods are always anxious to behold. But I am not to be seen, even as I have shown myself to thee, by study of the *Vedas,* nor by mortifications, nor alms-giving, nor sacrifices. I am to be approached and seen and known in truth by means of that devotion which has me alone as the object. He whose actions are for me alone, who esteemeth me the supreme goal, who is my servant only, without attachment to the results of action and free from enmity towards any creature, cometh to me, O son of Pāndu.''

Yoga and Samadhi

Swami Prabhavananda (1893–   ) was born Abani Ghosh in India. He received a B.A. from Calcutta University and joined the Ramakrishna Order in 1914. Ordained a swami, he came to the United States and founded Vedanta Societies both in Portland, Oregon (1925), and in Southern California (1929). A prolific author, he translated *The Song of God: Bhagavad Gita, Shankara's Crest-Jewel of Discrimination, How to Know God: The Yoga Aphorisms of Patanjali* (all with Christopher Isherwood) and *The Upanishads* (with Frederick Manchester). Among his other titles are *Religion in Practice, Vedic Religion and Philosophy, Yoga and Mysticism, Eternal Companion,* and *The Sermon on the Mount According to Vedanta.*

The reading selection that follows is drawn principally from "The Yoga of Meditation," with additional passages from "Samadhi or Transcendental Consciousness," both of which essays are in Christopher Isherwood (ed.), *Vedanta for the Western World.*

THE YOGA OF MEDITATION

Meditation is the very center and heart of spiritual life. It matters not whether you are a follower of the path of Karma, or of devotion or knowledge, whether you are a Christian or a Buddhist or a Hindu, sooner or later you have to practice meditation, you have to become absorbed in divine contemplation; there is no other way. You may begin in divergent ways according to your beliefs and temperament, but as you proceed, as you approach the center and heart of religion and religious practice, you come to that center which is called meditation.

The yoga of meditation was propounded by the great Yogi Patanjali. Patanjali was not the founder of this path of meditation. There were already existent different systems of spiritual practices which he studied and followed, and afterwards systematized, edited and compiled into aphoristic form which became known as the Yoga Aphorisms of Patanjali.

The outstanding peculiarity of this philosophy of Patanjali is that what he propounds has nothing to do with any theory or dogma or presupposition. Even whether you believe in God or not does not matter.

Patanjali was one of those philosophers who claimed that belief in God is not a necessary prerequisite for spiritual life. To him religion is experience;

therefore, whether you have theories, or preconceived ideas, whether you believe in God or not, does not matter.

To the seeker after truth, who follows certain principles and makes the experiment, the truth will be revealed, because truth is truth, an existent factor, not anything imaginary, but a matter of fact and experience. Patanjali, however, says that belief in God is one of the means to practice yoga.

What God is, what that Reality is, nobody has been able to express in words. To define God is to limit Him, to finitize Him.

So Patanjali tells us that our belief in God is one of the means, and not the only means, to reach the ultimate Reality, and also gives us various principles and methods of life and procedure to follow for the attainment of that reality. These principles can be accepted and practiced universally by the followers of any path or religion.

Yoga has been defined by Patanjali as the complete control of the waves of the mind. One who can control the waves of the mind attains Yoga, that state when the true nature of the Self becomes revealed.

This control of the waves of the mind is not so simple as it would at first appear. It is a complete transformation of the character, when the mind becomes absolutely pure and tranquil. St. Paul said: "Be ye transformed by the renewal of your own mind." That is it, and this control is the blessedness of purity which Jesus spoke of when He said: "Blessed are the pure in heart for they shall see God." He meant that complete transformation, that complete overhauling of the mind.

In every religion we find the same truth taught, that the Kingdom of God is within; the Reality is to be found within our own Self. As long as we forget this truth, as long as we seek the Reality outside of ourselves so long shall we be disappointed. We must learn to look within.

The question may well be asked, if the Kingdom of God is within, what obstructs our knowledge of that Kingdom? Why do we not experience that Heaven? The obstruction to this knowledge is the restlessness of the mind due to the waves or impressions that have accumulated there. There are innumerable impressions in the mind, because no thought, no action is ever lost. We send out a thought of love or a thought of hatred, and this thought creates a peculiar impression in the mind. A thought may be forgotten, but it is never lost. It leaves an impression in the mind. So we see that the mind is filled with countless impressions, not only of this life but of many past lives, and to control these impressions of the mind which we have accumulated by the very nature of our existence would seem a tremendous task.

These innumerable impressions have been classified by Patanjali into five divisions—the five causes of impurity that exist in the mind. The first is *avidya*, ignorance, which causes us to forget our true nature, and hides the vision of the real Self. From ignorance springs *ego*. With the sense of ego arise *attachment* or attraction, *repulsion* and the *will to live*. Buddha calls this *will to live, tanha,* or thirst for life and enjoyment. Christ referred to this thirst when He said: "He that loveth his life shall lose it."

These are the impurities, the impressions, the waves that exist in the mind and obstruct our vision of the Reality, our entrance into the Kingdom of God.

To show us how to overcome these distractions and achieve that blessed purity through which the truth of God may be revealed in our own souls, Patanjali evolved a system which he called the eight-limbed Yoga. These eight limbs are: *yama, niyama* (which include the ethical practices), *asana* (posture), *pranayama* (regulation of breath), *pratyahara* (the indrawing of the senses from sense objects), *dharana* (concentration), *dhyana* (meditation), and *samadhi* (absorption).

Before explaining these limbs of Yoga, it would be well to explain in brief the ideal of ethical life as taught by the Hindu seers. There have been scholars in the West who have brought charge against the Hindu philosophy that ethics play no important part in the religion of India: whereas, on the contrary, the Hindu philosophers and mystics clearly state that, in order to have the transcendental experience of the Reality, though it is necessary to go beyond both good and evil, beyond ethics, moral life is the very foundation of spiritual life. Nevertheless, we must rise above this foundation. This does not mean that we become unmoral. Just as a flower gives out fragrance without any consciousness of doing so, but because it is fragrant by its very nature, in the same way our natures must become such that we do what is good and moral without any consciousness of being good and moral; we become moral because holiness has become a part of our very nature. This is what is meant by transcending ethical life.

As a house that is built upon quicksand cannot stand, neither can a spiritual life stand unless it is built firmly on the rock foundation of ethical and moral life. All great spiritual teachers insist, however, the spiritual life is something far greater, far grander, far nobler than moral life.

Now let us consider *yama,* the first of these eight limbs of yoga. Yama includes *ahimsa* (not hurting any creature), *satya* (truthfulness), *asteya* (non-stealing), *brahmacharya* (chastity), and *aparigraha* (non-covetousness). In order that we can practice the virtue of *ahimsa,* we must not hurt any creature by word, thought or deed; we must learn to feel unity, oneness and sympathy with every living being.

Next comes *satya,* truthfulness in thought, word and deed. Speak the truth but do not tell a harsh truth. We must always consider why we are speaking the truth; is it to help or to hurt another? To tell a harsh truth which would hurt another is to go against the very first principle, *ahimsa,* and it is unethical. Truth must always be agreeable and beneficial.

Non-stealing comes next. This may seem quite strange to many, because the habit of stealing as we understand it belongs to a very few selfish individuals. Few of us would actually steal the possessions of another. Yet, according to Patanjali, we are all thieves at heart, every one of us. How? Every time we label anything as ours and call it our own, we are stealing. Nothing belongs to us. Everything belongs to Prakriti—nature. The idea of ownership comes through ignorance. Non-stealing therefore means the ideal of non-possession.

The next ideal that follows is *chastity, continence*. To attain the heights of spiritual realization there must be the practice of continence in thought, word and deed.

Then comes *non-covetousness*. We must covet nothing, possess nothing. These constitute the ethical practices of life.

To know about the ethical practices, to grasp their importance intellectu-ally is not enough. We must practice them. But the question is, how? We are all creatures of habit. If we are good it is because we have formed the habit of being good; if we are bad, we are bad in spite of ourselves, it has become our habit. Therefore, in order to rid ourselves of this present bundle of habits we have to create a new bundle of habits, which brings us to the next step:

Niyama consists of the practices of *purity, contentment, austerity,* and *self-surrender*.

The first of these regular habits which must be formed is *purity,* which means purification, both external and internal. External purification is a simple matter as we know. We bathe every day as a matter of course, but with little or no thought behind the action. Now our daily bathing must become a purification ceremony; the temple of God must be consciously purified that the God within may become manifest. That is the ideal of external purification.

As the body becomes unclean if it is not cleansed each day, so also does the mind. Therefore we must practice *inner purification* every day. Within everyone of us there is the sense of ego, of pride, jealousy, hatred, etc. The method of this inner purification by which we may be cleansed of these impurities is to feel the presence of the Divine within, and to feel that all the impurities and all ignorance have been consumed by that Presence. This must become a daily habit; we must feel that Presence, and meditate upon It.

Next comes *contentment*. Whenever conditions do not suit us we want to change them. We feel sure that if we but change our environment everything will be different, and we shall be happy. Outward conditions can never be changed. We cannot change the weather, so what do we do? We adapt ourselves to it. If it is cold outside we change the condition in the home. In the same way we must change our inner condition. The outward conditions exist because of the inner condition. Change that, reform yourself and the whole world becomes reformed. Before you try to reform another reform yourself.

Study is the next regular habit to be formed. By study is not meant merely the reading of books. The study of different books, of different scriptures and different philosophies is very good for a beginner, but when once we take to the spiritual life seriously and have a conclusive intellectual understanding, then study must be only of such as will help contemplation. Study also means *Japam,* or the repetition of the sacred word and meditation on its meaning. This practice of study brings great purity of heart.

Then comes the regular habit of *surrendering ourselves to the Reality.* Though you may not know what that Reality is, you must feel that there is a Reality, an infinite power, and you must surrender yourself to that. If you believe in God, surrender yourself to Him—every day. Make this self-surrender a regular habit.

The foregoing principles are the foundation of spiritual life.

The first step in the higher practices to be followed is called *Asana* or posture. Posture has been defined by Patanjali as that which is firm and pleasant. There are no gymnastics in this practice. The only principle is that the upper part of the body must be kept straight. As one proceeds, as one grows and there comes certain spiritual unfoldment, many experiences will be felt coming through the spiritual nerve in the spine. Therefore, the spine must be kept perfectly straight.

The next practice is known as *Pranayama* or regulation of breath. Breath controls thought. When you are restless, when you are angry, watch your breath. When you are calm, tranquil, watch your breath. As you watch your breathing, you will notice that there are different rhythms at different times, according to your thoughts. When you feel love you will see that the breath is different than when you feel anger or hatred. Therefore, Patanjali tells us that if we can change the regulation of our breath we can gain control over our thoughts, and to do this he gave certain methods for regulating the breath which would bring calmness and tranquility in our thoughts.

Pratyahara which is the next practice has been beautifully described by Sri Krishna in the Bhagavad-Gita: "When, like the tortoise withdrawing its limbs, he can withdraw his senses from their objects, then his wisdom becomes steady." The secret of this practice is that we must learn to be attached and at the same time detached. We must be able to apply our minds to whatever we do, and yet be able to withdraw the mind completely at will. When the tortoise withdraws its limbs nothing from outside can hurt it, so when we learn to withdraw our minds from sense objects they are freed from distracting thoughts. For this practice of *Pratyahara* Patanjali has given certain instructions and rules which, if followed, will lead to that "steady wisdom."

Now we come to the practice of *concentration.* Concentration does not mean fixing one's gaze upon any external object. It means we have to concentrate upon the Reality which is within. Within this body—which is the temple of God—there are spiritual centers of consciousness, not imaginary, but very real, and it is upon one or the other of these centers of consciousness that we have to concentrate.

For the practice of concentration it is very necessary to follow the instructions of a *Guru* or teacher who has known and realized these spiritual centers: and to follow these instructions one must have faith in the words of the teacher. Faith is an important factor in every department of life. Just as a student of physics, for instance, must have faith in the words of the professor until he has experimented and attained certain results for himself, so must the spiritual aspirant have faith in the words of his Guru, until he has experimented and attained certain results. The teacher will instruct him according to his growth and development, and if these instructions are followed faithfully and perseveringly, the aspirant will attain definite experiences for himself.

Patanjali did not insist upon one object of concentration for everybody, but suggested different forms to suit the beliefs and tendencies of the individual. One suggestion he gives is to concentrate upon the effulgent light which is within the heart. Another suggestion is to concentrate upon the heart of a perfected soul.

Patanjali also speaks of the knowledge which sometimes comes in dreams. These dreams are rare indeed, and in the heart of the spiritual aspirant who gets such a dream there is created a deep and lasting impression, and he points out that one blessed with such a dream could make that the object of his concentration.

Thus there are many ideals upon which to concentrate, depending upon the growth and the temperament of the individual. It is difficult for the student to decide for himself which ideal he should adopt. Concentration can never be learned from the study of books. There is not one method for all; what may help one may harm another. Therefore, the need of a spiritual teacher cannot be too strongly emphasized.

The next stage is reached through the practice of concentration. It is called *Dhyana,* meditation. Through the practice of meditation the mind flows towards the one object of concentration without a break.

The mind by its very nature is always in a state of flux. One thought follows another constantly. It is possible of course to limit the mind to one certain subject of thought. For instance, one may meditate upon the life of Christ or any great soul, or upon the ideas expressed in a beautiful poem, but that is not what is meant by meditation, though such practices are helpful aids to meditation. The mind is still in a flux, moving in a larger space, following a series of thoughts.

The practice of meditation is to hold the mind to one thought. In the beginning other thoughts will intrude, gaps will be created, but again it must be applied to the one thought, until gradually the gaps will be lessened and there will be no more intervals; the one thought will continue uninterruptedly. Just as each point of the electric current, though separate, flows in one continuous stream and produces a flickerless light, or just as oil being poured from one vessel to another does not break, so when the mind flows toward the object of concentration, toward the spiritual ideal, without break or interval, there comes that state known as *Dhyana* which has been translated as meditation or contemplation.

This state brings us to the next stage known as *Samadhi*. Ordinarily the word samadhi has been used to mean the transcendental consciousness, the revelation, but Patanjali uses it as a stage of absorption, the door that leads to the transcendental experience.

This samadhi means identity with the object of meditation. Thus we see how important it is that the object of our meditation be divine and uplifting.

From this absorption we reach the stage in spiritual progress which is technically called *Samyama,* which means the complete forgetfulness of everything external or internal; there remains nothing but the object of meditation. Time itself is annihilated.

At this point there come visions, spiritual experiences and sometimes occult powers. Many aspirants in the course of their progress stop here. When these visions and spiritual experiences come, when they experience that joy which the Christian mystics call ecstasy, they feel there is nothing greater, nothing superior to be experienced. So they stop, and make no further progress.

Visions, spiritual ecstasies, occult powers are great in themselves, but there is a realm far beyond visions and ecstasies. Occult powers may come, but if you are tempted to use them, the door to spiritual progress is closed and you have to learn the secrets by which these powers can be controlled, and become once more a simple and humble seeker.

By transcending these powers and visions, the door to spiritual life is opened, and we experience *samadhi,* the transcendental consciousness. We come face to face with the Reality; then we too can say with Christ, "I and my Father are one."

SAMADHI OR TRANSCENDENTAL CONSCIOUSNESS

[In the words of Sri Ramakrishna,] "When one attains samadhi (transcendental consciousness), then only comes to him the knowledge of Brahman. Then only does he attain the vision of God. In that ecstatic realisation all thoughts cease. Perfectly silent he becomes. No power of speech is left by which to express Brahman. He comes back from his ecstatic consciousness, and thereafter, it may be, talks: but he talks only that he may teach humanity. The bee buzzes until it lights in the heart of the flower. It becomes quiet as soon as it begins to sip the honey. Then again, after it has its fill, when it is at last drunk with honey, it makes a sweet, murmuring sound."

. . .

Samadhi is chiefly of two kinds: savikalpa, lower samadhi, and nirvikalpa, the higher kind. In the lower form of samadhi, there exists the sense of "I" as distinct though not separate from God, wherein is realised the personal aspect of God. God the Creator, God the Father, God the Mother, God the Friend, God the Beloved—any or all of these aspects of God may then be realised in their completeness.

Nirvikalpa is the higher form of samadhi, wherein no sense of the separate ego is left, and there is realised the oneness of the self with God, the Impersonal. In that experience, there is neither *I* nor *you,* neither *one* nor *many.* Patanjali defines it as the cessation of all waves of the mind, that is, the complete stoppage of all thoughts and impressions of the mind, conscious and subconscious. Patanjali advises that the means to the attainment of this samadhi is the practice of concentration through which may come cessation of all the waves of the mind. The Christian mystic Meister Eckhart mentions the same method of attainment in "Mystische Schriften." "Memory, understanding, will all tend toward diversity and multiplicity of thought, therefore you must leave them all aside, as well as perception, ideation, and everything in which you find yourself or seek yourself. Only then can you experience this new birth—otherwise never."[1]

. . .

The crucial test of nirvikalpa or of savikalpa samadhi is that when a man returns from samadhi, he is not the same ignorant man as before his experience, for his whole life has become transformed with the attainment of illumination, and he now lives always in God and experiences the joy and freedom of a man in whom the divine side of his nature is expressed. After unconscious trance, on the contrary, or after deep sleep wherein the ego seems to have vanished, when a man returns to normal consciousness, his ego returns and he is the same ignorant individual. In contrast to unconscious trance and sleep, nirvikalpa samadhi is full of light. It is consciousness *itself,* without the contents of consciousness, such as of me or thee or of outer objects.

That this contentless consciousness is not the same as the unconsciousness which occurs in sleep is brought out very clearly in the Upanishads.

The Mandukya Upanishad, for instance, speaks of the three states of consciousness—waking, dreaming, and dreamless sleep—and in contrast to these is the Turiya—the fourth, the transcendental consciousness. The Chandogya Upanishad, by the famous story of how Indra and Virochana went to learn of the knowledge of Brahman from the teacher Prajapati, reveals how the unconsciousness of deep sleep serves no purpose in the knowledge of the Self, but that if we would attain our goal we must rise above and beyond the three states into the Turiya, the fourth.

[1]Quoted by Professor Pratt in "Religious Consciousness."

What Vedanta Means to Me

Christopher Isherwood (1904–   ) is a distinguished man of letters. His novels include *The Last of Mr. Norris, Down There on a Visit, The World in the Evening,* and *Prater Violet.* A collection of his stories entitled *Goodbye to Berlin* inspired the play and movie "I Am a Camera" and, more recently, the musical "Cabaret." Born in England, Isherwood came to the United States in 1939 and settled in California, where he has long been associated with the Vedanta Society of Southern California. In addition to collaborating with Swami Prabhavananda on translations of Hindu scriptures, he has written the biography *Ramakrishna and His Disciples.* He edited and contributed to the anthologies *Vedanta for the Western World* and *Vedanta for Modern Man.*

"What Vedanta Means to Me" was originally published in the magazine *Vedanta and the West* (September–October, 1951). Reprinted in pamphlet form, it has been widely distributed.

In order to say what Vedanta means to me, I shall have to explain what it was that I meant by 'religion' in the days before I learned about Vedanta. To do this will be to describe a number of prejudices, some of them silly, some of them not without a certain justification, all of them held by thousands of fairly intelligent men and women in the world today.

By 'religion' I meant the Christian religion, or, more specifically, the Church of England, into which I had been received by baptism when I was a baby. Other Christian sects I had been encouraged to suspect or despise; the Catholics were traditionally 'un-English' and involved in sinister international politics, the Nonconformists were 'common' and lower-middle-class. As for the Hindus, Buddhists, and Mohammedans, they were merely picturesque heathens who wailed from minarets, spun prayer-wheels, and flung themselves under juggernauts. You couldn't count them as being 'religious' at all. Such were the attitudes I inherited as a member of an upper-class land-owning Protestant family living on a small island which was, at that time, the centre of an enormous colonial empire.

Infant baptism provides dissatisfied Christians with a ready-made grudge against the Church. Why, they ask, should you be conscripted into it before you are old enough to have a will of your own? The Church's answer is to offer the ceremony of confirmation, which enables the adolescent individual to make a voluntary act of accepting his already imposed Christianity. Unfortu-

Christopher Ishwerwood, "What Vedanta Means to Me." From *Vedanta and the West* (September–October, 1951). Reprinted by permission of the Vedanta Society of Southern California.

nately, in my case, as in the case of many others, confirmation was not entirely voluntary. At my school, it was tacitly understood that you would be confirmed, and a good deal of moral pressure was exerted to make you agree to this. You could refuse, of course—one of my best friends did—but that took considerable independence and courage. I hadn't enough of either virtue. So I agreed.

Soon after my confirmation, I began to discover that I had, as they say, 'lost my faith'; or, to be more exact, I discovered that I had never had any. By the time I was twenty, I declared myself an atheist, and I remained in that conviction for the next fifteen years. I said privately and publicly that I loathed religion; that it was evil, superstitious, reactionary nonsense; and I warmly agreed that it was indeed 'the opium of the people'. These statements were taken as a matter of course by my friends, who were, with one or two exceptions, all of the same opinion as myself. It was therefore seldom necessary for me even to discuss the subject in any detail. However, if I had done so, I should probably have argued more or less as follows.

In the first place, I hated Christianity because it was dualistic. God, high in heaven, ruled with awful justice over us, His abject and sinful subjects, here below. He was good. We were bad. We were so bad that, when He sent His Son down to live amongst us, we promptly crucified Him. For this act, committed nearly two thousand years ago, we had to beg forgiveness, generation after generation. If we begged hard enough and were sincerely sorry, we might qualify for heaven, instead of being sent to hell, where we naturally belonged.

Who wouldn't rebel against the idea of such a God? Who wouldn't denounce His tyranny? Who wouldn't protest against the utter unfairness of this test to which He had subjected us: one short earthly life in which to earn salvation or deserve damnation? Who wouldn't detest His Son, who had come to us as a sort of agent provocateur, wearing a hypocritical mask of meekness, in order to tempt us to betray Him? Such were the questions I asked myself, and my answer was that only slaves could accept such a religion. If hell existed (which I anyhow denied) then I would be proud to be damned. In hell one could expect to meet every honest and courageous man or woman who had ever lived.

Then again, Christianity (as I saw it) seemed to consist almost entirely of 'don'ts'; everything you could possibly want to do was forbidden as a sin. My family has a Puritan background, and there is enough Puritanism in me to set up a conflict whenever the word 'sin' is mentioned. I rebelled so violently against these 'don'ts' that I regarded every sin as an act of defiance and hence almost as a virtue. I would have been apt, for example, to smoke opium *on principle* if I had been able to get any.

When I looked at the Christians around me (I knew hardly any serious ones, and none of them intimately) I wilfully saw them as a collection of dreary, canting hypocrites, missionaries of ignorance and reaction, who opposed all social reform lest it should endanger the status and privileges of their Church, and all personal freedom lest people should discover for themselves that the 'don'ts' were unnecessary. I disliked their stiff Sunday clothes and grave Sunday faces, their sickly humility, their lack of humour, their special tone when speaking of God, their selfish prayers for rain, health, and national victory in war. I assumed, quite arbitrarily, that every Christian was secretly longing to indulge in forbidden pleasures, and that he was only prevented from doing so by his cowardice, ugliness, or impotence. I delighted in stories which told of clergymen being seduced, and monks or nuns having clandestine love affairs. My venom against them knew no bounds. At the same time, I declared that I myself needed no religion to keep me moral, according to my own standards. I would try to behave properly, not because of the Ten Commandments or a fear of hell, but because I freely chose to follow the advice of my conscience.

A psychiatrist could probably tell me to what extent these exaggerated reactions were produced by a father-complex, or by certain experiences in early childhood, resulting in a dread of authority. That does not matter, as far as my present subject is concerned. For my prejudices were not merely neurotic; they had a direct relation to actual facts. There are some aspects of organized religion which I still believe to be bad. What I am trying to show is that my view of religion, during that period of my life, was distorted and very ill-informed.

. . .

To suggest that I accepted Vedanta philosophy just because it convinced me intellectually would be to claim that I am a creature of pure reason. And, of course, I am nothing of the kind. We none of us are. The really decisive convictions of our lives are never arrived at through the power of arguments alone. The right teacher must appear at exactly the right moment in the right place; and his pupil must be in the right mood to accept what he teaches. But a description of the way in which these various factors combined, in my own case, to influence me, would be too long and complicated, and too frankly autobiographical, to fit the kind of article I am writing. All I can do here is to list some of the reasons why Vedanta appealed to me—reminding the reader, at the same time, that these reasons are only reasons; they really do not explain anything.

1. Vedanta is non-dualistic. Psychologically, this was of the greatest importance to me; because of my fear and hatred of God as the father-figure. I don't think I could ever have swallowed a philosophy that *began* with dualism. Vedanta began by telling me that I was the Atman, and that the Atman was Brahman; the Godhead was my own real nature, and the real

nature of all that I experienced as the external, surrounding universe. Having taught me this, it could go on to explain that this one immanent and transcendent Godhead may project all sorts of divine forms and incarnations which are, as the Gita says, its 'million faces'. To the eyes of this world, the One appears as many. Thus explained, dualism no longer seemed repulsive to me; for I could now think of the gods as mirrors in which man could dimly see what would otherwise be quite invisible to him, the splendour of his own immortal image. By looking deeply and single-mindedly into these mirrors, you could come gradually to know your own real nature; and, when that nature, that Atman, was fully known and entered into, the mirror-gods would no longer be necessary, since the beholder would be absolutely united with his reflection. This approach to dualism via non-dualism appealed so strongly to my temperament that I soon found myself taking part enthusiastically in the cult of Sri Ramakrishna, and even going into Christian churches I happened to be passing, to kneel for a while before the altar. Obviously, I had been longing to do this for years. I was a frustrated devotee.

2. The non-dualism of Vedanta taught me a better understanding of the true function of prayer. If I am really the Atman, the Godhead, then it is obvious that my basic prayer must be for self-knowledge. I must pray to be released from the delusion that I am this Christopher Isherwood, this little transient ego-personality. I must pray to know myself. 'O, my real Self, reveal yourself to me': how can I possibly ask more—or less?

This was a novel and most inspiring idea to me, for I had always supposed that religious people limited their prayer to material petitions. You asked for worldly advantages and possessions on behalf of yourself, your neighbours, or your nation. This 'give-me' attitude seemed, and still seems to me tragically presumptuous and silly. How can we dare to suppose that we—these restricted ego-intelligences—know what we really need? Of course, I was totally wrong in thinking that all Christians prayed like this, but my misconception had at least a partial excuse. For there are many people—some of them priests and ministers—who make wholesale demands for divine intervention in their personal, business, and political affairs, omitting Christ's saving clause, 'nevertheless, not as I will but as thou wilt'.

3. Vedanta provides us with a cosmology, an account of the working and nature of the universe, which seems extremely reasonable and which is, in fact, largely in agreement with the findings and hypotheses of modern science. Vedanta cosmology does not pretend to explain the Absolute, but it does draw a clear line around the area of our ignorance. And its theory of karma and reincarnation is a very helpful and unsentimental approach to our problems as human beings. By assuming that we have had previous lives and that the consequences of our actions in them determine the conditions of our present birth, it saves us from the danger of blaming God for what we are and thus deciding that we are all helpless puppets.

4. However, Vedanta merely offers this cosmology as an intellectual aid to spiritual practice, not as a necessary article of faith. Vedanta is not dogmatic. Previously, I had always thought of religion in terms of dogmas, commandments, and declarative statements. The teacher expounded the truth, the dogmatic ultimatum; you, the pupil, had only to accept it in its entirety. (Your sole alternative was to reject it altogether.) But Vedanta made me understand, for the first time, that a practical, working religion is experimental and empirical. You are always on your own, finding things out for yourself in your individual way. Vedanta starts you off with a single proposition, which is no more than a working hypothesis. 'The Atman can be known. We say so, on the basis of the past experience of others. But we don't ask you to believe that. We don't want you to believe anything. All we ask is that you make a serious effort to get some spiritual experience for yourself, using the techniques of meditation which we shall teach you. If, after a reasonable period of time, you have found nothing, then never mind Ramakrishna, never mind Christ, never mind anybody; you are entitled to say boldly that our teaching is a lie, and we shall respect you for saying so. We have no use for blind believers.' Who could decline such a challenge? 'This,' I said to myself, 'is what religion is really all about. Religion isn't a course of passive indoctrination; it is an active search for awareness. Why didn't somebody ever tell me so before?' The question was, of course, absurdly unfair. I had been 'told' this innumerable times. Every moment of my conscious existence had contained within itself this riddle—'What is life for?'—and its answer: 'To learn what life means.' Every event, every encounter, every person and object I had met, had restated question and answer in some new way. Only I hadn't been ready to listen. Now, as I came to learn something about practical mysticism, I was greatly astonished to find how closely the recorded experiences of Hindu and Christian (not to mention Buddhist and Taoist, Sufi and Jewish) mystics are inter-related. And thus another group of my anti-Christian prejudices was liquidated, along with my ignorance.

5. Vedanta does not emphasize the vileness of man's mortal nature or the enormity of sin. It dwells, rather, on the greatness of man's eternal nature, and refuses to dignify sin by allowing it too much dramatic value. Vivekananda warns us not to think of ourselves as sinners; such seeming humility can easily degenerate into masochism. We shall do better to remind ourselves continually of what is godlike in man, and try to be worthy of that. As for our sins, we shall not atone for them by sentimental orgies of contrition. What we have to understand is simply this: every act has consequences, good or bad or mixed, and we are paid for everything we think or say or do with an absolute, automatic fairness, neither too much nor too little. If we persist in performing acts which strengthen the ego-sense (i.e. sins) then we shall find that we are becoming increasingly alienated from knowledge of the Atman within us. Maybe we imagine we want to perform such acts? Maybe we think we would

rather live in ignorance of the Atman? Very well, we are at liberty to try it. The will is free. The wheel of rebirth will not cease to revolve; and if we demand another thousand or ten thousand lives of human experience, it will provide them. In the end we shall learn better, we shall know what we really want; and when we know, when we turn towards the Atman, we shall find it, as always, there. And there will be nobody but ourselves to blame for all the delay.

This is the message of Vedanta as Vivekananda preaches it. Like many others before me, I heard it with an almost incredulous joy. Here, at last, was a man who believed in God and yet dared to condemn the indecent grovellings of the sin-obsessed Puritans I had so much despised in my youth. I loved him at once, for his bracing self-reliance, his humour, and his courage. He appealed to me as the perfect anti-Puritan hero: the enemy of Sunday religion, the destroyer of Sunday gloom, the shocker of prudes, the breaker of traditions, the outrager of conventions, the comedian who taught the deepest truths in idiotic jokes and frightful puns. That humour had its place in religion, that it could actually be a mode of spiritual self-expression, was a revelation to me; for, like every small boy of Puritan upbringing, I had always longed to laugh out loud and make improper noises in church.

further reading

M. Hiriyanna's *The Essentials of Indian Philosophy* (1949) is a clear and admirable survey of Hindu thought by an eminent scholar. Another excellent introduction is Swami Nikhilananda's *Hinduism: Its Meaning for the Liberation of the Spirit* (1959).

Nikhilananda's *The Gospel of Sri Ramakrishna* (1942) and *Vivekananda: A Biography* (1953) are studies of two of the outstanding Hindus of modern times.

The thinking of the best-known Hindu of this century may be found in Mahatma Gandhi's *An Autobiography; or The Story of My Experiments with Truth* (1927). Selections from Gandhi's writings appear in *My Religion* (1955), edited by Bharatan Kumarappa.

Geoffrey Parrinder's *Upanishads, Gita and Bible* (1962) is an illuminating comparative study of Hindu and Christian scriptures.

Useful collections of materials are Kenneth Morgan (ed.), *The Religion of the Hindus* (1953); Sarvepalli Radhakrishnan and Charles A. Moore (eds.), *A Sourcebook in Indian Philosophy* (1957); and Wm. Theodore de Bary *et al.* (eds.), *Sources of Indian Tradition* (1958).

Lizelle Reymond's *To Live Within* (1971) is a first-hand account of life and ideas in a Himalayan hermitage.

Translations often differ significantly, and it is informative to compare them. Important translations of the Upanishads include those by Juan Mascaró, *The Upanishads* (1965); Radhakrishnan, *The Principal Upanishads* (1953); Robert E. Hume, *The Thirteen Principal Upanishads* (2d ed., 1931); Nikhilananda, *The Upanishads* (1949);and Swami Prabhavananda and Frederick Manchester, *The Upanishads: Breath of the Eternal* (1948).

Notable translations of the *Bhagavad Gita* are those by Mascaró, *The Bhagavad Gita* (1962); W. D. P. Hill, *The Bhagavad Gita* (1928); Franklin Edgerton, *The Bhagavad Gita* (1944); Radhakrishnan, *The Bhagavadgita* (1948); Nikhilananda, *The Bhagavad Gita* (1944); and Prabhavananda and Isherwood, *The Song of God: Bhagavad-Gita* (1945).

Buddhism

the path to nirvana

introduction _____

To become a Buddhist is to follow the way of a man named Siddhartha Gautama. It is to resolve to do what he did: to become a Buddha, an Enlightened One. The way leads from *dukkha,* the irremediable suffering that is the most fundamental condition of life, to Nirvana, an ineffable bliss.

The religion begins, then, with Siddhartha. Born a prince in Northern India about 560 B.C., he lived amid luxury, married, and had a son. At the age of twenty-nine, deeply disturbed by questions about the meaning of human existence, he left his palace and family to seek his answers in the "forest." A six-year period of arduous searching finally resulted in an ecstatic awakening. Tempted to retire to his own Nirvana, he determined instead to teach, and thereby was Buddhism born. He taught for forty-five years, dying at the age of eighty in 480 B.C.

The heart of the Buddha's teaching is contained in the Four Noble Truths, described in this chapter by Heinrich Zimmer. The description is framed in psychological terms, as it should be, for the Buddha's analysis of man's predicament was a masterpiece of insight into the nature of the self and its "pathological blend of unfulfilled cravings, vexing longings, fears, regrets, and pains." Man is, in effect, mentally and emotionally ill; the Eighfold Path is a prescription.

The teachings of Buddha did not appear in written form until approximately the first century B.C., at which time there were already several schools of Buddhist thought. Most of those schools developed their own sets of scriptures, and thus there is no authoritative canon. The scriptures of one group, the Theravada, are known as the Pali Canon (after the dialect in which it is written), and it has been favored by Western scholars. Edward Conze, however, has pointed out that this canon is not older than others, and Pali was not the dialect of the Buddha.* The Pali Canon, divided into three "baskets" (*pitaka*), is called "The Three Baskets" (*Tripitaka*). In an edition published in Tokyo in 1924, a Chinese version of the *Tripitaka* filled 100 volumes of 1,000 pages each.

The essay by Christmas Humphreys discusses the doctrines of Karma and Rebirth, ideas drawn from Hinduism but modified by the Buddhists. The law of Karma is a law of causation in the moral realm: "Whatsoever a man reaps, . . . that has he also sown." Combined with the belief in Rebirth, there is here one of the best answers to the perennial "Problem of Evil," the problem of seeming

Thirty Years of Buddhist Studies (Columbia: University of South Carolina Press, 1968), pp. 3-5.

CHAPTER TWO / *Buddhism*

injustices that abound in the lives of men. But just as the present is a result of the past, so the future is created by the present. Hence Karma is not fatalism: "Work out your own salvation with diligence" were the last words of the Buddha.

The early divisions of thought that developed in Buddhism resulted in a schism that may be broadly characterized as conservative and liberal (or Southern and Northern). The conservative wing came to be known as the Theravada ("The Way of the Elders"); the liberal school was the Mahayana ("The Great Vessel"). The Theravadins stressed self-mastery and wisdom. The ideal was the world-renouncing, liberated *Arahat* (saint), who, as the *Khaggavisana Sutta* urged, chose to "walk alone like a rhinoceros." The Mahayanists emphasized the way of compassion for others and the ideal of the Bodhisattva, whose portrait is drawn in these pages by Ananda Coomaraswamy. The Mahayana was "the overflowing of Buddhism from the limits of the Order into the life of the world," and it was a path more attractive to the majority than were the rigorous austerities of the *Arahat.*

The meditational practices of Buddhism are designed to lead the individual to his Enlightenment. They are, therefore, of the utmost importance, comparable to what yoga is to the Hindu and prayer to the Christian. Of some forty standard subjects of meditation, two are especially recommended: friendliness and death. The latter meditation is outlined here by Buddhaghosa.

The chapter concludes with Lobsang Phuntsock Lhalungpa's essay on Tibetan Buddhism (or *Tantrayana,* a name which emphasizes the role played in the religion by those scriptures known as the *Tantras.)*† Tibetan Buddhists accept as the basis of their religion the Four Noble Truths and the other essential doctrines of Theravada Buddhism. Meditation is practiced and the final goal is Nirvana, as it is for all Buddhists. But upon this foundation there arises a superstructure of beliefs as breathtaking as the high peaks and plateaus of Tibet itself.

---

†Tibetan Buddhism is also called *Lamaism,* but that term is misleading. "Lama" is a title of distinction given to some monks in Tibet.

Buddhahood

One of the great scholars of Indian philosophy and art, German-born Heinrich Zimmer (1890–1943) studied at the universities of Munich and Berlin. He was a professor of philology at Heidelberg, worked with Carl Jung at the University of Zurich, and, leaving Germany on the eve of World War II, taught briefly at Oxford. Coming to the United States in 1940, he lectured at Columbia University until shortly before his death. His books include *The Art of Indian Asia* and *Myths and Symbols in Indian Art and Civilization.* The reading selection which follows is from his *Philosophies of India,* a posthumous volume edited by Joseph Campbell.

Buddhism was the only religious and philosophical message of India to spread far beyond the borders of its homeland. Conquering Asia to the north and east, it became in those vast areas the creed of the masses and shaped the civilization for centuries. This tends to conceal the fact that in essence Buddhism is meant only for the happy few. The philosophical doctrine at the root of the numerous fascinating popular features is not the kind of teaching that one would have expected to see made readily accessible to all. In fact, of the numerous answers that have been offered, during the millenniums, in all quarters of the world, as solutions to life's enigmas, this one must be ranked as the most uncompromising, obscure, and paradoxical.

. . .

. . . from the beginning, by the nature of the problem, the doctrine had been meant only for those prepared to hear. It was never intended to interfere with either the life and habits of the multitude or the course of civilization. In time it might even vanish from the world, becoming incomprehensible and meaningless—for the lack of anyone capable of treading the path to understanding; and this, too, would be right. In contrast, in other words, to the other great teachers of mankind (Zarathustra preaching the religious law of Persia; Confucius commenting on the restored system of early Chinese thought; Jesus announcing Salvation to the world) Gautama, the prince of the royal Śākya clan, is known properly as Śākya-muni: the "silent sage (*muni*) of the Śākyas"; for in spite of all that has been said and taught about him, the Buddha remains the symbol of something beyond what can be said and taught.

In the Buddhist texts there is no word that can be traced with unquestionable authority to Gautama Śākyamuni. We glimpse only the enlightening shadow of his personality; yet this suffices to merge us in a spiritual atmosphere that is unique. For though India in his time, half a millennium before Christ, was a veritable treasure-house of magical-religious lore—to our eyes a jungle of mythological systems—the teaching of the Enlightened One offered no mythological vision, either of the present world or of a world beyond, and no tangible creed. It was presented as a therapy, a treatment or cure, for those strong enough to follow it—a method and a process of healing. Apparently Gautama, at least in his terminology, broke from all the popular modes and accepted methods of Indian religious and philosophical instruction. He offered his advice in the practical manner of a spiritual physician, as though, through him, the art of Indian medicine were entering the sphere of spiritual problems—that grand old arena where, for centuries, magicians of every kind had been tapping powers by which they and their disciples lifted themselves to the heights of divinity.

Following the procedure of the physician of his day inspecting a patient, the Buddha makes four statements concerning the case of man. These are the so-called "Four Noble Truths" which constitute the heart and kernel of his doctrine. The first, *All life is sorrowful,* announces that we members of the human race are spiritually unhealthy, the symptom being that we carry on our shoulders a burden of sorrow; the disease is endemic. No discussion of any question of guilt goes with this matter-of-fact diagnosis; for the Buddha indulged in no metaphysical or mythological dissertations. He inquired into the cause of the practical, psychological level, however, hence we have, as the second of the "Four Noble Truths," *The cause of suffering is ignorant craving* (tṛṣṇā).

As in the teaching of the Sāṅkhya,* an involuntary state of mind common to all creatures is indicated as the root of the world-disease. The craving of nescience, not-knowing-better (*avidyā*), is the problem—nothing less and nothing more. Such ignorance is a natural function of the life-process, yet not necessarily ineradicable; no more ineradicable than the innocence of a child. It is simply that we do not know that we are moving in a world of mere conventions and that our feelings, thoughts, and acts are determined by these. We imagine that our ideas about things represent their ultimate reality, and so we are bound in by them as by the meshes of a net. They are rooted in our own consciousness and attitudes; mere creations of the mind; conventional, involuntary patterns of seeing things, judging, and behaving; yet our ignorance accepts them in every detail, without question, regarding them and their contents as the facts of existence. This—this mistake about the true essence of reality—is the cause of all the sufferings that constitute our lives.

The Buddhist analysis goes on to state that our other symptoms (the familiar incidents and situations of our universal condition of non-well being)

*A system of Hindu philosophy which held that existence means suffering.—R.E.

are derivatives, one and all, of the primary fault. The tragedies and comedies in which we get ourselves involved, which we bring forth from ourselves and in which we act, develop spontaneously from the impetus of our innermost condition of non-knowing. This sends us forth in the world with restricted senses and conceptions. Unconscious wishes and expectations, emanating from us in the shape of subjectively determined decisions and acts, transcend the limits of the present; they precipitate for us the future, being themselves determined from the past. Inherited from former births, they cause future births, the endless stream of life in which we are carried along being greater far than the bounds of individual birth and death. In other words, the ills of the individual cannot be understood in terms of the individual's mistakes; they are rooted in our human way of life, and the whole content of this way of life is a pathological blend of unfulfilled cravings, vexing longings, fears, regrets, and pains. Such a state of suffering is something from which it would be only sensible to be healed.

This radical statement about the problems that most of us take for granted as the natural concomitants of existence, and decide simply to endure, is balanced in the doctrine of the Buddha by the third and fourth of the "Four Noble Truths." Having diagnosed the illness and determined its cause, the physician next inquires whether the disease can be cured. The Buddhist prognostication is that a cure is indeed possible; hence we hear: *The suppression of suffering can be achieved;* and the last of the Four Truths prescribes the way: *The way is the Noble Eightfold Path*–Right View, Right Aspiration, Right Speech, Right Conduct, Right Means of Livelihood, Right Endeavor, Right Mindfulness, and Right Contemplation.

The Buddha's thoroughgoing treatment is guaranteed to eradicate the cause of the sickly spell and dream of ignorance, and thus to make possible the attainment of a state of serene, awakened perfection. No philosophical explanation of man or the universe is required, only this spiritual physician's program of psycho-dietetics. And yet the doctrine can hardly appeal to the multitude; for these are not convinced that their lives are as unwholesome as they obviously are. Only those few who not only would like to try, but actually feel acutely a pressing need to undertake some kind of thoroughgoing treatment, would have the will and stamina to carry to the end such an arduous, self-ordained discipline as that of the Buddhist cure.

The way of Gautama Śākyamuni is called the "middle path"; for it avoids extremes. One pair of extremes is that of the outright pursuit of worldly desires, on the one hand, and the severe, ascetic, bodily discipline of such contemporaries of the Buddha as the Jainas, on the other, whose austerity was designed to culminate in annihilation of the physical frame. Another pair of extremes is that of skepticism, denying the possibility of transcendental knowledge, and the argumentative assertion of undemonstrable metaphysical doctrines. Buddhism eschews the blind alleys to either side and conduces to an attitude that will of itself lead one to the transcendental experience. It rejects explicitly *all* of the contending formulae of the intellect, as inadequate either to lead to or to express the paradoxical truth, which reposes far, far beyond the realm of cerebral conceptions.

A conversation of the Buddha, recorded among the so-called "Long Dialogues," enumerates an extended list of the practical and theoretical disciplines by which people master various skills, crafts, and professions, or seek some understanding of their own nature and the meaning of the universe. All are described and then dismissed without criticism, but with the formula: "Such knowledge and opinions, if thoroughly mastered, will lead inevitably to certain ends and produce certain results in one's life. The Enlightened One is aware of all these possible consequences, and also of what lies behind them. But he does not attach much importance to this knowledge. For within himself he fosters another knowledge—the knowledge of cessation, of the discontinuance of worldly existence, of utter repose by emancipation. He has perfect insight into the manner of the springing into existence of our sensations and feelings, and into the manner of their vanishing again with all their sweetness and bitterness, and into the way of escape from them altogether, and into the manner in which, by non-attachment to them through right knowledge of their character, he has himself won release from their spell."[1]

Buddhism attaches no serious importance to such knowledge as entangles men more tightly in the net of life, knowledge that adds a comfortable material or interesting spiritual background to existence and thereby only contributes additional substance to the maintenance of the personality. Buddhism teaches that the value attributed to a thing is determined by the particular pattern of life from which it is regarded and the personality concerned. The weight of a fact or idea varies with the unenlightenment of the observer—his spontaneous commitment to certain spheres of phenomena and ranges of human value. The atmosphere, nay the world, surrounding and overpowering him, is continually being produced from his own unconscious nature, and affects him in terms of his commitment to his own imperfections. Its traits are the phenomenal projections of his inner state of ignorance sent out into the realm of sense-perception and there, as it were, discovered by an act of empirical experience. Hence Buddhism denies, finally, the force and validity of everything that can be known.

A Tibetan author—a Buddhist Dalai-Lama—puts it this way: The one substance, which fundamentally is devoid of qualities, appears to be of various, completely differing flavors, according to the kind of being who tastes it. The same beverage which for the gods in their celestial realm will be the delightful drink of immortality, for men on earth will be mere water, and for the tormented inmates of hell a vile, disgusting liquid which they will be

[1] *Dīgha-nikāya 1.*

loath to swallow even though tortured with intolerable pangs of thirst. The three qualities of, or ways of experiencing, the one substance are here nothing more than the normal effects of three orders of karma. The senses themselves are conditioned by the subjective forces that brought them into being and hold them under strict control. The world without is no mere illusion—it is not to be regarded as nonexistent; yet it derives its enchanting or appalling features from the involuntary inner attitude of the one who sees it. The alluring hues and frightening shadows that form its very tissue are projected reflexes of the tendencies of the psyche.

One lives, in other words, enveloped by the impulses of the various layers of one's own nature, woven in the spell of their specific atmosphere, to which one submits as to an outside world. The goal of the techniques of the Buddhist therapy is to bring this process of self-envelopment to a stop. The living process is likened to a fire burning. Through the involuntary activity of one's nature as it functions in contact with the outer world, life as we know it goes on incessantly. The treatment is the extinction (*nirvāna*) of the fire, and the Buddha, the Awake, is the one no longer kindled or enflamed. The Buddha is far from having dissolved into non-being; it is not He who is extinct but the life illusion—the passions, desires, and normal dynamisms of the physique and psyche. No longer blinded, he no longer feels himself to be conditioned by the false ideas and attendant desires that normally go on shaping individuals and their spheres, life after life. The Buddha realizes himself to be void of the characteristics that constitute an individual subject to a destiny. Thus released from karma, the universal law, he reposes beyond fate, no longer subject to the consequences of personal limitations. What other people behold when they look upon his physical presence is a sort of mirage; for he is intrinsically devoid of the attributes that they venerate and are themselves striving to attain.

. . .

The Buddha's doctrine is called *yāna*. The word means "a vehicle," or, more to the point, "a ferryboat." The "ferryboat" is the principal image employed in Buddhism to render the sense and function of the doctrine. The idea persists through all the differing and variously conflicting teachings of the numerous Buddhist sects that have evolved in many lands, during the long course of the magnificent history of the widely disseminated doctrine. Each sect describes the vehicle in its own way, but no matter how described, it remains always the ferry.

To appreciate the full force of this image, and to understand the reason for its persistence, one must begin by realizing that in everyday Hindu life the ferryboat plays an extremely prominent role. It is an indispensable means of transportation in a continent traversed by many mighty rivers and where bridges are practically nonexistent. To reach the goal of almost any journey one will require a ferry, time and time again, the only possible crossing of the broad and rapid streams being by boat or by a ford. The Jainas called their way of salvation the ford *(tīrtha),* and the supreme Jaina teachers were . . . *Tīrthaṅkaras,* "those making, or providing, a ford." In the same sense, Buddhism, by its doctrine, provides a ferryboat across the rushing river of saṁsāra† to the distant bank of liberation. Through enlightenment *(bodhi)* the individual is transported.

The gist of Buddhism can be grasped more readily and adequately by fathoming the main metaphors through which it appeals to our intuition than by a systematic study of the complicated superstructure, and the fine details of the developed teaching. For example, one need only think for a moment about the actual, everyday experience of the process of crossing a river in a ferryboat, to come to the simple idea that inspires and underlies all of the various rationalized systematizations of the doctrine. To enter the Buddhist vehicle—the boat of the discipline—means to begin to cross the river of life, from the shore of the common-sense experience of non-enlightenment, the shore of spiritual ignorance *(avidyā),* desire *(kāma),* and death *(māra),* to the yonder bank of transcendental wisdom *(vidyā),* which is liberation *(mokṣa)* from this general bondage. Let us consider, briefly, the actual stages involved in any crossing of a river by ferry, and see if we can experience the passage as a kind of initiation-by-analogy into the purport of the stages of the Buddhist pilgrim's progress to his goal.

Standing on the nearer bank, this side the stream, waiting for the boat to put in, one is a part of its life, sharing in its dangers and opportunities and in whatever may come to pass on it. One feels the warmth or coolness of its breezes, hears the rustle of its trees, experiences the character of its people, and knows that its earth is underfoot. Meanwhile the other bank, the far bank, is beyond reach—a mere optical image across the broad, flowing waters that divide us from its unknown world of forms. We have really no idea what it will be like to stand in that distant land. How this same scenery of the river and its two shorelines will appear from the other side we cannot imagine. How much of these houses will be visible among the trees? What prospects up and down the river will unfold? Everything over here, so tangible and real to us at present—these real, solid objects, these tangible forms—will be no more than remote, visual patches, inconsequential optical effects, without power to touch us, either to help or to harm. This solid earth itself will be a visual, horizontal line beheld from afar, one detail of an extensive scenic view, beyond our experience, and of no more force for us than a mirage.

The ferryboat arrives; and as it comes to the landing we regard it with a feeling of interest. It brings with it something of the air of that yonder land which will soon be our destination. Yet when we are entering it we still feel like members of the world from which we are departing, and there is still that

†The world of becoming and change; the endless cycles of birth, death, and rebirth.—R.E.

feeling of unreality about our destination. When we lift our eyes from the boat and boatman, the far bank is still only a remote image, no more substantial than it was before.

Softly the ferryboat pushes off and begins to glide across the moving waters. Presently one realizes that an invisible line has been recently, imperceptibly passed, beyond which the bank left behind is assuming gradually the unsubstantiality of a mere visual impression, a kind of mirage, while the farther bank, drawing slowly nearer, is beginning to turn into something real. The former dim remoteness is becoming the new reality and soon is solid ground, creaking under keel—real earth—the sand and stone on which we tread in disembarking; whereas the world left behind, recently so tangible, has been transmuted into an optical reflex devoid of substance, out of reach and meaningless, and has forfeited the spell that it laid upon us formerly—with all its features, all its people and events—when we walked upon it and ourselves were a portion of its life. Moreover, the new reality, which now possesses us, provides an utterly new view of the river, the valley, and the two shores, a view very different from the other, and completely unanticipated.

Now while we were in the process of crossing the river in the boat, with the shore left behind becoming gradually vaguer and more meaningless—the streets and homes, the dangers and pleasures, drawing steadily away—there was a period when the shoreline ahead was still rather far off too; and during that time the only tangible reality around us was the boat, contending stoutly with the current and precariously floating on the rapid waters. The only details of life that then seemed quite substantial and that greatly concerned us were the various elements and implements of the ferryboat itself: the contours of the hull and gunwales, the rudder and the sail, the various ropes, and perhaps a smell of tar. The rest of existence, whether out ahead or left behind, signified no more than a hopeful prospect and a fading recollection—two poles of unrealistic sentimental association affiliated with certain clusters of optical effects far out-of-hand.

In the Buddhist texts this situation of the people in a ferryboat is compared to that of the good folk who have taken passage in the vehicle of the doctrine. The boat is the teaching of the Buddha, and the implements of the ferry are the various details of Buddhist discipline: meditation, yoga-exercises, the rules of ascetic life, and the practice of self-abnegation. These are the only things that disciples in the vehicle can regard with deep conviction; such people are engrossed in a fervent belief in the Buddha as the ferryman and the Order as their bounding gunwale (framing, protecting, and defining their perfect ascetic life) and in the guiding power of the doctrine. The shoreline of the world has been left behind but the distant one of release not yet attained. The people in the boat, meanwhile, are involved in a peculiar sort of middle prospect which is all their own.

Among the conversations of the Buddha known as the "Medium-length

Dialogues," there appears a discourse on the value of the vehicle of the doctrine. First the Buddha describes a man who, like himself or any of his followers, becomes filled with a loathing of the perils and delights of secular existence. That man decides to quit the world and cross the stream of life to the far land of spiritual safety. Collecting wood and reeds, he builds a raft, and by this means succeeds in attaining the other shore. The Buddha confronts his monks, then, with the question.

"What would be your opinion of this man," asks the Buddha, "would he be a clever man, if, out of gratitude for the raft that has carried him across the stream to safety, he, having reached the other shore, should cling to it, take it on his back, and walk about with the weight of it?"

The monks reply. "No, certainly the man who would do that would not be a clever man."

The Buddha goes on. "Would not the clever man be the one who left the raft (of no use to him any longer) to the current of the stream, and walked ahead without turning back to look at it? Is it not simply a tool to be cast away and forsaken once it has served the purpose for which it was made?"

The disciples agree that this is the proper attitude to take toward the vehicle, once it has served its purpose.

The Buddha then concludes. "In the same way the vehicle of the doctrine is to be cast away and forsaken, once the other shore of Enlightenment (*nirvāna*) has been attained."[2]

The rules of the doctrine are intended for beginners and advanced pupils, but become meaningless for the perfect. They can be of no service to the truly enlightened, unless to serve him, in his role of teacher, as a convenient medium by which to communicate some suggestion of the truth to which he has attained. It was by means of the doctrine that the Buddha sought to express what he had realized beneath the tree as inexpressible. He could communicate with the world through his doctrine and thus help his unprepared disciples when they were at the start, or somewhere in the middle, of the way. Talking down to the level of relative or total ignorance, the doctrine can move the still imperfect yet ardent mind; but it can say nothing any more, nothing ultimately real, to the mind that has cast away darkness. Like the raft, it must be left behind, therefore, once the goal has been attained; for it can thenceforth be no more than an inappropriate burden.

Moreover, not the raft only, but the stream too, becomes void of reality for the one who has attained the other shore. When such a one turns around to look again at the land left behind, what does he see? What *can* one see who has crossed the horizon beyond which there is no duality? He looks—and there *is* no "other shore"; there is no torrential separating river; there is no raft; there is no ferryman; there can have been no crossing of the nonexistent stream.

[2]*Majjhima-Nikāya* 3. 2. 22. 135.

The whole scene of the two banks and the river between is simply gone. There can be no such thing for the enlightened eye and mind, because to see or think of anything as something "other" (a distant reality, different from one's own being) would mean that full Enlightenment had not yet been attained. There can be an "other shore" only for people still in the spheres of dualistic perception; those this side the stream or still inside the boat and heading for the "other shore"; those who have not yet disembarked and thrown away the raft. Illumination means that the delusory distinction between the two shores of a worldly and a transcendental existence no longer holds. There *is* no stream of rebirths flowing between two separated shores: no saṁsāra and no nirvāna.

Thus the long pilgrimage to perfection through innumerable existences, motivated by the virtues of self-surrender and accomplished at the cost of tremendous sacrifices of ego, disappears like a landscape of dreams when one awakes. The long-continued story of the heroic career, the many lives of increasing self-purification, the picture-book legend of detachment won through the long passion, the saintly epic of the way to become a savior —enlightened and enlightening—vanishes like a rainbow. All becomes void; whereas once, when the dream was coming to pass step by step, with ever-recurrent crises and decisions, the unending series of dramatic sacrifices held the soul completely under its spell. The secret meaning of Enlightenment is that this titan-effort of pure soul-force, this ardent struggle to reach the goal by acts, ever-renewed, of beautiful self-surrender, this supreme, long strife through ages of incarnations to attain release from the universal law of moral causation (*karma*)—is without reality. At the threshold of its own realization it dissolves, together with its background of self-entangled life, like a nightmare at the dawn of day.

For the Buddha, therefore, even the notion of nirvāna is without meaning. It is bound to the pairs-of-opposites and can be employed only in opposition to saṁsāra—the vortex where the life-force is spellbound in ignorance by its own polarized passions of fear and desire.

The Buddhist way of ascetic training is designed to conduce to the understanding that there is no substantial ego—nor any object anywhere—that lasts, but only spiritual processes, welling and subsiding: sensations, feelings, visions. These can be suppressed or set in motion and watched at will. The idea of the extinction of the fire of lust, ill will, and ignorance becomes devoid of meaning when this psychological power and point of view has been attained; for the process of life is no longer experienced as a burning fire. To speak seriously, therefore, of nirvāna as a goal to be attained is simply to betray the attitude of one still remembering or experiencing the process as the burning of the fire. The Buddha himself adopts such an attitude only for the teaching of those still suffering, who feel that they would like to make the flames extinct. His famous Fire Sermon is an accommodation, not by any means the final word of the sage whose final word is silence. From the perspective of the Awake, the Illumined One, such opposed verbalizations as nirvāna and samsāra, enlightenment and ignorance, freedom and bondage, are without reference, void of content. That is why the Buddha refused to discuss nirvāna. The pointlessness of the connotations that would inevitably seem to be intended by his words would confuse those trying to follow his mysterious way. They being still in the ferryboat framed of these conceptions and requiring them as devices of transport to the shore of understanding, their teacher would not deny before them the practical function of such convenient terms; and yet would not give the terms weight, either, by discussion. Words like "enlightenment," "ignorance," "freedom," and "entanglement" are preliminary helps, referring to no ultimate reality, mere hints or signposts for the traveler, which serve to point him to the goal of an attitude beyond their own suggestions of a contrariety. The raft being finally left behind, and the vision lost of the two banks and the separating river, then there is in truth neither the realm of life and death nor that of release. Moreover, there is no Buddhism—no boat, since there are neither shores nor waters between. There is no boat, and there is no boatman—no Buddha.

henry clarke warren and paul carus (translators) _____

The Scriptures of Early Buddhism

The selections which follow are typical in both form and content of the scriptures of Buddhism. Sermons such as "The Sermon at Benares" and "The Fire Sermon" identify themselves as having been delivered at a definite place or on a particular occasion. Dialogues featuring someone who questions the Buddha or who requests clarification of concepts (as in "Questions Which Tend Not to Edification") are also common. The dialogue format is especially appropriate for the Socratic-type reasoning that characterized the Buddha's habit of thought. Perhaps most popular are the stories and parables ("The Three Woes" and "The Parable of the Mustard Seed") in which are embedded moral pronouncements.

In spite of deletions by translators and editors, it is still evident that the style of Buddhist scriptures is notable for its repetition of phrases and passages (some are repeated a dozen or more times within the space of a few pages). This repetitiveness is an outgrowth of the oral tradition that transmitted the scriptures for generations; it was an aid to the reciters who had to memorize the material.

THE THREE WOES

[*A famous episode in the traditional account of the life of Buddha, "The Three Woes" tells of Siddhattha's confrontation with the brutal facts of old age, sickness, and death; it was these experiences that led to his search for enlightenment. Although clearly dressed here in the language of legend, the story is no doubt true enough.*]

The palace which the king had given to the prince was resplendent with all the luxuries of India; for the king was anxious to see his son happy.

All sorrowful sights, all misery, and all knowledge of misery were kept away from Siddhattha, for the king desired that no troubles should come nigh him; he should not know that there was evil in the world.

But as the chained elephant longs for the wilds of the jungles, so the prince was eager to see the world, and he asked his father, the king, for permission to do so.

And Suddhodana ordered a jewel-fronted chariot with four stately horses to be held ready, and commanded the roads to be adorned where his son would pass.

The houses of the city were decorated with curtains and banners, and spectators arranged themselves on either side, eagerly gazing at the heir to the throne. Thus Siddhattha rode with Channa, his charioteer, through the streets of the city, and into a country watered by rivulets and covered with pleasant trees.

There by the wayside they met an old man with bent frame, wrinkled face and sorrowful brow, and the prince asked the charioteer: "Who is this? His head is white, his eyes are bleared, and his body is withered. He can barely support himself on his staff."

The charioteer, much embarrassed, hardly dared speak the truth. He said: "These are the symptoms of old age. This same man was once a suckling child, and as a youth full of sportive life; but now, as years have passed away, his beauty is gone and the strength of his life is wasted."

Siddhattha was greatly affected by the words of the charioteer, and he sighed because of the pain of old age. "What joy or pleasure can men take," he thought to himself, "when they know they must soon wither and pine away!"

And lo! while they were passing on, a sick man appeared on the way-side, gasping for breath, his body disfigured, convulsed and groaning with pain.

The prince asked his charioteer: "What kind of man is this?" And the charioteer replied and said: "This man is sick. The four elements of his body are confused and out of order. We are all subject to such conditions: the poor and the rich, the ignorant and the wise, all creatures that have bodies, are liable to the same calamity."

And Siddhattha was still more moved. All pleasures appeared stale to him, and he loathed the joys of life.

The charioteer sped the horses on to escape the dreary sight, when suddenly they were stopped in their fiery course.

Four persons passed by, carrying a corpse; and the prince, shuddering at the sight of a lifeless body, asked the charioteer: "What is this they carry? There are streamers and flower garlands; but the men that follow are overwhelmed with grief!"

The charioteer replied: "This is a dead man: his body is stark; his life is gone; his thoughts are still; his family and the friends who loved him now carry the corpse to the grave."

And the prince was full of awe and terror: "Is this the only dead man," he asked, "or does the world contain other instances?"

With a heavy heart the charioteer replied: "All over the world it is the same.

He who begins life must end it. There is no escape from death."

With bated breath and stammering accents the prince exclaimed: "O worldly men! How fatal is your delusion! Inevitably your body will crumble to dust, yet carelessly, unheedingly, ye live on."

THE SERMON AT BENARES

[*Tradition has it that this sermon was Buddha's first. It announces the "middle path" and the Four Noble Truths.*]

"There are two extremes, O bhikkhus, which the man who has given up the world ought not to follow—the habitual practice, on the one hand, of self-indulgence which is unworthy, vain and fit only for the worldly-minded—and the habitual practice, on the other hand, of self-mortification, which is a painful, useless and unprofitable.

"Neither abstinence from fish or flesh, nor going naked, nor shaving the head, nor wearing matted hair, nor dressing in a rough garment, nor covering oneself with dirt, nor sacrificing to Agni, will cleanse a man who is not free from delusions.

"Reading the Vedas, making offerings to priests, or sacrifices to the gods, self-mortification by heat or cold, and many such penances performed for the sake of immortality, these do not cleanse the man who is not free from delusions.

"Anger, drunkenness, obstinacy, bigotry, deception, envy, self-praise, disparaging others, superciliousness and evil intentions constitute uncleanness; not verily the eating of flesh.

"A middle path, O bhikkhus, avoiding the two extremes, has been discovered by the Tathāgata—a path which opens the eyes, and bestows understanding, which leads to peace of mind, to the higher wisdom, to full enlightenment, to Nirvāna!

. . .

"Now, this, O bhikkhus, is the noble truth concerning suffering:

"Birth is attended with pain, decay is painful, disease is painful, death is painful. Union with the unpleasant is painful, painful is separation from the pleasant; and any craving that is unsatisfied, that too is painful. In brief, bodily conditions which spring from attachment are painful.

"This, then, O bhikkhus, is the noble truth concerning suffering.

"Now this, O bhikkhus, is the noble truth concerning the origin of suffering:

"Verily, it is that craving which causes the renewal of existence, accompanied by sensual delight, seeking satisfaction now here, now there, the craving for the gratification of the passions, the craving for a future life, and the craving for happiness in this life.

"This, then, O bhikkhus, is the noble truth concerning the origin of suffering.

"Now this, O bhikkhus, is the noble truth concerning the destruction of suffering:

"Verily, it is the destruction, in which no passion remains, of this very thirst; it is the laying aside of, the being free from, the dwelling no longer upon this thirst.

"This, then, O bhikkhus, is the noble truth concerning the destruction of suffering.

"Now this, O bhikkhus, is the noble truth concerning the way which leads to the destruction of sorrow. Verily! it is this noble eightfold path; that is to say:

"Right views; right aspirations; right speech; right behavior; right livelihood; right effort; right thoughts; and right contemplation.

"This, then, O bhikkhus, is the noble truth concerning the destruction of sorrow.

THE FIRE SERMON

[*The "fire" of this famous sermon stands in contrast to Nirvana, which is literally a " 'waning away' (as of a flame) or 'cooling off.' "*\]

Then The Blessed One, having dwelt in Uruvelā as long as he wished, proceeded on his wanderings in the direction of Gayā Head, accompanied by a great congregation of priests, a thousand in number, who had all of them aforetime been monks with matted hair. And there in Gayā, on Gayā Head, The Blessed One dwelt, together with the thousand priests.

And there The Blessed One addressed the priests:—

"All things, O priests, are on fire. And what, O priests, are all these things which are on fire?

"The eye, O priests, is on fire; forms are on fire; eye-consciousness is on fire; impressions received by the eye are on fire; and whatever sensation, pleasant, unpleasant, or indifferent, originates in dependence on impressions received by the eye, that also is on fire.

"And with what are these on fire?

"With the fire of passion, say I, with the fire of hatred, with the fire of infatuation; with birth, old age, death, sorrow, lamentation, misery, grief, and despair are they on fire.

"The ear is on fire; sounds are on fire; . . . the nose is on fire; odors are on fire; . . . the tongue is on fire; tastes are on fire; . . . the body is on fire; things tangible are on fire; . . . the mind is on fire; ideas are on fire; . . mind-

---

*Ninian Smart, *Reason and Faiths* (London: Routledge & Kegan Paul, Ltd., 1958), p. 59.

consciousness is on fire; impressions received by the mind are on fire; and whatever sensation, pleasant, unpleasant, or indifferent, orginates in dependence on impressions received by the mind, that also is on fire.

"And with what are these on fire?

"With the fire of passion, say I, with the fire of hatred, with the fire of infatuation; with birth, old age, death, sorrow, lamentation, misery, grief, and despair are they on fire.

"Perceiving this, O priests, the learned and noble disciple conceives an aversion for the eye, conceives an aversion for forms, conceives an aversion for eye-consciousness, conceives an aversion for the impressions received by the eye; and whatever sensation, pleasant, unpleasant, or indifferent, originates in dependence on impressions received by the eye, for that also he conceives an aversion. Conceives an aversion for the ear, conceives an aversion for sounds, . . . conceives an aversion for the nose, conceives an aversion for odors, . . . conceives an aversion for the tongue, conceives an aversion for tastes, . . . conceives an aversion for the body, conceives an aversion for things tangible, . . . conceives an aversion for the mind, conceives an aversion for ideas, conceives an aversion for mind-consciousness, conceives an aversion for the impressions received by the mind; and whatever sensation, pleasant, unpleasant, or indifferent, originates in dependence on impressions received by the mind, for this also he conceives an aversion. And in conceiving this aversion, he becomes divested of passion, and by the absence of passion he becomes free, and when he is free he becomes aware that he is free; and he knows that rebirth is exhausted, that he has lived the holy life, that he has done what it behooved him to do, and that he is no more for this world."

Now while this exposition was being delivered, the minds of the thousand priests became free from attachment and delivered from the depravities.

QUESTIONS WHICH TEND NOT TO EDIFICATION

[*As Heinrich Zimmer noted in the previous essay, the Buddha chose not to discuss metaphysical questions. Later Buddhists, however, made up for his reticence.*]

Thus have I heard.

On a certain occasion The Blessed One was dwelling at Sāvatthi in Jetavana monastery in Anāthapindika's Park. Now it happened to the venerable Māluṅkyāputta, being in seclusion and plunged in meditation, that a consideration presented itself to his mind, as follows:—

"These theories which The Blessed One has left unelucidated, has set aside and rejected,—that the world is eternal, that the world is not eternal, that the world is finite, that the world is infinite, that the soul and the body are identical, that the soul is one thing and the body another, that the saint exists after death, that the saint does not exist after death, that the saint both exists and does not exist after death, that the saint neither exists nor does not exist after death,—these The Blessed One does not elucidate to me. And the fact that The Blessed One does not elucidate them to me does not please me nor suit me. Therefore I will draw near to The Blessed One and inquire of him concerning this matter.

[*Mālunkyāputta presents his questions and states also his resolve to lead the religious life under The Blessed One only if his questions are answered. The Blessed One replies:*]

"Mālunkyāputta, any one who should say, 'I will not lead the religous life under The Blessed One until The Blessed One shall elucidate to me either that the world is eternal, or that the world is not eternal, . . . or that the saint neither exists nor does not exist after death;'—that person would die, Mālunkyāputta, before The Tathāgata had ever elucidated this to him.

"It is as if, Mālunkyāputta, a man had been wounded by an arrow thickly smeared with poison, and his friends and companions, his relatives and kinsfolk, were to procure for him a physician or surgeon; and the sick man were to say, 'I will not have this arrow taken out until I have learnt whether the man who wounded me belonged to the warrior caste, or to the Brahman caste, or to the agricultural caste, or to the menial caste.'

"Or again he were to say, 'I will not have this arrow taken out until I have learnt the name of the man who wounded me, and to what clan he belongs.'

"Or again he were to say, 'I will not have this arrow taken out until I have learnt whether the man who wounded me was tall, or short, or of the middle height.'   . . .

"The religious life, Mālunkyāputta, does not depend on the dogma that the world is eternal; nor does the religous life, Mālunkyāputta, depend on the dogma that the world is not eternal. Whether the dogma obtain, Mālunkyāputta, that the world is eternal, or that the world is not eternal, there still remain birth, old age, death, sorrow, lamentation, misery, grief, and despair, for the extinction of which in the present life I am prescribing.

. . .

"Accordingly, Mālunkyāputta, bear always in mind what it is that I have not elucidated, and what it is that I have elucidated. And what, Mālunkyāputta, have I not elucidated? I have not elucidated, Mālunkyāputta, that the world is eternal; I have not elucidated that the world is not eternal; I have not elucidated that the world is finite; I have not elucidated that the world is infinite; I have not elucidated that the soul and the body are identical; I have not elucidated that the soul is one thing and the body another; I have not elucidated that the saint does not exist after death; I have not elucidated that the saint both exists and does not exist after death; I have not elucidated that the saint neither exists nor does not exist after death. And why, Mālunkyāputta, have I not elucidated this? Because, Mālunkyāputta, this profits not, nor has to do with the fundamentals of religion, nor tends to aversion, absence of passion, cessation, quiescence, the supernatural faculties, supreme wisdom, and Nirvana; therefore have I not elucidated it.

"And what, Mālunkyāputta, have I elucidated? Misery, Mālunkyāputta, have I elucidated; the origin of misery have I elucidated; the cessation of misery have I elucidated; and the path leading to the cessation of misery have I elucidated. And why, Mālunkyāputta, have I elucidated this? Because, Mālunkyāputta, this does profit, has to do with the fundamentals of religions, and tends to aversion, absence of passion, cessation, quiescence, knowledge, supreme wisdom, and Nirvana; therefore have I elucidated it. Accordingly, Mālunkyāputta, bear always in mind what it is that I have not elucidated, and what it is that I have elucidated."

Thus spake The Blessed One; and, delighted, the venerable Mālunkyāputta applauded the speech of The Blessed One.

THE MIDDLE DOCTRINE

The world, for the most part, O Kaccāna, holds either to a belief in being or to a belief in non-being. But for one who in the light of the highest knowledge, O Kaccāna, considers how the world arises, belief in the non-being of the world passes away. And for one who in the light of the highest knowledge, O Kaccāna, considers how the world ceases, belief in the being of the world passes away. The world, O Kaccāna, is for the most part bound up in a seeking, attachment, and proclivity [for the groups], but a priest does not sympathize with this seeking and attachment, nor with the mental affirmation, proclivity, and prejudice which affirms an Ego. He does not doubt or question that it is only evil that springs into existence, and only evil that ceases from existence, and his conviction of this fact is dependent on no one beside himself. This, O Kaccāna, is what constitutes Right Belief.

That things have being, O Kaccāna, constitutes one extreme of doctrine; that things have no being is the other extreme. These extremes, O Kaccāna, have been avoided by The Tathāgata, and it is a middle doctrine he teaches:—

On ignorance depends karma;
On karma depends consciousness;
On consciousness depend name and form;
On name and form depend the six organs of sense;
On the six organs of sense depends contact;
On contact depends sensation;
On sensation depends desire;

On desire depends attachment;
On attachment depends existence;
On existence depends birth;
On birth depend old age and death, sorrow, lamentation, misery, grief, and despair.
Thus does this entire aggregation of misery arise.

But on the complete fading out and cessation of ignorance ceases karma;
On the cessation of karma ceases consciousness;
On the cessation of consciousness cease name and form;
On the cessation of name and form cease the six organs of sense;
On the cessation of the six organs of sense ceases contact;
On the cessation of contact ceases sensation;
On the cessation of sensation ceases desire;
On the cessation of desire ceases attachment;
On the cessation of attachment ceases existence;
On the cessation of existence ceases birth;
On the cessation of birth cease old age and death, sorrow, lamentation, misery,
grief, and despair. Thus does this entire aggregation of misery cease.

THE THREE CHARACTERISTICS

Whether Buddhas arise, O priests, or whether Buddhas do not arise, it remains a fact and the fixed and necessary constitution of being, that all its constituents are transitory. This fact a Buddha discovers and masters, and when he has discovered and mastered it, he announces, teaches, publishes, proclaims, discloses, minutely explains, and makes it clear, that all the constituents of being are transitory.

Whether Buddhas arise, O priests, or whether Buddhas do not arise, it remains a fact and the fixed and necessary constitution of being, that all its constituents are misery. This fact a Buddha discovers and masters, and when he has discovered and mastered it, he announces, teaches, publishes, proclaims, discloses, minutely explains, and makes it clear, that all the constituents of being are misery.

Whether Buddhas arise, O priests, or whether Buddhas do not arise, it remains a fact and the fixed and necessary constitution of being, that all its elements are lacking in an Ego. This fact a Buddha discovers and masters, and when he has discovered and mastered it, he announces, teaches, publishes, proclaims, discloses, minutely explains, and makes it clear, that all the elements of being are lacking in an Ego.

THE DURATION OF LIFE

Strictly speaking, the duration of the life of a living being is exceedingly brief, lasting only while a thought lasts. Just as a chariot-wheel in rolling rolls only at one point of the tire, and in resting rests only at one point; in exactly the same way, the life of a living being lasts only for the period of one thought. As soon as that thought has ceased the being is said to have ceased. As it has been said:—

"The being of a past moment of thought has lived, but does not live, nor will it live.

"The being of a future moment of thought will live, but has not lived, nor does it live.

"The being of the present moment of thought does live, but has not lived, nor will it live."

THERE IS NO EGO

[*This and the following several excerpts are from the* Milindapanha (*"The Questions of Milinda"*), *an early Pali work. It is composed of the discussions between the Buddhist monk Nāgasena and the Greek King Milinda, who ruled in northwestern India in the second century* B.C.]

Then drew near Milinda the king to where the venerable Nāgasena was; and having drawn near, he greeted the venerable Nāgasena; and having passed the compliments of friendship and civility, he sat down respectfully at one side. And the venerable Nāgasena returned the greeting; by which, verily, he won the heart of king Milinda.

And Milinda the king spoke to the venerable Nāgasena as follows:—

"How is your reverence called? Bhante, what is your name?"

"Your majesty, I am called Nāgasena; my fellow-priests, your majesty, address me as Nāgasena: but whether parents give one the name Nāgasena, or Sūrasena, or Vīrasena, or Sīhasena, it is, nevertheless, your majesty, but a way of counting, a term, an appellation, a convenient designation, a mere name, this Nāgasena; for there is no Ego here to be found."

Then said Milinda the king,—

"Listen to me, my lords, ye five hundred Yonakas, and ye eighty thousand priests! Nāgasena here says thus: 'There is no Ego here to be found.' Is it possible, pray, for me to assent to what he says?"

And Milinda the king spoke to the venerable Nāgasena as follows:—

"Bhante Nāgasena, if there is no Ego to be found, who is it then furnishes you priests with the priestly requisites,—robes, food, bedding, and medicine, the reliance of the sick? who is it makes use of the same? who is it keeps the precepts? who is it applies himself to meditation? who is it realizes the Paths, the Fruits, and Nirvana? who is it destroys life? who is it takes what is not given him? who is it commits immorality? who is it tells lies? who is it drinks intoxicating liquor? who is it commits the five crimes that constitute 'proximate karma'? In that case, there is no merit; there is no demerit; there is no one who does or causes to be done meritorious or demeritorious deeds;

neither good nor evil deeds can have any fruit or result. Bhante Nāgasena, neither is he a murderer who kills a priest, nor can you priests, bhante Nāgasena, have any teacher, preceptor, or ordination. When you say, 'My fellow-priests, your majesty, address me as Nāgasena,' what then is this Nāgasena? Pray, bhante, is the hair of the head Nāgasena?"

"Nay, verily, your majesty."

"Is the hair of the body Nāgasena?"

"Nay, verily, your majesty."

"Are nails . . . teeth . . . skin . . . flesh . . . sinews . . . bones . . . marrow of the bones . . . kidneys . . . heart . . . liver . . . pleura . . . spleen . . . lungs . . . intestines . . . mesentery . . . stomach . . . faeces . . . bile . . . phlegm . . . pus . . . blood . . . sweat . . . fat . . . tears . . . lymph . . . saliva . . . snot . . . synovial fluid . . . urine . . . brain of the head Nāgasena?"

"Nay, verily, your majesty."

"Is now, bhante, form Nāgasena?"

"Nay, verily, your majesty."

"Is sensation Nāgasena?"

"Nay, verily, your majesty."

"Is perception Nāgasena?"

"Nay, verily, your majesty."

"Are the predispositions Nāgasena?"

"Nay, verily, your majesty."

"Is consciousness Nāgasena?"

"Nay, verily, your majesty."

"Are, then, bhante, form, sensation, perception, the predispositions, and consciousness unitedly Nāgasena?"

"Nay, verily, your majesty."

"Is it, then, bhante, something besides form, sensation, perception, the predispositions, and consciousness, which is Nāgasena?"

"Nay, verily, your majesty."

"Bhante, although I question you very closely, I fail to discover any Nāgasena. Verily, now, bhante, Nāgasena is a mere empty sound. What Nāgasena is there here? Bhante, you speak a falsehood, a lie: there is no Nāgasena."

Then the venerable Nāgasena spoke to Milinda the king as follows:—

"Your majesty, you are a delicate prince, an exceedingly delicate prince; and if, your majesty, you walk in the middle of the day on hot sandy ground, and you tread on rough grit, gravel, and sand, your feet become sore, your body tired, the mind is oppressed, and the body-consciousness suffers. Pray, did you come afoot, or riding?"

"Bhante, I do not go afoot: I came in a chariot."

"Your majesty, if you came in a chariot, declare to me the chariot. Pray, your majesty, is the pole the chariot?"

"Nay, verily, bhante."

"Is the axle the chariot?"

"Nay, verily, bhante."

"Are the wheels the chariot?"

"Nay, verily, bhante."

"Is the chariot-body the chariot?"

"Nay, verily, bhante."

"Is the banner-staff the chariot?"

"Nay, verily, bhante."

"Is the yoke the chariot?"

"Nay, verily, bhante."

"Are the reins the chariot?"

"Nay, verily, bhante."

"Is the goading-stick the chariot?"

"Nay, verily, bhante."

"Pray, your majesty, are pole, axle, wheels, chariot-body, banner-staff, yoke, reins, and goad unitedly the chariot?"

"Nay, verily, bhante."

"Is it, then, your majesty, something else besides pole, axle, wheels, chariot-body, banner-staff, yoke, reins, and goad which is the chariot?"

"Nay, verily, bhante."

"Your majesty, although I question you very closely, I fail to discover any chariot. Verily now, your majesty, the word chariot is a mere empty sound. What chariot is there here? Your majesty, you speak a falsehood, a lie: there is no chariot. Your majesty, you are the chief king in all the continent of India; of whom are you afraid that you speak a lie? Listen to me, my lords, ye five hundred Yonakas, and ye eighty thousand priests! Milinda the king here says thus: 'I came in a chariot;' and being requested, 'Your majesty, if you came in a chariot, declare to me the chariot,' he fails to produce any chariot. Is it possible, pray, for me to assent to what he says?"

When he had thus spoken, the five hundred Yonakas applauded the venerable Nāgasena and spoke to Milinda the king as follows:—

"Now, your majesty, answer, if you can."

Then Milinda the king spoke to the venerable Nāgasena as follows:—

"Bhante Nāgasena, I speak no lie: the word 'chariot' is but a way of counting, term, appellation, convenient designation, and name for pole, axle, wheels, chariot-body, and banner-staff."

"Thoroughly well, your majesty, do you understand a chariot. In exactly the same way, your majesty, in respect of me, Nāgasena is but a way of counting, term, appellation, convenient designation, mere name for the hair of my head, hair of my body . . . brain of the head, form, sensation, perception, the predispositions, and consciousness. But in the absolute sense there is no Ego here to be found. And the priestess Vajirā, your majesty, said as follows in the presence of The Blessed One:—

> " 'Even as the word of "chariot" means
> That members join to frame a whole;
> So when the Groups appear to view,
> We use the phrase, "A living being." ' "

"It is wonderful, bhante Nāgasena ! It is marvellous, bhante Nāgasena! Brilliant and prompt is the wit of your replies. If The Buddha were alive, he would applaud. Well done, well done, Nāgasena! Brilliant and prompt is the wit of your replies."

THE ROUND OF EXISTENCE

"Bhante Nāgasena," said the king, "when you say 'round of existence,' what is that?"

"Your majesty, to be born here and die here, to die here and be born elsewhere, to be born there and die there, to die there and be born elsewhere,—this, your majesty, is the round of existence."

"Give an illustration."

"It is as if, your majesty, a man were to eat a ripe mango, and plant the seed; and from that a large mango-tree were to spring and bear fruit; and then the man were to eat a ripe mango from that tree also and plant the seed; and from that seed also a large mango-tree were to spring and bear fruit; thus of these trees there is no end discernible. In exactly the same way, your majesty, to be born here and die here, to die here and be born elsewhere, to be born there and die there, to die there and be born elsewhere, this, your majesty, is the round of existence."

"You are an able man, bhante Nāgasena."

CAUSE OF REBIRTH

"Bhante Nāgasena," said the king, "are there any who die without being born into another existence?"

"Some are born into another existence," said the elder, "and some are not born into another existence."

"Who is born into another existence, and who is not born into another existence?"

"Your majesty, he that still has the corruptions is born into another existence; he that no longer has the corruptions is not born into another existence."

"But will you, bhante, be born into another existence?"

"Your majesty, if there shall be in me any attachment, I shall be born into another existence; if there shall be in me no attachment, I shall not be born into another existence."

"You are an able man, bhante Nāgasena."

REBIRTH IS NOT TRANSMIGRATION

Said the king: "Bhante Nāgasena, does rebirth take place without anything transmigrating [passing over]?"

"Yes, your majesty. Rebirth takes place without anything transmigrating."

"How, bhante Nāgasena, does rebirth take place without anything transmigrating? Give an illustration."

"Suppose, your majesty, a man were to light a light from another light; pray, would the one light have passed over [transmigrated] to the other light?"

"Nay, verily, bhante."

"In exactly the same way, your majesty, does rebirth take place without anything transmigrating."

"Give another illustration."

"Do you remember, your majesty, having learnt, when you were a boy, some verse or other from your professor of poetry?"

"Yes, bhante."

"Pray, your majesty, did the verse pass over [transmigrate] to you from your teacher?"

"Nay, verily, bhante."

"In exactly the same way, your majesty, does rebirth take place without anything transmigrating."

"You are an able man, bhante Nāgasena."

IS THIS TO BE MY LAST EXISTENCE?

"Bhante Nāgasena," said the king, "does a man know when he is not to be born into another existence?"

"Assuredly, your majesty, a man knows when he is not to be born into another existence."

"Bhante, how does he know it?"

"He knows it from the cessation of all cause or reason for being born into another existence."

"Give an illustration."

"It is as if, your majesty, a house-holding farmer were to plow and sow and fill his granary; and then were neither to plow nor sow, and were to use the grain previously stored up, or give it away, or do with it however else might suit him: your majesty, would this house-holding farmer know that his granary would not become filled up again?"

"Assuredly, bhante, would he know it."

"How would he know it?"

"He would know it from the cessation of all cause or reason for the filling up of the granary."

"In exactly the same way, your majesty, a man knows when he is not to be born into another existence, from the cessation of all cause or reason for being born into another existence."

"You are an able man, bhante Nāgasena."

THE CAUSE OF INEQUALITY IN THE WORLD

Said the king, "Bhante Nāgasena, what is the reason that men are not all alike, but some long-lived and some short lived, some healthy and some sickly, some handsome and some ugly, some powerful and some weak, some rich and some poor, some of high degree and some of low degree, some wise and some foolish?"

Said the elder, "Your majesty, why are not trees all alike, but some sour, some salt, some bitter, some pungent, some astringent, some sweet?"

"I suppose, bhante, because of a difference in the seed."

"In exactly the same way, your majesty, it is through a difference in their karma that men are not all alike, but some long-lived and some short-lived, some healthy and some sickly, some handsome and some ugly, some powerful and some weak, some rich and some poor, some of high degree and some of low degree, some wise and some foolish. Moreover, your majesty, The Blessed One has said as follows: 'All beings, O youth, have karma as their portion; they are heirs of their karma; they are sprung from their karma; their karma is their kinsman; their karma is their refuge; karma allots beings to meanness or greatness.' "

"You are an able man, bhante Nāgasena."

THE PARABLE OF THE MUSTARD-SEED

[*One of the best-known parables in Buddhist literature, the story of Kisā Gotamī, drives home relentlessly the fundamental principle in Buddhism that all things are impermanent.*]

. . . Kisā Gotamī had an only son, and he died. In her grief she carried the dead child to all her neighbors, asking them for medicine, and the people said: "She has lost her senses. The boy is dead."

At length Kisā Gotamī met a man who replied to her request: "I cannot give thee medicine for thy child, but I know a physician who can."

And the girl said: "Pray tell me, sir; who is it?" And the man replied: "Go to Sakyamuni, the Buddha."

Kisā Gotamī repaired to the Buddha and cried: "Lord and Master, give me the medicine that will cure my boy."

The Buddha answered: "I want a handful of mustard-seed." And when the girl in her joy promised to procure it, the Buddha added: "The mustard-seed must be taken from a house where no one has lost a child, husband, parent, or friend.''

Poor Kisā Gotamī now went from house to house, and the people pitied her and said: "Here is mustard-seed; take it!" But when she asked, "Did a son or daughter, a father or mother, die in your family?" They answered her: "Alas! the living are few, but the dead are many. Do not remind us of our deepest grief." And there was no house but some beloved one had died in it.

Kisā Gotamī became weary and hopeless, and sat down at the wayside, watching the lights of the city, as they flickered up and were extinguished again. At last the darkness of the night reigned everywhere. And she considered the fate of men, that their lives flicker up and are extinguished. And she thought to herself: "How selfish am I in my grief! Death is common to all; yet in this valley of desolation there is a path that leads him to immortality who has surrendered all selfishness."

Putting away the selfishness of her affection for her child, Kisā Gotamī had the dead body buried in the forest. Returning to the Buddha, she took refuge in him and found comfort in the Dharma, which is a balm that will soothe all the pains of our troubled hearts.

The Buddha said:

"The life of mortals in this world is troubled and brief and combined with pain. For there is not any means by which those that have been born can avoid dying; after reaching old age there is death; of such a nature are living beings.

"As ripe fruits are early in danger of falling, so mortals when born are always in danger of death."

Karma and Rebirth

Christmas Humphreys (1901–   ) was born in London and educated at Cambridge. In 1924 he founded the Buddhist Society in London, now the oldest and largest Buddhist organization in Europe. His lifelong interest in world Buddhism led to his formulation in 1945 of the "Twelve Principles of Buddhism,"* which have been widely accepted by Buddhist groups. Among his popular books on Buddhism are *The Way of Action, Concentration and Meditation, The Buddhist Way of Life, Karma and Rebirth,* and *Studies in the Middle Way.* He also edited *The Wisdom of Buddhism* and has written extensively on Zen. The present reading selection is from his *Buddhism.*

KARMA OR CAUSE-EFFECT

Karma (Pali: *Kamma)* is literally 'action', 'doing', 'deed'. It is at once cause, effect and the law which equilibrates the two. It is Newton's third law of motion, that Action and Reaction are equal and opposite, applied to the moral and all other realms of sentient life. For two thousand years have Christians heard it proclaimed from their pulpits: 'Be not deceived: God is not mocked, for whatsoever a man soweth, that shall he also reap', and Christ is reported to have said upon the Mount: 'Judge not that ye be not judged, for with what judgment ye judge ye shall be judged, and with what measure ye mete, it shall be measured to you again.'

From the Buddhist viewpoint, Karma stresses the converse of the Christian presentation of this law. Whatsoever a man reaps, say the Buddhists, that has he also sown. Believing in the operation of natural justice, Buddhism would say in reply to the Biblical enquiry: 'Who did sin, this man or his parents, that he was born blind?', that it was this man who had 'sinned', that is, had so behaved in a previous life as to cause in the life in question the effect of blindness. As Mrs Rhys Davids says, 'Afflictions are for Buddhists so many forms, not of pre-payment, by which future compensation may be claimed, but of settlement of outstanding debts accruing from bad, that is to say from evil-bringing, unhappiness-promoting acts, done either in this life or in previous lives'.[1] In Karma is to be found, in conjunction with its common-

---

*The "Twelve Principles" may be found in Humphreys' *Buddhism* (Harmondsworth: Penguin Books, 2nd ed., 1955), pp. 74-76.

[1]*Buddhism,* p. 124.

sense corollary, Rebirth, a natural and therefore reasonable answer to the apparent injustice of the daily round. Why should this man be born a beggar, this a prince? Why this a cripple, this a genius, that a fool? Why this a high-born Indian woman, that a low-born Englishman? These are effects. Do the causes lie in the hands of an irresponsible and finite God or, as the Buddhists say, within the lap of law? As it is man who suffers the effects, so it is man who generates the cause, and having done so he cannot flee the consequences. Says the *Dhammapada* (v. 165): 'By oneself evil is done; by oneself one suffers. By oneself evil is left undone; by oneself one is purified.' And, again, 'Not in the sky, not in the midst of the sea, nor anywhere else on earth is there a spot where a man may be freed from (the consequences of) an evil deed' (v. 127). Thus every man is the moulder and the sole creator of his life to come, and master of his destiny. 'Subsequents follow antecedents by a bond of inner consequence; no merely numerical sequence of arbitrary and isolated units, but a rational interconnection.' So said the Emperor Marcus Aurelius, and speaking of the abstract laws of the universe, Emerson said that they 'execute themselves . . . In the soul of man there is a justice whose retributions are instant and entire. He who does a good deed is instantly ennobled. He who does a mean deed is by the action itself contracted.' *(Miscellanies.)* And again: 'Secret retributions are always restoring the level, when disturbed, of the divine justice. It is impossible to tilt the beam. Settles for evermore the ponderous equator to its line, and man and mote, and star and sun, must range to it, or be pulverized by the recoil.'[2]

It is the mind which moulds man's destiny, action being but precipitated thought. It follows that one's lightest thought has vast effects, not only on the thinker, but on all that lives. Hence the tremendous power of hatred and love, which man, in childlike ignorance, is pouring out upon the world by night and day. Yet such dynamic qualities, controlled and cultivated, can make a man just what he wills to be. Karma is thus the very antithesis of fatalism. That which is done can by the doer be in time, as it were, neutralized. That which is yet to be depends on the deeds now being done. There is here no cruel Nemesis; only the slow and perfect action of an all-embracing law.

Omar Khayyam was a Buddhist when he wrote:

> The Moving Finger writes; and having writ,
> Moves on: nor all thy Piety nor Wit
> Shall lure it back to cancel half a line,
> Nor all thy Tears wash out a Word of it.

But though the record of a deed remains indelible, it is the sufferer whose finger wrote his destiny, and who had it in his power to choose whether the deed were good or bad. It is but just that he who disturbed should in the end restore the equilibrium.

---

[2]*Lectures and Biographical Studies.*

An individual's karma, in the sense of the sum of unexpended causes generated by him in the past, the burden which he has to bear upon life's pilgrimage, is classified with great precision in the various Schools, but can be analysed by any student for himself. Karma is an ever-generating force. It may be as a thundercloud, so fully charged that nothing can delay its equally complete discharge; it may be as a snowball on the mountain-side, so small and slowly moving at first that a slight expenditure of effort will bring its growing power to rest. Other analogies may be found with ease, but it is more important to understand the nature of Karma than to analyse its complex functioning.

The Buddhist, then, replaces Nemesis and Providence, Kismet, Destiny and Fate, with a natural law, by his knowledge of which he moulds his future hour by hour. In the words of an old jingle:

> Sow a thought, reap an act;
> Sow an act, reap a habit;
> Sow a habit, reap a character;
> Sow a character, reap a destiny.

But even as the causes generated by one man react upon that man, so the mass causation of a group, be it family, society or nation, reacts upon that group as such, and upon all whose karma placed them at the time therein. Each man has, therefore, several 'karmas', racial, national, family, and personal, yet all quite properly *his*, else he would not have found himself subject to their sway.

An understanding of the law of Karma leads to self-reliance, for in proportion as we understand its operation we cease to complain of our circumstances, and cease from turning with the weakness of a child to a man-made God to save us from the natural consequences of our acts. Karma is no God, for the gods themselves are subject to its sway. Only the ignorant personify Karma, and attempt to bribe, petition or cajole it; wise men understand it and conform to it.

The universe itself is an effect; hence all the units in it, viewed as events, are at once both cause and effect within a vast effect. Each is at once the result of all that has preceded it and a contributing cause of all to come. Yet, as we saw when studying causation, Karma is not only cause and effect in time; rather is it the law which governs the interrelation and solidarity of the Universe in all its parts, and hence, in a way, the karma of one such unit is the karma of all. It is 'the interdependence of Humanity which is the cause of what is called *Distributive Karma,* and it is this law which affords the solution to the great question of collective suffering and relief. No man can rise superior to his individual failings without lifting, be it ever so little, the whole body of which he is an integral part. In the same way no one can sin, nor suffer the effects of sin, alone.'[3]

[3]H. P. Blavatsky, *The Key to Theosophy,* p. 203.

REBIRTH

All action has its due result. A stone thrown into a pond causes wavelets to circle outwards to a distance proportionate to the initial disturbance; after which the initial state of equilibrium is restored. And since each disturbance must start from some particular point, it is clear that harmony can be restored only by the re-converging to that point of the forces set in motion. Thus the consequences of an act re-act, via all the universe, upon the doer with a force commensurate with his own.

Now Karma involves the element of time; and it is unreasonable to hold that all the causes generated in an average life will produce their full effect before the last day of that period. The oldest sage would admit that at the close of a life of study his wisdom was as a raindrop to the sea. Nor is the idea new. Almost every country of the East accepts the doctrine as too obvious to need proof, and anthropologists have traced its presence in the legends and indigenous ideas of nearly every country in the world. It is to be found in most of the greatest minds of Europe and America, from Plato to Origen, from Blake to Schopenhauer, from Goethe, Boehme, Kant, and Swedenborg to Browning, Emerson, Walt Whitman, and leading minds of the Western world today.[4]

It is clearly present in such fragments of Christ's teachings as are still extant. Consider, for example, the story of the man born blind, and the rumours that Christ was Jeremiah or Elias come again.[5] Even Herod seems to think that he was John the Baptist 'risen from the dead'.[6]

The truth of the doctrine cannot of course be 'proved', but it is at least immensely reasonable.

A life on earth is, to the Buddhist, as a wayside inn upon a road. At any moment there are many travellers therein, and even as we speak more enter through the doors of Birth, and others leave by one whose name is Death. Within the common meeting-rooms are men and women of every type whose relations to one another form that reaction to environment we call experience.

Such a belief affects all blood relationship. The child may be an older pilgrim than its parents, and is at least entitled to its point of view. In the West we say that the child of a musical father is musical (if it be so) because of heredity. In Buddhist lands it would be explained that the child was born into a musical family, because it (the child) had developed musical propensities in previous lives, and was attracted to an environment suitable for the expression of those 'gifts', a reversal of the Western view. The age of the body is thus no criterion of the age of the entity using it. In the same way, 'infant prodigies' are the outcome of a series of lives devoted to the development of a special

---

[4] See my *Karma and Rebirth* (Wisdom of the East Series) for a long series of quotations from Western writers who accept the doctrines of Rebirth.

[5] Matt. xvi, 13-16.

[6] Mark vi, 14-16.

CHAPTER TWO / *Buddhism*

faculty. The body alone is the product of its parents. So may a house be built by a landlord, but the tenant need not take it against his will. But even though the body be not the direct creation of that 'Self' which uses it, yet was it chosen as the instrument most suited to the needs of the informing consciousness. Karma is therefore, with Rebirth, a double key to unexplained phenomena. Life does not die at the body's death, nor do the consequences of a deed. Forms are created and destroyed; they come into being, serve their purpose and then die; but the life within knows no such limitation.

> Nay, but as when one layeth
> His worn-out robes away,
> And taking new ones, sayeth,
> 'These will I wear to-day!'
> So putteth by the spirit
> Lightly its garb of flesh,
> And passeth to inherit
> A residence afresh.

So wrote Sir Edwin Arnold in his verse translation of the *Bhagavad-Gita,* and, subject to understanding what it is which passes from life to life, the Buddhist would agree.

THE NATURE OF DEATH

Man alone, says the esoteric tradition, has an individual karma, but life is one, and passes unceasingly from form to form with intervals of rest between.

. . .

Death is the death of the body and its invisible counterpart. The body came into being; it must therefore one day die. Hence the Buddhist saying, 'The cause of death is not disease, but birth.' To mourn for the inevitable dissolution of a temporary garment is foolishness, and all the more so when the man who has thus cast off his outer clothing will return to earth to meet again, maybe, the friends he knew before. Karma takes no reckoning of time. A bond of love or hate between two persons is a cause that will need those 'persons' for the working out of its inevitable effect, and Karma can wait, if need be, for ten thousand years. Death is usually a well-earned rest, when the experience, great or small, of one life is quietly digested, to appear in later lives as faculty, ability, and innate tendency. It is but an incident of life, and viewed from the standpoint of a thousand lives, an incident of no more importance and finality than sleep.

What Chuang Tzŭ wrote of his Master, Lao Tzŭ, applies still more to us: 'When the Master came it was at the proper time; when he went away it was the simple sequence of his coming. Quiet acquiescence in what happens at its proper time and quietly submitting to its ceasing, afford no occasion for grief or joy.' Death, therefore, is the gateway to a different form of life, one which is strictly limited in duration by the thoughts and acts of the individual. How can the consequences of a finite life be infinite anything—Heaven or Hell? A man's hereafter is the aggregate effects of the causes generated by him in the past. The cause was limited; equally so will be the effects. The limited and finite cannot cause eternity. Each man, the Buddha taught, suffers in after life the hell or heaven which he was manufacturing every hour of his life on earth. The 'Day of Judgment' is at all times and for everyone — To-day.

It is often asked why we do not remember our past lives. The answer is clear. Because physical memory needs a physical brain, and the brain which remembers incidents of this life is different from that which registered the deeds of the one before. But in fact the bridge from life to life is often crossed. Students claim to have trained their memories to go back step by step until they arrive at an accurate memory of their previous life or lives. The subsequent verification of remembered scenery, surroundings and events, seems to prove the truth of the experimenters' claims, and the Buddhist Scriptures show examples of this interesting but unprofitable exercise.

WHAT IS REBORN

The nature of that which is reborn is the subject of much futile argument, but the details are of no importance in the treading of the Eightfold Path. The body dies at death, but the individual's karma, the resultant of all the causes generated by him in the past, lives on. This complex 'soul', the product of ten thousand lives, is clothed, as we have seen, with divers attributes or qualities, called *skandhas*. This it is which, in the intervening and subjective worlds, digests the lessons of the previous life until such causes as can take effect subjectively have been transmuted into faculty and innate tendency. That which remains to incarnate afresh may be regarded as an individual, as in the Northern school of Buddhism, or as a nameless complex residuum of karma, as in the Southern school. The danger of the former viewpoint lies in the tendency to look upon this individual as a 'separated soul' eternally distinct from other forms of life. The Southern viewpoint, on the other hand, anxious to enforce the doctrine of *anatta* in its literal sense, keeps to the letter rather than to the spirit of the Buddha's metaphors. One candle lighted from another—is the light of the second the same light as the first? Such imagery has its dangers to a certain type of mind, and leads them into a logical absurdity. Yet is the simile beautiful when understood. Light one candle from another and the light is the same, yet different; the same in essence yet seeming, maybe, to the outward eye, to shine more brightly than before. Perhaps the wax which formed the second candle was more purified, the wick of finer texture and the whole created from a finer mould. To that extent the second differs from the first, yet the Light or Life was one and the same, more brightly shining in the second case because of the purer *skandhas* of its form.

edward conze (translator) _____

Buddhaghosa on the Recollection of Death

Buddhaghosa was a great Indian scholar of the fifth century A.D. He is believed to have been the compiler of most of the ancient commentaries on the Pali Canon, which are second in importance only to the Canon itself, and he was the author of a treatise on Buddhist doctrine entitled *The Path of Purity* (the *Visuddhimagga*), from which the following selection is taken.

The translator is Edward Conze, whose voluminous studies of Buddhism include *Buddhism: Its Essence and Development, Buddhist Meditation, The Buddha's Law Among the Birds,* and *Thirty Years of Buddhist Studies.*

In "the recollection of death", the word "death" refers to the cutting off of the life-force which lasts for the length of one existence. Whoso wants to develop it, should in seclusion and solitude wisely set up attention with the words: "Death will take place, the life-force will be cut off", or (simply), "Death, death". But if somebody takes up an unwise attitude (to this problem of death), then sorrow will arise in him when he recalls the death of a loved person, like the grief of a mother when she thinks of the death of the dear child whom she has borne; and joy will arise when he recalls the death of an unloved person, like the rejoicing of a foe who thinks of an enemy's death; and when he recalls the death of an indifferent person, no perturbation will arise in him, just as the man who all day long burns corpses looks on dead bodies without perturbation; when, finally, he recalls his own death, violent trembling arises in him, as in a frightened man who sees before him a murderer with his sword drawn. And all this is the result of a lack in mindfulness, (reasonable) perturbation, and cognition.

Therefore the Yogin should look upon beings killed or dead here and there, and advert to the death of beings who died after having first seen prosperity. To this (observation) he should apply mindfulness, perturbation and cognition, and set up attention with the words, "Death will take place", and so on. When he proceeds thus, he proceeds wisely, i.e. he proceeds expediently. For only if someone proceeds in this way will his hindrances be impeded, will mindfulness be established with death for its object, and will some degree of concentration be achieved.

If this is not enough (to produce access), he should recall death from the following eight points of view:

1. As a murderer, standing in front of him.
2. From the (inevitable) loss of (all) achievement.
3. By inference.
4. Because one's body is shared with many others.
5. From the weakness of the stuff of life.
6. From the absence of signs.
7. Because the life-span is limited.
8. From the shortness of the moment.

1. "AS A MURDERER STANDING IN FRONT OF HIM" means, "as if a murderer were standing in front of him". One should recall that death stands in front of us just like a murderer, who confronts us with his drawn sword raised to our neck, intending to cut off our head. And why? Because death comes together with birth, and deprives us of life.

a) As a budding mushroom shoots upwards carrying soil on its head, so beings from their birth onwards carry decay and death along with them. For death has come together with birth, because everyone who is born must certainly die. Therefore this living being, from the time of his birth onwards, moves in the direction of death, without turning back even for a moment; b) just as the sun, once it has arisen, goes forward in the direction of its setting, and does not turn back for a moment on the path it traverses in that direction; c) or as a mountain stream rapidly tears down on its way, flows and rushes along, without turning back even for a moment. To one who goes along like that, death is always near; d) just as brooks get extinguished when dried up by the summer heat, e) as fruits are bound to fall from a tree early one day when their stalks have been rotted away by the early morning mists; f) as earthenware breaks when hit with a hammer; g) and as dewdrops are dispersed when touched by the rays of the sun. Thus death, like a murderer with a drawn sword, has come together with birth. Like the murderer who has raised his sword to our neck, so it deprives us of life. And there is no chance that it might desist.

2. "BY THE FAILURE OF ACHIEVEMENT", which means: Here in this world achievement prospers only so long as it is not overwhelmed by failure. And there is no single achievement that stands out as having transcended the (threat of) failure.

Moreover, all health ends in sickness, all youth in old age, all life in death; wherever one may dwell in the world, one is afflicted by birth, overtaken by old age, oppressed by sickness, struck down by death. Through realizing that the achievements of life thus end in the failure of death, he should recollect death from the failure of achievement.

3. "BY INFERENCE", means that one draws an inference for oneself from

others. And it is with seven kinds of person that one should compare oneself: those great in fame, great in merit, great in might, great in magical power, great in wisdom, Pratyekabuddhas, and fully enlightened Buddhas.

In what manner? This death has assuredly befallen even those (kings) like Mahasammata, Mandhatu, Mahasudassana, Dalhanemin and Nimippabhuti, who possessed great fame, a great retinue, and who abounded in treasures and might. How then could it be that it will not befall also me?

> "The greatly famous, noble kings,
> Like Mahasammata and others,
> They all fell down before the might of death.
> What need is there to speak of men like us?"

(And so for the other kinds of distinction.)

In this way he draws from others, who have achieved great fame, and so on, an inference as to himself, i.e. that death is common to himself and to them. When he recalls that, "as for those distinguished beings so also for me death will take place", then the subject of meditation attains to access.

4. "BECAUSE ONE'S BODY IS SHARED WITH MANY OTHERS:" This body is the common property of many. It is shared by the eighty classes of parasitic animals, and it incurs death as a result of their turbulence. Likewise it belongs to the many hundreds of diseases which arise within it, as well as to the outside occasions of death, such as snakes, scorpions, and so on.

For just as, flying from all directions, arrows, spears, lances, stones, and so on, fall on a target placed at the cross roads, so on the body also all kinds of misfortune are bound to descend. And through the onslaught of these misfortunes it incurs death. Hence the Lord has said: "Here, monks, a monk, when the day is over and night comes round, thinks to himself: many are, to be sure, for me the occasions of death: a snake, or a scorpion, or a centipede may bite me; thereby I may lose my life, and that may act as an obstacle (to my spiritual progress). Or I may stumble and fall, or the food I have eaten may upset me, or the bile may trouble me, or the phlegm, or the winds which cut like knives; and thereby I may lose my life, and that may act as an obstacle" (*Anguttara* III, 306).

5. "FROM THE WEAKNESS OF THE STUFF OF LIFE:" This life-force is without strength and feeble. For the life of beings is bound up with *a*) breathing in and out, *b*) the postures, *c*) heat and cold, *d*) the (four) great primaries, and *e*) with food.

a) It goes on only as long as it can obtain an even functioning of breathing in and out; as soon, however, as air issues from the nose without re-entering, or enters without going out again, one is considered dead. *b*) Again, it goes on only as long as it can obtain an even functioning of the four postures; but through the preponderance of one or the other of these the vital activities are cut off. *c*) Again, it goes on as long as it can obtain the even functioning of heat and cold; but it fails when oppressed by excessive heat or cold. *d*) Again, it goes on as long as it can obtain the even functioning of the (four) great primaries; but through the disturbance of one or the other of them (i.e.) of the solid, fluid, etc., element, the life of even a strong person is extinguished, be it by the stiffening of his body, or because his body has become wet and putrid from dysentery, and so on, or because it is overcome by a high temperature, or because his sinews are torn. *e*) Again, life goes on only as long as one obtains solid food, at suitable times; when one cannot get food, it gets extinguished.

6. "FROM THE ABSENCE OF SIGNS", because one cannot determine (the time of death, etc.). "From the absence of a definite limit", that is the meaning. For one says with regard to the death of beings:

a) Life's duration, *b*) sickness, *c*) time,
d) the place where the body is cast off, *e*) the future destiny.
These are five things about this animate world,
Which never can be known for certain, for no sign exists.

a) There is no sign (i.e. no clear indication) of the duration of life, because one cannot determine that so long will one live, and no longer. For beings may die in the first embryonic state, or in the second, third, or fourth, or after one month, or two, three, four, five or ten months, at the time when they issue from the womb, and further still at any time within or beyond one hundred years.

b) There is also no sign of the (fatal) sickness, insofar as one cannot determine that beings will die of this or that sickness, and no other; for beings may die from a disease of the eyes, or the ears, or any other.

c) There is also no sign of the time, insofar as one cannot determine that one will have to die just at this time of day and no other; for beings may die in the morning, or at midday, or at any other time.

d) There is also no sign as to the laying down of the body; for, when one is dying, one cannot determine that the body should be laid down just here and not anywhere else. For the body of those born within a village may fall away outside the village; and those born outside a village may perish inside one; those born on land may perish in water, those born in water may perish on land; and so this might be expanded in various ways.

e) There is also no sign of the future destiny, insofar as one cannot determine that one who has deceased there will be reborn here. For those who have deceased in the world of the gods may be reborn among men, and those deceased in the world of men may be reborn in the world of the gods, or anywhere else. In this way the world revolves round the five kinds of rebirth like an ox yoked to an oil-pressing mill.

7. "BECAUSE THE LIFE-SPAN IS LIMITED." Brief is the life of men at present; he lives long who lives for a hundred years, or a little more. Hence

the Lord has said: "Short, oh monks, is the life-span of men, transient, having its sequel elsewhere; one should do what is wholesome, one should lead a holy life, no one who is born can escape death; he lives long who lives for a hundred years, or a little more.

> Short is the life of men, the good must scorn it,
> And act as if their turban were ablaze.
> For death is surely bound to come" (*Samyutta* I, 108).

Furthermore, the whole Araka-Sutta (*Anguttara* IV, 136–8) with its seven similes should be considered in detail: (i.e. Life is fleeting, and passes away quickly, *a*) like dewdrops on the tips of blades of grass, which soon dry up when the sun rises; *b*) or like the bubbles which rain causes in water, and which burst soon; *c*) or like the line made by a stick in water, which vanishes soon; *d*) or like a mountain brook, which does not stand still for a moment; *e*) or like a gob of spittle spat out with ease; *f*) or like a lump of meat thrown into a hot iron pot, which does not last long; *g*) or like a cow about to be slaughtered; each time she raises her foot she comes nearer to death).

Furthermore, He said: "If, oh monks, a monk develops the recollection of death in such a way that he thinks—'may I just live for one day and night—for one day—for as long as it takes to eat an alms-meal—for as long as it takes to chew and swallow four or five lumps of food—and I will then attend to the Lord's religion, and much surely will still be done by me'—then such monks are said to lead heedless lives, and they develop in a sluggish way the recollection of death which aims at the extinction of the outflows. But if, oh monks, a monk develops the recollection of death in such a way that he thinks—'may I just live for so long as it takes to chew and swallow one lump of food—were I to live just long enough to breathe in after breathing out, or to breathe out after breathing in'—then such monks are said to lead watchful lives, and they develop keenly the recollection of death which aims at the extinction of the outflows" (*Anguttara* III, 305–6). And the span of life is brief like a mere swallowing of four or five lumps of food, and it cannot be trusted.

8. "FROM THE SHORTNESS OF THE MOMENT." In ultimate reality beings live only for an exceedingly brief moment, for it (life) lasts just as long as one single moment of thought. Just as a cart-wheel, whether it rolls along or stands still, always rests on one single spot of the rim; just so the life of beings lasts for one single moment of thought. As soon as that thought has ceased, the being also is said to have ceased. As it has been said: "In the past thought-moment one has lived, but one does not live and one will not live in it; in the future thought-moment one has not lived, but one does live, and one will live; in the present thought-moment one has not lived, but one does live, and one will not live in it.

> Our life and our whole personality,
> All our joys and all our pains,

Are bound up with one single thought,
And rapidly that moment passes.
And those skandhas which are stopped,
For one who's dying, or one remaining here,
They all alike have gone away,
And are no longer reproduced.
Nothing is born from what is unproduced;
One lives by that which is at present there.
When thought breaks up, then all the world is dead.
So't is when final truth the concept guides". (*Niddesa* I, 42.)

Result: When he recollects (death) from one or the other of these eight points of view, his mind by repeated attention becomes practised therein, mindfulness with death for its object is established, the hindrances are impeded, the Jhana-limbs become manifest. But, because of the intrinsic nature of the object and the agitation it produces, the Jhana only reaches access and not full ecstasy.

Benefits: And the monk who is devoted to this recollection of death is always watchful, he feels disgust for all forms of becoming, he forsakes the hankering after life, he disapproves of evil, he does not hoard up many things, and with regard to the necessities of life he is free from the taint of stinginess. He gains familiarity with the notion of impermanence, and, when he follows that up, also the notions of ill and not-self will stand out to him. At the hour of death, beings who have not developed the recollection of death, feel fear, fright and bewilderment, as if they were suddenly attacked by wild beasts, ghosts, snakes, robbers or murderers. He, on the contrary, dies without fear and bewilderment. If in this very life he does not win deathlessness, he is, on the dissolution of his body, bound for a happy destiny.

The Mahayana and the
Ideal of the Bodhisattva

Born in Ceylon of an English mother and Ceylonese father, Ananda Coomaraswamy (1877–1947) was raised and educated in England, receiving a Doctor of Science degree (in geology) from the University of London. From 1917 until his death, he was Fellow for Research in Indian, Persian, and Mohammedan Art at the Museum of Fine Arts in Boston. He lectured widely and pursued the scholarly interests which led to such books as *The Transformation of Nature in Art, Hinduism and Buddhism, A New Approach to the Vedas,* and *Am I My Brother's Keeper?* The selection which follows is from *Buddha and the Gospel of Buddhism* (originally published in 1916).

The Mahāyāna or Great Vessel is so-called by its adherents, in contradistinction to the Hīnayāna* or Little Vessel of primitive Buddhism, because the former offers to all beings in all worlds salvation by faith and love as well as by knowledge, while the latter only avails to convey over the rough sea of Becoming to the farther shore of Nibbāna those few strong souls who require no external spiritual aid nor the consolation of Worship. The Hīnayāna, like the 'unshown way' of those who seek the *'nirguna Brahman,'*† is exceeding hard;[1] whereas the burden of the Mahāyāna is light, and does not require that a man should immediately renounce the world and all the affections of humanity. The manifestation of the Body of the Law, says the Mahāyāna, is adapted to the various needs of the children of the Buddha; whereas the Hīnayāna is only of avail to those who have left their spiritual childhood far behind them. The Hīnayāna emphasizes the necessity of saving knowledge, and aims at the salvation of the individual, and refuses to develop the mystery of Nibbāna in a positive sense; the Mahāyāna lays as much or greater stress

---

*As Coomaraswamy goes on to say in a later paragraph, the designation "Hinayana" is not appreciated by followers of that branch of Buddhism; they prefer "Theravada."—R.E.

†"Nirguna" Brahman is the unknowable, impersonal Brahman of the early *Upanishads,* in contrast to the responsive, loving, and knowable "Saguna" Brahman of later *Upanishads.* The former is "It," Brahman "without attributes"; the latter is "He," Brahman "with attributes."—R.E.

[1] In the words of Behmen (*Supersensual Life,* Dialogue 2): *But, alas how hard it is for the Will to sink into nothing, to attract nothing, to imagine nothing.*

on love, and aims at the salvation of every sentient being, and finds in Nirvāna the One Reality, which is 'Void' only in the sense that it is free from the limitations of every phase of the limited or contingent experience of which we have empirical knowledge. The Buddhists of the primitive school, on the other hand, naturally do not accept the name of the 'Lesser Vessel,' and as true Protestants they raise objection to the theological and aesthetic accommodation of the true doctrine to the necessities of human nature.

Opinions thus differ as to whether we may regard the Mahāyāna as a development or a degeneration. Even the professed exponents of the Hīnayāna have their doubts. Thus in one place Professor Rhys Davids speaks of the Bodhisattva doctrine as the *bīrana*-weed which "drove out the doctrine of the Ariyan path," and the weed "is not attractive:"[2] while in another, Mrs Rhys Davids writes of the cool detachment of the Arahat, that perhaps "a yet more saintly Sāriputta would have aspired yet further, even to an infinite series of rebirths, wherein he might, with evergrowing power and self-devotion, work for the furtherance of the religious evolution of his fellows," adding that "social and religious ideals evolve out of, yea, and even beyond the finished work and time-straitened vision of the Arahants of old.'"[3] Perhaps we need not determine the relative value of either school: the way of knowledge will ever appeal to some, and the way of love and action to others, and the latter the majority. Those who are saved by knowledge stand apart from the world and its hopes and fears, offering to the world only that knowledge which shall enable others to stand aside in the same way: those others who are moved by their love and wisdom to perpetual activity—in whom the will to life is dead, but the will to power yet survives in its noblest and most impersonal forms—attain at last the same goal, and in the meanwhile effect a reconciliation of religion with the world, and the union of renunciation with action.

The development of the Mahāyāna is in fact the overflowing of Buddhism from the limits of the Order into the life of the world; into whatever devious channels Buddhism may have ultimately descended, are we to say that that identification with the life of the world, with all its consequences in ethic and aesthetic, was a misfortune? Few who are acquainted with the history of Asiatic culture would maintain any such thesis.

Mahāyānists do not hesitate to describe the Hīnayāna ideal as selfish; and we have indicated in several places to what extent it must in any case be called narrow. But the Mahāyānists—not to speak of Christian critics of the Hīnayāna—do not sufficiently realize that a selfish being could not possibly become an Arahat, who must be free from even the conception of an ego, and

---

[2]Dialogues of the Buddha, ii, p. 1. [But Edward Conze has written that "to regard all later Buddhist history as a record of the 'degeneration' of an 'original' gospel is like regarding an oak tree as a degeneration of an acorn." *Buddhism: Its Essence and Development* (New York: Harper Torchbook, 1959), p. 27.—R.E.]

[3]*Psalms of the Brethren*, p. xlviii.

still more from every form of ego-assertion. The selfishness of the would-be Arahat is more apparent than real. The ideal of self-culture is not opposed to that of self-sacrifice: in any perfectly harmonious development these seemingly opposite tendencies are reconciled. To achieve this reconciliation, to combine renunciation with growth, knowledge with love, stillness with activity, is the problem of all ethics. Curiously enough, though its solution has often been attempted by oriental religions, it has never been so clearly enunciated in the west as by the 'irreligious' Nietzsche—the latest of the mystics—whose ideal of the Superman combines the Will to Power . . . with the Bestowing Virtue . . . .

If the ideal of the Private Buddha seems to be a selfish one, we may reply that the Great Man can render to his fellows no higher service than to realize the highest possible state of his being. From the Unity of life we cannot but deduce the identity of (true) self-interest with the (true) interest of others. While therefore the Mahāyānists may justly claim that their system is indeed a greater vessel of salvation in the sense of greater convenience, or better adaptation to the needs of a majority of voyagers, they cannot on the other hand justly accuse the captain and the crew of the smaller ship of selfishness. Those who seek to the farther shore may select the means best suited to their own needs: the final goal is one and the same.

The most essential part of the Mahāyāna is its emphasis on the Bodhisattva ideal, which replaces that of Arahatta, or ranks before it. Whereas the Arahat strives most earnestly for Nirvāna, the Bodhisattva as firmly refuses to accept the final release. "Forasmuch as there is the will that all sentient beings should be altogether made free, I will not forsake my fellow creatures."[4] The Bodhisattva is he in whom the Bodhicitta or heart of wisdom is fully expanded. In a sense, we are all Bodhisattvas, and indeed all Buddhas, only that in us by reason of ignorance and imperfection in love the glory of the Bodhiheart is not yet made manifest. But those are specially called Bodhisattvas who with specific determination dedicate all the activities of their future and present lives to the task of saving the world. They do not merely contemplate, but feel, all the sorrow of the world, and because of their love they cannot be idle, but expend their virtue with supernatural generosity. It is said of Gautama Buddha, for example, that there is no spot on earth where he has not in some past life sacrificed his life for the sake of others, while the whole story of his last incarnation related in the *Vessantara Jātaka* relates the same unstinting generosity, which does not shrink even from the giving away of wife and children. But Buddhahood once attained, according to the old school, it remains for others to work out their salvation alone: "Be ye lamps unto yourselves," in the last words of Gautama. According to the Mahāyāna, however, even the attainment of Buddhahood does not involve indifference to

[4] *Avatamsaka Sūtra.*

the sorrow of the world; the work of salvation is perpetually carried on by the Bodhisattva emanations of the supreme Buddhas, just as the work of the Father is done by Jesus.

The Bodhisattvas are specially distinguished from the Srāvakas (Arahats) and Pacceka-Buddhas or 'Private Buddhas,' who have become followers of the Buddha 'for the sake of their own complete Nirvāna':[5] for the Bodhisattvas enter upon their course "out of compassion to the world, for the benefit, weal, and happiness of the world at large, both gods and men, for the sake of the complete Nirvāna of all beings. . . . Therefore they are called Bodhisattva Mahāsattva."[6]

A doctrine specially associated with the Bodhisattva ideal is that of the *parivarta* or turning over of ethical merit to the advantage of others, which amounts very nearly to the doctrine of vicarious atonement. Whereas in early Buddhism it is emphasized that each life is entirely separate from every other (also a Jaina doctrine, and no doubt derived from the Sāmkhya conception of a plurality of Purushas), the Mahāyāna insists on the interdependence and even the identity of all life; and this position affords a logical basis for the view that the merit acquired by one may be devoted to the good of others. This is a peculiarly amiable feature in late Buddhism; we find, for example, that whoever accomplishes a good deed, such as a work of charity or a pilgrimage, adds the prayer that the merit may be shared by all sentient beings.

. . .

The Mahāyānist doctors recognize ten stations in the spiritual evolution of the Bodhisattva, beginning with the first awakening of the Wisdom-heart (Bodhicitta) in the warmth of compassion (karunā) and the light of divine knowledge (prajñā). These stations are those of 'joy,' 'purity,' 'effulgence,' 'burning,' 'hard to achieve,' 'showing the face,' 'going afar off,' 'not moving to and fro,' 'good intelligence,' and 'dharma-cloud.' It is in the first station that the Bodhisattva makes those pregnant resolutions (pranidhāna) which determine the course of his future lives. An example of such a vow is the resolution of Avalokitesvara not to accept salvation until the least particle of dust shall have attained to Buddahood before him.

It may be mentioned that the course *(cariyā)* of the Bodhisattva has this advantage, that he never comes to birth in any purgatory, nor in any unfavourable condition on earth. Nor is the Bodhisattva required to cultivate a disgust for the conditions of life; he does not practise a meditation of Foul Things, like the aspirant for Arahatta. The Bodhisattva simply recognizes that the conditions of life have come to be what they are, that it is in the nature

[5]Hindus would express this by saying that Srāvakas and Pacceka-Buddhas choose the path of Immediate Salvation: Bodhisattvas, that of Ultimate Salvation. 'The deferred path of Liberation is the path of all Bhaktas. It is the path of compassion or service.'—P. N. Sinha, *Commentary on the Bhāgavata Purāna* p. 359.

[6]*Saddharmapundarīka Sūtra*.

(tattva, bhutathā, suchness) of things to be so, and he takes them accordingly for what they are worth. This position is nowhere more tersely summed up than in the well-known Japanese verselet—

Granted this dewdrop world be but a dewdrop world,
     This granted, yet . . .

Thus the new Buddhist law was in no way puritanical, and did not inculcate an absolute detachment. Pleasure indeed is not to be sought as an end in itself, but it need not be rejected as it arises incidentally. The Bodhisattva shares in the life of the world; for example, he has a wife, that his supernatural generosity may be seen in the gift of wife and children, and for the same reason he may be the possessor of power and wealth. If by reason of attachment and this association with the world some venial sins are unavoidably committed, that is of little consequence, and such sins are wiped away in the love of others: the cardinal sins of hatred and self-thinking cannot be imagined in him in whom the heart of wisdom has been awakened. It must not, however, be supposed that the Mahāyāna in any way relaxes the rule of the Order; and even in the matter of the remission of sins of the laity it is only minor and inevitable shortcomings that are considered, and not deliberate deeds of evil. And if the Mahāyāna doctors preach the futility of remorse and discourage-ment, on the other hand they are by no means quietists, but advocate a mysticism fully as practical as that of Ruysbroeck.

The idea of the Bodhisattva corresponds to that of the Hero, the Superman, the Saviour and the Avatār of other systems. In this connexion it is interesting to note that legitimate pride—the will to power, conjoined with the bestowing virtue—is by no means alien to the Bodhisattva character, but on the con-trary, "In respect of three things may pride be borne—man's works, his temptations, and his power," and the exposition follows: "The pride of works lies in the thought 'for me alone is the task.'[7] This world, enslaved by passion, is powerless to accomplish its own weal; then must I do it for them, for I am not impotent like them. Shall another do a lowly task while I am standing by? If I in my pride will not do it, better it is that my pride perish. . . . Then with firm spirit I will undo the occasions of undoing; if I should be conquered by them, my ambition to conquer the threefold world would be a jest. I will conquer all; none shall conquer me. This is the pride that I will bear, for I am the son of the Conqueror Lions![8] . . . Surrounded by the troop of the pas-sions man should become a thousand times prouder, and be as unconquerable to their hordes as a lion to flocks of deer . . . so, into whatever straits he may

---

[7] *Cf.* Blake:
             But when Jesus was crucified,
             Then was perfected His galling pride.
    [8] Buddha is often spoken of as Conqueror (Jina—a term more familiar in connexion with the followers of Mahāvīra, the 'Jainas') and as Lion (Sākyasinha, the lion of the Sākya race).

come, he will not fall into the power of the Passions. He will utterly give himself over to whatever task arrives, greedy for the work . . . how can he whose happiness is work itself be happy in doing no work? He will hold himself in readiness, so that even before a task comes to him he is prepared to turn to every course. As the seed of the cotton-tree is swayed at the coming and going of the wind, so will he be obedient to his resolution; and thus divine power is gained."[9]

We may remark here an important distinction between the Mahāyāna and the Hīnayāna lies in the fact that the former is essentially mythical and unhistorical; the believer is, indeed, warned—precisely as the worshipper of Krishna is warned in the Vaishnava scriptures that the Krishna Līlā is not a history, but a process for ever unfolded in the heart of man—that matters of historical fact are without religious significance. On this account, notwithstanding its more popular form, the Mahāyāna has been justly called 'more philosophical' than the Hīnayāna, "because under the forms of religious or mystical imagery it expresses the universal, whereas the Hīnayāna cannot set itself free from the domination of the historical fact."

[9]From the *Bodhicaryāvatāra* of Shānti Deva, translated by L. D. Barnett, 1902.

Tibetan Buddhism

It is almost invariably called the "mysterious" land of Tibet, and not without reason. A remote and isolated country, it has been hazily associated with the "Shangri-la" of James Hilton's *Lost Horizon* by a generation of readers in the West. Buddhism was introduced to Tibet in the seventh century A.D., and it gradually assimilated and superseded the ancient, indigenous Bon religion. One of the sects that have formed over the centuries is the Gelukpa. This is the so-called Yellow Hat school, in contrast to a rival sect, the Kagyupa, or Red Hat school. It was the third Grand Lama of the Gelukpa school who was given the title *Dalai* (Ocean Wide).

The doctrines and practices of Tibetan Buddhism are complex and elaborate, and its scriptures are lengthy indeed. The *Kagyur* is composed of materials comparable to those in the *Tripitaka*, to which have been added various Tantric works, and it runs to 108 volumes. The *Tangyur* is a 225-volume collection of commentaries on the *Kagyur* by Indian and Tibetan scholars.

Lobsang Phuntsok Lhalungpa is a former official of the Tibetan government who has passed through the major disciplines of Tibetan Buddhism. He now lives in Vancouver, British Columbia.

THE DALAI LAMA

For nearly three centuries the Dalai Lama has been the supreme temporal and spiritual power in Tibet.* The present Dalai Lama is the fourteenth in succession. Tibetans and Mongolians alike look upon him as being anxious to protect them from external enemies and injustices and as being their living Buddha—the one who will help them realize the Buddha and the Bodhisattva ideals. He is honored by all; all put their wholehearted faith in him; and all love him more dearly than anything else. To the Tibetans the Dalai Lama is not just a ruler or a teacher but a father, guide, protector, and above all, the great Bodhisattva. His words act upon them like magic, while his personality is so holy, so serene, and so forceful that they are thrilled and deeply moved whenever they happen to be in his presence. For his sake they are prepared to make any sacrifice. He is the unifying force of the country and as such is unmatched by any other spiritual teacher.

The Dalai Lama is looked upon as the incarnation of the Bodhisattva

*The invasion and conquest of Tibet by Communist China, begun in 1950, was climaxed in 1959 with a futile rebellion by the Tibetans. The Dalai Lama and some of his followers fled to India; others who managed to escape are scattered throughout the world.—R. E.

Avalokitesvara. According to certain of the twenty-one Sutras of Avalokitesvara—which were the first scriptures to be translated into Tibetan—the Bodhisattva Avalokitesvara made a solemn vow that instead of entering Nirvana he would remain in the world and help sentient beings attain the highest goal. . . .

To Tibetans the discovery of a new Dalai Lama is of vital importance for their material and spiritual well-being. The unity and sovereignty of the state depend upon the selection of the right person for their temporal and spiritual ruler. The process of selection is therefore extremely complicated and carefully checked. It rests chiefly on divine guidance given through visions and oracular predictions in which the physical characteristics, moral and spiritual qualities, and abnormal powers of the true candidate are clearly indicated. The first step is to find out from the State Oracle the locality in which the Dalai Lama has reincarnated. As soon as this important fact is known, search parties, which have been selected by lot or by the State Oracle, are sent out. On the basis of their reports the government draws up a list of possible candidates. In the meantime, the Regent of Tibet visits the sacred lake believed to be the abode of the Goddess Kali—for she appeared to the first Dalai Lama and solemnly vowed to watch over all his successors—and there he sees in the depths of the lake a vision indicating the location of the Dalai Lama's new birthplace.

In the case of the present Dalai Lama the vision seen by the late Regent Rading Rinpoche was, it is said, as clear as a movie film, showing not only the locality in which the reincarnation had taken place but the very house. In the second phase of the search the State Oracle gave the names of the parents and the district in which the child was to be found—and these directions coincided with those given by the Regent.

The searching mission disguised themselves as ordinary pilgrims and made their way into Amdo Province in China, and when they found the house they asked for lodging. When the boy turned up, he greeted the men with joy as if he were meeting some of his old followers. He pointed to one of the disguised men and identified him as a monk officer and to another and called him a lay officer, using the Tibetan language which none of his family could speak. The Lama who headed the mission then placed around his own neck two rosaries, one which had belonged to the late Dalai Lama and another which was an imitation. Without hesitation the boy snatched off the genuine one. He then selected the genuine walking stick and drum when they were shown to him, and, holding the stick in his left hand and the rosary and drum in his right, he recited the six-syllabled mantra of Avalokitesvara and retired.

The mission was deeply impressed by the manly character and intelligence of the child as well as by his power of bringing back memories of the past at such an early age. A confidential report was at once sent to the government. It was found that the mission's description of the locality, of the size and shape of the house, and even the color of the red dog there, tallied exactly with the vision seen by the Regent at the lake.

However, complications were caused by an omen which occurred at Lhasa. The horses of the late Dalai Lama galloped to the residence of the Prime Minister whose niece had just given birth to a son. According to the omen-loving people the gods had driven them there in order to indicate that the Dalai Lama had reincarnated in that particular family. At a secret ceremony, attended only by the Regent and the ministers, the State Oracle was asked to exhibit on his own body the sacred signs borne by the Guardian Deity who uses him as a mouthpiece. The Oracle, who was the course in a state of trance, thereupon took off his heavy golden helmet and showed on his head the mark of a sceptre. As another test, a paper containing the questions which the ministers wished to ask the Oracle was given to him rolled up in a scroll so that he could not read them. All the questions were answered point by point in elegant phrases such as the Oracle himself would have been quite incapable of composing. On this occasion the Guardian Deities disclosed that the boy at Amdo was the real Dalai Lama, they told his age, the names of his parents, and foretold his successful installation.

By way of an additional check, at a brief religious ceremony conducted by specially invited incarnate Lamas, lots were drawn in front of a sacred image of the Buddha. Out of the names of the numerous candidates, the boy's name was chosen. Thus all possible methods of ensuring the right choice were used.

According to Tibetan belief, the selection and installation of the right person is possible only by the combined efforts of men, gods, and Bodhisattvas. Good will among men and a variety of large-scale religious ceremonies are also essential to the success of the undertaking. Throughout the land the government and the people held prayers and performed special rites to guide the selection. The whole procedure may be described as the spiritual election of the spiritual and temporal ruler of a theocratic state, the holy land of Tibet where the lives of men are dominated and shaped by spiritual forces.

LAMAS, MONKS, LAYMEN, AND GURUS

The Buddhists of Tibet believe that the Buddha has continued to function in the world even after his passing into Nirvana and that, as he assured his followers, he will reappear as a Bodhisattva in innumerable worlds in order to help and to liberate living beings. To the Tibetans the Buddha is not only the supreme teacher but he is also their main support in their efforts to attain the final goal. There are, therefore, numerous Bodhisattvas who choose to remain with beings and share their sufferings in order to show them the true path to liberation. Such Bodhisattvas may be either recognized or unrecognized. In the recognized group belong the incarnate Lamas, the developed or nonincarnate Lamas, and those Bodhisattvas who, although they have acquiesced to the Great Compassion, have not yet acquired the actual state of Bodhisatt-vahood. The unrecognized Bodhisattvas are those living in various countries where they are destined to alleviate the sufferings of the people and reveal to them the principle of the Law without being recognized as Bodhisattvas.

. . .

Under these incarnate Lamas, who are highly respected and honored by all the people, are many thousands of monks who have voluntarily adopted the monastic life. The vows of a monk (monks are called *drapa* or *gedunpa*) are ordinarily for life, but if a monk should decide to leave the monastery he can go to the Lama who is his spiritual teacher and have him recite the mantras, the powerful words, which will release him from his vows. Such an action is not generally approved in Tibet.

. . .

Fifteen to twenty years must be devoted to the study of Buddhist literature and commentaries. A monk who completes the course of study and success-fully passes the public examination is given the title of Geshe, or Doctor in Literature and Philosophy, and permitted to go on to one of the tantric colleges for study. There he prepares for an examination in tantric literature, ritual, and the making of colored diagrams for the mandalas (thang-kas) which are used as an object of meditation. In addition, he must practice meditation for months and years and then must either retire to a hermitage or spend his time in teaching or preaching to the masses.

In this manner Tibet produces many spiritual masters. Some are incarnate Lamas, some are learned monks, and some are spiritual geniuses—self-developed Bodhisattvas. Monks are given a favored position in society, and respect is shown them by offering them food, money, and other necessities. But the highest honors go to the incarnate Lamas and spiritual geniuses who are the incarnate Bodhisattvas and the self-developed Bodhisattvas of Tibet.

. . .

In Tibet there are very many oracles who are consulted whenever it is necessary to know something of the future. Rarely are oracles monks; most of them are laymen and a few are laywomen. An oracle is a person who in a trance is connected with a particular spirit or deity and is able to predict future events.

The Tibetan people are highly respectful toward religion, for they regard it as the means for the realization of Enlightenment. Religion is for them the source of their culture, of the intellectual and spiritual illumination which has come to them. Every activity is connected with religion, whether it is a social gathering, leave-taking, building a new house, taking a new government post, concluding a business deal—all occasions of good or bad fortune are preceded by some kind of religious ceremony. Individual devotions are performed morning and evening in one's private shrine, which is decorated with images, offerings of flowers, perpetually burning lamps, and scented or pure water.

Books are considered to be more sacred than images, for, while images are only objects of recollection, books impart to us the Teaching. A private library usually consists of a complete set of Buddhist literature in more than 330 volumes.

Both monks and laymen use the thang-ka—which is sometimes called a mandala—as an aid to meditation. It is a picture of a Buddha or Bodhisattva, surrounded by other Bodhisattvas or guardian deities arranged in the form of a diagram which represents the universe, and decorated with symbols designed to aid recollection. In meditation the pictures serve as the object of concentration, and in the higher meditation the devotee concentrates on the higher nature of the deities pictured on the thang-ka.

The recitation of mantras is also prescribed for monks and laymen. A mantra is a word or series of words through which spiritual power is exercised. Some mantras are prescribed in the scriptures for getting good memory or for avoiding misfortune; the most important use is as an aid in concentration. Some mantras, like the six-syllabled mantra of Avalokitesvara, Om Mani Padme Hum, refer to a particular deity, and the recitation of such a mantra is the calling upon that deity. In Tantrayana, mantras are sometimes used for obtaining spiritual powers.

The prayer wheel is a means of repeating the mantras. Thousands of mantras are written and put in the center of the wheel after having been consecrated by rituals performed by Lamas; the turning of the wheel is the same as the recitation of the mantras. Often the mantras are also recited as the wheel is turned. The turning of the wheel by the wind or a water mill is a continuation of the recitation of the mantras in the wheel. Prayer flags are sometimes Bonist, but when used as a Buddhist devotion the flag has a mantra written on it, and as it blows in the wind it continues the recitation of the mantra.

. . .

Neither the monk nor the layman can attain Enlightenment by himself, however diligent he may be. Everyone must have a spiritual teacher, a guru, a noble and qualified teacher, whose precious instructions are followed with humble submission, wholehearted faith, and solemn resolve. By this means one is inspired and helped to acquire the intellectual and spiritual qualities which lead to Enlightenment.

There are different types of gurus for giving different types of instruction. Every layman has as many as five; Lamas and monks have many more, some of whom give instruction in simple practices, some in philosophy, some give inspiration, and some give training in Tantra. A guru is selected for his moral, intellectual, and spiritual qualities. The Vinaya recommends a teacher who is morally pure and spiritually developed, who knows the Vinaya ceremonies, loves patience, has good disciples, who is ready to assist his pupils morally, intellectually, and spiritually, and who gives timely instructions. The

Mahayana Sutras call for more advanced teachers who must be compassionate and able to draw others toward the Bodhisattva ideal. The tantric guru must be still more highly developed morally, intellectually, and spiritually. He must have a thorough knowledge of the Tantras and also know how to give instruction in accordance with the individual temperament and ability of each pupil.

. . .

THE DOCTRINE OF THE BUDDHA

The Doctrine of the Buddha, the Buddha Dharma, includes the two yanas—Hinayana and Mahayana. From the doctrinal point of view, *yana* means "burden" or "responsibility." Thus Hinayana, which is the doctrine dealing with self-emancipation, is called the Lesser Burden, while the doctrine which is concerned with the attainment of Enlightenment for the sake of all sentient beings is known as the Greater Burden.

After the Lord Buddha passed away, the Hinayana divided into many sects which, because of their greater prominence, claimed to be in the line of direct descent from the Buddha. Their Canon of the Buddha's teachings was written down in Pali in the first century B.C. The Mahayana followers, on the other hand, were more scattered and had neither organizations nor recognized institutions of their own for some time. Tibetans believe that the Mahayana teachings were handed down orally from generation to generation until they began committing them to writing in the first century B.C., beginning with the larger Prajnaparamita Sutra and the Saddharma Pundarika Sutra. The Mahayana came to include the yana based on the Prajnaparamita and the yana of the tantric teachings. Thus there are three yanas in Buddhist doctrine —Hinayana, Mahayana, and Tantrayana.

. . .

Practically speaking, Hinayana, Mahayana, and Tantrayana are interlinked in their essential principles and are the successive stages of one path. Each depends upon the others and serves as a stepping stone for the next higher. It is impossible to achieve the highest realization by sticking to one particular yana. Just as Mahayana is futile and dangerous unless it is based on the essential principles of Hinayana, so Hinayana is an incomplete approach to supreme realization unless it finds its consummation in Mahayana doctrines. . . .

. . .

The Three Precious Ones, that is, the Buddha, the Dharma, and the Sangha, have been known to the whole Buddhist world ever since the beginning of Buddhism. In temples and private shrines Tibetan Buddhists take devout and heartfelt refuge in the Three Precious Ones in the presence of their respective symbols, that is to say, before the images, the scriptures, and the congregation. This taking refuge in the Triple Gem is the most fundamental belief and most widely accepted practice in Buddhism. It precedes all other religious acts such as the reading of scriptures, making of solemn vows, receiving ordination, performance of ceremonies, and practice of meditation.

. . .

When a Tibetan takes refuge in the Buddha he is vowing to attempt to reach Buddhahood, to follow the career of a Bodhisattva. There have been in the past, are now in the present, and will be in the future, many Buddhas. When a human being has attained the highest development possible of the love, wisdom, intuition, resolution, spiritual power, and other qualities of a Buddha, such a human being can only be compared to other Buddhas. Bodhisattvas are those who have reached the middle stages of attainment, possessing the Buddha qualities to an extent which no ordinary human being can imagine. Tibetans believe that the Lord Buddha is still spiritually active and that he continues to guide, inspire, and protect the spiritual life, as do also the Bodhisattvas who appear again and again on the earth for the good of humanity.

. . .

Although the Mahayanists, like the Theravadins, believe that the Buddha was a man who reached the highest state of human perfection, they at the same time hold a different view that upon attaining the supreme Enlightenment he became one with the Triple Form of the Enlightened one *(Trikaya)*. At that point he ceased to be an ordinary man physically, mentally, and spiritually. This conception of the Triple Form, or Three Bodies of the Buddha, is a doctrine of paramount importance for understanding the Mahayana conception of the Buddha, and the ultimate goal of man.

The Triple Form includes the Earthly Body *(Nirmanakaya)*, the Subtle Body *(Sambhogakaya)*, and the Unmanifested Body *(Prajnadharmakaya)*. Therefore a Buddha may be defined as one who possesses these Three Bodies, together with all the qualities necessarily associated with them.

The Earthly Body (Nirmanakaya) appears in three different ways: as the Earthly Form of the Buddha proper, in various emanations as Bodhisattvas, and in concrete created forms.

When the Buddha himself appears in an Earthly Body, he bears upon his body the thirty-two major and eighty minor marks of an Enlightened One which are the result of his meritorious deeds in former existences—such as a curl of hair on the forehead, a knot of hair, and so on. But since his Earthly Body was in reality transcendental and not subject to the operation of natural law, including the law of karma, these marks only seem to be the result of his previous good actions. In reality they were deliberately assumed for the purpose of increasing the faith of his followers. This Earthly Body of the Buddha was mind-made and could be multiplied and transferred from place to place at will. It was majestic and dignified in appearance and clearly expressed gentleness and love. The Earthly Body plays the role of supreme spiritual guide, and as such plays a vitally important part in the progress and spiritual welfare of humanity.

The second aspect of the Earthly Body is the Bodhisattva. So great is the responsibility of the Buddha that he does not rest in the state of Nirvana but appears in the world again and again as an ordinary man who, inspired by universal love, compassion, and wisdom, shows the Path to all. A Buddha emanates as such Bodhisattvas as many times as he thinks necessary. Although Bodhisattvas are subject to the operation of natural law, there is no possibility that they can resort to evil deeds and wrong conceptions out of ignorance and selfishness. Their role, like that of the Buddhas, is to show the right Path to erring humanity, for they love to live in the world and serve beings. The numerous Bodhisattvas serve and direct mankind with motherly love and wisdom, and in all that they do they maintain without exception the course of natural law and are ready to suffer its consequences, however painful.

The third aspect of the Earthly Body is the concrete created form, of which there are very many. The concrete created forms can appear as paintings, images, or any other objects of religious art, or even as inanimate things such as hills and trees. The Buddha has stated in many Sutras that he would appear in the form of kings, ministers, priests, craftsmen, farmers, or even as birds and beasts.

The Subtle Body of the Buddha (Sambhogakaya), which is the second Body, is infinite in radiance, endowed with all the specific qualities of a Buddha, and sublimely beautiful. It is adorned with the splendid thirty-two major and eighty minor signs, all of unimaginable size. Although it is beyond the reach of human eyes, it appears to the highly developed Bodhisattvas. Aside from the fact that the Subtle Body immeasurably surpasses the Earthly Body in glory, the only difference between them is in location and duration and the relative scope of their duties. Of the different aspects of the Subtle Body one of the most difficult to understand is the fact that within it are contained all Buddhas. That is, in every particle of every Buddha can be contained all the other Buddhas, without there being any increase in the size of the particles or any decrease in the size of the Buddhas. This conception, which had its origin in the meditations of highly developed Bodhisattvas, is by no means easy to grasp until one has attained the same level of meditation. It is a way of saying that the Supreme Reality and all the specific qualities of the Buddhas are in essence identical.

The influence of the Subtle Form of the Buddha is so great that it extends over 10,000,000,000 worlds. Its work is nothing less than the liberation of all beings, including those Bodhisattvas who are not yet fully emancipated. Its tremendous task is summarized in the Five Perfect Attributes:

1. The subtle Body perfectly manifests all the acquired qualities of a Buddha.

2. Its abode is the whole universe.
3. It remains in manifestation until the end of existence of all beings.
4. It appears only to highly advanced Bodhisattvas.
5. It imparts to the Bodhisattvas the highest form of Mahayana doctrine.

The activity of this Subtle Body of the Buddha is perfect and incessant. It is a mistake, however, to think of it as governing the universe, or protecting beings from the consequences of their own deeds, or of forgiving evil deeds. All its actions, through its countless emanations as Bodhisattvas, aim at leading beings along the Path of the Buddha to the ultimate Enlightenment.

The third Body of the Buddha, the Unmanifested Body (*Prajnadharmakaya*), is difficult to define but something at least may be said concerning the complexities of its nature and functions. It is the Enlightened Mind in the sense of Supreme Reality, Supreme Wisdom combined with Infinite Compassion, and freedom from any obscurity caused by emotional defilements or false conceptions. The Supreme Reality of the Unmanifested Body is devoid of self-nature; it includes the other two Bodies of the Buddha. The Unmanifested Body is identical with the essential nature of all beings and things; within it there is no distinction, no origination, no cessation, no growth, no cause, no effect, and no condition. It is the Absolute Nature or the Supreme Reality of all individual persons and things, the goal to be realized through transcendental wisdom. It is to be attained by following the right Path shown to us by the Buddha on the basis of his personal experience.

The Unmanifested Body of the Buddha is endowed with a vast number of attributes which are the goal to be attained by those who follow the Path of the Buddha. Chief among the attributes in addition to Supreme Wisdom, Compassion, and Spiritual Power, are the Five Spiritual Faculties:

1. The Essential Wisdom, which perceives the Supreme Reality of all things and is devoid of growth and cessation
2. The Mirror-like Wisdom, which is pure and clear and free from obscurity
3. The Equality Wisdom, which frees the mind from all impediments
4. The All-discerning Wisdom, which sees things intuitively without going through the process of reasoning
5. The All-performing Wisdom, which accomplishes its purposes

All these attributes are the common heritage of all sentient beings. The attainment of the Triple Body of the Buddha is the goal of every form of life, the aim of every Tibetan Buddhist.

. . .

THE BOOK OF THE DEAD

Since there is no soul in beings, there cannot be any transmigration in the sense of an unchanging soul or ego moving from body to body. The rebirth is determined by the meritorious volitions of past lives, just as the plant grows from the seed. The actual process has been explained in the Buddhist doctrine of the twelve links in the chain of causation. In Tibetan Buddhism it is illustrated in the Wheel of Existence, which gives a vivid pictorial representation of how consciousness, obscured by ignorance, goes on accumulating all sorts of life-affirming activities. The Wheel of Existence symbolizes the unbroken circle of births and deaths which goes on in the various worlds.

In addition to the results of actions in past and present lives, the immediate cause determining the kind of rebirth one obtains is in each case the nature of the dying thoughts. If evil thoughts have defiled the consciousness at the time of dying, one will suffer rebirth in an inferior state, just as pure thoughts will bring rebirth in a superior state among men or the gods.

Those people who have committed neither highly meritorious nor highly demeritorious karma—whose consciousness is like a dried seed that needs heat and moisture—instead of being reborn at once, remain for some time in an intermediate state known as the Bardo. Such people, having failed to think good thoughts at the time of death, will have to experience subjective states which arouse emotions of fear, desire, and alarm, and these states partially determine the nature of their succeeding rebirth because they bring about the ripening of evil actions previously committed. The length of sojourn in Bardo varies from one week to seven. Tibetan Buddhists believe that while the consciousness is in this state it can be assisted by those with whom it had spiritual or physical relationship while on earth. It will be helped if such people will spend their property for the spiritual and material welfare of the masses and will perform various types of religious ceremonies for the benefit of the consciousnesses in Bardo.

The Old Translation school has a book called *The Liberation from the Intermediate State*—translated into English as *The Tibetan Book of the Dead*—which is read in front of the dying man or in front of the dead body by a celibate Lama. This practice is based on the Tibetan belief that after death the consciousness of the deceased person remains in or near the body for a week, or at least for three days, so that communication with it is still possible by means of the vibrations set up by the recitation of inspiring scriptures of this type or by the power of a spiritual genius.

. . .

Since the mental state of a dying person is, as it were, the steering wheel which guides the karmic vehicle to its destination, Tibetans attach great importance to what they call the art of dying, the transference of consciousness. This is one of the tantric practices. The people who are advanced in tantric practice can choose their deaths and rebirths at will. The friends and relatives, and his own Lama, have the special responsibility of giving the dying man the moral support which will enable him to restrain anger and tranquillize his disturbed mind. They must use all possible means to make sure that only good and pure thoughts are present in his mind. Any object or person for whom he has either a strong liking or dislike should be removed from the room. A faithful friend should assure him that he should not be anxious about his family, for the friend will look after them as if they were his own. The spiritual master should give instructions in the art of dying. The dying man is asked to have faith in the Triple Gem, to repent his evil actions with a pure heart, to resolve to keep the precepts, to make solemn vows, and to cultivate love toward all beings and a right understanding of phenomena. At the expiration of his last breath the Lama performs the ceremony called ''The Transference of Consciousness.''

Thus does the Wheel of Life turn for all beings.

further reading

Nancy Wilson Ross, *Three Ways of Asian Wisdom* (1966). Chapters on Hinduism, Buddhism, and Zen, with many reproductions of works of art that further enhance a delightful book.

Bhikshu Sangharakshita, *The Three Jewels: An Introduction to Modern Buddhism* (1967). The Three Jewels (and the three parts of this book) are the Buddha, the Dharma, and the Sangha.

Walpola Rahula, *What the Buddha Taught* (1959). An informed and readable introduction. Half of its eight chapters examine the Four Noble Truths.

James Bissett Pratt's *The Pilgrimage of Buddhism* (1928) has reached "standard work" status.

Allie M. Frazier (ed.), *Buddhism* (1969). A well-balanced anthology which contains both introductory essays by leading interpreters and readings from scriptures.

Edward J. Thomas, *The Life of the Buddha as Legend and History* (1927) and *The History of Buddhist Thought* (1933). Scholarly, authoritative, and detailed.

Chögyam Trungpa, *Born in Tibet* (1966). The autobiography of an incarnate Lama. The 1971 Penguin edition includes an Epilogue which carries the account further.

The Tibetan Book of the Dead (1927; many later revisions and editions), compiled and edited by W. Y. Evans-Wentz. Materials recited for the dead or dying, but relevant for the living.

The *Dhammapada,* a favorite part of the Pali Canon, is a collection of 423 aphorisms that epitomize the wisdom of early Buddhism. F. Max Müller's translation (1870) was the first of many; it is still among the best.

Sir Edwin Arnold's *The Light of Asia* (1879) is an enthusiastic poem relating the life and teachings of the Buddha. A phenomenal best-seller, it spurred Western interest in Buddhism.

With so much to choose from, anthologies of Buddhist scriptures vary widely. See Christmas Humphreys (ed.), *The Wisdom of Buddhism* (1960); Wm. Theodore de Bary (ed.), *The Buddhist Tradition* (1969); E. A. Burtt (ed.), *The Teachings of the Compassionate Buddha* (1955); Dwight Goddard (ed.), *A Buddhist Bible* (1938); Lucien Stryk (ed.), *The World of the Buddha* (1968); and Edward Conze (ed.), *Buddhist Scriptures* (1959), *Buddhist Texts Through the Ages* (1954), and *Buddhist Wisdom Books* (1958).

Zen Buddhism
_____ *the eternal in the now*

In walking, just walk.
In sitting, just sit.
Above all, don't wobble.

Yün-men

If religion could be called a kind of poetry, Zen would be *haiku,* that delightful form of poetry upon whose development in Japan Zen had a decisive influence. And those who are familiar with these simple, suggestive poems already know something of Zen. A good *haiku,* like Zen itself,

. . . is a hand beckoning, a door half-opened, a mirror wiped clean. It is a way of returning to nature, our moon nature, our cherry blossom nature, our falling leaf nature, in short to our Buddha nature. It is a way in which the cold winter rain, the swallows of evening, even the very day in its hotness, and the length of the night become truly alive, share in our humanity, speak their own silent and expressive language.*

In Zen and in *haiku* the sights and sounds of the everyday world are vivid and real, but they are also imbued with a sense of the Eternal. It is a kind of double vision: the concrete Here and Now is perceived as permeated with the Miraculous. Historically speaking, it is a blending of the visions of Taoist China and Indian Buddhism.

The name by which we know the religion is itself a thumbnail history: the Sanskrit term for meditation, *dhyana,* became *ch'an* in China[†] and *zen* in Japan; and it was from Japan that Zen came to the West. Zen's origins, then, were in India, but the details of its history there are speculative. Although Buddhist meditational practices were, of course, widespread, there seems to be no evidence of a distinctively Zen-type school in primitive Buddhism. The *traditional* history of Zen, nevertheless, begins with Gautama Buddha and claims an unbroken succession to the Twenty-eighth Patriarch, the Indian monk Bodhidharma, who brought Zen to China in the sixth century. (Scholars now believe that he had precursors in preceding centuries.) In China Bodhidharma became known as the First Patriarch, and with him appeared some of the signs of things to come. Later portraits of Bodhidharma convey a tigerlike disposition, and it is reported that he sat meditating before the wall of a cave for nine years. A disciple, Shen-kuang, is said to have cut off his left arm with a sword in order to demonstrate to Bodhidharma his sincerity. In time, Shen-kuang became the Second Patriarch.

But it was not until the seventh century and the Sixth Patriarch, Hui-neng (638–713), that Zen really bloomed. Hui-neng, a poor and illiterate youth, sold

*R. H. Blyth, quoted in Nancy Wilson Ross, *The World of Zen* (New York: Random House, 1960), p. 120.
†Hence most accounts of Zen in China refer to it as *Ch'an* Buddhism.

CHAPTER THREE / *Zen Buddhism*

firewood to support his widowed mother. One day while at work he overheard a customer reciting the *Diamond Sutra*. Profoundly impressed and inspired to learn more, he journeyed for a month to see the Fifth Patriarch, Hung-jen. The story of that meeting and the manner in which Hui-neng became the Sixth Patriarch is recounted in this chapter in *The Platform Sutra of the Sixth Patriarch*. Hui-neng was the last of the Patriarchs: in order to avoid jealousies and strife among his disciples, he did not name a successor.[‡]

The Golden Age of Zen followed Hui-neng and lasted until the beginning of the tenth century. There were a proliferation of sects and a series of great and original Zen masters. The literature of Zen abounds with stories of their wisdom and eccentricities. Ma-tsu (707–786) once suddenly twisted the nose of a disciple, who was abruptly enlightened. A deafening shout at another disciple left him stunned for three days—and precipitated his *satori* (awakening). Huang-po (d. 850) wrote *Treatise on the Essentials of the Transmission of Mind* and had among his disciples I-hsuan (d. 867), founder of the Lin-chi (Rinzai, in Japanese) school. Zen continued to thrive in China until about the seventeenth century, after which there began a long and steady decline.

In the twelfth and thirteenth centuries, however, two Japanese masters, Eisai (1141–1215) and Dogen (1200–1253), firmly established Zen in Japan, where over the centuries it has prospered and exerted a vast influence upon the thought and culture of that land. Eisai had studied Rinzai Zen in China, and he brought those teachings back to Japan. Dogen had also learned his Zen in China, but his wanderings there had led him to Soto teachings (the origins of which go back to one of the disciples of Hui-neng).

These two sects, the Rinzai and the Soto, are today the strongest of several in Japan. Both employ *zazen* (seated meditation), but the Rinzai more rigorously. As may be seen in the following essay by D. T. Suzuki, the greatest interpreter for the West of the Rinzai school, the use of the *koan* (a paradoxical, mind-snapping problem assigned to a student for meditation) as a means to *satori* is also a prominent feature of this "sudden awakening" school. Soto Zen, for which Shunryu Suzuki in these pages is an outstanding spokesman, holds that the awakening should come more naturally and spontaneously: this is the "gradual awakening" school. In the final selection of the chapter, Gary Snyder describes Zen training in a Rinzai school in Kyoto, Japan.

[‡]This traditional history of Zen has been challenged by Hu Shih, who says that Zen in China "arose not out of Indian yoga or dhyana but as a revolt against it." See his essay "The Development of Zen Buddhism in China" William Briggs (ed.), in *Anthology of Zen* (New York: Grove Press, 1961), pp. 7-30.

Zen, Satori, and the Koan

It may be said (and in fact always is said) that it was the writings of one Japanese scholar that opened up Zen to the West. Daisetz Teitaro Suzuki (1870–1966) lived most of his years in his native Japan, but he also traveled the world during his long lifetime. He came to the United States as early as 1897, working with Paul Carus and the Open Court Publishing Company as a writer and translator. In the late 1930s he lectured on Zen at Cambridge, Oxford, and other English universities. Under the auspices of the Rockefeller Foundation, he toured American universities and spent several years during the 1950s as a professor at Columbia University. Returning to Japan in 1958, he continued to work vigorously until his death.

Over the years he had published some 130 books and countless articles. His first book on Zen in English was *Essays in Zen Buddhism (First Series),* published in 1927. He began that volume with the memorable statement that "Zen in its essence is the art of seeing into the nature of one's own being, and it points the way from bondage to freedom." Other of his notable works on Zen included the Second and Third Series of essays on Zen, *The Training of the Zen Buddhist Monk,* and *Zen and Japanese Culture.*

WHAT IS ZEN?

Before proceeding to expound the teaching of Zen at some length in the following pages, let me answer some of the questions which are frequently raised by critics concerning the real nature of Zen.

Is Zen a system of philosophy, highly intellectual and profoundly metaphysical, as most Buddhist teachings are?

I have already stated that we find in Zen all the philosophy of the East

D. T. Suzuki, "Zen, Satori, and the Koan." Some notes have been omitted, and the remainder renumbered. Editor's title.

crystallized, but this ought not to be taken as meaning that Zen is a philosophy in the ordinary application of the term. Zen is decidedly not a system founded upon logic and analysis. If anything, it is the antipode to logic, by which I mean the dualistic mode of thinking. There may be an intellectual element in Zen, for Zen is the whole mind, and in it we find a great many things; but the mind is not a composite thing that is to be divided into so many faculties, leaving nothing behind when the dissection is over. Zen has nothing to teach us in the way of intellectual analysis; nor has it any set doctrines which are imposed on its followers for acceptance. In this respect Zen is quite chaotic if you choose to say so. Probably Zen followers may have sets of doctrines, but they have them on their own account, and for their own benefit; they do not owe the fact to Zen. Therefore, there are in Zen no sacred books or dogmatic tenets, nor are there any symbolic formulae through which an access might be gained into the signification of Zen. If I am asked, then, what Zen teaches, I would answer, Zen teaches nothing. Whatever teachings there are in Zen, they come out of one's own mind. We teach ourselves; Zen merely points the way. Unless this pointing is teaching, there is certainly nothing in Zen purposely set up as its cardinal doctrines or as its fundamental philosophy.

Zen claims to be Buddhism, but all the Buddhist teachings as propounded in the sutras and sastras are treated by Zen as mere waste paper whose utility consists in wiping off the dirt of intellect and nothing more. Do not imagine, however, that Zen is nihilism. All nihilism is self-destructive, it ends no-where. Negativism is sound as method, but the highest truth is an affirmation. When it is said that Zen has no philosophy, that it denies all doctrinal authority, that it casts aside all so-called sacred literature as rubbish, we must not forget that Zen is holding up in this very act of negation something quite positive and eternally affirmative. This will become clearer as we proceed.

Is Zen a religion? It is not a religion in the sense that the term is popularly understood; for Zen has no God to worship, no ceremonial rites to observe, no future abode to which the dead are destined, and, last of all, Zen has no soul whose welfare is to be looked after by somebody else and whose immortality is a matter of intense concern with some people. Zen is free from all these dogmatic and ''religious'' encumbrances.

When I say there is no God in Zen, the pious reader may be shocked, but this does not mean that Zen denies the existence of God; neither denial nor affirmation concerns Zen. When a thing is denied, the very denial involves something not denied. The same can be said of affirmation. This is inevitable in logic. Zen wants to rise above logic, Zen wants to find a higher affirmation where there are no antitheses. Therefore, in Zen, God is neither denied nor insisted upon; only there is in Zen no such God as has been conceived by Jewish and Christian minds. For the same reason that Zen is not a philosophy, Zen is not a religion.

As to all those images of various Buddhas and Bodhisattvas and Devas and other beings that one comes across in Zen temples, they are like so many pieces of wood or stone or metal; they are like the camellias, azaleas, or stone lanterns in my garden. Make obeisance to the camellia now in full bloom, and worship it if you like, Zen would say. There is as much religion in so doing as in bowing to the various Buddhist gods, or as sprinkling holy water, or as participating in the Lord's Supper. All those pious deeds considered to be meritorious or sanctifying by most so-called religiously minded people are artificialities in the eyes of Zen. It boldly declares that "the immaculate Yogins do not enter Nirvana and the precept-violating monks do not go to hell". This, to ordinary minds, is a contradiction of the common law of moral life, but herein lies the truth and life of Zen. Zen is the spirit of a man. Zen believes in his inner purity and goodness. Whatever is superadded or violently torn away, injures the wholesomeness of the spirit. Zen, therefore, is emphatically against all religious conventionalism.

Its irreligion, however, is merely apparent. Those who are truly religious will be surprised to find that after all there is so much of religion in the barbarous declaration of Zen. But to say that Zen is a religion, in the sense that Christianity or Mohammedanism is, would be a mistake. To make my point clearer, I quote the following. When Sakyamuni was born, it is said that he lifted one hand toward the heavens and pointed to the earth with the other, exclaiming, "Above the heavens and below the heavens, I alone am the Honoured One!" Ummon (Yun-men), founder of the Ummon School of Zen, comments on this by saying, "If I had been with him at the moment of his uttering this, I would surely have struck him dead with one blow and thrown the corpse into the maw of a hungry dog." What unbelievers would ever think of making such raving remarks over a spiritual leader? Yet one of the Zen masters following Ummon says: "Indeed, this is the way Ummon desires to serve the world, sacrificing everything he has, body and mind! How grateful he must have felt for the love of Buddha!"

Zen is not to be confounded with a form of meditation as practised by "New Thought" people, or Christian Scientists, or Hindu Sannyasins, or some Buddhists. Dhyana, as it is understood by Zen, does not correspond to the practice as carried on in Zen. A man may meditate on a religious or philosophical subject while disciplining himself in Zen, but that is only incidental; the essence of Zen is not there at all. Zen purposes to discipline the mind itself, to make it its own master, through an insight into its proper nature. This getting into the real nature of one's own mind or soul is the fundamental object of Zen Buddhism. Zen, therefore, is more than meditation and Dhyana in its ordinary sense. The discipline of Zen consists in opening the mental eye in order to look into the very reason of existence.

To meditate, a man has to fix his thought on something; for instance, on the oneness of God, or his infinite love, or on the impermanence of things. But this is the very thing Zen desires to avoid. If there is anything Zen strongly emphasizes it is the attainment of freedom; that is, freedom from all unnatural encumbrances. Meditation is something artificially put on; it does not belong to the native activity of the mind. Upon what do the fowl of the air meditate? Upon what do the fish in the water meditate? They fly; they swim. Is not that enough? Who wants to fix his mind on the unity of God and man, or on the nothingness of this life? Who wants to be arrested in the daily manifestations of his life-activity by such meditations as the goodness of a divine being or the everlasting fire of hell?

We may say that Christianity is monotheistic, and the Vedanta pantheistic; but we cannot make a similar assertion about Zen. Zen is neither monotheistic nor pantheistic; Zen defies all such designations. Hence there is no object in Zen upon which to fix the thought. Zen is a wafting cloud in the sky. No screw fastens it, no string holds it; it moves as it lists. *No amount of meditation will keep Zen in one place.* Meditation is not Zen. Neither pantheism nor monotheism provides Zen with its subjects of concentration. If Zen is monotheistic, it may tell its followers to meditate on the oneness of things where all differences and inequalities, enveloped in the all-illuminating brightness of the divine light, are obliterated. If Zen were pantheistic it would tell us that every meanest flower in the field reflects the glory of God. But what Zen says is "After all things are reduced to oneness, where would that One be reduced?" Zen wants to have one's mind free and unobstructed; even the idea of oneness or allness is a stumbling-block and a strangling snare which threatens the original freedom of the spirit.

Zen, therefore, does not ask us to concentrate our thought on the idea that a dog is God, or that three pounds of flax are divine. When Zen does this it commits itself to a definite system of philosophy, and there is no more Zen. Zen just feels fire warm and ice cold, because when it freezes we shiver and welcome fire. The feeling is all in all, as Faust declares; all our theorization fails to touch reality. But "the feeling" here must be understood in its deepest sense or in its purest form. Even to say that "This is the feeling" means that Zen is no more there. Zen defies all concept-making. That is why Zen is difficult to grasp.

Whatever meditation Zen may propose, then, will be to take things as they are, to consider snow white and the raven black. When we speak of meditation we in most cases refer to its abstract character; that is, meditation is known to be the concentration of the mind on some highly generalized proposition, which is, in the nature of things, not always closely and directly connected with the concrete affairs of life. Zen perceives or feels, and does not abstract nor meditate. Zen penetrates and is finally lost in the immersion. Meditation, on the other hand, is outspokenly dualistic and consequently inevitably superficial.

. . .

Zen is sometimes made to mean "mind-murder and the curse of idle reverie". This is the statement of Griffis, the well-known author of *Religions of Japan.*[1] By "mind-murder" I do not know what he really means, but does he mean that Zen kills the activities of the mind by making one's thought fix on one thing, or by inducing sleep? Mr. Reischauer in his book[2] almost endorses this view of Griffis by asserting that Zen is "mystical self-intoxication". Does he mean that Zen is intoxicated in the "Greater Self"; so called, as Spinoza was intoxicated in God? Though Mr. Reischauer is not quite clear as to the meaning of "intoxication", he may think that Zen is unduly absorbed in the thought of the "Greater Self" as the final reality in this world of particulars. It is amazing to see how superficial some of the uncritical observers of Zen are! In point of fact, Zen has no "mind" to murder; therefore, there is no "mind-murdering" in Zen. Zen has again no "self" as something to which we can cling as a refuge; therefore, in Zen again there is no "self" by which we may become intoxicated.

The truth is, Zen is extremely elusive as far as its outward aspects are concerned; when you think you have caught a glimpse of it, it is no more there; from afar it looks so approachable, but as soon as you come near it you see it even further away from you than before. Unless, therefore, you devote some years of earnest study to the understanding of its primary principles, it is not to be expected that you will begin to have a fair grasp of Zen.

"The way to ascend unto God is to descend into one's self";—these are Hugo's words. "If thou wishest to search out the deep things of God, search out the depths of thine own spirit";—this comes from Richard of St. Victor. When all these deep things are searched out there is after all no "self". Where you can descend, there is no "spirit", no "God" whose depths are to be fathomed. Why? Because Zen is a bottomless abyss. Zen declares, though in a somewhat different manner: "Nothing really exists throughout the triple world; where do you wish to see the mind (or spirit=*hsin*)? The four elements are all empty in their ultimate nature; where could the Buddha's abode be?—but lo! the truth is unfolding itself right before your eye. This is all there is to it—and indeed nothing more!" A minute's hesitation and Zen is irrevocably lost. All the Buddhas of the past, present, and future may try to make you catch it once more, and yet it is a thousand miles away. "Mind-murder" and "self-intoxication", forsooth! Zen has no time to bother itself with such criticisms.

The critics may mean that the mind is hypnotized by Zen to a state of unconsciousness, and that when this obtains, the favourite Buddhist doctrine of emptiness (*sunyata*) is realized, where the subject is not conscious of an objective world or of himself, being lost in one vast emptiness, whatever this may be. This interpretation again fails to hit Zen aright. It is true that there are some such expressions in Zen as might suggest this kind of interpretation, but to understand Zen we must make a leap here. The "vast emptiness" must be

[1] P. 255.
[2] *Studies of Buddhism in Japan*, p. 118.

traversed. The subject must be awakened from a state of unconsciousness if he does not wish to be buried alive. Zen is attained only when "self-intoxication" is abandoned and the "drunkard" is really awakened to his deeper self. If the mind is ever to be "murdered", leave the work in the hand of Zen; for it is Zen that will restore the murdered and lifeless one into a state of eternal life. "Be born again, be awakened from the dream, rise from the death, O ye drunkards!" Zen would exclaim. Do not try, therefore, to see Zen with the eyes bandaged; and your hands are too unsteady to take hold of it. And remember I am not indulging in figures of speech.

I might multiply many such criticisms if it were necessary but I hope that the above have sufficiently prepared the reader's mind for the following more positive statements concerning Zen. The basic idea of Zen is to come in touch with the inner workings of our being, and to do this in the most direct way possible, without resorting to anything external or superadded. Therefore, anything that has the semblance of an external authority is rejected by Zen. Absolute faith is placed in a man's own inner being. For whatever authority there is in Zen, all comes from within. This is true in the strictest sense of the word. Even the reasoning faculty is not considered final or absolute. On the contrary, it hinders the mind from coming into the directest communication with itself. The intellect accomplishes its mission when it works as an intermediary, and Zen has nothing to do with an intermediary except when it desires to communicate itself to others. For this reason all the scriptures are merely tentative and provisory; there is in them no finality. The central fact of life as it is lived is what Zen aims to grasp, and this in the most direct and most vital manner. Zen professes itself to be the spirit of Buddhism, but in fact it is the spirit of all religions and philosophies. When Zen is thoroughly understood, absolute peace of mind is attained, and a man lives as he ought to live. What more may we hope?

Some say that as Zen is admittedly a form of mysticism it cannot claim to be unique in the history of religion. Perhaps so; but Zen is a mysticism of its own order. It is mystical in the sense that the sun shines, that the flower blooms, that I hear at this moment somebody beating a drum in the street. If these are mystical facts, Zen is brim-full of them. When a Zen master was once asked what Zen was, he replied, "Your everyday thought." Is this not plain and most straightforward? It has nothing to do with any sectarian spirit. Christians as well as Buddhists can practise Zen just as big fish and small fish are both contentedly living in the same ocean. Zen is the ocean, Zen is the air, Zen is the mountain, Zen is thunder and lightning, the spring flower, summer heat, and winter snow; nay, more than that, Zen is the man. With all the formalities, conventionalisms, and superadditions that Zen has accumulated in its long history, its central fact is very much alive. The special merit of Zen lies in this: that we are still able to see into this ultimate fact without being biased by anything.

As has been said before, what makes Zen unique as it is practised in Japan is its systematic training of the mind. Ordinary mysticism has been too erratic a product and apart from one's ordinary life; this Zen has revolutionized. What was up in the heavens, Zen has brought down to earth. With the development of Zen, mysticism has ceased to be mystical; it is no more the spasmodic product of an abnormally endowed mind. For Zen reveals itself in the most uninteresting and uneventful life of a plain man of the street, recognizing the fact of living in the midst of life as it is lived. Zen systematically trains the mind to see this; it opens a man's eye to the greatest mystery as it is daily and hourly performed; it enlarges the heart to embrace eternity of time and infinity of space in its every palpitation; it makes us live in the world as if walking in the garden of Eden; and all these spiritual feats are accomplished without resorting to any doctrines but by simply asserting in the most direct way the truth that lies in our inner being.

Whatever else Zen may be, it is practical and commonplace and at the same time most living. An ancient master, wishing to show what Zen is, lifted one of his fingers, another kicked a ball, and a third slapped the face of his questioner. If the inner truth that lies deep in us is thus demonstrated, is not Zen the most practical and direct method of spiritual training ever resorted to by any religion? And is not this practical method also a most original one? Indeed, Zen cannot be anything else but original and creative because it refuses to deal with concepts but deals with living facts of life. When conceptually understood, the lifting of a finger is one of the most ordinary incidents in everybody's life. But when it is viewed from the Zen point of view it vibrates with divine meaning and creative vitality. So long as Zen can point out this truth in the midst of our conventional and concept-bound existence we must say that it has its reason of being.

SATORI

The essence of Zen Buddhism consists in acquiring a new viewpoint of looking at life and things generally. By this I mean that if we want to get into the inmost life of Zen, we must forgo all our ordinary habits of thinking which control our everyday life, we must try to see if there is any other way of judging things, or rather if our ordinary way is always sufficient to give us the ultimate satisfaction of our spiritual needs. If we feel dissatisfied somehow with this life, if there is something in our ordinary way of living that deprives us of freedom in its most sanctified sense, we must endeavour to find a way somewhere which gives us a sense of finality and contentment. Zen proposes to do this for us and assures us of the acquirement of a new point of view in which life assumes a fresher, deeper, and more satisfying aspect. This acquirement, however, is really and naturally the greatest mental cataclysm one can go through with in life. It is no easy task, it is a kind of fiery baptism, and one has to go through the storm, the earthquake, the overthrowing of the mountains, and the breaking in pieces of the rocks.

This acquiring of a new point of view in our dealings with life and the world is popularly called by Japanese Zen students 'satori' (*wu* in Chinese). It is really another name for Enlightenment (*annuttara-samyak-saṁbodhi*), which is the word used by the Buddha and his Indian followers ever since his realization under the Bodhi-tree by the River Nairañjanā. There are several other phrases in Chinese designating this spiritual experience, each of which has a special connotation, showing tentatively how this phenomenon is interpreted. At all events there is no Zen without satori, which is indeed the Alpha and Omega of Zen Buddhism. Zen devoid of satori is like a sun without its light and heat. Zen may lose all its literature, all its monasteries, and all its paraphernalia; but as long as there is satori in it it will survive to eternity. I want to emphasize this most fundamental fact concerning the very life of Zen; for there are some even among the students of Zen themselves who are blind to this central fact and are apt to think when Zen has been explained away logically or psychologically, or as one of the Buddhist philosophies which can be summed up by using highly technical and conceptual Buddhist phrases, Zen is exhausted, and there remains nothing in it that makes it what it is. But my contention is, the life of Zen begins with the opening of satori (*kai wu* in Chinese).

Satori may be defined as an intuitive looking into the nature of things in contradistinction to the analytical or logical understanding of it. Practically, it means the unfolding of a new world hitherto unperceived in the confusion of a dualistically-trained mind. Or we may say that with satori our entire surroundings are viewed from quite an unexpected angle of perception. Whatever this is, the world for those who have gained a satori is no more the old world as it used to be; even with all its flowing streams and burning fires, it is never the same one again. Logically stated, all its opposites and contradictions are united and harmonized into a consistent organic whole. This is a mystery and a miracle, but according to the Zen masters such is being performed every day. Satori can thus be had only through our once personally experiencing it.

. . .

Daie was a great advocate of satori, and one of his favorite sayings was, "Zen has no words; when you have satori, you have everything." Hence his strong arguments for it, which came, as has already been shown, from his own experience. Until then, he was quite ready to write a treatise against Zen in which he planned to disclaim everything accredited to Zen by its followers. His interview with his master Engo, however, crushed all his former determination, making him come out as a most intense advocate of the Zen experience. As I go on with this study of the *kōan* exercise, I shall have many occasions to make further references to Daie. In the meantime I wish to enumerate some of the most salient features of satori, which will later help us understand the role of *kōan* in the whole structure of Zen.

1. *Irrationality.* By this I mean that satori is not a conclusion to be reached by reasoning, and defies all intellectual determination. Those who have experienced it are always at a loss to explain it coherently or logically. When it is explained at all, either in words or gestures, its content more or less undergoes a mutilation. The uninitiated are thus unable to grasp it by what is outwardly visible, while those who have had the experience discern what is genuine from what is not. The satori experience is thus always characterized by irrationality, inexplicability, and incommunicability.

Listen to Daie once more: "This matter [i.e., Zen] is like a great mass of fire; when you approach it your face is sure to be scorched. It is again like a sword about to be drawn; when it is once out of the scabbard, someone is sure to lose his life. But if you neither fling away the scabbard nor approach the fire, you are no better than a piece of rock or of wood. Coming to this pass, one has to be quite a resolute character full of spirit." There is nothing here suggestive of cool reasoning and quiet metaphysical or epistemological analysis, but of a certain desperate will to break through an insurmountable barrier, of the will impelled by some irrational or unconscious power behind it. Therefore, the outcome also defies intellection or conceptualization.

2. *Intuitive Insight.* That there is noetic quality in mystic experiences has been pointed out by James in his *Varieties of Religious Experience,* and this applies also to the Zen experience known as satori. Another name for satori is *kenshō (chien-hsing)*, meaning "to see essence or Nature," which apparently proves that there is "seeing" or "perceiving" in satori. That this seeing is of quite a different quality from what is ordinarily designated as knowledge need not be specifically noticed. Eka is reported to have made this statement concerning his satori which was confirmed by Bodhidharma himself: "[As to my satori], it is not a total annihilation; it is knowledge of the most adequate kind; only it cannot be expressed in words." In this respect Jinne was more explicit, for he says that "the one character *chi* (knowledge) is the source of all mysteries *(myō).*"[3]

Without this noetic quality satori will lose all its pungency, for it is really the reason of satori itself. It is noteworthy that the knowledge contained in satori is concerned with something universal and at the same time with the individual aspect of existence. When a finger is lifted, the lifting means, from the viewpoint of satori, far more than the act of lifting. Some may call it symbolic, but satori does not point to anything beyond itself, being final as it is. Satori is the knowledge of an individual object and also that of Reality which is, if I may say so, at the back of it.

[3]Shūmitsu in "Zen Masters and Disciples." *Myō* is a difficult term to translate; it often means "exquisiteness," "indefinable subtlety." In this case *myō* is the mysterious way in which things are presented to this ultimate knowledge.

3. *Authoritativeness.* By this I mean that the knowledge realized by satori is final, that no amount of logical argument can refute it. Being direct and personal it is sufficient unto itself. All that logic can do here is to explain it, to interpret it in connection with other kinds of knowledge with which our minds are filled. Satori is thus a form of perception, an inner perception, which takes place in the most interior part of consciousness. Hence the sense of authoritativeness, which means finality. So, it is generally said that Zen is like drinking water, for it is by one's self that one knows whether it is warm or cold. The Zen perception being the last term of experience, it cannot be denied by outsiders who have no such experience.

4. *Affirmation.* What is authoritative and final can never be negative. For negation has no value for our life, it leads us nowhere; it is not a power that urges, nor does it give one a place to rest. Though the satori experience is sometimes expressed in negative terms, it is essentially an affirmative attitude toward all things that exist; it accepts them as they come along regardless of their moral values. Buddhists call this *kṣānti*, "patience," or more properly "acceptance," that is, acceptance of things in their suprarelative or transcendental aspect where no dualism of whatever sort avails.

Some may say that this is pantheistic. The term, however, has a definite philosophic meaning and I would not see it used in this connection. When so interpreted the Zen experience exposes itself to endless misunderstandings and "defilements." Daie says in his letter to Myōsō: "An ancient sage says that the Tao itself does not require special disciplining, only let it not be defiled. I would say: To talk about mind or nature is defiling; to talk about the unfathomable or the mysterious is defiling; to practice meditation or tranquillization is defiling; to direct one's attention to it, to think about it is defiling; to be writing about it thus on paper with a brush is especially defiling. What then shall we have to do in order to get ourselves oriented, and properly apply ourselves to it? The precious Vajra-sword is right here and its purpose is to cut off the head. Do not be concerned with human questions of right and wrong. All is Zen just as it is, and right here you are to apply yourself." Zen is Suchness—a grand affirmation.

5. *Sense of the Beyond.* Terminology may differ in different religions, and in satori there is always what we may call a sense of the Beyond; the experience indeed is my own but I feel it to be rooted elsewhere. The individual shell in which my personality is so solidly encased explodes at the moment of satori. Not, necessarily, that I get unified with a being greater than myself or absorbed in it, but that my individuality, which I found rigidly held together and definitely kept separate from other individual existences, becomes loosened somehow from its tightening grip and melts away into something indescribable, something which is of quite a different order from what I am accustomed to. The feeling that follows is that of a complete release or a complete rest—the feeling that one has arrived finally at the destination.

"Coming home and quietly resting" is the expression generally used by Zen followers. The story of the prodigal son in the *Saddharmapundarīka,* in the *Vajrasamādhi,* and also in the New Testament points to the same feeling one has at the moment of a satori experience.

As far as the psychology of satori is considered, a sense of the Beyond is all we can say about it; to call this the Beyond; the Absolute, or God, or a Person is to go further than the experience itself and to plunge into a theology or metaphysics. Even the "Beyond" is saying a little too much. When a Zen master says, "There is not a fragment of a tile above my head, there is not an inch of earth beneath my feet," the expression seems to be an appropriate one. I have called it elsewhere the Unconscious, though this has a psychological taint.

6. *Impersonal Tone.* Perhaps the most remarkable aspect of the Zen experience is that it has no personal note in it as is observable in Christian mystic experiences. There is no reference whatever in Buddhist satori to such personal and frequently sexual feelings and relationships as are to be gleaned from these terms: flame of love, a wonderful love shed in the heart, embrace, the beloved, bride, bridegroom, spiritual matrimony, Father, God, the Son of God, God's child, etc. We may say that all these terms are interpretations based on a definite system of thought and really have nothing to do with the experience itself. At any rate, alike in India, China, and Japan, satori has remained thoroughly impersonal, or rather highly intellectual.

Is this owing to the peculiar character of Buddhist philosophy? Does the experience itself take its colors from the philosophy or theology? Whatever this is, there is no doubt that in spite of its having some points of similitude to the Christian mystic experience, the Zen experience is singularly devoid of personal or human colorings. Chōben, a great government officer of the Sung dynasty, was a lay-disciple of Hōsen of Chiang-shan. One day after his official duties were over, he found himself leisurely sitting in his office, when all of a sudden a clash of thunder burst on his ear, and he realized a state of satori. The poem he then composed depicts one aspect of the Zen experience:

> Devoid of thought, I sat quietly by the desk in my official room,
> With my fountain-mind undisturbed, as serene as water;
> A sudden clash of thunder, the mind-doors burst open,
> And lo, there sitteth the old man in all his homeliness.

This is perhaps all the personal tone one can find in the Zen experience, and what a distance between "the old man in his homeliness" and "God in all His glory," not to say anything about such feelings as "the heavenly sweetness of Christ's excellent love," etc.! How barren, how unromantic satori is when compared with the Christian mystic experiences!

Not only satori itself is such a prosaic and non-glorious event, but the occasion that inspires it also seems to be unromantic and altogether lacking in super-sensuality. Satori is experienced in connection with any ordinary occurrence in one's daily life. It does not appear to be an extraordinary phenomenon as is recorded in Christian books of mysticism. Someone takes hold of you, or slaps you, or brings you a cup of tea, or makes some most commonplace remark, or recites some passage from a sutra or from a book of poetry, and when your mind is ripe for its outburst, you come at once to satori. There is no romance of love-making, no voice of the Holy Ghost, no plenitude of Divine Grace, no glorification of any sort. Here is nothing painted in high colors, all is gray and extremely unobtrusive and unattractive.

7. *Feeling of Exaltation.* That this feeling inevitably accompanies satori is due to the fact that it is the breaking up of the restriction imposed on one as an individual being, and this breaking up is not a mere negative incident but quite a positive one fraught with signification because it means an infinite expansion of the individual. The general feeling, though we are not always conscious of it, which characterizes all our functions of consciousness, is that of restriction and dependence, because consciousness itself is the outcome of two forces conditioning or restricting each other. Satori, on the contrary, essentially consists in doing away with the opposition of two terms in whatsoever sense—and this opposition is the principle of consciousness as before mentioned, while satori is to realize the Unconscious which goes beyond the opposition.

To be released of this, therefore, must make one feel above all things intensely exalted. A wandering outcast maltreated everywhere not only by others but by himself finds that he is the possessor of all the wealth and power that is ever attainable in this world by a mortal being—if this does not give him a high feeling of self-glorification, what could? Says a Zen master, "When you have satori you are able to reveal a palatial mansion made of precious stones on a single blade of grass; but when you have no satori, a palatial mansion itself is concealed behind a simple blade of grass."

Another Zen master, evidently alluding to the *Avatamsaka*, declares: "O monks, lo and behold! A most auspicious light is shining with the utmost brilliancy all over the great chiliacosm, simultaneously revealing all the countries, all the oceans, all the Sumerus, all the suns and moons, all the heavens, all the lands—each of which number as many as hundreds of thousands of koṭi. O monks, do you not see the light?" But the Zen feeling of exaltation is rather a quiet feeling of self-contentment; it is not at all demonstrative, when the first glow of it passes away. The Unconscious does not proclaim itself so boisterously in the Zen consciousness.

8. *Momentariness.* Satori comes upon one abruptly and is a momentary experience. In fact, if it is not abrupt and momentary, it is not satori. This abruptness (*tun*) is what characterizes the Enō school of Zen ever since its proclamation late in the seventh century. His opponent Jinshū was insistent on a gradual unfoldment of Zen consciousness. Enō's followers were thus

distinguished as strong upholders of the doctrine of abruptness. This abrupt experience of satori, then, opens up in one moment an altogether new vista, and the whole of existence is appraised from quite a new angle of observation.

THE KOAN

What the *kōan* proposes to do is to develop artificially or systematically in the consciousness of the Zen followers what the early masters produced in themselves spontaneously. It also aspires to develop this Zen experience in a greater number of minds than the master could otherwise hope for. Thus the *kōan* tended to the popularization of Zen and at the same time became the means of conserving the Zen experience in its genuineness. Aristocratic Zen was now turned into a democratic, systematized and, to a certain extent, mechanized Zen. No doubt it meant to that extent a deterioration; but without this innovation Zen might have died out a long time before. To my mind it was the technique of the *kōan* exercise that saved Zen as a unique heritage of Far-Eastern culture.

· · ·

What is a *kōan?*

A *kōan,* according to one authority, means "a public document setting up a standard of judgment," whereby one's Zen understanding is tested as to its correctness. A *kōan* is generally some statement made by an old Zen master, or some answer of his given to a questioner. The following are some that are commonly given to the uninitiated:

1. A monk asked Tōsan, "Who is the Buddha?"
"Three *chin* of flax."
2. Ummon was once asked, "When not a thought is stirring in one's mind, is there any error here?"
"As much as Mount Sumeru."
3. Jōshū answered, "*Mu!*" (Wu) to a monk's question, "Is there Buddha-nature in a dog?" *Mu* literally means "not" or "none," but when this is ordinarily given as a *kōan,* it has no reference to its literal signification; it is "*Mu*" pure and simple.
4. When Myo-jōza the monk overtook the fugitive Enō, he wanted Enō to give up the secret of Zen. Enō replied, "What are your original features which you have even prior to your birth?"
5. A monk asked Jōshū, "What is the meaning of the first patriarch's visit to China?"
"The cypress tree in the front courtyard."
6. When Jōshū came to study Zen under Nansen, he asked, "What is the Tao (or the Way)?"
Nansen replied, "Your everyday mind, that is the Tao."
7. A monk asked, "All things are said to be reducible to the One, but where is the One to be reduced?"

Jōshū answered, "When I was in the district of Ch'ing I had a robe made that weighed seven *chin.*"

8. When Hō-koji the old Zen adept first came to Baso in order to master Zen, he asked, "Who is he who has no companion among the ten thousand things of the world?"

Baso replied, "When you swallow up in one draught all the water in the Western River, I will tell you."

When such problems are given to the uninitiated for solution, what is the object of the master? The idea is to unfold the Zen psychology in the mind of the uninitiated, and to reproduce the state of consciousness, of which these statements are the expression. That is to say, when the *kōan* are understood the master's state of mind is understood, which is satori and without which Zen is a sealed book.

In the beginning of Zen history a question was brought up by the pupil to the notice of the master, who thereby gauged the mental state of the questioner and knew what necessary help to give him. The help thus given was sometimes enough to awaken him to realization, but more frequently than not puzzled and perplexed him beyond description, and the result was an ever-increasing mental strain or "searching and contriving" on the part of the pupil, of which we have already spoken in the foregoing pages. In actual cases, however, the master would have to wait for a long while for the pupil's first question, if it were coming at all. To ask the first question is to be more than half the way to its own solution, for it is the outcome of a most intense mental effort for the questioner to bring his mind to a crisis. The question indicates that the crisis is reached and the mind is ready to leave it behind. An experienced master often knows how to lead the pupil to a crisis and to make him successfully pass it. This was really the case before the *kōan* exercise came in vogue, as was already illustrated by the examples of Rinzai, Nangaku, and others.

As time went on there grew up many *mondō* which were exchanged between masters and pupils. And with the growth of Zen literature it was perfectly natural now for Zen followers to begin to attempt an intellectual solution or interpretation of them. The "questions-and-answers" ceased to be experiences and intuitions of Zen consciousness, and became subjects of logical inquiry. This was disastrous, yet inevitable. Therefore the Zen master who wished for the normal development of Zen consciousness and the vigorous growth of Zen tradition would not fail to recognize rightly the actual state of things, and to devise such a method as to achieve finally the attainment of the Zen truth.

The method that would suggest itself in the circumstances was to select some of the statements made by the old masters and to use them as pointers. A pointer would then function in two directions: (1) To check the working of the intellect, or rather to let the intellect see by itself how far it can go, and also that there is a realm into which it as such can never enter; (2) To effect the maturity of Zen consciousness which eventually breaks out into a state of satori.

When the *kōan* works in the first direction there takes place what has been called "searching and contriving." Instead of the intellect, which taken by itself forms only a part of our being, the entire personality, mind and body, is thrown out into the solution of the *kōan*. When this extraordinary state of spiritual tension, guided by an experienced master, is made to mature, the *kōan* works itself out into what has been designated as the Zen experience. An intuition of the truth of Zen is now attained, for the wall against which the Yogin has been beating hitherto to no purpose breaks down, and an entirely new vista opens before him. Without the *kōan* the Zen consciousness loses its pointer, and there will never be a state of satori. A psychological impasse is the necessary antecedent of satori. Formerly, that is, before the days of the *kōan* exercise, the antecedent pointer was created in the consciousness of the Yogin by his own intense spirituality. But when Zen became systematized owing to the accumulation of Zen literature in the shape of "questions-and-answers," the indispensability of the *kōan* had come to be universally recognized by the masters.

The worst enemy of Zen experience, at least in the beginning, is the intellect, which consists and insists in discriminating subject from object. The discriminating intellect, therefore, must be cut short if Zen consciousness is to unfold itself, and the *kōan* is constructed eminently to serve this end.

On examination we at once notice that there is no room in the *kōan* to insert an intellectual interpretation. The knife is not sharp enough to cut the *kōan* open and see what are its contents. For a *kōan* is not a logical proposition but the expression of a certain mental state resulting from the Zen discipline. For instance, what logical connection can there be between the Buddha and "three *chin* of flax"? or between the Buddha-nature and *"Mu"*? or between the secret message of Bodhidharma and "a cypress tree"? . . .

Technically speaking, the *kōan* given to the uninitiated is intended "to destroy the root of life," "to make the calculating mind die," "to root out the entire mind that has been at work since eternity," etc. This may sound murderous, but the ultimate intent is to go beyond the limits of intellection, and these limits can be crossed over only by exhausting oneself once for all, by using up all the psychic powers at one's command. Logic then turns into psychology, intellection into conation and intuition. What could not be solved on the plane of empirical consciousness is now transferred to the deeper recesses of the mind. So, says a Zen master, "Unless at one time perspiration has streamed down your back, you cannot see the boat sailing before the wind." "Unless once you have been thoroughly drenched in perspiration you cannot expect to see the revelation of a palace of pearls on a blade of grass."

The *kōan* refuses to be solved under any easier conditions. But once solved it is compared to a piece of brick used to knock at a gate; when the gate is opened the brick is thrown away. The *kōan* is useful as long as the mental doors are closed, but when they are opened it may be forgotten. What one sees after the opening will be something quite unexpected, something that has never before entered even into one's imagination. But when the *kōan* is reexamined from this newly acquired point of view, how marvellously suggestive, how fittingly constructed, although there is nothing artificial here!

wing-tsit chan (translator)

The Platform Sutra of the Sixth Patriarch

That Zen Buddhists disdain "sacred literature" was a point stressed by D. T. Suzuki in the preceding essay. A famous painting by Liang K'ai portrays an early Zen Patriarch gleefully tearing to shreds a scroll of scriptures. The way of Zen is not through mere words. But there are writings, some of which are quite ancient, which are highly regarded. Of these none is of greater significance than *The Platform Sutra of the Sixth Patriarch*. That it is called a *sutra* (discourse) is evidence of its revered status: the term is normally reserved for the teachings of the Buddha, and the *Platform Sutra* is the only Chinese work honored with that designation.

There are several extant versions of the *Platform Sutra*. The more recent ones tend to be longer and elaborate. The version which follows is believed to be the oldest; it was discovered in 1900 in Tun-huang (in northwest China).

The translator, Wing-tsit Chan (1901–   ), has had a long and distinguished academic career as a professor and author. Raised in South China, he received a Confucian education there and a Ph.D. from Harvard. He was Professor of Chinese Thought and Culture at Dartmouth College and held similar positions at the Universty of Hawaii and Columbia University. His books include *Religious Trends in Modern China, A Sourcebook in Chinese Philosophy,* and *The Way of Lao Tzu.*

Monk Hung-jen [601–675] asked Hui-neng: "Whence have you come to pay homage to me? What do you want from me?"

Hui-neng answered: "Your disciple is from Lingnan ["South of the Mountains Ranges," in the region of the present Canton]. A citizen of Hsin-chou, I have come a great distance to pay homage, without seeking anything except the Law of the Buddha."

The Great Master reproved him, saying: "You are from Lingnan and, furthermore, you are a barbarian. How can you become a Buddha?"

Hui-neng answered: "Although people are distinguished as northerners and southerners, there is neither north nor south in Buddha-nature. In physical body, the barbarian and the monk are different. But what is the difference in their Buddha-nature?"

The Great Master intended to argue with him further, but, seeing people around, said nothing. Hui-neng was ordered to attend to duties among the rest. It happened that one monk went away to travel. Thereupon Hui-neng was ordered to pound rice, which he did for eight months. [Sec. 3]

One day the Fifth Patriarch [Hung-jen] suddenly called all his pupils to come to him. As they assembled, he said: "Let me say this to you. Life and death are serious matters. You people are engaged all day in making offerings [to the Buddha], going after blessings and rewards only, and you make no effort to achieve freedom from the bitter sea of life and death. Your self-nature seems to be obscured. How can blessings save you? Go to your rooms and examine yourselves. He who is enlightened use his perfect vision of self-nature and write me a verse. When I look at his verse, if it reveals deep understanding, I shall give him the robe and the Law and make him the Sixth Patriarch. Hurry, hurry!" [Sec. 4]

At midnight Shen-hsiu, holding a candle, wrote a verse on the wall of the south corridor, without anyone knowing about it, which said:

> Our body is the tree of Perfect Wisdom,
> And our mind is a bright mirror.
> At all times diligently wipe them,
> So that they will be free from dust. [Sec. 6]

The Fifth Patriarch said: "The verse you wrote shows some but not all understanding. You have arrived at the front of the door but you have not yet entered it. Ordinary people, by practicing in accordance with your verse, will not degenerate. But it will be futile to seek the Supreme Perfect Wisdom while holding to such a view. One must enter the door and see his self-nature. Go away and come back after one or two days of thought. If you have entered the door and seen your self-nature, I shall give you the robe and the Law."

Shen-hsiu went away and for several days could not produce another verse. [Sec. 7]

Hui-neng also wrote a verse . . . which says:

> The tree of Perfect Wisdom is originally no tree.
> Nor has the bright mirror any frame.
> Buddha-nature is forever clear and pure.
> Where is there any dust?

Another verse:

> The mind is the tree of Perfect Wisdom.
> The body is the clear mirror.
> The clear mirror is originally clear and pure.
> Where has it been affected by any dust?

Monks in the hall were all surprised at these verses. Hui-neng, however, went back to the rice-pounding room. The Fifth Patriarch suddenly realized that Hui-neng was the one of good knowledge but was afraid lest the rest learn it. He therefore told them: "This will not do." [Sec. 8] The Fifth Patriarch waited till midnight, called Hui-neng to come to the hall, and expounded the *Diamond Sūtra*. As soon as Hui-neng heard this, he understood. That night the Law was imparted to him without anyone knowing it, and thus the Law and the robe [emblematic] of Sudden Enlightenment were transmitted to him. "You are now the Sixth Patriarch," said the Fifth Patriarch to Hui-neng. "The robe is the testimony of transmission from generation to generation. As to the Law, it is to be transmitted from mind to mind. Let people achieve understanding through their own effort."

The Fifth Patriarch told Hui-neng: "From the very beginning, the transmission of the Law has been as delicate as a hanging thread of silk. If you remain here, some one might harm you. You had better leave quickly." [Sec. 9]

[Hui-neng, having returned South, said]: I came and stayed in this place [Canton] and have not been free from persecution by government officials, Taoists, and common folk. The doctrine has been transmitted down from past sages; it is not my own idea. Those who wish to hear the teachings of the past sages should purify their hearts. Having heard them, they should first free themselves from their delusions and then attain enlightenment."

Great Master Hui-neng declared: "Good friends, perfection is inherent in all people. It is only because of the delusions of the mind that they cannot attain enlightenment by themselves. They must ask the help of the enlightened and be shown the way to see their own nature. Good friends, as soon as one is enlightened, he will achieve Perfect Wisdom." [Sec. 12]

"Good friends, in my system, meditation and wisdom are the bases. First of all, do not be deceived that the two are different. They are one reality and not two. Meditation is the substance (t'i) of wisdom and wisdom is the function (yung) of meditation.[1] As soon as wisdom is achieved, meditation is included in it, and as soon as meditation is attained, wisdom is included in it. Good friends, the meaning here is that meditation and wisdom are identified. A follower after the Way should not think wisdom follows meditation or vice versa or that the two are different. To hold such a view would imply that the dharmas possess two different characters. To those whose words are good but whose hearts are not good, meditation and wisdom are not identified. But to those whose hearts and words are both good and for whom the internal and external are one, meditation and wisdom are identified. Self-enlightenment and practice do not consist in argument. If one concerns himself about whether [meditation or wisdom] comes first, he is deluded. Unless one is freed from the consideration of victory or defeat, he will produce the [imagining of] dharmas and the self, and cannot be free from the characters [of birth, stagnation, deterioration, and extinction]." [Sec. 13]

"Good friends, there is no distinction between sudden enlightenment and gradual enlightenment in the Law, except that some people are intelligent and others stupid. Those who are ignorant realize the truth gradually, while the

[1]Technical terms of T'ien-t'ai philosophy denoting two aspects of a single reality.

CHAPTER THREE / *Zen Buddhism*

enlightened ones attain it suddenly. But if they know their own minds and see their own nature, then there will be no difference in their enlightenment. Without enlightenment, they will be forever bound in transmigration.'' [Sec. 16]

"Good friends, in my system, from the very beginning, whether in the sudden enlightenment or gradual enlightenment tradition, absence of thought has been instituted as the main doctrine, absence of phenomena as the substance, and nonattachment as the foundation. What is meant by absence of phenomena? Absence of phenomena means to be free from phenomena when in contact with them. Absence of thought means not to be carried away by thought in the process of thought. Nonattachment is man's original nature. [In its ordinary process], thought moves forward without a halt; past, present, and future thoughts continue as an unbroken stream. But if we can cut off this stream by an instant of thought, the Dharma-Body will be separated from the physical body, and at no time will a single thought be attached to any dharma. If one single instant of thought is attached to anything, then every thought will be attached. That will be bondage. But if in regard to all dharmas, no thought is attached to anything, that means freedom. This is the reason why nonattachment is taken as the foundation.

"Good friends, to be free from all phenomena means absence of phenomena. Only if we can be free from phenomena will the reality of nature be pure. This is the reason why absence of phenomena is taken as the substance.

"Absence of thought means not to be defiled by external objects. It is to free our thoughts from external objects and not to allow dharmas to cause our thoughts to rise. If one stops thinking about things and wipes out all thought, then as thought is terminated once and for all, there will be no more rebirth. Take this seriously, followers of the Path. It is bad enough for a man to be deceived himself through not knowing the meaning of the Law. How much worse is it to encourage others to be deceived! Not only does he fail to realize that he is deceived, but he also blasphemes against the scripture and the Law. This is the reason why absence of thought is instituted as the doctrine.

"All this is because people who are deceived have thoughts about sense-objects. With such thoughts, pervasive views arise, and all sorts of defilements and erroneous thoughts are produced from them.

"However, the school instituted absence of thought as the doctrine. When people are free from [erroneous] views, no thought will arise. If there are no thoughts, there will not even be 'absence of thought.' Absence means absence of what? Thought means thought of what? Absence means freedom from duality and all defilements. Thought means thought of Thusness and self-nature. True Thusness is the substance of thought and thought is the function of True Thusness. It is the self-nature that gives rise to thought. [Therefore] in spite of the functioning of seeing, hearing, sensing, and knowing the self-nature is not defiled by the many sense-objects and always remains as it truly is. As the *Vimalakīrti Scripture* says: 'Externally it skillfully differentiates the various dharma-characters and internally it abides firmly in the First Principle.' " [Sec. 17]

"Good friends, in this system sitting in meditation is at bottom neither attached to the mind nor attached to purity, and there is neither speech nor motion. Suppose it should be attached to the mind. The mind is at bottom an imagination. Since imagination is the same as illusion, there is nothing to be attached to. Suppose it were attached to purity, man's nature is originally pure. It is only because of erroneous thought that True Thusness is obscured. Our original nature is pure as long as it is free from erroneous thought. If one does not realize that his own nature is originally pure and makes up his mind to attach himself to purity, he is creating an imaginary purity. Such purity does not exist. Hence we know that what is to be attached to is imaginary." [Sec. 18]

"This being the case, in this system, what is meant by sitting in meditation? To sit means to obtain absolute freedom and not to allow any thought to be caused by external objects. To meditate means to realize the imperturbability of one's original nature. What is meant by meditation and calmness? Meditation means to be free from all phenomena and calmness means to be internally unperturbed. If one is externally attached to phenomena, the inner mind will at once be disturbed, but if one is externally free from phenomena, the inner nature will not be perturbed. The original nature is by itself pure and calm. It is only because of causal conditions that it comes into contact with external objects, and the contact leads to perturbation. There will be calmness when one is free from external objects and is not perturbed. Meditation is achieved when one is externally free from phenomena and calmness is achieved when one is internally unperturbed. Meditation and calmness mean that externally meditation is attained and internally calmness is achieved." [Sec. 19]

"All scriptures and writings of the Mahāyāna and Hīnayāna schools as well as the twelve sections of the Canon were provided for man. It is because man possesses the nature of wisdom that these were instituted. If there were no man, there would not have been any dharmas. We know, therefore, that dharmas exist because of man and there are all these scriptures because there are people to preach them.

"Among men some are wise and other stupid. The stupid are inferior people, whereas the wise ones are superior. The ignorant consult the wise and the wise explain the Law to them and enable them to understand. When the ignorant understand, they will no longer be different from the wise. Hence we know that without enlightenment, a Buddha is no different from all living beings, and with enlightenment, all living beings are the same as a Buddha. Hence we know that all dharmas are immanent in one's person. Why not seek in one's own mind the sudden realization of the original nature of True Thusness?" [Sec. 30]

CHAPTER THREE / *Zen Buddhism*

The Great Master said to Chi-ch'eng [pupil of Shen-hsiu]: "I hear that your teacher in his teaching transmits only the doctrine of discipline, calmness, and wisdom. Please tell me his explanation of these teachings."

Chi-ch'eng said: "The Reverend Shen-hsiu said that discipline is to refrain from all evil actions, wisdom is to practice all good deeds, and calmness is to purify one's own mind. These are called discipline, calmness, and wisdom. This is his explanation. I wonder what your views are."

Patriarch Hui-neng answered: "His theory is wonderful, but my views are different."

Chi-ch'eng asked: "How different?"

Hui-neng answered: "Some people realize [the Law] more quickly and others more slowly."

Chi-ch'eng then asked the Patriarch to explain his views on discipline, calmness, and wisdom. The Great Master said: "Please listen to me. In my view, freeing the mind from all wrong is the discipline of our original nature. Freeing the mind from all disturbances is the calmness of our original nature. And freeing the mind from all delusions is the wisdom of our original nature."

Master Hui-neng continued: "Your teacher's teaching of discipline, calmness, and wisdom is to help wise men of the inferior type but mine is to help superior people. When one realizes his original nature, then discipline, calmness, and wisdom need not be instituted."

Chi-ch'eng said: "Great Master, please explain why they need not be instituted."

The Great Master said: "The original nature has no wrong, no disturbance, no delusion. If in every instant of thought we introspect our minds with Perfect Wisdom, and if it is always free from dharmas and their appearances, what is the need of instituting these things? The original nature is realized suddenly, not gradually step by step. Therefore there is no need of instituting them."

Chi-ch'eng bowed, decided not to leave Ts'ao-li Mountain, but immediately became a pupil and always stayed close by the Master. [Sec. 41] *shunryu suzuki*

FROM *Zen Mind, Beginner's Mind*

A year or two before his death in 1971, Shunryu Suzuki was described as follows:

Short and slight, he appears to be in his early sixties; his head is shaved, and he wears the robes of a priest. One's overwhelming first impression is of openness and warmth. He laughs often, noiselessly—and when I was with him, trying to discuss "profound questions," I found myself laughing with him throughout the interview. Beneath the lightness and gentleness, however, one feels as well his tremendous rigor.*

A Zen master in Japan (and the son of a Zen master), Suzuki came to the United States in 1959 to head the Zen Center in San Francisco. In 1966 he founded the Zen Mountain Center at Tassajara Springs, a Soto Zen monastery in the mountains near Carmel on the California coast.

Zen Mind, Beginner's Mind, from which the following selections are taken, is composed of talks given by Suzuki and taped by Marian Derby. The tapes were edited by Trudy Dixon.

ZEN AND EXCITEMENT

It is necessary for us to keep the constant way. Zen is not some kind of excitement, but concentration on our usual everyday routine. If you become too busy and too excited, your mind becomes rough and ragged. This is not good. If possible, try to be always calm and joyful and keep yourself from excitement. Usually we become busier and busier, day by day, year by year, especially in our modern world. If we revisit old, familiar places after a long time, we are astonished by the changes. It cannot be helped. But if we become interested in some excitement, or in our own change, we will become completely involved in our busy life, and we will be lost. But if your mind is calm and constant, you can keep yourself away from the noisy world even though you are in the midst of it. In the midst of noise and change, your mind will be quiet and stable.

Zen is not something to get excited about. Some people start to practice Zen just out of curiosity, and they only make themselves busier. If your practice makes you worse, it is ridiculous. I think that if you try to do zazen once a week, that will make you busy enough. Do not be too interested in Zen. When young people get excited about Zen they often give up schooling and go

*Jacob Needleman, *The New Religions* (New York: Doubleday, 1970), p. 50.

CHAPTER THREE / *Zen Buddhism*

to some mountain or forest in order to sit. That kind of interest is not true interest.

Just continue in your calm, ordinary practice and your character will be built up. If your mind is always busy, there will be no time to build, and you will not be successful, particularly if you work too hard on it. Building character is like making bread—you have to mix it little by little, step by step, and moderate temperature is needed. You know yourself quite well, and you know how much temperature you need. You know exactly what you need. But if you get too excited, you will forget how much temperature is good for you, and you will lose your own way. This is very dangerous.

Buddha said the same thing about the good ox driver. The driver knows how much load the ox can carry, and he keeps the ox from being overloaded. You know your way and your state of mind. Do not carry too much! Buddha also said that building character is like building a dam. You should be very careful in making the bank. If you try to do it all at once, water will leak from it. Make the bank carefully and you will end up with a fine dam for the reservoir.

Our unexciting way of practice may appear to be very negative. This is not so. It is a wise and effective way to work on ourselves. It is just very plain. I find this point very difficult for people, especially young people, to understand. On the other hand it may seem as if I am speaking about gradual attainment. This is not so either. In fact, this is the sudden way, because when your practice is calm and ordinary, everyday life itself is enlightenment.

TO POLISH A TILE

Zen stories, or *koans,* are very difficult to understand before you know what we are doing moment after moment. But if you know exactly what we are doing in each moment, you will not find *koans* so difficult. There are so many *koans*. I have often talked to you about a frog, and each time everybody laughs. But a frog is very interesting. He sits like us, too, you know. But he does not think that he is doing anything so special. When you go to a zendo and sit, you may think you are doing some special thing. While your husband or wife is sleeping, you are practicing zazen! You are doing some special thing, and your spouse is lazy! That may be your understanding of zazen. But look at the frog. A frog also sits like us, but he has no idea of zazen. Watch him. If something annoys him, he will make a face. If something comes along to eat, he will snap it up and eat, and he eats sitting. Actually that is our zazen—not any special thing.

Here is a kind of frog *koan* for you. Baso was a famous Zen master called the Horse-master. He was the disciple of Nangaku, one of the Sixth Patriarch's disciples. One day while he was studying under Nangaku, Baso was sitting, practicing zazen. He was a man of large physical build; when he talked, his tongue reached to his nose; his voice was loud; and his zazen must have been very good. Nangaku saw him sitting like a great mountain or like a frog. Nangaku asked, "What are you doing?" "I am practicing zazen," Baso replied. "Why are you practicing zazen?" "I want to attain enlightenment; I want to be a Buddha," the disciple said. Do you know what the teacher did? He picked up a tile, and he started to polish it. In Japan, after taking a tile from the kiln, we polish it to give it a beautiful finish. So Nagaku picked up a tile and started to polish it. Baso, his disciple, asked, "What are you doing?" "I want to make this tile into a jewel," Nangaku said. "How is it possible to make a tile a jewel?" Baso asked. "How is it possible to become a Buddha by practicing zazen?" Nangaku replied. "Do you want to attain Buddhahood? There is no Buddhahood besides your ordinary mind. When the cart does not go, which do you whip, the cart or the horse?" the master asked.

Nangaku's meaning here is that whatever you do, that is zazen. True zazen is beyond being in bed or sitting in the zendo. If your husband or wife is in bed, that is zazen. If you think, "I am sitting here, and my spouse is in bed," then even though you are sitting here in the cross-legged position, that is not true zazen. You should be like a frog always. That is true zazen.

Dogen-zenji commented on his *koan*. He said, "When the Horse-master becomes the Horse-master, Zen becomes Zen." When Baso becomes Baso, his zazen becomes true zazen, and Zen becomes Zen. What is true zazen? When you become you! When you are you, then no matter what you do, that is zazen. Even though you are in bed, you may not be you most of the time. Even though you are sitting in the zendo, I wonder whether you are you in the true sense.

Here is another famous *koan*. Zuikan was a Zen master who always used to address himself. "Zuikan?" he would call. And then he would answer. "Yes!" "Zuikan?" "Yes!" Of course he was living all alone in his small zendo, and of course he knew who he was, but sometimes he lost himself. And whenever he lost himself, he would address himself, "Zuikan?" "Yes!"

If we are like a frog, we are always ourselves. But even a frog sometimes loses himself, and he makes a sour face. And if something comes along, he will snap at it and eat it. So I think a frog is always addressing himself. I think you should do that also. Even in zazen you will lose yourself. When you become sleepy, or when your mind starts to wander about, you lose yourself. When your legs become painful—"Why are my legs so painful?"—you lose yourself. Because you lose yourself, your problem will be a problem for you. If you do not lose yourself, then even though you have difficulty, there is actually no problem whatsoever. You just sit in the midst of the problem; when you are a part of the problem, or when the problem is a part of you, there *is* no problem, because you are the problem itself. The problem is you yourself. If this is so, there is no problem.

When your life is always a part of your surroundings—in other words, when you are called back to yourself, in the present moment—then there is no problem. When you start to wander about in some delusion which is something apart from you yourself, then your surroundings are not real anymore, and your mind is not real anymore. If you yourself are deluded, then your surroundings are also a misty, foggy delusion. Once you are in the midst of delusion, there is no end to delusion. You will be involved in deluded ideas one after another. Most people live in delusion, involved in their problem, trying to solve their problem. But just to live is actually to live in problems. And to solve the problem is to be a part of it, to be one with it.

So which do you hit, the cart or the horse? Which do you hit, yourself or your problems? If you start questioning which you should hit, that means you have already started to wander about. But when you actually hit the horse, the cart will go. In truth, the cart and the horse are not different. When you are you, there is no problem of whether you should hit the cart or the horse. When you are you, zazen becomes true zazen. So when you practice zazen, your problem will practice zazen, and everything else will practice zazen too. Even though your spouse is in bed, he or she is also practicing zazen—when *you* practice zazen! But when you do not practice true zazen, then there is your spouse, and there is yourself, each quite different, quite separate from the other. So if you yourself have true practice, then everything else is practicing our way at the same time.

That is why we should always address ourselves, checking up on ourselves like a doctor tapping himself. This is very important. This kind of practice should be continued moment after moment, incessantly. We say, "When the night is here, the dawn comes." It means there is no gap between the dawn and the night. Before the summer is over, autumn comes. In this way we should understand our life. We should practice with this understanding, and solve our problems in this way. Actually, just to work on the problem, if you do it with single-minded effort, is enough. You should just polish the tile; that is our practice. The purpose of practice is not to make a tile a jewel. Just continue sitting; that is practice in its true sense. It is not a matter of whether or not it is possible to attain Buddhahood, whether or not it is possible to make a tile a jewel. Just to work and live in this world with this understanding is the most important point. That is our practice. That is true zazen. So we say, "When you eat, eat!" You should eat what is there, you know. Sometimes you do not eat it. Even though you are eating, your mind is somewhere else. You do not taste what you have in your mouth. As long as you can eat when you are eating, you are all right. Do not worry a bit. It means you are you yourself.

When you are you, you see things as they are, and you become one with your surroundings. There is your true self. There you have true practice; you have the practice of a frog. He is a good example of our practice—when a frog becomes a frog, Zen becomes Zen. When you understand a frog through and through, you attain enlightenment; you are Buddha. And you are good for others, too: husband or wife or son or daughter. This is zazen!

NATURALNESS

There is a big misunderstanding about the idea of naturalness. Most people who come to us believe in some freedom or naturalness, but their understanding is what we call *jinen ken gedo,* or heretical naturalness. *Jinen ken gedo* means that there is no need to be formal—just a kind of "let-alone policy" or sloppiness. That is naturalness for most people. But that is not the naturalness we mean. It is rather difficult to explain, but naturalness is, I think, some feeling of being independent from everything, or some activity which is based on nothingness. Something which comes out of nothingness is naturalness, like a seed or plant coming out of the ground. The seed has no idea of being some particular plant, but it has its own form and is in perfect harmony with the ground, with its surroundings. As it grows, in the course of time it expresses its nature. Nothing exists without form and color. Whatever it is, it has some form and color, and that form and color are in perfect harmony with other beings. And there is no trouble. That is what we mean by naturalness.

For a plant or stone to be natural is no problem. But for us there is some problem, indeed a big problem. To be natural is something which we must work on. When what you do just comes out from nothingness, you have quite a new feeling. For instance, when you are hungry, to take some food is naturalness. You feel natural. But when you are expecting too much, to have some food is not natural. You have no new feeling. You have no appreciation for it.

The true practice of zazen is to sit as if drinking water when you are thirsty. There you have naturalness. It is quite natural for you to take a nap when you are very sleepy. But to take a nap just because you are lazy, as if it were the privilege of a human being to take a nap, is not naturalness. You think, "My friends, all of them, are napping; why shouldn't I? When everyone else is not working, why should I work so hard? When they have a lot of money, why don't I?" This is not naturalness. Your mind is entangled with some other idea, someone else's idea, and you are not independent, not yourself, and not natural. Even if you sit in the cross-legged position, if your zazen is not natural, it is not true practice. You do not have to force yourself to drink water when you are thirsty; you are glad to drink water. If you have true joy in your zazen, that is true zazen. But even though you have to force yourself to practice zazen, if you feel something good in your practice, that is zazen. Actually it is not a matter of forcing something on you or not. Even though you have some difficulty, when you want to have it, that is naturalness.

This naturalness is very difficult to explain. But if you can just sit and experience the actuality of nothingness in your practice, there is no need to explain. If it comes out of nothingness, whatever you do is natural, and that is true activity. You have the true joy of practice, the true joy of life in it. Everyone comes out from nothingness moment after moment. Moment after moment we have true joy of life. So we say *shin ku myo u,* "from true emptiness, the wondrous being appears." *Shin* is "true"; *ku* is "emptiness"; *myo* is "wondrous"; *u* is "being": from true emptiness, wondrous being.

Without nothingness, there is no naturalness—no true being. True being comes out of nothingness, moment after moment. Nothingness is always there, and from it everything appears. But usually, forgetting all about nothingness, you behave as if you have something. What you do is based on some possessive idea or some concrete idea, and that is not natural. For instance, when you listen to a lecture, you should not have any idea of yourself. You should not have your own idea when you listen to someone. Forget what you have in your mind and just listen to what he says. To have nothing in your mind is naturalness. Then you will understand what he says. But if you have some idea to compare with what he says, you will not hear everything; your understanding will be one-sided; that is not naturalness. When you do something, you should be completely involved in it. You should devote yourself to it completely. Then you have nothing. So if there is no true emptiness in your activity, it is not natural.

Most people insist on some idea. Recently the younger generation talks about love. Love! Love! Love! Their minds are full of love! And when they study Zen, if what I say does not accord with the idea they have of love, they will not accept it. They are quite stubborn, you know. You may be amazed! Of course not all, but some have a very, very hard attitude. That is not naturalness at all. Even though they talk about love, and freedom or naturalness, they do not understand these things. And they cannot understand what Zen is in that way. If you want to study Zen, you should forget all your previous ideas and just practice zazen and see what kind of experience you have in your practice. That is naturalness.

Whatever you do, this attitude is necessary. Sometimes we say *nyu nan shin,* "soft or flexible mind." *Nyu* is "soft feeling"; *nan* is something which is not hard"; *shin* is "mind". *Nyu nan shin* means a smooth, natural mind. When you have that mind, you have the joy of life. When you lose it, you lose everything. You have nothing. Although you think you have something, you have nothing. But when all you do comes out of nothingness, then you have everything. Do you understand? That is what we mean by naturalness.

gary snyder _____

Spring Sesshin at Shokoku-ji

The sympathies of Gary Snyder (1930–   ) lie with such people as the American Indians, early Taoists, Quakers, anarchists, and Bushmen. He advocates walking in the woods, cleaning up the streets, and bringing up children "as part of the wildlife." There is a need, he has written, "to live lightly on the earth, to be aware and alive, to be free of egoism, to be in contact with plants and animals."*

A San Franciscan by birth and a graduate of Reed College, Snyder has worked variously as a logger and merchant seaman, studied Chinese at Berkeley, visited India, and practiced Zen in Japan. In the 1950s, with Jack Kerouac, Allen Ginsberg, and Lawrence Ferlinghetti, he was one of those writers who spoke for the Beat Generation.

All this finds expression in his poetry (*Riprap and Cold Mountain Poems, The Back Country, Regarding Wave*) and occasional prose (*Earth House Hold: Technical Notes & Queries to Fellow Dharma Revolutionaries*).

_____

Shokoku Temple is in northern Kyoto, on level ground, with a Christian college just south of it and many blocks of crowded little houses and stone-edged dirt roads north. It is the mother-temple of many branch temples scattered throughout Japan, and one of the several great temple-systems of the Rinzai Sect of Zen. Shokoku-ji is actually a compound: behind the big wood gate and tile-topped crumbling old mud walls are a number of temples each with its own gate and walls, gardens, and acres of wild bamboo grove. In the center of the compound is the soaring double-gabled Lecture Hall, silent and airy, an enormous dragon painted on the high ceiling, his eye burning down on the very center of the cut-slate floor. Except at infrequent rituals the hall is unused, and the gold-gilt Buddha sits on its high platform at the rear untroubled by drums and chanting. In front of the Lecture Hall is a long grove of fine young pines and a large square lotus-pond. To the east is a wooden belltower and the unpretentious gate of the *Sodo,* the training school for Zen monks, or *Unsui.*[1] They will become priests of Shokoku-ji temples. A few, after years of *za-zen* (meditation), *koan* study, and final mastery of the

_____

[1] *Unsui.* The term is literally "cloud, water"—taken from a line of an old Chinese poem, "To drift like clouds and flow like water." It is strictly a Zen term. The Japanese word for Buddhist

*Gary Snyder and Friends, "Four Changes," in Theodore Roszak (ed.), *Sources* (New York: Harper Colophon Books, 1972), p. 383.

Gary Snyder, "Spring *Sesshin* at Shokoku-ji." From *Chicago Review,* Vol. 12, No. 2 (Summer, 1958). Reprinted by permission of the *Chicago Review.* A note has been omitted, and the remainder renumbered.

Avatamsaka (*Kegon*) philosophy, become *Roshi*[2] (Zen Masters), qualified to head Sodos, teach lay groups, or do what they will. Laymen are also permitted to join the Unsui in evening *Zendo* (meditation hall) sessions, and some, like the Unsui, are given a *koan* by the Roshi and receive regular *sanzen*—the fierce face-to-face moment where you spit forth truth or perish—from him. Thus being driven, through time and much *za-zen,* to the very end of the problem.

In the routine of Sodo life, there are special weeks during the year in which gardening, carpentry, reading, and such, are suspended, and the time given over almost entirely to *za-zen*. During these weeks, called *sesshin,* "concentrating the mind"—*sanzen* is received two to four times a day and hours of *za-zen* in the Zendo are much extended. Laymen who will observe the customs of Sodo life and are able to sit still are allowed to join in the *sesshin*. At Shokoku-ji, the spring *sesshin* is held the first week of May.

The *sesshin* starts in the evening. The participants single-file circle into the mat-floored Central Hall of the Sodo and sit in a double row in dim light. The Roshi silently enters, sits at the head, and everyone drinks tea, each fishing his own teacup out of the deep-sleeved black robe. Then the *Jikijitsu*—head Unsui of the Zendo (a position which revolves among the older men, changing every six months)—reads in formal voice the rules of Zendo and *sesshin,* written in archaic Sino-Japanese. The Roshi says you all must work very hard; all bow and go out, returning to the Zendo for short meditation and early sleep.

At three A.M. the *Fusu* (another older Zenbo who is in charge of food, finances and meeting people) appears in the Zendo ringing a hand-bell. Lights go on—ten-watt things tacked under the beams of a building lit for centuries by oil lamps—and everyone wordlessly and swiftly rolls up his single quilt and stuffs it in a small cupboard at the rear of his mat, leaps off the raised platform that rings the hall, to the stone floor, and scuffs out in straw sandals to dash icy water on the face from a stone bowl. They come back quickly and sit crosslegged on their *za-zen* cushions, on the same mat used for sleeping. The Jikijitsu stalks in and sits at his place, lighting a stick of incense and beginning

---

monks and priests of all sects is *bozu* (bonze). One takes no formal vows upon becoming an Unsui, although the head is shaved and a long Chinese-style robe called *koromo* is worn within Sodo walls. Unsui are free to quit the Zen community at any time. During the six months of the year in which the Sodo is in session (spring and fall) they eat no meat, but during the summer and winter off-periods they eat, drink, and wear what they will. After becoming temple priests (*Osho,* Chinese *Ho-shang*) the great majority of Zen monks marry and raise families. The present generation of young Unsui is largely from temple families.

[2] *Roshi.* Literally, "old master"—Chinese *Lao-shih.* A Roshi is not simply a person who "understands" Zen, but specifically a person who has received the seal of approval from his own Zen Master and is his "Dharma heir." A person may comprehend Zen to the point that his Roshi will say he has no more to teach him, but if the Roshi does not feel the student is intellectually and scholastically equipped to transmit Zen as well, he will not permit him to be his heir. Most Roshi are Zen monks, but laymen and women have also achieved this title.

the day with the rifleshot crack of a pair of hardwood blocks whacked together and a ding on a small bronze bell. Several minutes of silence, and another whack is heard from the Central Hall. Standing up and slipping on the sandals, the group files out of the Zendo trailing the Jikijitsu—who hits his bell as he walks—and goes down the roofed stone path, fifty yards long, that joins the Zendo and the Central Hall. Forming two lines and sitting on the mats, they begin to chant *sutras*. The choppy Sino-Japanese words follow the rhythm of a fish-shaped wooden drum and a deep-throated bell. They roar loud and chant fast. The Roshi enters and between the two lines makes deep bows to the Buddha-image before him, lights incense, and retires. The hard-thumping drum and *sutra*-songs last an hour, then suddenly stop and all return to the Zendo. Each man standing before his place, they chant the *Prajña-paramita-hridaya Sutra,* the Jikijitsu going so fast now no one can follow him. Then hoisting themselves onto the mats they meditate. After half an hour a harsh bell-clang is heard from the Roshi's quarters. The Jikijitsu bellows "Getout!" and the Zenbos dash out racing, feet slapping the cold stones and robes flying, to kneel in line whatever order they make it before the *sanzen* room. A ring of the bell marks each new entrance before the Roshi. All one hears from outside is an occasional growl and sometimes the whack of a stick. The men return singly and subdued from *sanzen* to their places.

Not all return. Some go to the kitchen, to light brushwood fires in the brick stoves and cook rice in giant black pots. When they are ready they signal with a clack of wood blocks, and those in the Zendo answer by a ring on the bell. Carrying little nested sets of bowls and extra-large chopsticks, they come down the covered walk. It is getting light, and at this time of year the camellia are blooming. The moss-floored garden on both sides of the walk is thick with them, banks under pine and maple, white flowers glowing through mist. Even the meal, nothing but salty radish pickles and thin rice gruel, is begun and ended by whacks of wood and chanting of short verses. After breakfast the Zenbos scatter: some to wash pots, others to mop the long wood verandas of the central hall and sweep and mop the Roshi's rooms or rake leaves and paths in the garden. The younger Unsui and the outsiders dust, sweep, and mop the Zendo.

The Shokoku-ji Zendo is one of the largest and finest in Japan. It is on a raised terrace of stone and encircled by a stone walk. Outside a long overhang roof and dark unpainted wood—inside round log posts set on granite footings—it is always cool and dark and very still. The floor is square slate laid diagonal. The raised wood platform that runs around the edge has mats for forty men. Sitting in a three-walled box that hangs from the center of the ceiling, like an overhead crane operator, is a lifesize wood statue of the Buddha's disciple Kasyapa, his eyes real and piercing anyone who enters the main door. In an attached room to the rear of the Zendo is a shrine to the founder of Shokoku-ji, his statue in wood, eyes peering out of a dark alcove.

By seven A.M. the routine chores are done and the Jikijitsu invites those cleaning up the Zendo into his room for tea. The Jikijitsu and the Fusu both have private quarters, the Fusu lodging in the Central Hall and the Jikijitsu in a small building adjoining the Zendo. The chill is leaving the air, and he slides open the paper screens, opening a wall of his room to the outside. Sitting on mats and drinking tea they relax and smoke and quietly kid a little, and the Jikijitsu—a tigerish terror during the *za-zen* sessions—is very gentle. "You'll be a Roshi one of these days" a medical student staying the week said to him. "Not me, I can't grasp *koans*," he laughs, rubbing his shaved head where the Roshi has knocked him recently. Then they talk of work to be done around the Sodo. During *sesshin* periods work is kept to a minimum, but some must be done. Taking off robes and putting on ragged old dungarees everyone spreads out, some to the endless tasks of weeding grass from the moss garden, others to the vegetable plots. The Jikijitsu takes a big mattock and heads for the bamboo-grove to chop out a few bamboo shoots for the kitchen. Nobody works very hard, and several times during the morning they find a warm place in the sun and smoke.

At ten-thirty they quit work and straggle to the kitchen for lunch, the main meal. *Misu*-soup full of vegetables, plenty of rice, and several sorts of pickles. The crunch of bicycles and shouts of children playing around the bell-tower can be heard just beyond the wall. After lunch the laymen and younger Unsui return to the Zendo. More experienced men have the greater responsibilities of running the Sodo, and they keep busy at accounts, shopping, and looking after the needs of the Roshi. Afternoon sitting in the Zendo is informal—newcomers take plenty of time getting comfortable, and occasionally go out to walk and smoke a bit. Conversation is not actually forbidden, but no one wants to talk.

Shortly before three, things tighten up and the Jikijitsu comes in. When everyone is gathered, and a bell heard from the Central-Hall, they march out for afternoon *sutra*-chanting. The *sutras* recited vary from day to day, and as the leader announces new titles some men produce books from their sleeves to read by, for not all have yet memorized them completely. Returning to the Zendo, they again recite the *Prajña-paramita-hridaya Sutra,* and the Jikijitsu chants a piece alone, his voice filling the hall, head tilted up to the statue of Kasyapa, hand cupped to his mouth as though calling across miles.

After sitting a few minutes the signal is heard for evening meal, and all file into the kitchen, stand, chant, sit, and lay out their bowls. No one speaks. Food is served with a gesture of "giving" and one stops the server with a gesture of "enough." At the end of the meal—rice and pickles—a pot of hot water is passed and each man pours some into his bowls, swashes it around and drinks it, wipes out his bowls with a little cloth. Then they are nested again, wrapped in their cover, and everyone stands and leaves.

It is dusk and the Zendo is getting dark inside. All the Zenbos begin to assemble now, some with their cushions tucked under arm, each bowing before Kasyapa as he enters. Each man, right hand held up before the chest flat like a knife and cutting the air, walks straight to his place, bows toward the center of the room, arranges the cushions, and assumes the crosslegged "half-lotus" posture. Other arrive too—teachers, several college professors, and half a dozen university students wearing the black uniforms that serve for classrooms, bars, and temples equally well—being all they own. Some enter uncertainly and bow with hesitation, afraid of making mistakes, curious to try *za-zen* and overwhelmed by the historical weight of Zen, something very "Japanese" and very "high class." One student, most threadbare of all, had a head shaved like an Unsui and entered with knowledge and precision every night, sitting perfectly still on his cushions and acknowledging no one. By seven-thirty the hall is half-full—a sizeable number of people for present-day Zen sessions—and the great bell in the bell-tower booms. As it booms the man ringing it, swinging a long wood beam ram, sings out a *sutra* over the shops and homes of the neighborhood. When he has finished, the faint lights in the Zendo go on and evening *za-zen* has begun.

The Jikijitsu sits at the head of the hall, marking the half-hour periods with wood clackers and bell. He keeps a stick of incense burning beside him, atop a small wood box that says "not yet" on it in Chinese. At the end of the first half-hour he claps the blocks once and grunts "*kinhin.*" This is "walking *za-zen*," and the group stands—the Unsui tying up sleeves and tucking up robes—and at another signal they start marching single file around the inside of the hall. They walk fast and unconsciously in step, the Jikijitsu leading with a long samurai stride. They circle and circle, through shadow and under the light, ducking below Kasyapa's roost, until suddenly the Jikijitsu claps his blocks and yells "Getout!"— the circle broken and everyone dashing for the door. Night *sanzen*. Through the next twenty minutes they return to resume meditation—not preparing an answer now, but considering the Roshi's response.

Za-zen is a very tight thing. The whole room feels it. The Jikijitsu gets up, grasps a long flat stick and begins to slowly prowl the hall, stick on shoulder, walking before the rows of sitting men, each motionless with eyes half-closed and looking straight ahead downward. An inexperienced man sitting out of balance will be lightly tapped and prodded into easier posture. An Unsui sitting poorly will be without warning roughly knocked off his cushions. He gets up and sits down again. Nothing is said. Anyone showing signs of drowsiness will feel a light tap of the stick on the shoulder. He and the Jikijitsu then bow to each other, and the man leans forward to receive four blows on each side of his back. These are not particularly painful—though the loud whack of them can be terrifying to a newcomer—and serve to wake one well. One's legs may hurt during long sitting, but there is no relief until the Jikijitsu rings his bell. The mind must simply be placed elsewhere. At the end of an hour the bell does ring and the second *kinhin* begins—a welcome twenty minutes of silent rhythmic walking. The walking ends abruptly and anyone not seated and settled when the Jikijitsu whips around the hall is knocked off his cushion. Zen aims at freedom but its practice is disciplined.

Several Unsui slip out during *kinhin*. At ten they return—they can be heard coming, running full speed down the walk. They enter carrying big trays of hot noodles, *udon*, in large lacquer bowls. They bow to the Jikijitsu and circle the room setting a bowl before each man; giving two or even three bowls to those who want them. Each man bows, takes up chopsticks, and eats the noodles as fast as he can. Zenbos are famous for fast noodle-eating and no one wants to be last done. As the empty bowls are set down they are gathered up and one server follows, wiping the beam that fronts the mats with a rag, at a run. At the door the servers stop and bow to the group. It bows in return. Then one server announces the person—usually a friend or patron of the Sodo—who footed the bill for the *sesshin* noodles that night. The group bows again. Meditation is resumed. At ten-thirty there is another rest period and men gather to smoke and chat a little in back. "Are there really some Americans interested in Zen?" they ask with astonishment—for their own countrymen pay them scant attention.

At eleven bells ring and wood clacks, and final *sutras* are chanted. The hall is suddenly filled with huge voices. The evening visitors take their cushions and leave, each bowing to the Jikijitsu and Kasyapa as he goes. The others flip themselves into their sleeping quilts immediately and lie dead still. The Jikijitsu pads once around, says "Take counsel of your pillow" and walks out. The hall goes black. But this is not the end, for as soon as the lights go out, everyone gets up again and takes his sitting cushion, slips outside, and practices *za-zen* alone wherever he likes for another two hours. The next day begins at three A.M.

This is the daily schedule of the *sesshin*. On several mornings during the week, the Roshi gives a lecture (*teisho*) based on some anecdote in the Zen textbooks—usually from *Mumonkan* or *Hekiganroku*. As the group sits in the Central Hall awaiting his entrance, one Zenbo stands twirling a stick around the edge-tacks of a big drum, filling the air with a deep reverberation. The Roshi sits crosslegged on a very high chair, receives a cup of tea, and delivers lectures that might drive some mad—for he tells these poor souls beating their brains out night after night that "The Perfect Way is without difficulty" and he means it and they know he's right.

In the middle of the week everyone gets a bath and a new headshave. There is a Zen saying that "while studying *koans* you should not relax even in the bath" but this one is never heeded. The bath-house contains two deep iron tubs, heated by brushwood fires stoked below from outside. The blue smoke and sweet smell of crackling *hinoki* and *sugi* twigs, stuffed in by a firetender, and the men taking a long time and getting really clean. Even in the bath-house you bow—to a small shrine high on the wall—both before and after bathing. The Jikijitsu whets up his razor and shaves heads, but shaves his own alone and without mirror. He never nicks himself any more.

On the day after bath they go begging (*takahatsu*). It rained this day, but putting on oiled-paper slickers over their robes and wearing straw sandals they splashed out. The face of the begging Zenbo can scarcely be seen, for he wears a deep bowl-shaped woven straw hat. They walk slowly, paced far apart, making a weird wailing sound as they go, never stopping. Sometimes they walk for miles, crisscrossing the little lanes and streets of Kyoto. They came back soaked, chanting a *sutra* as they entered the Sodo gate, and added up a meagre take. The rain sluiced down all that afternoon, making a green twilight inside the Zendo and a rush of sound.

The next morning during tea with the Jikijitsu, a college professor who rents rooms in one of the Sodo buildings came in and talked of *koans*. "When you understand Zen, you know that the tree is really *there*."—The only time anyone said anything of Zen philosophy or experience the whole week. Zenbos never discuss *koans* or *sanzen* experience with each other.

The *sesshin* ends at dawn on the eighth day. All who have participated gather in the Jikijitsu's room and drink powdered green tea and eat cakes. They talk easily, it's over. The Jikijitsu, who has whacked or knocked them all during the week, is their great friend now—compassion takes many forms.

further reading

Paul Reps' *Zen Flesh, Zen Bones* (1957) includes the wonderful "101 Zen Stories." Reps *does* Zen in his *Zen Telegrams* (1959), a brief book of "picture-poems."

The World of Zen (1960), edited by Nancy Wilson Ross, is an excellent anthology of koans, essays, photographs, and poetry. Included are materials on Zen in painting, gardening, the tea ceremony, psychology, and architecture.

For years Alan Watts has been one of the most popular interpreters of Zen. His *The Way of Zen* (1960) is a fine introduction. It should not be confused with his earlier *The Spirit of Zen* (1935).

More materials on Soto Zen, which has been overshadowed by D. T. Suzuki and Rinzai Zen, may be found in *A Primer of Sōtō Zen: A Translation of Dōgen's Shōbogenzō Zuimonki* (1971) and *The Sōtō Approach to Zen* (1958), both by Reiho Masunaga.

William Briggs (ed.), *Anthology of Zen* (1961). Thirty-five essays by the likes of Aldous Huxley, Rudolph Otto, Fung Yu-lan, Martin Buber, Reiho Masunaga, Nyogen Senzaki, and Ruth Fuller Sasaki.

Heinrich Dumoulin's *A History of Zen* (1959) is the outstanding history of the religion—and most readable, too.

Garma C. C. Chang, *The Practice of Zen* (1959). An introduction to Zen featuring discourses from Chinese Zen masters and an essay on meditation.

Lucien Stryk and Takashi Ikemoto (eds.), *Zen: Poems, Prayers, Sermons, Anecdotes, Interviews* (1965). All that, plus an introductory essay by Stryk, "Let the Spring Breeze Enter: The Quest of Zen."

Philip Kapleau (ed.), *The Three Pillars of Zen* (1965). Materials from both Rinzai and Soto Zen masters plus autobiographical accounts (including his own) of enlightenment experiences.

Zen in English Literature and Oriental Classics (1948) and other of R. H. Blyth's books are original contributions to Zen literature.

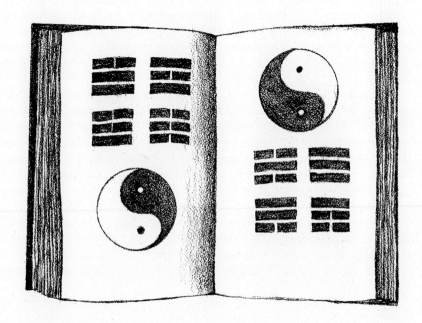

introduction _____

> For the Wise Man life is conformity to the motions of Heaven,
> death is but part of the common law of Change.
> At rest, he shares the secret powers of Yin;
> at work, he shares the rocking of the waves of Yang.
>
> *Chuang Tzu*

The use of the *I Ching* as a manual of divination has often caused the scientific-minded West to regard it as little more than a curious relic of China's most distant and primitive past. Contemporary thinking about it has been revived and modified principally by Richard Wilhelm's definitive translation and notes—portions of which are presented here. The *I Ching* is indeed a book of oracles, but it is also a compendium of ancient Chinese wisdom. Its "fortune-telling" is accompanied by abiding moral insight and guidance.

Presupposed by the *I Ching* is a cosmos of ceaseless movement, a dynamic but ordered flux. Nothing is static, but neither is there chaos. It is an organic world whose interrelated parts function harmoniously. Two elemental and complementary forces, or modes of energy, were termed *yang* and *yin*. The *yang* is that which is sunlit, active, hard—the positive, male principle. The *yin* is shaded, passive, yielding—the negative, female principle. These forces are in constant conjunction and interaction, and their ebb and flow comprise nature itself.

In the largest sense, it is the purpose of the *I Ching* to remind its readers of those rhythms of life, which are symbolically portrayed by the hexagrams. The alternating combinations of broken and unbroken lines lead from one hexagram to another: they reflect the constantly shifting and turning circumstances of life.

richard wilhelm _____

A Book of Oracles and of Wisdom

The *I* of its title is loosely translated as "change"; *"Ching"* means "classic" or "book." Hence it is the *Book of Change,* one of the *Five Classics* of ancient China, all but one of which antedate Confucius and Lao Tzu. The oldest elements of the *I Ching,* in fact, reportedly date back at least as far as the Hsia Dynasty (2205–1766, according to tradition). These elements are the linear signs that evolved into the sixty-four hexagrams.

_____

The Book of Changes—*I Ching* in Chinese—is unquestionably one of the most important books in the world's literature. Its origin goes back to mythical antiquity, and it has occupied the attention of the most eminent scholars of China down to the present day. Nearly all that is greatest and most significant in the three thousand years of Chinese cultural history has either taken its inspiration from this book, or has exerted an influence on the interpretation of its text. Therefore it may safely be said that the seasoned wisdom of thousands of years has gone into the making of the *I Ching.* Small wonder then that both of the two branches of Chinese philosophy, Confucianism and Taoism, have their common roots here. The book sheds new light on many a secret hidden in the often puzzling modes of thought of that mysterious sage, Lao-tse, and of his pupils, as well as on many ideas that appear in the Confucian tradition as axioms, accepted without further examination.

Indeed, not only the philosophy of China but its science and statecraft as well have never ceased to draw from the spring of wisdom in the *I Ching,* and it is not surprising that this alone, among all the Confucian classics, escaped the great burning of the books under Ch'in Shih Huang Ti.[1] Even the commonplaces of everyday life in China are saturated with its influence. In going through the streets of a Chinese city, one will find, here and there at a street corner, a fortune teller sitting behind a neatly covered table, brush and tablet at hand, ready to draw from the ancient book of wisdom pertinent counsel and information on life's minor perplexities. Not only that, but the very signboards adorning the houses—perpendicular wooden panels done in gold on black lacquer—are covered with inscriptions whose flowery language again and again recalls thoughts and quotations from the *I Ching.* Even the policy

[1] [213 B.C.]

Richard Wilhelm, "A Book of Oracles and of Wisdom." From Richard Wilhelm (trans.), *The I Ching: Or Book of Changes,* rendered into English by Cary F. Baynes, Bollingen Series XIX. Copyright © 1950 and 1967 by Bollingen Foundation. Reprinted by permission of Princeton University Press. Some notes have been omitted, and the remainder renumbered. Editor's title.

makers of so modern a state as Japan, distinguished for their astuteness, do not scorn to refer to it for counsel in difficult situations.

. . .

What is the Book of Changes actually? In order to arrive at an understanding of the book and its teachings, we must first of all boldly strip away the dense overgrowth of interpretations that have read into it all sorts of extraneous ideas. This is equally necessary whether we are dealing with the superstitions and mysteries of old Chinese sorcerers or the no less superstitious theories of modern European scholars who try to interpret all historical cultures in terms of their experience of primitive savages. We must hold here to the fundamental principle that the Book of Changes is to be explained in the light of its own content and of the era to which it belongs. With this the darkness lightens perceptibly and we realize that this book, though a very profound work, does not offer greater difficulties to our understanding than any other book that has come down through a long history from antiquity to our time.

THE BOOK OF ORACLES

At the outset, the Book of Changes was a collection of linear signs to be used as oracles. In antiquity, oracles were everywhere in use; the oldest among them confined themselves to the answers yes and no. This type of oracular pronouncement is likewise the basis of the Book of Changes. "Yes" was indicated by a simple unbroken line (——), and "No" by a broken line (— —). However, the need for greater differentiation seems to have been felt at an early date, and the single lines were combined in pairs:

$$\equiv \quad \equiv\equiv \quad \equiv\equiv \quad \equiv\equiv$$

To each of these combinations a third line was then added. In this way the eight trigrams came into being. These eight trigrams were conceived as images of all that happens in heaven and on earth. At the same time, they were held to be in a state of continual transition, one changing into another, just as transition from one phenomenon to another is continually taking place in the physical world. Here we have the fundamental concept of the Book of Changes. The eight trigrams are symbols standing for changing transitional states; they are images that are constantly undergoing change. Attention centers not on things in their state of being—as is chiefly the case in the Occident—but upon their movements in change. The eight trigrams therefore are not representations of things as such but of their tendencies in movement.

These eight images came to have manifold meanings. They represented certain processes in nature corresponding with their inherent character. Further, they represented a family consisting of father, mother, three sons, and three daughters, not in the mythological sense in which the Greek gods peopled Olympus, but in what might be called an abstract sense, that is, they represented not objective entities but functions.

A brief survey of these eight symbols that form the basis of the Book of Changes yields the following classification:

	Name	Attribute	Image	Family Relationship
☰ Ch'ien	the Creative	strong	heaven	father
☷ K'un	the Receptive	devoted, yielding	earth	mother
☳ Chên	the Arousing	inciting movement	thunder	first son
☵ K'an	the Abysmal	dangerous	water	second son
☶ Kên	Keeping Still	resting	mountain	third son
☴ Sun	the Gentle	penetrating	wind, wood	first daughter
☲ Li	the Clinging	light-giving	fire	second daughter
☱ Tui	the Joyous	joyful	lake	third daughter

The sons represent the principle of movement in its various stages —beginning of movement, danger in movement, rest and completion of movement. The daughters represent devotion in its various stages—gentle penetration, clarity and adaptability, and joyous tranquillity.

In order to achieve a still greater multiplicity, these eight images were combined with one another at a very early date, whereby a total of sixty-four signs was obtained. Each of these sixty-four signs consists of six lines, either positive or negative. Each line is thought of as capable of change, and whenever a line changes, there is a change also of the situation represented by the given hexagram. Let us take for example the hexagram K'un, THE RECEPTIVE, earth:

It represents the nature of the earth, strong in devotion; among the seasons it stands for late autumn, when all the forces of life are at rest. If the lowest line changes, we have the hexagram Fu, RETURN:

The latter represents thunder, the movement that stirs anew within the earth at the time of the solstice; it symbolizes the return of light.

As this example shows, all of the lines of a hexagram do not necessarily change; it depends entirely on the character of a given line. A line whose nature is positive, with an increasing dynamism, turns into its opposite, a negative line, whereas a positive line of lesser strength remains unchanged. The same principle holds for the negative lines.

More definite information about those lines which are to be considered so strongly charged with positive or negative energy that they move, is given in book II in the Great Commentary (pt. I, chap. IX), and in the special section on the use of the oracle at the end of book III. Suffice it to say here that positive lines that move are designated by the number 9, and negative lines that move by the number 6, while non-moving lines, which serve only as structural matter in the hexagram, without intrinsic meaning of their own, are represented by the number 7 (positive) or the number 8 (negative). Thus, when the text reads, "Nine at the beginning means . . ." this is the equivalent of saying: "When the positive line in the first place is represented by the number 9, it has the following meaning . . . ." If, on the other hand, the line is represented by the number 7, it is disregarded in interpreting the oracle. The same principle holds for lines represented by the numbers 6 and 8[2] respectively.

We may obtain the hexagram named in the example above—K'un, THE RECEPTIVE—in the following form:

8 at the top	— —
8 in the fifth place	— —
8 in the fourth place	— —
8 in the third place	— —
8 in the second place	— —
6 at the beginning	— —

Hence the five upper lines are not taken into account; only the 6 at the beginning has an independent meaning, and by its transformation into its opposite, the situation K'un, THE RECEPTIVE,

becomes the situation Fu, RETURN:

[2][For this reason, the numbers 7 and 8 never appear in the portion of the text dealing with the meanings of the individual lines.]

In this way we have a series of situations symbolically expressed by lines, and through the movement of these lines the situations can change one into another. On the other hand, such change does not necessarily occur, for when a hexagram is made up of lines represented by the numbers 7 and 8 only, there is no movement within it, and only its aspect as a whole is taken into consideration.

In addition to the law of change and to the images of the states of change as given in the sixty-four hexagrams, another factor to be considered is the course of action. Each situation demands the action proper to it. In every situation, there is a right and a wrong course of action. Obviously, the right course brings good fortune and the wrong course brings misfortune. Which, then, is the right course in any given case? This question was the decisive factor. As a result, the *I Ching* was lifted above the level of an ordinary book of soothsaying. If a fortune teller on reading the cards tells her client that she will receive a letter with money from America in a week, there is nothing for the woman to do but wait until the letter comes—or does not come. In this case what is foretold is fate, quite independent of what the individual may do or not do. For this reason fortune telling lacks moral significance. When it happened for the first time in China that someone, on being told the auguries for the future, did not let the matter rest there but asked, "What am I to do?" the book of divination had to become a book of wisdom.

It was reserved for King Wên, who lived about 1150 B.C., and his son, the Duke of Chou, to bring about this change. They endowed the hitherto mute hexagrams and lines, from which the future had to be divined as an individual matter in each case, with definite counsels for correct conduct. Thus the individual came to share in shaping fate. For his actions intervened as determining factors in world events, the more decisively so, the earlier he was able with the aid of the Book of Changes to recognize situations in their germinal phases. The germinal phase is the crux. As long as things are in their beginnings they can be controlled, but once they have grown to their full consequences they acquire a power so overwhelming that man stands impotent before them. Thus the Book of Changes became a book of divination of a very special kind. The hexagrams and lines in their movements and changes mysteriously reproduced the movements and changes of the macrocosm. By the use of yarrow stalks, one could attain a point of vantage from which it was possible to survey the condition of things. Given this perspective, the words of the oracle would indicate what should be done to meet the need of the time.

The only thing about all this that seems strange to our modern sense is the method of learning the nature of a situation through the manipulation of yarrow stalks. This procedure was regarded as mysterious, however, simply in the sense that the manipulation of the yarrow stalks makes it possible for the unconscious in man to become active. All individuals are not equally fitted to consult the oracle. It requires a clear and tranquil mind, receptive to the cosmic influences hidden in the humble divining stalks. As products of the vegetable kingdom, these were considered to be related to the sources of life. The stalks were derived from sacred plants.*

THE BOOK OF WISDOM

Of far greater significance than the use of the Book of Changes as an oracle is its other use, namely, as a book of wisdom. Lao-tse knew this book, and some of his profoundest aphorisms were inspired by it. Indeed, his whole thought is permeated with its teachings. Confucius too knew the Book of Changes and devoted himself to reflection upon it. He probably wrote down some of his interpretative comments and imparted others to his pupils in oral teaching. The Book of Changes as edited and annotated by Confucius is the version that has come down to our time.†

If we inquire as to the philosophy that pervades the book, we can confine ourselves to a few basically important concepts. The underlying idea of the whole is the idea of change. It is related in the Analects[3] that Confucius, standing by a river, said: "Everything flows on and on like this river, without pause, day and night." This expresses the idea of change. He who has perceived the meaning of change fixes his attention no longer on transitory individual things but on the immutable, eternal law at work in all change. This law is the tao of Lao-tse, the course of things, the principle of the one in the many. That it may become manifest, a decision, a postulate, is necessary. This fundamental postulate is the "great primal beginning" of all that exists, *t'ai chi*—in its original meaning, the "ridgepole." Later Chinese philosophers devoted much thought to this idea of a primal beginning. A still earlier beginning, *wu chi*, was represented by the symbol of a circle. Under this conception, *t'ai chi* was represented by the circle divided into the light and the dark, yang and yin, ☯.

This symbol has also played a significant part in India and Europe. However, speculations of a gnostic-dualistic character are foreign to the original thought of the *I Ching*; what it posits is simply the ridgepole, the line. With this line, which in itself represents oneness, duality comes into the world, for the line at the same time posits an above and a below, a right and left, front and back—in a word, the world of the opposites.

These opposites became known under the names yin and yang and created a great stir, especially in the transition period between the Ch'in and Han

---

*In the same volume from which these pages are taken, Wilhelm gave detailed directions for both the yarrow-stalk method and the more convenient coin method of approaching the *I Ching*. See "On Consulting the Oracle," pp. 721–724—R.E.

†Confucius came to the *I Ching* late in life and, apparently very impressed and mystified, wished that he had another lifetime in which to study it. The traditional claim that he edited the *I Ching* is doubted by contemporary scholars—R.E.

[3]*Lun Yü*, IX, 16. . . .

dynasties, in the centuries just before our era, when there was an entire school of yin-yang doctrine. At that time, the Book of Changes was much in use as a book of magic, and people read into the text all sorts of things not originally there. This doctrine of yin and yang, of the female and the male as primal principles, has naturally also attracted much attention among foreign students of Chinese thought. Following the usual bent, some of these have predicated in it a primitive phallic symbolism, with all the accompanying connotations.

To the disappointment of such discoverers it must be said that there is nothing to indicate this in the original meaning of the words yin and yang. In its primary meaning yin is "the cloudy," "the overcast," and yang means actually "banners waving in the sun," that is, something "shone upon," or bright. By transference the two concepts were applied to the light and dark sides of a mountain or of a river. In the case of a mountain the southern is the bright side and the northern the dark side, while in the case of a river seen from above, it is the northern side that is bright (yang), because it reflects the light, and the southern side that is in shadow (yin). Thence the two expressions were carried over into the Book of Changes and applied to the two alternating primal states of being. It should be pointed out, however, that the terms yin and yang do not occur in this derived sense either in the actual text of the book or in the oldest commentaries. Their first occurrence is in the Great Commentary, which already shows Taoistic influence in some parts. In the Commentary on the Decision the terms used for the opposites are "the firm" and "the yielding," not yang and yin.

However, no matter what names are applied to these forces, it is certain that the world of being arises out of their change and interplay. Thus change is conceived of partly as the continuous transformation of the one force into the other and partly as a cycle of complexes of phenomena, in themselves connected, such as day and night, summer and winter. Change is not meaningless—if it were, there could be no knowledge of it—but subject to the universal law, tao.

The second theme fundamental to the Book of Changes is its theory of ideas. The eight trigrams are images not so much of objects as of states of change. This view is associated with the concept expressed in the teachings of Lao-tse, as also in those of Confucius, that every event in the visible world is the effect of an "image," that is, of an idea in the unseen world. Accordingly, everything that happens on earth is only a reproduction, as it were, of an event in a world beyond our sense perception; as regards its occurrence in time, it is later than the suprasensible event. The holy men and sages, who are in contact with those higher spheres, have access to these ideas through direct intuition and are therefore able to intervene decisively in events in the world. Thus man is linked with heaven, the suprasensible world of ideas, and with earth, the material world of visible things, to form with these a trinity of the primal powers.

This theory of ideas is applied in a twofold sense. The Book of Changes shows the images of events and also the unfolding of conditions *in statu nascendi.*[‡] Thus, in discerning with its help the seeds of things to come, we learn to foresee the future as well as to understand the past. In this way the images on which the hexagrams are based serve as patterns for timely action in the situations indicated. Not only is adaptation to the course of nature thus made possible, but in the Great Commentary (pt. II, chap. II), an interesting attempt is made to trace back the origin of all the practices and inventions of civilization to such ideas and archetypal images. Whether or not the hypothesis can be made to apply in all specific instances, the basic concept contains a truth.

The third element fundamental to the Book of Changes are the judgments. The judgments clothe the images in words, as it were; they indicate whether a given action will bring good fortune or misfortune, remorse or humiliation. The judgments make it possible for a man to make a decision to desist from a course of action indicated by the situation of the moment but harmful in the long run. In this way he makes himself independent of the tyranny of events. In its judgments, and in the interpretations attached to it from the time of Confucius on, the Book of Changes opens to the reader the richest treasure of Chinese wisdom; at the same time it affords him a comprehensive view of the varieties of human experience, enabling him thereby to shape his life of his own sovereign will into an organic whole and so to direct it that it comes into accord with the ultimate tao lying at the root of all that exists.

[‡]"In the state of being created."—R.E.

richard wilhelm (translator) _____

The First Hexagram:
Ch'ien / The Creative

The *I Ching* opens with the Ch'ien hexagram, its unbroken lines representing the power of *yang*: great strength and creativity. The second hexagram (not included here) is K'un, "The Receptive," which consists of six broken lines symbolizing the passive energy of *yin*. These first and most important hexagrams thus delineate that polarity and tension within which all movement—all life—takes place.

---

above	CH'IEN	THE CREATIVE, HEAVEN
below	CH'IEN	THE CREATIVE, HEAVEN

The first hexagram is made up of six unbroken lines. These unbroken lines stand for the primal power, which is light-giving, active, strong, and of the spirit. The hexagram is consistently strong in character, and since it is without weakness, its essence is power or energy. Its image is heaven. Its energy is represented as unrestricted by any fixed conditions in space and is therefore conceived of as motion. Time is regarded as the basis of this motion. Thus the hexagram includes also the power of time and the power of persisting in time, that is, duration.

The power represented by the hexagram is to be interpreted in a dual sense—in terms of its action on the universe and of its action on the world of men. In relation to the universe, the hexagram expresses the strong, creative action of the Deity. In relation to the human world, it denotes the creative action of the holy man or sage, of the ruler or leader of men, who through his power awakens and develops their higher nature.[1]

THE JUDGMENT

> THE CREATIVE works sublime success,
> Furthering through perseverance.

According to the original meaning, the attributes [sublimity, potentiality of success, power to further, perseverance] are paired. When an individual

---

[1]The hexagram is assigned to the fourth month, May–June, when the light-giving power is at its zenith, i.e., before the summer solstice has marked the beginning of the year's decline. . . .

draws this oracle, it means that success will come to him from the primal depths of the universe and that everything depends upon his seeking his happiness and that of others in one way only, that is, by perseverance in what is right.

The specific meanings of the four attributes became the subject of speculation at an early date. The Chinese word here rendered by "sublime" means literally "head," "origin," "great." This is why Confucius says in explaining it: "Great indeed is the generating power of the Creative; all beings owe their beginning to it. This power permeates all heaven." For this attribute inheres in the other three as well.

The beginning of all things lies still in the beyond in the form of ideas that have yet to become real. But the Creative furthermore has power to lend form to these archetypes of ideas. This is indicated in the word success, and the process is represented by an image from nature: "The clouds pass and the rain does its work, and all individual beings flow into their forms."[2]

Applied to the human world, these attributes show the great man the way to notable success: "Because he sees with great clarity causes and effects, he completes the six steps at the right time and mounts toward heaven on them at the right time, as though on six dragons." The six steps are the six different positions given in the hexagram, which are represented later by the dragon symbol. Here it is shown that the way to success lies in apprehending and giving actuality to the way of the universe [tao], which, as a law running through end and beginning, brings about all phenomena in time. Thus each step attained forthwith becomes a preparation for the next. Time is no longer a hindrance but the means of making actual what is potential.

The act of creation having found expression in the two attributes sublimity and success, the work of conservation is shown to be a continuous actualization and differentiation of form. This is expressed in the two terms "furthering" (literally, "creating that which accords with the nature of a given being") and "preserving" (literally, "correct and firm"). "The course of the Creative alters and shapes beings until each attains its true, specific nature, then it keeps them in conformity with the Great Harmony. Thus does it show itself to further through perseverance."

In relation to the human sphere, this shows how the great man brings peace and security to the world through his activity in creating order: "He towers high above the multitude of beings, and all lands are united in peace."

Another line of speculation goes still further in separating the words "sublime," "success," "furthering," "perseverance," and parallels them with the four cardinal virtues in humanity. To sublimity, which, as the fundamental principle, embraces all the other attributes, it links love. To the attribute

[2]Cf. Gen. 2: 1 ff., where the development of the different creatures is also attributed to the fall of rain.

success are linked the mores,[3] which regulate and organize the expressions of love and thereby make them successful. The attribute furthering is correlated with justice, which creates the conditions in which each receives that which accords with his being, that which is due him and which constitutes his happiness. The attribute perseverance is correlated with wisdom, which discerns the immutable laws of all that happens and can therefore bring about enduring conditions. These speculations, already broached in the commentary called *Wên Yen,* later formed the bridge connecting the philosophy of the "five stages (elements) of change," as laid down in the Book of History (*Shu Ching*) with the philosophy of the Book of Changes, which is based solely on the polarity of positive and negative principles. In the course of time this combination of the two systems of thought opened the way for an increasingly intricate number symbolism.[4]

THE IMAGE

> The movement of heaven is full of power.
> Thus the superior man makes himself strong and untiring.

Since there is only one heaven, the doubling of the trigram Ch'ien, of which heaven is the image, indicates the movement of heaven. One complete revolution of heaven makes a day, and the repetition of the trigram means that each day is followed by another. This creates the idea of time. Since it is the same heaven moving with untiring power, there is also created the idea of duration both in and beyond time, a movement that never stops nor slackens, just as

---

[3]["Mores" is the word chosen to render the German word *Sitte*, when the latter refers, as in the present instance, to what the Chinese know as *li*. However, neither "mores" nor any other available English word, such as "manners" or "customs," conveys an adequate idea of what *li* stood for in ancient China, because none of them necessarily denotes anything more than behavior growing out of and regulated by tradition. The ideas for which *li* stands seem to have had their origin in a religious attitude to life and in ethical principles developing out of that attitude. On the religious side *li* meant the observance with true piety of the ritual through which the "will of heaven" was interpreted and made to prevail on earth. On the moral side it meant the sense of propriety—understood to be innate in man—that, through training, makes possible right relationships in personal life and in society. *Li* was the cornerstone upon which Confucius built in his effort to bring order out of chaos in his era (see *The Sacred Books of the East,* XXVII: *The Li Ki*). Obedience to the code of *li* was entirely self-imposed as regards the "superior man," who in feudal times was always a man of rank. The conduct of the "inferior man"—the lower-class individual—was governed by law.]

[4]The Creative causes the beginning and begetting of all beings, and can therefore be designated as heaven, radiant energy, father, ruler. It is a question whether the Chinese personified the Creative, as the Greeks conceived it in Zeus. The answer is that this problem is not the main one for the Chinese. The divine-creative principle is suprapersonal and makes itself perceptible only through its all-powerful activity. It has, to be sure, an external aspect, which is heaven, and heaven, like all that lives, has a spiritual consciousness, God, the Supreme Ruler. But all this is summed up as the Creative.

one day follows another in an unending course. This duration in time is the image of the power inherent in the Creative.

With this image as a model, the sage learns how best to develop himself so that his influence may endure. He must make himself strong in every way, by consciously casting out all that is inferior and degrading. Thus he attains that tirelessness which depends upon consciously limiting the fields of his activity.

THE LINES

> Nine at the beginning[5] means:
> Hidden dragon. Do not act.

In China the dragon has a meaning altogether different from that given it in the Western world. The dragon is a symbol of the electrically charged, dynamic, arousing force that manifests itself in the thunderstorm. In winter this energy withdraws into the earth; in the early summer it becomes active again, appearing in the sky as thunder and lightning. As a result the creative forces on earth begin to stir again.

Here this creative force is still hidden beneath the earth and therefore has no effect. In terms of human affairs, this symbolizes a great man who is still unrecognized. Nonetheless he remains true to himself. He does not allow himself to be influenced by outward success or failure, but confident in his strength, he bides his time. Hence it is wise for the man who consults the oracle and draws this line to wait in the calm strength of patience. The time will fulfill itself. One need not fear lest strong will should not prevail; the main thing is not to expend one's powers prematurely in an attempt to obtain by force something for which the time is not yet ripe.

> Nine in the second place means:
> Dragon appearing in the field.
> It furthers one to see the great man.

Here the effects of the light-giving power begin to manifest themselves. In terms of human affairs, this means that the great man makes his appearance in his chosen field of activity. As yet he has no commanding position but is still with his peers. However, what distinguishes him from the others is his seriousness of purpose, his unqualified reliability, and the influence he exerts

[5]The lines are counted from the bottom up, i.e., the lowest is taken as the first. If the person consulting the oracle draws a seven, this is important in relation to the structure of the hexagram as a whole, because it is a strong line, but inasmuch as it does not move [change] it has no meaning as an individual line. On the other hand, if the questioner draws a nine, the line is a moving one, and a special meaning is attached to it; this must be considered separately. The same principle applies in respect to all the other strong lines [and also as regards moving and nonmoving weak lines, i.e., sixes and eights]. The two lowest lines in each hexagram stand for the earth, the two in the middle for the world of man, and the upper two for heaven. . . .

on his environment without conscious effort. Such a man is destined to gain great influence and to set the world in order. Therefore it is favorable to see him.

> Nine in the third place means:
> All day long the superior man is creatively active.
> At nightfall his mind is still beset with cares.
> Danger. No blame.

A sphere of influence opens up for the great man. His fame begins to spread. The masses flock to him. His inner power is adequate to the increased outer activity.[6] There are all sorts of things to be done, and when others are at rest in the evening, plans and anxieties press in upon him. But danger lurks here at the place of transition from lowliness to the heights. Many a great man has been ruined because the masses flocked to him and swept him into their course. Ambition has destroyed his integrity. However, true greatness is not impaired by temptations. He who remains in touch with the time that is dawning, and with its demands, is prudent enough to avoid all pitfalls, and remains blameless.

> Nine in the fourth place means:
> Wavering flight over the depths.
> No blame.

A place of transition has been reached, and free choice can enter in. A twofold possibility is presented to the great man: he can soar to the heights and play an important part in the world, or he can withdraw into solitude and develop himself. He can go the way of the hero or that of the holy sage who seeks seclusion. There is no general law to say which of the two is the right way. Each one in this situation must make a free choice according to the inner law of his being. If the individual acts consistently and is true to himself, he will find the way that is appropriate for him. This way is right for him and without blame.

> O Nine in the fifth place[7] means:
> Flying dragon in the heavens.
> It furthers one to see the great man.

Here the great man has attained the sphere of the heavenly beings. His

---

[6][The upper trigram is considered to be "outside," the lower "inside". . . . This distinction underlies the constant juxtaposition, to be observed throughout bks. I and III, of inner, mental states and external actions or events, of subjective and objective experiences. From this also arise the frequent comparisons between ability and position, form and content, outer adornment and inner worth.]

[7][The circle indicates that this line is a governing ruler of the hexagram. Constituting rulers are marked by a square. . . .]

influence spreads and becomes visible throughout the whole world. Everyone who sees him may count himself blessed. Confucius says about this line:

Things that accord in tone vibrate together. Things that have affinity in their inmost natures seek one another. Water flows to what is wet, fire turns to what is dry. Clouds (the breath of heaven) follow the dragon, wind (the breath of earth) follows the tiger. Thus the sage arises, and all creatures follow him with their eyes. What is born of heaven feels related to what is above. What is born of earth feels related to what is below. Each follows its kind.

> Nine at the top means:
> Arrogant dragon will have cause to repent.

When a man seeks to climb so high that he loses touch with the rest of mankind, he becomes isolated, and this necessarily leads to failure. This line warns against titanic aspirations that exceed one's power. A precipitous fall would follow.

> When all the lines are nines, it means:
> There appears a flight of dragons without heads.
> Good fortune.

When all the lines are nines, it means that the whole hexagram is in motion and changes into the hexagram K'un, THE RECEPTIVE, whose character is devotion. The strength of the Creative and the mildness of the Receptive unite.* Strength is indicated by the flight of dragons, mildness by the fact that their heads are hidden. This means that mildness in action joined to strength of decision brings good fortune.

---

*A discussion of both of these important hexagrams may be found in Hellmut Wilhelm, *Change: Eight Lectures on the I Ching,* translated by Cary F. Baynes (Princeton, N.J.: Princeton University Press, 1960), Chap. 5, "The Hexagrams Ch'ien and K'un."—R.E.

further reading

John Blofeld (ed. and trans.), *I Ching* (1965). A shorter, simpler version, with practical guidelines for using the *I Ching* as a book of divination.

R. G. H. Siu, *The Man of Many Qualities: A Legacy of the I Ching* (1968). Some 700 quotations from almost as many authors are appended to the text of the *I Ching* to illustrate its meanings. Here the divinational aspect of the book is set aside in favor of its use as a "book of wisdom."

C. G. Jung's Foreword to the translation of the *I Ching* by Richard Wilhelm discusses "chance" as an important principle of the classic. Jung also describes the responses he received to questions he addressed to the *I Ching*.

Hellmut Wilhelm, *Change: Eight Lectures on the I Ching,* translated by Cary F. Baynes (1960). Brief, but thorough and very clear, this is the best introduction to the background, underlying philosophy, and purposes of the *I Ching*.

Confucianism

———————————————————————— the ideal of the true man

_____

> The superior man understands what is right;
> the inferior man understands what will sell.
>
> *The Analects*

The story of the life of Confucius is remarkable for its lack of those dramatic events one might expect in the career of the man who became the "First Teacher" of China and whose influence held sway for 2,500 years. Born in 551 B.C. in "humble circumstances," the young Confucius* received sufficient education to become a teacher, and he learned to enjoy hunting, fishing, and archery. An early marriage produced a son and a daughter, but otherwise went awry. Although he occasionally held minor posts in government, he mostly taught, and he excelled at it: students became disciples, and he was known by the rulers of states. He had, he said, a great love of learning and considered himself a diligent student, but he made no claim to wisdom nor even to unusual moral character. His ambition was to attain a significant position in government: he wanted to put into practice the ideas and ideals he taught. That ambition, however, was never realized, though he actively sought a position by traveling from one state to another for a number of years. He retired and spent his last years studying. He died, in Arthur Waley's phrase, "a disappointed itinerant tutor" in 479 B.C.

The substance of his teaching, described in the following essay by Huston Smith, dealt with those moral qualities which comprised the *chun tzu,* the superior man or "true gentleman." The *chun tzu* was a model of modest strength and decorum: gentle, poised, kind, sincere, dutiful, and trustworthy. He was not, however, an "individual." He was, of course, a person in his own right and deserving of happiness, but he was also and always a member of a family and of society—and it was this trinity of interests that concerned Confucius.

The preponderance of ethical and social content in the teachings of Confucius has often prompted two different (but related) responses. On the one hand, Confucianism is frequently termed a philosophy or, more specifically, "Chinese Humanism," rather than a religion. On the other hand, laborious attempts have been made to ferret out in Confucian literature those signs of "conventional" religious conviction and behavior which would prove Confucianism to be an authentic member of the world's family of religions. But each of these responses appears to rest on categories of thought more appropriate to Western than to Far Eastern religion.

*His family name was K'ung and given name Chung-ni; but as his reputation grew, he became known as K'ung Fu-tzu ("Master" K'ung). In the Latin of Jesuit missionaries, "K'ung Fu-tzu" was transformed into "Confucius."

Confucius was undeniably preoccupied with "down-to-earth" moral issues, but the term "humanism" implies "antisupernaturalism," and this type of dualism was foreign to Chinese thought. Confucianism is perhaps best understood as an expression of that older and larger vision in China of a cosmic harmony. The Confucian ideal of social order—of the rules of propriety observed by all, of tradition and ritual enhancing the lives of men—was a reflection of that Ultimate Order.[†] Heaven, earth, and man were, in China, a continuum: the ruler, for example, was the "Son of Heaven" and he ruled only by "decree" of Heaven. To restore harmony to the lives of men was to return to Tao, the Way. In ancient China, Joseph Kitagawa has written,

. . . the world of man and the world of nature constitute a seamless whole, governed by reciprocal relationships. . . . Chinese religion never made a distinction between sacred and secular. . . . The religious ethos of the Chinese must be found in the midst of their everyday life. . . . The meaning of life was sought in the whole of life, and not confined to any section of it called specifically "religious."[‡]

The readings of this chapter, apart from the introductory essay by Smith, include selections from three of the *Four Books* of Confucianism—all of which are products of the followers of Confucius. (Confucius said that he was "a transmitter and not a creator." It is not certain what, if anything, we have from his own hand.) The *Analects* is the most important source of the "sayings" and life of Confucius. *The Book of Mencius* is a collection of the teachings of the major figure in the centuries immediately following Confucius. *The Great Learning*, a brief summary of moral and social doctrines, is presented in its entirety. *The Doctrine of the Mean* (not included here), in addition to the subject named by its title, relates man to the Way of Heaven. The final selection is a contemporary reinterpretation of Confucius by Herbert Fingarette.

[†]The theme of a "cosmic harmony" has already been mentioned in connection with the *I Ching*. It is rarely explicit, however, in early Confucian literature, with the exception of *The Doctrine of the Mean*. ("Equilibrium is the great foundation of the world, and harmony its universal path," etc.) The Neo-Confucianists of the Middle Ages pursued the subject extensively.

[‡]*Religions of the East* (Philadelphia: Westminster Press, 1960), pp. 49-50.

huston smith

The Way of Deliberate Tradition

Born in Soochow, China, the son of missionaries, Huston Smith (1919–   ) lived in China for seventeen years. He received his Ph.D. from the University of Chicago and has taught philosophy at the University of Denver, Washington University, and, since 1958, the Massachusetts Institute of Technology. He is the author of *The Purposes of Higher Education, The Search for America, The Religions of Man,* and *Condemned to Meaning.*

The society in which Confucius lived had disintegrated into feuding states, and there were sporadic outbreaks of ferocious and devastating warfare. What was required first, therefore, was order, but Confucius knew that an inflexible regime of "law and order" was no solution. Hence the great Confucian virtue of *li* (the principle of propriety—the proper, structured way of doing things)was accompanied by *jen* (good-ness, human-heartedness, kindness). Orderliness and ceremony were to be observed, but they were to be balanced and kept alive by a sense of "humanity" and a concern for people.

Confucius found himself intrigued by tradition, man's original answer to the social problem. With others of his day, he believed that there had been in China's past a period of Grand Harmony. It was tradition that had effected this golden age; because the traditions had been powerful, people lived by them; because they had been finely wrought, in living by them the people lived well. Confucius may have idealized, even romanticized, China's past; he unquestionably envied it and wished to duplicate it as nearly as possible in his own time. As tradition held the secret then, so must it in some way now. . . .

This in no way implies that he was an antiquarian. He was a contemporary man alert to the new features which made his time unlike any before and so precluded all hope that a simple duplication of measures effective in the past would be equally effective in the present. The decisive difference that set off his age from that of the Grand Harmony was that men had become individu-als, self-conscious and reflective. This being so, spontaneous tradition—a tradition that had emerged unconsciously out of the trial and error of innum-erable generations and that held its power because men felt completely identified with the tribe—could not be expected to command their assent. The alternative was deliberate tradition. When tradition can no longer hold its own in the face of the eroding wash of critical self-consciousness, shore it up by giving it deliberate attention and reenforcement.

The answer held the appositeness of social genius. In times of transition an effective answer to the social problem must meet two conditions. It must preserve true continuity with the past, for only by tying in with what men have known and are accustomed to can it be widely accepted. "Think not that I came to destroy; I came not to destroy but to fulfill" must be the standard here. The answer must also take sufficient account of new factors that now render the old answers inapplicable. Confucius' answer met both requirements superbly. Continuity was preserved by keeping tradition in the center of the picture. Don't rush, Confucius seemed to be saying. Let's see how it was done in the past. "Myself, I am simply a lover of the ancients." With the regularity of a politician taking his stand on the Constitution, he appeals to the Classics as the sole basis for his proposal. And yet it wasn't the old answer. All the way through Confucius was reinterpreting, modifying. Unknown to his people, he was effecting a momentous reorientation by shifting tradition from an unconscious to a conscious base.

Unknown to his people—and for the most part unknown to himself we should add, for it would be a mistake to suppose that Confucius was fully aware of what he was doing. But genius does not depend upon full, self-conscious understanding of its acts. A poet may have less than a critic's awareness of why he chooses the words he does; the lack in no way precludes his words from being right. Probably all radical origination proceeds more by feel than by conscious design. It was clearly so with Confucius. He would not, he could not have justified or even described his answer in the frame of reference we have used. He merely conceived the answer in the first place, leaving to posterity the secondary task of trying to understand precisely what he had done and why it proved effective among the sons of the Middle Kingdom.

The shift from spontaneous to deliberate tradition requires that the powers of critical intelligence be turned both to continuing the force of tradition intact and to determining what ends tradition shall henceforth serve. A people must first decide what values are important to their collective well-being; this is why "among the Confucians the study of the correct attitudes was a matter of prime importance."[1] Then every device of education, formal and informal, should be turned to seeing that these values are internalized as far as possible by everyone. As one Chinese describes the process: "Moral ideas were driven into the people by every possible means—temples, theatres, homes, toys, proverbs, schools, history, and stories—until they became habits in daily life. . . . Even festivals and parades were always religious in

---

[1] Arthur Waley, *The Way and Its Power* (London: George Allen & Unwin, 1949), p. 161.

character."[2] By these means even a society composed of individuals can, if it puts itself to the task, spin a web of enveloping tradition, a power of suggestion, which its members will internalize and which will prompt them to behave socially even when out of sight of the law.

. . .

THE CONTENT OF DELIBERATE TRADITION

Deliberate tradition differs from spontaneous tradition in requiring attention. It requires attention first to maintain its force in the face of the increased individualism confronting it. This Confucius regarded as the main responsibility of education in its broadest terms. But, second, it requires that attention be given to the ends it is to serve.

What were Confucius' proposals on this second score? What was to be the content of deliberate tradition and what were the goals of character and social life it was to serve? The main outlines of his answer can be gathered under five key Confucian terms.

1. *Jen,* etymologically a combination of the character for "man" and for "two," names the ideal relationship which should pertain between people. Variously translated as goodness, man-to-man-ness, benevolence, and love, it is perhaps best rendered as human-heartedness. *Jen* was the virtue of virtues in Confucius' view of life. It was a sublime even transcendental perfection that he confessed he had never seen fully incarnated. Involving as it does the display of human capacities at their best, it is a virtue so exalted that one "cannot but be chary in speaking of it."[3] To the noble it is dearer than life itself. "The determined scholar and the man of *Jen* . . . will even sacrifice their lives to preserve their *Jen* complete."

Jen involves simultaneously a feeling of humanity toward others and respect for oneself, an indivisible sense of the dignity of human life wherever it appears. Subsidiary attitudes follow automatically; magnanimity, good faith, and charity. In the direction of *Jen* lies the perfection of everything that separates man from the beasts and makes him distinctively human. In public life the man of *Jen* is untiringly diligent. In private life he is courteous, unselfish, and gifted with empathy, "able to measure the feelings of others by his own." Stated negatively, this empathy leads to what the West, contrasting it with Jesus' parallel statement, has called the Silver Rule: "What you do not want done to yourself, do not do to others." There is no reason, however, to rest with this negative formulation, for Confucius puts the point positively as well: "The man who possesses *Jen,* wishing to be established himself, seeks

[2]Chiang Monlin, *Tides from the West* (New Haven: Yale University Press, 1947), pp. 9, 19.
[3]Confucius. Quoted in Arthur Waley, *The Analects of Confucius* (London: George Allen & Unwin), p. 28.

CHAPTER FIVE / *Confucianism*

also to enlarge others." Such largeness of heart knows no national boundaries for the man of *Jen* knows that "within the four seas all men are brothers."

2. The second concept is *Chun-tzu*. If *Jen* is the ideal relationship between human beings, *Chun-tzu* refers to the ideal term of such relations. It has been translated True Manhood, the Superior Man, and Manhood-at-its-Best. The word gentleman has declined to the point where it now denotes little but matters of etiquette—tipping the hat, pushing in ladies' chairs, and the like. But if we understand etiquette in its original French meaning as "the ticket on the outside of a package that indicates what's on the inside" we shall not be wrong in thinking of the *Chun-tzu* as a gentleman in the most significant sense.

The *Chun-tzu* is the opposite of the petty man, the mean man, the little man. Fully adequate, poised, he has toward life as a whole the approach of the ideal host who is so at home in his surroundings that he is completely relaxed and being so can turn his full attention to putting others at their ease. As he needs nothing himself, he is wholly at the disposal of others. Having come to the point where he is at home in the universe at large, the *Chun-tzu* carries these qualities of the ideal host with him through life generally. His approach to others is in terms not of what he can get but of what he can do to accommodate.

With the gentleman's adequacy go a pleasant air and good grace. Poised, confident, and competent, he is a man of perfect address. His movements are free of brusqueness and violence; his expression is open, his speech free of lewdness and vulgarity. The gentleman does not talk too much. He does not boast, push himself forward, or in any way display his superiority save perhaps at sports. Holding always to his own standards however others may forget theirs, he is never at a loss as to how to behave and can keep a gracious initiative where others are at sea. Schooled to meet any contingency "without fret or fear," his head is not turned by success nor his temper soured by adversity.

"It is only the man who is entirely real," Confucius thought, "who can establish the great foundations of civilized society." Only as the persons who make up society are transformed into *Chun-tzus* can the world move toward peace.

. . .

3. The third concept, *Li,* has two meanings.

Its first meaning is propriety, the way things should be done. Confucius thought individuals were not likely to achieve much in their search for beauty and goodness if starting from scratch. They needed precedent. Confucius wanted to lift to the collective attention of the community the finest precedents for social life that had been discovered, that everyone might gaze and memorize and duplicate. The French, whose culture not only in its love of cooking but in its attention to the art of life in general is China's nearest counterpart in the West, have several phrases that capture this idea so exactly that they have made their way into every Western vocabulary: *savoir faire,* the knowledge of how to comport oneself with grace and urbanity whatever the circumstance; *comme il faut,* the way things are done; *apropos,* that which is appropriate; and *esprit,* the right feel for things. Confucius wanted to cultivate the Chinese character in precisely the direction pointed by these idioms. Through maxims (burlesqued in the West by parodies of "Confucius say . . ."), anecdote (*The Analects* are full of them), and his own example ("Confucius, in his village, looked simple and sincere; . . . when in court he spoke minutely but cautiously . . .") he sought to order an entire way of life so that no one properly raised need ever be left to improvise his responses on momentary impulse because he is at a loss as to how to behave. "Manners maketh man" said a wise medieval bishop. To the extent that this is true, *Li* was to be the making of the Chinese character.

Propriety covers a wide range, but we can get the gist of what Confucius was concerned with if we look at his teachings on the Rectification of Names, the Mean, the Five Key Relationships, the Family, and Age.

Confucius said:

If names be not correct, language is not in accordance with the truth of things. If language be not in accordance with the truth of things, affairs cannot be carried on to success. . . . Therefore a superior man considers it necessary that the names he uses may be spoken appropriately, and also that what he speaks may be carried out appropriately. What the superior man requires is just that in his words there may be nothing incorrect.

This may sound like undue concern with words. But Confucius was grappling with a problem that in our time has spawned a whole new discipline, semantics; the inquiry into the relation between words, thought, and objective reality. All human thought proceeds through words. As long as words are askew, thought cannot be straight. When Confucius says that nothing is more important than that a father *be* a father, that a ruler *be* a ruler, this implies first that we know what we mean when we use the words father and ruler and that we mean the right things. Behind the concept of *Li,* therefore, stands the presumption that the various roles and relationships of life will have been normatively delineated and defined.

So important was the Doctrine of the Mean in Confucius' vision of the good life that an entire book by that title is an important part of the Confucian canon. The two Chinese words for Mean are *chung yung,* literally "middle" and "constant." The Mean, therefore, is the way that is "constantly in the middle" between life's extremes. With "nothing in excess" its guiding principle, its closest Western equivalent is the Golden Mean of Aristotle. The Mean balances a sensitive temperament against overdose and indulgence and checks depravity before it occurs. "Pride," admonishes the *Book of Li,* "should not be allowed to grow. The desires should not be indulged. The will should not be gratified to the full. Pleasure should not be carried to excess." Following the Mean brings harmony and balance. It disposes men to compromise, and issues in a becoming reserve. Never plunging to extremes, toward pure values "equally removed from enthusiasm as from indifference," China's regard for the Mean has come out in her recoil from everything approaching fanaticism.

The Five Relationships that make up the warp and woof of social life are in the Confucian scheme those between father and son, elder brother and junior brother, husband and wife, elder friend and junior friend, and ruler and subject. It is, therefore, vital to the health of society that they be rightly constituted. None of these relationships are transitive; in each case different responses are appropriate to the two terms. A father should be loving, a son reverential; an elder brother gentle, a younger brother respectful; a husband good, a wife "listening"; an elder friend considerate, a younger friend deferential; a ruler benevolent, a subject loyal. In effect Confucius is saying: You are never alone when you act. Every action affects someone else. Here in these five relationships is a frame within which you may achieve as much as is possible of individuality without doing damage or creating a bitter conflict with any other individual in the pattern of life.

That three of the Five Relationships pertain within the family is indicative of how important Confucius believed this institution to be. He was not inventing but continuing the Chinese assumption that the family is the basic unit of society, an assumption graphically embedded in Chinese legend which credits the hero who "invented" the family with bringing the Chinese from animal to human level by the discovery. Within the family, in turn, it is the children's respect for their parents that holds the key; hence the concept of filial piety. When the meanings of the father are no longer meaningful to the son, someone has recently written, civilization is in danger. Confucius could not have agreed more. "The duty of children to their parents is the fountain from whence all virtues spring." Accounts of devoted children pepper Confucian literature. They are simple stories, many of them, as for example that of the woman whose aged mother-in-law was pining for fish to eat in the depth of winter. The young woman prostrated herself on the ice of a pond and bared her bosom to melt the ice so she might catch the fish which immediately swam up to the hole.

Finally in this elaborate Confucian pattern of propriety that constituted *Li* there was respect for age. The West, accenting the physical, has eulogized youth as the best years of our lives. For the Chinese there is a wonder that only time can bestow. Age gives to all things, objects, institutions, and individual lives, their value, their dignity, their worth. As a consequence, esteem should always turn upward to those who have gone ahead and stand before us. Three of the Five Relationships prescribe that the bulk of respect flow from young to the old.

In the Rectification of Names, the Doctrine of the Mean, the Five Relationships, and attitudes toward Age and the Family we have sketched the main ingredients of Confucius' concept of *Li* in its first meaning, namely propriety. The other meaning of the word is ritual. When appropriate response is detailed to Confucian lengths, the individual's entire life becomes stylized into a vast, intricate, ceremonial rite. Life has become ordered completely. Every step of life's procession has been worked out leaving neither need nor room for improvisation. There is a pattern for every act, from the way thrice-yearly the Emperor renders to heaven an account of his mandate right down to the way you entertain the humblest guest in your home and serve him his tea.

Alfred North Whitehead's wife reported a Cambridge vicar who concluded his sermon by saying "Finally, my brethren, for well-conducted people life presents no problems."[4] *Li* was Confucius' blueprint for the well-conducted life.

4. The fourth pivotal concept Confucius sought to devise for his countrymen was *Te.*

Literally this word meant power, specifically the power by which men are ruled. But this is only the beginning of its definition. What is this power? Confucius disagreed with the Realists' thesis that the only effective rule is by physical might. How right he was in this dispute, history demonstrated through the one dynasty, Ch'in, that attempted to base its policy squarely on Realist principles. Fantastically successful in its early years, it conquered all of existing China within nine years and was the first dynasty to unite the nation only to collapse before the generation was out—vivid witness to Talleyrand's dictum that "You can do everything with bayonets except sit on them." One of the best known of all the stories of Confucius is how on the lonely side of Mount T'ai he heard the mourning wail of a woman. Asked why she wept, she replied, "My husband's father was killed here by a tiger, my husband also, and now my son has met the same fate."

"Then why," Confucius asked, "do you dwell in so dreadful a place?"

"Because here," she answered, "there is no oppressive ruler."

"Scholars," he said to his disciples, "remember this: oppressive rule is more cruel than a tiger."[5]

No state, Confucius was convinced, can constrain all its citizens all the time nor even any large fraction of them a large part of the time. It must depend on widespread acceptance of its will, which in turn requires a certain positive fund of faith in its total character. Observing that the three essentials of government were economic sufficiency, military sufficiency, and the confidence of the people, he added that popular trust is by far the most important since "if the people have no confidence in their government, it cannot stand."

[4]Lucien Price, ed., *Dialogues of Alfred North Whitehead,* p. 339. Quoted in Frederic Spiegelberg, *Living Religions of the World* (Englewood Cliffs: Prentice-Hall, 1956), p. 325.
[5]Related in Lady Hosie's Introduction to W. E. Soothill, *The Analects* (London: Oxford University Press, 1937), pp. xxxii-xxxiii.

CHAPTER FIVE / *Confucianism*

This spontaneous consent from its citizens, this morale without which the community cannot live, arises only when a people sense their leaders to be men of capacity, sincerely devoted to the common good and possessed of the kind of character which compels respect. Real *Te,* therefore, lies in the power of moral example. In the final analysis, goodness becomes embodied in society neither through might nor through law but through the impress of a great personality. Everything depends on the character of the man at the top. If he is crafty or worthless there is no hope for the social order. But if one can get as head of state a true King of Consent, the sanction of whose rule lies in his inherent righteousness, such a man will gather around him a cabinet of "unpurchaseable men." Their complete devotion to the public welfare will quicken in turn the public conscience of leaders in local communities and seep down from there to leaven the lives of the masses. In short, the imitation of the leader provides a new destination for society and a new set of values and purposes which start it moving on a new path. But men of this order are completely beyond personal ambition, which is why as the Confucians say "only those are worthy to govern who would rather be excused."

The following statements epitomize Confucius' idea of *Te:*

He who exercises government by means of his virtue [*te*] may be compared to the north polar star which keeps its place and all the stars turn toward it.

Asked by the Baron of Lu how to rule, Confucius replied: "To govern is to keep straight. If you, Sir, lead the people straight, which of your subjects will venture to fall out of line?"

When on another occasion the same ruler asked him whether the lawless should be executed, Confucius answered: "What need is there of the death penalty in government? If you showed a sincere desire to be good, your people would likewise be good. The virtue of the prince is like unto wind; that of the people like unto grass. For it is the nature of grass to bend when the wind blows upon it."

Justice Holmes used to say that he liked to pay taxes because he felt he was buying civilization. As long as there can be this kind of affirmative attitude toward the state, Confucius would have thought things were all right. But how is this positive attitude to be elicited? Among thinkers of the West, Confucius would have found his spokesman in Plato:

Then tell me, O Critias, how will a man choose the ruler that shall rule over him? Will he not choose a man who has first established order in himself, knowing that any decision that has its spring from anger or pride or vanity can be multiplied a thousand-fold in its effects upon the citizens?

The words of Thomas Jefferson would also have awakened in him a warm response: "The whole art of government consists in the art of being honest."

5. The final concept in the Confucian gestalt is *Wen.* This refers to "the arts

of peace," as contrasted to "the arts of war"; to music, art, poetry, the sum of culture in its esthetic mode.

Confucius valued the arts tremendously. A simple piece of music once cast such a spell over him that for three months he was unable to distinguish the taste of meat. If there is anyone who is totally immune to the power of art, he taught that such a one has no place in human society. Nevertheless Confucius was not on the whole an advocate of "art for art's sake." He cherished it primarily as an instrument for moral education.

By poetry the mind is aroused; from music the finish is received.
The odes stimulate the mind. They induce self-contemplation. They teach the art of sensibility. They help to regulate resentment. They bring home the duty of serving one's father and one's prince.[6]

The intriguing aspect of Confucius' doctrine of *Wen,* however, is neither his esteem for the arts in their own right nor his confidence in their didactic power but his insight into their relevance for international relations. What succeeds in interstate affairs? Here again the Realists answered in terms of physical might, victory goes to the state with the largest army. Confucius on the contrary contended that the ultimate victory goes to the state that develops the highest *Wen,* the most exalted culture—the state that has the finest art, the noblest philosophy, the grandest poetry, and gives evidence of realizing that "it is the moral character of a neighborhood that constitutes its excellence." For in the end it is these things that elicit the spontaneous admiration of men and women everywhere. The Gauls were fierce fighters and so crude of culture that they were considered barbarians; but once they experienced what Roman civilization meant, its superiority was so evident they never, after Caesar's conquest, had any general uprising against Roman rule. Confucius would not have been surprised.

Jen, Chun Tzu, Li, Te, and *Wen*—goodness, the gentleman, propriety, government by virtue, and the arts of peace—such were the values to which Confucius had given his heart. His entire life was lived under their spell. They, then, together were to comprise the content of deliberate tradition. Held before the individual from birth to death, they would furnish that "habitual vision of greatness" which Whitehead has called the essence of all true education—a continuum of public aspiration which alone can tie men together for good and in so doing initiate the individual into the mystery of true community.

[6]*The Analects,* XVII, 9.

FROM THE *Analects*

The *Analects* (*Lun Yü*, meaning "Selected Sayings") is the primary document of Confucianism. In it, however, are not the writings of Confucius himself, but rather his teachings as they were remembered and recorded by his followers. The selections presented here are from Books III through IX, which Waley believes represent the oldest and most authentic stratum. The remaining books of the total of twenty are of more uncertain quality.

Arthur Waley (1889–   ), born in England and educated at Cambridge, is this century's leading interpreter and translator of Chinese and Japanese literature. In his translation of poetry, he is himself a poet and brings to his work on classics such as the *Analects* and *Tao Te Ching* an awesome scholarship. Among his numerous titles are *Monkey, The Nō Plays of Japan, Chinese Poems* (5 vols.), *The Poetry and Career of Li Po, The Travels of an Alchemist,* and *The Tale of Genji*. Portions of his *Three Ways of Thought in Ancient China* appear in Chapter Six of this volume.

The Master said, High office filled by men of narrow views, ritual performed without reverence, the forms of mourning observed without grief—these are things I cannot bear to see! [*Book III, 26*]

The Master said, Without Goodness a man

> Cannot for long endure adversity,
> Cannot for long enjoy prosperity.

The Good Man rests content with Goodness; he that is merely wise pursues Goodness in the belief that it pays to do so.* [*Book IV, 2*]

Of the adage 'Only a Good Man knows how to like people, knows how to dislike them,' the Master said, He whose heart is in the smallest degree set upon Goodness will dislike no one. [*Book IV, 3,4*]

Wealth and rank are what every man desires; but if they can only be retained to the detriment of the Way he professes, he must relinquish them. Poverty and obscurity are what every man detests; but if they can only be avoided to the detriment of the Way he professes, he must accept them. The

*In the Introduction to his edition of the *Analects*, Waley notes that he translated the important term *jen* as "Good" or "Goodness." It is a "rare" and "sublime" moral attribute.—R.E.

gentleman who ever parts company with Goodness does not fulfil that name. Never for a moment does a gentleman quit the way of Goodness. He is never so harried but that he cleaves to this; never so tottering but that he cleaves to this. [*Book IV, 5*]

The Master said, I for my part have never yet seen one who really cared for Goodness, nor one who really abhorred wickedness. One who really cared for Goodness would never let any other consideration come first. One who abhorred wickedness would be so constantly doing Good that wickedness would never have a chance to get at him. Has anyone ever managed to do Good with his whole might even as long as the space of a single day? I think not. Yet I for my part have never seen anyone give up such an attempt because he had not the *strength* to go on. It may well have happened, but I for my part have never seen it. [*Book IV, 6*]

The Master said, A Knight whose heart is set upon the Way, but who is ashamed of wearing shabby clothes and eating coarse food, is not worth calling into counsel. [*Book IV, 9*]

The Master said, Those[1] whose measures are dictated by mere expediency will arouse continual discontent. [*Book IV, 12*]

The Master said, He[2] does not mind not being in office; all he minds about is whether he has qualities that entitle him to office. He does not mind failing to get recognition; he is too busy doing the things that entitle him to recognition. [*Book IV, 14*]

The Master said, Shên! My Way has one (thread) that runs right through it. Master Tsêng said, Yes. When the Master had gone out, the disciples asked, saying What did he mean? Master Tsêng said, Our Master's Way is simply this: Loyalty, consideration.[3] [*Book IV, 15*]

The Master said, A gentleman takes as much trouble to discover what is right as lesser men take to discover what will pay. [*Book IV, 16*]

The Master said, In the presence of a good man, think all the time how you may learn to equal him. In the presence of a bad man, turn your gaze within! [*Book IV, 17*]

[1]The rulers and upper classes in general.
[2]The gentleman. But we might translate 'I do not mind,' etc.
[3]Loyalty to superiors; consideration for the feelings of others, 'not doing to them anything one would not like to have done to oneself' . . . .

The Master said, In serving his father and mother a man may gently remonstrate with them. But if he sees that he has failed to change their opinion, he should resume an attitude of deference and not thwart them; may feel discouraged, but not resentful. [*Book IV, 18*]

The Master said, While father and mother are alive, a good son does not wander far afield; or if he does so, goes only where he has said he was going.[4] [*Book IV, 19*]

The Master said, If for the whole three years of mourning a son manages to carry on the household exactly as in his father's day, then he is a good son indeed. [*Book IV, 20*]

The Master said, In old days a man kept a hold on his words, fearing the disgrace that would ensue should he himself fail to keep pace with them. [*Book IV, 22*]

The Master said, Those who err on the side of strictness are few indeed! [*Book IV, 23*]

The Master said, A gentleman covets the reputation of being slow in word but prompt in deed. [*Book IV, 24*]

The Master said Moral force (*tê*) never dwells in solitude; it will always bring neighbours.[5] [*Book IV, 25*]

The Master gave Ch'i-tiao K'ai leave to take office, but he replied, 'I have not yet sufficiently perfected myself in the virtue of good faith.' The Master was delighted. [*Book V, 5*]

The Master said, The Way makes no progress. I shall get upon a raft and float out to sea.[6] I am sure Yu would come with me. Tzu-lu on hearing of this was in high spirits. The Master said, That is Yu indeed! He sets far too much store by feats of physical daring. It seems as though I should never get hold of the right sort of people. [*Book V, 6*]

The Master said, I have never yet seen a man who was truly steadfast.[7]

[4]Particularly in order that if they die he may be able to come back and perform the rites of mourning.

[5]Whenever one individual or one country substitutes *tê* for physical compulsion; other individuals or other countries inevitably follow suit.

[6]What Confucius proposes is, of course, to go and settle among the barbarians. . . .

[7]Impervious to outside influences, intimidations, etc.

Someone answered saying, 'Ch'êng.' The Master said, Ch'êng! He is at the mercy of his desires. How can *he* be called steadfast? [*Book V,10*]

Tzu-kung said, Our Master's views concerning culture and the outward insignia of goodness, we are permitted to hear; but about Man's nature and the ways of Heaven[8] he will not tell us anything at all. [*Book V, 12*]

Tzu-kung asked saying, Why was K'ung Wên Tzu called Wên ('The Cultured')? The Master said, Because he was diligent and so fond of learning that he was not ashamed to pick up knowledge even from his inferiors. [*Book V, 14*]

Of Tzu-ch'an the Master said that in him were to be found four of the virtues that belong to the Way of the true gentleman. In his private conduct he was courteous, in serving his master he was punctilious, in providing for the needs of the people he gave them even more than their due; in exacting service from the people, he was just. [*Book V, 15*]

Chi Wên Tzu used to think thrice before acting. The Master hearing of it said, Twice is quite enough.[9] [*Book V, 19*]

The Master said, How can we call even Wei-shêng Kao upright? When someone asked him for vinegar he went and begged it from the people next door, and then gave it as though it were his own gift.[10] [*Book V, 23*]

The Master said, Clever talk, a pretentious manner and a reverence that is only of the feet—Tso Ch'iu Ming was incapable of stooping to them, and I too could never stoop to them. Having to conceal one's indignation and keep on friendly terms with the people against whom one feels it—Tso Ch'iu Ming was incapable of stooping to such conduct, and I too am incapable of stooping to such conduct. [*Book V, 24*]

Once when Yen Hui and Tzu-lu were waiting upon him the Master said, Suppose each of you were to tell his wish. Tzu-lu said, I should like to have

[8]T'ien Tao. The Tao taught by Confucius only concerned human behaviour ('the ways of man'); he did not expound a corresponding Heavenly Tao, governing the conduct of unseen powers and divinities.

[9]Ch'êng Hao (A.D. 1032-1085) says that if one thinks more than twice, self-interest begins to come into play.

[10]Wei-shêng Kao (see *Chuang Tzu XXIX*, 1, *Chan Kuo Ts'ê*, Yen stories, Pt. 1, *Huai-nan Tzu* XVII, end) is the legendary paragon of truthfulness. . . . How rare, how almost non-existent a quality uprightness must be, Confucius bitterly says, if even into the legend of the most upright of all men there has crept an instance of falsity!

carriages and horses, clothes and fur rugs, share them with my friends and feel no annoyance if they were returned to me the worse for wear. Yen Hui said, I should like never to boast of my good qualities nor make a fuss about the trouble I take on behalf of others. Tzu-lu said, A thing I should like is to hear the Master's wish. The Master said, In dealing with the aged, to be of comfort to them; in dealing with friends, to be of good faith with them; in dealing with the young, to cherish them. [*Book V, 25*]

The Master said, In vain I have looked for a single man capable of seeing his own faults and bringing the charge home against himself. [*Book V, 26*]

The Master said, In an hamlet of ten houses you may be sure of finding someone quite as loyal and true to his word as I. But I doubt if you, would find anyone with such a love of learning.[11] [*Book V, 27*]

The Master said, Hui is capable of occupying his whole mind for three months on end with no thought but that of Goodness. The others can do so, some for a day, some even for a month; but that is all.[12] [*Book VI, 5*]

When Jan Kêng was ill, the Master went to enquire after him, and grasping his hand through the window said, It is all over with him! Heaven has so ordained it—But that such a man should have such an illness! That such a man should have such an illness![13] [*Book VI, 8*]

The Master said, Incomparable indeed was Hui! A handful of rice to eat, a gourdful of water to drink, living in a mean street—others would have found it unendurably depressing, but to Hui's cheerfulness it made no difference at all. Incomparable indeed was Hui! [*Book VI, 9*]

The Master said, Mêng Chih-fan is no boaster. When his people were routed he was the last to flee; but when they neared the city-gate, he whipped up his horses, saying, It was not courage that kept me behind. My horses were slow. [*Book VI, 13*]

The Master said, Who expects to be able to go out of a house except by the door? How is it then that no one follows this Way of ours?[14] [*Book VI, 15*]

[11]i.e. self-improvement in the most general sense. Not book-learning.

[12]On the strength of sayings such as this, the Taoists claimed Yen Hui as an exponent of *tso-wang* ('sitting with blank mind'), the Chinese equivalent of *yoga*.

[13]Later tradition very naturally explains the passage by saying that Jan Kêng's illness was leprosy. This fits in with the concluding words and also explains why Confucius did not enter the house.

[14]Though it is the obvious and only legitimate way out of all our difficulties.

The Master said, When natural substance prevails over ornamentation,[15] you get the boorishness of the rustic. When ornamentation prevails over natural substance, you get the pedantry of the scribe. Only when ornament and substance are duly blended do you get the true gentleman. [*Book VI, 16*]

The Master said, Man's very life is honesty, in that without it he will be lucky indeed if he escapes with his life. [*Book VI, 17*]

The Master said, To prefer it[16] is better than only to know it. To delight in it is better than merely to prefer it. [*Book VI, 18*]

The Master said, To men who have risen at all above the middling sort, one may talk of things higher yet. But to men who are at all below the middling sort it is useless to talk of things that are above them.[17] [*Book VI, 19*]

The Master said, A gentleman who is widely versed in letters and at the same time knows how to submit his learning to the restraints of ritual is not likely, I think, to go far wrong. [*Book VI, 25*]

The Master said, How transcendent is the moral power of the Middle Use![18] That it is but rarely found among the common people is a fact long admitted. [*Book VI, 27*]

The Master said, I have 'transmitted what was taught to me without making up anything of my own.' I have been faithful to and loved the Ancients. In these respects, I make bold to think, not even our old P'êng[19] can have excelled me. The Master said, I have listened in silence and noted what was said, I have never grown tired of learning nor wearied of teaching others what I have learnt. These at least are merits which I can confidently claim. The Master said, The thought that 'I have left my moral power (*tê*) untended, my learning unperfected, that I have heard of righteous men, but been unable to go to them; have heard of evil men, but been unable to reform them'—it is these thoughts that disquiet me. [*Book VII, 1, 2, 3*]

In his leisure hours the Master's manner was very free-and-easy, and his expression alert and cheerful. [*Book VII, 4*]

The Master said, Set your heart upon the Way, support yourself by its

[15]i.e. when nature prevails over culture.
[16]The Way.
[17]that belong to a higher stage of learning.
[18]Confucius's Way was essentially one of moderation: 'to exceed is as bad as to fall short.' . . .
[19]The Chinese Nestor. It is the special business of old men to transmit traditions.

power, lean upon Goodness, seek distraction in the arts.[20] [*Book VII, 6*]

The Master said, From the very poorest upwards—beginning even with the man who could bring no better present than a bundle of dried flesh—none has ever come to me without receiving instruction. [*Book VII, 7*]

The Master said, Only one who bursts with eagerness do I instruct; only one who bubbles with excitement, do I enlighten. If I hold up one corner and a man cannot come back to me with the other three, I do not continue the lesson. [*Book VII, 8*]

The Master said to Yen Hui, The maxim

> When wanted, then go;
> When set aside; then hide.

is one that you and I could certainly fulfil. Tzu-lu said, Supposing you had command of the Three Hosts,[21] whom would you take to help you? The Master said, The man who was ready to 'beard a tiger or rush a river' without caring whether he lived or died—that sort of man I should not take. I should certainly take someone who approached difficulties with due caution and who preferred to succeed by strategy. [*Book VII, 10*]

The Master said, He who seeks only coarse food to eat, water to drink and bent arm for pillow, will without looking for it find happiness to boot. Any thought of accepting wealth and rank by means that I know to be wrong is as remote from me as the clouds that float above. [*Book VII, 15*]

The 'Duke of Shê' asked Tzu-lu about Master K'ung (Confucius). Tzu-lu did not reply. The Master said, Why did you not say 'This is the character of the man: so intent upon enlightening the eager that he forgets his hunger, and so happy in doing so, that he forgets the bitterness of his lot and does not realize that old age is at hand.[22] That is what he is.' [*Book VII, 18*]

The Master said, I for my part am not one of those who have innate knowledge. I am simply one who loves the past and who is diligent in investigating it. [*Book VII, 19*]

The Master never talked of prodigies, feats of strength, disorders[23] or spirits. [*Book VII, 20*]

[20]Music, archery and the like.

[21]i.e. the whole army.

[22]According to the traditional chronology Confucius was sixty-two at the time when this was said.

[23]Disorders of nature; such as snow in summer, owls hooting by day, or the like.

The Master said, Even when walking in a party of no more than three I can always be certain of learning from those I am with. There will be good qualities that I can select for imitation and bad ones that will teach me what requires correction in myself. [*Book VII, 21*]

The Master said, Heaven begat the power (*tê*) that is in me. What have I to fear from such a one as Huan T'ui? [*Book VII, 22*]

The Master took four subjects for his teaching: culture, conduct of affairs, loyalty to superiors and the keeping of promises. [*Book VII, 24*]

The Master said, A Divine Sage I cannot hope ever to meet; the most I can hope for is to meet a true gentleman. The Master said, A faultless man I cannot hope ever to meet; the most I can hope for is to meet a man of fixed principles. Yet where all around I see Nothing pretending to be Something, Emptiness pretending to be Fullness, Penury pretending to be Affluence, even a man of fixed principles will be none too easy to find. [*Book VII, 25*]

The Master fished with a line but not with a net; when fowling he did not aim at a roosting bird. [*Book VII, 26*]

The Master said, There may well be those who can do without knowledge; but I for my part am certainly not one of them. To hear much, pick out what is good and follow it, to see much and take due note of it, is the lower[24] of the two kinds of knowledge. [*Book VII, 27*]

The Master said, Is Goodness indeed so far away? If we really wanted Goodness, we should find that it was at our very side. [*Book VII, 29*]

The Master said, As to being a Divine Sage or even a Good Man, far be it from me to make any such claim. As for unwearying effort to learn and unflagging patience in teaching others, those are merits that I do not hesitate to claim. Kung-hsi Hua said, The trouble is that we disciples cannot learn! [*Book VII, 33*]

When the Master was very ill, Tzu-lu asked leave to perform the Rite of Expiation. The Master said, Is there such a thing? Tzu-lu answered saying, There is. In one of the Dirges it says, 'We performed rites of expiation for

[24]The higher being innate knowledge, which Confucius disclaims above, VII, 19. He thus (ironically) places himself at two removes from the hypothetical people who can dispense with knowledge, the three stages being, (1) those who do not need knowledge; (2) those who have innate knowledge; (3) those who accumulate it by hard work.

you, calling upon the sky-spirits above and the earth-spirits below.' The Master said, My expiation began long ago![25] [Book VII, 34]

The Master said, Just as lavishness leads easily to presumption, so does frugality to meanness. But meanness is a far less serious fault than presumption. [Book VII, 35]

The Master said, A true gentleman is calm and at ease; the Small Man is fretful and ill at ease. [Book VII, 36]

The Master's manner was affable yet firm, commanding but not harsh, polite but easy. [Book VII, 37]

The Master said, Courtesy not bounded by the prescriptions of ritual becomes tiresome. Caution not bounded by the prescriptions of ritual becomes timidity, daring becomes turbulence, inflexibility becomes harshness.
The Master said, When gentlemen deal generously with their own kin, the common people are incited to Goodness. When old dependents are not discarded, the common people will not be fickle. [Book VIII, 2]

When Master Tsêng was ill, Mêng Ching Tzu came to see him. Master Tsêng spoke to him saying, When a bird is about to die its song touches the heart. When a man is about to die, his words are of note. There are three things that a gentleman, in following the Way, places above all the rest: from every attitude, every gesture that he employs he must remove all trace of violence or arrogance; every look that he composes in his face must betoken good faith; from every word that he utters, from every intonation, he must remove all trace of coarseness or impropriety. As to the ordering of ritual vessels and the like, there are those whose business it is to attend to such matters.   [Book VIII, 4]

Master Tsêng said, Clever, yet not ashamed to consult those less clever than himself; widely gifted, yet not ashamed to consult those with few gifts; having, yet seeming not to have; full, yet seeming empty; offended against, yet never contesting—long ago I had a friend whose ways were such as this. [Book VIII, 5]

Master Tsêng said, The man to whom one could with equal confidence entrust an orphan not yet fully grown or the sovereignty of a whole State,

[25]What justifies me in the eyes of Heaven is the life I have led. There is no need for any rite now. . . .

whom the advent of no emergency however great could upset—would such a one be a true gentleman? He I think would be a true gentleman indeed. [*Book VIII, 6*]

Master Tsêng said, The true Knight of the Way must perforce be both broad-shouldered and stout of heart; his burden is heavy and he has far to go. For Goodness is the burden he has taken upon himself; and must we not grant that it is a heavy one to bear? Only with death does his journey end; then must we not grant that he has far to go? [*Book VIII, 7*]

The Master said, Let a man be first incited by the *Songs,* then given a firm footing by the study of ritual, and finally perfected by music. [*Book VIII, 8*]

The Master said, The common people can be made to follow it;[26] they cannot be made to understand it. [*Book VIII, 9*]

The Master said, One who is by nature daring and is suffering from poverty will not long be law-abiding. Indeed, any men, save those that are truly Good, if their sufferings are very great, will be likely to rebel. [*Book VIII, 10*]

The Master said, If a man has gifts as wonderful as those of the Duke of Chou, yet is arrogant and mean, all the rest is of no account. [*Book VIII, 11*]

The Master said:

> One who will study for three years
> Without thought of reward[27]
> Would be hard indeed to find.

[*Book VIII, 12*]

The Master said, Learn as if you were following someone whom you could not catch up, as though it were someone you were frightened of losing. [*Book VIII, 17*]

The Master said, In Yü I can find no semblance of a flaw. Abstemious in his own food and drink, he displayed the utmost devotion in his offerings to spirits and divinities.[28] Content with the plainest clothes for common wear, he saw to it that his sacrificial apron and ceremonial head-dress were of the utmost magnificence. His place of habitation was of the humblest, and all his

---

[26]i.e. the Way.
[27]i.e. of obtaining a paid appointment.
[28]To ancestors, and spirits of hill, stream, etc.

CHAPTER FIVE / *Confucianism*

energy went into draining and ditching. In him I can find no semblance of a flaw. [*Book VIII, 21*]

There were four things that the Master wholly eschewed: he took nothing for granted, he was never over-positive, never obstinate, never egotistic. [*Book IX, 4*]

The Grand Minister (of Wu?) asked Tzu-kung saying, Is your Master a Divine Sage? If so, how comes it that he has many practical accomplishments?[29] Tzu-kung said, Heaven certainly intended[30] him to become a Sage; it is also true that he has many accomplishments. When the Master heard of it he said, The Grand Minister is quite right about me. When I was young I was in humble circumstances; that is why I have many practical accomplishments in regard to simple, everyday accomplishments? No, he is in no need of them at all.

Lao says that the Master said, It is because I have not been given a chance[31] that I have become so handy.   [*Book IX, 6*]

The Master said, Do I regard myself as a possessor of wisdom? Far from it. But if even a simple peasant comes in all sincerity and asks me a question, I am ready to thrash the matter out, with all its pros and cons, to the very end. [*Book IX, 7*]

Whenever he was visited by anyone dressed in the robes of mourning or wearing ceremonial head-dress, with gown and skirt, or a blind man, even if such a one were younger than himself, the Master on seeing him invariably rose to his feet, and if compelled to walk past him always quickened his step.[32] [*Book IX, 9*]

Yen Hui said with a deep sigh, The more I strain my gaze up towards it, [33] the higher it soars. The deeper I bore down into it, the harder it becomes. I see it in front; but suddenly it is behind. Step by step the Master skilfully lures one on. He has broadened me with culture, restrained me with ritual. Even if I wanted to stop, I could not. Just when I feel that I have exhausted every resource, something seems to rise up, standing out sharp and clear. Yet though I long to pursue it, I can find no way of getting to it at all.   [*Book IX, 10*]

[29]Gentlemen do not stoop to practical accomplishments; much less the Sage.
[30]But the wickedness of the world prevented it.
[31]In public life. . . .
[32]A sign of respect.
[33]Goodness.

The Master wanted to settle among the Nine Wild Tribes of the East. Someone said, I am afraid you would find it hard to put up with their lack of refinement. The Master said, Were a true gentleman to settle among them there would soon be no trouble about lack of refinement. [*Book IX, 13*]

The Master said, I have never yet seen anyone whose desire to build up his moral power was as strong as sexual desire. [*Book IX, 17*]

The Master said, The words of the *Fa Yü* (Model Sayings) cannot fail to stir us; but what matters is that they should change our ways. The words of the Hsüan Chü cannot fail to commend themselves to us; but what matters is that we should carry them out. For those who approve but do not change, I can do nothing at all. [*Book IX, 23*]

The Master said, First and foremost, be faithful to your superiors, keep all promises, refuse the friendship of all who are not like you; and if you have made a mistake, do not be afraid of admitting the fact and amending your ways. [*Book IX, 24*]

The Master said, 'Wearing a shabby hemp-quilted gown, yet capable of standing unabashed with those who wore fox and badger.' That would apply quite well to Yu, would it not?

> Who harmed none, was foe to none,
> Did nothing that was not right.

Afterwards Tzu-lu (Yu) kept on continually chanting those lines to himself. The Master said, Come now, the wisdom contained in them is not worth treasuring to that extent! [*Book IX, 26*]

The Master said, Only when the year grows cold do we see that the pine and cypress are the last to fade. [*Book IX, 27*]

The Master said, he that is really Good can never be unhappy. He that is really wise can never be perplexed. He that is really brave is never afraid.[34] [*Book IX, 28*]

> The flowery branch of the wild cherry
> How swiftly it flies back![35]
> It is not that I do not love you;
> But your house is far away.

[34]Goodness, wisdom and courage are the Three Ways of the true gentleman. Cf. XIV, 30. Confucius always ranks courage below wisdom and wisdom below Goodness. . . .

[35]When one pulls it to pluck the blossom. Cf. *Songs,* 268, I. Image of things that are torn apart after a momentary union. . . .

The Master said, He did not really love her. Had he done so, he would not have worried about the distance.[36] [*Book IX, 30*]

---

[36]Men fail to attain to Goodness because they do not care for it sufficiently, not because Goodness 'is far away.' . . .

w. a. c. h. dobson (translator)

FROM *The Book of Mencius*

Mencius (the Latinized form of Meng Tzu) was the most important of the early followers of Confucius, and he later became known as the "Second Sage" of China. Born in about 390 B.C., Mencius revered Confucius and sought to emulate him. And, indeed, his career paralleled very closely that of Confucius. He, too, was a teacher who tried without success to influence the rulers of his day.

His central idea was that man was by nature good, that those vital virtues of "humanity" (*jen*) and "justice" (*yi*) were *innate* qualities. There was required effort by the individual for the development and expression of his goodness, but it was only when he was coerced by adverse circumstances (the environment) that he acted wrongly.

Mencius taught with eloquence and courage, but his message—particularly his call for a government that exemplified humane principles—was too idealistic for those hardened and pragmatic rulers to whom he had to apply for a position. "[He] remained, as he began, an obscure teacher with a teaching that was out of joint with the times."* He died c. 305 B.C.

The translator, W. A. C. H. Dobson, is Professor of Chinese and Head of the Department of East Asiatic Studies, Massey College, the University of Toronto. He is also the author of *Early Archaic Chinese*.

Mencius was received in audience by King Hui of Liang. The King said, "Aged Sir! You have come, with no thought for so long a journey, to see me. You have, no doubt, some teaching by which I might profit my state?" Mencius replied, "Why must your Majesty use that word 'profit'? There is after all just Humanity and Justice, nothing more. If your Majesty asks 'How can I profit my state?' your nobles will ask 'How can we profit our estates?' and knights and commoners will ask 'How can we profit ourselves?' All ranks in society will be competing for profits. Such would undermine the state. In a 'ten-thousand-chariot state' [a major state] he who slew his prince might gain a 'thousand-chariot estate' [a large estate], and in a 'thousand-chariot state' he who slew his prince might gain a 'hundred-chariot estate.' A thousand in ten thousand, a hundred in a thousand is no small profit. If indeed you put profit first and relegate justice to a minor place, no one will be happy unless they are forever grabbing something. There has never been a Humane man abandoned

*W. A. C. H. Dobson (trans.), *Mencius* (University of Toronto Press, 1963), p. xvii.

CHAPTER FIVE / *Confucianism*

by his kin. There has never been a Just man who turned his back upon his prince. The king should speak of Justice and Humanity; why must he speak about profit?'' (*IA. 1*)

King Hui of Liang said, "No state, at one time, was greater than Tsin, and that, Sir, you know full well. But in my time we have been defeated by Ch'i in the east; my oldest son died in that campaign. We have lost seven hundred miles of territory to Ch'in in the west. Ch'u has humiliated us to the south. I feel the disgrace of this keenly, and hope before I die to expunge this disgrace in one fell swoop. What should I do to bring this about?" Mencius replied, "One could rule as a True King with a kingdom a hundred miles square. If the people saw your policies to be Humane, if you were to lighten the penal code, reduce taxes, encourage intensive ploughing and clearing of waste land, then the able bodied would have leisure to cultivate filial and fraternal duty, loyalty, and trust. On the one hand they could serve the elders of their families, and on the other serve their seniors in the state. They could oppose the stout mail and sharp weapons of Ch'in and Ch'u with sharpened sticks. Those great states deprive their people of labour in the farming seasons so that they can neither sow nor reap in season to feed their families. Parents freeze and starve to death. Brothers, wives, and children are separated. Those princes ensnare their people. If the King were to set out and punish them, who would dare oppose him? For this reason it is said, 'None can oppose the man of Humanity.' Let not your Majesty doubt this." (*IA. 5*)

. . . he who properly might be called a great man is one who dwells in the broad mansion of the world, takes his place in its seat of rectitude, pursues the Great Way of the world, who, gaining his ambition, shares it with the common people, but who, failing to gain his ambition, pursues his principles in solitude. He is one whom riches and honours cannot taint, poverty and lowly station cannot shift, majesty and power cannot bend. Such a one I call a great man." (*3B. 2*)

. . . only men of Humanity ought properly to occupy high position. To lack Humanity and to be highly placed is to spread abroad evil among the populace. When the prince has no principles by which to measure, his subordinates have no standards to maintain. If the Court does not remain true to principles, the workmen will not keep true to standards. If the ruler contravenes Justice, lesser men will contravene the penal code. It will then be a matter of sheer luck that the state survives. Truly it is said, 'It is not the imperfection of defensive walls, or the paucity of arms, that constitutes disaster for the state. It is neither a failure to increase the acreage of arable land, nor an inadequate accumulation of goods and wealth, that constitutes the losses of a state. . . . (*4A. 1*)

Mencius said, "People commonly speak of 'the Empire, the state, and the family.' The Empire lies rooted in the state, the state lies rooted in the family, and the family lies rooted in the individual." (4A. 5)

Mencius said, "The great man seeks no assurance that his words will be believed or that his course of action will get results. He is concerned only that in his words and actions Justice resides." (4B. 11)

The great man is one who never loses his child-like touch. (4B. 12)

Mencius said, "It is by what he guards in his thoughts that the True Gentleman differs from other men. He guards Humanity and propriety in his thoughts. The man of Humanity loves others. The man of propriety respects others. He who loves others is in turn loved by others. He who respects others is in turn respected by others. Suppose someone treats us badly. The True Gentleman will look for the reason within himself, feeling that he must have failed in Humanity or propriety, and will ask himself how such a thing could in fact have happened to him. If after examination he finds that he has acted Humanely and with propriety, and the bad treatment continues, he will look within himself again, feeling that he must have failed to do his best. But if on examination he finds that he has done his best, and the bad treatment continues, he will say, 'This person, after all, is an utter reprobate; I will have done with him. If he behaves like this, how does he differ from an animal? Why should I be put out by an animal?'
"Therefore the True Gentleman spends a lifetime of careful thought, but not a day in worrying. There are things to which he does give careful thought. 'Shun,' he says, 'was a man. I too am a man. But Shun became an examplar to the whole world, an example that has been passed down to us who come after, while I, as it were, am still a mere villager.' This is a matter about which he might take careful thought—taking careful thought only that he might be like Shun. As to those things about which the True Gentleman worries—they do not exist. What is contrary to Humanity he would not be. What is contrary to propriety he would not do. As to 'spending the day worrying,' the True Gentleman simply does not worry." (4B. 28)

Kao Tzu said, "The nature of man is comparable to water trapped in a whirlpool. Open a channel for it on the east side and it will flow away to the east. Open a channel for it on the west side and it will flow away to the west. This is because man's nature is neither inherently good nor bad, just as it is not inherently in the nature of water to flow to the east or to the west."
Mencius replied, "It is assuredly not in the nature of water to flow to the east or to the west, but can one say that it is not in the nature of water to flow upwards or downwards? Man's nature is inherently good, just as it is the

nature of water to flow downwards. As there is no water that flows upwards, so there are no men whose natures inherently are bad. Now you may strike forcefully upon water, and it will splash above your head. With a series of dams, you may force it uphill. But this is surely nothing to do with the nature of water; it happens only after the intrusion of some exterior force. A man can be made to do evil, but this is nothing to do with his nature. It happens only after the intrusion of some exterior force." (6A. 2)

Kung-tu Tzu said, "Kao Tzu says, 'Man's nature is neither good nor bad.' Others say man's nature may tend in either direction. They say in the reigns of the good kings Wen and Wu the people were disposed to do good. In the reigns of the bad kings Yu and Li the people were disposed to do evil. Still others say some men's natures are good while others are bad. These say that, under a good sovereign like Yao, a bad man like Hsiang appeared; and that, to a bad father like Ku-sou, a good son Shun was born; that, with a nephew of a senior branch as evil as Chou on the throne, such good uncles as Ch'i, Lord of Wei, and Prince Pi Kan lived.

"Now, Sir, you say, 'Man's nature is good.' I suppose that these others are wrong?"

Mencius said, "It is of the essence of man's nature that he do good. That is what I mean by good. If a man does what is evil he is guilty of the sin of denying his natural endowment. Every man has a sense of pity, a sense of shame, a sense of respect, a sense of right and wrong. From his sense of pity comes *jen* (Humanity); from his sense of shame comes *yi* (Justice); from his sense of respect, *li* (the observance of rites); from his sense of right and wrong, *chih* (wisdom). *Jen, yi, li,* and *chih* do not soak in from without; we have them within ourselves. It is simply that we are not always consciously thinking about them. So I say, 'Seek them and you have them. Disregard them and you lose them.' Men differ, some by twice, some by five times, and some by an incalculable amount, in their inability to exploit this endowment. The *Book of Songs* says,

> Heaven gave birth to all mankind
> Gave them life and gave them laws.
> In their holding to them
> They lean towards the virtue of excellence.

Confucius said, 'This poet really understood the Way,' Thus, to possess life is to possess laws. These are to be laid hold upon by the people, and thus they will love the virtue of excellence." (6A. 6)

Mencius said, "I am fond of fish, but, too, I am fond of bear's paws. If I cannot have both, then I prefer bear's paws. I care about life, but, too, I care about Justice. If I cannot have both, then I choose Justice. I care about life, but then there are things I care about more than life. For that reason I will not seek life improperly. I do not like death, but there there are things I dislike more than death. For that reason there are some contingencies from which I will not escape.

"If men are taught to desire life above all else, then they will seize it by all means in their power. If they are taught to hate death above all else, then they will avoid all contingencies by which they might meet it. There are times when one might save one's life, but only by means that are wrong. There are times when death can be avoided, but only by means that are improper. Having desires above life itself and having dislikes greater than death itself is a type of mind that all men possess—it is not only confined to the worthy. What distinguishes the worthy is that he ensures that he does not lose it.

"Even though it be a matter of life or death to him, a traveller will refuse a basket of rice or a dish of soup if offered in an insulting manner. But food that has been trampled upon, not even a beggar will think fit to eat. And yet a man will accept emoluments of ten thousand *chung* regardless of the claims of propriety and Justice. And what does he gain by that? Elegant palaces and houses, wives and concubines to wait on him, and the allegiance of the poor among his acquaintance! I was previously speaking of matters affecting life and death, where even there under certain conditions one will not accept relief, but this is a matter of palaces and houses, of wives and concubines, and of time-serving friends. Should we not stop such things? This is what I mean by 'losing the mind with which we originally were endowed.' " (*6A. 10*)

Mencius said, "There are patents of nobility bestowed by Heaven, and those bestowed by man. Such things as Humanity and Justice, loyalty and trustworthiness, and a tireless delight in the good—these are Heaven's patents of nobility. 'Duke,' 'minister,' 'noble'—these are noble ranks bestowed by man. In antiquity, men cultivated Heaven's titles, and the titles of man followed in due course. Today, men cultivate Heaven's titles as a means of gaining man's titles, and, once they obtain them, Heaven's titles are abandoned. This is the height of self-delusion. It ends only in the loss of all title." (*6A. 16*)

. . . Mencius replied, "The Way is like a great road; it is surely not difficult to understand. The sickness of men is that they do not seek it. If you, Sir, return to your home and seek for it, there will be teachers enough." (*6B. 2*)

Mencius said, "If a True Gentleman has not integrity, by what will he be governed?" (*6B. 12*)

It was proposed in the State of Lu to put Yo-cheng Tzu in charge of its government. Mencius said, "When I heard about the proposal, I was so delighted I could not sleep." Kung-sun Ch'ou said, "But is he forceful enough?" Mencius replied, "No." "But is he thoughtful enough?" Mencius replied, "No." "Then is he experienced enough?" Mencius replied, "No." "Then," said Kung-sun Ch'ou, "why were you so delighted that you could not sleep?" Mencius replied, "As a man he inclines towards the good." Kung-sun Ch'ou asked, "But is that enough?" Mencius replied, "In inclining towards the good, he would be adequate to govern the whole world, much less the State of Lu! For if he really inclines towards the good, all within the four seas will report to him, regarding a journey of one thousand miles as a light matter. But if it transpires that he does not incline towards the good, then men will say 'an upstart!' 'He thinks he knows everything.' The sight and sound of an upstart will drive men a thousand miles away. When True Gentlemen stay a thousand miles away, gossip-mongers and toadies gather. Can those who associate with gossip-mongers and toadies help to govern the state?" (6B. 13)

Mencius said, "Most people do things without knowing what they do, and go on doing them without any thought as to what they are doing. They do this all their lives without ever understanding the Way." (7A. 5)

Mencius said to Kou Chien of Sung, "You, Sir, like to travel from court to court. Let me tell you my views on this subject. If in doing so you gain recognition, then be content, but if you fail to gain recognition, then too be content."

Kou Chien said, "How can one always 'be content'?"

Mencius replied, "Honour virtue, delight in Justice; then you may be content. For a knight in financial straits does not lose sight of Justice, and in success he does not depart from the Way. In financial straits without losing sight of Justice—that is his satisfaction. In success and not departing from the Way—thus the people never lose their sense of expectation from him. In antiquity, when a man attained his goal, his beneficence flowed down to the common people; when he failed to attain it, he cultivated his person and so became famous in his generation. So that if you meet with financial straits, ensure that you are good yourself, and if you meet with success ensure that you do good to the whole world." (7A. 9)

Mencius said, "He who, rising at cock-crow, exerts every effort to be good is a disciple of Shun. He who, rising at cock-crow, exerts every effort in the pursuit of gain is a disciple of the brigand Ch'ih. If you wish to know what separates Shun from the brigand Ch'ih, it is no other than this: it is the margin that lies between making profits and being good." (7A. 25)

Prince Tien, son of King Hsüan, asked, "What are the duties of a knight?" Mencius replied, "To exalt his ideals." The Prince said, "What does that mean?" Mencius replied, "It means to exalt Justice and Humanity—nothing more. The murder of a single innocent man is contrary to Humanity. Taking things to which one has no right is contrary to Justice. Where is the knight to be found? Wherever Humanity is present. What road does he travel? The road that leads to Justice. In dwelling in Humanity and in the pursuit of Justice the duties of the great man are fulfilled." (*7A. 33*)

Kung-sun Ch'ou said, "As far as your teaching is concerned, it is lofty and admirable; indeed, it is like an ascent to Heaven—something one cannot quite attain to. Why not make it a little more attainable by daily unremitting effort?"

Mencius replied, "The Master Craftsman does not accommodate the inept workman by tampering with the measuring line. Yi the Archer did not accommodate an inept pupil by changing the target or the rules. The true gentleman leads. He does not turn aside. He leaps forward as it were, placing himself squarely in the centre of the Way. Those who can, follow him." (*7A. 41*)

Humanity (*jen*) is man (*jen*). Put together, the words spell out "the Way." (*7B. 16*)

Huo-sheng Pu-hai asked, "What sort of a man is Yo-cheng Tzu?"

Mencius replies, "He is good and reliable."

Huo-sheng said, "What do you mean 'good' and 'reliable'?"

Mencius replied, "By 'good,' I mean 'that which we properly may wish for'; by 'reliable' I mean 'having it within himself.' When goodness and reliability are fully realized in a man, I call him 'excellent'; when so realized as to dazzle the beholder, I call him 'a great man'; but when realized in such measure as to change the life of the beholder, I call him 'a Sage.' One with the attributes of a Sage, but who is unknowable, I call 'a god.' Yo-cheng Tzu I place among the 'good and reliable' but below the next four ['excellent,' 'great,' 'sage' and 'divine']." (*7B. 25*)

Mencius said, "In the nurturing of the mind, there is no better method than that of cutting down the number of desires. A man who has few desires, though he may have things in his mind which he should not have, will have but few of them. A man who has many desires, though he may have things in his mind which he should have, will have but few of them." (*7B. 35*)

The Great Learning

It was in the twelfth century that the Neo-Confucian scholar Chu Hsi grouped together the *Analects, The Book of Mencius, The Great Learning,* and *The Doctrine of the Mean* to form the *Four Books*, the "sacred" canon of Confucianism. Since that time the role of *The Great Learning* in the life of China has been enormous: until the present century, it was this essay with which all Chinese school children began their studies.*

The Great Learning is a concise, reasoned summary of Confucian ethical and political ideals. Its theme is that the health and well-being of individuals, the family, and the state are inextricably related. There is, in fact, no distinction to be made between ethics and politics: both private conduct and the affairs of empire are similarly moral issues, and these are to be resolved by the proper "cultivation" of the young.

Appearing throughout *The Great Learning* are editorial comments by Chu Hsi. He explains in one of his notes that he thought the first portion of the book was in the words of Confucius, as recorded by his disciple Tsang, and that the following chapters of commentary were by Tsang, as recorded by his disciples. It is now considered very unlikely that Confucius and Tsang were the sources of the book. *The Great Learning* was originally a chapter of the *Li Chi* (*The Book of Rites*) and possibly dates from the third century B.C.; the author is not known.

The translator is James Legge, whose work on the entire body of Confucian literature has long been the standard.

My master, the philospher Ch'ing, says;—"The Great Learning is a book left by Confucius, and forms the gate by which first learners enter into virtue. That we can now perceive the order in which the ancients pursued their learning, is solely owing to the preservation of this work, the Analects and Mencius coming after it. Learners must commence their course with this, and then it may be hoped they will be kept from error."

THE TEXT OF CONFUCIUS

1. What the Great Learning teaches, is—to illustrate illustrious virtue; to renovate the people; and to rest in the highest excellence.

2. The point where to rest being known, the object of pursuit is then determined; and, that being determined, a calm unperturbedness may be attained. To that calmness there will succeed a tranquil repose. In that repose there may be careful deliberation, and that deliberation will be followed by the attainment *of the desired end.*

*Lin Yutang, *The Wisdom of Confucius* (New York: Random House, 1938), p. 135.

James Legge (trans.), "The Great Learning." From James Legge (trans.), *The Chinese Classics* (New York: John B. Alden, Publisher, 1885).

3. Things have their root and their completion. Affairs have their end and their beginning. To know what is first and what is last will lead near to what is taught *in the Great Learning.*

4. The ancients who wished to illustrate illustrious virtue throughout the empire, first ordered well their own States. Wishing to order well their States, they first regulated their families. Wishing to regulate their families, they first cultivated their persons. Wishing to cultivate their persons, they first rectified their hearts. Wishing to rectify their hearts, they first sought to be sincere in their thoughts. Wishing to be sincere in their thoughts, they first extended to the utmost their knowledge. Such extension of knowledge lay in the investigation of things.

5. Things being investigated, knowledge became complete. Their knowledge being complete, their thoughts were sincere. Their thoughts being sincere, their hearts were then rectified. Their hearts being rectified, their persons were cultivated. Their persons being cultivated, their families were regulated. Their families being regulated, their States were rightly governed. Their States being rightly governed, the whole empire was made tranquil and happy.

6. From the emperor down to the mass of the people, all must consider the cultivation of the person the root of *every thing besides.*

7. It cannot be, when the root is neglected, that what should spring from it will be well ordered. It never has been the case that what was of great importance has been slightly cared for, and, at the same time, that what was of slight importance has been greatly cared for.

The preceding chapter of classical text is in the words of Confucius, handed down by the philosopher Tsang. The ten chapters of explanation which follow contain the views of Tsang, and were recorded by his disciples. In the old copies of the work, there appeared considerable confusion in these, from the disarrangement of the tablets. But now, availing myself of the decisions of the philosopher Ch'ing, and having examined anew the classical text, I have arranged it in order, as follows:—

COMMENTARY OF THE PHILOSOPHER TSANG

Chapter I

1. In the Announcement to K'ang it is said, "He was able to make his virtue illustrious."

2. In the T'ae Kea, it is said, "He contemplated and studied the illustrious decrees of heaven."

3. In the Canon of the emperor Yaou, it is said, "He was able to make illustrious his lofty virtue."

4. These *passages* all *show how those sovereigns* made themselves illustrious.

The above first chapter of commentary explains the illustration of illustrious virtue.

II

1. On the bathing-tub of T'ang, the following words were engraved:—"If you can one day renovate yourself, do so from day to day. Yea, let there be daily renovation."

2. In the Announcement to K'ang, it is said, "To stir up the new people."

3. In the Book of Poetry, it is said, "Although Chow was an ancient state, the ordinance which lighted on it was new."

4. Therefore, the superior man in every thing uses his utmost endeavours.

The above second chapter of commentary explains the renovating of the people.

III

1. In the Book of Poetry, it is said, "The imperial domain of a thousand le is where the people rest."

2. In the Book of Poetry, it is said, "The twittering yellow bird rests on a corner of the mound." The Master said, "When it rests, it knows where to rest. Is it possible that a man should not be equal to this bird?"

3. In the Book of Poetry, it is said, "Profound was King Wan. With how bright and unceasing a feeling of reverence did he regard his resting places!" As a sovereign, he rested in benevolence. As a minister, he rested in reverence. As a son, he rested in filial piety. As a father, he rested in kindness. In communication with his subjects, he rested in good faith.

4. In the Book of Poetry, it is said, "Look at that winding course of the K'e with the green bamboos so luxuriant! Here is our elegant and accomplished prince! As we cut and then file; as we chisel and then grind: *so has he cultivated himself.* How grave is he and dignified! How majestic and distinguished! Our elegant and accomplished prince never can be forgotten." *That expression*—"as we cut and then file," indicates the work of learning. "As we chisel, and then grind," indicates that of self culture. "How grave is he and dignified!" indicates the feeling of cautious reverence. "How commanding and distinguished," indicates an awe-inspiring deportment. "Our elegant and accomplished prince never can be forgotten," indicates how, when virtue is complete and excellence extreme, the people cannot forget them.

5. In the Book of Poetry, it is said, "Ah! the former kings are not forgotten." *Future* princes deem worthy what they deemed worthy, and love what they loved. The common people delight in what they delighted, and are benefited by their beneficial arrangements. It is on this account that the former kings, after they have quitted the world, are not forgotten.

The above third chapter of commentary explains resting in the highest excellence.

IV

The Master said, "In hearing litigations, I am like any other body. What is necessary is to cause the people to have no litigations?" *So,* those who are devoid of principle find it impossible to carry out their speeches, and a great awe would be struck into men's minds;—this is called knowing the root.

The above fourth chapter of commentary explains the root and the issue.

V

1. This is called knowing the root.
2. This is called the perfecting of knowledge.

The above fifth chapter of the commentary explained the meaning of "investigating things and carrying knowledge to the utmost extent," but it is now lost. I have ventured to take the views of the scholar Ch'ing to supply it, as follows:—The meaning of the expression,"The perfecting of knowledge depends on the investigation of things, is this:—If we wish to carry our knowledge to the utmost, we must investigate the principles of all things we come into contact with, for the intelligent mind of man is certainly formed to know, and there is not a single thing in which its principles do not inhere. But so long as all principles are not investigated, man's knowledge is incomplete. On this account, the Learning for Adults, at the outset of its lessons, instructs the learner, in regard to all things in the world, to proceed from what knowledge he has of their principles, and pursue his investigation of them, till he reaches the extreme point. After exerting himself in this way for a long time, he will suddenly find himself possessed of a wide and far-reaching penetration. Then, the qualities of all things, whether external or internal, the subtle or the coarse, will all be apprehended, and the mind, in its entire substance and its relations to things, will be perfectly intelligent. This is called the investigation of things. This is called the perfection of knowledge.

VI

1. What is meant by "making the thoughts sincere," is the allowing no self-deception, as *when* we hate a bad smell, and as when we love what is beautiful. This is called self-enjoyment. Therefore, the superior man must be watchful over himself when he is alone.

2. There is no evil to which the mean man, dwelling retired, will not proceed, but when he sees a superior man, he instantly tries to disguise himself, concealing his evil, and displaying what is good. The other beholds him, as if he saw his heart and reins:—of what use *is his disguise?* This is an instance of the saying—"What truly is within will be manifested without." Therefore, the superior man must be watchful over himself when he is alone.

3. The disciple Tsang said, "What ten eyes behold, what ten hands point to, is to be regarded with reverence!"

4. Riches adorn a house, and virtue adorns the person. The mind is expanded, and the body is at ease. Therefore, the superior man must make his thoughts sincere.

The above sixth chapter of commentary explains making the thoughts sincere.

VII

1. What is meant by, "The cultivation of the person depends on rectifying the mind," *may be thus illustrated:*—If a man be under the influence of passion, he will be incorrect in his conduct. He will be the same, if he is under the influence of terror, or under the influence of fond regard, or under that of sorrow and distress.

2. When the mind is not present, we look and do not see; we hear and do not understand; we eat and do not know the taste of what we eat.

3. This is what is meant by saying that the cultivation of the person depends on the rectifying of the mind.

The above seventh chapter of commentary explains rectifying the mind and cultivating the person.

VIII

1. What is meant by "The regulation of one's family depends on the cultivation of his person," is this:—Men are partial where they feel affection and love; partial where they despise and dislike; partial where they stand in awe and reverence; partial where they feel sorrow and compassion; partial where they are arrogant and rude. Thus it is that there are few men in the world, who love, and at the same time know the bad qualities of *the object of their love,* or who hate, and yet know the excellences of *the object of their hatred.*

2. Hence it is said, in the common adage, "A man does not know the wickedness of his son; he does not know the richness of his growing corn."

3. This is what is meant by saying that if the person be not cultivated, a man cannot regulate his family.

The above eighth chapter of commentary explains the cultivating the person and regulating the family.

IX

1. What is meant by "In order rightly to govern his State, it is necessary first to regulate his family," is this:—It is not possible for one to teach others, while he cannot teach his own family. Therefore, the ruler, without going beyond his family, completes the lessons for the State. There is filial piety:—therewith the sovereign should be served. There is fraternal submission:—therewith elders and superiors should be served. There is kindness:—therewith the multitude should be treated.

2. In the Announcement to K'ang, it is said, "*Act* as if you were watching over an infant." If a mother is really anxious about it, though she may not hit *exactly the wants of her infant,* she will not be far from doing so. There never has been *a girl* who learned to bring up a child, that she might afterwards marry.

3. From the loving *example* of one family, a whole State becomes loving, and from its courtesies, the whole State becomes courteous, while, from the ambition and perverseness of the one man, the whole State may be led to rebellious disorder;—such is the nature of the influence. This verifies the saying, "Affairs may be ruined by a single sentence; a kingdom may be settled by its one man."

4. Yaou and Shun led on the empire with benevolence, and the people followed them. Kee and Chow led on the empire with violence, and the people followed them. The orders which these issued were contrary to the practices which they loved, and so the people did not follow them. On this account, the ruler must himself be possessed of the *good* qualities, and then he may require them in the people. He must not have *the bad qualities* in himself, and then he may require that they shall not be in the people. Never has there been a man, who, not having reference to his own character and wishes in dealing with others, was able effectually to instruct them.

5. Thus we see how the government of the State depends on the regulation of the family.

6. In the Book of Poetry, it is said, "That peach tree, so delicate and elegant! How luxuriant is its foliage! This girl is going to her husband's house. She will rightly order her household." Let the household be rightly ordered, and then the people of the State may be taught.

7. In the Book of Poetry, it is said, "They can discharge their duties to their elder brothers. They can discharge their duties to their younger brothers." Let the ruler discharge his duties to his elder and younger brothers, and then he may teach the people of the State.

8. In the Book of Poetry, it is said, "In his deportment there is nothing wrong; he rectifies all the people of the State." *Yes;* when the ruler, as a father, a son, and a brother, is a model, then the people imitate him.

9. This is what is meant by saying, "The government of his kingdom depends on his regulation of the family."

The above ninth chapter of commentary explains regulating the family and governing the kingdom.

X

1. What is meant by "The making the whole empire peaceful and happy depends on the government of his State," is this:—When the sovereign behaves to his aged, as the aged should be behaved to, the people become filial; when the sovereign behaves to his elders, as elders should be behaved to, the people learn brotherly submission; when the sovereign treats compassionately the young and helpless, the people do the same. Thus the ruler has a principle with which, as with a measuring square, he may regulate his conduct.

2. What a man dislikes in his superiors, let him not display in the treatment of his inferiors; what he dislikes in inferiors, let him not display in the service of his superiors; what he hates in those who are before him, let him not therewith precede those who are behind him; what he hates in those who are behind him, let him not therewith follow those who are before him; what he hates to receive on the right, let him not bestow on the left; what he hates to receive on the left, let him not bestow on the right:—this is what is called "The principle, with which, as with a measuring square, to regulate one's conduct."

3. In the Book of Poetry, it is said, "How much to be rejoiced in are these princes, the parents of the people! When *a prince* loves what the people love, and hates what the people hate, then is he what is called the parent of the people.

4. In the Book of Poetry, it is said, "Lofty is that southern hill, with its rugged masses of rocks! Greatly distinguished are you, O *grand*-teacher Yin, the people all look up to you." Rulers of kingdoms may not neglect to be careful. If they deviate *to a mean selfishness,* they will be a disgrace in the empire.

5. In the Book of Poetry, it is said, "Before the sovereigns of the Yin *dynasty* had lost the *hearts of the* people, they could appear before God. Take warning from *the house of* Yin. The great decree is not easily *preserved.*" This shows that, by gaining the people, the kingdom is gained, and, by losing the people, the kingdom is lost.

6. On this account, the ruler will first take pains about *his own* virtue. Possessing virtue will give him the people. Possessing the people will give him the territory. Possessing the territory will give him its wealth. Possessing the wealth, he will have resources for expenditure.

7. Virtue is the root; wealth is the result.

8. If he make the root his secondary object, and the result his primary, he will *only* wrangle with his people, and teach them rapine.

9. Hence, the accumulation of wealth is the way to scatter the people; and the letting it be scattered among them is the way to collect the people.

10. And hence, the ruler's words going forth contrary to right, will come back to him in the same way, and wealth, gotten by improper ways, will take its departure by the same.

11. In the Announcement to K'ang, it is said, "The decree indeed may not always rest on *us;*" that is, goodness obtains the decree, and the want of goodness loses it.

12. In the Book of Ts'oo, it is said, "The kingdom of Ts'oo does not consider that to be valuable. It values, *instead,* its good men."

13. *Duke Wan's* uncle, Fan, said, "Our fugitive does not account that to be precious. What he considers precious, is the affection due to his parent."

14. In the Declaration *of the duke of* Ts'in, it is said, "Let me have but one

minister, plain and sincere, not *pretending to* other abilities, but with a simple, upright, mind; and possessed of generosity, *regarding* the talents of others as though he himself possessed them and, where he finds accomplished and perspicacious men, loving them in his heart more than his mouth expresses, and really showing himself able to bear them *and employ them:*–such a minister will be able to preserve my sons and grandsons, and black-haired people, and benefits likewise to the kingdom may well be looked for from him. But if *it be his character,* when he finds men of ability, to be jealous and hate them; and when he finds the accomplished and perspicacious men, to oppose them and not allow their advancement, showing himself really not able to bear them:—such a minister will not be able to protect my sons and grandsons and black-haired people; and may he not also be pronounced dangerous *to the State?*''

15. It is only the truly virtuous man, who can send away such a man and banish him, driving him out among the barbarous tribes around, determined not to dwell along with him in the Middle kingdom. This is in accordance with the saying, ''It is only the truly virtuous man who can love or who can hate others.''

16. To see men of worth and not be able to raise them to office; to raise them to office, but not to do so quickly:—this is disrespectful. To see bad men, and not be able to remove them; to remove them, but not to do so to a distance:—this is weakness.

17. To love those whom men hate, and to hate those whom men love;—this is to outrage the natural feeling of men. Calamities cannot fail to come down on him who does so.

18. Thus *we see that* the sovereign has a great course *to pursue.* He must show entire self-devotion and sincerity to attain it, and by pride and extravagance he will fail of it.

19. There is a great course *also* for the production of wealth. Let the producers be many and the consumers few. Let there be activity in the production, and economy in the expenditure. Then the wealth will always be sufficient.

20. The virtuous *ruler,* by means of his wealth, makes himself more distinguished. The vicious ruler accumulates wealth, at the expense of his life.

21. Never has there been a case of the sovereign loving benevolence, and the people not loving righteousness. Never has there been a case where the people have loved righteousness, and the affairs of the sovereign have not been carried to completion. And never has there been a case where the wealth in such a State, collected in the treasuries and arsenals, did not continue in the sovereign's possession.

22. The officer Mang Heen said, ''He who keeps horses and a carriage does not look after fowls and pigs. The family which keeps its stores of ice does not rear cattle or sheep. *So,* the house which possesses a hundred

chariots should not keep a minister to look out for imposts that he may lay them on the people. Than to have such a minister, it were better for that house to have one who should rob it *of its revenues.*" This is in accordance with the saying:—"In a State, *pecuniary* gain is not to be considered to be prosperity, but its prosperity *will* be found in righteousness."

23. When he who presides over a State or a family makes his revenues his chief business, he must be under the influence of some small, mean man. He may consider this man to be good; but when such a person is employed in the administration of a State of family, calamities *from Heaven,* and injuries *from men,* will befall it together, and, though a good man may take his place, he will not be able to remedy the evil. This illustrates *again* the saying, "In a State, gain is not to be considered prosperity, but its prosperity will be found in righteousness."

The above tenth chapter of commentary explains the government of the State, and the making the empire peaceful and happy.

There are thus, in all, ten chapters of commentary, the first four of which discuss, in a general manner, the scope of the principal topic of the Work; while the other six go particularly into an exhibition of the work required in its subordinate branches. The fifth chapter contains the important subject of comprehending true excellence, and the sixth, what is the foundation of the attainment of true sincerity. Those two chapters demand the especial attention of the learner. Let not the reader despise them because of their simplicity.

herbert fingarette _____

A Confucian Metaphor — the Holy Vessel

In a preface to the brief book from which the following selection is taken, Herbert Fingarette explains that he initially found Confucius "a prosaic and parochial moralizer." But continued study resulted in his coming to believe that Confucius was an original and provocative genius who, properly understood, still has much to teach in the twentieth century.

It is Fingarette's contention that Confucius was perhaps not as earthbound as he has been considered to be. The main thesis of Fingarette's book is that Confucius' great insight was into the "holiness in human existence" and that "the truly, distinctively human powers have, characteristically, a magical quality." Confucius found the means to capture and reveal this dimension of humanity in his doctrine of *li* ("holy rite," "sacred ceremony," in its earliest meaning).

Much of this theme is summarized and illustrated in "A Confucian Metaphor—the Holy Vessel," the final chapter of *Confucius—the Secular as Sacred.*

What is it that distinguishes man from the beasts and the inanimate? In what do man's peculiar dignity and power reside? Confucius offers an amazingly apt and generative image: Rite *(li).* But Rite and Ceremony would seem, off hand, to deemphasize the individual, whereas the tendency in much modern criticism is to stress the "discovery of the individual"[1] by Confucius. It is true that Hughes, who uses this particular phrase, adds a qualifying clause "man's ability to look at himself in relation to his fellows and in that light to integrate himself."

Wing-tsit Chan summarizes in a similar formula "the entire Confucian philosophy: . . . the realization of the self and the creation of a social order."[2] Although Hughes and Chan bring out the two poles "individual"—"society," Liu Wu-chi emphasizes even more the "individual" pole: "No matter from which angle we view it, the individual man is, after all, the hub of the universe. . . . Master K'ung discovered by a happy stroke of genius the ethical individual. . . . Individual man was now exalted

---

[1]E. R. Hughes (ed.), *The Individual in East and West* (London: Oxford University Press, 1937), p. 94.

[2]Wing-tsit Chan, "The Story of Chinese Philosophy," *Philosophy—East and West,* ed., C. A. Moore (Princeton: Princeton University Press, 1944), p. 27.

CHAPTER FIVE / *Confucianism*

to his new position as a social entity. . . . Thus for the first time in the history of man, the dignity of the individual was asserted. . . . The flowering of the individual is to be one's ultimate aim."[3] Creel, although he too elaborates on the social orientation of Confucius, nevertheless emphasizes in various contexts the "primacy and worth of the individual" in Confucius's thought.[4] And Lin Yutang, while stressing the social, says. " . . the kingdom of God is truly within man himself."[5]

In short, in these passages from a representative sample of modern writers we see a broadly recurring pattern of interpretation. In citing such brief phrases, one wrenches the remarks from contexts in which there is essential qualification and amplification. My aim in quoting, however, is not to provide a rounded report of the commentaries, but rather to note that when a brief and summary formula is finally required, the formula often tends to be formulated in terms of "society" and the "individual," with relative emphasis on the "individual" as primary. Self-realization, self-integrity, "self-flowering," the "ultimate worth of the individual"—these are supposed to reflect the characteristic discovery of Confucius. It is the thesis of the present remarks that we would do better to think of Confucius as concerned with the nature of "humanity" rather than with the polar terms "individual" and "society." The formulation in terms of individual and society reflects Western preoccupations and categories—and perhaps Taoist, Buddhist and neo-Confucian concerns.

Rather than arguing this point in the abstract, we cannot do better than to learn from Confucius himself, and more particularly from reflection on one of the illuminating images he presents to us.

Tzu-Kung asked: "What would you say about me as a person?"
The Master said: "You are a utensil."
"What sort of utensil?"
"A sacrificial vase of jade." (5:3)

[3]Liu Wu-chi, *Confucius, His Life and Times* (New York: Philosophical Library, 1955), pp. 155-56.

[4]H. G. Creel, *Confucius and the Chinese Way* (New York: Harper & Row, Torchbook No. 63, 1960), pp. 136, 138. My own interpretation follows Creel (and in some ways Kaizuka) [S. Kaizuka, *Confucius,* translated by G. Bournes (London: George Allen & Unwin, Ltd., 1956)] more than most in the way they stress the inseparability of man from society and the role of *li*. Without wishing to minimize this similarity or to enter into detailed comparative commentary, I might simply say that I have attempted to draw the philosophical and psychological implications of this view more stringently and more fully. I think that doing this puts Confucius's position in a new light. For one thing it helps to bring out the close logical connection between this view of man and the magical-reverential dimension of Confucius's thought—a dimension that I believe is seriously understated by Creel and "rationalized" (in spite of his evident *feeling* for it). See also: H.G. Creel, *Chinese Thought from Confucius to Mao Tse-Tung* (New York: New American Library, 1960), pp. 33-34.

[5]Lin Yutang, *The Wisdom of Confucius* (New York: Random House, Modern Library, 1938), p. 17.

This passage is usually read in the light of another passage in the *Analects* (2:II): "A noble man is not a utensil."

The general opinion among commentators, in the light of 2:II, seems to have been that Confucius is first putting Tzu-Kung in his place, and then, in his next response, softening the blow. These interpreters (whom I believe to be mistaken) might be supposed to read the cryptic passage along the lines of the following paraphrase.

"Master," we may suppose Tzu-Kung to be saying, "tell me where I stand with regard to the ideal." The Master replies, "You are still only a utensil, useful only for specific purposes. You are not the morally self-realized man, the man with broad (moral) capacities who is capable of governing or using the special (technical) capacities of others." Tzu-Kung, his eagerness and optimism shaken, does not give up. "But, Master, how do you mean that? Don't you have some qualifying or softening word with which you can give me more hope?" And the Master replies, in a paternalistic, encouraging tone: "Tzu-Kung, don't feel too bad about it. Even if you are still a man to be used and not yet one who is perfected and capable of using others, at least you are a very fine utensil of your kind. Indeed you are among the most handsome and valuable."

In my own opinion, as I have indicated, a reading along such lines is quite wrong. The only element of it that is acceptable is that Confucius does initially intend to dash cold water on Tzu-Kung's too-ready optimism. Confucius wants to bring him up short, to shake him, disturb him, puzzle him; Tzu-Kung must be made to feel the necessity to *think* his way through to a new insight. Confucius puts his answer in a manner best calculated to accomplish this end with a man of Tzu-Kung's character. It seems that this disciple was the most facilely successful and worldly of Confucius's disciples. With his learning and his worldly success, he might well feel pride in his personal achievement, might well be surprised and shaken at Confucius's initial response. For Tzu-Kung is well aware of the metaphor of the utensil and of the saying that a noble man is *not* a utensil. Confucius's initial response, like others he makes, is the first element, then, in a pedagogically effective paradox.[6]

However, the second statement by Confucius—"You are a sacrificial vessel of jade"—is not a mere sentimental softening of the blow. It both completes and resolves the paradox. It contains in a highly condensed image the central teaching which Confucius wishes to get across to the glib and self-satisfied Tzu-Kung. What is this central teaching?

Consider the sacrificial vessel: in the original text Confucius merely names

[6] For examples of Confucius's readiness to let an ironic comment stand without softening if irony is his intent and for his use of challenging, puzzling or paradoxical statements, see, for example, 3:8; 5:3; 6:1; 6:10; 6:22; 6:23; 7:10; 7:29; 10:26; 11:17; 11:21.

CHAPTER FIVE / *Confucianism*

a certain type of jade sacrificial vessel used for holding grain in connection with ceremonies for a bounteous harvest. Such a vessel is holy, sacred. Its outer appearance—the bronze, the carving, the jade—is elegant. Its content, the rich grain, expresses abundance.

Yet the vessel's sacredness does not reside in the preciousness of its bronze, in the beauty of its ornamentation, in the rarity of its jade or in the edibility of the grain. Whence does its sacredness come? It is sacred not because it is useful or handsome but because it is a constitutive element in the ceremony. It is sacred by virtue of its participation in rite, in holy ceremony. In isolation from its role in the ceremony, the vessel is merely an expensive pot filled with grain.

It is therefore a paradox as utensil, for unlike utensils in general, this has no (utilitarian) use external to ceremony itself but only a ritual function. (Indeed some ceremonial pots had holes in them in order to emphasize their ritual rather than utilitarian value.)

By analogy, Confucius may be taken to imply that the individual human being, too, has ultimate dignity, sacred dignity by virtue of his role in rite, in ceremony, in *li*. We must recall that Confucius expanded the sense of the word *li*, originally referring to religious ceremonial, in such a way as to envision society itself on the model of *li*. If the teaching about *li* is thus generalized, it is reasonable to follow through and generalize the analogy between Tzu-Kung and the ceremonial vessel. We will then see how this image deepens our understanding of Confucius's teaching about man and human relations.

Social etiquette in general, the father-son relation, the brother-brother relation, the prince-subject relation, the friend-friend relation and the husband-wife relation—persons and their relationships are to be seen as ultimately sanctified by virtue of their place in *li*. Society, at least insofar as regulated by human convention and moral obligations, becomes in the Confucian vision one great ceremonial performance, a ceremony with all the holy beauty of an elaborate religious ritual carried out with that combination of solemnity and lightness of heart that graces the inspired ritual performance. It is not individual existence *per se,* nor is it the existence of a group *per se* that is the condition sufficient to create and sustain the ultimate dignity of man. It is the ceremonial aspect of life that bestows sacredness upon persons, acts, and objects which have a role in the performance of ceremony.

Confucius does not see the individual as an ultimate atom nor society on the analogy of animal or mechanism, nor does he see society as a proving ground for immortal souls or a contractual or utilitarian arrangement designed to maximize individual pleasure. He does not talk in the *Analects* of society and the individual. He talks of what it is to be man, and he sees that man is a special being with a unique dignity and power deriving from and embedded in *li*.

Is it enough merely to be born, to eat, breathe, drink, excrete, enjoy sensual gratification and avoid physical pain and discomfort? Animals do this. To become civilized is to establish relationships that are not merely physical, biological or instinctive; it is to establish *human* relationships, relationships of an essentially symbolic kind, defined by tradition and convention and rooted in respect and obligation.

"Merely to feed one's parents well" . . . "even dogs and horses are fed." (2:7) To be devoted to one's parents is far more than to keep the parents alive physically. To serve and eat in the proper way, with the proper respect and appreciation, in the proper setting—this is to transform the act of mere nourishment into the human ceremony of dining. To obey the whip is to be not much more than a domestic animal; but to be loyal and faithful to those who rightly govern, to serve them and thus to serve *in* the human community, to do this out of one's own heart and nature—this is to be a true citizen of one's community.

Man's dignity, as does the dignity of things, lies in the ceremony rather than in individual biological existence, and this is evident in the fact that we understand a man who sacrifices his biological existence, his "life" in the biological but not the spiritual sense, if the "rite" demands it. Confucius makes the point succinctly when he responds to his disciple's concern over killing a sheep as an element in a sacrificial rite: "You love the sheep, but I love the ceremony," says Confucius. (3:17)

"Virtue does not exist in isolation; there must be neighbors," says Confucius. (4:25) Man is transformed by participation with others in ceremony which is communal. Until he is so transformed he is not truly man but only potentially so—the new-born infant, the wolf-boy of the forests or the "barbarian." Ceremony is justified when we see how it transforms the barbarian into what we know as man at his best. And, from the opposite direction, man at his best is justified when we see that his best is a life of holy ceremony rather than of appetite and mere animal existence. Whichever standpoint we take, we get a perspective on man and society which illuminates and deepens our vision of man's distinctive nature and dignity. When we see man as participant in communal rite rather than as individualistic ego, he takes on to our eyes a new and holy beauty just as does the sacrificial vessel.

Thus, in the *Analects,* man as individual is not sacred. However, he is not therefore to be thought of as a mere utensil to serve "society." For society is no more an independent entity than is ceremony independent of the participants, the holy vessels, the altar, the incantations. Society is men treating each other as men *(jen),* or to be more specific, according to the obligations and privileges of *li,* out of the love *(ai)* and loyalty *(chung)* and respect *(shu)* called for by their human relationships to each other. The shapes of human relationships are not imposed on man, not physically inevitable, not an instinct or reflex. They are rites learned and voluntarily participated in. The rite is self-justifying. The beings, the gestures, the words are not subordinate to rite, nor is rite subordinate to them. To "be self-disciplined and ever turning to *li*" (12:1) is to be no longer at the mercy of animal needs and demoralizing passion, it is to achieve that freedom in which the human spirit flowers; it is not, as Waley's translation may lead one to think, a matter of "submission" but of the triumph of the human spirit.

Confucius's theme, then, is not the "discovery of the individual" or of his ultimate importance. The *mere* individual is a bauble, malleable and breakable, a utensil transformed into the resplendent and holy as it serves in the ceremony of life. But then this does not deny *ultimate* dignity to men and to each man; he is not a meaningless ant serving the greater whole. His participation in divinity is as real and clearly visible as is that of the sacrificial vessel, for it *is* holy. And unlike the way he appears in the Christian view, man is not holy by virtue of his absolute possession, within himself and independently of other men, of a "piece" of the divine, the immortal soul. Nor is the "flowering" of the individual the central theme; instead it is the flowering of humanity in the ceremonial acts of men.

Although the individual must cultivate himself, just as the temple vessel must be carved and chiseled and polished, this self-cultivation is no more *central* to man's dignity, in Confucius's views, than the preparation of the vessel is central. Preparation and training are essential, but it is the ceremony that is central, and *all* the elements and relationships and actions in it are sacred though each has its special characteristics.

Nor should we suppose that Nature is cast out unless shaped into artifact for ritual use. The raiment of holiness is cast upon Nature as well as man, upon the river and the air as well as upon youth and song, when these are seen through the image of a ceremonial Rain Dance. (11:25)

The noble man is the man who most perfectly having given up self, ego, obstinacy and personal pride (9:4) follows not profit but the Way. Such a man has come to fruition as a person; he is the consummate Man. He is a Holy Vessel.

further reading

"At the age of 40 Lin Yutang was already an ancient Chinese sage," wrote Joseph Wood Krutch, and Lin's books reflect that estimation of him. His *My Country and My People* (1935; rev. ed., 1939) is an especially enjoyable portrait of China. He also edited and translated *The Wisdom of Confucius* (1938) and *The Wisdom of China and India* (1942).

Edward Herbert, *A Confucian Notebook* (1950). A very brief book which presents an "impression" of Confucianism by focusing on certain aspects of it.

Arthur Waley weaves together his own narrative and extracts from the Taoist Chuang Tzu, Mencius, and a "realist" philosopher, Han Fei Tzu, in his *Three Ways of Thought in Ancient China* (1939), which is recommended without the slightest reservation.

In his *Socrates, Buddha, Confucius, Jesus* (1957), Karl Jaspers writes of Confucius: "He had no fundamental religious experience, no revelation; he achieved no inner rebirth, he was not a mystic. . . . He was guided by the idea of an encompassing community through which man becomes man. His passion was for beauty, order, truthfulness, and happiness in the world."

The Story of Chinese Philosophy (1961), by Ch'u Chai and Winberg Chai, is a popular treatment of its subject. The same father-and-son team collaborated on *The Humanist Way in Ancient China: Essential Works of Confucianism* (1965), which is entitled *The Sacred Books of Confucius* in another edition.

Fung Yu-lan, *A History of Chinese Philosophy* (2 vols.; 1952, 1953) and *A Short History of Chinese Philosophy* (1948). These volumes from an outstanding Chinese scholar are authoritative but sometimes heavy reading.

Two massive and impressive anthologies, both featuring extensive introductory materials and scholarly notes, are those by Wm. Theodore de Bary, *et al.* (eds.), *Sources of Chinese Tradition* (1960), and Wing-tsit Chan (ed.), *A Source Book in Chinese Philosophy* (1963). Each of these books covers the full range of Chinese thought from pre-Confucian times to Mao Tse-tung.

Taoism

————————————————————————*the way to do is to be*

*introduction*_____

> Miraculous power and marvelous activity—
> Drawing water and hewing wood!
>
> P'ang-yun

Tao is the fundamental metaphysical concept of the Chinese and (as its name would suggest) the center of that way of life known as Taoism. In its deepest meaning, *Tao* is Reality, the Great Infinite. As with the Hindu's *Brahman,* there can be direct experience of *Tao*, but no mere words can describe it.

> Those who know do not speak;
> Those who speak do not know.*

The word "Tao," generally speaking, means Way and refers first to that inexpressible Way of Reality: the roots of life and of the world itself are grounded in mysterious Being. On a more accessible level, *Tao* is manifested in nature; its sublime rhythms are the seasons and the perennial processes of growth and decay, creation and destruction. And it is the *Tao* of nature which can be a guide for man. To know nature and to live an uncomplicated life in harmony with nature is the Way of the Taoist sage.

Intellectuality, on the other hand, is a freakish irrelevance: excessive reliance on ideas and words only clutters up the mind. "To be always talking is against nature" is a blunt admonition of the *Tao Te Ching*. The chatter of "progress" and of civilization is a crippling distraction. No "salvation" is sought by the Taoist, no liberation from this world.† We are children of cosmic nature, and we can follow and trust its ways. The *Tao Te Ching,* Huston Smith has commented, is "a testament to man's at-home-ness in the universe."‡

The Taoist way of life is largely epitomized in the concept of *wu-wei*. Defined variously as "actionless activity," "creative quietude," and "yielding to win," it means possessing such empathy with nature that its powers become one's own. The lightest touch, at the proper time and place, will do what heavy and forceful blows cannot. Movement can be so effortless that it seems not to be movement. This is neither a matter of mere technique nor

---

*Arthur Waley, *The Way and Its Power* (London: George Allen & Unwin, Ltd., 1934), Chap. LVI, p. 210. Another translation is that of Ho-shang Kung: "To know Tao and say you do not know is the best. Not to know Tao and say you know is a disease." Quoted in Wing-tsit Chan, *The Way of Lao Tzu* (Indianapolis: The Library of Liberal Arts, 1963), p. 225.

†Not discussed in this chapter is the "popular" Taoism which evolved in later times and featured belief in many deities, Heaven and Hell, magical practices, great concern over longevity and immortality, astrology, fortune-telling, and the like.

‡*The Religions of Man* (New York: Harper & Row, Perennial Library, 1965), p. 198.

even of knowledge: ultimately, it is accomplishing everything by *becoming* a certain type of person. The way to *do* is to *be*.

Frederic Spiegelberg's introductory essay reviews what little is known of Lao Tzu, the "Old Master," who was held by tradition (now doubted) to have been the author of the *Tao Te Ching* and hence the "founder" of Taoism. It is typical of the spirit of Taoism that it doesn't really matter whether he was the author of that work or not—or even whether he was a historical figure or not. In the world of Taoism nothing should be fussed about, much less an academic question of authorship or a distant detail of history. But the subtle themes of the *Tao Te Ching* do matter, and these are the subject of Spiegelberg's essay.

Then there are presented selections from the primary sources of Taoism, the *Tao Te Ching* and the *Chuang Tzu*. At once mystical and practical, simple and profound, the *Tao Te Ching* is both a literary and a philosophical classic that has prompted more translations than any other Chinese work. The *Chuang Tzu* is the "second" book of Taoism, but it is in many ways the equal of the *Tao Te Ching* in the brilliance of its style and thought. Perhaps more than anything else, there is reflected in the *Chuang Tzu* the essential spirit of freedom, of man liberated in *this* world.

Comparisons of China's two indigenous religions are inevitable: Confucianism and Taoism are so different and yet so complementary. Lin Tung-chi's approach in his "The Chinese Mind: Its Taoist Substratum" is to describe them as they are manifested as character traits in the individual. The Confucian impulse is social and politely aggressive; the Taoist is private and "yielding." The Confucian concern about the business of state is countered by the indifferent anarchism of the Taoist. The conformity and orderliness of the Confucianist stand in contrast to the "careless" Taoist, who moves with the moving world.

Alan Watts' "Flowing with the Tao" is an essay whose style itself exemplifies its subject matter. Because the essay meanders pleasantly and effortlessly, it may seem to have no particular direction. But, on finishing it, the reader is almost surprised to realize that he has indeed learned a good deal about the difficult concepts of *Tao* and *wu-wei,* not to mention the problems of translating the *Tao Te Ching.*

frederic spiegelberg _____

The Old Master and His Book

Frederic Spiegelberg, like Heinrich Zimmer and so many others, fled Nazi Germany in the 1930's for England and the United States. He taught at Columbia University, Union Theological Seminary, and Stanford University, and is the author of *The Religion of No Religion, Living Religions of the World,* and *Zen, Rocks, and Water.*

  The content of religious experience, he has written, is the Miracle of Being. Not miracles (in the plural), but *the* miracle, which is "the simple fact that we are, that the whole complex that we call the world is and has being." And "awakening to the Miracle of Being is the one and only true subject of all religions."* In China the Miracle of Being is called *Tao.*

_____

Lao Tse, which is not a proper name, but merely means Old Master, is generally considered to have been born circa 604 B.C. Sinologists place the date two or three hundred years either way, but 604 is the traditional date.[1] According to legend, Lao Tse was carried in his mother's womb not for 10 months, as in the case of the Buddha, but for 82 years. One way or another, some fable of miraculous birth gathers about any great religious leader. It is, however, the longest parturition on record. Lao Tse was thus born as an old man with a long white beard and a wrinkled face. Despite this appearance, he immediately went down on the floor and began to perform in the manner of a small child. He was carrying out the great Chinese principle of filial piety. He did not do so for long, but nonetheless, he conformed to the pattern society demanded. But having been born at the age of 82, when he began to grow older, he aged very rapidly and lived to a vast age. Since old men were rare in those days, as such he was exceptional and was considered a great sage. No doubt the legend about his age reflects an outward aspect of his wisdom. In China an old man is not merely a person who by chance has survived the ravages of time, disease, and his own offspring, and who no longer fulfills any useful social function. On the contrary, he is regarded as a person who, by reason of his longer experience, has much to teach.

  We are told very little about Lao Tse. We learn that he was a librarian in the

_____

Living Religions of the World (Englewood Cliffs, N.J.: Prentice-Hall, 1956), pp. 8-9, 17.

  [1]Modern scholars question whether he lived at all, a few claiming him to have been invented by Chuang-Tzu, his supposed disciple.

Court service, and legend would have it that in his old age he left China to travel westward, either to India, or to the glorious Buddhist paradise of Sukhavati. Clearly he went west in search of further wisdom, but since we do not know the exact date of the legends, we cannot say where this wisdom was thought to be located.

It is stated that the Chinese frontier officials would not allow Lao Tse to leave China without an export license for his possessions. Lao Tse had nothing with him, and explained that all he possessed was his philosophy, and that was in his mind. The customs inspector said that in that case he would have to leave his wisdom in China before departing, so Lao Tse sat at the border for three days and wrote down the *Tao te King.** The book is so succinct that it could easily have been written in three days, and could be read in half an hour. On the other hand, one could also spend a year on it, depending upon how thoroughly one read it. The *Tao te King* deals with the highest word concept of the Chinese language, the word tao.

It is not of importance that we know the doubtful English phonetic rendering of the word, but it is important that we know the Chinese ideogram and its meaning. Tao is, so to speak, the course of nature, or what we might call seasonableness; the agreement of circumstances with the needs of the hour. It might therefore just as well be placed in the center of the yang-yin hexagram of the *Yi-Ching*.

The ideogram: is supposedly a picture of a head. The other part of the ideogram is an abbreviation of the walking-man sign, so tao is a head-walking, or headway, or mainroad. There are several hundred translations of the expression tao in various European languages. The ramifications of any Chinese ideogram are so diverse, and the ramifications of its relation with other ideograms in a certain order so multiform, that no one translation can ever deal with all of them. It is as though we were to try to compress the twenty-four simple meanings of the French verb "garder," not to mention their cognate meanings, into one word, together with the twenty-one meanings, let us say, of the word "eau" to which it might be found in as many multiple relations. It is like that, but it is also worse. Thus one sees that even in a book as brief as the *Tao te King* the possibilities are almost infinite. Even in China the reading of ideograms, let alone the translation of them, is a great art. For that matter, to take an Occidental symbol at random, what does a cross with equidistant arms mean? It may mean any one of a hundred different things, or all of them, even though we understand it quite differently when it is a silent symbol than when we connect it with the word for which it stands. The difference between an original and a translation is always great. But when we are translating things that are both words *and* visual symbols, the difference is

*One of many variant spellings of *Tao Te Ching*.—R.E.

all the greater. The first sentence of the *Tao te King* may make this matter clear:

Tao ko Tao Feing Chang Tao, 　　道 可 道 非 常 道

We find the word tao itself three times. Ko is something like a genitive participle or relative pronoun, and means relation. Tao, insofar as it is termed tao is not the real tao, in other words. Fei means not. Chang; the real, eternal, or basically existent. So this sentence means that the Being of Being, insofar as it is expressed in terms of existence, is not the Being of Being that we really mean as the light that stands behind all things. Or, in the words of Meister Eckhart, "Our mind does not want God insofar as He is God. Why not? Because there He has names, and even if there would be a thousand, our mind penetrates them all more and more because it wants Him there where He has no names."

The very fact that tao is reflected in the mind means that the conception fails to be even the projection of the light we are talking about:

The name that can be named is not the enduring and unchanging name.[2]

Lao Tse goes on with his metaphysical exposition to prove that tao cannot be expressed in human terms or discussed, because once we try to do so, we lose it. As long as we do not try to conceive of it, however, it is there all the time. Thus we interpret the opening sentence of the *Tao te King*. But it could be interpreted in many other ways, for it is an arrangement of negatives and positives with no concrete root or externalized and specific statement.

There was something undefined and complete, coming into existence before Heaven and Earth. How still it was and formless, standing alone, and undergoing no change, reaching everywhere and in no danger *(of being exhausted)!* It may be regarded as the Mother of all things.

I do not know its name, and I give it the designation of the Tao *(the Way or Course).* Making an effort *(further)* to give it a name I call it The Great.

Great, it passes on *(in constant flow.)* Passing on, it becomes remote. Having become remote, it returns. Therefore the Tao is great; Heaven is great; Earth is great; and the *(sage)* king is also great. In the universe there are four that are great, and the *(sage)* king is one of them.

Man takes his law from the Earth; the Earth takes its law from Heaven; Heaven takes its law from the Tao. The law of the Tao is its being what it is.[3]

Nonetheless Lao Tse has written an entire book about the inexpressibility of tao. He endeavors to exposit this inexpressibility by means of parables, showing what Tao could be called if one wished to explain it, though it is better not to do so. The Buddha also used examples, in exactly the same way,

---

[2] James Legge, trans., *The Sacred Books of China, The Texts of Confucianism,* p. 47.
[3] Ibid., pp. 67-68.

in discussing nirvana without defining it, because he believed it to be undefinable. The Buddha says only that nirvana is like sparks that fly from the anvil when the hammer strikes it; like the oil lamp that burns out because one forgot to refuel it. Lao Tse uses the same technique:

There is nothing in the world more soft and weak than water, and yet for attacking things that are firm and strong there is nothing that can take precedence of it;—for there is nothing (so effectual) for which it can be changed.

Every one in the world knows that the soft overcomes the hard, and the weak the strong, but no one is able to carry it out in practice.

Therefore the sage has said:

> He who accepts his state's reproach,
> Is hailed therefore its altars' lord;
> To him who bears men's direful woes
> They all the name of King accord.

Words that are strictly true seem to be paradoxical.[4]

and:

The highest excellence is like (that of) water. The excellence of water appears in its benefiting all things, and in its occupying, without striving (to the contrary), the low place which all men dislike. Hence (its way) is near to (that of) the Tao.

It is necessary to speak of Tao in parabolic terms, for:

The Tao, considered as unchanging, has no name. As soon as it proceeds to action, it has a name.[5]

So he uses the simile of water. Tao is not water, but it is like water because it seeks the lowest places and never stands high: that is, it is humble, insofar as it knows and finds its own place, and does not aspire to be higher than it is. Also, like water, it is the strongest and most powerful element on earth, for through yielding, like water, you achieve success.

We all know some of the thousands of Taoist, Zen, and Buddhist brush paintings of a waterfall cascading down over rocks. Such pictures are not meant to be depictive. They have a quality that we sense, apart from what they show, for they are visible sermons and aids to meditation. They are designed to say that water tumbling over rocks yields entirely to the shape of the rocks, as it would to a vessel into which it might be poured. It takes the shape it is allowed, at least for a time; yet if you look again after a lapse of geologic time you would see that the rocks have taken on the shape of the water-flow, their corners are rounded off. Pictures of waterfalls are frequently given as wedding presents in the Orient, for what happens when a man (yang) and a woman (yin) live together? The man sets the pattern of living and the woman yields, but the more she yields, the more interesting and unexpected

[4]Ibid., p. 120.
[5]Ibid., pp. 52, 74.

will be the outcome. This attitude of not actually struggling to perform any action, out of conformity to passing circumstances, is the highest ethical principle of Taoism and is called the wu-wei. Usually, wu-wei is translated inaccurately as "not doing," giving the impression that Taoism is a doctrine of passive inactivity.

This is not the true meaning, for the word wu does not mean not in the sense of pure negation, as it does in English. The ideogram for wu originally meant: "forty men disappear in the woods." If you ask what happens to forty men who disappear in the woods, the answer is, nothing at all, they are merely no longer visible. So it is with wu as a negative. It does not mean a total negation, but rather an absence from the immediate scene. Wu-wei is therefore an imperative: act in such a way as forty men who disappear into the woods do. In other words, to translate the matter into the terms of Kant's categorical imperative, to act in such way that your action and the results of your actions are not noticeable, either to yourself or to others, for they should fit so smoothly into the surroundings and circumstances that they will not be egregious. If so:

He who does not fail in the requirements of his position continues long.[6]

On this matter Lao Tse is extremely explicit:

The skilful traveller leaves no traces of his wheels or footsteps; the skilful speaker says nothing that can be found fault with or blamed; the skilful reckoner uses no tallies; the skilful closer needs no bolts or bars, while to open what he has shut will be impossible.[7]

It is perhaps interesting that even when we discuss tao, we have to use such words as improper, proper, egregious, which are hardly ever used in current speech to define correct behavior. They were so used in the 18th century, when an appropriate and unostentatious conduct was emphasized by the social compact as highly as it has ever been in the Anglo-Saxon-American cultural stream.

Such conduct, to which nothing need be added, and from which nothing can be taken away without changing its nature, we found enunciated in the *Bhagavad-Gita,* or *Song of the Lord.* The God Krishna tells the hero, Arjuna, not to choose either akarma, or inactivity, or karma, which was vigorous action for the sake of specific ends, but to seek Nishkama karma, the kind of action that is gratuitous, performed for no goal of the self, but as an instrument of the divine force that acts through us, if we do not impede it with our personal selfishness.

In the literature that touches more or less directly upon any possible expression of the Being of Being by means of words, the book of tao stands as one of the best metaphysics. Unfortunately like all such pure sources, tao

[6] Ibid., p. 75.
[7] Ibid., p. 70.

hardens with the passage of time into an -ism, the colloidal suspension of its approach to the ineffable precipitating out into dogma and ritual. Mystical insight into the Being of Being is a personal, and not a social matter. So when such an insight is adjusted to the needs of those who cluster round the original master, very odd things are apt to happen. In the case of the system of Lao Tse, what happened was that his original insight solidified into a system of necromancy. Today most of the light-blue gowned Taoist monks and priests of China, far from being infallible philosophers, are sorcerers, soothsayers, and magicians of the lowest kind. Consequently there are very few enlightened persons who call themselves Taoists, and as Taoists, they are not appreciated as serious scholars. The hexagram of the *I-Ching,* from the form of a parable of the greater nature forces, deteriorated into a dream and magic book, and so too, did Tao.

A Chinese friend of the author's once took him to see a Taoist scholar, who lived in a tiny hermitage in the mountain ranges north of Hong Kong, in a condition of utmost simplicity. When asked if he thought the great spirit of the ancient tradition of tao was still alive, the scholar, who was fat, began to laugh until his belly shook. That was his only answer. Whether he was laughing at the impertinence of the question or at the irony of the answer was not clear. It is for the reader to decide. But no matter what Taoism is now, the book of tao remains. It is really a series of meditations upon the nature of tao, which, as we know from the first sentence of the *Tao te King,* cannot be the great tao if it can be expressed, the great tao being inexpressible. The second chapter of the *Tao te King* is particularly celebrated:

All in the world know the beauty of the beautiful, and in doing this they have *(the idea of)* what ugliness is; they all know the skill of the skilful, and in doing this they have *(the idea of)* what the want of skill is.

So it is that existence and non-existence give birth the one to *(the idea of)* the other; that difficulty and ease produce the one *(the idea of)* the other. . . .

Therefore the sage manages affairs without doing anything, and conveys his instructions without the use of speech.[8]

In other words, by overemphasizing one quality, we only serve to evoke its opposite. Or perhaps, as in all things, beauty in this sense is not the norm, but an extreme, on the eternal teeter-totter of yang and yin, so that by bearing all emphasis upon it, we only serve to drag it down and to make its opposite rise. In the last line, "teaching without words," is literally "not speaking talk," which is not quite the same thing. However, since we have seen that wu-wei does not mean without action, but acting in such a way that neither the action nor the result of the action is glaringly visible, we might reconsider the role of the sage. Emerson mentions somewhere that Socrates said: "All my good is

[8]Ibid., pp. 47-48. [The translation here by James Legge may be compared with the one that follows, by Gia-fu Feng and Jane English.—R.E.]

magnetic; and I educate not by lessons, but by going about my business." We also have the old saw about education consisting of Mark Hopkins at one end of a log and the pupil at the other. For education is not only an instruction in opinion and fact. It also deals with the transmission of a good deal of ineffable material that can only be conveyed by a form of osmosis. The Chinese sage, and in particular the sage envisioned by Lao Tse, did not only teach by example. He also taught by presence. This, clearly, was also the great strength of the Buddha, as it is of any revealed personality. When we read the great and momentous political speeches of the past, even of the immediate past, they make no impression on us at all. We wonder how they made their effect. If we have ever seen a first-rate actress in a fifth-rate play we would know how instantly. A great sage or teacher actually transmits, not information, except incidentally, but his personality, more or less intact. But this personality is not his personal ego, so much as it is a living mind modified by a special type of or series of experiences. Like a great artist, his skill consists in being able to transmit the insights he has received, which usually have little or nothing to do with the form in which he wraps them, so to speak, or even with his own ego. The artist, like the teacher, if inspired, has not only his own personal ego, but also an impersonal persona. It is the insights impressed upon this that he transmits. Rembrandt's *"Side of Beef"*; Chardin's pots and pans; Winslow Homer's trout streams, and Milton's *Paradise Lost* deal with matters far different than their subject matter. Thus, we can conjecture, the Buddha, though never describing nirvana, managed to convey its nature very well to his immediate disciples, for though we do not find the matter in his recorded texts, he had at his disposal the 84 principal mudras, or hand and body postures that, when we see them, still convey something to us, even if we do not know their precise symbolic meaning.

In this regard, it is not without interest that Buddhist sculpture in China, with the exception of the lotus postures, favored more than any other position "the posture of heavenly ease" of Kwannon.

In the *Tao te King,* Lao Tse mentions the god concept only once, in Section four:

The Tao is *(like)* the emptiness of a vessel; and in our employment of it we must be on our guard against all fulness. How deep and unfathomable it is, as if it were the Honoured Ancestor of all things!

. . . .

How pure and still the Tao is, as if it would ever so continue.[9]

This is very much like the hymn to creation in the *Rig Veda:*

Who verily knows and who can here declare it, whence it was born and whence comes this creation?

[9] Ibid., p. 50.

CHAPTER SIX / *Taoism*

The gods are later than this world's production. Who knows then whence it first came into being?[10]

The *Tao te King* is extremely sparse and laconic, much more succinct than anything to be found in the *Vedas*. Also, the general impression is one of more impersonality and detachment. Even the parables and similes are fleetingly brief.

The highest excellence is like *(that of)* water. The excellence of water appears in its benefiting all things, and in its occupying, without striving, *(to the contrary)*, the low place which all men dislike. Hence *(its way)* is near to *(that of)* the Tao.[11]

.   .   .

Clay is fashioned into vessels; but it is on their empty hollowness that their use depends.[12]

You don't want the glass or the brass or the clay, when you buy a vessel, you want the empty space, or capacity to carry liquid. The thing itself is worth nothing, but its ability, or emptiness, to receive is what is worth having. Man is worth nothing. His ability to receive insight is worth everything.

The door and windows are cut out *(from the walls)* to form an apartment; but it is on the empty space *(within)*, that its use depends.[13]

This sentence has been applied to Chinese and Japanese art, with their emphasis upon what is not to be seen in the picture, usually considered as more important than the actual lines the painter draws. Watch what he has left out, instead of concentrating on what he has drawn, and it usually becomes apparent that what he has drawn is there only so that what he left out may be noticed by contrast. Thus Hia Kouei's famous Landscape of a storm in autumn, shows only a man bending under an umbrella, a tree blowing in the wind, and grasses blowing on the edge of a cliff. The rest of the paper is bare. Ying Yu-Kien's "Fog Parting From A Village in the Mountains" consists of six rocks, three rooftops, and two bled-edge washes, plus two small figures each drawn with not more than three brushstrokes apiece; yet the picture is vast. The same is true of music. It is the interval, not the note, that is important there. Psychologically this idea is akin to some of the ideas behind the Yoga practices of India, in particular the attempt to abolish the personal ego, to act in an average way, and not to be noticed any longer insofar as one's work is no more worthy of notice than one is oneself.

.   .   .

[10] Ralph T. H. Griffith, trans., *Hymns of the Rig-Veda* (Benares: E. J. Lazarus and Co., 1896), p. 129.
[11] *The Sacred Books of China*, p. 52.
[12] Ibid., p. 55.
[13] Ibid., p. 55.

In the last entry of the *Tao te King* Lao Tse pokes fun at himself. After three days of writing, when he presents his written wisdom to the frontier official so that he may be permitted to leave China, what can he say but:

Sincere words are not fine; fine words are not sincere. Those who are skilled *(in the Tao)* do not dispute *(about it);* the disputatious are not skilled in it. Those who know *(the Tao)* are not extensively learned; the extensively learned do not know it.[14]

So Lao Tse laughs and mocks like the elderly Taoist scholar north of Hong Kong, for when one talks of profound matters, by talking one only makes them the more elusive. Such is the wisdom of Lao Tse. . . .

[14]Ibid., p. 123.

gia-fu feng and jane english (translators) _____

FROM THE *Tao Te Ching*

The *Tao Te Ching* consists of eighty-one poems which could easily fit within half that number of printed pages. Several of the poems are presented here in the recent and outstanding translation by Gia-fu Feng and Jane English. Terse and epigrammatic in style and paradoxical in thought, yet infinitely suggestive of mystery, the *Tao Te Ching* fits perfectly the Western image of the "Wisdom of the East."

The difficulties of translating the *Tao Te Ching,* commented upon by Spiegelberg, extend even to its title, which has been rendered as variously as *The Way and Its Power* (Arthur Waley) and *The Canon of Reason and Virtue* (D. T. Suzuki and Paul Carus). The key word "Tao" means "way" or "path," and hence, says Waley, "the way in which one does something; method, principle, doctrine." In Taoism, *Tao* refers to "the way the universe works," and "ultimately, something very like God, in the more abstract and philosophical use of that term."*

ONE

The Tao that can be told is not the eternal Tao.
The name that can be named is not the eternal name.
The nameless is the beginning of heaven and earth.
The named is the mother of ten thousand things.
Ever desireless, one can see the mystery.
Ever desiring, one can see the manifestations.
These two spring from the same source but differ in name; this appears as
    darkness.
Darkness within darkness.
The gate to all mystery.

*Arthur Waley, *The Way and Its Power* (London: George Allen & Unwin, Ltd., 1934), p. 30. Because of the theistic connotations of the word "God," it is probably not helpful to stress the comparison of that term with *Tao,* but one further reference is too interesting to omit. A translation of the Gospel of John into Chinese juxtaposed the two terms in this manner: "In the beginning was the *Tao,* and the *Tao* was with God, and the *Tao* was God." (Quoted in Chung-yuan Chang, "The Concept of Tao in Chinese Culture," *The Review of Religion,* Vol. 17 [March 1953], p. 116.)

TWO

Under heaven all can see beauty as beauty only because there is ugliness.
All can know good as good only because there is evil.

Therefore having and not having arise together.
Difficult and easy complement each other.
Long and short contrast each other;
High and low rest upon each other;
Voice and sound harmonize each other;
Front and back follow one another.

Therefore the sage goes about doing nothing, teaching no-talking.
The ten thousand things rise and fall without cease,
Creating, yet not possessing,
Working, yet not taking credit.
Work is done, then forgotten.
Therefore it lasts forever.

EIGHT

The highest good is like water.
Water gives life to the ten thousand things and does not strive.
It flows in places men reject and so is like the Tao.

In dwelling, be close to the land.
In meditation, go deep in the heart.
In dealing with others, be gentle and kind.
In speech, be true.
In ruling, be just.
In business, be competent.
In action, watch the timing.

No fight: No blame.

NINETEEN

Give up sainthood, renounce wisdom,
And it will be a hundred times better for everyone.

Give up kindness, renounce morality,
And men will rediscover filial piety and love.

Give up ingenuity, renounce profit,
And bandits and thieves will disappear.

These three are outward forms alone; they are not sufficient in themselves.
It is more important
To see the simplicity,
To realize one's true nature,
To cast off selfishness
And temper desire.

TWENTY-TWO

Yield and overcome;
Bend and be straight;
Empty and be full;
Wear out and be new;
Have little and gain;
Have much and be confused.

Therefore wise men embrace the one
And set an example to all.
Not putting on a display,
They shine forth.
Not justifying themselves,
They are distinguished.
Not boasting,
They receive recognition.
Not bragging,
They never falter.
They do not quarrel,
So no one quarrels with them.
Therefore the ancients say, "Yield and overcome."
Is that an empty saying?
Be really whole,
And all things will come to you.

TWENTY-FOUR

He who stands on tiptoe is not steady.
He who strides cannot maintain the pace.
He who makes a show is not enlightened.
He who is self-righteous is not respected.
He who boasts achieves nothing.
He who brags will not endure.
According to followers of the Tao,
    "These are extra food and unnecessary luggage."
They do not bring happiness.
Therefore followers of the Tao avoid them.

TWENTY-NINE

Do you think you can take over the universe and improve it?
I do not believe it can be done.

The universe is sacred.
You cannot improve it.
If you try to change it, you will ruin it.
If you try to hold it, you will lose it.

So sometimes things are ahead and sometimes they are behind;
Sometimes breathing is hard, sometimes it comes easily;
Sometimes there is strength and sometimes weakness;
Sometimes one is up and sometimes down.

Therefore the sage avoids extremes, excesses, and complacency.

THIRTY-THREE

Knowing others is wisdom;
Knowing the self is enlightenment.
Mastering others requires force;
Mastering the self needs strength.

He who knows he has enough is rich.
Perseverance is a sign of will power.
He who stays where he is endures.
To die but not to perish is to be eternally present.

CHAPTER SIX / *Taoism*

THIRTY-FIVE

All men will come to him who keeps to the one,
For there lie rest and happiness and peace.

Passersby may stop for music and good food,
But a description of the Tao
Seems without substance or flavor.
It cannot be seen, it cannot be heard,
And yet it cannot be exhausted.

FORTY

Returning is the motion of the Tao.
Yielding is the way of the Tao.
The ten thousand things are born of being.
Being is born of not being.

FORTY-THREE

The softest thing in the universe
Overcomes the hardest thing in the universe.
That without substance can enter where there is no room.
Hence I know the value of non-action.

Teaching without words and work without doing
Are understood by very few.

FORTY-SIX

When the Tao is present in the universe,
The horses haul manure.
When the Tao is absent from the universe,
War horses are bred outside the city.

There is no greater sin than desire,
No greater curse than discontent,
No greater misfortune than wanting something for oneself.
Therefore he who knows that enough is enough will always have enough.

FORTY-SEVEN

Without going outside, you may know the whole world.
Without looking through the window, you may see the ways of heaven.
The farther you go, the less you know.

Thus the sage knows without traveling;
He sees without looking;
He works without doing.

FORTY-EIGHT

In the pursuit of learning, every day something is acquired.
In the pursuit of Tao, every day something is dropped.

Less and less is done
Until non-action is achieved.
When nothing is done, nothing is left undone.

The world is ruled by letting things take their course.
It cannot be ruled by interfering.

FORTY-NINE

The sage has no mind of his own.
He is aware of the needs of others.

I am good to people who are good.
I am also good to people who are not good.
Because Virtue is goodness.
I have faith in people who are faithful.
I also have faith in people who are not faithful.
Because Virtue is faithfulness.

The sage is shy and humble—to the world he seems confusing.
Men look to him and listen.
He behaves like a little child.

FIFTY-SEVEN

Rule a nation with justice.
Wage war with surprise moves.
Become master of the universe without striving.
How do I know that this is so?
Because of this!

The more laws and restrictions there are,
The poorer people become.
The sharper men's weapons,
The more trouble in the land.
The more ingenious and clever men are,
The more strange things happen.
The more rules and regulations,
The more thieves and robbers.

Therefore the sage says:
    I take no action and people are reformed.
    I enjoy peace and people become honest.
    I do nothing and people become rich.
    I have no desires and people return to the good and simple life.

SEVENTY-SIX

A man is born gentle and weak.
At his death he is hard and stiff.
Green plants are tender and filled with sap.
At their death they are withered and dry.

Therefore the stiff and unbending is the disciple of death.
The gentle and yielding is the disciple of life.

Thus an army without flexibility never wins a battle.
A tree that is unbending is easily broken.

The hard and strong will fall.
The soft and weak will overcome.

FENG AND ENGLISH / *Tao Te Ching*

EIGHTY-ONE

Truthful words are not beautiful.
Beautiful words are not truthful.
Good men do not argue.
Those who argue are not good.
Those who know are not learned.
The learned do not know.

The sage never tries to store things up.
The more he does for others, the more he has.
The more he gives to others, the greater his abundance.
The Tao of heaven is pointed but does no harm.
The Tao of the sage is work without effort.

arthur waley (translator)

FROM THE *Chuang Tzu*

"Chuang Tzu" is used to refer to either the book by that title or the man, but of the man nothing is known except that he was a contemporary of Mencius in the fourth century B.C. Chuang Tzu did not author the book (which probably dates from the third century B.C.); it bears his name because he is the subject of, and inspiration for, many of its stories.

The *Chuang Tzu* pursues further the mystical themes of the *Tao Te Ching* and adds something else: the *Chuang Tzu* Taoist is also a delightfully light-hearted non-conformist who finds his free and easy way in the Way of nature and who laughs at pomp and circumstance and other foolishness. The later development of Ch'an (Zen) Buddhism in China owed much to Taoism in general and to Chuang Tzu in particular.

The selections which follow were translated by Arthur Waley (see biographical note in Chapter Five), excerpted from his *Three Ways of Thought in Ancient China*.

Hui Tzu said to Chuang Tzu, 'Your teachings are of no practical use.' Chuang Tzu said, 'Only those who already know the value of the useless can be talked to about the useful. This earth we walk upon is of vast extent, yet in order to walk a man uses no more of it than the soles of his two feet will cover. But suppose one cut away the ground round his feet till one reached the Yellow Springs,[1] would his patches of ground still be of any use to him for walking?' Hui Tzu said, 'They would be of no use.' Chuang Tzu said, 'So then the usefulness of the useless is evident.'

When Chuang Tzu's wife died, Hui Tzu came to the house to join in the rites of mourning. To his surprise he found Chuang Tzu sitting with an inverted bowl on his knees, drumming upon it and singing a song. 'After all,' said Hui Tzu, 'she lived with you, brought up your children, grew old along with you. That you should not mourn for her is bad enough; but to let your friends find you drumming and singing—that is going too far!' 'You misjudge me,' said Chuang Tzu. 'When she died, I was in despair, as any man well might be. But soon, pondering on what had happened, I told myself that in death no strange new fate befalls us. In the beginning we lack not life only, but form. Not form only, but spirit. We are blended in the one great featureless

[1]The world of the dead.

Arthur Waley, "From the *Chuang Tzu.*" From Arthur Waley (trans.), *Three Ways of Thought in Ancient China* (1939). Reprinted by permission of the publishers, George Allen & Unwin, Ltd. Acknowledgement is also made to Barnes & Noble. Some notes have been omitted, and the remainder renumbered.

indistinguishable mass. Then a time came when the mass evolved spirit, spirit evolved form, form evolved life. And now life in its turn has evolved death. For not nature only but man's being has its seasons, its sequence of spring and autumn, summer and winter. If some one is tired and has gone to lie down, we do not pursue him with shouting and bawling. She whom I have lost has lain down to sleep for a while in the Great Inner Room. To break in upon her rest with the noise of lamentation would but show that I knew nothing of nature's Sovereign Law. That is why I ceased to mourn.'

'Take the case of some words,' Chuang Tzu says, parodying the logicians, 'I do not know which of them are in any way connected with reality or which are not at all connected with reality. If some that are so connected and some that are not so connected are connected with one another, then as regards truth or falsehood the former cease to be in any way different from the latter. However, just as an experiment, I will now say them: If there was a beginning, there must have been a time before the beginning began, and if there was a time before the beginning began, there must have been a time before the time before the beginning began. If there is being, there must also be not-being. If there was a time before there began to be any not-being, there must also have been a time before the time before there began to be any not-being. But here am I, talking about being and not-being and still do not know whether it is being that exists and not-being that does not exist, or being that does not exist and not-being that really exists! I have spoken, and do not know whether I have said something that means anything or said nothing that has any meaning at all.

[*To be worked up about the difference between things that are really the same is called Three in the morning.*–Translator.]

What is meant by Three in the morning? In Sung there was a keeper of monkeys. Bad times came and he was obliged to tell them that he must reduce their ration of nuts. 'It will be three in the morning and four in the evening,' he said. The monkeys were furious. 'Very well then,' he said, 'you shall have four in the morning and three in the evening.' The monkeys accepted with delight.

When Confucius was in the West, he wanted to present copies of his works to the Royal House of Chou. A disciple advised him, saying, 'I have heard that there is a former Royal Librarian called Lao Tzu, who now lives in retirement at his home. If you, Sir, want to get your books accepted at the Library, you had better see if you can secure his recommendation.' 'A good idea,' said Confucius, and went to see Lao Tzu, who received the project very coldly. Whereupon Confucius unrolled a dozen treatises and began to expound them. Lao Tzu interrupted him, saying, 'This is going to take too long.

Tell me the gist of the matter.' 'The gist of the matter,' said Confucius, 'is goodness and duty.' 'Would you pray tell me,' said Lao Tzu, 'are these qualities natural to man?' 'Indeed these are,' said Confucius. 'We have a saying that gentlemen

> 'Without goodness cannot thrive,
> Without duty cannot live.

Goodness and duty are indeed natural to man. What else should they be?' 'And what pray, do you mean by goodness and duty?'

> To have a heart without guile,
> To love all men without partiality,

that,' said Confucius, 'is the true state of goodness and duty.'

'Hum,' said Lao Tzu, 'the second saying sounds to me dangerous. To speak of "loving all men" is a foolish exaggeration, and to make up one's mind to be impartial is in itself a kind of partiality. If you indeed want the men of the world not to lose the qualities that are natural to them, you had best study how it is that Heaven and Earth maintain their eternal course, that the sun and moon maintain their light, the stars their serried ranks, the birds and beasts their flocks, the trees and shrubs their station. Thus you too shall learn to guide your steps by Inward Power, to follow the course that the Way of Nature sets; and soon you will reach a goal where you will no longer need to go round laboriously advertising goodness and duty, like the town-crier with his drum, seeking for news of a lost child. No, Sir! What you are doing is to disjoint men's natures!'

Confucius visited Lao Tzu and began talking about goodness and duty. 'Chaff from the winnower's fan,' said Lao Tzu, 'can so blear our eyes that we do not know if we are looking north, south, east, or west; at heaven or at the earth. One gnat or mosquito can be more than enough to keep us awake a whole night. All this talk of goodness and duty, these perpetual pin-pricks, unnerve and irritate the hearer; nothing, indeed, could be more destructive of his inner tranquillity. . . . The swan does not need a daily bath in order to remain white; the crow does not need a daily inking in order to remain black. . . .

Confucius said to Lao Tzu, 'I have edited the Songs, the Book of History, the Rites, the Canon of Music, the Book of Changes, the Chronicle of Springs and Autumns—six scriptures in all—and I think I may say that I have thoroughly mastered their import. Armed with this knowledge I have faced seventy-two rulers, expounding the Way of former kings, the achievements of Chou and Shao; but there was not one ruler who made the slightest use of my teaching. It seems that either my hearers must have been singularly hard to convince, or the Way of the former kings is exceedingly difficult to understand.'

'It is a lucky thing,' said Lao Tzu, 'that you did not meet with a prince anxious to reform the world. Those six scriptures are the dim footprints of ancient kings. They tell us nothing of the force that guided their steps. All your lectures are concerned with things that are no better than footprints in the dust. Footprints are made by shoes; but they are far from being shoes.'

Tzu-lai fell ill. He was already at the last gasp; his wife and children stood weeping and wailing round his bed. 'Pst,' said Tzu-li, who had come to call, 'stand back! A great Change is at work; let us not disturb it.' Then, leaning against the door, he said to Tzu-lai, 'Mighty are the works of the Changer! What is he about to make of you, to what use will he put you? Perhaps a rat's liver, perhaps a beetle's claw!' 'A child,' said Tzu-lai, 'at its parents' bidding must go north and south, east or west; how much the more when those parents of all Nature, the great powers Yin and Yang command him, must he needs go where they will. They have asked me to die, and if I do not obey them, shall I not rank as an unmanageable child? I can make no complaint against them. These great forces housed me in my bodily frame, spent me in youth's toil, gave me repose when I was old, will give me rest at my death. Why should the powers that have done so much for me in life, do less for me in death?

How do I know that wanting to be alive is not a great mistake? How do I know that hating to die is not like thinking one has lost one's way, when all the time one is on the path that leads to home? Li Chi was the daughter of the frontier guardsman at Ai. When first she was captured and carried away to Chin, she wept till her dress was soaked with tears. But when she came to the king's palace, sat with him on his couch and shared with him the dainties of the royal board, she began to wonder why she had wept. How do I know that the dead do not wonder why they should ever have prayed for long life? . . .

Once Chuang Chou[2] dreamt that he was a butterfly. He did not know that he had ever been anything but a butterfly and was content to hover from flower to flower. Suddenly he woke and found to his astonishment that he was Chuang Chou. But it was hard to be sure whether he really was Chou and had only dreamt that he was a butterfly, or was really a butterfly, and was only dreaming that he was Chou.

It was the time when the autumn floods come down.* A hundred streams swelled the River, that spread and spread till from shore to shore, nay from island to island so great was the distance that one could not tell horse from bull. The god of the River felt extremely pleased with himself. It seemed to

[2] I.e. Chuang Tzu.
*This is the chapter called "The Autumn Flood," which is, states Waley, the most famous of Chuang Tzu's allegories.—R.E.

CHAPTER SIX / *Taoism*

him that all lovely things under heaven had submitted to his power. He wandered down-stream, going further and further to the east, till at last he came to the sea. He gazed eastwards, confidently expecting to see the further shore. He could discern no end to the waters. Then the god of the River began to turn his head, peering this way and that; but still he could see no shore. At last, addressing the ocean, he said with a deep sigh: 'There is a proverb which says,

> None like me
> Proves none so blind as he.

I fear it applies very well to myself . . . as I realize only too well when I gaze at your limitless immensity. Had I not this day enrolled myself as your disciple, I might well have made myself the laughing-stock of all who take the Wider View.'

. . . there are those whose thoughts are sublime without being strained; who have never striven after goodness, yet are perfect. There are those who win no victories for their State, achieve no fame, and yet perfect its policies; who find quietness, though far from streams and lakes; who live to great old age, though they have never practised Induction (tao-yin). They have divested themselves of everything, yet lack nothing. They are passive, seek no goal; but all lovely things attend them. Such is the way of Heaven and Earth, the secret power of the Wise. Truly is it said, 'Quietness, stillness, emptiness, not-having, inactivity—these are the balancers of Heaven and Earth, the very substance of the Way and its Power.' Truly is it said, 'The Wise Man rests therein, and because he rests, he is at peace. Because he is at peace, he is quiet.' One who is at peace and is quiet no sorrow or harm can enter, no evil breath can invade. Therefore his inner power remains whole and his spirit intact.

Truly is it said, 'For the Wise Man life is conformity to the motions of Heaven, death is but part of the common law of Change. At rest, he shares the secret powers of Yin; at work, he shares the rocking of the waves of Yang. He neither invites prosperity nor courts disaster. Only when incited does he respond, only when pushed does he move, only as a last resort will he rise. He casts away all knowledge and artifice, follows the pattern of Heaven. Therefore Heaven visits him with no calamity, the things of the world do not lay their trammels upon him, no living man blames him, no ghost attacks him. His life is like the drifting of a boat, his death is like a lying down to rest. He has no anxieties, lays no plans.

King Hui of Wei had a carver named Ting. When this carver Ting was carving a bull for the king, every touch of the hand, every inclination of the shoulder, every step he trod, every pressure of the knee, while swiftly and lightly he wielded his carving-knife, was as carefully timed as the movements of a dancer in the *Mulberry Wood*. . . . 'Wonderful,' said the king. 'I could never have believed that the art of carving could reach such a point as this.' 'I am a lover of Tao,' replied Ting, putting away his knife, 'and have succeeded in applying it to the art of carving. When I first began to carve I fixed my gaze on the animal in front of me. After three years I no longer saw it as a whole bull, but as a thing already divided into parts. Nowadays I no longer see it with the eye; I merely apprehend it with the soul. My sense-organs are in abeyance, but my soul still works. Unerringly my knife follows the natural markings, slips into the natural cleavages, finds its way into the natural cavities. And so by conforming my work to the structure with which I am dealing, I have arrived at a point at which my knife never touches even the smallest ligament or tendon, let alone the main gristle.

'A good carver changes his knife once a year; by which time the blade is dented. An ordinary carver changes it once a month; by which time it is broken. I have used my present knife for nineteen years, and during that time have carved several thousand bulls. But the blade still looks as though it had just come out of the mould. . . .

. . . 'Do not seek precision,' says Chuang Tzu, speaking of the realm of Tao . . . 'I myself have traversed it this way and that; yet still know only where it begins. I have roamed at will through its stupendous spaces. I know how to get to them, but I do not know where they end.'

When Chuang Tzu was angling in the river P'u, the king of Ch'u sent two high officers of state, who accosting Chuang Tzu announced that the king wished to entrust him with the management of all his domains. Rod in hand and eyes still fixed upon his line, Chuang Tzu replied, 'I have been told that in Ch'u there is a holy tortoise that died three thousand years ago. The king keeps it in the great hall of his ancestral shrine, in a casket covered with a cloth. Suppose that when this tortoise was caught, it had been allowed to choose between dying and having its bones venerated for centuries to come or going on living with its tail draggling in the mud, which would it have preferred?' 'No doubt,' said the two officers, 'it would have preferred to go on living with its tail draggling in the mud.' 'Well then, be off with you,' said Chuang Tzu, 'and leave me to drag my tail in the mud.'

CHAPTER SIX / *Taoism*

lin tung-chi

The Chinese Mind: Its Taoist Substratum

As Lin Tung-chi suggests in the following essay, Confucianism and Taoism are the *yang* and *yin* of Chinese personality. Confucianism turns outward toward society and duty; Taoism thrives in individual solitude and freedom. The Confucianist shoulders responsibilities and stands on ceremony, while the Taoist philosophy is that of "an artist, of a rustic and vagabond"; the cool reasonableness of the one is balanced by the poetical intuitiveness of the other.

Clearly, these are not rival religions. They are, as Burton Watson has written, "complementary doctrines, an ethical and political system for the conduct of public and family life, and a mystical philosophy for the spiritual nourishment of the individual, with the metaphysical teachings of the *Book of Changes* acting as a bridge between the two."*

I

Are Chinese Confucian? Yes, indeed. Every Chinese, if tutored at all, cannot help being Confucian, more or less.

And yet, there is necessarily the other side—the counterpoise. For every Chinese is likewise a Taoist, and the definition of a Taoist is, normally, what a Confucianist is not!

Most Westerners are at a loss in understanding Chinese personality. Not a little of the difficulty, I suggest, has come from ignoring this dual nature of the Chinese.

The fact is: we are socially Confucian and individually Taoist. For all the imposing superstructures of our society, with its intricate family ties and relations and its myriad conventions and mannerisms to which we submit as good Confucianists, we as individuals *per se* are irreducibly Taoists.

There is such a thing as personality in solitude as distinguished from personality in association—the intimate self that we feel at home with and are ever inclined to be, as distinguished from the public self that we will to be or have to be. The psychologist has perhaps a word for it—the subconscious. Consciously we are Confucianists, but deep in the obscure subconscious we

Chuang Tzu: Basic Writings (New York: Columbia University Press, 1964), pp. 10-11. Watson's reference here to the *Book of Changes* recalls Richard Wilhelm's observation that Confucianism and Taoism have "their common roots" in that classic.

Lin Tung-chi, "The Chinese Mind: Its Taoist Substratum." From *Journal of the History of Ideas*, Vol. 8, No. 3 (June, 1947) pp. 259-266. Reprinted by permission of *Journal of the History of Ideas*.

feel with alternate fear and joy the blatant Taoist in us all. We fear because we believe we *should be* Confucian in toto. We rejoice because we know we *are* not.

Confucianism is a practical, prosaic affair. Society, social control, gregariousness, and reciprocity of action guided by accepted rules and expressed through a code of decorum—these are but elementary requirements for any decent communal living. The underlying spirit is Duty—namely, the duty of the individual towards his fellowmen and society.

Taoism, on the other hand, is not concerned with society and social order. In direct antithesis to these and other man-made institutions, the Taoist upholds Nature and the State of Nature, wherein the individual and his free expression become the end and justification of everything. What Taoism represents is manifestly a spirit of Freedom—freedom to behave as one pleases irrespective of what society may say and how it may be affected. We are here speaking of Taoism as that subtle but abiding psychic mood in an educated Chinese, and not of the superstitious hodgepodge of the same name with its bewildering hierarchy of gods and fairies concocted and spread by the magician-priests. The latter is a form of popular religion, and hence a social institution. The former is a philosophic attitude or even an aesthetic temperament which, while perpetually seeking expression, ever refuses to actualize itself in any institutional form, religious or otherwise.

Confucianism, with its command of duty, calls for cooperation and conformity; socially speaking, it unites, conserves and perpetuates. Taoism, as an embodiment of individual free will, ever tends toward dissent and dissociation. The contrast between the two is glaring indeed. Yet, like so many paradoxes of life, opposites dwell closest together. The combination of these two modes of thought in one culture, nay, in one person, is not an unhappy mixture in many ways. They supply, shall we say, the positive and the negative elements in Chinese life—the *yin* and the *yang* which complement each other and operate dialectically to lead life out of its periodic impasse; and thanks to them, China is no nation of monomaniacs and monotones.

II

One should be on one's guard against confounding Taoism facilely with Western individualism. True, both advocate individual freedom. But it would be sheer naïveté to assume that they mean the same thing. Taoist freedom is the freedom of a pre-social or an asocial being, while the libertarian freedom of the West is the freedom of a socially conscious man.

Broadly speaking, the gulf that separates the two is perhaps one that separates romanticism from realism in general. There was a time in Europe when the first romantic flush of the Rousseauean indictment against civilization carried with it an advocacy of freedom à la Taoiste—idyllic, abstract and generalized. But that stage was an effervescence: it soon gave way to something organically different. Libertarian individualism of post-Rousseauean days smacks less of romanticism than of practical levelheadedness. The actual question at issue has never been generalized freedom as such, which concept the consensus of Western opinion, even among theoreticians, has long abandoned as untenable. The real issue in each case has always been freedom from something specific and for something specific. Hence, freedom of speech, freedom of assemblage, freedom of belief and worship and, characteristically enough, freedom of contract. There is an unerring move to a definition of position and a specification of concrete objectives which makes the libertarian individualism of the West a realistic and calculated drive almost from the very start. . . .

In Taoism, however, specific objectives do not exist. Taoism postulates generalized freedom without giving it content; it proposes wholesale destruction of civilization without offering an attainable substitute. Freedom to a Taoist does not mean the struggle to free oneself from somebody or something specific; it means freedom of all from all. . . .

Western individualism is essentially the battling creed of a social group in pursuit of power, a rising bourgeoisie demanding liberties to undo the *ancien régime* in order to bring about its reconstruction. Taoism is the philosophy of an artist, of a rustic and vagabond, who feels physiologically incompatible with the congested and sordid atmosphere of over-urbanized life and who impatiently shouts "Air! air!" simply because air is the immediate relief he needs. If he proposes to abandon a stuffy room for deep breathing in the open, he has not the slightest intention of building a sanitorium with scientific ventilation and contrivances for himself or for his fellow-sufferers. Western individualism is born of a new unfolding technology, irresistibly oriented toward a new order. Taoism, impelled by no technological changes, derives its inspiration purely from a retrospective glance over the enchanting simplicities of societies which are either non-existent or have, technologically speaking, been more or less irrevocably superseded. The one is pregnant with an urge for social action; the other remains a lyrical note, expressive of private likes and dislikes, which, however intense, operates basically within the frame of a single individual.

This brings us to a fundamental point: Western individualism is a faith and Taoism is scepticism *par excellence*.

The impulse to social action makes every Western individualist forever conscious of the need of a following. He craves an audience. He is out for converts. Not only is he obliged to demonstrate how profitable and workable his schemes are, but he must of necessity become a zealous missionary, bearing a new standard of revealed truth. Here, the law of psychic action operates. Intent upon hypnotizing, the zealot becomes self-hypnotized. Practically motivated, he soon comes to be convinced of the righteousness of his cause. Interests are transformed into rights and rights are further sanctified as eternal verities. Despite its hard-headed utilitarian origin, libertarian individualism is destined to become a faith, a new faith enthroned to displace an old idol. The average Western individualist can hardly doubt for a moment that God is on his side. He is dead certain—certain of his moral superiority and of his inevitable triumph.

A Taoist is anything but certain. In the last analysis, a Taoist is a sceptic —by temperamental necessity. Basically an artist, he has little use for a faith. The motivation of group interests is absent in him. Nor is he prone to view things in terms of moral significance. Freed from social considerations such as these, he is left with a lone, detached eye which, "seeing through things," as the favorite Taoist phrase has it, does seem to possess the devilish faculty of divesting faith of its staunchness and reducing social symbols to mere shams. A Taoist is persistently tempted to question the ultimate values of things. Suspicious as an old fox, he looks behind and beneath every object he comes upon. He mistrusts, especially where trust is taken for granted. There gleams a native mischievousness in his sidelong glances that makes him forever an uncomfortable companion to the credulous and the faithful.

III

Taoism may be defined as romantic individualism baptized in the fire of what Nietzsche calls "the grand distrust." It is the natural and necessary counterpart to the complacent gregariousness of Confucianism. Come what may, the first prompting of a Taoist is to "debunk," so much folly and ill taste does he see in this all-too-human world.

The urge to debunk is probably the most basic of Taoist traits. Yet, to debunk just the world would make but half a Taoist. A mature Taoist will start with a debunking of humanity and end with a thorough debunking of *himself*.

One can perhaps best describe the working of the Taoist mentality in terms of a psychic curve.

It begins with an ascending movement, whereby the discharging energy of debunking is directed outward to the external objects around until it reaches a point where the fire of debunking turns into a white flame of defiance. Here, one sees the Taoist rise to the full stature of a man as the West commonly conceives it. He looks the world straight in the eye, with the aroused strength of an ego entrenched for battle. It is the moment most surcharged with possibility of action, the juncture at which a Chinese intellectual may most readily turn a revolutionary if ever his defiant mood finds the way to combine with the popular discontent of his age.

A typical Taoist nature does not, however, become a revolutionary as a rule. He does not easily mix with the populace. A proud artist, he stands alone, contemplating no comrades. His predestined fight is of one against all and one against everything. And a more exalted and tense state of mind cannot be imagined.

Yet, there is no vent. Totally unable to view the impending battle in terms of practical interests and concrete issues, he is at a loss as to where and on whom to deal his blows. The intensity of his charged feeling, thus blocked, soon recoils upon itself. A mental crisis develops when an involuntary repression compresses the rising temper on a narrow plateau, which, foundering at this tremulous height, quickly turns into a state of Dionysian drunkenness. The Taoist revolt at this stage takes on the character of an emotional self-abandonment. He gives himself up to himself, having lost sight of the non-ego world and then of the ego itself. He no longer defies, he simply disregards. A sort of ecstasy takes place, in which the half-conscious bitterness and the half-felt rapture combine to produce a vent peculiarly Taoist—the devastating laugh of the intoxicated.

But this blessed stage cannot stay long. A mental numbness born of helpless desperation is foredoomed to come to a *dénouement*—the beginning of the descending curve.

The effects of intoxication clearing away, the last possibility of action disappears. The tension between the ego and the non-ego drops as his facial muscles resume their normal expression. He cannot but question, now, the worth of it all. "Why excitement and fury?" asks the erstwhile rebel. If the Dionysian drunkenness still suggests faintly the pride of one who thinks himself the wisest, this ensuing sobriety of mind brings him to doubts. *Que sais-je?* And he begins to debunk *himself.* He discovers the folly of it all and the fool in himself. With a chuckle, he drops the gauntlet and retires to the mountains. The boisterous rebel becomes the saintly recluse. After the tempest, the serene sunset.

IV

It is important not to confuse Taoist retirement with Buddhist resignation. The Buddhist becomes resigned out of pity for the sufferings of life; he does so with a laden heart. The Taoist retires out of scorn for all; but it is a scorn without bitterness, a departure in high spirits. The one is Gravity personified, heavy, dead serious, full of pathos and tragic forebodings. The other is Emancipation achieved through a whirling dance and celebrated with perfumed wine. For the Taoist fairies are light-footed immortals who tread bird-like on the undulant surface of floating clouds—laughing as they move on, sleeves in the wind, carefree, nonchalant, and altogether oblivious of humanity swarming below.

Unlike the Buddhist with Nirvana as his last hope and belief, a true Taoist neither hopes nor believes. He retires from the world with no Paradise in view, no Finality to attain. He retires simply because he sees the folly of quibbling about anything. He will live and let live the remainder of his life—wishing nothing and doing nothing, a disbeliever at heart to the last, but a disbeliever who, having found the limitations of everything on earth, decides to leave them as they are. And he will not dogmatize on his disbelief. There is in him something of the Pyrrhonian imperturbability which denies knowledge even as regards one's own ignorance or doubt. Thus, between believing and disbelieving, he rests in equilibrium. In this non-committal silence, he has found his Freedom.

A Taoist recluse has all the ease and gracefulness of the truly free. He is truly free because he is so thoroughly the Child of the Present. He lives from moment to moment, taking life as it comes and giving it up as it passes. So completely is his spirit of the Here-and-Now that he escapes altogether the crushing weight of Time and Space which, for all the salvation devices of transmigrations and redemptions of the world-famed religions, persists in hanging heavily on the waking consciousness of man. It is left to the Taoist to achieve the strange spirituality of ethereal diffuseness, which seems to envelop the silhouettes of Time and Space, not by vainly reaching for eternity and infinitude, but by breaking them into myriad atomic bits and fusing himself with these one by one as he chances upon them. The result is the attainment of a *pantheistic repose,* at once immanent and transcendental —like a fish lying listlessly on the surface of undulating waves, or a bird resting its wings on the air currents, rising and falling as the atmospheric pressure changes. There is an elasticity of adjustment in the apparent stillness of position, which definitely makes the word "static" altogether inadequate to describe the subtle relations involved.

It is here that one divines the spiritual fountain-head of Chinese landscape painting.

Chinese landscape painting is the world-feeling of the Taoist recluse, expressed in a form providential in its fitness and with instruments that permit of no substitutes. Take up, if you will, any of the existent masterpieces by the Sung and Ming artists. As the scroll unfolds, one is instantaneously transported body and soul, as it were, to a sphere where Man and Nature palpably merge. What pre-eminently satisfies is the pantheistic repose which the art affords. It is the repose of one who, having debunked everything, realizes debunking itself is vain, and who therefore, while withdrawing from all, will yet diffuse into all. In thus diffusing, he is able to obliterate in his art as in his soul the awareness of the finite ego and, hence, the tension of Time and Space.

Flowing with the Tao

In his autobiography, writing about the suffocating atmosphere of the boarding schools he attended as a boy in England, Alan Watts (1915–1973) described finally leaving school in mid-year: "I was reading Suzuki, Keyserling, Nietzsche, Vivekananda, Lao-tzu, the *Upanishads,* Feuchtwanger, Bergson, Blavatsky, the *Bhagavad-Gita,* Lafcadio Hearn, Anatole France, Havelock Ellis, Bernard Shaw, the *Diamond Sutra,* . . . all the literature which was 'oddball' and screened out of the curriculum. I was seventeen, and all set to go."* He went his own way all his life. Physically, he found his home on the central coast of California—in Big Sur, Sausalito, and similar "pockets of irregularity that are essential to a free people." Spiritually, he moved to the East and mysticism, but he abhorred absolute allegiances to particular creeds.

Watts' very serious but free-wheeling interests and studies found perfect expression in his writing. He became, especially, an infinitely ingenious interpreter of the East, writing with insight, wit, and seeming ease of abstruse ideas in a score of books from *The Spirit of Zen* (1935) to *Cloud-hidden, Whereabouts Unknown* (1973).

JULY 10, 1970

The Chinese characters which I have written on this page are the opening words of the Old Boy's Book of *The Way and Its Power,* otherwise known as Lao-tzu's *Tao Te Ching.* I do not write Chinese very well; an Oriental person looking at my writing knows at once that it was done by a Westerner. Still,

---

In My Own Way (New York: Vintage Books, 1973), p. 121.

they sometimes say that my brushwork is pretty good (for a Westerner), and the young Japanese who are now using ball-point pens instead of brushes say I do it extraordinarily well. But they are a very polite people, and though I have played with the writing brush for many years I am well aware that my technique is nowhere near that of the great masters.

Nevertheless, I have always been in love with Chinese writing. Each character, or ideogram, is an abstract picture of some feature of the process of nature—that is, of the Tao, the Way or Course of the universe. When translated very literally into English, Chinese reads like a telegram. *"Tao* can *tao* not eternal *Tao,"* or "Way can speak-about not eternal Way." In contrast with English, and particularly German or Japanese, Chinese is the fastest and shortest way of saying things, both in speech and writing. If, as seems possible, Mao-tse Tung's people shift to an alphabetic form of writing, they will be at a great disadvantage, for, as their own proverb says, "One picture is worth a thousand words."

The very mechanics of writing Chinese is an aesthetic delight. It requires a pointed brush with a bamboo handle, the hairs of the brush being lightly impregnated with glue, and brushes come in a delicious variety of sizes and designs—from tiny twigs for writing characters like the footprints of spiders to immense three-inch-wide swabbers for making posters. The ink comes in hard flattened sticks made, essentially, of carbon, glue and perfume, and is embossed with dragons in the clouds or bamboos by the water, or with its brand name in gold characters. A fine old stick of Chinese or Korean ink may fetch as much as $500 on the Japanese market, and I am speaking of a small black object never much more than 6" x 2" x 1". Why? Because of the aesthetic and meditative pleasure of rubbing a fine ink into liquid form upon an ink-stone, which is usually a black rectangular block with rounded corners like a small swimming pool, with a short deep end and a long shallow end. Water is poured upon the stone, and the ink-stick is then rubbed gently and lovingly upon the shallow end until the mixture has just the right viscosity and color, for, under reflected light, the black pigment has to look blue, and the ink-stick has to slide through the water with a certain amiable greasiness. The rubbing takes at least fifteen minutes, and, with the perfume of sandalwood or aloes-wood, an artist or calligrapher gets himself in the proper frame of mind to begin his work. Rubbing ink is a form of *za-zen,* or Zen Buddhist meditation in which verbal and conceptual thinking is temporarily suspended. Inferior artists make their apprentices rub the ink. Truly vulgar and depraved artists use bottled ink.

There is a street in Kyoto named Tera-machi (i.e., Temple Street) where, from very small shops, one may buy implements for the tea ceremony, ancient pottery, rosaries, mushrooms, second-hand books, and the most excellent tea in the world. There is also a British-style pub. But the largest shop on the street sells writing brushes, ink, fine paper, and incense. It is one of my paradises, and whenever I get to Kyoto I go there immediately to buy aloeswood (which has, as Dr. Suzuki told me, the essential smell of Buddhism), ink and writing brushes. I just can't resist them. Last time I found a small stick of vermilion ink covered with gold leaf. It should be rubbed on a window sill, early in the morning, using a drop of dew for the water.

It is said to be "difficult" to master the art of Chinese writing, but this means only that the art must grow on you over many years. We use the word "difficult" for tasks which require extreme force or effort, and over which we must perspire, grunt, and groan. But the difficulty of writing Chinese with the brush is to make the brush write by itself, and the Taoists call this the art of *wu-wei*—which may be translated variously as "easy does it," "roll with the punch," "go with the stream," "don't force it," or, more literally, "not pushing." I suppose the Taoist way of life is the polar opposite of Billy Graham's muscular Christianity. *Wu-wei* is the understanding that energy is gravity, and thus that brush writing, or dancing, or judo, or sailing, or pottery, or even sculpture is following patterns in the flow of liquid. Lao-tzu was perhaps the contemporary of that marvelous and neglected Greek philosopher Heraclitus, and both taught exactly the same principles. *Panta rhei*—everything flows, and therefore the understanding of water is the understanding of life. Fire is water falling upwards.

Thus another advantage of Chinese is that, although brief in form, it can say so many things at once. There must be at least eighty English translations of Lao-tzu's book. All differ, and most are to some extent correct. Let us compare differing versions of these six first words:

> The Way that can be described is not the eternal Way.
> The Course that can be discoursed is not the eternal Course.
> The Way that can be Weighed is not the regular Way.
> The Flow that can be followed is not the real Flow.
> Energy which is energetic is not true energy.
> Force forced isn't force.

The fourth and fifth characters appear, surprisingly, on planes and trains in the Far East followed by a character which is simply a square, signifying "mouth" or "door." The three put together mean "Emergency exit." Thus:

> The Go that can be gone is an emergency Go.

Most scholars translate the second use of the ideogram *tao* as "to speak about," although Duyvendak has argued that this is a late meaning of the word. But in my own feeling this kind of laconic and aphoristic Chinese is best translated by giving, in parallel, many of the different ways in which it may be understood: for it means all of them. Linear languages like English, German, and Sanskrit have to stretch out Chinese indefinitely. It has thus more or less come to the point where we have simply adopted the word *tao* into English (like karma and curry) and those who call it "tay-o" should realize that in Peking it is called "dow," in Canton "toe," and in Tokyo "daw," and of course Tokyo itself is something like "Tawkyaw."

Tao (which we shall therefore no longer print in different type as a foreign word) signifies the energy of the universe as a way, current, course, or flow which is at once intelligent and spontaneous, but not personal like a Western god. It would be absurd to worship or pray to the Tao because it's your own true self, the very energy and patterning of your bones, muscles, and nerves. Lao-tzu's first statement about it is that it cannot be defined—for the simple reason that you cannot make what is basically you and basically real an *object* of knowledge. You cannot stand aside from it and examine it as something out there. Although, then, we cannot define it, we must not assume that it is something bleary like the "blind energy" of nineteenth-century scientists. From our own points of view our heads themselves are blind spots, but were it otherwise we should be looking only at neurons and dendrites and would never see mountains and trees. (But, of course, when neurons and dendrites are *seen from the inside* they become mountains and trees.)

Yet although Tao cannot be examined and pinned down, it has a characteristic atmosphere which may be sensed in the life-styles of various Far Eastern poets, artists, and sages, and which is indicated by the term *feng-liu* in Chinese and *furyu* in Japanese, and which means something like flowing with or following with the wind. It is also translated as elegance, which is not quite right, because in English an elegant person is refined and fussy, and perpetrates an atmosphere of haughty disdain—whereas the Chinese poet is sometimes amiably drunken, wandering aimlessly in the mountains, and laughing at falling leaves. One gathers that this sort of person is no longer allowed in China. But he is typified by Pu-tai, the fat, laughing tramp-buddha who carries a gnarled staff and a huge bag of interesting rubbish which he gives away to children.

Poets like Su Tungp'o and Tu Fu were a little more on the side of elegance as we think of it, for they relished drinking fine tea on lazy afternoons, tea made with the best of clear waters from springs and wells, boiled over carefully chosen wood, and served in porcelain or in ceramic bowls with a glaze like jade. On the other hand, a young American Buddhist sought out an extremely holy and magical hermit in the mountains of Japan and, after finding him with extreme difficulty, was served hot water without tea. He had the sense to appreciate the high compliment which he had been offered. Frederic Spiegelberg, philospher and Orientalist, visited a Taoist hermit like Pu-tai on an island near Hong Kong. When he was introduced as an American university professor traveling under a Rockefeller grant to find out whether Asian spirituality was still vital, the hermit began to chuckle very gently, and this gradually developed into uproarious laughter at which his whole glutaneous mass shook like jelly. That was the end of the interview.

A more ancient Taoist sage, whose name I forget, was approached by a Chinese emperor to be an adviser to the government. He declined the offer with extreme courtesy, but when the emissary had departed he washed out his ears—and also those of the donkey on which he customarily rode. There was also a Chinese Zen priest famed as a great painter, but who, unlike other priests, grew his hair long. After getting sufficiently drunk, he would dip his hair into a bowl of ink and then slosh it over a scroll of paper. The next day he would give himself a Rorschach test on the splosh and see in it images of mountains, rivers, and forests which needed only a few touches of the brush to bring them out for all to see. When I was invited to the tea ceremony by the artist and printmaker Saburo Hasegawa he pointed out the subtle beauty of cigarette ash on a tile made by J. B. Blunk, which we were using for an ashtray.

These are vignettes to give some suggestion of the atmosphere of flowing with the Tao. The principle of the thing is also recognized by our own surf riders, some of whom know very well that their sport is a form of yoga or Taoist meditation in which the whole art is to generate immense energy from going with your environment, from the principle of *wu-wei,* or following the gravity of water and so making yourself one with it. For, as Lao-tzu himself said, ''Gravity is the root of lightness.''

further reading

Huston Smith, "Tao Now," in Ian G. Barbour (ed.), *Earth Might Be Fair* (1972). The West's sense of alienation from nature, with its dire ecological implications, is contrasted with the Taoist's feeling for the relatedness, interdependence, and unity of all things.

Herrymon Maurer, *The Old Fellow* (1943). A kind of biographical novel, this portrait of Lao Tzu reads like fiction but has a scholarly basis. Maurer elaborates on the traditions about the "Old Fellow" and borrows from the *Tao Te Ching* for portions of his dialogue.

Holmes Welch, *Taoism: The Parting of the Way* (1957; rev. ed., 1965). A popular and successful introduction. Its final chapter compares Taoism and the American way of life.

Burton Watson (trans.), *Chuang Tzu: Basic Writings* (1964) and *The Complete Works of Chuang Tzu* (1968). Apart from Arthur Waley, who translated only excerpts from Chuang Tzu in his *Three Ways of Thought in Ancient China,* Watson is the best source for this philosopher.

Chang Chung-yuan, *Creativity and Taoism: A Study of Chinese Philosophy, Art and Poetry* (1963). Topics include "Invisible Ground of Sympathy," "Immeasurable Potentialities of Creativity," and "Processes of Self-Realization."

Chang Chung-yuan is also the author of two notable journal articles. "The Concept of Tao in Chinese Culture" (*The Review of Religion,* Vol. 17 [March 1953], pp. 115-132) is a thorough review of the multiple meanings of "Tao" in both Confucianism and Taoism. "An Introduction to Taoist Yoga" (*The Review of Religion,* Vol. 20 [March 1956], pp. 131–148) holds that Chinese yoga had origins in Lao Tzu and Chuang Tzu which were independent of Indian influences.

The much-discussed difficulties of translating the *Tao Te Ching* make it evident that a comparison of the translations is interesting and revealing. Among the best are Witter Bynner, *The Way of Life According to Lao Tzu* (1944); Wing-tsit Chan, *The Way of Lao Tzu* (1963); Arthur Waley, *The Way and Its Power* (1934); D. T. Suzuki and Paul Carus, *The Canon of Reason and Virtue* (1913); Lin Yutang, *The Wisdom of Lao Tzu* (1948); and John C. H. Wu, *Lao Tzu / Tao Te Ching* (1961).

chapter seven

Judaism

the people of the book

> More flesh, more worms; more wealth, more worry.
> More women, more witchery; more maids, more unchastity. . . .
> But more Torah, more life; more study, more wisdom. . . .

Hillel

Judaism is the hallowing of life for the glory of God, and it is God's covenant with a chosen people. It is a history of God's revelation through great prophets and events; it is the Torah and the Talmud and a profound love of learning. Mordecai Kaplan called it a civilization. It is a religion rich in tradition and ritual, but the prophet Micah was able to ask so very simply, "What does the Lord require of you but to do justice, and to love kindness and to walk humbly with your God?"

In all this wealth of vision and wisdom, Genesis suggests a starting place: "In the beginning God . . . ." And it is with the concept of God that Will Herberg begins, in the first reading of this chapter. For the Jews, God is a transcendent Person, a Creator who is the source of this very real and meaningful world. And because man is also a person, a relationship—a *loving* relationship—with God is possible; a man "can hear God's word and respond to it" with a good life dedicated to the service of God. Finally, although the primary goal in this world is the sanctification of life itself, there is at the end of time an ultimate Kingdom of God, "a new heaven and new earth," and the fulfillment of God's plan.

The crucial theme of the covenant—of God's pact with the Hebrews —recurs throughout the Old Testament, and this is the subject of Leo Baeck's essay. The covenant gave to the Jews their essential identity and mission: it meant they were chosen by God to serve Him and to serve mankind. As the "chosen people," they would be watched over by God. They could live in righteousness, in keeping with God's commandments, and prosper, or they could sin and suffer punishment; and they were to face unusual challenges.

The prophets of old appeared like embodied voices of conscience, condemning corrupt ways and reminding the Hebrews of the true nature of their religion and destiny. And so it is with a modern "prophet", Abraham Heschel: Religion has declined in our times, he writes, "not because it was refuted, but because it became irrelevant, dull, oppressive, insipid." Religion fails "when faith is completely replaced by creed, worship by discipline, love by habit." Authentic religion is a vital response to ultimate questions; it is a sense of continuing wonder and amazement at the mystery of being. Religion is man's search for God, but God is also searching for man. The covenant is mutually binding.

Hasidism is a unique and colorful variety of Jewish mysticism which exalts

God by exalting life, so that life is thereby transformed. This is mysticism without asceticism and without withdrawal—an earthly mysticism. In Elie Wiesel's words, Hasidism is "a smiling Judaism, . . . a resounding call to joy."*

What cannot but astound us is that Hasidim ["the pious ones," adherents of Hasidism] remained Hasidim inside ghetto walls, inside the death camps. In the shadow of the executic er, they celebrated life. Startled Germans whispered to each other of Jews dancing in the cattle cars rolling toward Birkenau.†

Hasidism attained prominence as a movement during the eighteenth and nineteenth centuries in eastern Europe. As the essay by Martin Buber in this chapter demonstrates, the lore and traditions of Hasidism are embedded in lively stories and anecdotes about the Zaddikim ("holy men" or leaders) and their disciples. In Hasidism, as in Zen Buddhism, the teacher–disciple relationship is of vital importance, and the literature of Hasidism abounds with accounts of questions by disciples and of the incisive but oblique answers by the Zaddikim. ‡

The faith of Jews has been challenged through the centuries by incredible calamity and continual persecution, but what happened to them at the hands of the Nazis in this century is unprecedented and incomprehensible. Jews were systematically collected in concentration camps and subjected to inhuman and sometimes unspeakable terrors. More than six million were methodically murdered. The concentration camp at Auschwitz was only one of many, but its name has come to represent the other camps as well and, more generally, the horror of all those years. Emil Fackenheim's essay, "Jewish Faith and the Holocaust," is an attempt to confront Auschwitz, for, as he explains, it *must* be confronted. To ignore Auschwitz or to simply join it with the other nightmares of our age would be to betray every victim of the holocaust.

Souls on Fire (New York: Random House, 1972), p. 209.
†*Ibid.,* p. 38.
‡Zen Buddhism and Hasidism are compared by Martin Buber in "The Place of Hasidism in the History of Religion," in his *Origin and Meaning of Hasidism,* edited and translated by Maurice Friedman (New York: Horizon Press, 1960).

will herberg

The Fundamental Outlook
of Hebraic Religion

Will Herberg (1906–   ), a graduate of Columbia University and Professor of Judaic Studies and Social Philosophy at Drew University, is the author of *The Writings of Martin Buber*, *Protestant–Catholic–Jew*, and *Four Existentialist Theologians*. The essay which follows is from his *Judaism and Modern Man*, a book Herberg describes as being "in the nature of a confession of faith." Its subtitle is *An Interpretation of Jewish Religion* because "to stand witness to one's faith and to try to communicate a sense of its meaning, power and relevance . . . [is] all that theology can pretend to do without falling into the delusion that it is speaking 'objectively' from the throne of God."

An initial understanding of what the Jewish religious commitment really signifies as an attitude to life may perhaps best be obtained by comparing the Hebraic world-outlook with the outlook of the very different type of religion manifested in Greco-Oriental spirituality. This comparison is not arbitary, nor is it merely conceived as an explanatory device. It really goes to the heart of the matter. For whatever may be thought of the so-called primitive religions, it seems to be the case that the higher religions of mankind fall into two main groups distinguished by widely different, often diametrically opposed preconceptions and attitudes. One group we may quite properly call Hebraic, for it includes Judaism, Christianity and Islam. The other group consists, as Moore points out, of "the soteric religions and philosophies of India and of Greece and the native and foreign mysteries of the Hellenistic-Roman world."[1] Perhaps the most appropriate designation for this type would be Greco-Oriental; Buddhism and Yoga are its best-known modern representatives.

It is not suggested that these religious types are manifested in pure form in any existing empirical religion; every existing religion would probably show, in its doctrine and practice, a varying mixture of elements stemming from both sources. But it is maintained that normative Judaism through the centuries has remained remarkably close to its Hebraic center, and that its "essence" can best be understood from this point of view. A brief presentation of the nature of the Hebraic religious outlook, in contrast to the outlook we have

[1]G. F. Moore, *The Birth and Growth of Religion* (Scribner's: New York, 1923), pp. 126-27.

called Greco-Oriental, will therefore serve as our point of departure for an account of the structure of faith in Judaism.

Hebraic and Greco-Oriental religion, as religion, agree in affirming some Absolute Reality as ultimate, but they differ fundamentally in what they say about this reality. To Greco-Oriental thought, whether mystical or philosophic, the ultimate reality is some primal impersonal force. To call it God, as so many have done, would be misleading; it is more nearly "godness" than God, an all-engulfing divine quality, the ground and end of everything. Whether one names it Brahma or the All-Soul or Nature (as Spinoza does) or nothing at all (as is the way of many mystics) does not really matter; what is meant is very much the same in all cases—some ineffable, immutable, impassive divine substance that pervades the universe or rather *is* the universe insofar as the latter is at all real. This, of course, is pantheism: the All is "God." Greco-Oriental religion, whatever its specific form, irresistibly tends towards a pantheistic position.

Nothing could be further from normative Hebraic religion. To Hebraic religion, God is neither a metaphysical principle nor an impersonal force. God is a living Will, a "living, active Being. . .endowed with personality."[2] As against the Greco-Oriental conception of *immanence,* of divinity permeating all things and constituting their reality, Hebraic religion affirms God as a *transcendent* Person, who has indeed created the universe but who cannot without blasphemy be identified with it. Where Greco-Oriental thought sees continuity between God and the universe, Hebraic religion insists on discontinuity. "Hebrew religion," Frankfort declares, "rejects precisely this doctrine [that the divine is immanent in nature]. The absolute transcendence of God is the foundation of Hebrew religious thought. God is absolute, unqualified, transcending every phenomenon. . . . God is not in sun and stars, rain and wind; they are his creatures and serve him."[3]

This radical difference in the conception of God makes for an equally profound divergence in attitude to life and the world. Both Greco-Oriental and Hebraic religion draw some distinction between the Absolute Reality that they affirm as ultimate and the empirical world of everyday experience. To the Buddhist theologian, the Hindu mystic or the Platonic philosopher, the empirical world is illusion, an unreal, shifting flux of sensory deception: only the Absolute, which is beyond time and change, is real. Life and history are therefore essentially meaningless; as temporal processes, they are hopelessly infected with the irrational and the unreal. True knowledge—saving knowledge—consists in breaking through the "veil of illusion" of empirical life, in sweeping this shadow world aside, in order to obtain a glimpse of the unchanging reality which it hides. This is the way of salvation.

To the Hebraic mind, on the other hand, the empirical world is real and significant, though not, of course, self-subsistent since it is ultimately depen-

[2] Meyer Waxman, *A Handbook of Judaism* (Bloch: New York, 1947), p. 134.
[3] Henri Frankfort, *Kingship and the Gods* (University of Chicago: Chicago, 1948), p. 343.

dent on God as Creator. Life and history, too, are real and meaningful, though again not in their own terms. As against Greco-Oriental otherworldliness, Hebraic religion strikes an unmistakably *this*-worldly note: this world, the world in which we pass our lives, the world in which history is enacted, the world of time and change and confusion, is the world in which the divine Will is operative and in which, however strange it may seem, man encounters God. Depreciation of this world in favor of some timeless world of pure being or essence is utterly out of line with the realistic temper of Hebraism.[4]

Since man is of course in some sense part of the empirical world, one's fundamental attitude to the world will find reflection in the conception one has of man and his nature. The drift of Greco-Oriental thought is quite clear: it affirms a body-soul dualism according to which the body—that is, matter—is held to be the principle of evil, and the soul—the mind or reason—the principle of good. In the Platonic figure, the body is the "prison-house of the soul";[5] as a result of its confinement in its carnal dungeon, the soul is confused and stupefied and dragged down into the mire of immorality. "For the Greeks," Moore writes, and what he says applies to all within the sphere of Greco-Oriental spirituality, "the soul is a fallen divinity . . . imprisoned in a material mortal body . . . [In earthy life] the soul is subject to physical and moral defilement; the body is the tomb of the soul or its prison-house, its transient tabernacle, its vesture of flesh, its filthy garment."[6] Death, which releases the immortal soul, is liberation.

However familiar and plausible this dualistic view may seem to many religious people today, it is nevertheless utterly contrary to the Hebraic outlook. In authentic Hebraism, man is not a compound of two "substances" but a dynamic unity. It is indeed necessary to distinguish between the natural and the spiritual dimensions of human life, but this is not a distinction between body and soul, much less between good and evil. The body, its impulses and passions, are not evil; as parts of God's creation, they are innocent and, when properly ordered, positively good. Nor, on the other hand, is human spirit the "fallen divinity" of the Greeks. Spirit is the source of *both* good and evil, for spirit is will, freedom, decision. It is impossible to imagine a more profound difference in orientation and outlook than is here revealed.

Equally profound is the divergence between the two religious outlooks in their view of man's spiritual condition and need. They agree, of course, in finding men in this world to be lost, forlorn, sunk in evil from which they must be saved. But they are poles apart in their conception of the nature of the evil and the way of salvation.

---

[4]"To the Hebrew, the world of phenomena, so far from being illusion, is the field of values. . . . And from this flows a correlated diversity in their fundamental conceptions of the role of religion. To the Indian, this is the attainment of peace; to the Jew, it is the realization of value." B. H. Streeter, *The Buddha and the Christ* (Macmillan: New York, 1933), p. 49.

[5]Plato *Phaedo* 66B, 67C, 67D; *Cratylus* 400C; *Phaedrus* 250C.

[6]Moore, *op. cit.,* p. 120.

Greco-Oriental religion finds the evil besetting men to be error and illusion. Men are so bedazzled by the empirical world that they actually take it for reality. They thus become involved in the world and attached to it; they develop cravings for its illusory "goods," thereby inviting pain and suffering. All the ills that afflict men are, in the view of Plato and the Buddha alike, the result of the benightedness that mistakes illusion for reality.

Perhaps the most dangerous of the errors that bedevil mankind, in this view, is the notion of individuality. Individuality is born out of illusion since the separateness of one man from another is simply an aspect of the world of empirical unreality; in its turn, individuality generates craving and greed, a grasping after things, a clinging to personality, which effectually blocks the hope of liberation from evil. "Individuality," Moore says, describing this type of religion, "is the great error, the cause of all man's ills . . . The real self, mistakenly imagined to be individual, is identical with the All-Soul and the end of man's being is to realize this identity."[7]

When we approach the same problem through Hebraic eyes, we move in an entirely different universe. Man's personality is taken as the inexpugnable reality of his being; it is because man is a person that he can hear God's word and respond to it. Nor, as we have seen, is the world itself unreal. That is not the source of evil. The evil condition, the lost state, from which man seeks salvation is, in the Hebraic view, his alienation from God. Man's proper condition is fellowship with God in faith and obedience. It is when man denies his faith and forgets his obedience, when he falls into egocentricity and self-absolutization, that he brings disorder to his own soul and confusion to the world. This self-absolutization in rebellion against God is *sin,* a concept central of Hebraic religion but, in its proper sense, quite unknown to Greek and Eastern thought.

We shall, of course, discuss in detail below this basic conception as well as the doctrine of salvation which it implies. But it may be said here that in Hebraic religion salvation for the individual consists essentially in repentance and reconciliation, in his abandoning his sinful pretensions and thankfully accepting the privilege of walking humbly with his God. Salvation is thus not the denial of personality but its enhancement through the power of personal communion in which all barriers of alienation are removed.

To the Yogi, Buddhist or neo-Platonic philosopher, this goal must seem both fantastic and delusive. How can personal relationship be established with the Ultimate Reality when personality itself is unreal and illusory? And what sort of salvation would it be, even if it were possible, since it would leave man actively involved in the things of this world? No, to Greco-Oriental religion, salvation is first of all "nonattachment," the breaking of all ties with the world of desire and body and matter, the annihilation of personality and ultimately its dissolution in the All-Soul as a drop of water is dissolved in the

[7]Moore, *op. cit.,* pp. 160, 99.

ocean. Only in the East, however, where there is no Hebraic heritage to restrain it, has mystic religion gone that far; but even where it stops halfway and speaks of salvation as the "beatific vision" or the "vision of God" after death, the tendency toward flight from the world and personal self-annihilation through "nearness to God" is unmistakable.[8]

If the question were put to the Buddhist or Hindu: "What am I? What shall I do to be saved?" his answer would be: "You are a fragment of the All-Soul whose effort it must be to find its way back to the Divine Whole." But if the same question were asked of one who holds to the biblical standpoint, the answer would be very different indeed. Man is a person, so the answer would run, a dynamic center of action, yet at the same time a creature, brought into being to serve his Creator in faith and love and thus achieve his salvation.[9] In one case, salvation is *from* life and *from* the world; in the other, it is *for* life and *for* the world.

There is still another radical distinction. For the Greek philosopher, as for the Hindu mystic, salvation is essentially self-salvation. "Primitive Buddhism and some other contemporary and cognate religions," Moore states, "acknowledge no power whose aid man can enlist to deliver him from the endless round of rebirth . . . ; he alone can be his own deliverer and by his own effort attain release in Nirvana. . . . They lodge in man the power to emancipate himself from the bondage of empirical humanity and the cycle of mundane existence."[10] The role of philosophy as conceived in neo-Platonic tradition is not essentially different.

To the Hebraic mind, such confident claims to self-salvation are nothing short of blasphemy. They amount to self-absolutization in its most presumptuous form. For man is thus held to be entirely self-sufficient; he does not need God, not even for his eternal salvation. What is this but outright atheism?[11]

The good life for man is life ordered to the Absolute. But what does this life imply? In Greco-Oriental view, the good life is a life of contemplation, in which all attachments to the empirical world are broken and all illusions as to

[8]"If at first he [Buber] regarded himself as a mystic, he later came to the conclusion that mysticism, which seeks through 'nearness to God' to submerge and efface man's individual character is essentially anti-religious and therefore non-Jewish." A. Steinberg, "The History of Jewish Religious Thought," *The Jewish People: Past and Present* (Central Yiddish Culture Organization: New York, 1946), I, 305.

[9]See the very significant article by John A. Hutchison, "The Biblical Idea of Vocation," *Christianity and Society,* Vol. XIII (Spring, 1948), No. 2.

[10]Moore, *op. cit.,* p. 19.

[11]Indeed, original Buddhism and many varieties of present-day Yoga must be regarded as explicitly atheistic. Speaking of Yoga and associated cults, Moore writes: "They worship no gods and they own no Lord (personal supreme God) . . . they undertake to show a man what he must do to achieve his own deliverance from the round of rebirth and its endless misery, to be his own savior without the aid of god or man." Moore, *op. cit.,* p. 149. "Nor [in primitive Buddhism] was there any god who could further a man in his pursuit of salvation, much less bestow it upon him." p. 153.

its reality dissipated; it is a life of total self-absorption, with illumination and finally mystic union as its goal. To the Hebraic mind, the good life is the life of action in the service of God and therefore of one's fellow-men. Nowhere is the contrast sharper than between the passionless quietism of the one and the active service of love of the other. The mystic or philosopher "sees and enjoys"; the man of the Bible "hears and obeys."[12]

Greco-Oriental religion is "beyond good and evil." In its view, ethics is instrumental, useful to clear the way for higher things. Obviously, no man can regard himself as "detached" from the world and free from craving if he still harbors hate or anger or envy; these therefore must be removed to start with. But the higher stages of the mystic way transcend ethical considerations of every kind: compassion and loving concern are likewise obstacles to self-liberation since they, too, are bonds that tie the aspirant down to the world of change and desire.

In Hebrew religion, ethics is central and ultimate for man, though God himself, of course, transcends ethical categories as he does all others. For man, the moral life, the life of personal concern and loving service, is not something to be left behind at any stage of spiritual development: man stands ever active in the service of the Absolute who is Lord of life.

That there is and must be a fulfilment beyond immediate life is an insight common to all higher religion. But as to what this fulfilment is and how it is related to our present life there is the very sharpest disagreement. Greek and Oriental religions contemplate not so much the fulfilment of life and history as escape from it. What is passionately longed for is the liberation of the soul from the body, from time and empirical existence, and its translation to an immaterial above-world out of time: "the emancipation of the soul," as Moore puts it, "from bondage to matter and sense and the realization of its divine nature."[13] The immortality of an immaterial soul by virtue of its own imperishable quality is the characteristic doctrine of the more familiar varieties of this type of religion.

In the Hebraic scheme, the great goal is not escape from life but its fulfilment. The prophetic proclamation of the Messianic Age and the "end of days" speaks of "a new heaven and new earth" in which all the possibilities of life will be realized and all human enterprises judged and fulfilled. The Hebraic outlook, which in its attitude to the world is so pronouncedly this-worldly, is here deepened and completed in a *trans*-worldly, *trans*-historical vision—a vision in which the ultimate meaning of life is revealed in terms of an

---

[12]"For the Bible, the fundamental religious encounter is God's call to man—a call not primarily to communion or contemplation but to action. . . . God calls us, puts us under orders, and sets us tasks in such a way that we become his servants, the instruments by which the divine purpose is accomplished in the world. And for us men, the meaning of our existence consists in responding to this call." Hutchison, *ibid.*

[13]Moore, *op. cit.,* p. 125.

"end" which ever confronts it. And this fulfilment is conceived as the fulfilment of the *whole man,* not merely of a disembodied soul; that is why rabbinic tradition is so insistent on the dogma of the resurrection of the dead, to the scandal of all modern minds. As in the beginning, so in the end: like the affirmation of a transcendent personal God, this hope of a "last day" on which life and history will achieve their fulfilment defines the unbridgeable gulf between Hebraic and Greco-Oriental spirituality. Here there can be no reconciliation, no compromise.[14]

Let us now summarize briefly the picture thus hastily sketched. Greco-Oriental religion affirms an impersonal immanent reality; Hebraism proclaims its allegiance to the Lord of life and history, the Creator of the universe, a transcendent Person with whom man can establish genuinely personal relations. Greco-Oriental thought negates the empirical world and urges that it be brushed aside as unreal and delusive. It finds the principle of evil in the body and in personal "separateness," which it associates with the body. It has no sense of sin or guilt, since it finds the root of man's trouble in the benighted state that leads him to take illusion for reality. It can assign no meaning to life or history since both are immersed in time while only the eternal is real. It assures man that he can achieve salvation—liberation from the world—through his own efforts without God. It holds out mystic illumination, the contemplative "vision of God" and, in its extreme form, even absorption in the All-Soul as the final goal. In the strictest sense of the term, it is self-annihilating and life-denying.

Hebraic religion, on the other hand, is self-affirming and life-enhancing. It sees in human personality the "image of God" and the source of spiritual creativity. "It is not the I that is given up," Martin Buber declares, speaking of Judaism, "but the false self-asserting impulse. . . . There is no self-love that is not self-deceit, but without being and remaining oneself, there is no love."[15] It does not split man into body and soul, but sees him whole, as a dynamic unity immersed in nature, yet transcending it by virtue of his freedom. Evil it finds not in matter or body or the natural impulses of life, but in a certain spiritual perversity which tempts man to try to throw off his allegiance to the Absolute and to make himself the center of his universe. From this sinful self-absolutization stems the disorder and misery of life, individual and

[14]Sikhism, which makes a deliberate effort to combine Hinduism with Christianity and Islam, has gone far in the direction of Hebraism but has stopped short at these two points: (1) it affirms an "Impersonal Formless God," and (2) it "looks to no decisive Day of Judgment with eternal reward and punishment, but rather to the continued development of the soul through countless rebirths, as in Hinduism, until it becomes at last ready for absorption in the Infinite Soul." H. W. Boulter, "Sikhism," *Religion in the Twentieth Century* (Philosophical Library: New York, 1948), pp. 197-98. On these two points there could be no syncretism.

[15]Buber, "The Question to the Single One," *Between Man and Man* (Kegan Paul: London, 1947), p. 43.

collective. There is no salvation except return to God in faith and repentance, no salvation except through the grateful acceptance of the divine forgiveness that alone can heal the soul rent with guilt and despair. Hebraic religion declares the life of moral action, the life of service to God in this world, to be the ultimate duty of man. It knows how to prize the inexhaustible resources of authentic communion with God in prayer, contemplation and study, but it never sees in this experience the ultimate end of human existence. It sees it rather as a never-failing source of spiritual power in the struggle of life and a sure refuge for the weary soul amidst the futilities and frustrations of existence. The "end" of life and history Hebraic religion envisions as the Kingdom of God, in which all our efforts, all our hopes and enterprises, will come to fruition and judgment.

Greco-Oriental spirituality is selfcentered and individualistic: "Salvation is in the strictest sense an achievement of the individual for himself and by himself."[16] Hebraism, on the other hand, holds salvation, like life itself, to be communal, and sees man's self-transcending service to fellow-man as the true service of God. Yet such is the ultimate paradox of life, that the self-absorption of the Buddhist or Yogi culminates in self-annihilation, while the sacrificial service enjoined by prophet and rabbi turns out to be the way toward personal fulfilment: "Identify your will with the will of God, that he may identify his will with yours."[17]

Such are the two world-outlooks. At bottom, they are irreconcilable, for what one affirms the other denies, and what one denies the other affirms. Between them, too, in their various forms and combinations, they exhaust the field of significant religious expression. How, then, is one to choose between them? By what criterion are we to make our choice? In the last analysis, there is no such criterion, for since these world-views are in fact ultimate orientations, there is nothing beyond in terms of which they can be judged. Affirmation of one or the other is concretely a matter of total existential commitment, a staking of our life and the "lives of all the generations" on the truth-for-us. Yet even here a less ultimate consideration may be allowed some weight. After explaining that, in the Greco-Oriental view, "salvation is an achievement of the individual for himself and by himself," Moore adds: "Buddha discovered the way and taught it to men." But *why?* Why, having discovered it, did he teach it to others? This question would seem to constitute an insurmountable stumbling block to Buddhism and to lead it to what in effect is a repudiation of itself. For if the highest good is, as Buddhism affirms, liberation of the self from empirical existence and the attainment of the "endless peace" of Nirvana and if, as Buddhism further affirms, the Buddha had acquired the knowledge necessary to achieve this goal, why then did he

[16]Moore, *op. cit.*, p. 153.
[17]*M.* Abot 2.4.

not make use of this saving knowledge "for himself and by himself"? Why, instead of liberating himself immediately as he might have done, did he suspend or postpone his liberation and go about preaching to his fellow-men? What was his concern with his fellowmen? In the Buddhist system, such behavior on the part of the Buddha and countless Buddhist preachers after him simply makes no sense; indeed, it seems to amount, as I have suggested, to a fundamental repudiation of Buddhism. It looks very much as if, at the crucial moment of decision, the Buddha acted not in accord with the imperative of Buddhism: "Save yourself by your own effort," but in accordance with the Hebraic imperative: "Thou shalt love thy neighbor as thyself." The very first act of Buddhism was thus in a basic sense a refutation of itself. In this self-contradiction, which permeates Greco-Oriental spirituality in all its forms, may perhaps be found the clue for a final judgment between the two irreconcilable religious world-views.

FROM *The Holy Scriptures*

The Holy Scriptures of Judaism are the thirty-nine books commonly known to Christians and others as the Old Testament. The concept of revelation, of God's revealing his will to men through prophets and through history, attaches a tremendous significance to these books, which chronicle that revelation and the Hebrews' response to it. Jews differ over the degree to which the Scriptures are to be considered the Word of God, but to all, in one sense or another, the Scriptures are inspired writings and they guide the life of Judaism.

The ancient Hebrews first committed some of their traditions to writing as early, perhaps, as the tenth century B.C., and the canon was not closed until early in the second century A.D. The Scriptures are thus the work of many authors, and they were edited and re-edited over the ages. Some books, such as Genesis, are themselves compilations of materials from different centuries. Until the recent discovery of the Dead Sea Scrolls, the oldest existing copies of the Old Testament in Hebrew dated from only the ninth or tenth century A.D.—remarkably late. But with the Scrolls of the Qumran Community by the Dead Sea were large portions of the Old Testament in Hebrew, dating from the last centuries before the time of Christ.

GENESIS

[*The first five books of the Scriptures are together called the Pentateuch, and tradition long held that Moses was their author. In Genesis alone, however, modern scholarship has discerned the work of three or more authors. The clearest evidence of multiple authorship appears early in Chapter 2, where there begins a* second *account of creation—which is believed to have been written centuries earlier than the creation account of Chapter 1.*]

Chapter 1

In the beginning God created the heaven and the earth. And the earth was without form, and void; and darkness was upon the face of the deep. And the spirit of God moved upon the face of the waters. And God said, "Let there be light": and there was light. And God saw the light, that it was good: and God divided the light from the darkness. And God called the light Day, and the darkness he called Night. And the evening and the morning were the first day.

And God said, "Let there be a firmament in the midst of the waters, and let it divide the waters from the waters". And God made the firmament, and divided the waters which were under the firmament from the waters which were above the firmament: and it was so. And God called the firmament Heaven. And the evening and the morning were the second day.

And God said, "Let the waters under the heaven be gathered together unto one place, and let the dry land appear": and it was so. And God called the dry land Earth; and the gathering together of the waters called he Seas: and God saw that it was good. And God said, "Let the earth bring forth grass, the herb yielding seed, and the fruit tree yielding fruit after his kind, whose seed is in itself, upon the earth": and it was so. And the earth brought forth grass, and herb yielding seed after his kind, and the tree yielding fruit, whose seed was in itself, after his kind: and God saw that it was good. And the evening and the morning were the third day.

And God said, "Let there be lights in the firmament of the heaven to divide the day from the night; and let them be for signs, and for seasons, and for days, and years: and let them be for lights in the firmament of the heaven to give light upon the earth": and it was so. And God made two great lights; the greater light to rule the day, and the lesser light to rule the night: he made the stars also. And God set them in the firmament of the heaven to give light upon the earth, and to rule over the day and over the night, and to divide the light from the darkness: and God saw that it was good. And the evening and the morning were the fourth day.

And God said, "Let the waters bring forth abundantly the moving creature that hath life, and fowl that may fly above the earth in the open firmament of heaven". And God created great whales, and every living creature that moveth, which the waters brought forth abundantly, after their kind, and every winged fowl after his kind: and God saw that it was good. And God blessed them, saying, "Be fruitful, and multiply, and fill the waters in the seas, and let fowl multiply in the earth". And the evening and the morning were the fifth day.

And God said, "Let the earth bring forth the living creature after his kind, cattle, and creeping thing, and beast of the earth after his kind": and it was so. And God made the beast of the earth after his kind, and cattle after their kind, and every thing that creepeth upon the earth after his kind: and God saw that it was good. And God said, "Let us make man in our image, after our likeness: and let them have dominion over the fish of the sea, and over the fowl of the air, and over the cattle, and over all the earth, and over every creeping thing that creepeth upon the earth". So God created man in his own image, in the image of God created he him; male and female created he them. And God blessed them, and God said unto them, "Be fruitful, and multiply, and replenish the earth, and subdue it: and have dominion over the fish of the sea, and over the fowl of the air, and over every living thing that moveth upon the earth". And God said, "Behold, I have given you every herb bearing seed, which is upon the face of all the earth, and every tree, in the which is the fruit of a tree yielding seed; to you it shall be for meat. And to every beast of the earth, and to every fowl of the air, and to every thing that creepeth upon the earth, wherein there is life, I have given every green herb for meat:'' and it was so. And God saw every thing that he had made, and, behold, it was very good. And the evening and the morning were the sixth day.

Chapter 2

Thus the heavens and the earth were finished, and all the host of them. And on the seventh day God ended his work which he had made; and he rested on the seventh day from all his work which he had made. And God blessed the seventh day, and sanctified it: because that in it he had rested from all his work which God created and made.

These are the generations of the heavens and of the earth when they were created, in the day that the LORD God made the earth and the heavens, and every plant of the field before it was in the earth, and every herb of the field before it grew: for the LORD God had not caused it to rain upon the earth, and there was not a man to till the ground. But there went up a mist from the earth, and watered the whole face of the ground. And the LORD God formed man of the dust of the ground, and breathed into his nostrils the breath of life; and man became a living soul. And the LORD God planted a garden eastward in Eden; and there he put the man whom he had formed. And out of the ground made the LORD God to grow every tree that is pleasant to the sight, and good for food; the tree of life also in the midst of the garden, and the tree of knowledge of good and evil. And a river went out of Eden to water the garden; and from thence it was parted, and became into four heads. The name of the first is Pison: that is it which compasseth the whole land of Havilah, where there is gold; and the gold of that land is good: there is bdellium and the onyx stone. And the name of the second river is Gihon: the same is it that compasseth the whole land of Ethiopia. And the name of the third river is Hiddekel: that is it which goeth toward the east of Assyria. And the fourth river is Euphrates. And the LORD God took the man, and put him into the garden of Eden to dress it and to keep it. And the LORD God commanded the man, saying, ''Of every tree of the garden thou mayest freely eat: but of the tree of the knowledge of good and evil, thou shalt not eat of it: for in the day that thou eatest thereof thou shalt surely die''.

And the LORD God said, ''It is not good that the man should be alone; I will make him an help meet for him''. And out of the ground the LORD God formed every beast of the field, and every fowl of the air; and brought them unto Adam to see what he would call them: and whatsoever Adam called every living creature, that was the name thereof. And Adam gave names to all cattle, and to the fowl of the air, and to every beast of the field; but for Adam there was not found an help meet for him. And the LORD God caused a deep sleep to fall upon Adam, and he slept: and he took one of his ribs, and closed up the flesh instead thereof; and the rib, which the LORD God had taken from man, made he a woman, and brought her unto the man. And Adam said, "This is now bone of my bones, and flesh of my flesh: she shall be called Woman, because she was taken out of Man". Therefore shall a man leave his father and his mother, and shall cleave unto his wife: and they shall be one flesh. And they were both naked, the man and his wife, and were not ashamed.

EXODUS

[*Moses, who is believed to have lived in the thirteenth century B.C., was a figure of epic dimensions. He led the Exodus itself, the great escape of the Israelites from the bondage of Egypt; but of even greater significance were the events he participated in at Mount Sinai. The covenant formed there, many would agree, represented the transformation of the early religion of the Israelites into the religion of Judaism.*]

Chapter 19

In the third month, when the children of Israel were gone forth out of the land of Egypt, the same day came they into the wilderness of Sinai. For they were departed from Rephidim, and were come to the desert of Sinai, and had pitched in the wilderness; and there Israel camped before the mount. And Moses went up unto God, and the LORD called unto him out of the mountain, saying, "Thus shalt thou say to the house of Jacob, and tell the children of Israel; 'Ye have seen what I did unto the Egyptians, and how I bare you on eagles' wings, and brought you unto myself. Now therefore, if ye will obey my voice indeed, and keep my covenant, then ye shall be a peculiar treasure unto me above all people: for all the earth is mine: and ye shall be unto me a kingdom of priests, and an holy nation.' These are the words which thou shalt speak unto the children of Israel." And Moses came and called for the elders of the people, and laid before their faces all these words which the LORD commanded him. And all the people answered together, and said, "All that the LORD hath spoken we will do". And Moses returned the words of the people unto the LORD. And the LORD said unto Moses, "Lo, I come unto thee in a thick cloud, that the people may hear when I speak with thee, and believe thee for ever". And Moses told the words of the people unto the LORD. And the LORD said unto Moses, "Go unto the people, and sanctify them to day and to morrow, and let them wash their clothes, and be ready against the third day: for the third day the LORD will come down in the sight of all the people upon mount Sinai. And thou shalt set bounds unto the people round about, saying, 'Take heed to yourselves, that ye go not up into the mount, or touch the border of it: whosoever toucheth the mount shall be surely put to death: there shall not an hand touch it, but he shall surely be stoned, or shot through; whether it be beast or man, it shall not live: when the trumpet soundeth long, they shall come up to the mount'." And Moses went down from the mount unto the people, and sanctified the people; and they washed their clothes. And he said unto the people, "Be ready against the third day: come not at your wives". And it came to pass on the third day in the morning, that there were thunders and lightnings, and a thick cloud upon the mount, and the voice of the trumpet exceeding loud; so that all the people that was in the camp trembled. And Moses brought forth the people out of the camp to meet with God; and they stood at the nether part of the mount. And mount Sinai was altogether on a smoke, because the Lord descended upon it in fire: and the smoke thereof ascended as the smoke of a furnace, and the whole mount quaked greatly. And when the voice of the trumpet sounded long, and waxed louder and louder, Moses spake, and God answered him by a voice. And the Lord came down upon mount Sinai, on the top of the mount: and the Lord called Moses up to the top of the mount; and Moses went up. And the Lord said unto Moses, "Go down, charge the people, lest they break through unto the Lord to gaze, and many of them perish. And let the priests also, which come near to the Lord, sanctify themselves, lest the Lord break forth upon them." And Moses said unto the Lord, "The people cannot come up to mount Sinai: for thou chargedst us, saying, 'Set bounds about the mount, and sanctify it'". And the Lord said unto him, "Away, get thee down, and thou shalt come up, thou, and Aaron with thee: but let not the priests and the people break through to come up unto the Lord, lest he break forth upon them". So Moses went down unto the people, and spake unto them.

Chapter 20

And God spake all these words, saying,

"I am the Lord thy God, which have brought thee out of the land of Egypt, out of the house of bondage.

"Thou shalt have no other gods before me.

"Thou shalt not make unto thee any graven image, or any likeness of anything that is in heaven above, or that is in the earth beneath, or that is in the water under the earth: thou shalt not bow down thyself to them, not serve them: for I the Lord thy God am a jealous God, visiting the iniquity of the fathers upon the children unto the third and fourth generation of them that hate me; and shewing mercy unto thousands of them that love me, and keep my commandments.

"Thou shalt not take the name of the Lord thy God in vain; for the Lord will not hold him guiltless that taketh his name in vain.

"Remember the sabbath day, to keep it holy. Six days shalt thou labour, and do all thy work: but the seventh day is the sabbath of the Lord thy God: in it thou shalt not do any work, thou, not thy son, nor thy daughter, thy manservant, nor thy maidservant, nor thy cattle, nor thy stranger that is within thy gates: for in six days the LORD made heaven and earth, the sea, and all that in them is, and rested the seventh day: wherefore the LORD blessed the sabbath day and hallowed it.

"Honour thy father and thy mother: that thy days may be long upon the land which the LORD thy God giveth thee.

"Thou shalt not kill.

"Thou shalt not commit adultery.

"Thou shalt not steal.

"Thou shalt not bear false witness against thy neighbour.

"Thou shalt not covet thy neighbour's house, thou shalt not covet thy neighbour's wife nor his manservant, nor his maidservant, nor his ox, nor his ass, nor any thing that is thy neighbour's."

. . .

ISAIAH

[*The great prophets appeared over a period of centuries. They exhorted the Hebrews to return to the path of righteousness, and they pronounced dire warnings of catastrophes to come if their words were not heeded. Through them the old faith was renewed with fresh insight, and the ethical conscious-ness of the religion was heightened.*

Chapters 1 through 39 of the Book of Isaiah *are from an eighth-century prophet, the "Isaiah of Faith." But from Chapter 40 on, a different style and tone and other internal evidence suggest a sixth-century* second *Isaiah, the "Prophet of the Exile."*]

Chapter 1

The vision of Isaiah the son of Amoz, which he saw concerning Judah and Jerusalem in the days of Uzziah, Jotham, Ahaz, and Hezekiah, kings of Judah.

Hear, O heavens, and give ear, O earth:
For the LORD hath spoken,
"I have nourished and brought up children,
And they have rebelled against me.
The ox knoweth his owner,
And the ass his master's crib:
But Israel doth not know,
My people doth not consider."
Ah sinful nation, a people laden with iniquity,
A seed of evil doers, children that are corrupters:
They have forsaken the LORD,

They have provoked the Holy One of Israel unto anger,
They are gone away backward.
Why should ye be stricken any more?
Ye will revolt more and more:
The whole head is sick, and the whole heart faint.
From the sole of the foot even unto the head there is no soundness in it;
But wounds, and bruises, and putrifying sores:
They have not been closed, neither bound up, neither mollified with ointment.
Your country is desolate,
Your cities are burned with fire:
Your land, strangers devour it in your presence,
And it is desolate, as overthrown by strangers.
And the daughter of Zion is left as a cottage in a vineyard,
As a lodge in a garden of cucumbers,
As a besieged city.
Except the LORD of hosts had left unto us a very small remnant,
We should have been as Sodom,
And we should have been like unto Gomorrah.

Hear the word of the LORD, ye rulers of Sodom;
Give ear unto the law of our God, ye people of Gomorrah.
"To what purpose is the multitude of your sacrifices unto me?" saith the
  LORD?
"I am full of the burnt offerings of rams, and the fat of fed beasts;
And I delight not in the blood of bullocks, or of lambs, or of he goats.
When ye come to appear before me,
Who hath required this at your hand, to tread my courts?
Bring no more vain oblations; incense is an abomination unto me;
The new moons and sabbaths, the calling of assemblies, I cannot away with;
It is iniquity, even the solemn meeting.
Your new moons and your appointed feasts my soul hateth:
They are a trouble unto me;
I am weary to bear them.
And when ye spread forth your hands, I will hide mine eyes from you:
Yea, when ye make many prayers, I will not hear:
Your hands are full of blood.
Wash you, make you clean; put away the evil of your doings from before mine
  eyes;
Cease to do evil; learn to do well;
Seek judgment, relieve the oppressed,
Judge the fatherless, plead for the widow.

"Come now, and let us reason together," saith the LORD:
"Though your sins be as scarlet, they shall be as white as snow;
Though they be red like crimson, they shall be as wool.

If ye be willing and obedient, ye shall eat the good of the land:
But if ye refuse and rebel,
Ye shall be devoured with the sword:"
For the mouth of the LORD hath spoken it.

How is the faithful city become an harlot!
It was full of judgment; righteousness lodged in it;
But now murderers.
Thy silver is become dross,
The wine mixed with water:
Thy princes are rebellious, and companions of thieves:
Every one loveth gifts, and followeth after rewards:
They judge not the fatherless,
Neither doth the cause of the widow come unto them.

Therefore saith the Lord, the LORD of hosts, the Mighty One of Israel,
"Ah, I will ease me of mine adversaries,
And avenge me of mine enemies:
And I will turn my hand upon thee,
And purely purge away thy dross,
And take away all thy tin:
And I will restore thy judges as at the first,
And thy counsellors as at the beginning:
Afterward thou shalt be called,
The city of righteousness, the faithful city".
Zion shall be redeemed with judgment,
And her converts with righteousness.
And the destruction of the transgressors and of the sinners shall be together,
And they that forsake the LORD shall be consumed.
For they shall be ashamed of the oaks which ye have desired,
And ye shall be confounded for the gardens that ye have chosen.
For ye shall be as an oak whose leaf fadeth,
And as a garden that hath no water.
And the strong shall be as tow,
And the maker of it as a spark,
And they shall both burn together, and none shall quench them.

Chapter 40

"Comfort ye, comfort ye my people," saith your God.
"Speak ye comfortably to Jerusalem, and cry unto her,
That her warfare is accomplished,
That her iniquity is pardoned:
For she hath received of the LORD's hand double for all her sins."

The voice of him that crieth in the wilderness, "Prepare ye the way of the
    LORD,
Make straight in the desert a highway for our God.
Every valley shall be exalted,
And every mountain and hill shall be made low:
And the crooked shall be made straight,
And the rough places plain:
And the glory of the LORD shall be revealed,
And all flesh shall see it together:
For the mouth of the LORD hath spoken it."
The voice said, "Cry".
And he said, "What shall I cry?"
"All flesh is grass,
And all the goodliness thereof is as the flower of the field:
The grass withereth, the flower fadeth:
Because the spirit of the LORD bloweth upon it:
Surely the people is grass.
The grass withereth, the flower fadeth:
But the word of our God shall stand for ever."

O Zion, that bringest good tidings, get thee up into the high mountain;
O Jerusalem, that bringest good tidings, lift up thy voice with strength;
Lift it up, be not afraid;
Say unto the cities of Judah, "Behold your God!"
Behold, the Lord GOD will come with strong hand,
And his arm shall rule for him:
Behold, his reward is with him,
And his work before him.
He shall feed his flock like a shepherd:
He shall gather the lambs with his arm,
And carry them in his bosom,
And shall gently lead those that are with young.

Who hath measured the waters in the hollow of his hand,
And meted out heaven with the span,
And comprehended the dust of the earth in a measure,
And weighed the mountains in scales,
And the hills in a balance?
Who hath directed the spirit of the LORD,
Or being his counsellor hath taught him?
With whom took he counsel, and who instructed him,
And taught him in the path of judgment,
And taught him knowledge,
And shewed to him the way of understanding?

Behold, the nations are as a drop of a bucket,
And are counted as the small dust of the balance:
Behold, he taketh up the isles as a very little thing.
And Lebanon is not sufficient to burn,
Nor the beasts thereof sufficient for a burnt offering.
All nations before him are as nothing;
And they are counted to him less than nothing, and vanity.
To whom then will ye liken God?
Or what likeness will ye compare unto him?
The workman melteth a graven image,
And the goldsmith spreadeth it over with gold,
And casteth silver chains.
He that is so impoverished that he hath no oblation chooseth a tree that will
not rot;
He seeketh unto him a cunning workman
To prepare a graven image, that shall not be moved.
Have ye not known? have ye not heard?
Hath it not been told you from the beginning?
Have ye not understood from the foundations of the earth?
It is he that sitteth upon the circle of the earth,
And the inhabitants thereof are as grasshoppers;
That stretcheth out the heavens as a curtain,
And spreadeth them out as a tent to dwell in:
That bringeth the princes to nothing;
He maketh the judges of the earth as vanity.
Yea, they shall not be planted;
Yea, they shall not be sown:
Yea, their stock shall not take root in the earth:
And he shall also blow upon them, and they shall wither,
And the whirlwind shall take them away as stubble.
"To whom then will ye liken me, or shall I be equal?" said the Holy One.
Lift up your eyes on high,
And behold who hath created these things,
That bringeth out their host by number:
He calleth them all by names
By the greatness of his might, for that he is strong in power;
Not one faileth.

Why sayest thou, O Jacob, and speakest, O Israel,
"My way is hid from the LORD,
And my judgment is passed over from my God"?
Hast thou not known? hast thou not heard,
That the everlasting God, the LORD,
The Creator of the ends of the earth,

CHAPTER SEVEN / *Judaism*

Fainteth not, neither is weary?
There is no searching of his understanding.
He giveth power to the faint;
And to them that have no might he increaseth strength.
Even the youths shall faint and be weary,
And the young men shall utterly fall:
But they that wait upon the LORD shall renew their strength;
They shall mount up with wings as eagles;
They shall run, and not be weary;
And they shall walk, and not faint.

PSALMS

[*The Psalms are the hymns or songs of the Israelites, most of them composed from the fifth through the first century B.C. Their beauty and simplicity have contributed to their perennial popularity, as has the fact that they represent the voices of individuals addressing God. Otherwise, the ideas contained in the Psalms are as varied as those of the* Old Testament *in its entirety*.]

Psalm 1

Blessed is the man
That walketh not in the counsel of the ungodly,
Nor standeth in the way of sinners,
Nor sitteth in the seat of the scornful.
But his delight is in the law of the LORD;
And in his law doth he meditate day and night.
And he shall be like a tree planted by the rivers of water,
That bringeth forth his fruit in his season;
His leaf also shall not wither;
And whatsoever he doeth shall prosper.
The ungodly are not so:
But are like the chaff which the wind driveth away.
Therefore the ungodly shall not stand in the judgment,
Nor sinners in the congregation of the righteous.
For the LORD knoweth the way of the righteous:
But the way of the ungodly shall perish.

Psalm 96

O sing unto the LORD a new song:
Sing unto the LORD, all the earth.
Sing unto the LORD, bless his name;
Shew forth his salvation from day to day.

Declare his glory among the heathen,
His wonders among all people.
For the LORD is great, and greatly to be praised:
He is to be feared above all gods.
For all the gods of the nations are idols:
But the LORD made the heavens.
Honour and majesty are before him:
Strength and beauty are in his sanctuary.
Give unto the LORD, O ye kindreds of the people,
Give unto the LORD glory and strength.
Give unto the LORD the glory due unto his name:
Bring an offering, and come into his courts.
O worship the LORD in the beauty of holiness:
Fear before him, all the earth.
Say among the heathen that the LORD reigneth:
The world also shall be established that it shall not be moved:
He shall judge the people righteously.
Let the heavens rejoice, and let the earth be glad;
Let the sea roar, and the fulness thereof.
Let the field be joyful, and all that is therein:
Then shall all the trees of the wood rejoice
Before the LORD: for he cometh,
For he cometh to judge the earth:
He shall judge the world with righteousness,
And the people with his truth.

leo baeck _____

The Covenant

Leo Baeck (1873–1956) was a scholarly rabbi whose religious commitments were also commitments to action. Born in Poland, Baeck earned a Ph.D. at the University of Berlin and served as an army chaplain on both the eastern and western fronts in World War I. During the years prior to World War II he became the leader of German Jewry. Rejecting opportunities to flee from Germany, he chose instead to share the fate of those Jews who could not escape, and he spent the war years in a concentration camp. "Late at night, the prisoners would crowd into one of the barracks and listen to Baeck lecture on a variety of subjects. They would listen—and they ceased being numbers and once again became human beings. In the daytime, Baeck would walk around the camp, and peace and comfort walked with him."* After the war he taught in the United States and in England.

One of his most important books, *The Essence of Judaism,* was published in 1905, and over the years a flood of books poured from his pen. *This People Israel,* from which the following selection is taken, was his last work, finished only days before his death. It was a book "written during dark times," Baeck explained in the Preface. A large portion of the book was originally composed in the concentration camp, "on any scrap of paper that came to hand, whenever a quiet hour was to be found."

THE INNER AND THE OUTER WORLD

Every people, particularly in its youth, wishes to possess the account of its beginning; its legends and poems sing of it, and many peoples desire to be descended from gods and heroes. But it is unique that one people found its special origin, its foundation, in the origin of all origins, in the foundation of the universe. Coming forth from the precincts of the eternal and the infinite, the revelation of the One who exists behind all multiplicity assigned to it the task of life. The world beyond spoke of the beginning and the essence of this people, and proclaimed to it the conditions and the goal of its history. Out of all peoples, only the people of Israel experienced this in its youth and preserved it for all time. God, the One and Eternal, the Creator and Ruler, had become central to all that Israel experienced, and He was therefore the measure for all its action and striving. In Him, Israel had the explanation for its special life. The word which He had spoken, the demand He had made,

*Albert Friedlander, in his introduction to Leo Baeck, *This People Israel* (New York: Holt, Rinehart and Winston, 1964), p. xiv.

had increasingly become to this people the constant and only answer whenever it desired to inquire about the meaning of its particular fate. To this people, its beginning thus became an idea. In a sense it knew itself as a people emerging out of the beyond, as a people of metaphysical existence, a people brought into existence by a revelation of God and on behalf of a revelation of God.

Ever since men began to reflect, ever since they began to search for reasons and relationships in what they experienced and observed, and philosophy and religion began to develop, they came to understand that human life moves in two spheres. At times this insight was obscured; at times it was clear. Life disclosed itself to them from without, through the senses, and was quantified by measuring, weighing, and counting. Life also opened itself to them from within, through feelings and desires which became doubts, certainties, and decisions. At times men turned outwards; at times they harked within. Intellectual developments were carried by both spheres through the centuries. In both realms, certain proprieties, relationships, and anticipations have become knowledge: from without, certainty comes through rationality, through measuring, weighing, and building; from within, something different, the unmeasurable, the unweighable, the irrational, shows the way.

Men who reflect are at times more capable of entering the one sphere, at times more capable of penetrating the other. The same division is found in the talents of peoples. It is the characteristic genius through which the Jewish people defined its uniqueness that it constantly refined its knowledge; it attempted and succeeded in understanding both spheres. It understood them not only in terms of their own specific actuality, but also, above all, in terms of the relationships existing between them. The Jewish spirit has always sought to grasp the oneness of all of reality. All reality, whether unfolding itself in one sphere or in the other, expresses one great unity to the Jewish spirit. It comes from the One God, is created by Him, and reveals Him. Only the One God exists, and therefore there is only one order, no matter how manifold its appearances, how contradictory its representations. The natural and the spiritual, the external and the internal, cannot be separated from one another if they are to become known. They arise from the One. They are His creation, His revelation.

The rational and the irrational do not contradict one another here; they are related. They cannot be understood without each other. The irrational is the root of the rational, the predicate of its existence and its validity; and the rational is an expression of the irrational, a form in which the irrational reveals itself. An irrational reality that sought to be self-validating would remain formless and void of development; and a rational reality, limited to itself, would ever remain without solid foundation, without deep security. The unity of the rational and irrational was always recognized in the Jewish spirit, even though the ways and means of expressing this unity in a definite fashion took time to develop. But once begun, the forms which it unfolded were ever fresh and new.

This people Israel came to have a particular understanding of this view of reality through its history, and was persuaded by it. Its history is something clear to this people, a clear way, a clear task, a clear commandment; but it rises out of the world of the mystery, out of the supernal unity, out of the deepest foundation of everything that is.

In this perspective Israel received the form of its spiritual being. Little was given to it by way of external security or protected days. In place of such, it received inner security and certainty. It knew that the root of its being is in the One and Eternal, that the integrity and meaning of its life emanates from this source. He alone had become Israel's great certainty. A *beyond* sustained the moment; that which had been was the foundation of what Israel was becoming. Because it found its source in Him, Israel was often considered rootless by those who wanted to draw their strength from the terrestrial; and, at times, Israel was accounted godless and atheistic by those whose powers and deities had established their altars upon the earth. For this people, history—its own and that of all peoples—developed out of final causes. Historical consciousness was first of all knowledge of the One God, and, at the same time, a knowledge of the beginning and the totality of all men, of humanity. What it experienced in itself became a testimony and an instruction that reached far beyond its own boundaries. Israel could thus appear to be without history to those peoples who had entrapped themselves in self-contemplation and regarded only their own soil and surroundings as having the power to speak to them of history's meaning.

THE TASK OF EXISTENCE

The religion of this people, in which its genius matured, in which alone it could flourish, is marked by a unique concept: human existence elevated into the realm of the task and the chosenness of man. Everything given to man in his existence becomes a commandment; all that he has received means "Thou shalt!" The word "life" acquired a different content from that which it received in other cultures. Not only the conduct of individual life, but the form of communal life in which the individual participates, is converted into a matter of personal decision. Man is born both into individual life and into communal life, without his willing it and without any action on his part. Man, with his own will and actions, with the self given to him by God, stands amidst both his lives and makes them into his task. They are now the meaning which God has assigned for him. Because he was born, they became the place in which he lives, they are the path he walks, the way which God commands him; and it is also God's ways that are to radiate outward from this place. Human existence becomes a task assigned by God. By the fulfillment of

God's commandment a people must truly become itself. It must make itself into a people. In Israel this task was fully experienced and exhibited. The idea of the beginning of the people and the idea of God's choice cohered as one. This people was given a direction. It had been chosen by the One, the Eternal; and the One, the Eternal, was to renew the choice. It could only understand its existence and its history as God's mission among men.

One verse therefore became almost a title for this people, a motto for its beginning: "Thou hast avouched Him-Who-Is this day to be thy God. . . . And He-Who-Is hath avouched thee this day to be His own treasure . . ." (Deut. 26:17—18).[1] It is thus that Moses, the servant of Him-Who-Is, spoke to this people whom he was the first to form. A poetic prophet later found a tender personal expression by which to let God address the people:

And I will betroth thee unto Me for ever;
Yea, I will betroth thee unto Me in righteousness, and in justice,
And in lovingkindness, and in compassion.
And I will betroth thee unto Me in faithfulness;
And thou shalt know Him-Who-Is. (*Hosea 2:21–22*)

The knowledge of God and the knowledge of self became a unity that remains indivisible in this people. Whether Israel lived through bright or dark days, it always knew who was above it and who was before it. It was embraced by the "everlasting arms" (Deut. 33:27), the *brachia sempiterna*. Its history thereby assumed the kind of meaning that signifies greatness.

At this moment its history is a history of millennia, and understandably it comprehends a diversity of times and persons. At some times and in various places the people were few and their achievements small. The saying that the corruption of the best is the worst corruption—*corruptio optimi pessima*—was a palimpsest of many a line of this history. Nonetheless, someone who views the whole becomes aware of what might almost be termed a sublimity. That great trait, that trait of ultimate loyalty toward the Eternal and His word, remains in constant evidence. Through each of the many centuries, no matter how this or that person in the House of Israel acquitted himself, despite every divergent way, including wrong ways and detours, the idea that Israel had to be a people before God continued to shine clearly. It is for this reason that the existence of Israel has historic value.

Only as a people of meaning could, and can, this people Israel be. Only thus can it exist before God and before itself. It can consider its history only from

[1]*Er, der ist,* Baeck's rendering of the Tetragrammaton, usually given in English as "Lord," I have translated throughout as "He-Who-Is." Otherwise, biblical quotations are taken from *The Holy Scriptures According to the Masoretic Text: A New Translation* (The Jewish Publication Society of America: Philadelphia, 1917), except where Baeck's translation of Scriptures, which is always his own, requires, in context, a different rendering. [Translator]

the perspective of God. It is to be a people in relation to God, not simply a people in relation to other peoples. One of its historians, in the days when its individuality was first brought to view before the world, Flavius Josephus, created the word theocracy. This people's constitution is founded in God's commandment; it is to be a people that is predisposed to God, one that in all its development, its wandering, in all of the ebb and flow of history, must remain within its relationship toward the One-Who-Is. Israel is not only to be a people within history, but the people of history. And with the desire to be this, it becomes at the same time the people of humanity. As it cannot and may not think of itself without God, it cannot see itself without all of humanity. Universal history and Israel's particular history become one. "I will . . . give thee for a covenant of the people" (Is. 42:6; 49:8). This people stands on earth within a covenant that encloses all people and is valid for everyone.

Its ways have led it, perhaps had to lead it, through days and even epochs in which it was fated to seek humanity and not to find it. A foreign world confronted it, bitter and hard, cold and cruel, a world of injustice, of incomprehension, of blasphemy. A moral chasm, a spiritual abyss, seemed to have opened up; Israel lived alone. When it looked about, it could not see where humanity dwelt. For the sake of humanity it had to feel separate from the many peoples. To the author of the Book of Daniel, the father of the apocalypse, the great kingdoms, the rulers of might and culture once appeared in the form of wild animals; he saw only his people in the likeness of human beings.

In such days, when this people meditated concerning the future of humanity, it could look only toward its own future. It had no other choice. If it had no future, humanity had none. And when it looked about for a way which would lead to a time of humanity, the idea of judgment had to awaken within it, the idea of the avenging, eternal judgment which alone would create a place for humanity. For the sake of humanity, this idea had to come to life. For only if the punishing judgment of God would fall on all of these masters and servants of blasphemy, only then would those lands once again become pure and free and wide, so that humanity would be able to live there. It is anger, often fiery anger, which speaks here, but humanity's yearning and conscience seek expression in it. It contains more true humanness than is found in many a sweet song of man. The soul of a people of humanity wrestles here. At this point the call "for a covenant of the people" has captured the soul.

The word covenant (*berit* in Hebrew), which now confronts us, has a consistent emphasis within the sacred scriptures of Israel. The book became the Bible, the book of humanity, and with it this word, covenant, assumed its place among the great words of humanity. Following the period of Alexander the Great, at a time when East and West sought to find each other, the Bible was translated into Greek; and this word was reproduced by a Greek expression which belonged in essence to legal terminology. It could and did happen in the Greco-Christian world that the word became a juristic-theological concept with all of the formality and occasional artificiality of such a concept. But in the Bible the word is elemental, alive, filled with a germinating and unfolding meaning. Through the religion of this people, a unique power developed within its language, enabling it to unfold new and living content out of archaic words. A language of religion and of humanity developed. In it, the word covenant, too, was taken far beyond it beginnings.

In the inscriptions of old Arabian tribes, the Sabeans and the Minaens, this word was already used as a general term indicating the relationship of a tribe to its deity, a contract between them, binding upon both parties. But in the language of the Bible it was lifted into the sphere of revolutionary meaning. It became a characteristic religious word, one of those words in which the idea of the great interrelatedness, the great unity of all, of mystery and ordered certainty, seeks to express itself. The God-given order was to find expression in this term—the here and the beyond, the near and the far, earth and heaven. This order is equally a covenant, for man and his free will are introduced into the covenant so that the *berit* might become the rule of man's domain. Poetry dared even the bolder image that the covenant was also a decision of nature to recognize and to accept this order.

Whatever its linguistic origins, the word *berit* entered the Bible. Through the religious power which it contains, the word became the expression of this order. It is the expression of that which is to endure because God has made it part of the beings and forms which He has created, the condition for their unity and interrelatedness, the prerequisite for reality itself. This makes it possible for a psalm to parallel the word *berit* with: "The word which He commanded to a thousand generations" (Ps. 105:8); and, then, with the word "statute" (Ps. 105:10). Later, the old Aramaic translation of the Bible, more concerned with the inner content than with the outer form of the word, translated *berit* as *kayama,* the established, the firmly founded, the enduring, the existing, indicating that which is above all change, above all that comes and goes.

The closest approximation to the meaning of the word *berit* is the word "law." Or, we could say that the concept of law (no matter how it has been developed in other languages) has here been given in the Hebrew a more vigorous, more inclusive sense, a more dynamic content. A comparison will clarify this. In the Greek language the word "law," *nomos,* indicated something functional within a totality, an effectively forming and defining force. To the Romans, the word "law," *lex,* indicated, rather, something organic, constructive, the great coordination, the secure structure of human relations.

In the Bible, the idea of law, as suggested by the word *berit,* encompasses the idea of the living creation through the One, and the living revelation of the One, the idea of the beyond entering the present. Law, creation, revelation—all are fused in a single word.

What is law? In it and through it, all endures that has been created and revealed; that is, this creation, this revelation. Law is the continually active order of creation and revelation, which find in law their ever-new and yet ever-identical expression. Ground and appearance are related through the law. The law is that in which and through which the changing and the abiding, the visible-audible and the invisible-inaudible, the rational and the irrational, are one. In the world of nature it confronts us as the cosmos which is simply there; in the human world it confronts us as a cosmos which, ever again, ought to come into being. Law, creation, revelation, they are the same, they are God's "covenant." The word "covenant" first signified a contract. The contract became the law in which creation and revelation find expression. Above, below, before and after, all that comes and goes is that which is and remains, the covenant of the One.

That this *berit* lives, that it binds and rules eternally and everywhere, has become the faith of Israel. Ever again it has ascertained this. All comes from the One and is oriented toward the One—law is established by the One God. He has established it in the universe and among men. Nothing is outside this enduring covenant, nothing exists without it—this became the particular certainty of Israel within an encompassing metaphysical certainty. The law of this people endures—this people is called by the One God to the law so that the law might become its life and its future. Within the covenant made with the world and all its creatures, there is God's covenant with this people and its history.

Prophets experience the certitude of God and His covenant. This certitude went forth from them and became the experience of their people, and afterward an experience for the peoples of the world. Within every thing, therefore, there exists an inner reality—unique, one, concealed, unfathomable, infinite, eternal—which is its foundation. It is the all-embracing, so that no one and no thing can exist beside it or outside it. No one may suppose that he exists only for himself or within his own realm. Man is always in this oneness and of it, lost in it and yet facing it. He is seemingly embraced, seen, and heard by it, and can never elude nor evade it. He is never able to make his way solely on his own, nor can he be related only to himself. He is always recognized, he is taken, he is held. Always and everywhere, man is encompassed by an eternal certainty, embraced by the arms of eternity. He is therefore never forsaken and never lost, nowhere alone, nowhere condemned forever. He is never surrendered or wholly abandoned to anyone. Rather, he is always supported by the One, the unfathomable. At all hours, in all places, this was the living experience. We human beings can therefore strive toward the nearness and the power of this Incomprehensible, Eternal One. We can aspire toward union with it, yearn for it, and trust in it. This eternal *I* that speaks to us, this I of all I's, from which all emanates, is that which creates all, determines all, beholds all, analyzes all. This I is for all at once the enduring *Thou,* a Thou of all Thous. Everyone can look to it, call to it, can elevate himself to it, and can bring his anguish and fears to it. The eternal, infinite covenant is sealed.

Anyone who has fully experienced how he has come to be, how he is sustained, how he is guided, cannot fail to see something else. He learns that simultaneously a demand is affirmed that can no longer be ignored. The direction has been shown. He has been given a task, and with it, a promise has been granted him. Out of the concealed, the distant, the beyond, out of the unique, the One, out of the eternal, infinite I, the inexorable *Thou shalt* reaches every man, quite intimate, quite clear. He now becomes Thou, named thus by the One. To everyone, wherever he might be, the word of the One God comes as a command, and simultaneously as a promise.

THE LAW AND THE COMMANDMENT

The experience of the One revealed to Israel that a commandment confronts man. It is always the same commandment, because it is the commandment of God. Yet it is also always new, because it is the commandment of each and every hour. Man is to fulfill it; a purpose is set before him. As long as he lives, he is on the way; as long as he lives, the way lies before him. Fulfillment itself can be found only at the end of the way. Man can only direct his vision toward it, for man is finite. But that is the great design, man's answer to the limitations of human existence. Wherever a man travels on the right way, achievement is already his, for he fulfills there and then a commandment of God.

God demands from man, and with this the greatest has already been given to him. God has awaited him, and with this the greatest has already been assured. It is a paradox that God's will can be realized through man. The Eternal's everlasting will can be, and is to be, the will of mortal man. What is demanded is the pledge; the commandment is the promised possession. Through the fulfillment of the commandment man becomes as I out of God's I: I by the grace of God. The individual becomes a personality, becomes a chosen one. The language of the Bible attempts to express this by saying that man is made in the image of God. Every *Thou art* is also a *Thou shalt*. Man is the image of Him who is the eternal, infinite I. Through God, man becomes I, his particular self, someone special within the world. He is that because he is someone to whom God calls "Thou," someone called forward by God and addressed by Him. God says to him, "Thou," and thus makes him I. From the eternal I, through the "Thou shalt," a particular uniqueness enters into his life and makes him conscious of his I. Now he can also speak to God, can say to Him, "Thou art my God."

The law becomes a reality by the fact that man realizes it. He now shares the law, shares God's covenant. This vision of decision, this moral imagery given to this people to take along its way, went forth from it to all the world. And because such an experience existed, because an historical decision grew out of it, this people, throughout the process of having to become I, possesses a clear beginning and a clear way. It always learned anew in order to know the covenant. It always had the living experience of this totality, the one, the decisive. It always held to the truth that every final condition and limitation, every true demand and certainty, is rooted in a metaphysical reality, in a world beyond the terrestrial. It understood this beyond, this domain of the eternal and the unending, because it was able to comprehend how the beyond entered into the here and now as the creation and the revelation of the One. It comprehended how the beyond, as the foundation that supports all, as the order which determines all, lives in all that changes and moves. Thus was it experienced: there is something permanent in everything, *one* standard is given for all, *one* law sealed into all. A covenant exists and endures.

This covenant is God's covenant with Noah and his descendants. "Noah was in his generations a man righteous and whole-hearted; Noah walked with God" (Gen. 6:9). He alone survived the destruction of a world that had become corrupt and had been destroyed to clear it for a renewed creation. This covenant, within the new humanity, is also the covenant with the father of this people, Israel, with Abraham, and with his descendants. God had spoken to Abraham: "Get thee out of thy country, and from thy kindred, and from thy father's house . . . and be thou a blessing . . . and in thee shall all the families of the earth be blessed" (Gen. 12:1–3). God had "Known him, to the end that he may command his children and his household after him, that they may keep the way of Him-Who-Is, to do righteousness and justice" (Gen. 18:19).

The covenant with the world and with the human race is, logically and theologically, first in the order of experience; psychologically, however, the covenant with Noah was within Israel from the very beginning. The sense of humanity and of the world as universe was experienced by this people as its own history.

The Way of Man According to the Teachings of Hasidism

Martin Buber (1878–1965) is the best-known and most widely praised Jewish philosopher in this century. Born in Vienna, he spent his youth in Poland and received a traditional Jewish upbringing and education. It was in Poland that he first came into contact with Hasidim, and they made an indelible impression on him. Buber was later to stress the influence upon him of some of the forerunners of existentialism (Kierkegaard, Dostoyevsky, Nietzsche), and he studied intensively Christian mystics such as Jacob Boehme and Meister Eckhart. But it was in and through Hasidism that the existential and mystical aspects of his thought were able to blend with his own Jewish heritage.

Buber's interests and work ranged wide. He studied at the University of Vienna and received a doctorate in philosophy from the University of Berlin. He spent a period of years immersed in Hasidic writings, eventually publishing a long series of works full of the lore and wisdom of the Hasidim. An early leader in the Zionist movement, he was also a professor at the University of Frankfort until Nazi pressure forced him to resign. In Jerusalem he was a professor at the Hebrew University; at the age of seventy-three he came to the United States for a lecture tour. At eighty he gave a series of lectures at Princeton. And then there are his books, far too many to be listed here. They include his translation of the Hebrew Bible into German, the celebrated *I and Thou, The Eclipse of God, Two Types of Faith, Paths in Utopia, Israel and the World,* and *Tales of the Hasidim.*

INTRODUCTION

In most systems of belief the believer considers that he can achieve a perfect relationship to God by renouncing the world of the senses and overcoming his own natural being. Not so the hasid. Certainly, "cleaving" unto God is to him the highest aim of the human person, but to achieve it he is not required to abandon the external and internal reality of earthly being, but to affirm it in its true, God-oriented essence and thus so to transform it that he can offer it up to God.

Hasidism is no pantheism. It teaches the absolute transcendence of God, but as combined with his conditioned immanence. The world is an irradiation of God, but as it is endowed with an independence of existence and striving, it is apt, always and everywhere, to form a crust around itself. Thus, a divine spark lives in every thing and being, but each such spark is enclosed by an isolating shell. Only man can liberate it and re-join it with the Origin: by holding holy converse with the thing and using it in a holy manner, that is, so that his intention in doing so remains directed toward God's transcendence. Thus the divine immanence emerges from the exile of the "shells."

But also in man, in every man, is a force divine. And in man far more than in all other beings it can pervert itself, can be misued by himself. This happens if he, instead of directing it toward its origin, allows it to run directionless and seize at everything that offers itself to it; instead of hallowing passion, he makes it evil. But here, too, a way to redemption is open: he who with the entire force of his being "turns" to God, at this his point of the universe lifts the divine immanence out of its debasement, which he has caused.

The task of man, of every man, according to hasidic teaching, is to affirm for God's sake the world and himself and by this very means to transform both.

HEART-SEARCHING

Rabbi Shneur Zalman, the *rav*[1] of Northern White Russia (died 1813), was put in jail in Petersburg, because the *mitnagdim*[2] had denounced his principles and his way of living to the government. He was awaiting trial when the chief of the gendarmes entered his cell. The majestic and quiet face of the rav, who was so deep in meditation that he did not at first notice his visitor, suggested to the chief, a thoughtful person, what manner of man he had before him. He began to converse with his prisoner and brought up a number of questions which had occurred to him in reading the Scriptures. Finally he asked: "How are we to understand that God, the all-knowing, said to Adam: 'Where art thou?' "

"Do you believe," answered the rav, "that the Scriptures are eternal and that every era, every generation and every man is included in them?"

"I believe this," said the other.

"Well then," said the zaddik, "in every era, God calls to every man: 'Where are you in your world? So many years and days of those allotted to you have passed, and how far have you gotten in your world?' God says something like this: 'You have lived forty-six years. How far along are you?'"

When the chief of the gendarmes heard his age mentioned, he pulled himself together, laid his hand on the rav's shoulder, and cried: "Bravo!" But his heart trembled.

What happens in this tale?

At first sight, it reminds us of certain Talmudic stories in which a Roman or some other heathen questions a Jewish sage about a Biblical passage, with a view to exposing an alleged contradiction in Jewish religious doctrine, and

[1]Rabbi.
[2]adversaries (of Hasidism).

receives a reply which either explains that there is no such contradiction or refutes the questioner's arguments in some other way; sometimes, a personal admonition is added to the actual reply. But we soon perceive an important difference between those Talmudic stories and this Hasidic one, though at first the difference appears greater than it actually is. It consists in the fact that in the Hasidic story the reply is given on a different plane from that on which the question is asked.

The chief wants to expose an alleged contradiction in Jewish doctrine. The Jews profess to believe in God as the all-knowing, but the Bible makes him ask questions as they are asked by someone who wants to learn something he does not know. God seeks Adam, who has hidden himself. He calls into the garden, asking where he is; it would thus seem that He does not know it, that it is possible to hide from Him and, consequently, that He is not all-knowing. Now, instead of explaining the passage and solving the seeming contradiction, the rabbi takes the text merely as a starting point from where he proceeds to reproach the chief with his past life, his lack of seriousness, his thoughtlessness and irresponsibility. An impersonal question which, however seriously it may be meant in the present instance, is in fact no genuine question but merely a form of controversy, calls forth a personal reply or, rather, a personal admonition in lieu of a reply. It thus seems as if nothing had remained of those Talmudic answers but the admonition which sometimes accompanied them.

But let us examine the story more closely. The chief inquires about a passage from the Biblical story of Adam's sin. The rabbi's answer means, in effect: "You yourself are Adam, you are the man whom God asks: 'Where art thou?'" It would thus seem that the answer gives no explanation of the passage as such. In fact, however, it illuminates both the situation of the Biblical Adam and that of every man in every time and in every place. For as soon as the chief hears and understands that the Biblical question is addressed to him, he is bound to realize what it means when God asks: "Where art thou?" whether the question be addressed to Adam or to some other man. In so asking, God does not expect to learn something he does not know; what he wants is to produce an effect in man which can only be produced by just such a question, provided that it reaches man's heart—that man allows it to reach his heart.

Adam hides himself to avoid rendering accounts, to escape responsibility for his way of living. Every man hides for this purpose, for every man is Adam and finds himself in Adam's situation. To escape responsibility for his life, he turns existence into a system of hideouts. And in thus hiding again and again "from the face of God," he enmeshes himself more and more deeply in perversity. A new situation thus arises, which becomes more and more questionable with every day, with every new hideout. This situation can be precisely defined as follows: Man cannot escape the eye of God, but in trying to hide from Him, he is hiding from himself. True, in him too there is something that seeks him, but he makes it harder and harder for that "something" to find him. This is the situation into which God's question falls. This question is designed to awaken man and destroy his system of hideouts; it is to show man to what pass he has come and to awake in him the great will to get out of it.

Everything now depends on whether man faces the question. Of course, every man's heart, like that of the chief in the story, will tremble when he hears it. But his system of hideouts will help to overcome this emotion. For the Voice does not come in a thunderstorm which threatens man's very existence; it is a "still small voice," and easy to drown. So long as this is done, man's life will not become a *way*. Whatever success and enjoyment he may achieve, whatever power he may attain and whatever deeds he may do, his life will remain way-less, so long as he does not face the Voice. Adam faces the Voice, perceives his enmeshment, and avows: "I hid myself"; this is the beginning of man's way. The decisive heart-searching is the beginning of the way in man's life; it is, again and again, the beginning of a human way.

But heart-searching is decisive only if it leads to the way. For there is a sterile kind of heart-searching, which leads to nothing but self-torture, despair and still deeper enmeshment. When the Rabbi of Ger,[3] in expounding the Scriptures, came to the words which Jacob addresses to his servant: "When Esau my brother meets thee, and asks thee, saying, Whose art thou? and whither goest thou? and whose are these before thee?" he would say to his disciples: "Mark well how similar Esau's questions are to the saying of our sages: 'Consider three things. Know whence you came, whither you are going, and to whom you will have to render accounts.' Be very careful, for great caution should be exercised by him who considers these three things: lest Esau ask in him. For Esau, too, may ask these questions and bring man into a state of gloom."

There is a demonic question, a spurious question, which apes God's question, the question of Truth. Its characteristic is that it does not stop at: "Where art thou?" but continues: "From where you have got to, there is no way out." This is the wrong kind of heart-searching, which does not prompt man to turn or put him on the way, but, by representing turning as hopeless, drives him to a point where it appears to have become entirely impossible and lets him go on living only by demonic pride, the pride of perversity.

THE PARTICULAR WAY

Rabbi Baer of Radoshitz once said to his teacher, the "Seer" of Lublin: "Show me one general way to the service of God."

The zaddik replied: "It is impossible to tell men what way they should take. For one way to serve God is through learning, another through prayer,

[3]Góra Kalwarya near Warsaw.

BUBER / *Way of Man According to Hasidism*

another through fasting, and still another through eating. Everyone should carefully observe what way his heart draws him to, and then choose this way with all his strength."

In the first place, this story tells us something about our relationship to such genuine service as was performed by others before us. We are to revere it and learn from it, but we are not to imitate it. The great and holy deeds done by others are examples for us, since they show, in a concrete manner, what greatness and holiness is, but they are not models which we should copy. However small our achievements may be in comparison with those of our forefathers, they have their real value in that we bring them about in our own way and by our own efforts.

The *maggid*[4] of Zlotchov[5] was asked by a Hasid: "We are told: 'Everyone in Israel is in duty bound to say: When will my work approach the works of my fathers, Abraham, Isaac and Jacob?' How are we to understand this? How could we ever venture to think that we could do what our fathers did?"

The rabbi expounded: "Just as our fathers founded new ways of serving, each a new service according to his character: one the service of love, the other that of stern justice, the third that of beauty, so each of us in his own way shall devise something new in the light of teachings and of service, and do what has not yet been done."

Every person born into this world represents something new, something that never existed before, something original and unique. "It is the duty of every person in Israel to know and consider that he is unique in the world in his particular character and that there has never been anyone like him in the world, for if there had been someone like him, there would have been no need for him to be in the world. Every single man is a new thing in the world and is called upon to fulfill his particularity in this world. For verily: that this is not done is the reason why the coming of the Messiah is delayed." Every man's foremost task is the actualization of his unique, unprecedented and never-recurring potentialities, and not the repetition of something that another, and be it even the greatest, has already achieved.

. . .

BEGINNING WITH ONESELF

Once when Rabbi Yitzhak of Vorki was playing host to certain prominent men of Israel, they discussed the value to a household of an honest and efficient servant. They said that a good servant made for good management and cited Joseph at whose hands everything prospered. Rabbi Yitzhak objected. "I once thought that too," he said. "But then my teacher showed me that everything depends on the master of the house. You see, in my youth my wife gave me a great deal of trouble and, though I myself put up with her as

[4]preacher.
[5]town in Eastern Galicia.

best I could, I was sorry for the servants. So I went to my teacher, Rabbi David of Lelov, and asked him whether I should oppose my wife. All he said was: 'Why do you speak to me? Speak to yourself!' I thought over these words for quite a while before I understood them. But I did understand them when I recalled a certain saying of the Baal-Shem: 'There is thought, speech and action. Thought corresponds to one's wife, speech to one's children, and action to one's servants. Whoever straightens himself out in regard to all three will find that everything prospers at his hands.' Then I understood what my teacher had meant: everything depended on myself.''

This story touches upon one of the deepest and most difficult problems of our life: the true origin of conflict between man and man.

Manifestations of conflict are usually explained either by the motives of which the quarreling parties are conscious as the occasion of their quarrel, and by the objective situations and processes which underlie these motives and in which both parties are involved; or, proceeding analytically, we try to explore the unconscious complexes to which these motives relate like mere symptoms of an illness to the organic disturbances themselves. Hasidic teaching coincides with this conception in that it, too, derives the problematics of external from that of internal life. But it differs in two essential points, one fundamental and one practical, the latter of which is even more important than the former.

The fundamental difference is that Hasidic teaching is not concerned with the exploration of particular psychical complications, but envisages man as a whole. This is, however, by no means a quantitative difference. For the Hasidic conception springs from the realization that the isolation of elements and partial processes from the whole hinders the comprehension of the whole, and that real transformation, real restoration, at first of the single person and subsequently of the relationship between him and his fellow men, can only be achieved by the comprehension of the whole as a whole. (Putting it paradoxically: the search for the center of gravity shifts it and thereby frustrates the whole attempt at overcoming the problematics involved.) This is not to say that there is no need to consider all the phenomena of the soul; but no one of them should be made so much the center of attention as if everything else could be derived from it; rather, they shall all be made starting points—not singly but in their vital connection.

The practical difference is that in Hasidism man is not treated as an object of examination but is called upon to "straighten himself out." At first, a man should himself realize that conflict-situations between himself and others are nothing but the effects of conflict-situations in his own soul; then he should try to overcome this inner conflict, so that afterwards he may go out to his fellow men and enter into new, transformed relationships with them.

Man naturally tries to avoid this decisive reversal—extremely repugnant to him in his accustomed relationship to the world—by referring him who thus appeals to him, or his own soul, if it is his soul that makes the appeal, to the fact that every conflict involves two parties and that, if he is expected to turn his attention from the external to his own internal conflict, his opponent should be expected to do the same. But just this perspective, in which a man sees himself only as an individual contrasted with other individuals, and not as a genuine person, whose transformation helps toward the transformation of the world, contains the fundamental error which Hasidic teaching denounces. The essential thing is to begin with oneself, and at this moment a man has nothing in the world to care about other than this beginning. Any other attitude would distract him from what he is about to begin, weaken his initiative, and thus frustrate the entire bold undertaking.

Rabbi Bunam taught:

"Our sages say: 'Seek peace in your own place.' You cannot find peace anywhere save in your own self. In the psalm we read: 'There is no peace in my bones because of my sin.' When a man has made peace within himself, he will be able to make peace in the whole world."

However, the story from which I started does not confine itself to pointing out the true origin of external conflicts, i.e., the internal conflict, in a general way. The quoted saying of the Baal-Shem states exactly in what the decisive inner conflict consists. It is the conflict between three principles in man's being and life, the principle of thought, the principle of speech, and the principle of action. The origin of all conflict between me and my fellow men is that I do not say what I mean, and that I do not do what I say. For this confuses and poisons, again and again and in increasing measure, the situation between myself and the other man, and I, in my internal disintegration, am no longer able to master it but, contrary to all my illusions, have become its slave. By our contradiction, our lie, we foster conflict-situations and give them power over us until they enslave us. From here, there is no way out but by the crucial realization: Everything depends on myself; and the crucial decision: I will straighten myself out.

But in order that a man may be capable of this great feat, he must first find his way from the casual, accessory elements of his existence to his own self; he must find his own self, not the trivial ego of the egotistic individual, but the deeper self of the person living in a relationship to the world. And that is also contrary to everything we are accustomed to.

· · ·

HERE WHERE ONE STANDS

Rabbi Bunam used to tell young men who came to him for the first time the story of Rabbi Eizik, son of Rabbi Yekel of Cracow. After many years of great poverty which had never shaken his faith in God, he dreamed someone bade him look for a treasure in Prague, under the bridge which leads to the king's palace. When the dream recurred a third time, Rabbi Eizik prepared for the journey and set out for Prague. But the bridge was guarded day and night and he did not dare to start digging. Nevertheless he went to the bridge every morning and kept walking around it until evening. Finally the captain of the guards, who had been watching him, asked in a kindly way whether he was looking for something or waiting for somebody. Rabbi Eizik told him of the dream which had brought him here from a faraway country. The captain laughed: "And so to please the dream, you poor fellow wore out your shoes to come here! As for having faith in dreams, if I had had it, I should have had to get going when a dream once told me to go to Cracow and dig for treasure under the stove in the room of a Jew—Eizik, son of Yekel, that was the name! Eizik, son of Yekel! I can just imagine what it would be like, how I should have to try every house over there, where one half of the Jews are named Eizik and the other Yekel!" And he laughed again. Rabbi Eizik bowed, traveled home, dug up the treasure from under the stove, and built the House of Prayer which is called "Reb Eizik Reb Yekel's Shul."

"Take this story to heart," Rabbi Bunam used to add, "and make what it says your own: There is something you cannot find anywhere in the world, not even at the zaddik's, and there is, nevertheless, a place where you can find it."

This, too, is a very old story, known from several popular literatures, but thoroughly reshaped by Hasidism. It has not merely—in a superficial sense—been transplanted into the Jewish sphere, it has been recast by the Hasidic melody in which it has been told; but even this is not decisive: the decisive change is that it has become, so to speak, transparent, and that a Hasidic truth is shining through its words. It has not had a "moral" appended to it, but the sage who retold it had at last discovered its true meaning and made it apparent.

There is something that can only be found in one place. It is a great treasure, which may be called the fulfillment of existence. The place where this treasure can be found is the place on which one stands.

Most of us achieve only at rare moments a clear realization of that fact that they have never tasted the fulfillment of existence, that their life does not participate in true, fulfilled existence, that, as it were, it passes true existence by. We nevertheless feel the deficiency at every moment, and in some measure strive to find—somewhere—what we are seeking. Somewhere, in some province of the world or of the mind, except where we stand, where we have been set—but it is there and nowhere else that the treasure can be found. The environment which I feel to be the natural one, the situation which has been assigned to me as my fate, the things that happen to me day after day, the things that claim me day after day—these contain my essential task and such fulfillment of existence as is open to me. It is said of a certain Talmudic master that the paths of heaven were as bright to him as the streets of his native town. Hasidism inverts the order: It is a greater thing if the streets of a man's native town are as bright to him as the paths of heaven. For it is here, where we stand, that we should try to make shine the light of the hidden divine life.

If we had power over the ends of the earth, it would not give us that fulfillment of existence which a quiet devoted relationship to nearby life can give us. If we knew the secrets of the upper worlds, they would not allow us so much actual participation in true existence as we can achieve by performing, with holy intent, a task belonging to our daily duties. Our treasure is hidden beneath the hearth of our own home.

The Baal-Shem teaches that no encounter with a being or a thing in the course of our life lacks a hidden significance. The people we live with or meet with, the animals that help us with our farm work, the soil we till, the materials we shape, the tools we use, they all contain a mysterious spiritual substance which depends on us for helping it toward its pure form, its perfection. If we neglect this spiritual substance sent across our path, if we think only in terms of momentary purposes, without developing a genuine relationship to the beings and things in whose life we ought to take part, as they in ours, then we shall ourselves be debarred from true, fulfilled existence. It is my conviction that this doctrine is essentially true. The highest culture of the soul remains basically arid and barren unless, day by day, waters of life pour forth into the soul from those little encounters to which we give their due; the most formidable power is intrinsically powerlessness unless it maintains a secret covenant with these contacts, both humble and helpful, with strange, and yet near, being.

Some religions do not regard our sojourn on earth as true life. They either teach that everything appearing to us here is mere appearance, behind which we should penetrate, or that it is only a forecourt of the true world, a forecourt which we should cross without paying much attention to it. Judaism, on the contrary, teaches that what a man does now and here with holy intent is no less important, no less true—being a terrestrial indeed, but none the less factual, link with divine being—than the life in the world to come. This doctrine has found its fullest expression in Hasidism.

Rabbi Hanokh said: "The other nations too believe that there are two worlds. They too say: 'In the other world.' The difference is this: They think that the two are separate and severed, but Israel professes that the two worlds are essentially one and shall in fact become one."

In their true essence, the two worlds are one. They only have, as it were, moved apart. But they shall again become one, as they are in their true essence. Man was created for the purpose of unifying the two worlds. He contributes toward this unity by holy living, in relationship to the world in which he has been set, at the place on which he stands.

Once they told Rabbi Pinhas of the great misery among the needy. He listened, sunk in grief. The he raised his head. "Let us draw God into the world," he cried, "and all need will be stilled."

But is this possible, to draw God into the world? Is this not an arrogant, presumptuous idea? How dare the lowly worm touch upon a matter which depends entirely on God's grace: how much of Himself He will vouchsafe to His creation?

Here again, Jewish doctrine is opposed to that of other religions, and again it is in Hasidism that it has found its fullest expression. God's grace consists precisely in this, that He wants to let Himself be won by man, that He places Himself, so to speak, into man's hands. God wants to come to His world, but He wants to come to it through man. This is the mystery of our existence, the superhuman chance of mankind.

"Where is the dwelling of God?"

This was the question with which the Rabbi of Kotzk surprised a number of learned men who happened to be visiting him.

They laughed at him: "What a thing to ask! Is not the whole world full of His glory?"

Then he answered his own question:

"God dwells wherever man lets Him in."

This is the ultimate purpose: to let God in. But we can let Him in only where we really stand, where we live, where we live a true life. If we maintain holy intercourse with the little world entrusted to us, if we help the holy spiritual substance to accomplish itself in that section of Creation in which we are living, then we are establishing, in this our place, a dwelling for the Divine Presence.

abraham heschel _____

FROM *God in Search of Man*

A great scholar and philosopher of Judaism, Abraham Heschel (1907–1972) was born in Warsaw and earned his doctorate at the University of Berlin. In 1938 he and other Polish Jews were expelled from Germany by the Nazis; he was briefly in Poland and England before coming to the United States in 1940. He taught at Hebrew Union College and was for many years Professor of Jewish Ethics and Mysticism at the Jewish Theological Seminary.

Some sense of Heschel's intensity and personal involvement in the issues of religion and of his times is suggested by his marching with Martin Luther King in Selma, Alabama. And less than a week before his death, in spite of a weak heart and heavy schedule, he stood in the snow in Danbury, Connecticut, to greet war-protestor Father Philip Berrigan upon his release from prison.

Heschel's books are grounded in a profound learning, but his style, as will be seen in the selection that follows, is very close to poetry. His many titles include *The Prophets, The Insecurity of Freedom, The Sabbath, The Earth Is the Lord's, Man Is Not Alone, Man's Quest for God, Israel: An Echo of Eternity,* and *Who Is Man?*

TO RECOVER THE QUESTIONS

It is customary to blame secular science and anti-religious philosophy for the eclipse of religion in modern society. It would be more honest to blame religion for its own defeats. Religion declined not because it was refuted, but because it became irrelevant, dull, oppressive, insipid. When faith is completely replaced by creed, worship by discipline, love by habit; when the crisis of today is ignored because of the splendor of the past; when faith becomes an heirloom rather than a living fountain; when religion speaks only in the name of authority rather than with the voice of compassion—its message becomes meaningless.

Religion is an answer to man's ultimate questions. The moment we become oblivious to ultimate questions, religion becomes irrelevant, and its crisis sets in. The primary task of philosophy of religion is to rediscover the questions to which religion is an answer. The inquiry must proceed both by delving into the consciousness of man as well as by delving into the teachings and attitudes of the religious tradition.

There are dead thoughts and there are living thoughts. A dead thought has been compared to a stone which one may plant in the soil. Nothing will come out. A living thought is like a seed. In the process of thinking, an answer without a question is devoid of life. It may enter the mind; it will not penetrate the soul. It may become a part of one's knowledge; it will not come forth as a creative force.

. . .

TWO KINDS OF WONDER

Wonder or radical amazement is the chief characteristic of the religious man's attitude toward history and nature. One attitude is alien to his spirit: taking things for granted, regarding events as a natural course of things. To find an approximate cause of a phenomenon is no answer to his ultimate wonder. He knows that there are laws that regulate the course of natural processes; he is aware of the regularity and pattern of things. However, such knowledge fails to mitigate his sense of perpetual surprise at the fact that there are facts at all. Looking at the world he would say, "This is the Lord's doing, it is marvelous in our eyes" (Psalms 118:23).

That "wonder is the feeling of a philosopher, and philosophy begins in wonder" was stated by Plato[1] and maintained by Aristotle: "For it is owing to their wonder that men both now begin and at first began to philosophize."[2] To this day, rational wonder is appreciated as *"semen scientiae,"* as the seed of knowledge, as something conducive, not indigenous to cognition.[3] Wonder is the prelude to knowledge; it ceases, once the cause of a phenomenon is explained.[4]

But does the worth of wonder merely consist in its being a stimulant to the acquisition of knowledge? Is wonder the same as curiosity? To the prophets

---

[1]*Theaetetus,* 155d.

[2]*Metaphysica,* 12, 982b, 12.

[3]"The special philosophical disposition consists primarily in this, that a man is capable of wonder beyond the ordinary and everyday degree . . . the lower a man stands in an intellectual regard the less of a problem is existence itself to him; everything, how it is, and that it is, appears to him rather a matter of course." Schopenhauer, *Supplements to the World as Will and Idea,* ch. xvii.

"The feeling of wonderment is the source and inexhaustible fountainhead of [the child's] desire for knowledge. It drives the child irresistibly on to solve the mystery, and if in his attempt he encounters a causal relationship, he will not tire of repeating the same experiment ten times, a hundred times, in order to taste the thrill of discovery over and over again. . . . The reason why the adult no longer wonders is not because he has solved the riddle of life, but because he has grown accustomed to the laws governing his world picture. But the problem of why these particular laws and no others hold, remains for him just as amazing and inexplicable as for the child. He who does not comprehend this situation, misconstrues its profound significance, and he who has reached the stage where he no longer wonders about anything, merely demostrates that he has lost the art of reflective reasoning." Max Planck, *Scientific Autobiography,* New York, 1949, pp. 91-93.

[4]*Mechanica,* 847a, 11.

wonder is *a form of thinking.* It is not the beginning of knowledge but an act that goes beyond knowledge; it does not come to an end when knowledge is acquired; it is an attitude that never ceases. There is no answer in the world to man's radical amazement.

. . .

"FAR OFF AND DEEP"

In the Book of Ecclesiastes we read the account of a man who sought wisdom, who searched for insight into the world and its meaning. "I said, I will be wise" (7:23), and "I applied my mind to know wisdom and to see what is done on earth" (8:16). Did he succeed? He claims, "I have acquired great wisdom, surpassing all who were over Jerusalem before me" (1:16). But he ultimately realized "that *man cannot find out* the work that is done under the sun. However much man may toil in seeking, he will not find it out; even though a wise man claims to know, he cannot find it out" (8:17).

"I said, I will be wise, but it was *far from me.* That which *is, is far off and deep, exceedingly deep.* Who can find it out?" (7:23-24). Ecclesiastes is not only saying that the world's wise are not wise enough, but something more radical. What *is,* is more than what you see; what *is,* is "far off and deep, exceedingly deep." *Being is mysterious.*

This is one of Ecclesiastes' central insights: "I have seen the task that God has given to the sons of men. . . . He has made all things beautiful in its time; but he has also *implanted in the hearts of men the mystery,* so that man cannot find out what God has done from the beginning to the end" (3:10-11).[5]

Wisdom is beyond our reach. We are unable to attain insight into the ultimate meaning and purpose of things. Man does not know the thoughts of his own mind nor is he able to understand the meaning of his own dreams (see Daniel 2:27).

IN AWE AND AMAZEMENT

In awe and amazement the prophets stand before the mystery of the universe:

> Who has measured the waters in the hollow of his hand,
> And marked off the heavens with a span,
> Enclosed the dust of the earth in a measure,
> And weighed the mountains in scales,
> And the hills in a balance? (*Isaiah 40:12*)

[5]The difficult word here is *ha'olam* which has been rendered by the Septuagint with "eternity," by the Vulgate with "world," and by others with "knowledge" (on the basis of the Arabic cognate). Rashi, following rabbinic sources (*Kohelet Rabba* 3, 15; *Tanhuma,* Kedoshim, 8; *Midrash Tehillim* 9, 1), explains it as "hiddenness" or mystery.

An even deeper sense of humility is expressed in the words of Agur:

> Surely I am too stupid to be a man.
> I have not the understanding of a man.
> I have not learned wisdom,
> Nor have I knowledge of the Holy One.
> Who has ascended to heaven and come down?
> Who has gathered the wind in his fists?
> Who has wrapped up the waters in a garment?
> Who has established all the ends of the earth?
> What is his name, and what is his son's name,
> If thou knowest? *(Proverbs 30:2– 4)*

. . .

TWO KINDS OF IGNORANCE

There are two kinds of ignorance. The one is "dull, unfeeling, barren," the result of indolence; the other is keen, penetrating, resplendent; the one leads to conceit and complacency, the other leads to humility. From the one we seek to escape, in the other the mind finds repose.

The deeper we search the nearer we arrive at knowing that we do not know. What do we truly know about life and death, about the soul or society, about history or nature? "We have become increasingly and painfully aware of our abysmal ignorance. No scientist, fifty years ago, could have realized that he was as ignorant as all first-rate scientists now know themselves to be."[6] "Can we not see that exact laws, like all the other ultimates and absolutes, are as fabulous as the crock of gold at the rainbow's end?"[7] "Beware lest we say, we have found wisdom" (Job 32:13).[8] "They who travel in pursuit of wisdom, walk only in a circle; and after all their labor, at last return to their pristine ignorance."[9] "No illumination," remarks Joseph Conrad in *The Arrow of Gold*, "can sweep all mystery out of the world. After the departed darkness the shadows remain."

. . .

THE BEGINNING OF WISDOM IS AWE

Ultimate meaning and ultimate wisdom are not found within the world but in God, and the only way to wisdom is, as said above, through our relationship to God. That relationship is *awe*. Awe, in this sense, is more than an emotion;

---

[6] Abraham Flexner, *Universities,* New York, 1930, p. 17.

[7] Gilbert N. Lewis, *The Anatomy of Science,* New Haven, 1926, p. 154.

[8] According to Socrates, "God only is wise," and the man who claimed actual possession of wisdom was guilty of presumption, if not blasphemy. He called himself a lover of wisdom. *Apology,* 20ff.

[9] Oliver Goldsmith, *The Citizen of the World,* letter 37.

it is a way of understanding. Awe is itself an act of insight into a meaning greater than ourselves.

The question, therefore, *where shall wisdom be found?* is answered by the Psalmist: *the awe of God is the beginning of wisdom.*[10] The Bible does not preach awe as a form of intellectual resignation; it does not say, awe is the end of wisdom. Its intention seems to be that awe is a way to wisdom. In Job we encounter a complete equation: *the awe of God is wisdom.*[11]

The beginning of awe is wonder, and the beginning of wisdom is awe.

THE MEANING OF AWE

Awe is a way of being in rapport with the mystery of all reality. The awe that we sense or ought to sense when standing in the presence of a human being is a moment of intuition for the likeness of God which is concealed in his essence. Not only man; even inanimate things stand in a relation to the Creator. The secret of every being is the divine care and concern that are invested in it. Something sacred is at stake in every event.[12]

Awe is an intuition for the creaturely dignity of all things and their preciousness to God; a realization that things not only are what they are but also stand, however remotely, for something absolute. Awe is a sense for the transcendence, for the reference everywhere to Him who is beyond all things. It is an insight better conveyed in attitudes than in words. The more eager we are to express it, the less remains of it.

The meaning of awe is to realize that life takes place under wide horizons, horizons that range beyond the span of an individual life or even the life of a nation, a generation, or an era. Awe enables us to perceive in the world intimations of the divine, to sense in small things the beginning of infinite significance, to sense the ultimate in the common and the simple; to feel in the rush of the passing the stillness of the eternal.

In analyzing or evaluating an object, we think and judge from a particular point of view. The psychologist, economist, and chemist pay attention to different aspects of the same object. Such is the limitation of the mind that it can never see three sides of a building at the same time. The danger begins when, completely caught in one perspective, we attempt to consider a part as the whole. In the twilight of such perspectivism, even the sight of the part is distorted. What we cannot comprehend by analysis, we become aware of in

[10]Psalms 111:10; Proverbs 9:10; see Proverbs 1:7; 15:33; Ecclesiastes 12:13; Sirach 25:12-13; and *The Sayings of the Fathers,* III, 21:

> Where there is no wisdom, there is no awe;
> Where there is no awe, there is no wisdom.

[11]Job 28:28.
[12]*See Man is Not Alone,* p. 286.

awe. When we "stand still and consider," we face and witness what is immune to analysis.

Knowledge is fostered by curiosity; wisdom is fostered by awe. True wisdom is participation in the wisdom of God. Some people may regard as wisdom "an uncommon degree of common sense." To us, wisdom is the ability to look at all things from the point of view of God, sympathy with the divine pathos, the identification of the will with the will of God. "Thus says the Lord: Let not the wise man glory in his wisdom, let not the mighty man glory in his might, let not the rich man glory in his riches; but let him who glories glory in this, that he understands and knows Me, that I am the Lord who practises kindness, justice, and righteousness on the earth; for in these things I delight, says the Lord" (Jeremiah 9:22-23).

There are, of course, moments of higher or lower intensity of awe. When a person becomes alive to the fact that God "is the great ruler, the rock and foundation of all worlds, before Whom all existing things are as nought, as it has been said, all the inhabitants of the earth are as nought" (Daniel 4:32),[13] he will be overwhelmed by a sense of the holiness of God. Such awe is reflected in the exhortation of the prophets: "Enter into the rock, hide thee in the dust, from before the terror of the Lord, from the splendor of His majesty" (Isaiah 2:10).

We find a classical expression of the meaning and expression of awe in Maimonides:

When a man is in the presence of a mighty king, he will not sit, move, and behave in the same way as he would when he is alone in his own house; nor will he speak in the king's audience chamber in the same easy-going manner as he would in his own family circle or among his relatives. Therefore any man who is keen on attaining human perfection and wishes to be a true "man of God" must awake to the fact that the great King who constantly protects him and is near to him is mightier than any human individual, even if it were David or Solomon. That King and constant guardian is the spirit emanated upon us which is the bond between us and God. Just as we perceive Him in that light which He emanates upon us—as it is said: *In thy light we see light* (Psalm 36:9)—so God looks down upon us by the same light. Because of it God is perpetually with us looking down upon us from above, *Can any hide himself in secret places that I shall not see him, saith the Lord* (Jeremiah 23:24).[14]

. . .

[13]*Zohar,* vol. I, 11b. In the opening paragraph of the *Shulchan Aruch,* the Code of Laws, the word of the Psalmist, *I keep the Lord always before me* (16:8) is described as *"the basic principle of the Torah"* (according to Rabbi Moshe Isserles). It was a requirement in Jewish piety to be constantly aware of His presence. As an aid to such remembrance, it was suggested that one constantly keep before the inner eye the four letters of the Ineffable Name. Paraphrasing the verse in Psalm 32:2, it was said, that blessed is he to whom not to think of God for one moment is a sin.

[14]Maimonides, *The Guide of the Perplexed,* vol. III, ch. 52. Translated by Ch. Rabin, London, 1952.

METAPHYSICAL LONELINESS

The ideals we strive after, the values we try to fulfill, have they any significance in the realm of natural processes? The sun spends its rays upon the just and the wicked, upon flowers and snakes alike. The heart beats normally within those who torture and kill. Is all goodness and striving for veracity but a fiction of the mind to which nothing corresponds in reality? Where are the spirit's values valid? Within the inner life of man? But the spirit is a stranger in the soul. A demand such as "love thy neighbor as thyself" is not at home in the self.

We have in common a terrible loneliness. Day after day a question goes up desperately in our minds: Are we *alone* in the wilderness of the self, alone in this silent universe, of which we are a part, and in which we feel at the same time like strangers?

It is such a situation that makes us ready to search for a voice of God in the world of man: the taste of utter loneliness; the discovery that unless God has a voice, the life of the spirit is a freak; that the world without God is a torso; that a soul without faith is a stump.

. . .

THE ARGUMENT FROM DESIGN

Of the various ways in which the existence of a supreme intelligence has been demonstrated, the teleological proof or the argument from design is one which according to Kant "must always be mentioned with respect." It claims that the order and arrangement of the universe cannot be adequately explained without assuming the activity of an intelligent God.[15]

The argument from design infers the existence of a divine power from the purposeful structure of nature. Order implies intelligence. That intelligence is God. A classic formulation is found in a familiar passage in Paley's *Natural Theology* (1803), ch. 1. "Suppose I had found a watch upon the ground. . . . The mechanism being observed . . . the inference we think is inevitable that the watch must have a maker; that there must have existed, at some time, and at some place or other, an artificer or artificers, who formed it for the purpose which we find it actually to answer; who comprehended its construction, and designed its use." The universe stands to God in the relation in which a watch is related to the mechanic who constructed it. The heavens are the works of His hands, just as the watch is the work of the watchmaker.

This comparison regards the universe as it does the watch as a separate, independent and absolute entity. Nature is a thing in itself, complete and

[15]An impressive restatement of the teleological argument is found in Frederick Robert Tennant's *Philosophical Theology,* Cambridge, 1929-30, vol. II, pp. 78ff. Compare also Frederick J. E. Woodbridge, *Nature and Mind,* New York, 1937, pp. 29-36.

self-sufficient at this present moment. The problem thus faced concerns not the existence of the universe but its cause; not its present, but its past. Since the ultimate structure and order of nature were thought of in mechanical terms, its origin or creation was also conceived of as a mechanical process, comparable to the process of constructing a watch.

The shortcomings of this view lie in its taking both the watch and all of reality for granted. The ultimate problem is not only how it came into being, but also how is it that it is. The problem extends furthermore not only to the substance of the question, but to the act of asking that question. We cannot take the existence of the watch as a safe starting point and merely ask the question of who brought it into being. *Is not the watch itself a mystery? Is not the act of my perceiving the watch and of my comprehending its design a most incomprehensible fact?*

RELIGION BEGINS WITH WONDER AND MYSTERY

The value of the proof from design lies in its being an answer to a speculative problem; its weakness lies in its failure to answer the religious problem. The first problem comes out of the quest of those who are sure of what they know (the fact of the design of the universe); the latter problem comes out of the amazement of those who know that they do not know. The speculative mind seeks to explain the known; the religious mind seeks a way by which to account for the unknown. If the world is taken for granted, then all we need is to know its cause; but if the world is a mystery, then the most pressing problem is, what does it stand for? What is its meaning? All reference to ideas that are analogous to this-worldly acts becomes utterly inadequate.

There is no answer in the world for man's ultimate wonder at the world. There is no answer in the self to man's ultimate wonder at the self. The question, Who created these? cannot be answered by referring to a cause or a power, since the question would remain, who created the power or the cause? There is nothing in the world to deserve the God. The world is a mystery, a question, not an answer. Only an idea that is greater than the world, an idea not borrowed from either experience or speculation, is adequate and worthy to be related to the religious problem. The mystery of creation rather than the concept of design; a God that stands above the mystery rather than a designer or a master mind; a God in relation to Whom the world here and now may gain meaning—these are answers that are adequate to the religious problem. The admission that we do not comprehend the origin of the universe is more honest than the acceptance of a designer.

.   .   .

. . . Religion is the result of what man does with his ultimate wonder, with the moments of awe, with the sense of mystery.

.   .   .

"WHERE ART THOU?"

Most theories of religion start out with defining the religious situation as man's search for God and maintain the axiom that God is silent, hidden and unconcerned with man's search for Him. Now, in adopting that axiom, the answer is given before the question is asked. To Biblical thinking, the definition is incomplete and the axiom false. The Bible speaks not only of man's search for God but also of *God's search for man*. "Thou dost hunt me like a lion," exclaimed Job (10:16).

"From the very first Thou didst single out man and consider him worthy to stand in Thy presence."[16] This is the mysterious paradox of Biblical faith: *God is pursuing man.*[17] It is as if God were unwilling to be alone, and He had chosen man to serve Him. Our seeking Him is not only man's but also His concern, and must not be considered an exclusively human affair. His will is involved in our yearnings. All of human history as described in the Bible may be summarized in one phrase: *God is in search of man.* Faith in God is a response to God's question.

. . .

When Adam and Eve hid from His presence, the Lord called: *Where art thou* (Genesis 3:9). It is a call that goes out again and again. It is a still small echo of a still small voice, not uttered in words, not conveyed in categories of the mind, but ineffable and mysterious, as ineffable and mysterious as the glory that fills the whole world. It is wrapped in silence; concealed and subdued, yet it is as if all things were the frozen echo of the question: *Where art thou?*

Faith comes out of awe, out of an awareness that we are exposed to His presence, out of anxiety to answer the challenge of God, out of an awareness of our being called upon. Religion consists of *God's question and man's answer*. The way *to* faith is the way *of* faith. The way to God is a way of God. Unless God asks the question, all our inquiries are in vain.

The answer lasts a moment, the commitment continues. Unless the awareness of the ineffable mystery of existence becomes a permanent state of mind, all that remains is a commitment without faith. To strengthen our alertness, to

[16]The liturgy of the Day of Atonement.

[17]"Said Rabbi Yose: Judah used to expound, *The Lord came from Sinai* (Deuteronomy 33:2). Do not read thus, but read, *The Lord came to Sinai*. I, however, do not accept this interpretation, but, *The Lord came from Sinai*, to welcome Israel as a bridegroom goes forth to meet the bride." *Mechilta, Bahodesh* to 19:17. God's covenant with Israel was an act of grace. "It was He who initiated our delivery from Egypt in order that we should become His people and He our King," *Kuzari* II, 50. "The first man would never have known God, if He had not addressed, rewarded and punished him. . . . By this he was convinced that He was the Creator of the world, and he characterized Him by words and attributes and called Him *the Lord*. Had it not been for this experience, he would have been satisfied with the name *God;* he would not have perceived what God was, whether He is one or many, whether He knows individuals or not." *Kuzari,* IV, 3.

CHAPTER SEVEN / *Judaism*

refine our appreciation of the mystery is the meaning of worship and observance. For faith does not remain stationary. We must continue to pray, continue to obey to be able to believe and to remain attached to His presence.

Recondite is the dimension where God and man meet, and yet not entirely impenetrable. He placed within man something of His spirit (see Isaiah 63:10), and "it is the spirit in a man, the breath of the Almighty, that makes him understand" (Job 32:8).

.   .   .

THE MEANING OF SPIRIT

Religion becomes sinful when it begins to advocate the segregation of God, to forget that the true sanctuary has no walls. Religion has always suffered from the tendency to become an end in itself, to seclude the holy, to become parochial, self-indulgent, self-seeking; as if the task were not to ennoble human nature but to enhance the power and beauty of its institutions or to enlarge the body of doctrines. It has often done more to canonize prejudices than to wrestle for truth; to petrify the sacred than to sanctify the secular. Yet the task of religion is to be a challenge to the stabilization of values.

emil l. fackenheim _____

Jewish Faith and the Holocaust

Emil L. Fackenheim is a professor of philosophy at the University of Toronto and the author of *The Religious Dimension in Hegel's Thought, God's Presence in History,* and *Quest for Past and Future: Essays in Jewish Theology.* In "Jewish Faith and the Holocaust," he asks how a Jew ought to respond to Auschwitz. No *explanation* of Auschwitz is sought for, because none is conceivable: the utter irrationality of Auschwitz defies every type of explanation. "Auschwitz is a unique descent into hell," Fackenheim writes. "It is an unprecedented celebration of evil. It is evil for evil's sake." But how is one to be faithful to those who suffered? To merely despair or to forget "would be further victories to Hitler, and are thus impossible." No *redeeming* Voice will ever be heard from Auschwitz, Fackenheim believes, but there is a *commanding* Voice.

Within the past two centuries, three events have shaken and are still shaking Jewish religious existence—the Emancipation and its after-effects, the Nazi Holocaust, and the rise of the first Jewish state in two thousand years—and of these, two have occured in our own generation. From the point of view of Jewish religious existence, as from so many other points of view, the Holocaust is the most shattering. Doubtless the Emancipation and all its works have posed and continue to pose powerful challenges, with which Jewish thought has been wrestling all along—scientific agnosticism, secularism, assimilation, and the like. The Emancipation represents, however, a challenger *ab extra,* from without, and for all its well-demonstrated power to weaken and undermine Jewish religious existence, I have long been convinced that the challenge can be met, religiously and intellectually. The state of Israel, by contrast, is a challenge *ab intra,* from within—at least to much that Jewish existence has been throughout two millennia. But this challenge is positive—the fact that in one sense (if not in many others) a long exile has ended. That it represents a positive challenge was revealed during and immediately after the Six-Day War, when biblical (i.e., pre-exilic) language suddenly came to life.

The Holocaust, too, challenges Jewish faith from within, but the negativism of its challenge is total, without light or relief. After the events associated with the name of Auschwitz, everything is shaken, nothing is safe.

To avoid Auschwitz, or to act as though it had never occurred, would be blasphemous. Yet how face it and be faithful to its victims? No precedent exists either within Jewish history or outside it. Even when a Jewish religious thinker barely begins to face Auschwitz, he perceives the possibility of a desperate choice between the faith of a millennial Jewish past, which has so far persisted through every trial, and faithfulness to the victims of the present. But at the edge of this abyss there must be a great pause, a lengthy silence, and an endurance.

II

Men shun the scandal of the particularity of Auschwitz. Germans link it with Dresden; American liberals, with Hiroshima. Christians deplore anti-Semitism-in-general, while Communists erect monuments of victims-of-Fascism-in-general, depriving the dead of Auschwitz of their Jewish identity even in death. Rather than face Auschwitz, men everywhere seek refuge in generalities, comfortable precisely because they are generalities. And such is the extent to which reality is shunned that no cries of protest are heard even when in the world community's own forum obscene comparisons are made between Israeli soldiers and Nazi murderers.

The Gentile world shuns Auschwitz because of the terror of Auschwitz —and because of real or imagined implication in the guilt for Auschwitz. But Jews shun Auschwitz as well. Only after many years did significant Jewish responses begin to appear. Little of real significance is being or can be said even now. Perhaps there should still be silence. It is certain, however, that the voices, now beginning to be heard, will grow ever louder and more numerous. For Jews now know that they must ever after remember Auschwitz, and be its witnesses to the world. Not to be a witness would be a betrayal. In the murder camps the victims often rebelled with no other hope than that one of them might escape to tell the tale. For Jews now to refrain from telling the tale would be unthinkable. Jewish faith still recalls the Exodus, Sinai, the two destructions of the Temple. A Judaism which survived at the price of ignoring Auschwitz would not deserve to survive.

It is because the world shrinks so fully from the truth that once a Jew begins to speak at all he must say the most obvious. Must he say that the death of a Jewish child at Auschwitz is no more lamentable than the death of a German child at Dresden? He must say it. And in saying it, he must also refuse to dissolve Auschwitz into suffering-in-general, even though he is almost sure to be considered a Jewish particularist who cares about Jews but not about mankind. Must he distinguish between the mass-killing at Hiroshima and that at Auschwitz? At the risk of being thought a sacrilegious quibbler, he must, with endless patience, forever repeat that Eichmann was moved by no such ''rational'' objective as victory when he diverted trains needed for military purposes in order to dispatch Jews to their death. He must add that there was no "irrational" objective either. Torquemada burned bodies in order to save souls. Eichmann sought to destroy both bodies and souls. Where else and at what other time have executioners ever separated those to be murdered now from those to be murdered later to the strain of Viennese waltzes? Where else has human skin ever been made into lampshades, and human body-fat into soap—not by isolated perverts but under the direction of ordinary bureaucrats? Auschwitz is a unique descent into hell. It is an unprecedented celebration of evil. It is evil for evil's sake.

A Jew must bear witness to this truth. Nor may he conceal that fact that Jews in their particularity were the singled-out victims. Of course, they were by no means the sole victims. And a Jew would infinitely prefer to think that to the Nazis, Jews were merely a species of the genus "inferior race." This indeed was the theme of Allied wartime propaganda, and it is still perpetuated by liberals, Communists, and guilt-ridden Christian theologians. Indeed, "liberal"-minded Jews themselves perpetuate it. The superficial reason is that this view of Auschwitz unites victims of all races and creeds: it is "brotherly" propaganda. Under the surface, however, there broods at least in Jewish if not in some Gentile minds[1] an idea horrible beyond all description. Would even Nazis have singled out Jews for such a terrible fate unless Jews had done *something* to bring it upon themselves? Most of the blame attaches to the murderers: must not at least some measure of blame attach to the victims as well? Such are the wounds which Nazism has inflicted on some Jewish minds. And such is the extent to which Nazism has defiled the world that, while it should have destroyed every vestige of anti-Semitism in every Gentile mind on earth, Auschwitz has, in some Gentile minds, actually increased it.

These wounds and this defilement can be confronted only with the truth. And the ineluctable truth is that Jews at Auschwitz were not a species of the genus "inferior race," but rather the prototype by which "inferior race" was defined. Not until the Nazi revolution had become an anti-Jewish revolution did it begin to succeed as a movement;[2] and when all its other works came crashing down only one of its goals remained: the murder of Jews. This is the scandal which requires, of Germans, a ruthless examination of their whole history; of Christians, a pitiless reckoning with the history of Christian anti-Semitism; of the whole world, an inquiry into the grounds of its indifference for twelve long years. Resort to theories of suffering-in-general or persecution-in-general permits such investigations to be evaded.

---

[1]Witness the recent Polish propaganda campaign—tantamount to a rewriting of Holocaust history—in which it was suggested that the Jews had cooperated with the Nazis in their own destruction.

[2]See, e.g., George L. Mosse, *The Crisis of German Ideology;* especially chapter 17.

CHAPTER SEVEN / *Judaism*

Yet even where the quest for explanations is genuine there is not, and never will be, an adequate explanation. Auschwitz is the scandal of evil for evil's sake, an eruption of demonism without analogy; and the singling-out of Jews, ultimately, is an unparalleled expression of what the rabbis call groundless hate. This is the rock on which throughout eternity all rational explanations will crash and break apart.

How can a Jew respond to thus having been singled out, and to being singled out even now whenever he tries to bear witness? Resisting rational explanations, Auschwitz will forever resist religious explanations as well. Attempts to find rational causes succeed at least up to a point, and the search for the religious, ideological, social, and economic factors leading to Auschwitz must be relentlessly pressed. In contrast, the search for a purpose in Auschwitz is foredoomed to total failure. Not that good men in their despair have not made the attempt. Good Orthodox Jews have resorted to the ancient "for our sins are we punished," but this recourse, unacceptable already to Job, is in this case all the more impossible. A good Christian theologian sees the purpose of Auschwitz in a divine reminder of the sufferings of Christ, but this testifies to a moving sense of desperation—and to an incredible lapse of theological judgment. A good Jewish secularist will connect the Holocaust with the rise of the state of Israel, but while to see a causal connection here is possible and necessary, to see a purpose is intolerable. A total and uncompromising sweep must be made of these and other explanations, all designed to give purpose to Auschwitz. No purpose, religious or non-religious, will ever be found in Auschwitz. The very attempt to find one is blasphemous.

Yet it is of the utmost importance to recognize that seeking a purpose is one thing, but seeking a response quite another. The first is wholly out of the question. The second is inescapable. Even after two decades any sort of adequate response may as yet transcend the power of any Jew. But his faith, his destiny, his very survival will depend on whether, in the end, he will be able to respond.

How can a Jew begin to seek a response? Looking for precedents, he finds none either in Jewish or in non-Jewish history. Jewish (like Christian) martyrs have died for their faith, certain that God needs martyrs. Job suffered despite his faith, able to protest within the sphere of faith. Negro Christians have died for their race, unshaken in a faith which was not at issue. The one million Jewish children murdered in the Nazi Holocaust died neither because of their faith, nor in spite of their faith, nor for reasons unrelated to faith. They were murdered because of the faith of their great-grandparents. Had these great-grandparents abandoned their Jewish faith, and failed to bring up Jewish children, then their fourth-generation descendants might have been among the Nazi executioners, but not among their Jewish victims. Like Abraham of old, European Jews some time in the mid-19th century offered a human sacrifice, by the mere minimal commitment to the Jewish faith of bringing up

Jewish children. But unlike Abraham they did not know what they were doing, and there was no reprieve. This is the brute fact which makes all comparisons odious or irrelevant. This is what makes Jewish religious existence today unique, without support from analogies anywhere in the past. This is the scandal of the particularity of Auschwitz which, once confronted by Jewish faith, threatens total despair.

I confess that it took me twenty years until I was able to look at this scandal, but when at length I did, I made what to me was, and still is, a momentous discovery: that while religious thinkers were vainly struggling for a response to Auschwitz, Jews throughout the world—rich and poor, learned and ignorant, religious and non-religious—had to some degree been responding all along. For twelve long years Jews had been exposed to a murderous hate which was as groundless as it was implacable. For twelve long years the world had been lukewarm or indifferent, unconcerned over the prospect of a world without Jews. For twelve long years the whole world had conspired to make Jews wish to cease to be Jews wherever, whenever, and in whatever way they could. Yet to this unprecedented invitation to group-suicide Jews responded with an unexpected will-to-live—with, under the circumstances, an incredible commitment to Jewish group survival.

In ordinary times, a commitment of this kind may be a mere mixture of nostalgia and vague loyalties not far removed from tribalism; and, unable to face Auschwitz, I had myself long viewed it as such, placing little value on a Jewish survival which was, or seemed to be, only survival for survival's sake. I was wrong, and even the shallowest Jewish survivalist philosophy of the postwar period was right by comparison. For in the age of Auschwitz a Jewish commitment to Jewish survival is in itself a monumental act of faithfulness, as well as a monumental, albeit as yet fragmentary, act of faith. Even to do no more than remain a Jew after Auschwitz is to confront the demons of Auschwitz in all their guises, and to bear witness against them. It is to believe that these demons cannot, will not, and must not prevail, and to stake on that belief one's own life and the lives of one's children. To be a Jew after Auschwitz is to have wrested hope—for the Jew and for the world—from the abyss of total despair. In the words of a speaker at a recent gathering of Bergen-Belsen survivors, the Jew after Auschwitz has a second *Shema Yisrael:* no second Auschwitz, no second Bergen-Belsen, no second Buchenwald—anywhere in the world, for anyone in the world!

What accounts for this commitment to Jewish existence when there might have been, and by every rule of human logic should have been, a terrified and demoralized flight from Jewish existence? Why, since Auschwitz, have all previous distinctions among Jews—between religious and secularist, Orthodox and liberal—diminished in importance, to be replaced by a new major distinction between Jews committed to Jewish survival, willing to be singled out and counted, and Jews in flight, who rationalize this flight as a rise to humanity-in-general? In my view, nothing less will do than to say that a commanding Voice speaks from Auschwitz, and that there are Jews who hear it and Jews who stop their ears.

The ultimate question is: where was God at Auschwitz? For years I sought refuge in Buber's image of an eclipse of God. This image, still meaningful in other respects, no longer seems to me applicable to Auschwitz. Most assuredly no *redeeming* Voice is heard from Auschwitz, or ever will be heard. However, a commanding Voice is being heard, and has, however faintly, been heard from the start. Religious Jews hear it, and they identify its source. Secularist Jews also hear it, even though perforce they leave it unidentified. At Auschwitz, Jews came face to face with absolute evil. They were and still are singled out by it, but in the midst of it they hear an absolute commandment: *Jews are forbidden to grant posthumous victories to Hitler.* They are commanded to survive as Jews, lest the Jewish people perish. They are commanded to remember the victims of Auschwitz, lest their memory perish. They are forbidden to despair of man and his world, and to escape into either cynicism or otherworldliness, lest they cooperate in delivering the world over to the forces of Auschwitz. Finally, they are forbidden to despair of the God of Israel, lest Judaism perish. A secularist Jew cannot make himself believe by a mere act of will, nor can he be commanded to do so; yet he can perform the commandment of Auschwitz. And a religious Jew who has stayed with his God may be forced into new, possibly revolutionary, relationships with Him. One possibility, however, is wholly unthinkable. A Jew may not respond to Hitler's attempt to destroy Judaism by himself cooperating in its destruction. In ancient times, the unthinkable Jewish sin was idolatry. Today, it is to respond to Hitler by doing his work.

In the Midrash, God is, even in time of unrelieved tragedy, only "seemingly" powerless, for the Messiah is still expected. In Elie Wiesel's *Night,* God hangs on the gallows, and for the hero of Wiesel's *The Gates of the Forest,* A Messiah who is able to come, and yet at Auschwitz failed to come, is not to be conceived. Yet this same hero asserts that precisely because it is too late we are commanded to hope. He also says the Kaddish, "that solemn affirmation, filled with grandeur and serenity, by which man returns to God His crown and His scepter." But how a Jew after Auschwitz can return these to God is not yet known. Nor is it yet known how God can receive them.

III

The Nazi Holocaust has brought Jews and Christians closer together—and set them further apart. The first truth is comforting and obvious. The second is painful, complex, and obscure, but perhaps in the end more necessary to confront. The gulf between Jews and Christians which Hitler succeeded in creating can be bridged only if it is recognized. But to bridge it is of incalculable importance for the future of both Judaism and Christianity.

Since an objective grasp of this issue is almost impossible, I had better state my views in terms of my own subjective development. Twenty years ago I believed that what once separated Jew and Christian was now dwarfed by what united them—namely their opposition to Nazism. I was of course not unaware of phenomena like the Nazi "German-Christian" church, or of the fact that respectable and indeed outstanding theologians were part of it. But so far as my native Germany was concerned, it was not the Christian Nazis who mattered to me; it was rather the Christian anti-Nazis, however small their number—not the "German-Christian" but rather the German confessional church. And what mattered theologically was thinkers like Barth and Tillich, able to recognize Nazi idolatry and to fight it courageously and unequivocally. To this day I still revere Kierkegaard, the first Christian thinker to perceive the nature and extent of modern idolatry, who would surely have been put into a concentration camp had he lived and written in Nazi Germany. To this day I am supported in my Judaism by the faithfulness of Christians to their Christianity. And when a new generation of Christian theologians arises to proclaim the death of God I feel, as a Jew, abandoned and betrayed.

The ancient rabbis recognized "righteous Gentiles" as being equal to the high priest in the sight of God; but they had no real acquaintance with Christianity and, of course, none with Islam. Medieval Jewish thinkers recognized Christianity and Mohammedanism as valid monotheistic religions, and considering the state of medieval Jewish-Christian and Jewish-Moslem relations, it is surprising that they did. But since the experience of Nazism and of Christian opposition to Nazism (which goes back to my adolescence), I have been convinced that there is now a need for Jewish recognition that the Christian (and the Mohammedan) not only affirms the One God but also stands in a living relation to Him. Where to go from here I cannot say. I never could accept Rosenzweig's famous "double covenant" doctrine, according to which all except Jews (who are already "with the Father") need the Son in order to find Him. How can a modern Jew pray for the conversion of the whole non-Jewish world to Christianity when even pre-modern Jews could pay homage to Moslem monotheism? Rosenzweig's doctrine seems altogether outmoded at a time when Christians themselves are beginning to replace missionary efforts with inter-religious dialogue, and I wonder whether even for Rosenzweig this doctrine was more than a stage in his self-emancipation from modern paganism.

Thus, though I very much feel the need for a Jewish doctrine of Christianity, I am left without one and must for the time being rest content only with openness to Jewish-Christian dialogue. As regards the prospect of such dialogue, I confess that I have over the years become less optimistic in the hope that the long age of Christian triumphalism over Judaism is truly being superseded by an age of Jewish-Christian dialogue. In view of recent Christian developments, such as ecclesiastical declarations deploring anti-Semitism and absolving Jews of the charge of deicide, this may seem a strange, and even perverse, personal opinion. Yet I think that recent events have shown it to be realistic.

To most impartial observers it has always been a plain fact that, ever since the Age of Enlightenment, it was secularists who spearheaded the struggle for Jewish emancipation; organized Christian forces sometimes accepted emancipation, often opposed it, but rarely if ever led the fight. This fact, plain to so many, I myself failed to see (or refused to accept) until quite recently. I saw the distinction between the new Nazi and the old Christian anti-Semitism, but could not bear to admit a relation between them. In the grim years of Nazism and immediately thereafter, I found it humanly impossible to see enemies on every side. Twenty-five years later, however, it is necessary to confront yet another painful truth.

I will confine myself to two examples, both concerning German Christians opposed to Nazism. In 1933, many Jews then in Germany, myself included, made a veritable saint of Cardinal Faulhaber, crediting him with opposing both Nazism and Nazi anti-Semitism. This image remained with me for many years. I had read the Cardinal's relevant sermons, but had somehow not noticed what they said. Not until about three years ago, when I came upon Guenter Lewy's masterful *The Catholic Church and Nazi Germany,* did I realize that Faulhaber had confined his defense to the Jews of the Old Testament, and had gone out of his way to make clear that he was not defending his Jewish contemporaries. To quote Lewy:

We must distinguish, he told the faithful, between the people of Israel before the death of Christ, who were vehicles of divine revelation, and the Jews after the death of Christ, who have become restless wanderers over the earth. But even the Jewish people of ancient times could not justly claim credit for the wisdom of the Old Testament. So unique were these laws that one was bound to say: "People of Israel, this did not grow in your own garden of your own planting. This condemnation of usurious land-grabbing, this war against the oppression of the farmer by debt, this prohibition of usury, is not the product of your spirit."

Rarely has the Christian belief in the revealed character of the Hebrew Bible been put to so perverse a use.

My second example is even more painful, for it involves none other than the universally beloved Dietrich Bonhoeffer, brave anti-Nazi Christian witness and martyr to his cause. Even now I find it hard to believe that he should have confined his attack on Nazi Aryan legislation to its application to converted Jews; and I find it even harder to believe that these words were written by Bonhoeffer in Nazi Germany in response to Nazi anti-Semitism:

Now the measures of the state toward Judaism in addition stand in quite special context for the church. The church of Christ has never lost sight of the thought that the "chosen people," who nailed the redeemer of the world to the cross, must bear the curse for its action through a long history of suffering. . . .

Rather than comment myself, I prefer to cite the comment of the American Christian theologian, J. Coert Rylaarsdam:

We all think of Dietrich Bonhoeffer as a good Christian, even a martyr, perhaps. With great courage he insisted on "the crown rights of the Redeemer" within his own church. Moreover, he insisted that Jews who had converted to Christianity were entitled to the same rights in the church as other Christians, a position by no means unanimously held in the church of Hitler's Germany. Nevertheless, standing in the Christian tradition of the curse, Bonhoeffer did not hesitate to appeal to it to rationalize Hitler's program for Jews faithful to their own faith.

To keep the record straight, one must add that the passages in question were written in 1933 (when, according to his friend Eberhard Bethge, Bonhoeffer still suffered from "lack of reality-relatedness"), that his opposition to Nazism became more complete as it came to assume secular-political expression, and, indeed, that he took personal risks to save Jewish lives. Even so, I know of no evidence yet (though I would dearly love to hear of any) to the effect that Bonhoeffer ever totally repudiated the Christian "tradition of the curse." From the very beginning he opposed the encroachment of racism upon the church and spoke up for Jews converted to Christianity. By 1940 he charged that the church "was silent when she should have cried out because the blood of the innocent was crying aloud to heaven . . . she is guilty of the deaths of the weakest and most defenseless brothers of Jesus Christ." But during the most grievous Jewish martyrdom in all of history, did he ever repudiate a millennial Christian tradition, and seek a bond (even if only in his own mind) with "Jews faithful to their own faith," because, and not in spite of, their faithfulness? How different would Bonhoeffer's struggle have been if he had repudiated the "Christian tradition of the curse" from the start! How different would Jewish fate have been in our time had his whole church repudiated it!

In America, to be sure, it has always been different, and the churches of the 1960's differ everywhere from those of the 1940's, there being historic changes in the making in Christian attitudes toward Jews. The question is, however, whether American differences are not mainly due to the effect of secular democracy, and also whether the changes in Christian attitudes toward Jews possess the radicalism which, after Auschwitz, is a categorical imperative. Here again, only ruthless truthfulness can save the future of Jewish-Christian dialogue. And the truth, as I am now forced to see it, is that the organized Christian forces will find it easiest to drop the ancient charge of deicide, harder to recognize roots of anti-Semitism in the New Testament, and hardest of all to face up to the fact that Jews and Judaism are both still alive. Confronted with the awkward fact of Jewish survival after the advent of Christianity, theologians have looked upon Judaism as a fossil, an anachronism, a shadow. It is not easy to reverse a doctrine which has persisted for two millennia (assuming not only religious, but also, as in Toynbee, secular, and, as in Marx, anti-religious forms), and to recognize that both Jews and Judaism have maintained an unbroken existence throughout the entire Christian era. But how can a Jew, however he may strain his ears, hear God speak to the Christian church, if even after Auschwitz this ancient calumny is not at length totally and categorically rejected? And how, he wonders, can a Christian enter into dialogue with a Jew unless he recognizes that the person across the table is no shadow but alive?

These questions became traumatically vivid for any Jew committed to Jewish-Christian dialogue during the momentous events of May and June 1967, when the state of Israel, the most incontestable proof that the Jewish people still lives, was threatened with destruction. The secular Western press understood well enough that Israel was fighting for her life. Yet only a handful of Christian spokesmen showed the same understanding. Why should Christian spokesmen have remained neutral as between Israel's claim to the right to live and Arab claims to the right to destroy her—if not because of old, unconscious, theologically-inspired doubts as to whether the "fossil" Israel did indeed have the right to live? Why has there always been much Christian concern for Arab refugees from Israel, but none whatever for Jewish refugees from Arab countries—if not because of old, no longer consciously remembered ecclesiastical doctrines to the effect that Jews (unlike Arabs) must be kept landless, and therefore rightless? Why were ecclesiastical authorities untroubled by two decades of Moslem control of the Christian holy places (and of Arab desecration of Jewish holy places), and yet now so deeply distressed by Jewish control?

But a still more ultimate question is raised by the events of 1967. For two long weeks in May the worldwide Jewish community perceived the specter of a second Jewish Holocaust in a single generation. For two weeks it listened to the same words emanating from Cairo and Damascus which had once emanated from Berlin, largely composed, one may be sure, by pupils of Joseph Goebbels. For two weeks it longed for Christian words of apprehension and concern. But whereas some such words came from secular sources, from the churches there was little but silence.[3] Once again, Jews were alone. This fact, transcending as it does all politics, is a trauma for Jews regardless of political persuasion—non-Zionists and even anti-Zionists as well as Zionists.

[3]See A. Roy and Alice L. Eckardt, "Again, Silence in the Churches," *The Christian Century*, July 26 and August 2, 1967.

Moreover, it stands between Jews and Christians even now, for when Jews ask why there was no moral Christian outcry against a second Auschwitz they are still widely misunderstood, as demanding of Christians that they side politically with Israel against the Arab states.

Any Jew pondering this ultimate question must surely reject the idea that the Christian churches abandoned Jews knowingly to a second Holocaust. What, then, was revealed by the Christian silence in the spring of 1967? Not, I believe, an old Christian anti-Semitism, but rather a new Jewish-Christian problem—the fearful truth that Hitler, against his will bringing Jews and Christians closer, also had his will in setting them further apart.

A Jew at Auschwitz was murdered because he was a Jew; a Christian was murdered only if he was a saint: but there are few saints among either Jews or Christians. Hitler gave a new and perverse reality to the ancient Jewish doctrine that anyone born a Jew is a Jew. He also gave a new and perverse reality to the ancient Christian doctrine that one becomes a Christian only through an act of voluntary commitment—and, with diabolical cunning as well as terror, he led Christians into temptation. Hitler tried to create an abyss between Jews and Christians; he succeeded; and—this is the horror—he continues to enjoy posthumous successes. The Jew after Auschwitz exists with the knowledge of abandonment; the Christian cannot bear to face his responsibility for this abandonment. He knows that, as a Christian, he should voluntarily have gone to Auschwitz, where his own Master would have been dragged, voluntarily or involuntarily, and he is wracked by a sense of guilt the deeper the less he has cause to feel it. Hence the Christian failure to face Auschwitz. Hence Christian recourse to innocuous generalities. Hence, too, Christian silence in May 1967. If in May 1967 the Christian community did not cry out against a second Auschwitz, it was not because of its indifference to the words emanating from Cairo and Damascus, but rather because it did not hear them. It failed to recognize the danger of a second Holocaust because it has yet to recognize the fact of the first.

To bridge the Jewish-Christian gulf which Hitler has succeeded in creating is a task of incalculable importance, and at a Jewish-Christian colloquium prior to the events of May 1967 I attempted a hesitant step in that direction. I said there that if every Christian in Hitler's Europe had followed the example of the King of Denmark and decided to put on the yellow star, there would today be neither confusion nor despair in the church, nor talk of the death of God. I said with every emphasis at my command that, as a Jew after Auschwitz, I did not and could not speak as a judge, but only as a witness. To remove every trace of ambiguity or doubt I stated not politely, but quite truthfully, that I had been sixteen years of age when Hitler came to power, and had not known then, any more than I knew now, whether I would have become a Nazi had I been born a Gentile. Yet a leading Christian thinker, himself a lifelong anti-Nazi, mistook my statement for a case of Jewish triumphalism. So wide still is the gulf between Jews and Christians which Hitler opened decades ago. So close are we to handing him further, posthumous victories.

IV

On another Public occasion, in March 1967, I asked the following question:

Would we [like Job] be able to say that the question of Auschwitz will be answered in any sense whatever in case the eclipse of God were ended and He appeared to us? An impossible and intolerable question.

Less than three months later this purely hypothetical question had become actual, when at Jerusalem the threat of total annihilation gave way to sudden salvation, atheists spoke of miracles, and hardboiled Western reporters resorted to biblical images.

The question *is* impossible and intolerable. Even Job's question is not answered by God's presence, and to him children are restored. The children of Auschwitz will not be restored, and the question of Auschwitz will not be answered by a saving divine presence.

And yet, is a Jew after Auschwitz permitted to despair of salvation because of Auschwitz? Is it permitted him to cast out all hope and all joy? But on the other side, can there be any hope and any joy, purchased at the price of forgetting? Any one of these responses would be further victories handed to Hitler, and are thus impossible.

It was into precisely this impossible and intolerable contradiction that believing Jews were placed by the events at Jerusalem in May and June 1967. Those events cast into clear relief the whole as yet unassimilated fact of an embattled, endangered, but nevertheless free Jewish state, emerging from ashes and catastrophe. Solely because of the connection of the events of May and June with Auschwitz did a military victory (rarely applauded in Judaism, and never for its own sake) acquire an inescapable religious dimension.

In this context, let me quote from a letter I recently received from Professor Harold Fisch of Bar-Ilan University in Israel:

May I report to you a conversation I had last summer with a colleague, a psychologist, who had served during the war as an artillery officer in Sinai. I asked him how he accounted for the remarkable heroism of the quite ordinary soldier of the line, for, as you may know, exemplary heroism was the normal thing at that time; mere carrying out of duty was the exception. Where, I asked him, was the psychological spring? To my surprise, he answered that what deeply motivated each and every solider was the memory of the Holocaust, and the feeling that *above all this must never happen again*. There had been an ominous similarity between the statements of Arab leaders, their radio, and newspapers, and the remembered threats of the Nazis: we had entered into a *Shoah* (holocaust) psychosis, all around us enemies threatening us with extermination and having both the means and the will to carry out their threat. As the ring closed in and help seemed far, one noticed one's neighbors who had been in Auschwitz and Bergen-Belsen going about white-faced. It was all too obvious what was the source of their dread. The years in between had momentarily fallen away, and they were back in that veritable nightmare world. The dark night of the soul was upon us. *And it was the commandment which the Lord of history had, so to speak, pronounced at Auschwitz which saved us.* [Italics added.] I told my friend that I could not entirely accept his explanation because I knew that a majority of the soldiers had no personal or family recollections of the European Holocaust: they had come from North Africa or Yemen, or even the neighboring Arab countries where at that time such horrors were unknown. How could they feel the force of the analogy as could the survivors of Buchenwald? He told me that the intervening twenty years had brought it about that the Holocaust had become a collective experience pressing consciously and unconsciously on the minds of all, even the young, for whom Jewish history in the Diaspora had come to an end with the beginnings of Israeli independence.

It is solely because of this connection of the events of May and June with Auschwitz that a Jew must both tremble and rejoice. He must tremble lest he permit any light after Auschwitz to relieve the darkness of Auschwitz. He must rejoice, lest he add to the darkness of Auschwitz. Rejoicing after Auschwitz and because of Auschwitz, the Jew must be a Jew, *am Yisrael chai* ("the people Israel, alive"), a witness to the world, preparing a way for God.

further reading

Elie Wiesel spent part of his youth in the camps at Auschwitz and Buchenwald: his autobiographical *Night* (1964) is an unforgettable account of those years. See also his *Souls on Fire* (1972), an exceptional book about Hasidism.

Richard L. Rubenstein, *After Auschwitz* (1966). In contrast to the essay by Emil Fackenheim in this chapter, Rubenstein hears no "Voice" at all from Auschwitz. Judaism, he writes, will ultimately "pass away, for omnipotent Nothingness is Lord of All Creation."

Milton Steinberg, *Basic Judaism* (1947). A very clear and nontechnical introduction. There are chapters on the Torah, God, "The Good Life," and other major topics.

Herman Wouk, *This Is My God* (1959). The author of *The Caine Mutiny* and other works of fiction here turns to his own Orthodox Jewish faith and describes it with great feeling.

Max I. Dimont, *Jews, God and History* (1962). A popular history of the Jews. Its author argues that the topic is "too fascinating, too interesting, too incredible to remain the private property of Jews and scholars."

Herbert Weiner's *9½ Mystics: The Kabbala Today* (1969) is a good introduction to the difficult subject of Jewish mysticism. Gershon Scholem is the outstanding scholar of the topic: see his *Major Trends in Jewish Mysticism* (3rd ed., 1954). Leo Schaya's *The Universal Meaning of the Kabbalah* (1971) is written by a man who is himself within the mystical tradition.

Lewis Browne (ed.), *The Wisdom of Israel* (1945). Excerpts from the Old Testament, the Talmud, Maimonides, the Zohar, Hasidic teachings, and scores of other authors and sources—all with helpful introductory notes.

Judah Goldin, *The Living Talmud* (1957). Selections from the Talmud, which is a vast body of commentary on the Law and "legends, folklore, . . . theosophical and theological speculation, homilies, parables prayers, gnomic sayings, historical reminiscence."

THIS DISTANCE MEASURED IN MILLIMETERS
VERIFIES THE PERCENTAGE OF YOUR
ENLARGEMENT / REDUCTION

The Dead Sea Scrolls

from forgotten caves

> I will sing Thy mercies,
> > and on Thy might I will meditate all day long.
> I will bless Thy Name evermore.

> Dead Sea Scrolls

The most spectacular discovery of modern times in the field of biblical archaeology was made in 1947 by a Bedouin shepherd boy who was looking for a stray goat. Climbing the cliffs near the shore of the Dead Sea, he noticed an odd hole in the cliff face and threw a rock into it. Hearing the crack of pottery, he retreated, fearful of desert spirits. But later he and a friend returned to enter the cave, and there they found several jars containing what turned out to be the first of the Dead Sea Scrolls.

The harrowing story of how the priceless scrolls were haphazardly carried about and finally sold is too long to be recounted here, but they eventually drifted into the hands of scholars who recognized the nature of the discovery. Archaeological expeditions then scoured the area examining other caves, often competing in the search with Bedouins who had also learned the value of the scrolls. Further important scroll finds were made, and at the same time excavations revealed the nearby Qumran settlement and monastery. Evidence found during the course of the digging suggested that the Qumran community had flourished until about 68 A.D. It is theorized that at the approach of a Roman legion, known to have entered the area at that time, members of the community had hidden their sacred books in the caves prior to fleeing.

The scrolls contained large portions of the Old Testament in Hebrew, which are of immense significance: these documents are a thousand years older than any other manuscript of the Hebrew Bible. Also in the scrolls are commentaries on the Bible and writings distinctive to the Qumran settlement. The Hebrew sect represented at Qumran, according to majority opinion, was the ascetic Essenes. The community lived by strict rules of discipline under a hierarchy of priests and believed that in the world and in man there raged a war between the forces of righteousness and the forces of evil. That war, moreover, was drawing to a close: the "last days" had come, and it was a time of intense expectations.

john allegro

The Life and Discipline of the Sect

John Allegro (1923–   ) is a Lecturer in Old Testament and Intertestamental Studies at the University of Manchester. He was one of the original members of the international editing team that first worked on the scrolls. Among his books are *The People of the Dead Sea Scrolls, The Treasure of the Copper Scroll,* and *The Dead Sea Scrolls: A Reappraisal,* from which the following selection is taken.

The scrolls were found in varying states of deterioration, and some were damaged by their subsequent handling. One of the tasks of the scholars was to attempt to piece together the many thousands of manuscript fragments that were found. Thus in the translations of scroll material in Allegro's essay, and again in the translation by Geza Vermes of the "Hymns of Thanksgiving," the words placed within brackets [ ] are reconstructions of missing materials. Within parentheses ( ) are words added by the translator for the sake of coherence.

The Sect knew itself primarily as the 'Covenant' (*bĕrīth*), and specifically as the 'New Covenant' (*bĕrīth hădāshah*). Other names were the 'Congregation' (*'ēdah*), 'Assembly' (*qahal*), 'Party' (*'ēsah,* sometimes also meaning 'Council'), and 'Community' (*yahad),* a word conveying the idea of 'unity', and these last two are often combined into 'Party of the Community' (*'ēsath ha-yahad*). This idea of unity lay very close to the heart of the Sect, and the same word *yahad* is used very often adverbially meaning 'in common'. Thus they shared all the necessities of life, spiritual as well as material:

For everything shall be (held) in common, Truth and fair humility, and faithful love, and just consideration for one's fellow in the holy Council . . .

There was no place for the egoist in such a gathering:

No man shall walk in the stubbornness of his heart to err after his own will, eyes and purpose.

They took their meals communally, and sang their praises to God together, and in joint session held their deliberate councils. When one became a full member of the Sect, he 'mixed' his worldly possessions in the common pool, and he received back only the necessities of life. However, it should not be thought that this was an egalitarian society, where each man was as good as his fellow. We have frequent mention of their 'ranks', and according to their

John Allegro, "The Life and Discipline of the Sect." From John Allegro, *The Dead Sea Scrolls: A Reappraisal* (Pelican Original, 1964). © John Allegro, 1956, 1964. By permission of Penguin Books, Ltd.

respective status in the society was their order of seating in the deliberative assemblies, of their speaking, and in fact of practically every communal activity. And in everything the priests had precedence. It is true that in a special sense the whole Community saw themselves as a joint priesthood,

an eternal planting, a holy house of Israel, an assembly of supreme holiness for Aaron . . .

but beginning as a priestly society, founded by a priestly Teacher, it was the priestly element which held the casting vote in matters of moment concerning the whole of the Community. . . .

.   .   .

The executive head of the Party seems to have been a special Council of twelve men and three priests, ideally representing the twelve tribes of Israel and the three priestly families descended through the three sons of Levi. There were also panels of judges, twelve in number according to one document from Cave Four, and ten in the *Damascus Document,* consisting in this case of four priests and six laymen, all of whom must be well versed in the Book of Meditation and the Law of Moses, and none younger than twenty-five or older than sixty.

Here is a summary of the penal code as given in the *Manual.* Exclusion from the 'Purity of the Many' means a temporary or permanent excommunication from full initiation, so that the offender is reduced, as it were, to the ranks, being of no higher status than that of a probationer. 'Fining' means a deprivation of rations, serious enough in a Community which would in any case be living on the bare necessities of life.

For deliberate lying in the matter of personal possessions—exclusion from the Purity of the Many for one year, and one quarter rations.

Bearing a grudge unjustly against one's fellow—six months (a later hand has written above the line 'one year'), and taking personal vengeance—the same.

Foolish speech—three months.

Interrupting another person speaking—ten days.

Sleeping during a session of the Many—thirty days.

Leaving a session without permission or good reason, up to three times in a single session—ten days.

Unnecessary self-exposure—six months.

Indecent exposure during bodily movement—thirty days.

Spitting during a session of the Many—thirty days.

Foolish laughter—thirty days.

Slandering one's fellow—exclusion for one year; slandering the Many—banishment for ever.

Murmuring against the institution of the Community—banishment for ever; against one's fellow—six months.

A man who is so overawed by the institution of the Community as to betray the truth and walk obstinately alone, and yet he returns—two years. In the first he will not touch the Purity of the Many, and in the second he will not approach the Banquet of the Many but shall take his place after all the others. When his two years are completed, his case will be investigated and if they admit him, he will be enrolled according to his rank, and may therefore be consulted in judgement. A veteran of more than ten years, however, who shall similarly default, shall return no more, and anybody associating with such a person will suffer the same fate.

That women and children had some place in the Community is shown by the heading of the *Manual:*

when they come they will gather together all the arrivals, women and children, and will recite (in their ears) all the statutes of the Covenant.

Then, in discussing the upbringing of boys, it lays down that a lad may not take a woman to wife until he is twenty, by which time he should know the difference between good and evil. Then he must realize the responsibilities involved, for, from that time, the wife may witness against him in process of law and may take part in the deciding of the issue. More material evidence of the presence of women at Qumran has been the discovery of female skeletons in the cemetery. Furthermore, some of the rules of the *Damascus Document* seem to have been formulated with a view to family life and speak of orphans and unmarried women requiring help.

. . .

All in all, it seems the Covenanters had none too high an opinion of the fair sex, believing them all potential seducers of men from the strait and narrow way. . . .

. . .

This apparent distrust of women may have been carried by some sections of the Order to the point of avoiding marriage altogether. In this we have one of the many correspondences between the Scrolls Community and an ancient Jewish sect known as the *Essenes,* described to us by Josephus and other historians. We shall have occasion to refer to them frequently, and most scholars believe that the Covenanters of the Scrolls are to be identified with at least one branch of the Essene movement. A section of the Essenes were celibate, and it is interesting to find that one of the Qumran documents seems to modify certain biblical ordinances with just this kind of situation in mind. Thus, although Exodus xxii. 16—17 requires a man seducing an unbetrothed virgin to marry her and pay her father an appropriate dowry (Deuteronomy xxii. 29 adding that he should not thereafter be allowed to divorce her), the Qumran document says that the offender should merely be fined two minas (i.e. a hundred shekels, the fine required by Deuteronomy xxii. 19 from a husband falsely accusing his newly-wed wife of unchastity) and be expelled from the community for life. . . .

. . .

INITIATION

The *Manual* lays down three stages through which the initiate must pass. The first, of unspecified period, is a matter of becoming acquainted with the spirit and practices of the Sect and is preceded by an examination, by the Inspector, of his motives and general outlook. At the conclusion of this stage, the Many debate his case and may, if satisfied, admit him to the next stage, or alternatively, can reject him altogether. If promoted, he will then pass into the Party of the Community, but without touching the Purity of the Many. At the end of a further year, a general session of the Community will deliberate on his suitability for further promotion and if favourably inclined, may admit him to the last stage, which again will last one year. In this last stage he will hand over to the Overseer all his worldly wealth, and it will be marked to his credit but not yet 'mixed' in with the common pool. He is still excluded from the Messianic Banquet, but is now apparently admitted to the Purity of the Many. If, on his completion of this stage, he is adjudged fit to enter full membership, he is enrolled and assigned a rank amongst brethren. Now, and only now, may he take his share in the Community decisions, be asked for his counsel, and permitted to pool his possessions with the Sect's. He has now entered the Covenant before God,

to do all that He has commanded, and to remain constant in following Him even in the face of terror, fright, or ordeal which may face him during the dominion of Belial.

At the initiation ceremony the priests and the Levites pronounce their blessings, praising 'the God of deliverances and all His deeds of faithfulness', and all the members say 'Amen! Amen!' Then follows a recitation of the wondrous works of God, His compassionate works of grace towards Israel, whilst the Levites recount the rebelliousness of the people and their sin under the dominion of Belial. Then those entering the Covenant make a general confession:

W₋ have been perverse [. . .], we have done wickedly, we and our forefathers before us, walking [. . .] truth. But [God] is righteous, [who has executed] His judgements upon us and upon our fathers; and His faithful mercies he has bestowed upon us from everlasting to everlasting.

Following this, the priests bless the 'men of God's lot, who walk perfectly in all His ways', and say:

May He bless thee with every good: may He keep thee from all evil, and illumine thy heart with the knowledge of life, and favour thee with eternal wisdom. And may He lift up the face of His sure mercies upon you to everlasting peace.

The Levites than take up their curses upon the men of Belial's party, condemn them to eternal fire, and proceed to give a solemn warning to those who would enter this sacred Covenant that, should they prove unfaithful to it,

their lot will be placed in the midst of the eternally accursed.

Again the new members respond with the two-fold Amen. This, we may be sure, is the service for reception of new members, but we actually meet it in the *Manual* as the annual Covenant service, where the membership of each initiate is renewed by this service of self-dedication every year, 'all the days of the dominion of Belial', in the order of priests, Levites, and then the people, according to their respective ranks. Thus the Community is kept constantly aware of its blessings and responsibilities and the ever present struggle between the ultimate rule or kingdom of God and the temporary dominion of Belial.

This rite of initiation into the full membership of the Community was probably accompanied by an initial baptism ceremony. . . . Salvation could come to the Qumran Covenanter only by complete separation of himself and his possessions from the world. This was not prompted by any smug self-righteousness on his part, but because he sincerely believed that pollution from the non-purified world meant the risk of contact with the dominion of Belial or the Devil, which might compromise the constant battle he was fighting within himself against the powers of evil. We shall have more to say on this matter when discussing the theology of the Sect, but the same idea prompted their strict disciplinary measures against any defaulting member on what might seem to us trivial faults. To the Sect, the slightest falling away from their very high standards of conduct and ritual purity meant that the member responsible had been brought into the power of the Devil, even though only for a fleeting moment of weakness, but yet in that time had proved himself a weak link in the chain of their defence against the dominion of Belial. Once let the powers of evil get a hold on a man, and he might prove a source of added temptation to other brethren, who must at all costs be protected in this critical time preceding the end of the present world order. Thus the initiate

will not unite himself with him in his work or his wealth lest he cause him to incur the guilt of transgression: for he must keep far from him in every matter . . . for all who are not reckoned in His Covenant are to be separated, they and all their possessions, and the holy man is not to rely on vain works, for vain are all those who know not His Covenant.

For this reason the rules for initiation are very exacting. This was no missionary Sect, going out into the world looking for members. People who desired the hard and pure life of the Covenanters with its promised blessings of the messianic age came to them and devoted themselves entirely to the cause, withholding nothing. If they came merely because they had suffered disappointments in life or had personal troubles or the like, the chances were that they would soon tire of the tremendous sacrifices demanded of the Sectarian, and fall by the wayside. Such people had to be rooted out before they came near the Purity of full members, hence the long and searching probation. One cannot doubt that at this stage many were turned away, and few reached the full initiation.

THE DAILY LIFE OF THE COVENANTER

There is little in the literature so far recovered from Qumran which tells us much about the secular activities of the Covenanter, but a certain amount can be reconstructed from the excavations of the Khirbet. There were certainly the usual domestic tasks to perform, such as cleaning the communal rooms and kitchens, sweeping the plaster floors, raking over those of beaten earth. Some would work in the pottery workshops, preparing the clay, turning the vessels on the wheel, or firing the fashioned jars. The kitchen ovens have been found where the cooks prepared the communal meals, and the pantry where the simple crockery was stacked for the use of the Sectarians in the long dining-hall next door. Continual attention must have been given to building repairs and alterations, and in the winter the water conduits would need to be kept clear of mud and other blockages preventing the desperately needed supply to the cisterns. No doubt the repair of the aqueduct itself was an annual task round about October after eight or nine months of summer drought. At this time the empty cisterns would be examined for cracks in the plaster which, if not repaired in time, would allow the precious water to seep away into the ground. The simple reed and marl roofs would require attention after the summer's sun, if they were to withstand the heavy winter showers. And all through the year the shepherds and goatherds tended their flocks in the vicinity and particularly by the fresh vegetation of the 'Ain Feshkha, where doubtless simple farming also was carried on by the members to provide food for their Community.

From the Scriptorium would come the steady scratching of pens, as the scribes copied their precious scrolls, and near by their fellows prepared the inks and skins for their use. Perhaps the women of the Community would be weaving the flaxen cloths for wrapping scrolls for storage, and either in the Settlement or in the caves a librarian was at his task of sorting and classifying the texts.

And all the time, day and night, came the chant of the recited Law or the hymns of thanksgiving. The duty of studying the Mosaic Law was taken very seriously. God's command to Joshua that

this book of the Law shall not depart out of thy mouth, but thou shalt meditate therein day and night . . .

was carried out to the letter by the Community:

Let the Many keep awake in community a third of all the nights in the year in order to read aloud from the Book and to expound Judgement and to sing blessings altogether.

. . .

During the night, as some slept in their tents and huts under the cliffs round about, and their brethren in the Settlement kept up this continual chant of hymns and readings, some of the elders would be standing in the watchtower, gazing at the skies, noting the movements of the moon and stars. We have a number of their works referring to the movements of the heavenly bodies, and not all their study was of purely academic interest. For them the stars and their positions could affect men's lives, and amongst their esoteric documents we have one giving the signs of the Zodiac distributed over the days of the month. Natural phenomena occurring at those times could be used to predict certain events. Thus:

if it thunders in the sign of the Twins—terror and distress caused by foreigners . . .

Another such astrological work, written this time in a secret code of their own devising, portrays the influence of the heavenly bodies on the physical and spiritual characteristics of those born in certain sections of the Zodiac. Thus, for example, a person born under Taurus, the Bull, will have long and lean thighs, narrow toes, and a humble demeanour. He will have inherited a balance of good spirit against bad, in the proportion of six to three. On the other hand, a rascal cursed with a proportion of eight parts of bad spirit to only one of good may be expected to display a somewhat coarse appearance with broad, hairy thighs and short, stubby toes and fingers.

. . .

We know of one rite peculiar to Qumran which probably became the sacramental focus of their worship, just as basically the same act did for the Christian Church. This was the Messianic Banquet, which is described for us in some detail in the *Rule for all the Congregation:*

[This is (the order of) the ses]sion of men of repute, [who are called] to meet for the Council of the Community. When [God] begets the Messiah with them, there shall come [the Priest], head of all the Congregation of Israel, and all the priests, e[lders of the children of] Aaron, [invited] to the Meeting as men of repute. And they shall sit be[fore him, each] according to his rank, corresponding to his st[ation] in the camps and marches. And all the heads of the el[ders of the Congregation] shall sit before them, each man according to his rank. And [when] they are gathered at the communion ta[ble, or to drink] the new wi[ne], and the communion table is laid out, and the new wine [mixed] for drinking, [let no man stretch forth] his hand on the first of the bread or the [wine] before the Priest; for [he will bl]ess the first of the bread and win[e, and will stretch forth] his hand on the bread first.

And after[wards], the Messiah will str[etch forth] his hands upon the bread, [and then] all the Congregation of the Community [will give bles]sings, each [according to] his rank. And after this prescription shall they act for every ass[embly where] at least ten men are assembled.

The chief actors in the Qumran Sect's Messianic Banquet, then, are the two Messiahs, i.e., the High Priest and the lay or Davidic Messiah, of whom we shall speak later, the priests, the heads of the thousands of Israel, the elders, and the Congregation. This will be the pattern of the Banquet to be held for the Elect who survive the great purging of the world in the last days. The last sentence, however, makes it clear that it could be a frequently observed ceremony involving far fewer participants than the numbers of the true Israel in the apocalyptic ideal, and since elsewhere in the *Manual* we have reference to the customary blessing of the bread and wine before partaking of the daily meal, it seems probable that every communal repast was considered to some extent a rehearsal of the Messianic Banquet. On the other hand, there is some evidence for a periodic observance of this act which exceeds in scope and importance the day-to-day communal feeding. . . .

THE DOCTRINES OF THE SECT

The basic philosophical and religious conception of the Sect is contained in their doctrine of the Two Spirits. Briefly this implies that there are in the Universe two spirits, one of good and the other of evil, respectively symbolized as Light and Darkness. Both are under the same supreme rule of God who will eventually give the victory to Good, but only after a prolonged cosmic battle. The war of the Spirits is reflected on earth in the tensions within every man for good and evil, as the *Manual* says:

And He assigned to Man two Spirits in which he should walk until the time of His visitation. They are the spirits of Truth and Perversity: Truth born out of the spring of Light, Perversity from the well of Darkness. The dominion of all the children of righteousness is in the hands of the Prince of Light so that they walk in the ways of Light, whereas the government of the children of Perversity is in the hands of the Angel of Darkness, to walk in the ways of Darkness. The purpose of the Angel of Darkness is to lead all the children of righteousness astray, and all their sin, their iniquities, their guilt and their rebellious works are the result of his domination, in accordance with God's mysteries until His appointed time. And all their stripes and seasons of affliction are consequent upon the rule of his (Satan's) hostility.

Thus the whole cosmos is divided for the time being into two camps, and as Man is apportioned these two spirits so will he behave:

Until now the Spirits of Truth and Perversity struggle within the heart of Man, behaving with wisdom and folly. And according as a man inherits truth and righteousness, so will he hate Perversion, but in so far as his heritage is rather from the side of perversion and wickedness, so shall he loathe the Truth.

As we have seen, another document tells us that his 'inheriting' of these Spirits depends on the stars at his birth, and even that the proportions within a man can be numerically reckoned.

Here are the fruits of the Spirit of Truth as enumerated in the *Manual:*

To enlighten the heart of Man and to make straight before him all the ways of true righteousness, to make his heart fearful for the judgements of God; a humble spirit, an even temper, a freely compassionate nature, an eternal goodness, and understanding and insight and mighty wisdom which believes in all God's works, and a confident trust in His many mercies, and a spirit of knowledge in every ordered work, and zeal for righteous judgements, and a determined holiness with steadfast mind; loyal feelings towards all the children of Truth, and a radiant purity which loathes every impure idol; a humble bearing and a discretion regarding all the hidden things of Truth and secrets of Knowledge.

The reward to those who show these qualities in their lives is

healing and abundant peace, length of life and fruitful seed with everlasting blessings, and eternal joy in immortality, a crown of glory and a robe of majesty in eternal light.

To be contrasted with this sublime state is the lot of those led by the Spirit of Perversion. Among the fruits of their Spirit are greed, injustice, wickedness, falsehood, pride, deceit, hasty temper, jealousy, lechery, blasphemy, spiritual obtuseness, and obstinacy, and vile cunning. No wonder that the best he can expect in the 'Day of Visitation' is

many stripes from the Angels of Destruction, in the everlasting Pit, through the overwhelming God of Vengeance, in everlasting terror and perpetual disgrace, with the shame of extermination in the Fire of the dark regions. And all their times for all generations will be in grievous mourning and bitter misfortune, in the dark calamities until they are destroyed with no chance to escape.

Since the Spirits are apportioned at birth, this apparent determinism may seem to override the bounds of justice. If a man, by his stars, is given a balance of evil in his character it seems hardly fair to condemn him to such punishment for eternity. The argument will have a familiar ring in these days of popular psychology, but the Qumran Covenanter, at least, had his answer. For all men there was one way of salvation, depending on his own will and the mercy of God. If he would but apply himself to the study of God's Word in humility and pious devotion, God would answer by granting him a restored cleanliness, a sense of perfection.

For it is . . . through the submission of his soul to the statutes of God that his flesh may be cleansed ('flesh' being here exactly the Pauline *sarx,* the debased moral nature of Man) . . . He will order his steps in the perfect Way and in all the paths of God . . . not transgressing a single one of His words.

Man must prepare himself by self-discipline, but the action of cleansing is entirely dependent on the will of God. Man has no claim to justification merely on the grounds of his good works; it is an act of divine grace, as much in the eyes of the Covenanter as of Paul.

As for me [says the psalmist at the end of the *Manual*], my justification belongs to God, and in His hand is the perfection of my way . . . and from the fountain of His righteousness (springs) my justification, a light in my heart.

And again,

if I totter, the covenant love of God is my eternal salvation, and if I stumble in the crookedness of my flesh, my justification depends on the righteousness of God, which is eternal.

The word used here for 'justification' is *mishpat,* which also means 'judge-ment'. Man's justification is the pronounced verdict of God, a legal 'clearing' which by no means implies sinlessness. Rather, Man's iniquity has been cleansed by the grace of God: he is restored into true sonship and, in the words of another passage of the *Manual,* 'estimated perfect'.

g. vermes (translator) ⸺⸺⸺⸺⸺⸺⸺⸺⸺⸺⸺⸺⸺⸺⸺

Hymns of Thanksgiving

There are about twenty-five hymns, or psalms, in the scrolls, and they are a part of those nonbiblical writings that originated in the community itself. As such, they reflect the doctrines and feelings of the group, and may have been regularly recited or sung as part of particular ceremonies. But whatever their doctrinal basis or public use, the hymns remain essentially the voices of individuals addressing their God in a troubled age.

Hungarian-born Geza Vermes (1924–   ) is a Fellow of Wolfson College, Oxford University, and was one of the major translators and interpreters of the scrolls. His *Dead Sea Scrolls in English*, from which the following hymns are taken, presents all of the nonbiblical scrolls with notes on the community and the texts.

5

I thank Thee, O Lord,
   for Thou hast redeemed my soul from the Pit,
and from the Hell of Abaddon
   Thou hast raised me up to everlasting height.

I walk on limitless level ground,
and I know there is hope for him
   whom Thou hast shaped from dust
   for the everlasting Council.
Thou hast cleansed a perverse spirit of great sin
   that it may stand with the host of the Holy Ones,
and that it may enter into community
   with the congregation of the Sons of Heaven.

Thou hast allotted to man an everlasting destiny
   amidst the spirits of knowledge,
that he may praise Thy Name in a common rejoicing
   and recount Thy marvels before all Thy works.

And yet I, a creature of clay,
   what am I?
Kneaded with water,
   what is my worth and my might?

For I have stood in the realm of wickedness
    and my lot was with the damned;
the soul of the poor one was carried away
    in the midst of great tribulation.
Miseries of torment dogged my steps
while all the snares of the Pit were opened
    and the lures of wickedness were set up
    and the nets of the damned (were spread) on the waters;
while all the arrows of the Pit
    flew out without cease,
    and striking, left no hope;
while the rope beat down in judgement
    and a destiny of wrath (fell) upon the abandoned
    and a venting of fury upon the cunning.
It was a time of the wrath of all Satan
    and the bonds of death tightened without any escape.

The torrents of Satan shall reach
    to all sides of the world.
In all their channels
    a consuming fire shall destroy
    every tree, green and barren, on their banks;
unto the end of their courses
    it shall scourge with flames of fire,
and shall consume the foundations of the earth
    and the expanse of dry land.
The bases of the mountains shall blaze
    and the roots of the rocks shall turn
    to torrents of pitch;
it shall devour as far as the great Abyss.

The torrents of Satan shall break into Abaddon,
    and the deeps of the Abyss shall groan
    amid the roar of heaving mud.
The land shall cry out because of the calamity
    fallen upon the world,
    and all its deeps shall howl.
And all those upon it shall rave
    and shall perish amid the great misfortune.
For God shall sound His mighty voice,
    and His holy abode shall thunder
    with the truth of His glory.
The heavenly hosts shall cry out
    and the world's foundations
    shall stagger and sway.

The war of the heavenly warriors shall scourge the earth;
    and it shall not end before the appointed destruction
    which shall be for ever and without compare.

10

                    .   .   .

[I am] as a sailor in a ship
    amid furious seas;
their waves and all their billows
    roar against me.
[There is no] calm in the whirlwind
    that I may restore my soul,
no path that I may straighten my way
    on the face of the waters.
The deeps resound to my groaning
    and [my soul has journeyed] to the gates of death.

But I shall be as one who enters a fortified city,
    as one who seeks refuge behind a high wall
    until deliverance (comes);
    I will [lean on] Thy truth, O my God.
For Thou wilt set the foundation on rock
    and the framework by the measuring-cord of justice;
and the tried stones [Thou wilt lay]
    by the plumb-line [of truth],
to [build] a mighty [wall] which shall not sway;
    and no man entering there shall stagger.

For no enemy shall ever invade [it
    since its doors shall be] doors of protection
    through which no man shall pass;
and its bars shall be firm
    and no man shall break them.
No rabble shall enter in with their weapons of war
    until all the [arrows] of the war of wickedness
    have come to an end.

                    .   .   .

12

I [thank Thee, O Lord],
    for Thou hast enlightened me through Thy truth.
In Thy marvellous mysteries,
and in Thy lovingkindness to a man [of vanity,
and] in the greatness of Thy mercy to a perverse heart
    Thou hast granted me knowledge.

Who is like Thee among the gods, O Lord,
  and who is according to Thy truth?
Who, when he is judged,
  shall be righteous before Thee?
For no spirit can reply to Thy rebuke
  nor can any withstand Thy wrath.

Yet Thou bringest all the sons of Thy truth
  in forgiveness before Thee,
[to cleanse] them of their faults
  through Thy great goodness,
and to establish them before Thee
  through the multitude of Thy mercies
  for ever and ever.

For Thou art an eternal God;
  all Thy ways are determined for ever [and ever]
 and there is none other beside Thee.
And what is a man of Naught and Vanity
  that he should understand Thy marvellous mighty deeds? . . .

17

I thank Thee, my God,
  for Thou hast dealt wondrously to dust,
  and mightily towards a creature of clay!
I thank Thee, I thank Thee!

What am I, that Thou shouldst [teach] me
  the counsel of Thy truth,
and give me understanding
  of Thy marvellous works;
that Thou shouldst lay hymns of thanksgiving
  within my mouth
  and [praise] upon my tongue,
and that of my circumcised lips
  (Thou shouldst make) a seat of rejoicing?

I will sing Thy mercies,
  and on Thy might I will meditate all day long.
I will bless Thy Name evermore.
I will declare Thy glory in the midst of the sons of men
  and my soul shall delight in Thy great goodness.

I know that Thy word is truth,
  and that righteousness is in Thy hand;

that all knowledge is in Thy purpose,
　　and that all power is in Thy might,
　　and that every glory is Thine.

19

　　　　　　　　　　　　. . .

Behold, [I was taken] from dust
　　[and] fashioned [out of clay]
as a source of uncleanness,
　　and a shameful nakedness,
a heap of dust,
　　and a kneading [with water,]
. . .

　　and a house of darkness,
　　a creature of clay returning to dust,
returning [at the appointed time
　　to dwell] in the dust whence it was taken.

How then shall dust reply [to its Maker,
　　and how] understand His [works]?
How shall it stand before Him who reproves it?
. . .

　　[and the Spring of] Eternity,
the Well of Glory
　　and the Fountain of Knowledge.
Not even [the wonderful] Heroes [can] declare all Thy glory
　　or stand in face of Thy wrath,
and there is none among them
　　that can answer Thy rebuke;
for Thou art just and none can oppose Thee.
How then can (man) who returns to his dust?

I hold my peace;
　　what more shall I say than this?
I have spoken in accordance with my knowledge,
　　out of the righteousness given to a creature of clay.
And how shall I speak unless Thou open my mouth;
　　how understand unless Thou teach me?
How shall I seek Thee unless Thou uncover my heart,
　　and how follow the way that is straight
　　unless [Thou guide me?
How shall my foot] stay on [the path
　　unless Thou] give it strength;
and how shall I rise . . .

*further reading*_____

Yigael Yadin, *The Message of the Scrolls* (1957). Yadin was another of those who played a central role in the early work on the scrolls. He designed this book for the general reader.

Edmund Wilson's *The Dead Sea Scrolls, 1947–1969* is the latest edition of a very popular work which was first published in 1955 both in *The New Yorker* magazine and in book form. It has been criticized by some scholars, but there is little written in this controversial area that is not subject to criticism.

Krister Stendahl (ed.), *The Scrolls and the New Testament* (1957). An outstanding collection of essays by leading scholars.

Theodore H. Gaster's *The Dead Sea Scriptures* (1956; rev. ed., 1964) is a translation of the scrolls (excluding the Old Testament manuscripts), with introductions and notes.

The eminent Oxford historian Cecil Roth is one of those who dissent from the prevailing view that the members of the Qumran community were Essenes. Roth argues that they were Zealots, and he summarizes his case in "New Light on the Dead Sea Scrolls," *Commentary*, Vol. 37, No. 6 (June 1964), pp. 27-32.

Other major authors include Millar Burrows, *The Dead Sea Scrolls* (1955) and *More Light on the Dead Sea Scrolls* (1961); Frederick F. Bruce, *Second Thoughts on the Dead Sea Scrolls* (1961); William Hugh Brownlee, *The Meaning of the Qumran Scrolls for the Bible* (1964); and Frank Cross, *The Ancient Library of Qumran* (1958).

Christianity

_____ *taking up the cross*

> In the Cross is salvation, in the Cross is life. . . .
> Take up therefore thy Cross and follow Jesus:
> and thou shalt go into life eternal.
>
> Thomas à Kempis

There is really just one topic for a student of Christianity: the life and teaching of Jesus of Nazareth—and that life and those teachings have been the subject of incredibly intensive research. The basic documents pertaining to Jesus were long ago collected in the New Testament, and every syllable of that book has been examined in microscopic detail. The age and the area in which Jesus lived and every possibly relevant scrap of information have been discussed in countless volumes.

It is obvious, however, that little agreement has been reached. Interpretations of Christianity are notoriously diverse, and the best scholars have succeeded principally in uncovering new and ever more perplexing questions. At the heart, perhaps, of all the disagreements and questions is the fact that Jesus himself wrote nothing. The materials in the New Testament are from a variety of authors writing at different times and places and with diverse purposes in mind. Matthew, Mark, and Luke are "major theologians in their own right, with viewpoints every bit as distinctive as those of John and Paul," Norman Perrin has written. Thus the New Testament itself

. . . represents the whole spectrum of possibilities of what it means to be a Christian in the world, and either anticipates or inspires every subsequent development within the Christian churches. The Roman Catholic and the Lutheran, the liberal Protestant and the fundamentalist, the contemplative mystic and the apocalyptic visionary, all find themselves at home in one part or another of this collection from the literature of earliest Christianity.*

Morton Scott Enslin's "Jesus and the Galilee Mission," the first reading selection in this chapter, is written from the point of view of "higher criticism," a method of approach to the New Testament that employs the tools of historical and literary research.† Enslin's essay illustrates that every inch of the way to Jesus is fraught with difficulties. Even the reports of Jesus' birthplace provide fuel for disputation, and beyond such biographical details are the issues pregnant with religious significance. What was the meaning of

---

*Norman Perrin, *The New Testament: An Introduction* (New York: Harcourt Brace Jovanovich, 1974), pp. v, 19.

†It is termed "higher" criticism in contrast to "lower," or textual, criticism, which attempts to reconstruct the texts themselves as they were originally composed.

CHAPTER NINE / *Christianity*

Jesus' encounter with John the Baptist? Did Jesus himself believe that he was the Messiah? What does the phrase "son of man" refer to?

Another of the approaches to Christianity is through human reason, and its master was St. Thomas Aquinas. A thirteenth-century Dominican monk, St. Thomas granted that there were certain mysteries (including the Incarnation) that could be known only by revelation, but in support of the bulk of Christian doctrine he provided logical arguments and proofs. His *Summa Theologica* is a monument to rational thought, and it and other of his writings became the basis for subsequent Roman Catholic theology. In this century Jacques Maritain is the leading Neo-Thomist: his work is a contemporary interpretation of St. Thomas and of Christianity. Maritain's essay in the following pages demonstrates his conviction that issues such as "The Immortality of the Soul" may be resoved with "rational certainty."

Mysticism is that expression of the religious life which culminates in an essentially indescribable *experience* of the Divine. The mystical conscious-ness, it is held, transcends the rational intellect, and the mystical experience is an overwhelming and indubitable sense of the *presence* of God. Very prevalent in the East, particularly in Hinduism, mysticism in the West is at some variance with the orthodox belief (in Judaism, Christianity, and Islam) that there is a vast "abyss" between God and man. Nevertheless, there have been many Western mystics who (with God's grace, they would insist) have bridged that abyss to achieve an ecstatic "union" with God. Among the Christian mystics is St. John of the Cross, portions of whose "The Dark Night of the Soul" appear in this chapter.

Rigorously and sternly Protestant, Søren Kierkegaard spent his brief life grappling with the challenge of becoming an authentic Christian. That goal was for him absolutely crucial ("Christianity is the frightful earnestness that your eternity is decided in this life"), and it was an almost unbearably difficult undertaking. "To be a Christian," he wrote, "is the most appalling of all agonies." Thus he was infuriated by the comfortable "Christians" he saw all about him who easily conformed to a watered-down Christianity. Kierkegaard said they were merely "playing at Christianity," and he thought that kind of hypocrisy was so frightful that it should not even be listed with the other heresies.

The last two readings of the chapter could not be much further apart in the views they express. Billy Graham, in the tradition of American revivalism and Protestant fundamentalism, holds that the Scriptures are eternally and literally true. Satan and his demons, for example, are very real, and Graham cites "chapter and verse" time and again in support of his position. Rudolf Bult-mann, on the other hand, is a very liberal Protestant theologian who believes that such talk as that of a "devil" reflects the thought and language of a prescientific and archaic world view. The task today, according to Bultmann, is to translate the "mythical" elements of the New Testament into twentieth-century concepts that can be understood and appreciated by modern man.

morton scott enslin _____

Jesus and the Galilee Mission

Morton Scott Enslin (1897–   ) was born in Massachusetts. He received his B.A. and Th.D. degrees from Harvard and a B.D. from Newton Theological Seminary. Enslin taught at Crozer Theological Seminary in Pennsylvania for thirty years. At the Theological School, St. Lawrence University, he was appointed Craig Professor of Biblical Languages and Literature, and at Bryn Mawr he has been chairman of the Department of the History of Religion. He served as editor of the *Crozer Quarterly* and the *Journal of Biblical Literature,* and as president of both the Society of Biblical Literature and the American Theological Society. Among his books are *The Ethics of Paul, Christian Beginnings, The Prophet from Nazareth, Letters to Churches,* and *From Jesus to Christianity.*

For the beginning of Christianity we must look to Galilee, for it was there that Jesus "began both to do and to teach," for he must be seen as the point of departure for the movement which came eventually to regard itself as a new religion and to be called by his name. Regardless of the differences between his point of view and that of his early followers; regardless of the fact that many of the words attributed to him in the gospels were coloured if not actually produced by the outlook of the age in which they were written; regardless of the practical difficulties encountered in striving to apply these words literally in this twentieth century—none the less, Jesus is to be seen as the centre of the movement, and however he may be portrayed, however much we seek to prove that he was a first-century Jew in outlook and belief, this must not obscure the fact that it was his tremendous personality that gripped those first disciples, that wrested a man like Saul of Tarsus from the things formerly dear to him, and that has continued to the present day in unabated power. The emphasis of the Fourth Gospel is right: The living, deathless person of Christ is the ultimate force in Christianity.

This is not the place for a detailed study of Jesus' life or teaching. It is more than doubtful if either is possible of reconstruction, as is abundantly evidenced by the many attempts; certainly not without a thorough and exact knowledge of the literary relationship and problems of the gospels . . . . Accordingly, this chapter must be rigidly limited to a consideration of his direct influence, in so far as we may with reasonable confidence discover it, in the movement later to be called by his name.

Jesus was born and brought up in the hills of Galilee, in the quiet town of

Nazareth, the very name of which is unknown to us in that period outside the gospels and Acts. The Bethlehem stories, regardless of their homiletic beauty, apparently rest upon no historical foundation, but must be regarded as pure legend. A critical examination of the two accounts—the one assuming the fixed residence of the parents in Bethlehem, the homage of Magi guided from the East by a miraculous star, the edict of a cruel king (strangely akin to that told of the infant Moses), the flight into Egypt, and subsequent return to Palestine, but to Nazareth, not Bethlehem; the other telling of a most unusual journey from Nazareth to Bethlehem, undertaken by the expectant mother in compliance with the requirement of a supposed census,[1] the inability to find lodgings, the resultant birth in a stable, the vision of angels granted to shepherds, and their visit to the manger—reveals that they are mutually exclusive, contradicting each other at every point. Their value is real; none the less, this value does not lie in the realm of history.

Nor do we know more of his boyhood or young manhood. At a very early date Christians were struck by these "hidden years" and sought to remedy the lack. The so-called Apocryphal Gospels, of which the Protevangelium of James, the Gospel of Thomas, and the various Infancy gospels are conspicuous examples, plainly evidence the utter lack of information that made the resultant grotesque and repellent stories possible. They simply depict a wonder child, endowed with limitless magical power but destitute of any ethical sense. In this connexion the one story which occurs in the accepted gospels[2] is significant. Due in part to the fact that it occurs in a *canonical* gospel, in part to the chasteness and restraint of the account in contrast to the tales of the malicious and malignant little boy of the other narratives, this story of the visit of the twelve-year-old Jesus to the temple has been often accepted, but usually with the entire evacuation of its meaning. Attempts to understand it as the normal attitude of the respectful little boy, awed by his elders, and thrilled at the thought that he is now a "son of the Law," quite miss the point. In essence the story is of precisely the same character as those in the Apocryphal Gospels. It portrays a unique child, wise beyond his years, aware of his vocation in life, asking his questions quite as a full-grown Socrates might have done, or as Jesus himself later did.

Attempts to probe back into the years before the ministry are utterly fruitless. The utmost that can be said has already been said by Luke, and said magnificently:

And the child grew, and waxed strong, filled with wisdom: and the grace of God was upon him.

[1] Attempts to establish the accuracy of the Lucan account by postulating this earlier census, also conducted by Quirinius, as was the other one, definitely known to us . . . as one in a regular fourteen-year cycle, have been made, notably by Ramsay, *Was Christ Born in Bethlehem?* but have little probability and have not commended themselves to scholars generally.

[2] Luke 2:41-51.

And Jesus advanced in wisdom and stature, and in favor with God and men.[3]

More than this we can never know.

The gospel accounts begin with the story of the baptism of Jesus by John the Baptist. This story has been widely considered, even by critical historians, as resting upon an essentially trustworthy tradition of an actual occurrence, and many fanciful conclusions have been drawn from it: Jesus was started on his mission as a prophet by the Baptist—an explanation which would have scandalized the older conservative scholars, hard put to explain the inappropriateness of the sinless Christ deigning to accept baptism[4]—whose disciple he became. It was not until John's imprisonment that he started a really independent mission. He returned to Galilee to avoid encroaching upon the Master's territory. Thus the similarity of the teaching of the two was explained: Jesus' early message was essentially a repetition of the Baptist's. Such an explanation might account for the entrance of Jesus in the rôle of a prophet; however, it simply pushes the difficulty one stage further back by failing to provide a similar impetus for John.

Reasons have already been given in a previous chapter for viewing the whole story of the contact of Jesus and John as the creation of later Christian thinking. It is surely no less arbitrary to assume this relationship of master and pupil and to explain the similarity of teaching as due to the borrowing by Jesus of the message of John than it is to reverse the procedure and to consider the possibility that all the words found in the mouth of the Baptist in the gospel narrative are the result of Christian tradition and actually have as much right to be regarded as words, not of John, but of Jesus, as do the words actually attributed to the latter in the gospel pages. In addition to the reasons already suggested for hesitating to consider the account of the baptism of Jesus by John historical is the utter disregard of baptism, both in practice and in injunction, during the ministry and not improbably in the months—perhaps years—which followed.[5] As the account stands in Mark it was a critical experience for Jesus, a turning point in his career. Then it was that God's Holy Spirit descended upon him, transforming him into God's own prophet, commissioned from on high to sound the clarion call to repentance in preparation for the new age soon to dawn. It is astonishing that an experience of such moment to himself should not have commended itself to him as valuable for others as well. Finally, there is the problem of the source of knowledge of the event—and this applies equally to the subsequent narrative of the Temptation. According to the narratives of the Synoptic gospels—and probability

[3]Luke 2:40, 52.
[4]Ignatius (ad Eph. 18:2) remarks that his baptism was "to cleanse the water."
[5]For a discussion of such passages as Matt. 28:19; Mark 16:16; John 3.22; 4:1-2; Acts 2:38-41 which are in apparent contradiction to this statement, see . . . pp. 194 ff. [of Enslin's Christian Beginnings].

bears them out—Jesus' first contact with followers was in Galilee; the notion of a ministry in Judea with disciples recruited there who followed him into Galilee is sheer assumption. Accordingly the information, if authentic, must have come from Jesus himself. That such information was given by him is also sheer assumption, and, as Origen early pointed out,[6] out of keeping with the character of the one who "on all occasions avoided unnecessary talk about himself." The presumption is that no information prior to the ministry in Galilee was available when the first traditions began to take form. Nor is it surprising that there was an occasional early attempt to push the prehistory farther back into a period before the time the central figure had come into the public eye. Flat and arbitrary denial of the possibility of the narrative being historic would of course be rash. But in history, as in engineering, one can never be too critical towards bricks destined for the growing edifice. Traditions which we can safely consider reliable do not appear to antedate the preaching in Galilee.

That something occurred in the course of the years before his appearance by the lake that led him to assume the rôle of prophet, confident that he had insights into the heart and purposes of God that the rest of Jewry did not have; confident that when he revealed the coming of the Kingdom—God's most precious boon for men—they, like him, would lay their tasks aside and prepare themselves for the blessed day—all this is perhaps intrinsically possible. But what led to that conviction—sudden or the result of years of reflection—we shall never know. That following his conviction, like the prophet of old, "As Jehovah liveth, what Jehovah saith unto me, that will I speak," he passed through a reaction of doubt and questioning from which he emerged to speak with a confidence which could not be daunted is also not unlikely. This we can assume from the common experience of mankind, not because of the conventional narratives of this period of initial temptation through which the heroes of both legend and history were supposed to have passed. Not only does the balanced structure of the triad of trials found in Matthew and Luke with their apposite quotation of Scripture appear the product of Christian meditation, but the simpler narrative of Mark appears designed for a distinct and practical end. The wild beasts with whom he spent forty days apparently would signify to the Jewish reader evil demons. These Jesus had conquered at the very beginning. Their power was broken; they alone, of all whom Jesus later approached, knew who he was, and feared but must obey him.

With his public appearance in the towns of Galilee on the shore of the lake our information about him begins, although it is far less definite than could be desired. In a curiously obscure phrase,[7] which has caused difficulty from the

[6]c. *Celsum* i,48 (end).
[7]Luke 3:23.

earliest days, Luke apparently says he was about thirty at the start of his ministry. Whether that rests upon a definite tradition or is a conjecture that when he started his work he was already a mature man is uncertain. Furthermore, although most scholars are agreed that his ministry was limited to Galilee until he "stedfastly set his face to go to Jerusalem," it is impossible to say how long this ministry was. The traditional view that it occupied three years rests upon the Fourth Gospel, which arbitrarily transforms this ministry into a series of visits to attend feasts. The Fourth Gospel is invaluable for an understanding of later Christian thought; it is valueless to the historian seeking information regarding the nature or the length of the ministry. The other three gospels set no time. Their failure to mention any going to Jerusalem prior to the one ending in his crucifixion would perhaps heighten the probability that the ministry was limited to a few months, scarcely more than a single year. It is to be observed that many of the early writers, including Clement of Alexandria and Origen, reached the same conclusion, although on other grounds.[8] Jesus' words were such that opposition soon flared up against him. All the data preserved by our first three gospels could easily fall within a twelvemonth period. The elaborate synchronism of dates (Luke 3:1,2) apparently suggests 28 A.D. as the time of his public appearance; the spring of 29 A.D. is perhaps the most probable date for the crucifixion.

His message was simple. Mark summarizes it: "The time is fulfilled, and the kingdom of God is at hand: repent ye, and believe in the gospel;" that is, believe that this good news that the Father's greatest gift to men is at hand is true. It can scarcely be doubted that he sounded his message with full confidence that the nation would hearken and rejoice. It was all so clear to him; nothing else in life mattered. The Father had spoken. Of course God's children would obey as soon as they heard his voice. As the weeks went by and as he saw the initial enthusiasm giving way first to apathy, then to bitter opposition, he became quickly disillusioned; soon it was borne home to him that so strait was the gate and narrow the way that few would enter in. By the kingdom of God—Matthew alone prefers kingdom of heaven—he did not apparently mean the gradual amelioration of society, as is often imagined today. His message was pitched in terms of the first century, not the twentieth. The kingdom of God, soon to appear, was the Age to Come, the new age which would suddenly and spectacularly follow the cataclysmic end of the present age. Attempts to soften or alter his message to make it more acceptable to our way of thinking and to make it conform to the verdict of history are utterly superfluous. Much confusion has been caused by the endless debate as to whether the kingdom is present or future. The evidence of the gospels as well as the outlook of early Christianity, as revealed not alone by the opening

[8]They understood the phrase, "the acceptable year of the Lord" of Luke 4:19 (Isa. 61:1 f.) literally.

chapters of Acts but by the letters of Paul, would appear unmistakably to indicate that in his thinking the kingdom was still in the future, but that it would appear at any moment. It was present only in the sense that the coming clouds in the heavens cast their shadow upon the earth. Israel was incessantly talking about God, deluding itself that it was obeying his commands. They must cease this playing at life; must turn back to the Father and recognize his sovereignty at once. Life must be made to conform to the pattern that soon would be introduced. Men must start now to live the kind of lives they would live in the coming kingdom—if they were fortunate enough to have a share in it. "The kingdom of God is among you"[9] does not signify an "inward and invisible power in the hearts of men" wooing them to a growth in righteousness. It is a vivid announcement of the immediacy of the approach of this kingdom and its attendant judgment. It is so near at hand, that for added vividness it may be spoken of as actually here. The purposes of God are inevitable; he has spoken and will fulfil. The shadow of the approaching cloud is even now upon the land. The parable of the Seed Growing Secretly,[10] which has often been interpreted in the sense of the present kingdom, appears to yield exactly the opposite meaning. The seed has been sown; nothing that man can do to thwart it will avail; the harvest must come.

By the word "repent," Jesus meant, as did every other Jew, change of conduct as well as of heart. Everything incompatible with the kingdom—this new age soon to be set up—must be laid aside resolutely. As the merchant gladly sells all his other pearls to purchase the one of great price, or the man who has discovered a treasure hidden in a field sells all his possessions to gain that treasure; so the wise man will consider everything in life, not alone his immediate comfort, but his actual physical well-being, of secondary importance. What is an eye or a hand—parts of a perishable body—worth in comparison with acceptance or rejection by Almighty God at the Judgment soon to be set up! Words which must be watered down when the teaching of Jesus is forced into terms of modern thought are perfectly intelligible without appeal to "oriental hyperbole" when he who lived in the first century is allowed to think and speak as such. Thus there are few matters connected with the gospels clearer or more certain than that Jesus believed in the near approach[11] of this universal sovereignty of God, that is, the near approach of the apocalyptic Age to Come. This was the good news which he and his helpers were to proclaim.

. . .

Did Jesus feel that he was the Messiah, the son of David destined for Israel's throne? In recent years this question has been hotly debated. The

---

[9] . . . —Luke 17:21.
[10] Mark 4:26 ff.
[11] See also pp. 165 f. . . . [of Enslin's *Christian Beginnings*—p. 378 in this volume].

answer to it is by no means as simple as has often been supposed. The conventional answer has been, Yes; but it rested in no small measure upon the mistaken notion that all popular Jewish thinking in the first century centered about the person of the Messiah. Accordingly, it was argued: Any one to gain a popular hearing must pitch his message in these terms. Thus, although Jesus was by no means satisfied with the conventional thinking on the subject, he must for want of a better designation make such claims for himself. But if, as has been argued in a preceding chapter, the figure of the Davidic King Messiah did not bulk so large in popular thinking, there seems little reason to assume that Jesus felt compelled to accept the rôle unless it was perfectly congenial. As soon as this cardinal point is observed, it becomes highly significant that Jesus appears to have laid his emphasis upon the coming kingdom, not upon the one who was to be king in it. It is the Fourth Gospel which represents Jesus as habitually discoursing at length about himself, the king. That the representation in the Synoptic gospels is more primitive and more probably historic is almost universally conceded. That Matthew and Luke felt that Jesus was the Davidic Messiah is clear. However such a passage as Matt. 11:25-30 was originally intended, it now stands as embodying distinct and unique claims in the mouth of Jesus. Luke is very particular to make clear that Jesus' death was due to this claim alone. On the contrary, Mark 12:35-37 (‖ Matt. 22:41-46; Luke 20:41-44) can only be understood as denying that Jesus, although anointed, was the scion of David. Such a denial must have been primitive; it clashes too directly with early Christian thinking. The most natural interpretation of it is that it reflects Jesus' own attitude. Although he conceived himself anointed by God for his service, he rejected the notion that this meant that he was the anointed Davidic king.

Nor is it by any means certain that he claimed to be the supernatural figure, destined to be the Final Judge of men, namely the son of man, although his followers soon after his death were confident that he was that figure and had claimed to be. Indeed, the evangelists are so confident that he had made this claim for himself that they use the phrase as a substitute for "I". A striking example of this editorial revision is afforded by Matthew's alteration of Mark 8:27. In Mark the query reads, "Who do men say that I am?" Matthew (16:13) has "Who do men say that the son of man is?" Again, such passages as Mark 2:10 f.; 27 f. can scarcely be understood save as mistranslations into Greek, where the original Aramaic *bar nasha,* that is, human being,[12] has been mistakenly rendered "son of man," thus giving a specific application to Jesus not originally intended. The second of these passages is particularly clear. Jesus says, "The Sabbath was made for man, and not man for the Sabbath: therefore *man* is lord even of the Sabbath." This is balanced and intelligible; substitution of *son of man,* making a specific reference to Jesus, makes the

[12]See . . . pp. 141 f. [of Enslin's *Christian Beginnings*].

"therefore" unintelligible. A third type of passage is illustrated by Mark 8:38—

For whosoever shall be ashamed of *me* and of *my* words in this adulterous and sinful generation, the *Son of man* also shall be ashamed of him, when *he* cometh in the glory of *his* Father with the holy angels.

There would seem to be no compelling reason to identify here the "me" and "my" with the "son of man," "he," and "his." Indeed, it is not failure to believe in or to adopt a correct attitude toward him (Jesus) that Jesus is here condemning, but the rejection of the message which he is sounding. This rejection can only result in condemnation when the son of man appears in the very near future to sit upon his judgment throne.

That the phrase "son of man" was constantly upon Jesus' lips is highly probable. That he meant himself by the phrase is far less certain. That his disciples eventually came to the conclusion that by the enigmatic phrase he had meant himself is certain; that they made this identification after his death rather than during his ministry would appear not unlikely. Thus primitive tradition which revealed too clearly for the growing theological estimates of Jesus' person that he, as God's prophet, had heralded the coming of the supernatural son of man, his successor, soon to appear to set up the Final Judgment and inaugurate the Age to Come, gradually came to be put into the mouth of John the Baptist. The whole imagery of final judgments, of supernatural figures coming on the clouds of heaven, was as natural to the first century as it is unnatural to ours. A man in those days could hold such views without raising the suspicion of mental disturbance. None the less, it is one thing for a first-century Jew to have expected such a figure soon to appear; a totally different thing for him to believe that he himself would be miraculously transformed from a flesh-and-blood man into this figure. With all allowances made, it is hard to conceive how such a view could have been held save at the expense of mental sanity. There seems no reason from the accounts to postulate this last conclusion. But views, which if held by himself before his death can scarcely be understood of a sane and balanced man, are easily understood for the disciples after his death. Then the obstacle was removed. He was now, they were confident, in heaven. There was now no reason why he might not come from heaven on the clouds.

· · ·

What then was the authority which he claimed for himself? The most obvious answer is not improbably the correct one, namely, the one preserved in the gospels themselves, that he was a prophet of God. This was apparently the impression he made upon his hearers. It is highly probable that this impression was due to his own belief. If this is the case, he must have believed himself to be inspired by the Holy Spirit, for in the thinking of Judaism the Holy Spirit is specifically the spirit of prophecy. "All the prophets spoke by

CHAPTER NINE / *Christianity*

the holy spirit. The holy spirit is so specifically prophetic inspiration that when Haggai, Zechariah, and Malachi, the last prophets, died, the holy spirit departed from Israel."[13]

Once more God was speaking to his people in the old and accredited way. The prophet like unto Moses long expected had now appeared. As the mouthpiece of God he uttered his clarion call, confident that it was not he but God who was calling men to repent and to watch for the appearance of the Final Judge who would baptize the nation with a baptism of fire. This passionate confidence may well have caused him to appear "beside himself."[14] To his opponents it was the frenzy of a man possessed by an evil spirit; to his followers the mark of that divine madness that proclaimed the power of God. To folk accustomed to explain everything out of the ordinary as the result of the presence of a *daimon,* good or bad, Jesus with his scathing denunciations and his impossible demands, his power to quiet the insane, his genial attitude toward children and those in distress, his absolute self-confidence, may well have seemed a most unusual and amazing character, one from the past sent by God to herald a new age.

And this catastrophic end was near at hand. It might come at any moment; when, he did not know. It could not, however, be long delayed. It would come before the present generation had died.[15] It is useless to try to smooth this difficulty away. To attempt to explain this as a misunderstanding of his meaning by his hearers or as a view later developed and attributed to him is most unfortunate. On the one hand, this would demand such an amazing lack of intelligence on the part of his hearers or inability on his own part to express himself clearly on a point of vital importance that we would be justified in doubting whether any reputed recollection from such sources could approach historical probability; on the other, each succeeding year made the difficulty of the expectation more acute, for the generation was dying. Why should his earliest followers have come to such an expectation and have believed he had taught them so, had their leader not so taught?

More impressive, however, than an appeal to any specific passage, which after all may be open to legitimate critical doubt, is the consistent tone and undercurrent of his reported teaching. Were men to follow implicitly the instruction not alone to the rich ruler but as recorded in the Sermon on the Mount—"And if any man would go to law with thee, and take away thy coat, let him have the cloak also. . . . Give to him that asketh thee, and from him that would borrow of thee turn not thou away. . . . Resist not him that is evil: but whosoever smiteth thee on thy right cheek, turn to him the other also"—it would mean the collapse of society. It is possible to water these words—and there are many more like them—down into more or less innocuous admoni-

[13]G. F. Moore, *Judaism,* Vol. 1, p. 237.
[14]Mark 3:21.
[15]Mark 9:1 and parallels (Matt. 16:28; Luke 9:27).

tion to be generous and even-tempered, but the result of this popular means of justifying present-day ideals by the appeal to the fancied support of Jesus are, to say the least, not impressive nor particularly convincing. The demands *are* impossible if life is to continue as it is. But in the thinking of Jesus this is precisely the point. Life was not to continue. The end was at hand. This might well be an ideal preparation for the Age to Come. Thus it would seem wiser not to call these teachings an "interim ethic." Rather they are a "kingdom ethic." This is to be the kind of life lived in the new age soon to appear. To achieve entrance men must begin to live as though the change had actually taken place. In the short time of waiting matters which have seemed of so great concern pale into insignificance. Why concern oneself about wealth, clothing, position, bodily comfort, dignity, national pride which is affronted by subjection to a foreign power? The time is too short for indulging in such idle trivialities. Certainly his earliest followers in Jerusalem, who pooled their property in confidence that before it was expended the kingdom would dawn, appear to have understood him in this sense.

. . .

After a time of itinerant preaching in Galilee, he turns south to the nation's capital. In Luke's fine phrase, "he stedfastly set his face to go to Jerusalem." Why did he go? The answer is by no means easy. It may well be that the increasing opposition had convinced him that his earlier dreams for the nation were not to be realized, that, like the prophets before him, he must fall before the blind prejudice of those to whom he had been sent. But if he were to die, he must first stand in Jerusalem and herald God's word in Zion. A prophet might not die save in Jerusalem. So he turned to the south. But this is easily over-emphasized. From the time of his transfiguration near Caesarea Philippi the gospels represent him as speaking openly of his death, but invariably appending the mention of his resurrection three days later. This view obviously reflects the thinking of Christians at the time the gospels were written. That it accurately portrays the actual fact is far less certain. The stubborn fact of the dismay of his disciples, their flight back to Galilee, their feeling that the last word had been spoken and that that word was failure make very difficult the view that he had foreseen and openly predicted an event which was to vindicate in so startling a manner his mission, and which could scarcely fail to arouse joyful anticipation, not abject terror. As suggested on a previous page, such a view can scarcely fail to reduce the intelligence of his closest followers to the vanishing-point or to necessitate seeing him speaking in riddles, intelligible only to a later age. It is far wiser not to endeavour to give a fictitious clarity to those days known to us at best at a far remove, but to allow them to remain hidden. Whatever the motives which led him to leave the Galilean hills for the nation's capital, he apparently turned to the south with the confidence that, though he could not see the end from the beginning, God was directing his steps; God's will could not be thwarted; so long as it was day, he would do the will of him who had sent him.

He enters the city of Jerusalem. The gospels represent the pilgrim throngs hailing him joyfully. But any such enthusiasm was at best short-lived. His preaching soon disillusioned them. The opposition in the nation's capital was far more intense than in Galilee. Those in control saw in him a most dangerous figure, the potential source of all sorts of difficulties, a disturber of the *status quo,* a troubler of Israel. With his eye fixed on the coming kingdom, impatient toward any such makeshift remedies as the Home Rule Party were crying for, he dashed any hopes they might have had for him to the ground. His outspoken attitude, which made possible the story told of the cleansing of the temple, sealed his doom. His life was forfeit. A short time—how long we do not know, for there seem to be hints in the gospels of a longer stay in Jerusalem than the traditional week—and he died on a Roman cross. His friends who had accompanied him scattered in dismay and fled back to their old homes. They had hoped in vain that it was he who should restore Israel. But the comradeship of the months with him could not be so quickly broken. He had built himself too vitally into their lives for that. Their first grief gave way; they experienced him again, became convinced that he had not been defeated, and returned to Jerusalem in joy and confidence. The true triumphal entry into Jerusalem was not on the ninth of Nisan but sometime later when these men, in whose hearts had dawned a new confidence, without display reëntered the city that a little earlier had seen the downfall of the prophet of Galilee.

FROM THE *New Testament*

The Bible used by Jesus and his disciples was, of course, the Old Testament.* The writings which came to comprise the New Testament were composed during the second half of the first century and the early second century. It was only gradually that they came to be regarded as Scripture. The third century saw widespread agreement about which documents were to be included in the New Testament, but it was not until the fourth century that the present twenty-seven books were definitely settled upon.

The sequence in which the books appear in almost all editions of the New Testament is not the order in which they were written. The letters of Paul, for example, are the oldest materials. Most scholars are convinced that Mark was the first of the gospels, followed by Matthew and Luke (both of which incorporated much of Mark). The similarities among these three gospels in content and point of view have caused them to be designated the "Synoptic" Gospels. The Gospel of John, the last of the gospels to be written, is different in its perspective and style.

The selections presented here are from the Authorized (or King James) Version of the Bible, easily the most familiar and beloved of all the English versions.

THE GOSPEL ACCORDING TO JOHN

Chapter 1

In the beginning was the Word, and the Word was with God, and the Word was God. The same was in the beginning with God. All things were made by him; and without him was not any thing made that was made. In him was life; and the life was the light of men. And the light shineth in darkness; and the darkness comprehended it not. There was a man sent from God, whose name was John. The same came for a witness, to bear witness of the Light, that all men through him might believe. He was not that Light, but was sent to bear witness of that Light. That was the true Light, which lighteth every man that cometh into the world. He was in the world, and the world was made by him, and the world knew him not. He came unto his own, and his own received him not. But as many as received him, to them gave he power to become the sons of God, even to them that believe on his name: which were born, not of blood, nor of the will of the flesh, nor of the will of man, but of God. And the Word

---

*In the first century A.D. the Old Testament canon was not yet closed. Hence the Old Testament known to Jesus was not quite the one known today.

was made flesh, and dwelt among us, (and we beheld his glory, the glory as of the only begotten of the Father,) full of grace and truth. John bare witness of him, and cried, saying, "This was he of whom I spake, He that cometh after me is preferred before me: for he was before me". And of his fulness have all we received, and grace for grace. For the law was given by Moses, but grace and truth came by Jesus Christ. No man hath seen God at any time; the only begotten Son, which is in the bosom of the Father, he hath declared him.

. . .

Chapter 3

There was a man of the Pharisees, named Nicodemus, a ruler of the Jews: the same came to Jesus by night, and said unto him, "Rabbi, we know that thou art a teacher come from God: for no man can do these miracles that thou doest, except God be with him". Jesus answered and said unto him, "Verily, verily, I say unto thee, Except a man be born again, he cannot see the kingdom of God". Nicodemus saith unto him, "How can a man be born when he is old? can he enter the second time into his mother's womb, and be born?" Jesus answered, "Verily, verily, I say unto thee, Except a man be born of water and of the Spirit, he cannot enter into the kingdom of God. That which is born of the flesh is flesh; and that which is born of the Spirit is spirit. Marvel not that I said unto thee, Ye must be born again. The wind bloweth where it listeth, and thou hearest the sound thereof, but canst not tell whence it cometh, and whither it goeth: so is every one that is born of the Spirit." Nicodemus answered and said unto him, "How can these things be?" Jesus answered and said unto him, "Art thou a master of Israel, and knowest not these things? Verily, verily, I say unto thee, We speak that we do know, and testify that we have seen; and ye receive not our witness. If I have told you earthly things, and ye believe not, how shall ye believe, if I tell you of heavenly things? And no man hath ascended up to heaven, but he that came down from heaven, even the Son of man which is in heaven. And as Moses lifted up the serpent in the wilderness, even so must the Son of man be lifted up: that whosoever believeth in him should not perish, but have eternal life."

For God so loved the world, that he gave his only begotten Son, that whosoever believeth in him should not perish, but have everlasting life. For God sent not his Son into the world to condemn the world; but that the world through him might be saved. He that believeth on him is not condemned: but he that believeth not is condemned already, because he hath not believed in the name of the only begotten Son of God. And this is the condemnation, that light is come into the world, and men loved darkness rather than light, because their deeds were evil. For every one that doeth evil hateth the light, neither cometh to the light, lest his deeds should be reproved. But he that doeth truth cometh to the light, that his deeds may be made manifest, that they are wrought in God.

THE GOSPEL ACCORDING TO MATTHEW

Chapter 5

And seeing the multitudes, he went up into a mountain: and when he was set, his disciples came unto him: and he opened his mouth, and taught them, saying,

"Blessed are the poor in spirit: for theirs is the kingdom of heaven.

"Blessed are they that mourn: for they shall be comforted.

"Blessed are the meek: for they shall inherit the earth.

"Blessed are they which do hunger and thirst after righteousness: for they shall be filled.

"Blessed are the merciful: for they shall obtain mercy.

"Blessed are the pure in heart: for they shall see God.

"Blessed are the peacemakers: for they shall be called the children of God.

"Blessed are they which are persecuted for righteousness' sake: for theirs is the kingdom of heaven. Blessed are ye, when men shall revile you, and persecute you, and shall say all manner of evil against you falsely, for my sake. Rejoice, and be exceeding glad: for great is your reward in heaven: for so persecuted they the prophets which were before you.

"Ye are the salt of the earth: but if the salt have lost his savour, wherewith shall it be salted? it is thenceforth good for nothing, but to be cast out, and to be trodden under foot of men. Ye are the light of the world. A city that is set on an hill cannot be hid. Neither do men light a candle, and put it under a bushel, but on a candlestick; and it giveth light unto all that are in the house. Let your light so shine before men, that they may see your good works, and glorify your Father which is in heaven.

"Think not that I am come to destroy the law, or the prophets: I am not come to destroy, but to fulfil. For verily I say unto you, Till heaven and earth pass, one jot or one tittle shall in no wise pass from the law, till all be fulfilled. Whosoever therefore shall break one of these least commandments, and shall teach men so, he shall be called the least in the kingdom of heaven: but whosoever shall do and teach them, the same shall be called great in the kingdom of heaven. For I say unto you, that except your righteousness shall exceed the righteousness of the scribes and Pharisees, ye shall in no case enter into the kingdom of heaven.

"Ye have heard that it was said by them of old time, 'Thou shalt not kill; and whosoever shall kill shall be in danger of the judgment': but I say unto you, that whosoever is angry with his brother without a cause shall be in danger of the judgment: and whosoever shall say to his brother, 'Raca,' shall be in danger of the council: but whosoever shall say, 'Thou fool,' shall be in danger of hell fire. Therefore if thou bring thy gift to the altar, and there rememberest that thy brother hath aught against thee; leave there thy gift before the altar, and go thy way; first be reconciled to thy brother, and then come and offer thy gift. Agree with thine adversary quickly, whiles thou art in the way with him; lest at any time the adversary deliver thee to the judge, and the judge deliver thee to the officer, and thou be cast into prison. Verily I say unto thee, Thou shalt by no means come out thence, till thou hast paid the uttermost farthing.

"Ye have heard that it was said by them of old time, 'Thou shalt not commit adultery': but I say unto you, that whosoever looketh on a woman to lust after her hath committed adultery with her already in his heart. And if thy right eye offend thee, pluck it out, and cast it from thee: for it is profitable for thee that one of thy members should perish, and not that thy whole body should be cast into hell. And if thy right hand offend thee, cut it off, and cast it from thee: for it is profitable for thee that one of thy members should perish, and not that thy whole body should be cast into hell. It hath been said, 'Whosoever shall put away his wife, let him give her a writing of divorcement': but I say unto you, that whosoever shall put away his wife, saving for the cause of fornication, causeth her to commit adultery: and whosoever shall marry her that is divorced committeth adultery.

"Again, ye have heard that it hath been said by them of old time, 'Thou shalt not forswear thyself, but shalt perform unto the Lord thine oaths': but I say unto you, Swear not at all; neither by heaven; for it is God's throne: nor by the earth; for it is his footstool: neither by Jerusalem; for it is the city of the great King. Neither shalt thou swear by the head, because thou canst not make one hair white or black. But let your communication be, 'Yea, yea'; 'Nay, nay': for whatsoever is more than these cometh of evil.

"Ye have heard that it hath been said, 'An eye for an eye, and a tooth for a tooth': but I say unto you, that ye resist not evil: but whosoever shall smite thee on thy right cheek, turn to him the other also. And if any man will sue thee at the law, and take away thy coat, let him have thy cloke also. And whosoever shall compel thee to go a mile, go with him twain. Give to him that asketh thee, and from him that would borrow of thee turn not thou away.

"Ye have heard that it hath been said, 'Thou shalt love thy neighbour, and hate thine enemy'. But I say unto you, Love your enemies, bless them that curse you, do good to them that hate you, and pray for them which despitefully use you, and persecute you; that ye may be the children of your Father which is in heaven: for he maketh his sun to rise on the evil and on the good, and sendeth rain on the just and on the unjust. For if ye love them which love you, what reward have ye? do not even the publicans the same? And if ye salute your brethren only, what do ye more than others? do not even the publicans so? Be ye therefore perfect, even as your Father which is in heaven is perfect."

Chapter 6

"Take heed that ye do not your alms before men, to be seen of them: otherwise ye have no reward of your Father which is in heaven.

"Therefore when thou doest thine alms, do not sound a trumpet before thee, as the hypocrites do in the synagogues and in the streets, that they may have glory of men. Verily I say unto you, They have their reward. But when thou doest alms, let not thy left hand know what thy right hand doeth: that thine alms may be in secret: and thy Father which seeth in secret himself shall reward thee openly.

"And when thou prayest, thou shalt not be as the hypocrites are: for they love to pray standing in the synagogues and in the corners of the streets, that they may be seen of men. Verily I say unto you, They have their reward. But thou, when thou prayest, enter into thy closet, and when thou hast shut thy door, pray to thy Father which is in secret; and thy Father which seeth in secret shall reward thee openly. But when ye pray, use not vain repetitions, as the heathen do: for they think that they shall be heard for their much speaking. Be not ye therefore like unto them: for your Father knoweth what things ye have need of, before ye ask him. After this manner therefore pray ye: 'Our Father which art in heaven, Hallowed be thy name. Thy kingdom come. Thy will be done in earth, as it is in heaven. Give us this day our daily bread. And forgive us our debts, as we forgive our debtors. And lead us not into temptation, but deliver us from evil: For thine is the kingdom, and the power, and the glory, for ever. Amen.' For if ye forgive men their trespasses, your heavenly Father will also forgive you: but if ye forgive not men their trespasses, neither will your Father forgive your trespasses.

"Moreover when ye fast, be not, as the hypocrites, of a sad countenance: for they disfigure their faces, that they may appear unto men to fast. Verily I say unto you, They have their reward. But thou, when thou fastest, anoint thine head, and wash thy face; that thou appear not unto men to fast, but unto thy Father which is in secret: and thy Father, which seeth in secret, shall reward thee openly.

"Lay not up for yourselves treasures upon earth, where moth and rust doth corrupt, and where thieves break through and steal: but lay up for yourselves treasures in heaven, where neither moth nor rust doth corrupt, and where thieves do not break through nor steal: for where your treasure is, there will your heart be also. The light of the body is the eye: if therefore thine eye be single, thy whole body shall be full of light. But if thine eye be evil, thy whole body shall be full of darkness. If therefore the light that is in thee be darkness, how great is that darkness! No man can serve two masters: for either he will hate the one, and love the other; or else he will hold to the one, and despise the other. Ye cannot serve God and mammon. Therefore I say unto you, Take no thought for your life, what ye shall eat, or what ye shall drink; not yet for your body, what ye shall put on. Is not the life more than meat, and the body than raiment? Behold the fowls of the air: for they sow not, neither do they reap, nor gather into barns; yet your heavenly Father feedeth them. Are ye not much better than they? Which of you by taking thought can add one cubit unto his stature? And why take ye thought for raiment? Consider the lilies of the field, how they grow; they toil not, neither do they spin: and yet I say unto you, that even Solomon in all his glory was not arrayed like one of these. Wherefore, if God so clothe the grass of the field, which to day is, and to morrow is cast into the oven, shall he not much more clothe you, O ye of little faith? Therefore take no thought, saying, 'What shall we eat?' or, 'What shall we drink?' or, 'Wherewithal shall we be clothed?' (for after all these things do the Gentiles seek:) for your heavenly Father knoweth that ye have need of all these things. But seek ye first the kingdom of God, and his righteousness; and all these things shall be added unto you. Take therefore no thought for the morrow: for the morrow shall take thought for the things of itself. Sufficient unto the day is the evil thereof.''

Chapter 7

"Judge not, that ye be not judged. For with what judgment ye judge, ye shall be judged: and with what measure ye mete, it shall be measured to you again. And why beholdest thou the mote that is in thy brother's eye, but considerest not the beam that is in thine own eye? Or how wilt thou say to thy brother, 'Let me pull out the mote out of thine eye'; and, behold, a beam is in thine own eye? Thou hypocrite, first cast out the beam out of thine own eye; and then shalt thou see clearly to cast out the mote out of thy brother's eye.

"Give not that which is holy unto the dogs, neither cast ye your pearls before swine, lest they trample them under their feet, and turn again and rend you.

"Ask, and it shall be given you; seek, and ye shall find; knock, and it shall be opened unto you: for every one that asketh receiveth; and he that seeketh findeth; and to him that knocketh it shall be opened. Or what man is there of you, whom if his son ask bread, will he give him a stone? Or if he ask a fish, will he give him a serpent? If ye then, being evil, know how to give good gifts unto your children, how much more shall your Father which is in heaven give good things to them that ask him? Therefore all things whatsoever ye would that men should do to you, do ye even so to them: for this is the law and the prophets.

"Enter ye in at the strait gate: for wide is the gate, and broad is the way, that leadeth to destruction, and many there be which go in thereat: because strait is the gate, and narrow is the way, which leadeth unto life, and few there be that find it.

"Beware of false prophets, which come to you in sheep's clothing, but inwardly they are ravening wolves. Ye shall know them by their fruits. Do men gather grapes of thorns, or figs of thistles? Even so every good tree bringeth forth good fruit; but a corrupt tree bringeth forth evil fruit. A good tree cannot bring forth evil fruit, neither can a corrupt tree bring forth good fruit. Every tree that bringeth not forth good fruit is hewn down, and cast into the fire. Wherefore by their fruits ye shall know them. Not every one that saith unto me, 'Lord, Lord, have we not prophesied in thy name? and in thy name have cast out devils? and in thy name done many wonderful works?' And then will I profess unto them, I never knew you: depart from me, ye that work iniquity. Therefore whosoever heareth these sayings of mine, and doeth them, I will liken him unto a wise man, which built his house upon a rock: and the rain descended, and the floods came, and the winds blew, and beat upon that house; and it fell not: for it was founded upon a rock. And every one that heareth these sayings of mine, and doeth them not, shall be likened unto a foolish man, which built his house upon the sand: and the rain descended, and the floods came, and the winds blew, and beat upon that house; and it fell: and great was the fall of it.''

And it came to pass, when Jesus had ended these sayings, the people were astonished at his doctrine: for he taught them as one having authority, and not as the scribes.

THE EPISTLE OF PAUL TO THE ROMANS
Chapter 8

There is therefore now no condemnation to them which are in Christ Jesus, who walk not after the flesh, but after the Spirit. For the law of the Spirit of life in Christ Jesus hath made me free from the law of sin and death. For what the law could not do, in that it was weak through the flesh, God sending his own Son in the likeness of sinful flesh, and for sin, condemned sin in the flesh: that the righteousness of the law might be fulfilled in us, who walk not after the flesh, but after the Spirit. For they that are after the flesh do mind the things of the flesh; but they that are after the Spirit the things of the Spirit. For to be carnally minded is death; but to be spiritually minded is life and peace. Because the carnal mind is enmity against God: for it is not subject to the law of God, neither indeed can be. So then they that are in the flesh cannot please God. But ye are not in the flesh, but in the Spirit, if so be that the Spirit of God dwell in you. Now if any man have not the Spirit of Christ, he is none of his. And if Christ be in you, the body is dead because of sin; but the Spirit is life because of righteousness. But if the Spirit of him that raised up Jesus from the dead dwell in you, he that raised up Christ from the dead shall also quicken your mortal bodies by his Spirit that dwelleth in you.

Therefore, brethren, we are debtors, not to the flesh, to live after the flesh. For if ye live after the flesh, ye shall die: but if ye through the Spirit do mortify the deeds of the body, ye shall live. For as many as are led by the Spirit of God, they are the sons of God. For ye have not received the spirit of bondage again to fear; but ye have received the Spirit of adoption, whereby we cry, ''Abbba, Father''. The Spirit itself beareth witness with our spirit, that we are the children of God: and if children, then heirs; heirs of God, and joint-heirs with Christ; if so be that we suffer with him, that we may be also glorified togther.

For I reckon that the sufferings of this present time are not worthy to be compared with the glory which shall be revealed in us. For the earnest expectation of the creature waiteth for the manifestation of the sons of God. For the creature was made subject to vanity, not willingly, but by reason of him who hath subjected the same in hope, because the creature itself also shall be delivered from the bondage of corruption into the glorious liberty of the children of God. For we know that the whole creation groaneth and travaileth in pain together until now. And now only they, but ourselves also, which have the firstfruits of the Spirit, even we ourselves groan within ourselves, waiting for the adoption, to wit, the redemption of our body. For we are saved by hope: but hope that is seen is not hope: for what a man seeth, why doth he yet hope for? But if we hope for that we see not, then do we with patience wait for it.

Likewise the Spirit also helpeth our infirmities: for we know not what we should pray for as we ought: but the Spirit itself maketh intercession for us with groanings which cannot be uttered. And he that searcheth the hearts knoweth what is the mind of the Spirit, because he maketh intercession for the saints according to the will of God. And we know that all things work together for good to them that love God, to them who are the called according to his purpose. For whom he did foreknow, he also did predestinate to be conformed to the image of his Son, that he might be the firstborn among many brethren. Moreover whom he did predestinate, them he also called: and whom he called, them he also justified: and whom he justified, them he also glorified.

What shall we then say to these things? If God be for us, who can be against us? He that spared not his own Son, but delivered him up for us all, how shall he not with him also freely give us all things? Who shall lay anything to the charge of God's elect? It is God that justifieth. Who is he that condemneth? It is Christ that died, yea rather, that is risen again, who is even at the right hand of God, who also maketh intercession for us. Who shall separate us from the love of Christ? shall tribulation, or distress, or persecution, or famine, or nakedness, or peril, or sword? As it is written,

> "For thy sake we are killed all the day long;
> We are accounted as sheep for the slaughter".

Nay, in all these things we are more than conquerors through him that loved us. For I am persuaded, that neither death, nor life, nor angels, nor principalities, nor powers, nor things present, nor things to come, nor height, nor depth, nor any other creature, shall be able to separate us from the love of God, which is in Christ Jesus our Lord.

Chapter 12

I beseech you therefore, brethren, by the mercies of God, that ye present your bodies a living sacrifice, holy, acceptable unto God, which is your reasonable service. And be not conformed to this world: but be ye transformed by the renewing of your mind, that ye may prove what is that good, and acceptable, and perfect, will of God.

For I say, through the grace given unto me, to every man that is among you, not to think of himself more highly than he ought to think; but to think soberly according as God hath dealt to every man the measure of faith. For as we have many members in one body, and all members have not the same office: so we, being many, are one body in Christ, and every one members one of another. Having then gifts differing according to the grace that is given to us, whether prophecy, let us prophesy according to the proportion of faith; or ministry, let us wait on our ministering: or he that teacheth, on teaching; or he that exhorteth, on exhortation: he that giveth, let him do it with simplicity; he that ruleth, with diligence; he that giveth, let him do it with simplicity; he that ruleth, with diligence; he that sheweth mercy, with cheerfulness. Let love be without dissimulation. Abhor that which is evil; cleave to that which is good. Be kindly affectioned one to another with brotherly love; in honour preferring one another; not slothful in business; fervent in spirit; serving the Lord; rejoicing in hope; patient in tribulation; continuing instant in prayer; distributing to the necessity of saints; given to hospitality. Bless them which persecute you: bless, and curse not. Rejoice with them that do rejoice, and weep with them that weep. Be of the same mind one toward another. Mind not high things, but condescend to men of low estate. Be not wise in your own conceits. Recompense to no man evil for evil. Provide things honest in the sight of all men. If it be possible, as much as lieth in you, live peaceably with all men. Dearly beloved, avenge not yourselves, but rather give place unto wrath: for it is written, "Vengeance is mine; I will repay, saith the Lord". Therefore if thine enemy hunger, feed him; if he thirst, give him drink: for in so doing thou shalt heap coals of fire on his head. Be not overcome of evil, but overcome evil with good.

Chapter 13

Let every soul be subject unto the higher powers. For there is no power but of God: the powers that be are ordained of God. Whosoever therefore resisteth the power, resisteth the ordinance of God: and they that resist shall receive to themselves damnation. For rulers are not a terror to good works, but to the evil. Wilt thou then not be afraid of the power? do that which is good, and thou shalt have praise of the same: for he is the minister of God to thee for good. But if thou do that which is evil, be afraid; for he beareth not the sword in vain: for he is the minister of God, a revenger to execute wrath upon him that doeth evil. Wherefore ye must needs be subject, not only for wrath, but also for conscience sake. For for this cause pay ye tribute also: for they are God's ministers, attending continually upon this very thing. Render therefore to all their dues: tribute to whom tribute is due; custom to whom custom; fear to whom fear; honour to whom honour.

Owe no man any thing, but to love one another: for he that loveth another hath fulfilled the law. For this, "Thou shalt not commit adultery, Thou shalt not kill, Thou shalt not steal, Thou shalt not bear false witness, Thou shalt not covet"; and if there be any other commandment, it is briefly comprehended in this saying, namely, "Thou shalt love thy neighbour as thyself". Love worketh no ill to his neighbour: therefore love is the fulfilling of the law.

And that, knowing the time, that now it is high time to awake out of sleep: for now is our salvation nearer than when we believed. The night is far spent, the day is at hand: let us therefore cast off the works of darkness, and let us put on the armour of light. Let us walk honestly, as in the day; not in rioting and drunkenness, not in chambering and wantonness, not in strife and envying. But put ye on the Lord Jesus Christ, and make not provision for the flesh, to fulfil the lusts thereof.

Chapter 14

Him that is weak in the faith receive ye, but not to doubtful disputations. For one believeth that he may eat all things: another, who is weak, eateth herbs. Let not him that eateth despise him that eateth not; and let not him which eateth not judge him that eateth: for God hath received him. Who art thou that judgest another man's servant? to his own master he standeth or falleth. Yea, he shall be holden up: for God is able to make him stand. One man esteemeth one day above another: another esteemeth every day alike. Let every man be fully persuaded in his own mind. He that regardeth the day, regardeth it unto the Lord; and he that regardeth not the day, to the Lord he doth not regard it. He that eateth, eateth to the Lord, for he giveth God thanks; and he that eateth not, to the Lord he eateth not, and giveth God thanks. For none of us liveth to himself, and no man dieth to himself. For whether we live, we live unto the Lord; and whether we die, we die unto the Lord: whether we live therefore, or die, we are the Lord's. For to this end Christ both died, and rose, and revived, that he might be Lord both of the dead and living. But why dost thou judge thy brother? or why dost thou set at nought thy brother? for we shall all stand before the judgment seat of Christ. For it is written,

> "As I live, saith the Lord, every knee shall bow to me,
> And every tongue shall confess to God".

So then every one of us shall give account of himself to God.

Let us not therefore judge one another any more: but judge this rather, that no man put a stumblingblock or an occasion to fall in his brother's way. I know, and am persuaded by the Lord Jesus, that there is nothing unclean of itself: but to him that esteemeth any thing to be unclean, to him it is unclean. But if thy brother be grieved with thy meat, now walkest thou not charitably. Destroy not him with thy meat, for whom Christ died. Let not then your good be evil spoken of: for the kingdom of God is not meat and drink: but righteousness, and peace, and joy in the Holy Ghost. For he that in these things serveth Christ is acceptable to God, and approved of men. Let us therefore follow after the things which make for peace, and things wherewith one may edify another. For meat destroy not the work of God. All things indeed are pure; but it is evil for that man who eateth with offence. It is good neither to eat flesh, nor to drink wine, nor any thing whereby thy brother stumbleth, or is offended, or is made weak. Hast thou faith? have it to thyself before God. Happy is he that condemneth not himself in that thing which he alloweth. And he that doubteth is damned if he eat, because he eateth not of faith: for whatsoever is not of faith is sin.

THE FIRST EPISTLE OF PAUL TO THE CORINTHIANS

Chapter 13

Though I speak with the tongues of men and of angels, and have not charity, I am become as sounding brass, or a tinkling cymbal. And though I have the gift of prophecy, and understand all mysteries, and all knowledge; and though I have all faith, so that I could remove mountains, and have not charity, I am nothing. And though I bestow all my goods to feed the poor, and though I give my body to be burned, and have not charity, it profiteth me nothing. Charity suffereth long, and is kind; charity envieth not; charity vaunteth not itself, is not puffed up, doth not behave itself unseemly, seeketh not her own, is not easily provoked, thinketh no evil; rejoiceth not in iniquity, but rejoiceth in the truth; beareth all things, believeth all things, hopeth all things, endureth all things. Charity never faileth: but whether there be prophecies, they shall fail; whether there be tongues, they shall cease; whether there be knowledge, it shall vanish away. For we know in part, and we prophesy in part. But when that which is perfect is come, then that which is in part shall be done away. When I was a child, I spake as a child, I understood as a child, I thought as a child: but when I became a man, I put away childish things. For now we see through a glass, darkly; but then face to face: now I know in part; but then shall I know even as also I am known. And now abideth faith, hope, charity, these three; but the greatest of these is charity.

Chapter 15

Moreover, brethren, I declare unto you the gospel which I preached unto you, which also ye have received, and wherein ye stand; by which also ye are saved, if ye keep in memory what I preached unto you, unless ye have believed in vain. For I delivered unto you first of all that which I also received, how that Christ died for our sins according to the scriptures; and that he was buried, and that he rose again the third day according to the scriptures: and that he was seen of Cephas, then of the twelve: after that, he was seen of above five hundred brethren at once; of whom the greater part remain unto this present, but some are fallen asleep. After that, he was seen of James; then of all the apostles. And last of all he was seen of me also, as of one born out of due time. For I am the least of the apostles, that am not meet to be called an apostle, because I persecuted the church of God. But by the grace of God I am what I am: and his grace which was bestowed upon me was not in vain; but I laboured more abundantly than they all: yet not I, but the grace of God which was with me. Therefore whether it were I or they, so we preach, and so ye believed.

Now if Christ be preached that he rose from the dead, how say some among you that there is no resurrection of the dead? But if there be no resurrection of the dead, then is Christ not risen: and if Christ be not risen, then is our preaching vain, and your faith is also vain. Yea, and we are found false witnesses of God; because we have testified of God that he raised up Christ: whom he raised not up, if so be that the dead rise not. For if the dead rise not, then is not Christ raised: and if Christ be not raised, your faith is vain; ye are yet in your sins. Then they also which are fallen asleep in Christ are perished. If in this life only we have hope in Christ, we are of all men most miserable.

·   ·   ·

jacques maritain _____

The Immortality of the Soul

Born in Paris in 1882, Jacques Maritain was in his mid-twenties when he was converted from his liberal Protestantism to Catholicism. He became a professor of philosophy and lectured at major universities throughout Europe and the United States. Over the years he has composed a small library of books, and has come to be generally regarded as the greatest Roman Catholic philosopher of this century.

Maritain is a philosopher in the "classic" sense: his thought ranges wherever reason can reach and a significant question exists. He has dealt in his writings with logic, metaphysics, ethics, and epistemology; art and poetry; democracy and freedom; and education and the state.

It is true that death is but a second birth, and that our life on earth is a kind of uterine life, in the obscure womb of the griefs and dreams and passing images of this enigmatic world. "Life is changed, life is not taken away." That is why, in the liturgy of the Catholic Church, the feasts of the saints are celebrated on the anniversary of their death, that is, of their real and definite birth. But this is so only because the soul of man is an individual substance, existing by and unto itself as a perfectly defined unit; because it is destined to objective immortality, genuine personal immortality, not in time and history, but in eternity.

THE EXISTENCE OF THE SOUL

It is of this immortality, and of the way in which the Scholastics* established its rational certainty, that I should now like to speak.

We must of course realize that we have a soul before we can discuss whether it is immortal. How does St. Thomas Aquinas proceed in this matter?

He observes first that man has an activity, the activity of the intellect, which is in itself immaterial. The activity of the intellect is immaterial because the proportionate or "connatural" object of the human intellect is not, like the object of the senses, a particular and limited category of things, or rather a particular and limited category of the qualitative properties of things. The proportionate or "connatural" object of the intellect is the nature of the

---

*The Scholastics were the Catholic theologians (St. Thomas among them) of the Middle Ages, noted for their rigorous reasoning. Hence Jacques Maritain is sometimes termed also a "Neo-Scholastic."—R.E.

sense-perceivable things considered in an all-embracing manner, whatever the sense concerned may be. It is not only—as for sight—color or the colored thing (which absorbs and reflects such or such rays of light) nor—as for hearing—sound or the sound-source; it is the whole universe and texture of sense-perceivable reality which can be known by the intellect, because the intellect does not stop at qualities, but pierces beyond, and proceeds to look at essence (that which a thing *is*). This very fact is a proof of the spirituality, or complete immateriality of our intellect; for every activity in which matter plays an intrinsic part is limited to a given category of material objects, as is the case for the senses, which perceive only those properties which are able to act upon their physical organs.

There is already, in fact, a certain immateriality in sense-knowledge; knowledge, as such, is an immaterial activity, because when I am in the act of knowing, I become, or am, the very thing that I know, a thing other than myself, insofar as it is other than myself. And how can I be, or become, other than myself, if it is not in a supra-subjective or immaterial manner? Sense-knowledge is a very poor kind of knowledge; insofar as it is knowledge, it is immaterial, but it is an immaterial activity intrinsically conditioned by, and dependent upon, the material functioning of the sense-organs. Sense-knowledge is the immaterial achievement, the immaterial actuation and product of a living bodily organ; and its very object is also something half material, half immaterial, I mean a physical quality *intentionally* or immaterially present in the medium by which it acts on the sense-organ (something comparable to the manner in which a painter's idea is immaterially present in his paint-brush).

But with intellectual knowledge we have to do with an activity which is in itself completely immaterial. The human intellect is able to know whatever participates in being and truth; the whole universe can be inscribed in it; this means that, in order to be known, the object known by the intellect has been stripped of any existential condition of materiality. This rose, which I see, has contours; but Being, of which I am thinking, is more spacious than space. The object of the intellect is universal, for instance that universal or de-individualized object which is apprehended in the idea of man, of animal, of atom; the object of the intellect is a universal which remains what it is while being identified with an infinity of individuals. And this is only possible because things, in order to become objects of the mind, have been entirely separated from their material existence. To this it must be added that the operation of our intellect does not stop at the knowledge of the nature of sense-perceivable things; it goes further; it knows by analogy the spiritual natures; it extends to the realm of merely possible things; its field has infinite magnitude.

Thus, the objects known by the human intellect, taken not as things existing in themselves, but precisely as objects determining the intellect and united with it, are purely immaterial.

Furthermore, just as the condition of the *object* is immaterial, so is the condition of the *act* which bears upon it, and is determined or specified by it. The object of the human intellect is, as such, purely immaterial; the act of the human intellect is also purely immaterial.

And, moreover, if the act of the intellectual power is purely immaterial, that *power* itself is also purely immaterial. In man, this thinking animal, the intellect is a purely spiritual power. Doubtless it depends upon the body, upon the conditions of the brain. Its activity can be disturbed or hindered by a physical disorder, by an outburst of anger, by a drink or a narcotic. But this dependence is an *extrinsic* one. It exists because our intelligence cannot act without the joint activity of the memory and the imagination, of the internal senses and external senses, all of which are organic powers residing in some material organ, in some special part of the body. As for the intellect itself, it is not *intrinsically* dependent upon the body since its activity is immaterial; the human intellect does not reside in any special part of the body. It is not contained by the body, but rather contains it. It uses the brain, since the organs of the internal senses are in the brain; yet the brain is not an organ of the intelligence; there is no part of the organism whose act is intellectual operation. The intellect has no organ.

Finally, since intellectual power is spiritual, or purely immaterial in itself, its *first substantial root,* the subsisting principle from which this power proceeds and which acts through its instrumentality, is also spiritual.

So much for the spirituality of the intellect. Now, thought or the operation of the intellect is an act and emanation of man as a unit; and when I think, it is not only my intellect which thinks: it is *I*, my own self. And my own self is a bodily self; it involves matter; it is not a spiritual or purely immaterial subject. The body is an essential part of man. The intellect is not the whole man.

Therefore the intellect, or rather the substantial root of the intellect, which must be as immaterial as the intellect, is only a part, albeit an essential part, of man's substance.

But man is not an aggregate, a juxtaposition of two substances; man is a natural whole, a single being, a single substance.

Consequently, we must conclude that the essence or substance of man is single, but that this single substance itself is a compound, the components of which are the body and the spiritual intellect: or rather matter, of which the body is made, and the spiritual principle, one of the powers of which is the intellect. Matter—in the Aristotelian sense of prime matter, or of that root potentiality which is the common stuff of all corporeal substance—matter, substantially united with the spiritual principle of the intellect, is onto-logically molded, shaped from within and in the innermost depths of being, by this spiritual principle as by a substantial and vital impulse, in order to constitute that body of ours. In this sense, Saint Thomas, after Aristotle, says that the intellect is the form, the substantial form of the human body.

That is the Scholastic notion of the human soul. The human soul, which is the root principle of the intellectual power, is the first principle of life of the human body, and the substantial form, the *entelechy,* or that body. And the human soul is not only a substantial form or entelechy, as are the souls of plants and animals according to the biological philosophy of Aristotle; the human soul is also a spirit, a spiritual substance able to exist apart from matter, since the human soul is the root principle of a spiritual power, the act of which is intrinsically independent of matter. The human soul is both a soul and a spirit, and it is its very substantiality, subsistence and existence, which are communicated to the whole human substance, in order to make human substance be what it is, and to make it subsist and exist. Each element of the human body is human, and exists as such, by virtue of the immaterial existence of the human soul. Our body, our hands, our eyes exist by virtue of the existence of our soul.

The immaterial soul is the first substantial root not only of the intellect, but of all that which, in us, is spiritual activity; and it is also the first substantial root of all our other living activities. It would be inconceivable that a non-spiritual soul, that kind of soul which is not a spirit and cannot exist without informing matter—namely, the souls of plants or animals in Aristotelian biology—should possess a power or faculty *superior* to its own degree in being, that is, immaterial, or act through a supra-material instrumentality independent of any corporeal organ and physical structure. But when it is a question of a spirit which is a soul, or of a *spiritual soul,* as the human soul is, then it is perfectly conceivable that such a soul should have, aside from immaterial or spiritual faculties, other powers and activities which are organic and material, and which, relating to the union between soul and body, pertain to a level of being *inferior* to that of the spirit.

THE SPIRITUALITY OF THE HUMAN SOUL

Thus, the very way in which the Scholastics arrived at the existence of the human soul also established its spirituality. Just as the intellect is spiritual, that is to say intrinsically independent of matter in its operation and in its nature, so also, and for the same reason, the human soul, the substantial root of the intellect, is spiritual, that is, intrinsically independent of matter in its nature and in its existence; it does not live by the body, the body lives by it. The human soul is a spiritual substance which, by its substantial union with matter, gives existence and countenance to the body.

That is my second point. As we have seen, the Scholastics demonstrated it by a metaphysical analysis of the intellect's operation, carefully distinguished from the operation of the senses. They adduced, of course, much other evidence in support of their demonstration. In their consideration of the intellect, they observed, for instance, that the latter is capable of *perfect reflection,* that is, of coming back entirely upon itself—not in the manner of a sheet of paper, half of which can be folded on the other half, but in a complete manner, so that it can grasp its whole operation and penetrate it by knowledge, and can contain itself and its own principle, the existing self, in its own knowing activity, a perfect reflection or self-containing of which any material agent, extended in space and time, is essentially incapable. Here we are confronted with that phenomenon of self-knowledge, of *prise de conscience* or becoming aware of oneself, which is a privilege of the spirit, as Hegel (after St. Augustine) was to emphasize, and which plays so tremendous a part in the history of humanity and the development of its spiritual energies.

In the same way it is possible to show that the human will, which is rooted in the intellect, and which is able to determine itself, or to master the very motive or judgment which determines it and is made efficacious by the will itself, is spiritual in its operation and nature. Every material agent is subject to the universal determinism. Free will is the privilege, the glorious and weighty privilege, of an agent endowed with immaterial power.

We are responsible for ourselves; we choose for ourselves and decide on our own ends and our own destinies. We are capable of spiritual, suprasensuous love, and desire and joy, which are naturally intermingled with our organic and sensuous emotions, but which are in themselves affections of the spiritual will, and are awakened through the immaterial light of intellectual insight. We delight in beauty, we desire perfection and justice, we love truth, we love God, we love all men—not only the members of our social group, or our family, our class or nation—but all men because they are human beings, and children of God. The saints, those men who are called everywhere spiritual men, experience a contemplation which establishes their souls in a peace superior to and stronger than the whole world, and they go through inner trials, crucifixions and deaths which only a life superior to and stronger than biological existence can suffer and go through—and still remain alive. And we ourselves know that we can deliberate about ourselves, judge our own actions, cling to what is good because it is good and for no other reason; all of us know more or less obscurely that we are persons, that we have rights and duties, that we preserve human dignity within ourselves. Each one of us can, at certain moments in his existence, descend into the innermost depths of the Ego, to make there some eternal pledge or gift of himself, or face some irrefutable judgment of his conscience; and each one of us, on such occasions, alone with himself, feels that he is a universe unto himself, immersed in, but not dominated by, the great star-studded universe.

Through all these convergent ways, we may realize and experience in a certain measure, and in a concrete fashion, that living reality of our spiritual

CHAPTER NINE / *Christianity*

roots, or of what is above time in us, which the philosophical proofs make intellectually certain, but in the abstract manner of scientific knowledge.

THE IMMORTALITY OF THE HUMAN SOUL

The third point follows immediately from the second. The immortality of the human soul is an immediate corollary of its spirituality. A soul which is spiritual in itself, intrinsically independent of matter in its nature and existence, cannot cease existing. A spirit—that is, a "form" which needs nothing other than itself (save the influx of the Prime Cause) to exercise existence —once existing cannot cease existing. A spiritual soul cannot be corrupted, since it possesses no matter; it cannot be disintegrated, since it has no substantial parts; it cannot lose its individual unity, since it is self-subsisting, nor its internal energy, since it contains within itself all the sources of its energies. The human soul cannot die. Once it exists, it cannot disappear; it will necessarily exist forever, endure without end.

Thus, philosophic reason, put to work by a great metaphysician like Thomas Aquinas, is able to prove the immortality of the human soul in a demonstrative manner. Of course, this demonstration implies a vast and articulate network of metaphysical insights, notions and principles (relating to essence and nature, substance, act and potency, matter and form, operation, etc.) the validity of which is necessarily presupposed. We can appreciate fully the strength of the Scholastic demonstration only if we realize the significance and full validity of the metaphysical notions involved. If modern times feel at a loss in the face of metaphysical knowledge, I fancy that it is not metaphysical knowledge which is to blame, but rather modern times and the weakening of reason they have experienced.

. . . .

THE CONDITION AND DESTINY OF THE IMMORTAL SOUL

What can philosophy tell us about the natural condition of the immortal soul after the death of its body? That is my fourth and last point. Philosophy can tell us very little indeed on this subject. Let us try to summarize the few indications there are. All the organic and sensuous powers of the human soul remain dormant in a separated soul, for they cannot be brought into play without the body. The separated soul is itself engulfed in a complete sleep with regard to the material world; the external senses and their perceptions have vanished; the images of memory and imagination, the impulses of instinct and passion have vanished. But this sleep is not like the sleep we know, obscure and filled with dreams; it is lucid and intelligent, alive to spiritual realities. For now light shines from within. The intellect and the spiritual powers are awake and active. From the very fact of its separation from the body, the soul now knows itself through itself; its very substance has become transparent to its intellect; it is intellectually penetrated to its innermost depths. The soul knows itself in an intuitive manner; it is dazzled by its own beauty, the beauty of a spiritual substance, and it knows other things through its own substance already known, in the measure in which other things resemble it. It knows God through that image of God which the soul itself is. And in accordance with its state of incorporeal existence, it receives from God, the sun of the spirits, certain ideas and inspirations which directly enlighten it, and help the natural light of the human intellect, of that intellect which is, as Saint Thomas Aquinas phrased it, the lowest in the hierarchy of spirits.

Saint Thomas teaches also that all that is of the intellect and the spirit, and especially the intellectual memory, which is but one with the intellect, keeps alive, in the separated soul, the whole treasure of knowledge acquired during our bodily life. The intellectual knowledge, the intellectual virtues acquired here below subsist in the separated soul. Whereas the images of the sense-memory, which had its seat in the brain, disappear, that which has penetrated into the intellectual memory is preserved. Thus, in an intellectual and spiritual manner, the separated soul ever knows those whom it loved. And it loves them spiritually. And it is able to converse with other spirits by opening to them what abides in its inner thoughts and is taken hold of by its free will.

We may thus imagine that, at the moment when it leaves the body, the soul is suddenly immersed into itself as into a shining abyss, where all that was buried within it, all its dead, rise up again in full light, insofar as all this was encompassed in the subconscious or supraconscious depths of the spiritual life of its intellect and will. Then all that is true and good in the soul becomes a blessing for it at the touch of this all-pervading revelatory light; all that is warped and evil becomes a torment for it under the effect of the very same light.

I do not believe that natural reason can go further in its understanding of the natural condition of the separated soul. What would be the life and happiness of souls if their state after death were a purely natural state? Their supreme good would consist in wisdom, untrammeled spiritual life, mutual friendship, and first and foremost in advancing constantly in their natural knowledge and love of God, Whom they would, however, never see face to face. It would be happiness in motion, never absolutely fulfilled—what Leibniz called *un chemin par des plaisirs,* "a road amidst spiritual pleasures."

But if we wish to know more, can we not go beyond philosophy? Philosophy itself will then entrust us to the guidance of a knowledge whose sources are superior to its own. Christians know that man does not live in a state of pure nature. They know that he was created in a state of grace, and that, after the first sin which wounded our race, he has been living in a state of fallen and redeemed nature; they know that he is made for supernatural blessedness. In answer to the question of the separated soul's destiny, the

Scholastic doctors spoke not as philosophers, but as theologians whose knowledge rests on the data of Revelation.

Insofar as man participates in the metaphysical privileges of spirit and personality, he has aspirations which transcend human nature and its possibilities, and which consequently may be called transnatural aspirations: the longing for a state in which he would know things completely and without error, in which he would enjoy perfect communion with spirits, in which he would be free without being able to fail or to sin, in which he would inhabit a realm of unfading justice, in which he would have the intuitive knowledge of the First Cause of being.

Such a longing cannot be fulfilled by nature. It can be fulfilled by grace. The immortal soul is involved and engaged in the great drama of the Redemption. If, at the moment of its separation from the body, at the moment when its choice is immutably fixed forever, the immortal soul prefers its own will and self-love to the will and gift of God, if it prefers misery with pride to the blessing of grace, then it is granted what it has wished for. It has it, and it will never cease wanting and preferring it, for a free choice made in the condition of a *pure* spirit is an eternal choice. If the soul opens itself to the will and gift of God, Whom it loves more than its own existence, then it is granted what it has loved, it enters forever into the joy of the uncreated Being, it sees God face to face and knows Him as it is known by Him, intuitively. Thus, it becomes God by participation, as Saint John of the Cross phrased it, and, through grace, it attains that communion in divine life, that blessedness for the sake of which all things have been created. And the degree of its blessedness itself, the degree of its vision, will correspond to the degree of the inner impetus which projects it into God, in other words, to the degree of love to which it has attained in its life on earth. In the last analysis, therefore, we must say with Saint John of the Cross: It is upon our love that we shall be judged. In its state of blessedness the immortal soul will know creation in the Creator, by that kind of knowledge which Saint Augustine called "matutinal" knowledge, because it is produced in the eternal morning of Creative Ideas; the immortal soul will be equal to the angels, and will communicate freely with the whole realm of spirits; it will love God, henceforth clearly seen, with a sovereign necessity; and it will exert free will with regard to all its actions concerning creatures, but its free will shall no longer be liable to failure and sin; the soul will inhabit the realm of unfading justice, that of the three divine Persons and of the blessed spirits; it will grasp and possess the divine Essence which, infinitely clearer and more intelligible than any of our ideas, will illumine the human intellect from within and will itself be the intelligible medium, the actuating form through which it will be known. According to a line of the Psalms which Saint Thomas loved and often quoted: "In Thy light shall we see light."

Such are the teachings of Saint Thomas, both as a philosopher and as a theologian, about the condition and destiny of the human soul. Immortality is not a more or less precarious, successful or unsuccessful survival in other men, or in the ideal waves of the universe. Immortality is a nature-given, inalienable property of the human soul as a spiritual substance. And grace makes eternal life possible to all, to the most destitute as well as to the most gifted. The eternal life of the immortal soul is its transforming union with God and His intimate life, a union which is to be accomplished inchoatively here below, by love and contemplation and, after the body's death, in a definite and perfect manner, by the beatific vision. For eternal life begins here upon earth, and the soul of man lives and breathes where it loves; and love, in living faith, has strength enough to make the soul of man experience unity with God—"two natures in a single spirit and love, *dos naturalezas en un espiritu y amor de Dios.*"

I do not believe that a philosopher can discuss the immortality of the soul without taking into consideration the complementary notions which religious thought adds to the true and inadequate answers which reason and philosophy can furnish by themselves.

FROM *The Dark Night of the Soul*

St. John of the Cross (1542–1591), one of the most remarkable of Christian mystics, has been described by F. C. Happold as "a spirit of flame, on fire with the love of God, the supreme spiritual mountaineer."* Born into an impoverished family in Spain, he felt at an early age the call of a religious vocation and at twenty-one joined the Carmelite Order. Sent to the University of Salamanca for study in theology and philosophy, he was ordained a priest in 1576. Although his own inclinations were toward solitude and the contemplative life, he became involved in an effort to reform the Carmelite Order, which had fallen away from its disciplines. Meeting fierce resistance, he was imprisoned for almost nine months in a small cell in a dungeon before managing to escape. Life in the dungeon had been physically punishing but spiritually rewarding: it was there that he wrote some of his most inspired poetry. Throughout his remaining years, he held various positions in the order and continued his efforts at reform, meeting occasionally with further persecution. In the last year of his life he was threatened with removal from the order.

THE MAIN THEME AND FINAL GOAL:
THE SOUL'S UNION WITH GOD

This treatise deals with the manner in which a soul may prepare itself to attain to union with God. It gives useful advice and instruction, both to beginners and to those more advanced in the spiritual life, so that they may learn how to free themselves from all that is temporal and not weigh themselves down with the spiritual, and remain in that complete nakedness and freedom of the spirit which are necessary for union with God.

The entire doctrine which I intend to discuss . . . is contained in the following stanzas, and they describe also the manner of ascending to the peak of the mountain, that is, that high state of perfection which we here designate as the union of the soul with God. The poem reads as follows:

1

In a dark night,
My longing heart aglow with love,
—Oh, blessed lot!—
I went forth unseen
From my house that was at last in deepest rest.

Mysticism (Baltimore: Penguin Books, 1970), p. 356.

2

Secure and protected by darkness,
I climbed the secret ladder, in disguise,
—Oh, blessed lot!—
In darkness, veiled and concealed I went
Leaving behind my house in deepest rest.

3

Oh, blissful night!
Oh, secret night, when I remained unseeing and unseen,
When the flame burning in my heart
Was my only light and guide.

4

This inward light,
A safer guide than noonday's brightness,
Showed me the place where He awaited me
—My soul's Beloved—
A place of solitude.

5

Oh, night that guided me!
Oh, night more lovely than the rosy dawn!
Oh, night whose darkness guided me
To that sweet union,
In which the lover and Beloved are made one.

6

Upon the flower of my breast,
Kept undefiled for Him alone,
He fell asleep,
While I was waking,
Caressing Him with gentle cedars' breeze.

7

And when Aurora's breath
Began to spread His curled hair,
His gentle hand
He placed upon my neck,
And all my senses were in bliss suspended.

8

Forgetful of myself,
My head reclined on my Beloved,
The world was gone
And all my cares at rest,
Forgotten all my grief among the lilies.

.   .   .

THE CONQUERING OF THE DESIRES

The counsels for the conquering of the desires, which now follow, though brief and few in number, I believe to be as helpful and efficacious as they are concise. He who earnestly wishes to make practical use of them will need no others, for he will find them all implied therein.

First, he should have an habitual inclination to imitate Christ in everything he does, trying to conform himself to His life. Let him meditate on the life of Christ, so that he may learn how to imitate it and to behave in all things as Christ would behave.

Secondly, to be able to do this well, every pleasure that presents itself to the senses, if it be not purely for the honor and glory of God, must be renounced; he must cast it out for the love of Christ, Who in this life had and desired no other pleasure than to do the will of His Father.

Let me give you the following example: If a person were offered the pleasure of listening to things which are of no value for the service and honor of God, he must neither desire this pleasure nor desire to hear of these things; and if he were offered the pleasure of looking at things which do not help him on his journey toward God, he must not desire this pleasure nor look at such things. And he should behave in like manner with respect to all the senses. If this is beyond his power, it suffices that he desire not to have this pleasure whenever his sensory perception encounters these things. In this manner he will succeed in depriving and emptying his senses of all such pleasure, leaving them, as it were, in darkness. In carefully following this counsel, he will soon make much progress.

The Silencing of the Passions

To silence and tranquillize the four natural passions—joy, hope, fear, and grief—the following counsels are very helpful, conducive to great merit, and the source of great virtues:

Take care that you always choose
  Not the easiest, but the hardest;
  Not the most delectable, but the most distasteful;
  Not what gives most pleasure, but what is less pleasing;

Not what allows you much rest, but what requires great exertion;

Not what consoles, but what deprives you of consolation;

Not the loftiest and the most precious, but the lowest and the most despised;

Not the desire for anything, but a desire for nothing.

Do not go about seeking the best of temporal things, but the worst.

Desire nothing but to enter for Christ's sake into total nakedness, emptiness, and poverty with respect to all the things of this world.

These counsels, if well heeded and put into practice, are quite sufficient for entering into the night of sense.

"Todo y Nada": All and Nothing

In concluding this enumeration of counsels and rules, it is fitting to set down . . . instructions intended to teach the manner of ascending and thus attaining to the height of Divine union.

These lines read as follows:

If you want to have pleasure in everything,
   You must desire to have pleasure in nothing.

If you want to possess everything,
   You must desire to possess nothing.

If you want to become all,
   You must desire to be nothing.

If you want to know all,
   You must desire to know nothing.

If you want to arrive at that which you know not,
   You must go by a way which you know not.

If you want to arrive at that which you possess not,
   You must go by a way which you possess not.

If you want to arrive at that which you are not,
   You must pass through that which you are not.

The Way Not to Obstruct
the Efficacy of the All

If you allow yourself to be detained by anything,
   You desist from casting yourself upon the All.

For, in order to proceed from all things to the All,
   You must deny yourself wholly in all things.

If you are to attain to the possession of All,
   You must learn to possess it without desiring anything.

For, if you desire to possess anything at all,
   You cannot have your treasure in God alone.

In this nakedness the spiritual soul finds its quietude and rest; since it covets nothing, nothing wearies it in its upward flight, (and nothing oppresses it when it is cast down; for the soul then abides in the center of its humility.)

THE DARK NIGHT

This dark night is an inflowing of God into the soul, which purges it from its ignorance and its habitual—natural and spiritual—imperfections. The theologians call it *infused contemplation* and treat of it in *mystical theology*. In this state God mysteriously teaches the soul the perfection of love, without its doing anything and without its understanding the nature of this infused contemplation. For what produces such striking effects in the soul is the loving wisdom of God, which by its purifying and illuminating action prepares the soul for the union of love with God. And this loving wisdom is the same which also purifies and illumines the blessed spirits.

But now the question arises: Why does the soul call this Divine light a dark night? The answer is that for two reasons this Divine wisdom is for the soul not only night and darkness, but also affliction and torment. The first reason is the sublime grandeur of Divine Wisdom, which transcends the capacity of the soul and is therefore darkness to it. The second reason is the lowliness and impurity of the soul, and in this respect Divine Wisdom is for the soul painful, bitter, and dark.

In order to prove the first point, we must refer to a doctrine of the Philosopher [i.e., Aristotle], which says that, the clearer and more manifest Divine things are in themselves, the darker and more hidden they are to the soul; just as, the brighter the light is, the more it blinds and darkens the eye of the night-owl. When, therefore, this Divine light of contemplation invades a soul which is not yet wholly illumined, it causes spiritual darkness in it; for it not only transcends the soul's natural intellectual capacity, but it also drowns out and darkens the act of intellection. This is why Dionysius [the Areopagite] and other mystical theologians call this infused contemplation a ray of darkness for the soul that is not yet wholly purified and illumined.

And [with respect to the second point] it is clear that this dark contemplation is in its early stages very painful to the soul; for, as this Divine infused contemplation comprises in itself a plentitude of the highest perfections, and since the soul which receives them is not yet wholly purified and thus still engulfed in a sea of miseries, it follows that—because two contraries cannot coexist in one subject—the soul must of necessity endure much pain and suffering. Thus, when this pure light invades the soul, in order to expel its impurity, the soul feels its own impurity so intensely that it believes God to be its enemy and comes to think of itself as an enemy of God. This causes it so much grief and sadness that it feels actually rejected and forsaken by God. And what gives it the greatest pain is the fear that it will never be worthy of God and that therefore all its blessings are lost for ever. For this Divine and dark light now reveals to the soul's sight all its faults and miseries, so that it may see clearly how by its own powers it can never have anything else.

The second kind of torment which the soul suffers is caused by its natural, moral, and spiritual weakness; for, when this Divine contemplation takes hold of the soul with some degree of violence, in order to strengthen it and make it obedient, it suffers so much pain in its weakness that it almost faints. Both sense and spirit suffer such pain and agony as if they were weighed down by some immense load, so that even death would appear as a release and relief. And it is indeed very strange and very sad that the soul is so weak and impure that the light and gentle hand of God appears to it as such a prodigious weight and such a hostile force, since this hand does not really weigh the soul down, but only touches it mercifully, in order to bestow favors and graces upon it.

THE MYSTICAL LADDER

There are, as we have said, ten steps on this ladder of love, by which the soul ascends, one by one, to God. The *first step* of love causes the soul to become sick, and this is for its own good. On this step stood the Bride [in the Song of Solomon] when she said: "I adjure you, daughters of Jerusalem, if you find my Beloved, tell Him that I am sick with love" (Canticles 5:8). This sickness, however, is not unto death, but for the glory of God; for in this sickness the soul dies only to sin and to all things that are not God. And the soul does not fall into this sickness unless an excess of love is communicated to it. And now it can no longer find any pleasure, support, consolation, and rest in anything. It therefore begins at once to climb to the second step.

The *second step* causes the soul to seek God without ceasing. And thus, when the Bride says that she sought her Beloved as she was lying upon her bed, and found Him not, she immediately adds: "I will rise and seek Him Whom my soul loves" (Cant. 3:2). On this step the soul is so filled to overflowing with love that it seeks the Beloved in all things, and in all its thoughts it has in mind the Beloved. When it eats, when it sleeps, in its night-watches, and in whatever else it does, all its care is for the Beloved. And now, as love gradually recovers its health and is gaining new strength on this second step, it begins at once to climb to the third, by means of a new purgation in this dark night.

The *third step* of the ladder of love activates the soul and fills it with a burning zeal to work without wearying. On this step the valiant deeds which the soul may have done for its Beloved appear to it as very small, and the long hours which it may have spent in serving Him appear as very short. The soul considers itself quite useless in all that it does, and thinks that it is wasting its life in idleness. And from this springs another admirable effect, namely, the firm conviction that it is far worse than all other souls; first and foremost, because love makes it realize more and more how much it owes to God; and second, because it recognizes how faulty and imperfect are the many works which it does for God in this state. And this anxious care, together with many similar effects that are produced in the soul on this third step of love, impart to it the courage and strength to mount to the fourth step.

The *fourth step* of this ladder of love produces in the soul a continuous suffering for the sake of the Beloved, but a suffering which the soul endures without wearying. For, as St. Augustine says, love makes all things that are burdensome and painful so easy that they appear as nothing. In this state the spirit gains so much strength that it is capable of keeping the flesh in complete subjection and is as little encumbered by it as a tree is by one of its leaves.

Exceedingly lofty, then, is this fourth step of love; for, as the soul in this state goes ever after God with truest love and with the spiritual resolve to suffer for His sake, His Majesty frequently grants it the sweet joys of a visitation in the spirit; for the boundless love of Christ, the Word, cannot allow the loving soul to suffer without coming to its aid. This He affirmed through the mouth of Jeremiah, where we read: "I have remembered you, and have pitied your tender youth, when you went after Me through desert land" (Jer. 2:2). This fourth step, then, enkindles the soul and makes it burn with such desire for God that it causes it to rise to the fifth step.

The *fifth step* of this ladder of love causes in the soul an impatient striving and yearning for God. On this step the longing of the loving soul for the possession of the Beloved and for union with Him has become so vehement that every delay, however brief it be, appears to the soul very long, wearisome, and oppressive, since its only thought is how to find the Beloved. On this step the lover must either behold the Beloved, or die. The soul is thus languishing with hunger, and its only nourishment is love; and hence it rises to the sixth step.

The *sixth step* causes the soul to run swiftly to meet God and to experience His nearness in many palpable touches. Its hope runs after Him without wearying; for hope has been made strong by love, so that it may fly swiftly. And the cause of this swiftness is that the soul's love is greatly enlarged on this step, and its purification is almost complete; and thus the soul at once advances to the seventh step.

The *seventh step* of this ladder makes the soul very daring. Here love is no longer guided by prudent judgment or daunted in its hope, nor does it accept any counsel to draw back. For the grace which God here grants the soul causes it to become very determined in its boldness. By this attitude it confirms what the Apostle says, namely, that love believes all things, hopes all things, and is capable of doing and enduring all things (cf. 1 Cor. 13:7). On this step the Bride grew bold, and said: "I thirst for a kiss from these lips" (Cant. 1:1). To this the soul could never dare to aspire unless it had first received the inward grace bestowed upon it "by the sceptre of the King"; for otherwise it would fall from the other steps which it has mounted and to which it must cling with humility. From the daring and freedom which God grants to the soul on this seventh step follows the eighth, on which the soul is united with the Beloved.

The *eighth step* of love, then, causes the soul to seize the Beloved and hold Him fast without letting Him go, according to the words of the Bride: "I found Him Whom my heart and soul love; and now that He is mine I will never let Him go" (Cant. 3:4). On this step of union the longing of the soul is satisfied, but not continuously; for some souls gain a temporary foothold on this step and then lose it again. If it were otherwise and this union were to continue, they would in fact attain to a certain state of glory in this life.

The *ninth step* of love causes the soul to burn with sweet rapture. This is the state of perfection, that is, the state of those perfect souls who are aflame with the sweet love of God. This blissful flame of love is caused by the Holy Ghost, by virtue of the union which these souls have with God. And there are no words with which the abundant graces and treasures of God which the soul enjoys on this step can be described.

The *tenth and last step* of this secret ladder of love causes the soul to become wholly assimilated to God, by virtue of the *clear vision of God* to which the soul that has ascended to the ninth step in this life, attains immediately after it has gone forth from the flesh. For these souls, who are few, enter not into purgatory, since they have already been wholly purged by love. Of these souls St. Matthew speaks when he says: "Blessed are the pure of heart; they shall see God" (Matt. 5:8). And this vision is the cause of the perfect likeness of the soul to God, for, according to the words of St. John, "we know that we shall be like Him" (1 John 3:2). Not because the soul will have the capacity of God, for this is impossible; but because all that the soul is will be like to God, so that the soul will be *God by participation*.

On this last step of pure vision, which is also the last step on this ladder, nothing is any longer hidden from the soul, because it has now been wholly assimilated to God. In this manner, then, the soul—by this mystical Divine Wisdom and this mystical love—rises above all things and above itself, and ascends to God.

FROM THE *Journal*

Søren Kierkegaard (1813–1855) was born and lived almost all of his life in Copenhagen. Physically, he was "slight, spindly and with so pronounced a stoop that he was regarded as a hunchback. The curvature of his spine . . . made him lean back as he walked, and gave him a dislocated, mechanical, crab-like gait.* Intellectually, he was brilliant, and socially he could be witty, charming, and a fascinating conversationalist.

But Kierkegaard himself was a complex and often enigmatic man who was subject to periods of melancholy and despair. Dark crises were precipitated by his relationship with his father, a severely religious man tormented by a sense of guilt, and by his engagement to Regina Olsen. Kierkegaard broke that engagement, possibly because he thought such renunciation was necessary for his single-minded religious quest. He agonized over the decision and his love for Regina for the rest of his life. Thus he led a solitary, introverted life, set apart both by a malformed body and an endlessly reflective and deliberative mind. There are 10,000 pages in his journal, twice the number he published. He died at the age of only forty-two.

It is the same with Christianity or with becoming a Christian as it is with all radical cures. One postpones it as long as possible. (*1835*)

There is a most remarkable saying, I know not where, but one which bears the inward stamp of being the kind of utterance which, so to speak, is spoken with the mouth of a whole people. A desperate sinner wakes up in hell and cries out, "What time is it?" The devil answers, "Eternity." (*1836*)

What is the nourishment offered one by all the world's knowledge in comparison to what is given by Christianity, which pours out the very body and blood of its founder. (*1837*)

To need God is man's highest perfection. (*1844*)

Deep within every human being there still lives the anxiety over the possibility of being alone in the world, forgotten by God, overlooked among the millions and millions in this enormous household. One keeps this anxiety at a distance by looking at the many round about who are related to him as kin and friends, but the anxiety is still there, nevertheless, and one hardly dares think of how he would feel if all this were taken away. (*1847*)

The Journal of Kierkegaard, translated and selected by Alexander Dru (New York: Harper Torchbooks, 1959), p. 8.

From *Søren Kierkegaard's Journal and Papers,* Vol. 1, trans. and ed. by Howard V. Hong and Edna H. Hong. Copyright © 1967 by Howard V. Hong. Reprinted by permission of Indiana University Press, Bloomington. Notes have been omitted.

It is claimed that arguments against Christianity arise out of doubt. This is a total misunderstanding. The arguments against Christianity arise out of insubordination, reluctance to obey, mutiny against all authority. Therefore, until now the battle against objections has been shadow-boxing, because it has been intellectual combat with doubt instead of being ethical combat against mutiny. *(1847)*

It is easy enough to show how false and basically traitorous, even though unconscious, all this defense of Christianity is—yes, even the very form which discourse about Christianity ordinarily takes. The fact of the matter is that pastors and scholars, etc., do not believe in Christianity at all. If a person himself firmly believes that the good he is discoursing about is the highest good, if he almost sags under the impression of its exceedingly abundant blessedness—how in all the world could he ever come to defend it, to conduct a defense of its really being a good, or even to talk in the following manner: This is a great good for three reasons—this supreme good, this good which makes the wisest of men's understanding dizzy and reduces it to tiny sparrow-like understanding, this is a great good—for three reasons. What an anticlimax! Imagine a lover. Yes, he can keep on talking day in and day out about the gloriousness of his beloved. But if anyone demands him to prove it with three reasons, or even defend it—I wonder if he would not regard this as a demented proposal; or if he were a bit more sagacious, he no doubt would say to the person who suggested this to him: Oho, you do not know what it is to be in love at all, and you half believe that I am not either. *(1848)*

The fact of the matter is that Christianity is really all too joyous, and therefore really to stick to Christianity a man must be brought to madness by suffering. Most men, therefore, will be able to get a real impression of Christianity only in the moment of their death, because death actually takes away from them what must be surrendered in order to get an impression of Christianity. *(1848)*

There is something almost cruel about the Christian's being placed in a world which in every way wants to pressure him to do the opposite of what God bids him to do with fear and trembling in his innermost being. It would be something like the cruelty of parents if they were to threaten and sternly order their child to do thus and so—and then place the child together with the kind of children who would pressure him in every way to do just the opposite. *(1848)*

"Seek first the kingdom of God"—these words could be presented in such a way that one negatively examines everything else and shows that this is what one should not do, or in such a way that one shows that the first manifestation of seeking God's kingdom first is, in a certain sense, to do nothing; for to seek the kingdom of God first is at first the same as to renounce everything. *(1848)*

Seek first the kingdom of God. But what am I supposed to do? Shall I seek an office in order to be influential? No, first you shall seek God's kingdom. Shall

I give all my fortune to the poor? No, first you shall seek God's kingdom and his righteousness. Shall I go out in the world as an apostle and proclaim this? No, first you shall seek God's kingdom. But isn't this in a certain sense doing nothing at all? Yes, to be sure, in a certain sense this is what it is. (*1848*)

Being a Christian is neither more nor less, without a doubt neither more nor less, than being a martyr; every Christian, that is, every true Christian, is a martyr.

But I hear one of those shabby pastors (by shabby I mean one of those who is shabby enough to accept two or three thousand rix-dollars a year, prestige with decorations, etc.—in order to betray Christianity) say: But, of course, we cannot all be martyrs. To this God would reply: Stupid man, do you not think I know how I have arranged the world. Fear only that it will never happen that all become Christians, that only 1/10, only 1/1000 become Christians.

The point is this—becoming a Christian is an examination given by God. But for this very reason in every age (year 1 and year 1848) it must continually be equally difficult to become a Christian. In a certain sense God has squandered so much upon existence[*Tilvaerelsen*] that at any and every moment there will be thousands upon thousands in abundance to persecute the true Christians—and yet in another sense it continues to be possible for every one of these thousands also to become a Christian.

The purpose (and this will also be the end of the matter) of Christendom's suddenly being called out for inspection is that in a more serious way all the sweat will be tormented out of all those shabby, profusely sweating clergymen.

Let us then once again in a noble Christian sense get shabby pastors, poor men who walk about in poor clothing, despised men whom all ridicule, mock, and spit upon. I hope and believe that with the assistance of God I would be able to preach fearlessly even if someone spat in my face as I climbed the stairs to the pulpit. But if I were to be dressed up in a velvet cloak with stars and ribbons and then name the name of Christ—I would die of shame. (*1848*)

After all, many people think that the Christian message (i.e., to love one's neighbor as oneself) is purposely a little too rigorous—something like the household alarm clock which runs a half-hour fast so that one does not get up too late in the morning. (*1848*)

There is only one, and quite rightly pathological, proof of the truth of Christianity—when the anxiety of sin and the burdened conscience constrain a man to cross the narrow line between despair unto madness—and Christianity.

There lies Christianity. (*1849*)

Humanly speaking, there is an almost mad self-contradiction in Christianity's requirement, which is the anguish of being a Christian. It sets a task and says: In the same degree as you succeed, you will come to suffer more and more. You will continually think: "But, Lord God, if I rightly love men— then . . . . ." The Christian answer to this must be: Stupid man, or presumptuous man, did not the Savior of the world rightly love men, and he was mocked, spit upon, etc.; has it not been this way for all true Christians, and if not, it merely indicates that they were not Christians, for the prototype settles everything. (*1849*)

. . . if you desire, humanly speaking, pleasant and happy days, then never get involved *in earnest* with Christianity.

If you do, there is humanly only one consolation for you: death, for which you will learn to long more impatiently than the most amorous girl longs to see her lover again. Yet death is no consolation either. But truly there is, there is one consolation—the eternal. Love the eternal, then you hate this life—this is Christianity. Love God, then you hate this world—this is Christianity. Love Christ, then you are hated by all men—this is Christianity.

See, this is Christianity. If you are not conscious of being a sinner to the degree that in the anxiety of the anguished conscience you do not dare anything other than to commit yourself to Christ—then you never will become a Christian. Only the agony of the consciousness of sin can explain the fact that a person will submit to this radical cure. To become a Christian is the most fearful operation of all, of all. Just as unlikely as it is for a person who merely feels a little indisposed to think of submitting to the most painful operation, just as unlikely is it for a man to think of getting involved with Christianity if sin did not pain him inordinately—if, note well, he then knows what Christianity is and has not been talked into some nonsense about Christianity's gentle, life-beautifying, and ennobling ground of comfort. (*1849*)

There are so and so many children baptized every year, so and so many confirmed, so many become theological professors; there are a thousand pastors; there are theological professors, bishops, deans, custodians, sub-custodians—everything is as it should be—if only Christianity also existed. (*1850*)

There was a time when one could almost be afraid to call himself a disciple [*Discipel*] of Christ, because it meant so much. Now one can do it with complete ease, because it means nothing at all. (*1851*)

It is frequently said that if Christ were to come again now he would once more be slain. This is perfectly true; but qualified more precisely, it would have to be added that he would be sentenced to death and slain because what he proclaimed was NOT CHRISTIANITY but a lunatic, wicked, blasphemous, misanthropic exaggeration and caricature of that gentle doctrine, Christianity, the true Christianity, which is found in Christendom and whose founder was Jesus Christ. (*1850*)

Above all, read the N.T. without a commentary. Would it ever occur to a lover to read a letter from his beloved with a commentary!

In connection with everything which qualitatively makes a claim of having purely personal significance to me, a commentary is a most hazardous meddler.

If the letter from the beloved were in a language I do not understand—well, then I learn the language—but I do not read the letter with the aid of commentaries by others. I read it, and since the thought of my beloved is vividly present and my purpose in everything is to will according to her will and wishes, I understand the letter all right. It is the same with the Scriptures. With the help of God I understand it all right. (*1850*)

As soon as the awakened get together they immediately chatter about nothing else but Christianity.

This is disgusting frivolousness. But didn't the first Christians do it? Indeed. Why was it not frivolousness then? Because the sword of persecution hung over their heads every hour, because it was constantly a matter of life and death, because everything was event and action, so that it was impossible to talk about anything else than that, just as it is impossible to talk about anything else than a fire—as long as it lasts.

But the awakened nowadays suffer nothing, do nothing—and that is why this continual chatter is frivolousness. (*1852*)

Christianity has become complete nonsense. We are all Christians by birth—in "Christendom" a child is not merely born in sin but also in nonsense. (*1853*)

Anselm prays in all inwardness that he might succeed in proving God's existence. He thinks he has succeeded, and he flings himself down in adoration to thank God. Amazing. He does not notice that this prayer and this expression of thanksgiving are infinitely more proof of God's existence than—the proof. (*1853*)

A young girl "16 summers old"—it is her confirmation day. Among various elegant and beautiful gifts she also receives a beautifully bound New Testament.

Look, this is what they call Christianity! Actually they do not expect her to read it, now any more than the others, of course, or read it in any primitive way. She receives this book as a consolation in her life: Here you will find consolation if you should need it. Of course they do not expect her to read it, no more than the other young girls, and above all not primitively, otherwise she would discover that here are all the terrors, compared to which the ordinary terrors found in the world are almost a jest.

But look, this is Christianity. And this, too, is Christianity, this foolishness with Bible societies which distribute New Testaments by the millions.

No, I could be tempted to make another proposal to Christendom. Let us collect all the New Testaments there are and bring them out to an open place or up on a mountain and then, while we all kneel, let someone talk to God in this manner: Take this book back again. We human beings, such as we are, are not fit to involve ourselves with such a thing; it only makes us unhappy. I suggest that we, like those inhabitants (Matt. 8:34), beg Christ "to leave the neighborhood." This would be honest and human talk—something different from this nauseating, hypocritical preacher-prattle about life being worthless to us without this priceless good, which is Christianity. (*1854*)

To be a Christian in Christendom in plain and simple conformity is just as impossible as doing gymnastics in a straitjacket. (*1854*)

Whenever I think of the insipid, mawkish, syrupy concept of the Savior of the world which Christendom adores and offers for sale, reading his own words about himself has a strange effect: "I have come to set afire," come to produce a split which can tear the most holy bonds, the bonds God himself has sanctified, the bonds between father and son, wife and husband, parents and children, etc. (*1854*)

Have you seen people at a fire? How do they look? Is it not true that everyone in death-anxiety thinks only of saving himself.

But according to the Christian view a man lives at every moment in far greater danger than in the most raging fire, in danger of forfeiting an eternity: do they look like it? (*1854*)

Take 1/10 of the essentially Christian, add this ingredient to what man has invented—and you will find (what thousands and thousands of clergymen and professors of lies have found) that this kind of "Christianity" tastes so sweet to men, so delicious, so indescribably delightful, that they do not know what they should concoct in return as a treat for such a professor or preacher.

Take Christianity whole—and you will find (what you, glorious martyrs and witnesses of the truth, have found!) that even the most good-natured man becomes as if he were infuriated, furiously embittered, by this kind of "Christianity," that it is a matter of life and death.

Alas, but God knows man, and since, according to the New Testament, to love God is to hate the world, God has intentionally established Christianity in such a way that it completely shocks those who, merely humanly speaking, might be called the most good-natured of men, as well as the most obstinate of men. For God wants no man to have direct transition into being a Christian. Men do not, according to Christianity, live in a pretty world which God loves—in such a case to become a Christian could be a direct transition for natural human goodness and kindness. No, born in sin, every man, according to Christianity, lives in a sinful world which God hates, and to become a Christian is anything but direct transition; Christianly, this so-called natural human goodness and kindness is just as bad as defiance, etc., and this shows up, also, as soon as Christianity in its truth is brought into contact with this natural human goodness and kindness, for then it becomes just as infuriated with Christianity as defiance, etc. (*1854*)

Christianity is the frightful earnestness that your eternity is decided in this life. (*1854*)

We play at Christianity. We use all the orthodox Christian terminology—but everything, everything without character. Yes, we are not fit at all to shape a heresy or a schism, for which some character is always necessary, after all.

No, the whole thing survives: the Christian sacraments and customs, the Christian terminology—but it is all decoration, a way of speaking, the preacher-actor, the artist.

But then Christianity is nothing but mythology, poetry—and the difference between the orthodox clergyman and the free-thinker is this—the free-thinker comes out and says it, but the orthodox clergyman says: For the sake of God in heaven let's not talk about it, let's just keep our ears open—otherwise the whole thing goes to pot.

There is something frightful in the fact that the most dangerous thing of all, playing at Christianity, is never included in the list of heresies and schisms. Still, of course, it is too frightful to be included this way on a list with other heresies. No, this frightful thing has to have a rubric for itself. The question is whether this is not precisely what the New Testament means by "the fall from Christianity." (*1854*)

To be a Christian is the most appalling of all agonies; it is, so it must be, to have one's hell here on earth. (*1855*)

The Devil Is Alive

The world-famous evangelist Billy Graham was born in 1918 in North Carolina, and he made his own "decision for Christ" at the age of sixteen during a revival meeting. He was graduated from the Florida Bible Institute, received a B.A. from Wheaton College, and by the mid-1940's was preaching at Youth for Christ rallies. In 1949 the great success of a "Canvas Cathedral" meeting in Los Angeles brought him national attention, and in the years that followed the size of his audiences grew to phenomenal numbers. Graham and his expert team of associates launched citywide crusades throughout the United States and in several other countries; the mass media brought him to millions of people. Copies of his books also number in the millions: they include *World Aflame, Peace with God, The Secret of Happiness, My Answer, Seven Deadly Sins,* and *The Jesus Generation.*

"Satan is alive and well," according to a recent survey. And it certainly seems evident from the number of articles about the devil that have appeared recently in national magazines. One publication featured thirty-five pages about the devil as he appears in Satan worship, witchcraft, sorcery, spiritistic seances, demonology, wizardry, black magic, yoga masters, psychic seers, poltergeistry, and voodoo priests.

A few years ago, the idea of the existence of the devil had gone out of style along with "fire and brimstone" preaching. Today, while there is a statistical drift from the organized church, an ever-increasing percentage of Americans—now sixty-five percent—believe in a personal devil. At a time when the educational system of our nation has virtually excluded the Bible and God from the classroom, parapsychology has worked its way into the center of the curricula.

Nor is the devil enthroned only in our academic institutions. Churches dedicated to Satan worship are springing up all over the country. Their services include black masses, goat's horns, demon imagery, nudity, and songs lauding Lucifer. The film world has moved from the mere use of such catch titles as "The Devil's Doorway" to themes which actually center around Satan, such as "Rosemary's Baby" (Satan is the father).

And this devilish trend has taken to the streets to propagate Satan worship through psychic music, grabbing rituals, "Process" propagating proclamations, and the aggressive distribution of literature. You meet them on the sidewalks of Seattle, San Francisco, Omaha, Atlanta, Toronto, or New York. On Easter weekend, 1971, 5,000 Satan worshipers gathered in Chicago to celebrate the rise of the devil. Early in 1971, 450 "Ministers of Satan" were "ordained" in one week in a small city in the Northwest.

Satan worship is now a world-wide phenomenon. Recently, a Presbyterian minister in Britain informed me that the occult and witchcraft are even more pronounced there than in America. In England, a nation which many had thought of as perhaps the world's most rational society, a legislator now claims that a majority of the secondary school students have been in touch with either a witch or a wizard. Nor is this phenomenon limited to the West. The *Los Angeles Times* news service has been carrying stories about whole villages in Russia being taken over by witchcraft and wizardry. There is a great revival of Satan worship in Northern Europe, especially in Germany.

The Bible teaches that *the devil and his demons are real.* The word "Satan" comes from the Greek word "diabolos"; the word "devils" or "demons" comes from "diamonia." The Bible teaches that demons are capable of entering and controlling people. They are spoken of as unclean, violent, and malicious. All outside of Christ are in danger of demon possession. The Bible teaches that these demons continue to harass Christians, even after their conversion. "For we wrestle not against flesh and blood, but against principalities, against powers, against the rulers of the darkness of this world, against spiritual wickedness in high places" (Ephesians 6:12).

Jesus and His apostles frequently cast out demons. Peter was addressing "younger men" when he cautioned: " . . . be on the alert! Your enemy the devil, like a roaring lion, prowls around looking for someone to devour. Stand up to him, firm in the faith . . . " (1 Peter 5:8 NEB).* James urged us to "Be submissive then to God. Stand up to the devil and he will turn and run" (James 4:7 NEB). Paul taught that the devil is a tricky tactician: " . . . Satan himself masquerades as an angel of light. It is therefore a simple thing for his agents to masquerade as agents of good" (2 Corinthians 11:14, 15 NEB). He also predicted that as the end of the age approached all this would worsen, reaching a "final rebellion against God when wickedness will be revealed" in "the work of Satan" to "be attended by all the powerful signs and miracles of THE LIE."

So the pressure is on, and the onus of responsibility rests upon you to seek complete victory over the devil in the Lordship of Jesus Christ. The devil has supernatural power but not total power or knowledge. Jesus said, "All power is given unto me in heaven and earth." Satan's power is limited. He can act only under the permissive will of God. There is a mystery to this that no theologian totally understands. Paul called it the "mystery of iniquity."

Satan engages us in spiritual warfare. To understand more about his power and tactics, let's consider the encounter which Jesus had with the maniac of Gadara (Mark 5). For a long time this man had been troubled by demons who

*NEB = *The New English Bible.*—R.E.

had implanted an "unclean spirit" in him. When he was transformed by the power of Christ, it says that he was in his "right mind."

Satan can affect the mind. There is more derangement in the world today than ever before, with millions of Americans struggling to maintain a balanced mind. Could some of this be satanic activity? I think so. This does not mean that everyone who is mentally deranged is possessed by demons. However, I do believe that some of it is Satan, especially in those who have yielded their lives to lust, drugs, alcohol, etc.

The devil will also attack people morally. The maniac whom Christ met in the wilderness wore no clothes. He ran naked through a desolate cemetery. What is it that creates the craze in our day for nudity? Movies and magazines, nudist camps and pop festivals are constantly accentuated by nudity as a life style. This is not new. The maniac of Gadara did it because the devil got into him. He not only tore off his clothing, but also the chains and restraints which were imposed upon him by society. And he abused his body by cutting himself with jagged stones. All this was the work of the devil.

Perhaps you find that you abuse yourself. You don't protect your body which, if you are Christ's, is the temple of the Holy Spirit. Youth who mainline drugs are pushing a self-destruct button. Fornication, Paul says, is sin against your own body. This is true also of gluttony, drunkenness, and smoking. These are slow suicide. The devil promotes anything which tends immediately or ultimately to destroy you.

Mark says that the maniac became *violent,* and this, too, was the work of the devil. Until God chains the devil, man will be hopelessly intimidated by this recurring resort to violence. Man cannot control himself, and if he will not be controlled by Jesus Christ, then he will be controlled by Satan.

We read that this demon-possessed man was compelled to live in a cemetery. He lived with the dead. The Bible teaches that we "were dead in trespasses and sins" (Ephesians 2:1). Your body may be alive, but your soul is dead toward God until you are born from above. However, a wonderful phrase in Psalm 88:5 says, "Free among the dead." When you come to Jesus Christ, He frees you from the dominating power of Satan. While the world around you may be spiritually dead, you can be spiritually free and alive!

We have seen that Satan is a threat. *How does the Christian meet this threat?* By keeping Jesus Christ enthroned in his life as Savior and Lord. Thus he excludes the devil from a place in his life. "Greater is he that is in you, than he that is in the world," promised John. And an ancient Hebrew prophet promised: "When the enemy shall come in like a flood, the spirit of the Lord shall lift up a standard against him." As long as the Christian invokes the Name of Jesus, and insofar as he yields himself fully and constantly to Him and studies the Scriptures, he will enjoy spiritual triumph. "The Son of God," we read in the New Testament, "came to earth with the express purpose of liquidating the devil's activities" (1 John 3:8, Phillips).

CHAPTER NINE / *Christianity*

A Christian must rely on the Word of God. When Jesus was tempted by the devil, He answered Satan's temptation with: "It is written. . . . " Three of history's most attractive propositions were made by Satan, but each time Jesus replied with, "It is written." God has exalted His Word to be equal to His own Name. Is it any wonder that the devil always retreats in the face of the Word of God? He hates and fears its power.

The Bible teaches that every Christian is tempted, but it also teaches that temptation is not a sin. It is the yielding that is sin. All temptation is from the devil. God will test us, but He will never tempt us to sin! "There hath no temptation taken you but such as is common to man: but God is faithful, who will not suffer you to be tempted above that ye are able; but will with the temptation also make a way to escape, that ye may be able to bear it" (1 Corinthians 10:13).

An illustration I like is of the housewife chasing a mouse with her broom. The mouse wastes no time eyeing the broom—he is looking for a hole. Get your eyes off the temptation and look for the way of escape.

The Bible says we are to *"resist the devil"* and "fight the good fight of faith." You reply, "But the devil does such fascinating things." Yes, we read in the Book of Revelation that there will be "spirits of devils working miracles" and, hence, those who "worship devils." This prophecy is behind much of the current Satan worship. But the Christian is to "resist the devil." Tell him to get off your back.

This can be done through prayer. In our Lord's model prayer, He commanded us to pray daily: "Deliver us from the Evil One"—that is the devil. "We are not ignorant of his devices," said Paul, and Peter spoke of "your adversary the devil." He is always lurking in the shadows and crouching under a nearby bush. And he is rough! In the gospels we read such things as "the devil threw him down"; "when the devil had thrown him in the midst"; a man "was driven of the devil into the wilderness"; and "my daughter is grievously vexed with a devil." Is it any wonder that Martin Luther threw an inkwell at the devil? Hudson Taylor, the great pioneer missionary to China, when asked how one can know there is a devil, suggested, "Resist him for a day and you'll soon find out."

In the final book of the Bible we read that *"they overcame him by the blood of the Lamb."* The reason Jesus came to die on the cross was: "to destroy the works of the devil." When you find yourself unable to triumph over the devil through your own strength, claim your victory in the name of the Lord Jesus.

On a number of occasions in my ministry I have met people in various parts of the world whom I was convinced were demon possessed. Missionaries encounter them frequently. We read of them in the news today. How else can one account for a Hitler or the mass killers of our generation?

And finally we read, *"They overcame him . . . by the word of their testimony."* You cannot maintain an upper hand over the devil unless you are prepared to witness constantly for Christ. Personal witnessing is an integral part of Christian victory. When Jesus had cast the demons out of the maniac of Gadara, the healed Gadarene wanted to go with Him. But Jesus said no. He told him: "Go home to your friends and tell them the great things the Lord has done for you." I would urge you to do the same.

Yes, the devil is alive and kicking. But if you are in Christ and follow the simple rules of daily Bible study, prayer, and witnessing, *he has no power over you!* "In all these things we are more than conquerors through him that loved us" (Romans 8:37).

rudolf bultmann _____

The New Testament and Mythology

The Protestant (Lutheran) theologian Rudolf Bultmann (1884–   ) was born and educated in Germany, and he taught at the University of Marburg for over thirty years. During those years he became one of the world's most influential and controversial New Testament scholars, particularly with his call for "demythologizing" the New Testament. Among his books are *The Presence of Eternity, Jesus Christ and Mythology, The History of the Synoptic Tradition, Jesus and the Word, Theology of the New Testament,* and *Primitive Christianity in Its Contemporary Setting.*

A. THE PROBLEM

1. The Mythical View of the World and the Mythical Event of Redemption

The cosmology of the New Testament is essentially mythical in character. The world is viewed as a three-storied structure, with the earth in the centre, the heaven above, and the underworld beneath. Heaven is the abode of God and of celestial beings—the angels. The underworld is hell, the place of torment. Even the earth is more than the scene of natural, everyday events, of the trivial round and common task. It is the scene of the supernatural activity of God and his angels on the one hand, and of Satan and his daemons on the other. These supernatural forces intervene in the course of nature and in all that men think and will and do. Miracles are by no means rare. Man is not in control of his own life. Evil spirits may take possession of him. Satan may inspire him with evil thoughts. Alternatively, God may inspire his thought and guide his purposes. He may grant him heavenly visions. He may allow him to hear his word of succour or demand. He may give the supernatural power of his Spirit. History does not follow a smooth unbroken course; it is set in motion and controlled by these supernatural powers. This aeon is held in bondage by Satan, sin, and death (for "powers" is precisely what they are), and hastens towards its end. That end will come very soon, and will take the form of a cosmic catastrophe. It will be inaugurated by the "woes" of the last time. Then the Judge will come from heaven, the dead will rise, the last judgement will take place, and men will enter into eternal salvation or damnation.

This then is the mythical view of the world which the New Testament presupposes when it presents the event of redemption which is the subject of

Rudolf Bultmann, "The New Testament and Mythology." From Hans Werner Bartsch, ed., *Kerygma and Myth: A Theological Debate.* Reprinted by permission of the publishers, S.P.C.K. (The Society for Promoting Christian Knowledge), London. Notes have been renumbered.

its preaching. It proclaims in the language of mythology that the last time has now come. "In the fulness of time" God sent forth his Son, a pre-existent divine Being, who appears on earth as a man.[1] He dies the death of a sinner[2] on the cross and makes atonement for the sins of men.[3] His resurrection marks the beginning of the cosmic catastrophe. Death, the consequence of Adam's sin, is abolished,[4] and the daemonic forces are deprived of their power.[5] The risen Christ is exalted to the right hand of God in heaven [6] and made "Lord" and "King".[7] He will come again on the clouds of heaven to complete the work of redemption, and the resurrection and judgement of men will follow.[8] Sin, suffering and death will then be finally abolished.[9] All this is to happen very soon; indeed, St Paul thinks that he himself will live to see it.[10]

All who belong to Christ's Church and are joined to the Lord by Baptism and the Eucharist are certain of resurrection to salvation,[11] unless they forfeit it by unworthy behaviour. Christian believers already enjoy the first instalment of salvation, for the Spirit[12] is at work within them, bearing witness to their adoption as sons of God,[13] and guaranteeing their final resurrection.[14]

2. The Mythological View of the World Obsolete

All this is the language of mythology, and the origin of the various themes can be easily traced in the contemporary mythology of Jewish Apocalyptic and in the redemption myths of Gnosticism. To this extent *the kerygma* is incredible to modern man, for he is convinced that the mythical view of the world is obsolete.* We are therefore bound to ask whether, when we preach the Gospel to-day, we expect our converts to accept not only the Gospel message, but also the mythical view of the world in which it is set. If not, does the New Testament embody a truth which is quite independent of its mythical setting? If it does, theology must undertake the task of stripping the kerygma from its mythical framework, of "demythologizing" it.

Can Christian preaching expect modern man *to accept the mythical view of*

[1]Gal. 4. 4; Phil. 2. 6ff.; 2 Cor. 8. 9; John 1. 14, etc.
[2]2 Cor. 5. 21; Rom. 8. 3.
[3]Rom. 3. 23–26; 4. 25; 8. 3; 2 Cor. 5. 14, 19; John 1. 29; 1 John 2. 2, etc.
[4]1 Cor. 15. 21f.; Rom. 5. 12ff.
[5]1 Cor. 2. 6; Col. 2. 15; Rev. 12. 7ff., etc.
[6]Acts 1. 6f.; 2. 33; Rom. 8. 34, etc.
[7]Phil. 2. 9–11; 1 Cor. 15. 25.
[8]1 Cor. 15. 23f., 50ff., etc.
[9]Rev. 21. 4, etc.
[10]1 Thess. 4. 15ff.; 1 Cor. 15. 51f.; cf. Mark 9. 1.
[11]Rom. 5. 12ff.; 1 Cor. 15. 21ff., 44b, ff.
[12] Ἀπαρχή: Rom. 8.23, ἀρραβών: 2 Cor. 1. 22; 5. 5.
[13]Rom. 8. 15; Gal. 4. 6.
[14]Rom. 8. 11.
*The "proclamation," or central message, of the New Testament.—R.E.

the world as true? To do so would be both senseless and impossible. It would be senseless, because there is nothing specifically Christian in the mythical view of the world as such. It is simply the cosmology of a pre-scientific age. Again, it would be impossible, because no man can adopt a view of the world by his own volition—it is already determined for him by his place in history. Of course such a view is not absolutely unalterable, and the individual may even contribute to its change. But he can do so only when he is faced by a new set of facts so compelling as to make his previous view of the world untenable. He has then no alternative but to modify his view of the world or produce a new one. The discoveries of Copernicus and the atomic theory are instances of this, and so was romanticism, with its discovery that the human subject is richer and more complex than enlightenment or idealism had allowed, and nationalism, with its new realization of the importance of history and the tradition of peoples.

It may equally well happen that truths which a shallow enlightenment had failed to perceive are later rediscovered in ancient myths. Theologians are perfectly justified in asking whether this is not exactly what has happened with the New Testament. At the same time it is impossible to revive an obsolete view of the world by a mere fiat, and certainly not a mythical view. For all our thinking to-day is shaped irrevocably by modern science. A blind acceptance of the New Testament mythology would be arbitrary, and to press for its acceptance as an article of faith would be to reduce faith to works. Wilhelm Herrmann pointed this out, and one would have thought that his demonstration was conclusive. It would involve a sacrifice of the intellect which could have only one result—a curious form of schizophrenia and insincerity. It would mean accepting a view of the world in our faith and religion which we should deny in our everyday life. Modern thought as we have inherited it brings with it criticism of *the New Testament view of the world.*

Man's knowledge and mastery of the world have advanced to such an extent through science and technology that it is no longer possible for anyone seriously to hold the New Testament view of the world—in fact, there is no one who does. What meaning, for instance, can we attach to such phrases in the creed as "descended into hell" or "ascended into heaven"? We no longer believe in the three-storied universe which the creeds take for granted. The only honest way of reciting the creeds is to strip the mythological framework from the truth they enshrine—that is, assuming that they contain any truth at all, which is just the question that theology has to ask. No one who is old enough to think for himself supposes that God lives in a local heaven. There is no longer any heaven in the traditional sense of the word. The same applies to hell in the sense of a mythical underworld beneath our feet. And if this is so, the story of Christ's descent into hell and of his Ascension into heaven is done with. We can no longer look for the return of the Son of Man on the clouds of heaven or hope that the faithful will meet him in the air (1 Thess. 4. 15ff.).

Now that the forces and the laws of nature have been discovered, we can no longer believe in *spirits, whether good or evil.* We know that the stars are physical bodies whose motions are controlled by the laws of the universe, and not daemonic beings which enslave mankind to their service. Any influence they may have over human life must be explicable in terms of the ordinary laws of nature; it cannot in any way be attributed to their malevolence. Sickness and the cure of disease are likewise attributable to natural causation; they are not the result of daemonic activity or of evil spells.[15] The *miracles of the New Testament* have ceased to be miraculous, and to defend their historicity by recourse to nervous disorders or hypnotic effects only serves to underline the fact. And if we are still left with certain physiological and psychological phenomena which we can only assign to mysterious and enigmatic causes, we are still assigning them to causes, and thus far are trying to make them scientifically intelligible. Even occultism pretends to be a science.

It is impossible to use electric light and the wireless and to avail ourselves of modern medical and surgical discoveries, and at the same time to believe in the New Testament world of spirits and miracles.[16] We may think we can manage it in our own lives, but to expect others to do so is to make the Christian faith unintelligible and unacceptable to the modern world.

The mythical eschatology is untenable for the simple reason that the parousia†of Christ never took place as the New Testament expected. History did not come to an end, and, as every school-boy knows, it will continue to run its course. Even if we believe that the world as we know it will come to an end in time, we expect the end to take the form of a natural catastrophe, not of a mythical event such as the New Testament expects. And if we explain the parousia in terms of modern scientific theory, we are applying criticism to the New Testament, albeit unconsciously.

But natural science is not the only challenge which the mythology of the New Testament has to face. There is still more serious challenge presented by *modern man's understanding of himself.*

[15]It may of course be argued that there are people alive to-day whose confidence in the traditional scientific view of the world has been shaken, and others who are primitive enough to qualify for an age of mythical thought. And there are also many varieties of superstition. But when belief in spirits and miracles has degenerated into superstition, it has become something entirely different from what it was when it was genuine faith. The various impressions and speculations which influence credulous people here and there are of little importance, nor does it matter to what extent cheap slogans have spread an atmosphere inimical to science. What matters is the world view which men imbibe from their environment, and it is science which determines that view of the world through the school, the press, the wireless, the cinema, and all the other fruits of technical progress.

[16]Cp. the observations of Paul Schütz on the decay of mythical religion in the East through the introduction of modern hygiene and medicine.

†The anticipated coming of Christ as Judge and Redeemer of the world.—R.E.

Modern man is confronted by a curious dilemma. He may regard himself as pure nature, or as pure spirit. In the latter case he distinguishes the essential part of his being from nature. In either case, however, *man is essentially a unity*. He bears the sole responsibility for his own feeling, thinking, and willing.[17] He is not, as the New Testament regards him, the victim of a strange dichotomy which exposes him to the interference of powers outside himself. If his exterior behaviour and his interior condition are in perfect harmony, it is something he has achieved himself, and if other people think their interior unity is torn asunder by daemonic or divine interference, he calls it schizophrenia.

Although biology and psychology recognize that man is a highly dependent being, that does not mean that he has been handed over to powers outside of and distinct from himself. This dependence is inseparable from human nature, and he needs only to understand it in order to recover his self-mastery and organize his life on a rational basis. If he regards himself as spirit, he knows that he is permanently conditioned by the physical, bodily part of his being, but he distinguishes his true self from it, and knows that he is independent and responsible for his mastery over nature.

In either case he finds *what the New Testament has to say about the "Spirit"* ($\pi\nu\epsilon\hat{\upsilon}\mu\alpha$) *and the sacraments utterly strange and incomprehensible.* Biological man cannot see how a supernatural entity like the $\pi\nu\epsilon\hat{\upsilon}\mu\alpha$ can penetrate within the close texture of his natural powers and set to work within him. Nor can the idealist understand how a $\pi\nu\epsilon\hat{\upsilon}\mu\alpha$ working like a natural power can touch and influence his mind and spirit. Conscious as he is of his own moral responsibility, he cannot conceive how baptism in water can convey a mysterious something which is henceforth the agent of all his decisions and actions. He cannot see how physical food can convey spiritual strength, and how the unworthy receiving of the Eucharist can result in physical sickness and death (1 Cor. 11. 30). The only possible explanation is that it is due to suggestion. He cannot understand how anyone can be baptized for the dead (1. Cor. 15. 29).

We need not examine in detail the various forms of modern *Weltanschauung,*‡ whether idealist or naturalist. For the only criticism of the New Testament which is theologically relevant is that which arises *necessarily* out of the situation of modern man. The biological *Weltanschauung* does not, for instance, arise necessarily out of the contemporary situation. We are still free to adopt it or not as we choose. The only relevant question for the theologian is the basic assumption on which the adoption of a biological as of every other *Weltanschauung* rests, and that assumption is the view of the world which has been moulded by modern

[17]Cp. Gerhardt Krüger, *Einsicht und Leidenschaft, Das Wesen des platonischen Denkens,* Frankfort, 1939, p. 11 f.

‡A comprehensive world view or philosophy.—R.E.

science and the modern conception of human nature as a self-subsistent unity immune from the interference of supernatural powers.

Again, the biblical doctrine that *death is the punishment of sin is* equally abhorrent to naturalism and idealism, since they both regard death as a simple and necessary process of nature. To the naturalist death is no problem at all, and to the idealist it is a problem for that very reason, for so far from arising out of man's essential spiritual being it actually destroys it. The idealist is faced with a paradox. On the one hand man is a spiritual being, and therefore essentially different from plants and animals, and on the other hand he is the prisoner of nature, whose birth, life, and death are just the same as those of the animals. Death may present him with a problem, but he cannot see how it can be a punishment for sin. Human beings are subject to death even before they have committed any sin. And to attribute human mortality to the fall of Adam is sheer nonsense, for guilt implies personal responsibility, and the idea of original sin as an inherited infection is sub-ethical, irrational, and absurd.

The same objections apply to *the doctrine of the atonement.* How can the guilt of one man be expiated by the death of another who is sinless—if indeed one may speak of a sinless man at all? What primitive notions of guilt and righteousness does this imply? And what primitive idea of God? The rationale of sacrifice in general may of course throw some light on the theory of the atonement, but even so, what a primitive mythology it is, that a divine Being should become incarnate, and atone for the sins of men through his own blood! Or again, one might adopt an analogy from the law courts, and explain the death of Christ as a transaction between God and man through which God's claims on man were satisfied. But that would make sin a juridical matter; it would be no more than an external transgression of a commandment, and it would make nonsense of all our ethical standards. Moreover, if the Christ who died such a death was the pre-existent Son of God, what could death mean for him? Obviously very little if he knew that he would rise again in three days!

The *resurrection of Jesus* is just as difficult for modern man, if it means an event whereby a living supernatural power is released which can henceforth be appropriated through the sacraments. To the biologist such language is meaningless, for he does not regard death as a problem at all. The idealist would not object to the idea of a life immune from death, but he could not believe that such a life is made available by the resuscitation of a dead person. If that is the way God makes life available for man, his action is inextricably involved in a nature miracle. Such a notion he finds incomprehensible, for he can see God at work only in the reality of his personal life and in his transformation. But, quite apart from the incredibility of such a miracle, he cannot see how an event like this could be the act of God, or how it could affect his own life.

Gnostic influence suggests that this Christ, who died and rose again, was not a mere human being but a God-man. His death and resurrection were not isolated facts which concerned him alone, but a cosmic event in which we are all involved.[18] It is only with effort that modern man can think himself back into such an intellectual atmosphere, and even then he could never accept it himself, because it regards man's essential being as nature and redemption as a process of nature. And as for the pre-existence of Christ, with its corollary of man's translation into a celestial realm of light, and the clothing of the human personality in heavenly robes and a spiritual body—all this is not only irrational but utterly meaningless. Why should salvation take this particular form? Why should this be the fulfilment of human life and the realization of man's true being?

B. THE TASK BEFORE US

1. Not Selection or Subtraction

Does this drastic criticism of the New Testament mythology mean the complete elimination of the kerygma?

Whatever else may be true, we cannot save the kerygma by selecting some of its features and subtracting others, and thus reduce the amount of mythology in it. For instance, it is impossible to dismiss St Paul's teaching about the unworthy reception of Holy Communion or about baptism for the dead, and yet cling to the belief that physical eating and drinking can have a spiritual effect. If we accept *one* idea, we must accept everything which the New Testament has to say about Baptism and Holy Communion, and it is just this one idea which we cannot accept.

It may of course be argued that some features of the New Testament mythology are given greater prominence than others: not all of them appear with the same regularity in the various books. There is for example only one occurrence of the legends of the Virgin birth and the Ascension; St Paul and St John appear to be totally unaware of them. But, even if we take them to be later accretions, it does not affect the mythical character of the event of redemption as a whole. And if we once start subtracting from the kerygma, where are we to draw the line? The mythical view of the world must be accepted or rejected in its entirety.

At this point absolute clarity and ruthless honesty are essential both for the academic theologian and for the parish priest. It is a duty they owe to themselves, to the Church they serve, and to those whom they seek to win for the Church. They must make it quite clear what their hearers are expected to accept and what they are not. At all costs the preacher must not leave his people in the dark about what he secretly eliminates, nor must he be in the dark about it himself. In Karl Barth's book *The Resurrection of the Dead* the

[18]Rom. 5. 12ff.; 1 Cor. 15. 21ff., 44b.

cosmic eschatology§ in the sense of "chronologically final history" is eliminated in favour of what he intends to be a non-mythological "ultimate history". He is able to delude himself into thinking that this is exegesis of St Paul and of the New Testament generally only because he gets rid of everything mythological in I Corinthians by subjecting it to an interpretation which does violence to its meaning. But that is an impossible procedure.

If the truth of the New Testament proclamation is to be preserved, the only way is to demythologize it. But our motive in so doing must not be to make the New Testament relevant to the modern world at all costs. The question is simply whether the New Testament message consists exclusively of mythology, or whether it actually demands the elimination of myth if it is to be understood as it is meant to be. This question is forced upon us from two sides. First there is the nature of myth in general, and then there is the New Testament itself.

2. The Nature of Myth

The real purpose of myth is not to present an objective picture of the world as it is, but to express man's understanding of himself in the world in which he lives. Myth should be interpreted not cosmologically, but anthropologically, or better still, existentially.[19] Myth speaks of the power or the powers which man supposes he experiences as the ground and limit of his world and of his own activity and suffering. He describes these powers in terms derived from the visible world, with its tangible objects and forces, and from human life, with its feelings, motives, and potentialities. He may, for instance, explain the origin of the world by speaking of a world egg or a world tree. Similarly he may account for the present state and order of the world by speaking of a primeval war between the gods. He speaks of the other world in terms of this world, and of the gods in terms derived from human life.[20]

Myth is an expression of man's conviction that the origin and purpose of the world in which he lives are to be sought not within it but beyond it—that is, beyond the realm of known and tangible reality—and that this realm is perpetually dominated and menaced by those mysterious powers which are its source and limit. Myth is also an expression of man's awareness that he is not lord of his own being. It expresses his sense of dependence not only within the visible world, but more especially on those forces which hold sway beyond

§That area of theology concerned with "last things," such as death, the end of the world, heaven and hell.—R.E.

[19]Cp. Gerhardt Krüger, *Einsicht und Leidenschaft,* esp. p. 17f., 56f.

[20]Myth is here used in the sense popularized by the 'History of Religions' school. Mythology is the use of imagery to express the other worldly in terms of this world and the divine in terms of human life, the other side in terms of this side. For instance, divine transcendence is expressed as spatial distance. It is a mode of expression which makes it easy to understand the cultus as an action in which material means are used to convey immaterial power. Myth is not used in that modern sense, according to which it is practically equivalent to ideology.

the confines of the known. Finally, myth expresses man's belief that in this state of dependence he can be delivered from the forces within the visible world.

Thus myth contains elements which demand its own criticism—namely, its imagery with its apparent claim to objective validity. The real purpose of myth is to speak of a transcendent power which controls the world and man, but that purpose is impeded and obscured by the terms in which it is expressed.

Hence the importance of the New Testament mythology lies not in its imagery but in the understanding of existence which it enshrines. The real question is whether this understanding of existence is true. Faith claims that it is, and faith ought not to be tied down to the imagery of New Testament mythology.

3. The New Testament Itself

The New Testament itself invites this kind of criticism. Not only are there rough edges in its mythology, but some of its features are actually contradictory. For example, the death of Christ is sometimes a sacrifice and sometimes a cosmic event. Sometimes his person is interpreted as the Messiah and sometimes as the Second Adam. The kenosis[||] of the pre-existent Son (Phil. 2. 6ff.) is incompatible with the miracle narratives as proofs of his messianic claims. The Virgin birth is inconsistent with the assertion of his pre-existence. The doctrine of the Creation is incompatible with the conception of the "rulers of this world" (I Cor. 2. 6ff.), the "gold of this world" (2 Cor. 4. 4) and the "elements of this world" $\sigma\tau o\iota\chi\epsilon\tilde{\iota}\alpha\ \tau o\tilde{\upsilon}\ \kappa\acute{o}\sigma\mu o\upsilon$, Gal. 4. 3). It is impossible to square the belief that the law was given by God with the theory that it comes from the angels (Gal. 3. 19f).

But the principal demand for the criticism of mythology comes from a curious contradiction which runs right through the New Testament. Sometimes we are told that human life is determined by cosmic forces, at others we are challenged to a decision. Side by side with the Pauline indicative stands the Pauline imperative. In short, man is sometimes regarded as a cosmic being, sometimes as an independent "I" for whom decision is a matter of life or death. Incidentally, this explains why so many sayings in the New Testament speak directly to modern man's condition while others remain enigmatic and obscure. Finally, attempts at demythologization are sometimes made even within the New Testament itself. But more will be said on this point later.

4. Previous Attempts at Demythologizing

How then is the mythology of the New Testament to be reinterpreted? This is not the first time that theologians have approached this task. Indeed, all we

||Christ's relinquishment of the form of God to become a man and to suffer death.—R.E.

have said so far might have been said in much the same way thirty or forty years ago, and it is a sign of the bankruptcy of contemporary theology that it has been necessary to go all over the same ground again. The reason for this is not far to seek. The liberal theologians of the last century were working on the wrong lines. They threw away not only the mythology but also the kerygma itself. Were they right? Is that the treatment the New Testament itself required? That is the question we must face to-day. The last twenty years have witnessed a movement away from criticism and a return to a naïve acceptance of the kerygma. The danger both for theological scholarship and for the Church is that this uncritical resuscitation of the New Testament mythology may make the Gospel message unintelligible to the modern world. We cannot dismiss the critical labours of earlier generations without further ado. We must take them up and put them to constructive use. Failure to do so will mean that the old battles between orthodoxy and liberalism will have to be fought out all over again, that is, assuming that there will be any Church or any theologians to fight them at all! Perhaps we may put it schematically like this: whereas the older liberals used criticism to *eliminate* the mythology of the New Testament, our task to-day is to use criticism to *interpret* it. Of course it may still be necessary to eliminate mythology here and there. But the criterion adopted must be taken not from modern thought, but from the understanding of human existence which the New Testament itself enshrines.[21]

To begin with, let us review some of these earlier attempts at demythologizing. We need only mention briefly the allegorical interpretation of the New Testament which has dogged the Church throughout its history. This method spiritualizes the mythical events so that they become symbols of processes going on in the soul. This is certainly the most comfortable way of avoiding the critical question. The literal meaning is allowed to stand and is dispensed with only for the individual believer, who can escape into the realm of the soul.

It was characteristic of the older liberal theologians that they regarded mythology as relative and temporary. Hence they thought they could safely eliminate it altogether, and retain only the broad, basic principles or religion and ethics. They distinguished between what they took to be the essence of religion and the temporary garb which it assumed. Listen to what Harnack has to say about the essence of Jesus' preaching of the Kingdom of God and its coming: "The kingdom has a triple meaning. Firstly, it is something supernatural, a gift from above, not a product of ordinary life. Secondly, it is a purely religious blessing, the inner link with the living God; thirdly, it is the most important experience that a man can have, that on which everything else depends; it permeates and dominates his whole existence, because sin is

[21] As an illustration of this critical re-interpretation of myth cf. Hans Jonas, *Augustin und das paulinische Freiheitsproblem,* 1930, pp. 66–76.

forgiven and misery banished." Note how completely the mythology is eliminated: "The kingdom of God comes by coming to the individual, by entering into his *soul* and laying hold of it."[22]

It will be noticed how Harnack reduces the kerygma to a few basic principles of religion and ethics. Unfortunately this means that *the kerygma has ceased to be kerygma:* it is no longer the proclamation of the decisive act of God in Christ. For the liberals the great truths of religion and ethics are timeless and eternal, though it is only within human history that they are realized, and only in concrete historical processes that they are given clear expression. But the apprehension and acceptance of these principles does not depend on the knowledge and acceptance of the age in which they first took shape, or of the historical persons who first discovered them. We are all capable of verifying them in our own experience at whatever period we happen to live. History may be of academic interest, but never of paramount importance for religion.

But the New Testament speaks of an *event* through which God has wrought man's redemption. For it, Jesus is not primarily the teacher, who certainly had extremely important things to say and will always be honoured for saying them, but whose person in the last analysis is immaterial for those who have assimilated his teaching. On the contrary, his person is just what the New Testament proclaims as the decisive event of redemption. It speaks of this person in mythological terms, but does this mean that we can reject the kerygma altogether on the ground that it is nothing more than mythology? That is the question.

Next came the History of Religions school. Its representatives were the first to discover the extent to which the New Testament is permeated by mythology. The importance of the New Testament, they saw, lay not in its teaching about religion and ethics but in its actual religion and piety; in comparison with that all the dogma it contains, and therefore all the mythological imagery with its apparent objectivity, was of secondary importance or completely negligible. The essence of the New Testament lay in the religious life it portrayed; its high-watermark was the experience of mystical union with Christ, in whom God took symbolic form.

These critics grasped one important truth. Christian faith is not the same as religious idealism; the Christian life does not consist in developing the individual personality, in the improvement of society, or in making the world a better place. The Christian life means a turning away from the world, a detachment from it. But the critics of the History of Religions school failed to see that in the New Testament this detachment is essentially eschatological and not mystical. Religion for them was an expression of the human yearning to rise above the world and transcend it: it was the discovery of a supramun-

---

[22]*What is Christianity?* Williams and Norgate, 1904, pp. 63–4 and 57.

dane sphere where the soul could detach itself from all earthly care and find its rest. Hence the supreme manifestation of religion was to be found not in personal ethics or in social idealism but in the cultus regarded as an end in itself. This was just the kind of religious life portrayed in the New Testament, not only as a model and pattern, but as a challenge and inspiration. The New Testament was thus the abiding source of power which enabled man to realize the true life of religion, and Christ was the eternal symbol for the cultus of the Christian Church.[23] It will be noticed how the Church is here defined exclusively as a worshipping community, and this represents a great advance on the older liberalism. This school rediscovered the Church as a *religious* institution. For the idealist there was really no place for the Church at all. But did they succeed in recovering the meaning of the Ecclesia in the full, New Testament sense of the word? For in the New Testament the Ecclesia is invariably a phenomenon of salvation history and eschatology.

Moreover, if the History of Religions school is right, the kerygma has once more ceased to be kerygma. Like the liberals, they are silent about a decisive act of God in Christ proclaimed as the event of redemption. So we are still left with the question whether this event and the person of Jesus, both of which are described in the New Testament in mythological terms, are nothing more than mythology. Can the kerygma be interpreted apart from mythology? Can we recover the truth of the kerygma for men who do not think in mythological terms without forfeiting its character as kerygma?

5. An Existentialist Interpretation the Only Solution

The theological work which such an interpretation involves can be sketched only in the broadest outline and with only a few examples. We must avoid the impression that this is a light and easy task, as if all we have to do is to discover the right formula and finish the job on the spot. It is much more formidable than that. It cannot be done single-handed. It will tax the time and strength of a whole theological generation.

The mythology of the New Testament is in essence that of Jewish apocalyptic and the Gnostic redemption myths. A common feature of them both is their basic dualism, according to which the present world and its human inhabitants are under the control of daemonic, satanic powers, and stand in need of redemption. Man cannot achieve this redemption by his own efforts; it must come as a gift through a divine intervention. Both types of mythology speak of such an intervention: Jewish apocalyptic of an imminent world crisis in which this present aeon will be brought to an end and the new aeon ushered in by the coming of the Messiah, and Gnosticism of a Son of God sent down from the realm of light, entering into this world in the guise of a

[23]Cp. e.g. Troeltsch, *Die Bedeutung der Geschichtlichkeit Jesu für den Glauben*, Tübingen, 1911.

man, and by his fate and teaching delivering the elect and opening up the way for their return to their heavenly home.

The meaning of these two types of mythology lies once more not in their imagery with its apparent objectivity but in the understanding of human existence which both are trying to express. In other words, they need to be interpreted existentially. A good example of such treatment is to be found in Hans Jonas's book on Gnosticism.[24]

Our task is to produce an existentialist interpretation of the dualistic mythology of the New Testament along similar lines. When, for instance, we read of daemonic powers ruling the world and holding mankind in bondage, does the understanding of human existence which underlies such language offer a solution to the riddle of human life which will be acceptable even to the non-mythological mind of today? Of course we must not take this to imply that the New Testament presents us with an anthropology like that which modern science can give us. It cannot be proved by logic or demonstrated by an appeal to factual evidence. Scientific anthropologies always take for granted a definite understanding of existence, which is invariably the consequence of a deliberate decision of the scientist, whether he makes it consciously or not. And that is why we have to discover whether the New Testament offers man an understanding of himself which will challenge him to a genuine existential decision.

[24]*Gnosis und spätantiker Geist. I. Die mythologische Gnosis,* 1934.

further reading

Thomas Merton, *No Man Is an Island* (1955), *New Seeds of Contemplation* (1961), *Raids on the Unspeakable* (1965), and many other of his books. A Trappist monk, Merton wrote in the meditative tradition of St. John of the Cross.

Oxford scholar C. S. Lewis argued brilliantly (and with wit) for a conservative interpretation of Christianity in such books as *The Screwtape Letters* (1942), *Miracles* (1947), and *Mere Christianity* (1952).

Dom Aelred Graham's *Zen Catholicism* (1963) contains fine insights, prompted by a study of Zen Buddhism, into the author's Catholicism. William Johnston's *Christian Zen* (1971) advocates Zen meditation techniques as a means of renewing one's Christianity "at its very heart, that is to say, at the mystical level."

Robert McAfee Brown, *The Spirit of Protestantism* (1961). The topic would appear to be unmanageable, but in Brown's hands it is perceptively reduced to principles and presented, moreover, in a most felicitous style.

Paul Tillich, *The Courage to Be* (1952). A distinguished Protestant theologian and "Apostle of the Skeptics," Tillich defines faith in existentialist terms.

Paul van Buren's *The Secular Meaning of the Gospel* (1963) is a "radical" and important interpretation that reflects the methods of linguistic analysis, a major school of thought in modern philosophy.

Albert Schweitzer, *The Quest for the Historical Jesus* (1906). A classic study, one of the turning points in the history of New Testament scholarship.

Robert M. Grant, in collaboration with David Noel Freedman, *The Secret Sayings of Jesus* (1960). A study of the Gospel of Thomas, one of the gospels excluded from the New Testament, with a translation of that gospel by William R. Schoedel.

Early Christian Fathers (1953), translated and edited by Cyril C. Richardson. Important Christian documents from the first two centuries, including materials by Clement, Irenaeus, and Athenagoras. Anne Fremantle's *A Treasury of Early Christianity* (1953) contains a wide range of brief selections dating through the eighth century.

Maurice Nicoll, in *The New Man* (1950), offers an arrestingly fresh interpretation of the parables of Jesus and opens up the whole idea of a contemplative language that contains hidden existential meanings.

Islam
_____ *no god but allah*

introduction _____

In the name of the merciful and compassionate God.
Say, "He is God alone!
God the Eternal!
He begets not and is not begotten!"

Koran

For most of its followers over the course of the centuries, Islam has been an uncomplicated but profoundly demanding way of life. Its teachings, as the orthodox have understood them, are simple, explicit, and comprehensive, and they require a total commitment. The word "Islam" itself suggests the dominating theme of the religion: it means *submission* to the will of Allah. A Muslim is one who submits, who *surrenders* himself to God. It is as "simple" as that.

Islam had its origins in the seventh century with a single remarkable prophet, whose life and dramatic career are described in the following pages by Philip K. Hitti. Muhammad never claimed to be more than a prophet; in fact, at first he was amazed to find himself in that role. But the voice of the archangel Gabriel persisted: Muhammad was indeed to serve as God's messenger. Through ancient prophets—Abraham, Moses, and Jesus among them—God had spoken to other peoples. Those earlier revelations, however, had been incomplete, and they had been somewhat obscured and confused in their passage through time. Now the message was to be clarified and completed: Muhammad was to be the last and the greatest, the "seal," of the prophets.

Most of the teachings revealed through Muhammad may have been recorded by scribes during Muhammad's lifetime; certainly all were committed to memory by men who had perfected that art. Shortly after the death of Muhammad in 632 an effort was initiated to collect and preserve the revelations, and during the Caliphate of Ulthman (644–653) an authorized collection was established. This, of course, is the Koran (or Qur'an), "that inimitable symphony, the very sounds of which move men to tears and ecstasy."* Devout Muslims—who are the rule rather than the exception—consider the Koran a standing miracle, the absolutely infallible word of God, and many are able to recite it in its entirety.

The principal beliefs and practices of Muslims are outlined in this chapter by H. A. R. Gibb. Beginning with Islam's "uncompromising monotheism," they include doctrines regarding angels and devils, prophecy, the Last Judgment, Heaven, and Hell. Many of these and other Muslim doctrines are

---

*Marmaduke Pickthall (translator), *The Meaning of the Glorious Koran* (New York: New American Library, 1953), p. vii.

CHAPTER TEN / *Islam*

held in common with Jews and Christians, but all are cast in a new and different light. The religious and moral obligations of Muslims, spelled out in painstaking detail in the Koran, are headed by the five "Pillars of the Faith." Taken together, the doctrine and ritual of Islam comprise a stern and rigorously disciplined religion.

The relationship between Islam and Christianity has been a decidedly difficult one, to say the very least. Each has considered itself *the* true religion, and each has accordingly been impatient with, and critical of, the other. The physical proximity of the spheres of influence of the two religions and the ambitions of both to win over new souls and lands have further increased the friction. That the "new" religion of Islam enjoyed such phenomenal success was a bitter pill for the older religion, and Christians in the past have typically looked upon Muhammad as an imposter, a false prophet, or the antichrist. In *The Inferno* Dante "bisected the trunk of Muhammad's body and consigned it to the ninth hell as befits the chief of the damned souls, bringers of schism into religion."† In the pages that follow, Ameer Ali's essay "Islam and Christianity" presents the Muslim point of view on the theological differences between the two religions. Ali notes the surprising number of beliefs shared by Muslims and Christians, but he discusses especially the sharp disagreements—the foremost of which is the Muslim denial of the Christian's cardinal doctrine that Jesus was "the only begotten Son of God."

Islamic mysticism is known as Sufism (probably from a word denoting the coarse woollen garments worn by early Sufi ascetics), and it has been a vital force within Islam. Described in the following pages by Seyyed Hossein Nasr, Sufism is the "marrow of the bone or the inner dimension of the Islamic revelation." Complementing the stress upon the prescribed and "formal" responsibilities that characterize much of the traditional practice of Islam, the aspiring Sufi embarks upon an arduous and private spiritual journey. "Sufism reminds man to seek all that he needs inwardly within himself, to tear his roots from the outer world and plunge them in the Divine nature, which resides at the centre of his heart.‡ Sufi masters have variously outlined the spiritual "stations" (which can be achieved with great effort and self-discipline) and "states" (which come only with God's grace) that mark the path to God, but it is understood that the soul's quest for God cannot really be charted. Such accounts serve primarily to suggest the immensity of the undertaking. The climactic end of the journey, as in all mysticism, is the experience of the Divine: the Sufi's quest and separateness are dissolved in the bliss of union with God.

†Philip K. Hitti, *Islam: A Way of Life* (Minneapolis: University of Minnesota Press, 1970), p. 23.
‡Seyyed Hossein Nasr, *Sufi Essays* (Albany: State University of New York Press, 1972), p. 33.

philip k. hitti ————————————————————————————————————

The Prophet and the Man

Born in Lebanon, Philip K. Hitti earned his B.A. at the American University of Beirut and, in 1915, his Ph.D. at Columbia University. There followed an exceptional academic career: he served as chairman of the Department of Oriental Studies at Princeton, and he was the founder and first director of Princeton's program in Near Eastern Studies. Over the years he lectured at Columbia University, the American University of Beirut, Harvard University, and the University of São Paulo in Brazil. Now Professor Emeritus of Semitic Literature at Princeton, he is the author of *History of the Arabs, History of Syria, Lebanon in History, The Near East in History, The Arabs: A Short History,* and *Islam: A Way of Life.*

It all started with one man. The name given that man by his parents remains uncertain. The one by which he is generally known, Muhammad ("highly praised"), sounds like an honorary title. Hardly anyone before him bore that name. In his youth he was known to his people as al-Amin ("the trustworthy").

The name of the city of Muhammad's birth in 570, Makkah (Mecca), has become well known thanks to the hundreds of thousands of his followers who through the ages have annually flocked to its shrine. Yathrib, the city of his burial, has been designated al-Madinah (Medina), "the city," and shares with its sister Mecca the interest of the annual pilgrims.

. . .

The first glimpse of Muhammad offered by history is of an orphan child born to an impoverished family, a fact corroborated in an early chapter (surah, 93:6–7) of the Koran. This book provides the best source of facts about his life. Muhammad's father died on a caravan journey to Syria before the child's birth. His mother died when he was about six years old. The grandfather who took charge of him died two years later leaving the troubled child in the custody of his uncle abu-Talib. The clan into which Muhammad was born, the banu-Hashim ("children of Hashim"), had fallen on bad times and did not share with its tribe, the Quraysh, the prosperity that tribe enjoyed and the power it possessed.

Years pass before history records a second glimpse of Muhammad. He is by then twenty-five years old, married to his employer, a wealthy Qurayshite widow who was then forty. Her business involved trade and caravans, the most lucrative commerce of the day. For the first time in his life Muhammad had sufficient income, a fact of such importance that it was cited in the Koran (93:4–5, 8).

. . .

In the performance of his new duties the future prophet must have had personal contacts with Syrian and Abyssinian Christian merchants, travelers, and slaves. Besides, there was an ancient Christian community in Najran, on the southern border of Hijaz, and two Christianized Arabian tribes on the northeast and northwest margins of the peninsula. This means there were Christian Arabs before Moslem Arabs. Then there were Arabicized Jewish tribes in and near Medina. From such sources Muhammad must have gained the impression that while Christians and Jews had each a "book" (scripture) and were more advanced, his people had no book and lagged behind.

The third historical snapshot of the man showed him to be moody and distraught. The year was 610. Torn between doubts and aspirations he indulged in retreats while seeking a solution for the obsessing problem of what to do about the lag between his people and the Christians and Jews. On one of these occasions, while contemplating in his favorite hill cave outside of Mecca, he heard a voice exhorting him:

> Recite, in the name of thy Lord, who created,
> Created man from a clot of blood.

And as if the confused man questioned his ability to recite, the voice continued:

> Recite, for thy Lord is the most bounteous,
> Who teacheth by the pen,
> Teacheth man what he did not know. (96:1–5)

After a brief interval the voice came again like the "reverberating of bells." Muhammad must have been in a state of ecstasy accompanied by chills, for he rushed home and asked his wife to put more covers on him. As if in a trance he then heard:

> O thou, enwrapped in thy mantle,
> Arise and warn! (74:1–2)

No more doubt about it, the voice was that of an angel, later identified as Gabriel. And so the Prophet was born. The day is still commemorated throughout the world of Islam, usually on the twenty-seventh of Ramadan. (A holy period in pre-Islam, Ramadan is the only month mentioned in the Koran [2:181].) A surah (97) is dedicated to the episode. In its introduction the entire revelation of the Koran, which was recorded over a period of twenty-two years, is telescoped in one vision, in one night: "Lo, We have sent it down on the night of power." That night is further described as more worthy than "a thousand months."

Islam shares with Judaism and Christianity the concept of revelation, but in a different form. The concept is prompted by man's feeling of insecurity and inability to cope with the besetting problems of life and his desire for guidance and support from a supreme source. More than inspiration in the Christian sense, as the process by which the divine mind works through human consciousness, the Moslem view of revelation (*wahy*) is tantamount to dictation. Word form and contents are God's. The process is described as "sending down," down from heaven where lay an archetype. It entails a passive recipient to whom God communicates his thought and will. When thus commissioned, the recipient is "sent forth" to announce the message. He becomes God's messenger. Accordingly Allah, on one of several occasions, commissioned Muhammad:

We have given revelation to thee just as We gave revelation to Noah and the prophets after him. We also gave revelation to Abraham, to Ishmael, to Isaac, to Jacob, to the Tribes [patriarchs descended from Jacob], to Jesus, to Job, to Jonah, to Aaron, and to Solomon; while to David We gave a Psalter [*zabur,* from Heb. *mizmor*]. *(4:161–2)*

There were also messengers whose stories We have told thee before, and messengers whose stories We have not told thee.

To each people God sends one messenger (10:48; 16:38; cf. 23:46). In each case the messenger is entrusted with a book, confirmatory of the preceding books. Muhammad was sent to a people lacking a book, a people to whom God had not yet sent a messenger. The Koran is revealed in Arabic, and Arabic thus became an integral part of the revelation. Arabs refer to is as "the tongue of the angels," meaning, in the opinion of one struggling to learn it, no one can master it until he dies and becomes an angel. Additionally, Arabic, the language of the Koran, served as a basis for a new nation to be created by Muhammad from motley, unruly Arabian tribes that had never united before. Thus, the founder of Islam added a new dimension to his triple contribution of religion, state, and culture.

Lo, We have made it an Arabic Koran, so that ye may understand
And lo, it is in the Mother of the Book [the heavenly archetype] in Our presence, exalted, wise. *(43:2–3)*

Again and again the divine nature of the Koran is emphasized and Muhammad is ordered to proclaim nothing but what is revealed (43:42). Meantime the messenger's audience is duly notified:

Thus have We sent to you a messenger from amongst yourselves to recite to you Our revelation, to purify you and to instruct you in the book and the wisdom and to teach you what ye do not know. *(2:146)*

And as if eager to remove all possibility of misunderstanding, Allah adds: "And Muhammad is naught but a messenger" (3:138).

Messengership was a Christian concept that had been institutionalized for centuries. Jesus "sent forth" his twelve disciples, who became apostles, or envoys. An apostle was one sent by God. The title was later applied to other than disciples, like Paul, who carried on the message. The Koran bestows on Muhammad another title—"prophet." In several verses he is commissioned as a prophet and is so addressed by Allah:

O prophet, We have sent thee as a witness, a bringer of good tidings and a warner,
A summoner to Allah by His permission and a light-giving lamp. *(33:44–5)*

In another surah the prophet is characterized as *ummi*.

Say: "O mankind, I am Allah's messenger to you all,
Of Him to whom belongeth the kingdom of the heavens and of the earth.

There is no god but He.
He giveth life and causeth to die.
Believe then in Allah and in His messenger,
The *ummi* prophet, who himself believeth in Allah and His words, and follow him;
Haply so ye will be guided." *(7:157–8; cf. 7:156)*

Moslem commentators are in agreement that *ummi* means "unlettered," or "illiterate." Modern scholars, however, argue that Muhammad, as one engaged in trade, could probably read and write, and that the term, judged by the context, probably means one belonging to a community without a book and therefore uninstructed in scriptures (cf. 3:19).

. . .

Consecrated and fired by the new task assigned him, the Messenger-Prophet began with his own people. He taught, preached, and admonished as he delivered the new message. It was initially as clear as it was simple. There is only one God, Allah. He is all-powerful, the creator of all, the everlasting. There is a paradise and there is a hell. Splendid rewards await those who obey His commands. Terrible punishment awaits those who disregard them. Disappointed with the lack of receptivity to his message, the teacher-preacher turned to warning people that the day of judgment was imminent. But his was another voice in the wilderness. Neither fear nor reward proved to be an effective motivator.

The Allah he preached about was not new to Meccans. Indeed He was the principal deity of a group enshrined in their al-Ka'bah (Kaabah), the leading sanctuary of Hijaz. The objection was not to him as such but to this exclusiveness required in worshiping him. Acceptance of the new doctrine would eliminate all other deities and would thereby alienate the people from their fathers, who worshiped many deities. Besides, the new teaching would consign all those fathers to hell. The Quraysh—particularly its Umayyad clan —custodians of the Kaabah and the Zamzam, controllers of the caravan trade, and oligarchic masters of the city, had special reasons for resistance.

The new preaching might jeopardize pilgrimages to the Kaabah, next to trade their main source of income. Moreover, the once-poor orphan was introducing such dangerous economic doctrines as the rightful claim of beggars and the destitute to a share in the wealth of the rich (70:24–5). Additionally he advocated a dangerous doctrine, one that substitute faith for blood as the social bond of community life. If "the believers are naught but brothers" (49:10) was acted upon, the entire family, clan, and tribal unity would be undermined and replaced by religious unity. Then there were dangerous political implications in Muhammad's teaching. Religious success could entail political success, and the new prophet was a potential new ruler. Shrewd merchants that they were, they found nothing in what he offered that they cared to buy.

The opposition at first did not take the upstart seriously. Silence was followed by verbal attacks. He was "possessed by jinn" (81:22) said some; no, he was "a falsifying magician" (38:3) claimed others; "a soothsayer" (69:42) asserted still others. In this discouraging debut on the stage of prophethood, Muhammad was sustained and encouraged by his first convert, his wife Khadijah. As long as she lived, he had no other wife. His cousin 'Ali, son of abu-Talib in whose house he was brought up, was probably his second convert. Another early and valuable recruit from the Quraysh was abu-Bakr, the future father-in-law and first successor of the Prophet. But the bulk of followers were from the lowest classes—the poor and the slaves—the "meanest" in the koranic phrase (26:111).

At last the time came for the aristocracy of his tribe, the banu-U-mayyah, to engage in active persecution. This necessitated the migration (in 615) of eighty-three families of his followers to Christian Abyssinia, considered safe because its people believed in one God. But Muhammad himself held out. His patron abu-Talib refused to deliver him to his enemies because the clannish code of honor so dictated. A new weapon was devised: economic and social boycott. A quarantine was imposed on the recalcitrant clan. For three years the entire tribe refused to deal with members of Muhammad's clan. Toward the end of this period (619) both Muhammad's noble-minded wife Khadijah and his chivalrous uncle died.

Muhammad's position as a prophet was deteriorating, despite the addition of a few fresh recruits. Outstanding among them was another Qurayshite, 'Umar ibn-al-Khattab, who was to become another of Muhammad's successors as well as his father-in-law. The core of the opposition, the Umayyads, remained adamant in its hostility. Muhammad felt it necessary to seek a new field for his missionary activity. Taif, a fertile settlement on a high plateau seventy-five miles southeast of Mecca, was chosen. But the move, to use an Arabic figure of speech, was from under the leak to under the main. The city was a favorite summer resort for rich Meccans. It housed a shrine for the exalted goddess Allat. But the Lady of Taif was not ready for dethronement, and the intruder's teaching ran counter to other established interests here no less than in Mecca. The town gave its guest a rude welcome. A mob flung stones at him. The garden in which he sought refuge offered no refuge; it was owned by a leader of the opposition. The expatriate had to return from where he came. No other course seemed open. Dejected, he turned his back on Taif and faced Mecca, the city that had earlier rejected him, with the following moving Davidian prayer on his lips:

O Lord, unto Thee do I complain of my helplessness, paucity of resourcefulness and insignificance vis-à-vis other men. O most merciful of the merciful, Thou art the lord of the helpless and Thou art my lord. To whom wilt Thou abandon me? To one who would abuse me? Or to one who has been given power over me? Assuredly if Thy wrath is not upon me, I have no worry. For Thy favor then encompasseth me. I therefore seek refuge in the light of Thy countenance, the light by which darkness is illumined and all affairs of this world and the world to come are rightly ordered. May it never be that I should incur Thy anger or fail to satisfy Thee. For there is no resource and no power save in Thee.[1]

The second period of residence in Mecca was productive of no better results than the first, but occasional visits to the annual fairs held in the city opened up new prospects. These fairs attracted pilgrims to the great sanctuary as well as buyers and sellers from neighboring desert camps and settlements. They also provided opportunities for competitive poetical contests. On one of his visits Muhammad got acquainted with a group from Yathrib, two hundred and fifty miles north, who seemed to be mildly interested in him. Perhaps they thought Muhammad was the great religious leader their Jewish fellow townsmen were expecting to appear. Muhammad's negotiations with a delegation of seventy-two representatives of Yathrib resulted in an invitation and a guarantee of security and protection for the guest and his followers.

To escape the Umayyad vigilance Muhammad had about two hundred of his followers slip quietly out of Mecca. Accompanied by 'Ali and abū-Bakr, Muhammad followed and arrived on September 24, 622. In 639 the second caliph, 'Umar ibn-al-Khattab, fixed this hijrah date—he, however, made it begin with July 16, 622—rather than the birth date, as the starting point of the new calendar. With this migration (*hijrah,* wrongly translated as "flight") one period—the Meccan—ended and another—the Medinese—began.

More than that the hijrah marks the end of the pre-Islamic era and the start of the Islamic. For Muhammad it was the point in his career when he turned from a pattern of frustration to self-realization. . . .

. . .

[1] Ibn-Hisham, *Sirah,* ed. Ferdinand Wüstenfeld (Gottingen, 1858–9), p. 280; cf. Alfred Guillaume, tr., *The Life of Muhammad* (London, 1955), p. 193.

For the newcomers the first two years were especially difficult. They had problems obtaining food and housing and adjusting to a new environment. The immediate solution lay in having each newly converted family extend full hospitality to an emigrant family. Thereby the proclaimed theory that the new religion was a fraternal order was put into practice. But the economic condition of Medina was getting progressively worse. New sources of revenue had to be discovered. Meccan caravans returning from Syria with cash and goods offered an easy target as well as a chance to injure the lifeline of Mecca.

The first raid was well timed and well located. It occurred during Ramadan (mid-March 624), one of the four "sacred months" (9:36) in which warring was prohibited except in self-defense. The location was a watering place southwest of Medina, named Badr, at which the next caravan was sure to stop. The caravan numbered a thousand camels; Muhammad, according to ibn-Hisham, could muster only 312 men. The caravan leader and Umayyad chief, abu-Sufyan, had got wind of the contemplated attack and sent for aid from Mecca. His reinforcement included nine hundred men, accompanied by female singers to spark the fighters' enthusiasm. Following the usual procedure the combat began with single challenges between champions. Confident of victory the Quraysh fought with no plan and under no discipline. The attackers were given instructions about formation and method by their leader. They fought for survival and Allah; the will to conquer was on their side. The foe fought for its possessions and was routed, losing seventy dead and seventy prisoners. The Moslems lost fourteen men, the first martyrs to the cause of Allah. Against the advice of 'Umar ibn-al-Khattab and other sanguinary men, ransom was accepted. It was more useful than bloodshed.

There could be no question about it: the feat was accomplished with divine support. In fact the Koran (9:9–12, 17) gives the exact number of angels, a thousand, sent to participate in the battle. The first encounter between monotheism and polytheism ended in victory, a divine sanction of the new faith. Badr, distinguished by a mention in the Koran (3:119), became the source of inspiration for future wars. In the distribution of the booty God and his Messenger received one fifth (8:42); that set a precedent for future conquests.

The defeat was humiliating to the Meccans but not annihilating. Twelve months later the same foe, led by the same man, was again ready to measure swords. The encounter took place at Uhud on the side of the valley opposite Medina. Abu-Sufyan scored a victory. During the battle a stone hit the Prophet, and when he fell he smashed a tooth and cut his lip. But the victory was not enough to tarnish the glamour of Badr, and both sides expected a final round.

It came. Muhammad could muster only three thousand troops. In 627 at the head of a coalition of Meccans, mercenary Bedouins, black slaves, and allied Jews—ten thousand in all—abu-Sufyan moved against Medina and found it defended by a series of trenches, an innovation in Arabian warfare suggested by a Persian follower of Muhammad. The effect of the innovation must have been as demoralizing as the introduction of the tank was in World War I. The trench rendered the six hundred cavalrymen ineffective. Especially disgusted were the Bedouins, whose main interest in fighting was pay and booty. The loosely held confederation began to fall apart. The encounter was a match between number and wits. Moslem leadership was not only more intelligent, it also had a better intelligence agency. After a month's siege the invaders withdrew, leaving twenty dead, and never again challenged Islam. The battle, commemorated in the Koran by surah 33 ("The Confederates") is commonly styled that of the "trench" (khandaq).

The way was now open for Moslem hegemony in the area. The Quraysh lost not only their prestige, but their hold on the trade route to Syria as well. Throughout his Meccan period Muhammad had acted on the assumption that his religion was ideologically so closely related to the two older monotheisms—particularly Judaism—that there could be no difficulty in establishing it organically within their framework (2:127–31). Abraham's religion was the mother of Islam, and Abraham himself was the father of the Arabians through Hagar and Ishmael. It was he who rebuilt and purified the Kaabah as the "house [bayt] of Allah" (2:119) after its destruction by the Deluge. The women of the "people of the book" were made legitimate as wives to Moslems, and their food was also legitimized (5:7). Muhammad's harem included a Christian (Mariyah) and a Jewish wife. He prayed toward Jerusalem and his followers were ordered to do so. It was not long, however, after his landing at Medina that he began to be disillusioned. The Jews, he came to realize, considered themselves God's chosen people, the only seed of Abraham; they neither accepted others into Judaism nor themselves left it in favor of other religions. The expected Messiah could rise from no other tribe but theirs.

However, the break with the Jews had an economic aspect as well as a religious one. Early in the second year at Medina the mounting need for rehabilitating the expatriates was augmented by military preparations. Muhammad expected his Jewish neighbors, as quasi-brothers of Moslems, to contribute freely to the community chest. But a unilateral brotherhood is no brotherhood, and since they did not agree to Muhammad's request they were denounced in several koranic passages. The cold war that ensued was bound to lead to a hot war. A silly trick by a Jewish merchant on a Moslem woman customer sparked the conflict. Those of the Jewish tribe who survived found refuge in Syria. The weapons and other possessions they left behind supplied a much needed relief to the Moslems. The next year (625) saw the expulsion of the second tribe of Jews. Their houses and palm gardens were no less welcome than the possessions of the first tribe. The Moslems next turned (in 628) against Khaybar, a fertile Jewish oasis a hundred miles north of Medina.

Khaybar had served as an asylum for exiled Medinese Jews and as a source of that contingent of Jews which took part in the "battle of the trench." Its defenses against Bedouin attacks rendered it, in the eyes of its inhabitants, impregnable. But the forthcoming was not a Bedouin attack, and it took only two weeks to force a surrender. The terms included the annual delivery of one half of the yield of the oasis' gardens and fields. The Jewish problem of Arabia was thus solved.

In the meantime a movement to Islamize the religious practices that had been borrowed from Judaism was under way. The direction of the ritual prayer (kiblah, Ar. *qiblah*) was changed from Jerusalem to Mecca (2:139, 114–5). The human voice calling for prayer replaced the trumpet and the gong used by Jews and Christians. It was certainly a more effective means. Friday was ordained as the only day for congregational prayer (62:9–11). That day (*Jum'ah*, "assembly day") was chosen because it was the weekly shopping day when Jews particularly flocked to the market to buy provisions for their Sabbath. Once begun, the Arabization, the nationalization of Islam, continued. Ramadan was fixed as a month of fasting. Pilgrimage to the Kaabah was authorized and the kissing of the Black Stone—a pre-Islamic fetish housed in the Kaabah's corner—was sanctioned. In the pilgrimage Islam accepted its richest heritage from polytheistic Arabia and thereby alienated itself further from its two historic sisters.

While Islam was in its formative state Muhammad lacked the opportunity of establishing firsthand contact with a Christian community comparable to that established with the Jewish—hence the preponderant Jewish imprint on his religion. His contacts with Christians were limited to personal contacts with a few Christian individuals. Besides a Christian (Coptic) concubine, he had a Christian (Abyssinian) ex-slave and a Christian adopted son, Zayd. Besides the historic contacts with Christians, there is a Moslem legend that Muhammad had for a teacher a Syrian monk, Bahira, whom young Muhammad met when on a caravan to Damascus. The nearest Arabian Christian communities were on the southern border of Hijaz (Najranites), the northeastern border of Syria (Ghassanids), and the northwestern frontier of Persia (Lakhmids). All three communities belonged to the Syrian Church, whose views on the nature of Christ and the relation of his humanity to his divinity were considered equally heretical by both Catholic and Orthodox churches. Even so, no Christian Arabic texts were available to Muhammad, and his sources of information were oral and secondhand with an inextricable mixture of biblical and pseudo-biblical material. The Gospels (*Injil*, from Gr. *Evangel*) are mentioned eleven times in five different surahs, but there is no reference to Paul or the Epistles. In principle the Koran takes the position of confirming and rectifying the Christian Scriptures; in practice it abrogates them.

· · ·

CHAPTER TEN / *Islam*

Shortly before the subjugation of Khaybar, Muhammad conceived the brilliant idea of undertaking, at the head of a band of followers, a holy pilgrimage to Mecca in the hope of convincing its people that there was a place in his scheme for their sanctuary and its associated institution. But the Quraysh, learning that he was leading fifteen hundred men, put a different interpretation on the move. With two hundred cavalry they went out ready to battle the invaders. At al-Hu-daybiyah (nine miles north of Mecca) the two parties met. Messengers shuttled back and forth. After some bargaining a pact of nonaggression was signed, providing for cessation of hostility and future coexistence. Muhammad returned to Medina after scoring this significant peaceful victory. He could now, with no fear from an enemy at his back, proceed to consolidate what he had, expand it, and extend his Pax Islamica over it. In the two years following he sent bands led by his lieutenants on more than a dozen expeditions against tribes and settlements in the north as far as southern Palestine. The farthest point reached was Mu'tah near the southern end of the Dead Sea. . . .

. . .

Events moved quickly to a climax. The long-awaited hour came. In January 630 Muhammad, backed by a thousand followers, made his triumphal entry into the city of his birth. Realizing the futility of any further opposition the Quraysh yielded. Even abu-Sufyan, the archenemy of Islam, was ready to embrace the faith he had fought violently for so long. Before this time two other Qurayshites, Khalid ibn-al-Walid and 'Amr ibn-al-'As, had been recruited to the cause. Against the advice of 'Umar ibn-al-Khattab and other aides, the victor proscribed only ten of the opposition leaders. Abu-Sufyan was spared. Such self-restraint and statemanship have few parallels in the annals of that time. Muhammad, predictably, lost no time in making his way into the Kaabah, there to smash the three hundred and sixty idols while exclaiming, "Truth hath come, and falsehood hath vanished!"

. . .

In spring 632 the sixty-two-year-old chief led a large body of believers to undertake the annual pilgrimage to Mecca. After going through the rites prescribed in the Koran, he delivered one of the noblest sermons of his career. It began:

Harken, O ye men, unto my words and take ye them to heart. Know ye that every Moslem is a brother unto every Moslem, and that ye are now one brotherhood [cf. sur. 49:10]. It is, therefore, not legitimate for any one of you to appropriate unto himself anything that belongs to his brother unless it is willingly given by that brother.[2]

Substituting the religious for the centuries-old blood bond as the basis for

---

[2] Ibn-Hisham, *Sirah* (Cairo, 1929), p. 26. Cf. Philip K. Hitti, *History of the Arabs,* 10th ed. (London and New York, 1970), p. 120.

social cohesion was, indeed, a daring and original accomplishment of the Prophet of Arabia.

Three months later, on June 8, 632, Muhammad took ill in his home at Medina and died complaining of severe headache. He was buried under the floor of the mud hut of his favorite wife, 'A'ishah.

edward herbert palmer (translator) _____

FROM THE *Koran*

The 114 chapters (*suras*) of the Koran are arranged merely according to length: the longest chapter opens the book. It is now thought that some of the shorter chapters were the first to be revealed, but the chronological order of the chapters is in the main entirely problematical. Some chapters are themselves composites of teachings delivered at different times. Hence to non-Muslims the Koran typically appears formless, and it is in fact repetitious. Those who know the Koran in the original Arabic, however, insist that much of its force and beauty is lost in every translation. "The rhetoric and rhythm of the Arabic of the Koran," A. J. Arberry has written, "are so characteristic, so powerful, so highly emotive, that any version whatsoever is bound in the nature of things to be but a poor copy of the glittering splendour of the original."[*]

The translator here is Cambridge scholar Edward Herbert Palmer, whose well-known translation of the Koran first appeared in *The Sacred Books of the East* and later in such series as *The Harvard Classics*.

_____

THE OPENING . . .

In the name of the merciful and compassionate God.

Praise belongs to God, the Lord of the worlds, the merciful, the compassionate, the ruler of the day of judgment! Thee we serve and Thee we ask for aid. Guide us in the right path, the path of those Thou art gracious to; not of those Thou art wroth with; nor of those who err.

THE CHAPTER OF UNITY

In the name of the merciful and compassionate God.
Say, 'He is God alone!
God the Eternal!
He begets not and is not begotten!
Nor is there like unto Him any one!'

THE CHAPTER OF 'NECESSARIES'

In the name of the merciful and compassionate God.
Hast thou considered him who calls the judgment a lie? He it is who pushes

The Koran Interpreted (New York: Macmillan, 1955), p. 24.

Reprinted from *The Sacred Books of the East,* ed. by F. Max Müller, Vols. VI and IX *(The Qur'an,* trans. by Edward Herbert Palmer), 1900. By permission of The Clarendon Press, Oxford. Some notes have been omitted, and the remainder renumbered.

the orphan away; and urges not (others) to feed the poor.

But woe to those who pray and who are careless in their prayers,
Who pretend and withhold necessaries.[1]

THE CHAPTER OF THE SMITING

In the name of the merciful and compassionate God.
The smiting!
What is the smiting?
And what shall make thee know what the smiting is?
The day when men shall be like scattered moths; and the mountains shall be like flocks of carded wool!
And as for him whose balance is heavy, he shall be in a well-pleasing life.
But as for him whose balance is light, his dwelling shall be the pit of hell.
And who shall make thee know what it is?—a burning fire!

THE CHAPTER OF THE CLEAVING ASUNDER

In the name of the merciful and compassionate God.
When the heaven is cleft asunder,
And when the stars are scattered,
And when the seas gush together,
And when the tombs are turned upside down,
The soul shall know what it has sent on or kept back!

O man! what has seduced thee concerning thy generous Lord, who created thee, and fashioned thee, and gave thee symmetry, and in what form He pleased composed thee?

Nay, but ye call the judgment a lie! but over you are guardians set,[2]—noble, writing down! they know what ye do!

Verily, the righteous are in pleasure, and, verily, the wicked are in hell; they shall broil therein upon the judgment day; nor shall they be absent therefrom!

And what shall make thee know what is the judgment day? Again, what shall make thee know what is the judgment day? a day when no soul shall control aught for another; and the bidding on that day belongs to God!

THE CHAPTER OF THE FOLDING UP

In the name of the merciful and compassionate God.
When the sun is folded up,
And when the stars do fall,

[1]Or, 'alms.' The word might be rendered 'resources.'
[2]The recording angels.

And when the mountains are moved,
And when the she-camels ten months' gone with young shall be neglected,[3]
And when the beasts shall be crowded together,[4]
And when the seas shall surge up,
And when souls shall be paired with bodies,
And when the child who was buried alive shall be asked for what sin she was
    slain,
And when the pages shall be spread out,
And when the heaven shall be flayed,
And when hell shall be set ablaze,
And when Paradise shall be brought nigh.
The soul shall know what it has produced!
I need not swear by the stars that slink back, moving swiftly, slinking into
    their dens!
Nor by the night when darkness draws on!
Nor by the morn when it first breathes up!
Verily, it is the speech of a noble apostle, mighty, standing sure with the Lord
    of the throne, obeyed and trusty too!
Your comrade is not mad; he saw him[5] on the plain horizon, nor does he
    grudge to communicate the unseen.
Nor is it the speech of a pelted devil.
Then whither do ye go?
It is but a reminder to the worlds, to whomsoever of you pleases to go
    straight:—but ye will not please, except God, the Lord of the world,
    should please.

THE CHAPTER OF THE INEVITABLE

In the name of the merciful and compassionate God.
When the inevitable[6] happens; none shall call its happening a lie!—abasing—
    exalting!
When the earth shall quake, quaking! and the mountains shall crumble,
    crumbling, and become like motes dispersed!
And ye shall be three sorts;
And the fellows of the right hand—what right lucky fellows!
And the fellows of the left hand—what unlucky fellows!
And the foremost foremost[7]!

---

[3]Such camels being among the most valuable of an Arab's possessions, neglect of them must
imply some terribly engrossing calamity.
[4]The terrors of the judgment day will drive all the wild beasts together for mutual shelter.
[5]Gabriel.
[6]I.e. the day of judgment.
[7]I.e. the foremost in professing the faith on earth shall be the foremost then.

These are they who are brought nigh,
In gardens of pleasure!
A crowd of those of yore,
And a few of those of the latter day!
And gold-weft couches, reclining on them face to face.
Around them shall go eternal youths, with goblets and ewers and a cup of
flowing wine; no headache shall they feel therefrom, nor shall their wits
be dimmed!
And fruits such as they deem the best;
And flesh of fowl as they desire;
And bright and large-eyed maids like hidden pearls;
A reward for that which they have done!
They shall hear no folly there and no sin;
Only the speech, 'Peace, Peace!'
And the fellows of the right—what right lucky fellows!
Amid thornless lote trees.
And tal'h[8] trees with piles of fruit;
And outspread shade,
And water out-poured;
And fruit in abundance, neither failing nor forbidden;
And beds upraised!
Verily, we have produced them[9] a production.
And made them virgins, darlings of equal age (with their spouses) for the
fellows of the right!
A crowd of those of yore, and a crowd of those of the latter day!
And the fellows of the left—what unlucky fellows!
In hot blasts and boiling water;
And a shade of pitchy smoke,
Neither cool nor generous!
Verily, they were affluent ere this, and did persist in mighty crime; and used to
say, 'What, when we die and have become dust and bones, shall we then
indeed be raised? or our fathers of yore?'
Say, 'Verily, those of yore and those of the latter day shall surely be gathered
together unto the tryst of the well-known day.'
Then ye, O ye who err! who say it is a lie! shall eat of the Zaqqûm tree! and fill
your bellies with it! and drink thereon of boiling water! and drink as
drinks the thirsty camel.
This is their entertainment on the judgment day!
We created you, then why do ye not credit?
Have ye considered what ye emit?

[8]The mimosa gummifera is generally so called in Arabia; but the banana is said to be meant in
this passage.
[9]The celestial damsels.

Do we create it, or are we the creators?

We have decreed amongst you death; but we are not forestalled from making the likes of you in exchange, or producing you as ye know not of.

Ye do know the first production—why then do ye not mind?

Have ye considered what ye till?

Do ye make it bear seed, or do we make it bear seed?

If we pleased we could make it mere grit, so that ye would pause to marvel:

'Verily, we have got into debt[10] and we are excluded.'[11]

Have ye considered the water which ye drink?

Do ye make it come down from the clouds, or do we make it come down?

If we pleased we could make it pungent—why then do ye not give thanks?

Have ye considered the fire which ye strike?

Do ye produce the tree that gives it,[12] or do we produce it?

We have made it a memorial and a chattel for the traveller of the waste?

Then celebrate the grand name of thy Lord!

So I will not swear by the positions of the stars; and, verily, it is a grand oath if ye did but know—that, verily, this is the honourable Qur'ân—in the laid-up Book!

Let none touch it but the purified!

A revelation from the Lord of the worlds.

What! this new discourse will ye despise?

And make for your provison, that you call it a lie?

Why then—when it[13] comes up to the throat, and ye at that time look on, though we are nearer to him than you are, but ye cannot see,—why, if ye are not to be judged, do ye not send it back, if ye do tell the truth?

But either, if he be of those brought nigh to God,—then rest and fragrance and the garden of pleasure!

Or, if he be of the fellows of the right! then 'Peace to thee!' from the fellows of the right!

Or, if he be of those who say it is a lie,—who err! then an entertainment of boiling water! and broiling in hell!

Verily, this is surely certain truth!

So celebrate the grand name of thy Lord!

THE CHAPTER OF MARY

. . .

And mention, in the Book, Mary; when she retired from her family into an eastern place; and she took a veil (to screen herself) from them; and we sent unto her our spirit; and he took for her the semblance of a well-made man.

[10]I.e. for seed and labour.
[11]From reaping the fruits of it.
[12]The ancient Arabs produced fire by the friction of a stick in a hollow piece of wood.
[13]The soul of a dying man.

Said she, 'Verily, I take refuge in the Merciful One from thee, if thou art pious.' Said he, 'I am only a messenger of Thy Lord to bestow on thee a pure boy.'

Said she, 'How can I have a boy when no man has touched me, and when I am no harlot?' He said, 'Thus says thy Lord, It is easy for Me! and we will make him a sign unto man, and a mercy from us; for it is a decided matter.'

So she conceived him, and she retired with him into a remote place. And the labour pains came upon her at the trunk of a palm tree, and she said 'O that I had died before this, and been forgotten out of mind!' and he called[14] to her from beneath her, 'Grieve not, for thy Lord has placed a stream beneath thy feet; and shake towards thee the trunk of the palm tree, it will drop upon thee fresh dates fit to gather; so eat, and drink, and cheer thine eye; and if thou shouldst see any mortal say, "Verily, I have vowed to the Merciful One a fast, and I will not speak to-day with a human being." '

Then she brought it to her people, carrying it; said they, 'O Mary! thou hast done an extraordinary thing! O sister of Aaron! thy father was not a bad man, nor was thy mother a harlot!'

And she pointed to him, and they said, 'How are we to speak with one who is in the cradle a child?' He said, 'Verily, I am a servant of God; He has brought me the Book, and He has made me a prophet, and He has made me blessed wherever I be; and He has required of me prayer and almsgiving so long as I live, and piety towards my mother, and has not made me a miserable tyrant; and peace upon me the day I was born, and the day I die, and the day I shall be raised up alive.'

That is, Jesus the son of Mary,—by the word of truth whereon ye do dispute!

God could not take to himself any son! celebrated be His praise! when He decrees a matter He only says to it 'BE,' and it is; and, verily, God is my Lord and your Lord, so worship Him; this is the right way.

. . .

THE CHAPTER OF WOMEN

In the name of the merciful and compassionate God.

O ye folk! fear your Lord, who created you from one soul, and created therefrom its mate, and diffused from them twain many men and women. And fear God, in whose name ye beg of one another, and the wombs; verily, God over you doth watch.[15]

And give unto the orphans their property, and give them not the vile in exchange for the good, and devour not their property to your own property;

---

[14]Either the infant himself or the angel Gabriel; or the expression 'beneath her' may be rendered 'beneath it,' and may refer to the palm tree.

[15]That is, fear God, and pay respect to your mothers and wives.

verily, that were a great sin. But if ye fear that ye cannot do justice between orphans, then marry what seems good to you of women, by twos, or threes, or fours; and if ye fear that ye cannot be equitable, then only one, or what your right hands possess.[16] That keeps you nearer to not being partial.

And give women their dowries freely; and if they are good enough to remit any of it of themselves, then devour it with good digestion and appetite.[17]

But do not give up to fools[18] their property which God has made you to stand by; but maintain them from it, and clothe them, and speak to them with a reasonable speech. Prove orphans until they reach a marriageable age, and if ye perceive in them right management, then hand over to them their property, and do not devour it extravagantly in anticipation of their growing up. And he who is rich, let him abstain; but he who is poor, let him devour in reason, and when ye hand over to them their property, then take witnesses against them; but God sufficeth for taking account.

Men should have a portion of what their parents and kindred leave, and women should have a portion of what their parents and kindred leave, whether it be little or much, a determined portion. And when the next of kin and the orphans and the poor are present at the division, then maintain them out of it, and speak to them a reasonable speech. And let these fear lest they leave behind them a weak seed, for whom they would be afraid; and let them fear God, and speak a straightforward speech. Verily, those who devour the property of orphans unjustly, only devour into their bellies fire, and they shall broil in flames.

God instructs you concerning your children; for a male the like of the portion of two females, and if there be women above two, then let them have two-thirds of what (the deceased) leaves; and if there be but one, then let her have a half; and as to the parents, to each of them a sixth of what he leaves, if he has a son; but if he have no son, and his parents inherit, then let his mother have a third, and if he have brethren, let his mother have a sixth after payment of the bequest he bequeaths and of his debt.

Your parents or your children, ye know not which of them is nearest to you in usefulness:—an ordinance this from God; verily, God is knowing and wise! And ye shall have half of what your wives leave, if they have no son; but if they have a son, then ye shall have a fourth of what they leave, after payment of the bequests they bequeath or of their debts. And they shall have a fourth of what ye leave, if ye have no son; but if ye have a son, then let them have an

---

[16]That is, female slaves.

[17]The Arabic idiom for the enjoyment of property being to eat it up, Mohammed here gives the men permission to enjoy such portion of their wives' dowries as the latter might be pleased to remit, and adds, with a sort of humour, the colloquial expression used by the Arabs when any one is eating. The sentence might be paraphrased 'and if they are kind enough to remit any portion of it of their own accord, then enjoy it, and much good may it do you!'

[18]To idiots or persons of weak intellect.

eighth of what ye leave, after payment of the bequest ye bequeath and of your debts.

And if the man's or the woman's (property) be inherited by a kinsman who is neither parent nor child, and he have a brother or sister, then let each of these two have a sixth; but if they are more than that, let them share in a third after payment of the bequest he bequeaths and of his debts, without prejudice,[19]—an ordinance this from God, and God is knowing and clement!

These be God's bounds, and whoso obeys God and the Apostle He will make him enter into gardens beneath which rivers flow, and they shall dwell therein for aye;—that is the mighty happiness.

But whoso rebels against God and His Apostle, and transgresses His bounds, He will make him enter into fire, and dwell therein for aye; and for him is shameful woe.

Against those of your women who commit adultery, call witnesses four in number from among yourselves; and if these bear witness, then keep the women in houses[20] until death release them, or God shall make for them a way.

And if two of you commit it, then hurt them both[21]; but if they turn again and amend, leave them alone, verily, God is easily turned, compassionate.

God is only bound to turn again towards those who do evil through ignorance and then turn again. Surely, these will God turn again to, for God is knowing, wise. His turning again is not for those who do evil, until, when death comes before one of them, he says, 'Now I turn again;' nor yet for those who die in misbelief. For such as these have we prepared a grievous woe.

O ye who believe! it is not lawful for you to inherit women's estates against their will; nor to hinder them,[22] that ye may go off with part of what ye brought them, unless they commit fornication manifestly; but associate with them in reason, for if ye are averse from them, it may be that ye are averse from something wherein God has put much good for you.

But if ye wish to exchange one wife for another, and have given one of them a talent,[23] then take not from it anything. What! would you take it for a calumny and a manifest crime[24]?

How can ye take it when one of you has gone in unto the other, and they have taken from you a rigid compact?

---

[19]I.e. to the heirs.

[20]Women taken in adultery or fornication were at the beginning of Islâm literally immured.

[21]The commentators are not agreed as to the nature of the offence here referred to. The text, however, speaks of two of the masculine gender. The punishment to be inflicted is also the subject of dispute, the original merely saying, as I have translated it, 'hurt them.'

[22]That is, from marrying again.

[23]That is, a large dowry.

[24]This question is ironical, and intended as a warning against bringing a false accusation of infidelity against a wife for the sake of keeping her dowry when divorced.

And do not marry women your fathers married,—except bygones,—for it is abominable and hateful, and an evil way; unlawful for you are your mothers, and your daughters, and your sisters, and your paternal aunts and maternal aunts, and your brother's daughters, and your sister's daughters, and your foster mothers, and your foster sisters, and your wives' mothers, and your step daughters who are your wards, born of your wives to whom ye have gone in; but if ye have not gone in unto them, then it is no crime in you; and the lawful spouses of your sons from your own loins, and that ye form a connexion between two sisters,—except bygones,—verily, God is forgiving, merciful; and married women, save such as your right hands possess,—God's Book against you!—but lawful for you is all besides this, for you to seek them with your wealth, marrying them and not fornicating; but such of them as ye have enjoyed, give them their hire as a lawful due; for there is no crime in you about what ye agree between you after such lawful due, verily, God is knowing and wise.

But whosoever of you cannot go the length of marrying marriageable women who believe, then take of what your right hands possess, of your maidens who believe;—though God knows best about your faith. Ye come one from the other; then marry them with the permission of their people, and give them their hire in reason, they being chaste and not fornicating, and not receivers of paramours.

But when they are married, if they commit fornication, then inflict upon them half the penalty for married women; that is for whomsoever of you fears wrong; but that ye should have patience is better for you, and God is forgiving and merciful.

h. a. r. gibb _____

Doctrine and Ritual in the Koran

Sir Hamilton A. R. Gibb (1895–1971) was born in Egypt but educated at the University of Edinburgh, the University of London, and the University of Oxford. He went on to hold positions of great distinction in both England and the United States. He was Laudian Professor of Arabic at the University of Oxford and Professor of Arabic and Director of the Center for Middle Eastern Studies at Harvard University. A Fellow of the British Academy, he was also an Honorary Member of the American Academy of Arts and Sciences. Among his books are *The Arab Conquests in Central Asia, Arabic Literature, Studies in Contemporary Arabic Literature, Modern Trends in Islam, Studies on the Civilization of Islam,* and *Mohammedanism.*

Although it would be vain to look in the Koran for a systematic exposition of Muslim beliefs or ritual, yet there emerges from it, taken as a whole, a consistent body of doctrine and of practical obligations. These have remained in all ages the core and inspiration of the Muslim religious life, and as such will be summarized in this chapter . . . .

Rather surprisingly, the famous *shahāda* or profession of faith: *lā ilāha illa'llāh muhammadun rasūlu'llāh,* 'There is but one God, Mohammed is the Apostle of God,' is not found in this composite form anywhere in the Koran, but its two halves occur separately. What may be taken, however, as the outline of a *credo*—and often is so taken by Muslims—is given in Sūra iv, v. 135:

O ye who believe, believe in God and His Apostle and the Book which He hath sent down to His Apostle and the Scripture which He hath sent down formerly. Whosoever denieth God and His Angels and His Books and His Apostles and the Last Day hath strayed far from the Truth.

(i) *God.* The Arabic word *Allāh* is a shortened form of *al-ilāh,* '*The* god'. Both the concept of a supreme God and the Arabic term have been shown to be familiar to the Arabs in Mohammed's time. What Mohammed did was to give a new and fuller content to the concept, to purify it from the elements of polytheism which still clustered round it, and to substitute for acceptance of a vague and distant figure belief in an intensely real, if transcendent, Being, Creator and Sustainer of the universe, the all-knowing and all-powerful Arbiter of good and evil, and final Judge of all men.

H. A. R. Gibb, "Doctrine and Ritual in the *Koran.*" From H. A. R. Gibb, *Mohammedanism* (2nd ed., 1953). By permission of The Clarendon Press, Oxford. Notes have been renumbered.

To give even in outline all the teaching about God which is explicit or implicit in the Koran would be impossible here. Much of it is expressed in the form of epithets and adjectives, such as Hearer, Seer, Bestower, Reckoner, Pardoner, Keeper, Guide, from which Muslims have put together the ninety-nine 'most beautiful names' of God. But occasionally there are longer passages of exposition, the most impressive of which, in its sustained eloquence, is the famous Throne-verse (Sūra ii, v. 256):

God—there is no god but He, the Living, the Self-subsistent. Slumber seizeth Him not, neither sleep. To Him belongeth whatsoever is in the Heavens and whatsoever is in the Earth. Who is there that shall intercede with Him save by His Will? He knoweth what is present with men and what shall befall them, and nought of His knowledge do they comprehend, save what He willeth. His Throne is wide as the Heavens and the Earth, and the keeping of them wearieth Him not. And He is the High, the Mighty One.

For Mohammed the essential element of true belief was an uncompromising monotheism. At Mecca he rejected the pretension that the goddesses worshipped by the Arabs were 'daughters of Allah', as later on he rejected the worship of Jesus and of Mary as 'lords' and upbraided the Jews for calling their religious teachers by the title of *rabbi* ('my lord'). True belief demands *ikhlās,* the giving of one's whole and unmixed allegiance to God, and its opposite is *shirk,* the ascribing of partners to God and the worship of any creature. This is the one unforgivable sin: 'Verily God forgiveth not the giving of partners to Him; other than this will He forgive to whom He pleaseth, but whosoever giveth a partner to God hath conceived a monstrous sin' (iv, v. 51).

God exists from all eternity to all eternity. He is the only reality: 'Call not on any other god but Allah; there is no god but He. Everything shall perish except His Face.[1] To Him belongeth the rule and to Him shall ye be brought back for judgement' (xxviii, v. 88). All else from the Seven Heavens downwards comes into existence by His Will and at His creative Word 'Be!' He alone gives life and death, His Decree is inescapable, and all things are determined and disposed by His foreknowledge, pictorially expressed as written on a 'Preserved Tablet'. Men are His creatures, *'ibād* (a plural of *'abd*, 'slave', already employed as a technical religious term by the Arab Christians), and must submit their wills to His ways, however mysterious. 'Peradventure ye may dislike some thing, yet God setteth in it abundant good' (iv, v. 18). He 'misleads whom He will and guides whom He will' (lxxiv, v. 34). Man must live in constant fear and awe of Him, and always be on his guard against Him (such is the idomatic meaning of the term for 'fearing God' which runs through the Koran from cover to cover), yet he is bidden to adore Him, to magnify and praise Him, and ever to commemorate His Name.

[1]'Face' is the term which in the Koran corresponds to *persona* or 'being'.

For alongside the terrible and majestic aspects of God as Creator, Supreme Power, Judge, and Avenger, the Koran stresses also His bounty and loving-kindness. He is not only 'the Compassionate One, the Merciful', but also the Protector, the Provider, the Pardoner, the Clement, ever ready to turn to the repentant sinner. He is the Subtle, Who is 'closer to man than his own neck-vein' (l, v. 15), 'the First and the Last, the Manifest and the Hidden' (lvii, v. 3). And finally the mystical indwelling of God in His universe is suggested in the parable of the 'Light-verse' (xxiv, v. 35):

God is the Light of the Heavens and of the Earth. The similitude of His Light is as it were a niche wherein is a lamp, the lamp within a glass, the glass as though it were a pearly star. It is lit from a blessed Tree, an olive-tree neither of the East nor of the West, the oil whereof were like to shine even though no fire were applied to it; Light upon Light; God guideth to His Light whom He will.

(ii) *Angels*. In the imagery of the Koran the angels are represented generally as God's messengers. They are, like men, His creatures and servants and worship Him continually; they bear up His Throne, descend with His Decrees on the Night of Power, record men's actions, receive their souls when they die, and witness for or against them at the Last Judgement, and guard the gates of Hell. At the battle of Badr they assisted the Muslims against the vastly superior forces of the Meccans.

Although the term Archangels is not found in the Koran, the idea seems to be implied in the mention of the Angel of Death, who is set in authority over men (xxxii, v.11), and of Michael alongside Gabriel in one verse (ii, v. 92). But it is above all Gabriel who is God's chief messenger; and it is certain that the early Muslims identified Gabriel with that 'illustrious messenger, lord of power' who communicated the Koran to Mohammed (lxxxi, vv. 19–21), and again with the 'Holy Spirit' who announced the birth of Jesus to the Virgin Mary and is said in three passages to have 'strengthened' Jesus.

With the doctrine of angels goes also the doctrine of devils, although the devils are represented as rebellious *jinn* rather than fallen angels. The *jinn* are, like men, created, but of fire instead of earth; there are believers and infidels amongst them, and the unbelievers will be judged with men and condemned to Hell. The rebellious *jinn* are called *shaitāns*; they lead men astray, oppose the Prophets, and try to overhear what is discussed in Heaven but are driven off by shooting stars. They teach men sorcery, and were made subject to Solomon, for whom they dived and built.

The leader of these evil spirits is called 'the *Shaitān*' or Iblīs. His fall from a place among the angels was due to his refusal to worship Adam on God's command; for this he was accursed, but respited till the Day of Resurrection and given authority over those of mankind who should be seduced by him.

(iii) *Books and Apostles*. The doctrine of Apostles is, as the *shahāda* shows, next to the Unity of God the central doctrine of the Koran. At all times and to all peoples, including the *jinn,* God has sent messengers or prophets to preach the unity of God and to warn men of the Judgement. Most, if not all, were rejected and persecuted by the majority of their fellow-citizens, who were subsequently visited by a terrible punishment. They were not workers of miracles, except when God endowed them with special powers as 'signs'. Muslims are required to believe in them all without distinction, although only a few are mentioned by name, or their histories related, in the Koran. Several received special endowments and rank above others, particularly Adam, Noah, the house of Abraham, Moses, and Jesus. The last or 'Seal' of the Prophets is Mohammed, who is God's Apostle to all mankind.

Altogether, twenty-eight Prophets are mentioned in the Koran. Of these, four (if Luqmān be included) are Arabian, eighteen are Old Testament figures, three (Zechariah, John the Baptist, and Jesus) are of the New Testament, and two are personages denoted by epithets—one being Dhu'l-Qarnain, 'The two-horned', commonly identified with the hero of the Alexander-legend. The prophetic narratives are almost all contained in Meccan passages, and in the case of the Biblical figures they correspond, with many variations, to the Biblical narratives. The story of Joseph occupies the whole of Sūra xii, and Sūra xviii contains three independent stories, those of the Seven Sleepers, of the meeting of Moses with 'one of Our servants' (identified by Muslim tradition with the wandering saint al-Khidr), and of Dhu'l-Qarnain and the building of the wall of Gog and Magog. In the story of Jesus, which is found both in a Meccan and in a Medinian version, particular stress is laid on the Virgin Birth, his miracles, and the denial of his divinity or claim to divinity. The crucifixion is rejected as a Jewish fable, another in his semblance having been crucified in his stead.

The doctrine preached by all the Prophets is essentially one and the same, although in matters of detail there has been a gradual evolution in their messages towards the final and perfect revelation. These stages are represented also by the various 'books' or scriptures granted to several of the major Prophets. Several earlier scriptures are referred to anonymously, but four are singled out by name. To Moses was given by Divine inspiration the *Tawrāh*, the Jewish *Tōrah,* corresponding to the Pentateuch; to David the *Zabūr*, identified with the Psalms by a verbal quotation of Psalm xxxvii, v. 29 in Sūra xxi, v. 105; to Jesus the *Injīl*, the Evangel or Gospel; and to Mohammed the *Qur'ān* or Recital. All these scriptures were written revelations, and all alike are to be believed and accepted, since they all confirm one another and the Koran in particular not only confirms earlier scriptures, but, as the final revelation, clears up all uncertainties and is the repository of perfect Truth.

Furthermore, it is declared that the coming of Mohammed was foretold by Jesus under the name of Ahmad, and that his name is specifically recorded in the *Tawrāh* and *Injīl* as the 'Prophet of the Gentiles' (*an-nabī al-ummī,* interpreted by later orthodoxy as 'the unlettered Prophet'). Nevertheless, the Jews (and perhaps, by implication, the Christians also) seek to conceal the witness of their scriptures and are guilty of misquoting and even of wilfully perverting them.

As for Mohammed himself, the Koran repeatedly disclaims on his behalf anything that savours of the superhuman. He is but a mortal man, commissioned with the sole duty of conveying God's warning and message of salvation. He has no knowledge beyond what is revealed to him, and has been granted no miraculous powers. He is commanded to seek pardon for his faults and to be patient under adversity. Yet he is a noble pattern to those who hope in God, his decisions must be accepted in matters of faith and conduct, belief in his revelation and obedience to him are necessary to salvation.

(iv) *The Last Day*. [The Last Judgement] . . . is presented always as a cataclysmic event, coming suddenly at a time known only to God. The Trumpet will be sounded, the heavens shall be split asunder and the mountains ground to dust, the graves will open, and men and *jinn* will be called to account. Each man's guardian angels will bear witness to his record, his deeds will be weighed in the Balance, and his book will be placed in his hand, the right hand of the blessed, the left hand of the damned.

Then the blessed, the godfearing men and women, the humble and charitable, the forgiving, those who have suffered and been persecuted for God's sake, those who have fought in the way of God, shall be summoned to enter the Garden of Paradise, the Abode of Peace, the abiding mansion, where they shall dwell for ever by flowing rivers, praising God, reclining on silken couches, enjoying heavenly food and drink and the company of dark-eyed maidens and wives of perfect purity, and yet greater bliss which no soul knoweth.

But the covetous, the unbelieving, the worshippers of gods other than Allah, shall be cast into the Fire, to abide therein for ever, with no release from its torments, fed with boiling water and the fruit of the *zaqqūm*, resembling the heads of *shaitāns* and like molten brass in the belly. No description can indeed convey the terror of the Koranic portrayal of Hell, backed up as it is by the sombre asseveration 'Verily I shall fill Hell with *jinn* and men altogether,' or the horror of the day 'when We shall say to Hell "Art thou filled?" and Hell shall answer "Are there yet more?" ' (l, v. 29).

Yet this presentation of the awful reckoning is lightened by repeated assurances of the Divine Mercy and by hints of the power of intercession which God will grant to those whom He pleases, save on behalf of the evildoers in Hell. In no passage of the Koran, however, is the power of intercession specifically attributed to Mohammed, nor any suggestion that the profession of Islam in itself is a sure passport to Paradise. Apart from martyrs for the Faith, the only promise of Paradise is made to 'those who repent and believe and are righteous in act'.

Islamic orthodoxy has, accordingly, always coupled faith with works, and in particular with those 'acts of devotion' (*'ibādāt*) which are enjoined on Believers in the Koran.

(v) *Prayer*. The observance of the ritual prayers (*salāh*) is repeatedly emphasized as one of the essential religious duties. Although neither the ceremonies nor the five set times of prayer are precisely stated in the Koran, it is certain that they were well established before Mohammed's death. Each consists of a fixed number of 'bowings' (called *rak'ah*), the 'bowing' itself consisting of seven movements with their appropriate recitations: (i) the recitation of the phrase *Allāhu akbar*, 'God is most Great', with the hands open on each side of the face; (2) the recitation of the *Fātihah* or opening sūra of the Koran, followed by another passage or passages, while standing upright; (3) bowing from the hips; (4) straightening up; (5) gliding to the knees and a first prostration with face to the ground; (6) sitting back on the haunches; (7) a second prostration. The second and later 'bowings' begin with the second of these movements, and at the end of each pair of 'bowings' and the conclusion of the whole prayer the worshipper recites the *shahāda* and the ritual salutations.

The set times are at daybreak (2 *rak'ahs*), noon (4 *rak'ahs*), mid-afternoon (4 *rak'ahs*), after sunset (3 *rak'ahs*), and in the early part of the night (4 *rak'ahs*). At these times prayers should be said and the ritual observed by every Believer wherever he may be; but by preference they should be performed congregationally in a mosque (*masjid*, 'place of prostration') under the leadership of an *imām*, a man who, standing in front of the lines of worshippers, sets the timing of each movement. It seems that at Medina women joined in the congregational prayers, standing in rows behind the men. The *imām* and the worshippers face towards the *qibla*, the prescribed 'direction', which was defined in an early Medinian verse as the Sacred Mosque of Mecca. In times of sickness or danger the ritual may be relaxed, but not otherwise. Additional or 'supererogatory' prayers are frequently recommended, especially during the night.

The Koran also mentions the noon prayer on Friday, the principal congregational prayer of the week, and enjoins the suspension of work during it. In the same connexion mention is made of the call to prayer (*adhān*). This replaced the use of bells or clappers, which Mohammed abhorred; and the first muezzin (*mu'adhdhin*, reciter of the *adhān*) was his Abyssinian slave Bilāl. Minarets were as yet unknown, and were first adopted, as it would seem, in Syria during the Caliphate of the Umayyads.

Ablution before prayers is strictly enjoined, and the ritual is defined in Sūra v, v. 9: 'When ye rise up to prayer, wash your faces and your hands [and arms] to the elbows, and wipe your heads and your feet to the ankles.' This is the 'lesser ablution' (*wudhū*). The 'greater ablution' (*ghusl*) is a complete washing of the body after major pollutions. If no water is at hand, hands and face may be wiped with fine clean sand. While personal cleanliness is formally demanded of worshippers, the Koran clearly indicates the symbolic meaning which underlies the practice of ablution.[2]

(vi) *Alms*. With the observance of prayer the Koran regularly enjoins the giving of alms (*zakāh*), as the outward sign of piety and means of salvation. In the earlier years the recommendation of almsgiving seems to have referred rather to free-will offerings (*sadaqāt*); but a late passage (lviii, vv. 13–14) clearly distinguishes *sadaqāt* from *zakāh*. This would imply that the latter was already established as an obligatory contribution, presumably at the rate (prescribed in the later law-books) of one-fortieth of the annual revenue in money or kind. It is to be exacted from all who, whether voluntarily or under constraint, enter into the brotherhood of Islam; but it is not a tax. Rather is it to be regarded as a loan made to God, which He will repay many-fold. Free-will offerings are also a means of expiating offences, and are to be given to relations, orphans, the needy, and travellers (ii, v. 211). The objects upon which the revenue from *zakāh* is to be spent are defined (in Sūra ix, v. 60, though the term used here is *sadaqāt*) as: the poor, the needy, those employed in its collection, those who are to be conciliated, slaves and prisoners, debtors, wayfarers, and the 'Way of God' (see section ix below).

(vii) *Fasting* was prescribed at Medina 'as it was prescribed for those who were before you' (ii, vv. 179–183). It is laid down that the month of Ramadān, the ninth month of the lunar year, is to be observed as a period of fasting, with complete abstinence from food and drink during the hours of daylight. Those sick or on a journey at this time are exempted, but must make compensation by fasting an equal number of days later. In addition, fasting is included amongst the expiations for various offences.

(viii) *Pilgrimage (Hajj)* to the Sacred Mosque at Mecca was also definitely regulated at Medina. The traditional days in Dhu'l-Hijja (the twelfth month) and the traditional ceremonies of going in circuit round the Kaaba, running between the two small eminences of Safa and Marwa in the vicinity, assembling on the ninth day of the month at the hill of Arafāt (some twelve miles east of Mecca), offering sacrifices of sheep and camels at Minā on the way back to Mecca—all these were retained and prescribed in the Koran. Other traditional usages, including the kissing of the Black Stone set in one of the walls of the Kaaba, and the stoning of the pillars representing the Devil in the vicinity of Minā, though not mentioned explicitly, were observed by Mohammed in his pilgrimages, and so were incorporated into the Muslim rite.

As before praying the worshipper must be ritually clean, so also before making the Pilgrimage the worshipper must be in a state of ritual consecration (*ihrām*). This involves firstly the shaving of the head and the discarding of

[2] It is a curious fact that circumcision, though generally regarded as obligatory upon Muslims, is not mentioned in the Koran.

ordinary clothing before entering the territory of Mecca, putting on instead two plain unsewn sheets, so as to leave the head and face uncovered. Thereafter the pilgrim may not hunt, cut his hair or nails, use perfume, cover his head (except in the case of women), or have sexual relations, until after the sacrifice at Minā, when he resumes his normal condition of life.

Although the Pilgrimage constitutes a religious obligation on every Muslim, the obligation is explicitly limited by possession of the necessary means and the physical possibility of getting to Mecca. With this exception, the duties summed up in the four preceding paragraphs constitute the four universally obligatory 'acts of devotion', and together with the *shahāda* or profession of faith form the five 'Pillars of the Faith'.

(ix) *Jihād in the Way of God*. In addition to these obligations, however, the Koran further enjoins Believers in many passages to 'strive in the Way of God'. The duty is formulated in general terms in Sūra ii, vv. 186 sqq., between the regulations for the Fast and the Pilgrimage.

Fight in the Way of God against those who fight against you, but do not commit aggression. . . . Slay them wheresoever ye find them, and expel them from whence they have expelled you, for sedition is more grievous than slaying. . . . fight against them until sedition is no more and allegiance is rendered to God alone; but if they make an end, then no aggression save against the evildoers.

While the context suggests that these verses refer primarily to Mohammed's Meccan opponents, two later passages draw a distinction between warfare against the pagans on the one hand and against Jews and Christians on the other.

When the Sacred Months[3] are over, kill those who ascribe partners to God wheresoever ye find them; seize them, encompass them, and ambush them; then if they repent and observe prayer and pay the alms, let them go their way (ix, v. 5).

Fight against those who believe not in God nor in the Last Day, who prohibit not what God and His Apostle have prohibited, and who refuse allegiance to the True Faith from among those who have received the Book, until they humbly pay tribute out of hand (ix, v. 29).

As for those who are slain on the Way of God, they are not dead but 'living in the presence of their Lord, their needs supplied, rejoicing in the bounty which God hath given them' (iii, vv. 163–4).

(x) Besides these major issues of doctrine, ritual, and obligation, the Koran contains also a large body of religious and ethical teaching and of legal injunctions. Wine, swine's flesh, gambling, and usury, for example, are forbidden, along with a number of superstitious usages of the pagan Arabs and the making of images or representations. Dowries, divorce, the guardianship

---

[3]The Sacred Months were the seventh, eleventh, twelfth, and first months of the Arabian year, when by immemorial custom no raiding or fighting was done.

of orphans, and inheritance are regulated in detail. Penalties are laid down for certain crimes, such as stealing, homicide, and murder, as well as for a few minor offences. Slavery is accepted as an institution, but certain limitations are placed on the rights of owners over slaves and their good treatment is enjoined. Fraud, perjury, and slander are repeatedly and severely condemned, and rules of social behaviour are laid down in several passages. . . .

In the light of this summary of Koranic religion, some conclusions may be reached on the relation of Islam to Judaism and Christianity and the disputed question of its originality. If by originality is meant an entirely new system of ideas about God and humanity, the relation between them, and the spiritual significance of the universe, then Mohammed's intuition was in no way original. But originality in such a sense has neither place nor value in monotheistic religion. All religion has developed by a gradual process of revaluation of existing ideas, as religious thinkers and seers in later genrations have reinterpreted elements present in the thought of earlier generations, giving them fuller significance or setting them in a fresh relation to the common structure of religious thinking and experience.

So far from professing to bring a new revelation Mohammed insisted that the Scripture given to him was but a restatement of the faith delivered to the Prophets before him, confirming their Scriptures and itself confirmed by them. Yet the originality of Islam is none the less real, in that it represents a further step in the logical (if not philosophical) evolution of monotheistic religion. Its monotheism, like that of the Hebrew Prophets, is absolute and unconditioned, but with this it combines the universalism of Christianity. On the one hand, it rejects the nationalist taint from which Judaism as a religion did not succeed in freeing itself; for Islam never identified itself with the Arabs, although at times Arabs have identified themselves with it. On the other hand, it is distinguished from Christianity, not so much (in spite of all outward appearances) by its repudiation of the trinitarian concept of the Unity of God, as by its rejection of the soteriology of Christian doctrine and the relics of the old nature cults which survived in the rites and practices of the Christian Church. . . .

In thus setting man as it were face to face with God, without any mediating spiritual or personal elements, Islam necessarily emphasized the contrast between them. In spite of the passages of mystical intuition in the Koran, the dogmatic derived from it could not but start from the postulate of the opposition between God and man, and (as a necessary corollary) the equality of all men in their creaturely relation to God. In this stark contrast lies the original tension of Islam. And however the concrete and literalist minds of the desert-men may have conceived the power and majesty of God, the pleasures of Paradise, and the terrors of Hell, the effect of this tension in rousing religious minds to a sense of responsibility is proved by the explosive and creative force which it manifested century after century.

Islam and Christianity

Born in India, Ameer Ali* (1849–1928) was graduated from Calcutta University, and became Judge of the Calcutta High Court. In 1885 he went to England, where he was appointed to the Judicial Committee of the Privy Council. His very influential *The Spirit of Islam* (originally entitled *The Life and Teachings of Mohammed*) was published in 1891. That book, a forcefully written review of ideals and theology, "furnished the awakening political consciousness of Muslims with the reasoned basis of self-esteem which it required in the face of the Western world."† Similarly, the essay which follows is a comparison of Islamic and Christian doctrines in which Ali's purpose is to demonstrate that it is the *Muslim* position that is philosophically sound.

Ever since it seated itself on the throne of the Caesars, Christianity has claimed to exercise, and has in fact exercised, a potent influence over large masses of mankind. Within certain limits it has furthered civilisation and the development of humanitarian ideas. And although its humanity has been at all times of an exclusive character, even in its mediaeval phase it produced many generous and noble natures. Whilst it burnt, regardless of age and sex, witches and heretics, it gave birth to a Las Casas and a St. Xavier. In spite of the inroads of science and freethought into the domains of orthodoxy, its demand to be regarded as the sole means of salvation is great and persistent. How its principles, tenets, and doctrines appeal to the religious consciousness of outsiders must always form an interesting subject of study.

I propose, therefore, to examine . . . the dogmas and ethics of Christianity from the standpoint of a cognate religion. The following pages give frank expression to the Islâmic views, without implying the smallest disparagement or disrespect to the Christian faith or its professors. In common with all Moslems, I entertain the profoundest veneration for the Prophet of Nazareth, and I should be grieved if my remarks were taken in a spirit other than philosophical, having for its sole object the elucidation of the thesis entrusted to me.

Both Islâm and Christianity have identical aims and ideals; both agree in their general principles. Even in matters of dogma the agreement is often

---

*His name is spelled here as it was in the 1906 issue of the *Hibbert Journal*, from which this essay was taken. In more recent editions of his work, his name is more often given as Sayyid Amīr Alī.

†H. A. R. Gibb, *Mohammedanism* (New York: Oxford University Press, 1962), p. 182.

Reprinted from Ameer Ali, "Christianity from the Islamic Standpoint," *Hibbert Journal,* Vol. IV, No. 2 (January, 1906). By permission of the Hibbert Trust. Editor's title. Notes have been renumbered.

astonishing. The belief in "one living and true God, everlasting, without body, parts or passions, of infinite wisdom and goodness, the Maker of all things visible and invisible," is common to both; they are agreed that the immutable laws which regulate human relations emanate from a divine source. The orthodox Moslem, like the orthodox Christian, accepts Jesus as the Messiah of the Jews, and even designates him as "the Spirit of God." And what is most noteworthy is that they both believe in the mystery of the "Immaculate Conception." And yet an impassable gulf, as it seems, of bitterness and misunderstanding divides the two religions so closely allied to each other, and makes all communion in the work of humanitarian development well-nigh impossible.

To the question what can be the cause of this divergence, the answer is not difficult. It consists primarily in the Christian dogma of the Sonship of Jesus—that he was "the only begotten Son of God."

The Moslem denies that there is any warrant for this doctrine in the teachings of the Nazarene Prophet. He asserts that the idea is borrowed from foreign sources and interpolated with his sayings. The Arabian Prophet regards the very notion as preposterous, that Jesus claimed divine worship: "It beseemeth not a man," warns the Koran, "that God should give him the Scriptures and the wisdom and the gift of prophecy, and then he should say to his followers, 'Be ye worshippers of mine as well as of God,' but rather be ye perfect in things pertaining to God, since ye know the Scriptures and have studied deep."[1] The conception that God should have issue is viewed with a feeling akin to horror. "They say the God of mercy hath begotten a son. Now have ye uttered a grievous thing; and it wanteth but little that the heavens should be torn open and the earth cleave asunder, and the mountains fall down, for that they attribute children unto the Merciful; whereas it is not meet for God to have children. Verily there is none in heaven or earth but shall approach the Merciful as His servant."[2]

It is an article of faith among Moslems of all shades of opinion that the Christian Gospels in their present shape give an imperfect and erroneous view of the life and preachings of Jesus, and that his sayings have been garbled and tampered with according to the idiosyncrasies of individual compilers or the environments of the times and the requirements of factions and sects. That this view is not altogether unwarranted is amply borne out by the results of modern Biblical criticism, which shows how age after age everything human, everything not purely ideal, has been smoothed away from the adored image of an incarnate God, "the essentially pathetic story of Jesus has been converted into a fairy-tale," and his life so surrounded with myths that it is now impossible for us to know what he really was and did.

[1]Sura iii. 7.
[2]Sura xix. 91–94.

The religious consciousness of the Islâmist repels all idea of associating another in the worship of God. "Your God is one God, there is no God but He, the Most Merciful. In the creation of heaven and earth and the alternation of night and day, and in the ship which saileth on the sea . . . ; and in the rain which God sendeth from heaven, quickening again the dead earth . . . and in the change of winds and the clouds balanced between heaven and earth, are signs to people of understanding."[3] "God, there is no God but He, the Living, the Eternal. . . . Whatever is in heaven or earth is His. Who can intercede with Him but by His own permission? . . . He alone is God, God the Eternal. He begetteth not and He is not begotten; there is none like unto Him."[4]

Again, the idea of an "Intercessor" between God and man, either to purge him of his sins or to reconcile him to an angry Deity, is repugnant to the Islâmic conception. The relations between the Creator and His creatures are such that all human beings can obtain "nearness" to Him by the practice of self-sacrifice, self-denial, and obedience to His commands. If they sin, they can obtain forgiveness by appealing direct to Him and by *"abandoning their evil ways."*

Nor can the Moslem reconcile the humility of spirit which pervades most of the sayings of Jesus, even as they have reached us, with the pretensions that are often attributed to him. Whilst Islâm accepts Jesus as one of the greatest teachers of the world, the Messiah of the Jews, sent to regenerate and reform a backsliding race, it regards him strictly as a human personality. The "Immaculate Conception" is the only mystery it recognises.

. . .

Thoroughly acquainted with the [Hebrew] poet-prophets, whom he frequently quotes, Jesus was naturally imbued with the Messianic hopes and aspirations which filled the air in which he lived and moved. The "visions" of Daniel and the preachings of Yahya (John), his immediate predecessor, could not but make a deep impression on a sensitive and mystical mind. The whole atmosphere was charged with the expectation of the coming Messiah, and all the conditions, social and political, inspired the Teacher with the faith that he was destined to fulfil in his person the presagings of the nation's seers. Thus does the voice of God speak to the souls of His servants.

There is ample warrant for the Islâmic belief that Jesus considered himself as the Messiah of his people, and his answer to the piteous appeal of the Canaanite woman would indicate that he regarded his mission as exclusively confined to the Jews. But it is by no means proven that he ever *claimed* to be the "Son of God"; whilst the discrepancy between the statements of Matthew and Mark regarding the answer of Peter to the question put by Jesus

[3]Sura ii. 158–160.
[4]Sura cxii.

in the neighbourhood of Caesarea Philippi suggest a doubt if the apostle ever called him "the son of the living God."

According to Islâm, the conception of Jesus as to his own personality, when divested of the "Aberglaube" of his followers, was singularly free from exaggeration.[5] His idea of the "Fatherhood" of God embraced all humanity. Even if it were assumed that he made use of the expressions attributed to him, do they prove that he claimed to be "the only begotten Son of the Father"?

. . .

It is not the "unique life of Jesus" which makes him, in the Moslem mind, one of the greatest landmarks in the history of religious development. It is the message he brought to humanity—the message the Almighty entrusts to His chosen ones only at intervals, to recall mankind from the worship of their passions, symbolised in the idols of their infancy.

The Moslem belief probably is in accord with that of the primitive Christians—of the Ebionites, "the.sect of the poor," to whom Jesus had preached and among whom he had lived. It has nothing in common with Pauline Christianity. To Paul, Jew by birth, Greek by education, who had never felt the influence of the great Prophet, is due the present divergence between Islâm and Christianity.[6] He took up the idea of the man at whose martyrdom he had assisted, and spread it abroad. The educated classes had been trained by Alexandrian philosophy to the conception of a Demiurgus between God and man; Syria and Palestine were permeated by the Essenic doctrine of the Angel-Messiah borrowed from the further East; the blood of Stephen the martyr blossomed into the faith of Christianity, and his defence before the "council" became the fountain of Pauline inspiration.

So far from being an angel or the Son of God, the great Teacher, in the sublimity of his character, like all prophets, was eminently human. His *humanity* was one of the most attractive features of his character. He was neither free from the human frailty of anger,[7] nor that excess of religious zeal which borders on exclusiveness.

Although the Moslem does not accept the doctrine of "Sonship," his veneration for the mother of Jesus is profound. She is regarded as one of the purest and holiest of women, only two others taking rank with her—Khadîja, the wife of the Prophet of Islâm, and Fâtima, his daughter, "the mother of the Syeds," the nobility of Islâm.

. . .

[5] When a man called him "Good Master," Jesus replied, "Why dost thou call me good? None is good save one, even God." This is an instance of his conception regarding his own personality, that he was no more than a man.

[6] "And straightway he preached Christ in the synagogues, that he is the Son of God" (Acts ix. 20).

[7] His anger with the Phraisees and Sadducees who had come to ask for a "sign" was not without cause; but the curse on the fig-tree seems strange.

The Moslems, in common with the Docetic Christians, do not believe that Jesus died on the cross. The Docetic belief regarding his disappearance is more consistent with his Sonship than the orthodox doctrine. For it seems somewhat difficult to understand that the Father would allow his beloved Son to die on the cross without bringing about a convulsion of nature. "These Christians believe that the man who suffered on the cross was a different person from the divine Christ, who escaped from the hands of his persecutors, and went away to the regions whence he had come."[8] According to the Moslem traditions, the Jewish Messiah was at the last moment saved by divine agency from an ignominious death. The orthodox belief is that he was translated to heaven, whilst the rationalist explains the disappearance on more intelligible hypotheses.

The story relating to the crucifixion and resurrection of Jesus in the Christian Gospels is poetical but hardly convincing. It reads more like a myth than a historical account. We know of the intense desire of Pilate, whom Tertullian calls a Christian at heart, to save Jesus; we know that outside the circle of his disciples he had many sympathisers; we are told also that a preternatural gloom overshadowed the earth at the most awful part of the drama. There is no inherent improbability in the belief that the innocent escaped and the guilty suffered. And this probability grows into a conviction when we consider the circumstantial account given in the Gospel of Luke, how after the Resurrection Jesus called for and partook of food. "And as they thus spake," says the chronicler, "Jesus himself stood in the midst of them, and saith unto them, Peace be unto you. But they were terrified and affrighted, and supposed that they had seen a spirit. And he said unto them, Why are ye troubled? and why do thoughts arise in your hearts? Behold my hands and my feet, that it is myself: handle me, and see; for a spirit hath not flesh and bones, as ye see me have. And when he had thus spoken, he showed them his hands and his feet. And while they yet believed not for joy, and wondered, he said unto them, Have ye here any meat? And they gave him a piece of a broiled fish, and of an honey-comb. And he took it, and did eat before them." From this it is quite clear that "the Resurrection" was corporeal. Then, the Moslem asks, what became of the wounds Jesus is said to have received on the cross, which caused his death?

The accounts in the several chronicles regarding "the Resurrection" are so discrepant that they may safely be treated as "unhistorical," and the stories of the women relating what they saw at the tomb, as the Apostles treated them, "idle tales"[9]

The rationalistic Moslem belief that Jesus was rescued, if not by his lukewarm disciples, by persons who were in sympathy with him and revered

[8]*The Spirit of Islâm*, p. 57.
[9]Luke xxiv. 11.

his character, is based on some solid facts. He was apparently kept concealed for a time from his enemies. But the atmosphere of Jerusalem was fraught with the greatest danger. Accordingly, after giving his final instructions, the Prophet betook himself to the regions of the East, where, safe from Jewish persecution, he could peacefully pursue his great mission, and where he eventually died.[10]

In order to reconcile the two conflicting theories—the Sonship of Jesus with his death on the cross—Pauline Christianity formulated the doctrine of Atonement, which again is based on the dogma that "mankind sinned in Adam."[11] Islâm absolutely repudiates the doctrine of original sin. Hereditary depravity and "natural sinfulness" are emphatically denied. Every child of man is born pure; every departure in after life from the path of truth and rectitude is due to education. "Every child of man," declared the Prophet of Islâm, "is born religiously constituted; it is his parents who make him afterwards a Jew, a Christian, or a Sabean. . . . Every human being has two inclinations—one prompting him to good and impelling him thereto, and the other prompting him to evil, and thereto impelling him"; but "the Godly assistance is nigh, and he who asks for the help of God in contending with the evil promptings of his own heart obtains it." The Moslem cannot naturally conceive that the Almighty Creator of the universe, the All-good, the All-wise, should create a world abounding in sin; that, not successful in rooting it out, He should send His "sole begotten Son" to offer himself as a sacrifice to save mankind from eternal perdition. It seems somewhat absurd that, because the first man was unreasonable or disobedient enough to eat the forbidden fruit of the tree of knowledge, he should not only be expelled from the Garden of Eden, but an awful doom should be passed on all his posterity, from which they would not be extricated until the Son of God should sacrifice himself.[12] To the Moslem mind, it is incomprehensible that, if the Father accepted the life of the Son as a forfeit for the sins of mankind, the bulk of humanity should still not be exempt from divine wrath, nor those who believe in the Son be free from sin.

The Moslem believes that the idea of atonement in Christianity is a survival of the conception which prevailed among all the nations of antiquity, and which is in vogue even now among some races, that an angry God can only be appeased by the "sacrifice" of human beings, particularly someone especially dear or especially precious. The Islâmist does not believe that Jesus

[10]A recent Moslem writer asserts that the tomb of a prophet called Nabi Isa is still pointed out in the country north of Cashmere.

[11]Romans v. 12.

[12]The writer is aware that many modern Christians do not hold these doctrines in the form described above. At the same time, these doctrines remain unaltered in the official formularies of the Christian religion, and so long as they remain there, Moslems will be justified in taking them as truly representative of Christianity.

ever wished his followers to understand his death as a sacrificial offering for the sins of mankind in general or *their* sins in particular. . . .

. . .

The doctrine of "justification by faith," an important feature in Protestantism, may be said to derive support from the sayings of Jesus as reported in the Christian Gospels. Literally construed, they would convey the idea that, so long as people believe in him, conduct is immaterial. And this view Paul has interwoven into his system as an integral part of Christianity.[13]

The Prophet of Islâm declared the present life to be a seedground of the future. To work in all humility of spirit for the human good, to strive with all energy to approach the perfection of the All-perfect, is the essential principle if Islâm. Each man will be judged at the Great Account by the work he has done in this life. "Verily those who believe (Moslems) and those who are Jews, Christians or Sabeans, whoever hath faith in God and the last day, and *worketh that which is right and good,* for them shall be the reward with their Lord."[14]

"To every man we have given a law and way . . . and if God had pleased He would have made you all one people (people of one religion). But He hath done otherwise that He might try you in that which He hath severally given unto you; wherefore strive in good works. Unto God shall ye return, and He will tell that concerning which ye disagree." "There is no piety in turning the face to the east or the west, but in placing trust in God and in *doing good.*" The Moslem naturally regards the doctrine of "justification by faith" as disastrous to human morality.

In this connection arises the question, what did Jesus actually teach? The Islâmic belief is that his mission, like that of Mohammed, was to re-enunciate the eternal truths of God, and to recall humanity to the inevitable track of spiritual evolution. His ethical precepts, whether direct in form or dressed in parables, are thus common to all higher religions. There is no question of borrowing from one source or another, for God imparts His truths to all He chooses for His work. Jesus was thus not the first to impress on the conscience of mankind the duties of self-sacrifice, self-abnegation, devotion to God, love of humanity. There were others before him, as others after him, to preach the practice of peace, humility, charity, good works, submission to God's will, forgiveness of injuries, and the denial of self. . . .

. . .

. . . filial devotion and reverence to parents are inculcated in the strongest terms in the Koran. "Defer humbly to your parents; with humility and tenderness say: O Lord, be merciful to them even as they brought me up when

[13]But to him that worketh not, but believeth on him that justifieth the ungodly, his faith is reckoned for righteousness" (Rom. iv. 5).
[14]Koran, Sura v. 73.

I was helpless." "Moreover, we have enjoined on man to show kindness to his parents. With pain his mother beareth him; with pain she bringeth him forth; and he saith: O my Lord! stir me up to be grateful for thy favours wherewith thou hast favoured me and my parents, and to do good works which shall please thee, and prosper me in my offspring: for to thee am I turned, and am resigned to thy will."

To the Moslem, therefore, the attitude of Jesus towards his mother—the mother who had so tenderly watched over him in infancy and youth, and whose maternal devotion shone forth at the last crisis of his life—when she, accompanied by his brothers, came to see him,[15] is utterly incomprehensible, and only explainable by an exalted enthusiasm in his own mission.

. . .

Withal, the Moslems regard Jesus as one of the greatest moral teachers of the world, and love and revere him as such. The Jews had turned the Levitical law, with all its minutiae, into a fetish: Jesus redeemed them from its bondage. He was the first among his nation to teach in the truest sense that the kernel was of greater value than the shell, the spirit than the letter. In an age when hardness of heart was a virtue, and poverty a crime, he preached charity and love, compassion to the poor, pity for the orphan. He taught the sacredness of truth, justice and purity, the blessedness of humility. He widened the narrow horizon of Judaism, and raised its ideal. His messengership was essentially a link in the chain of man's spiritual development. . . .

. . .

In view of the denunciations of the Nazarene Prophet against the rich, and the promise of the kingdom of heaven to the poor and the humble, the Moslem fails to understand the feverish pursuit of wealth in the Western world, the devotion to luxury, the unregulated dispensing of charity, the callousness to distress and suffering, the contempt for the virtues which Jesus inculcated —patience, meekness, and humility of spirit; or why the system which styled its founder "the Prince of Peace" should not be able to suppress war and rapine among his followers. The fanaticism which threw its dark shadow over the whole of Europe for centuries, and made holocausts of innumerable beings, was not inconsistent with the religious sentiment of the times. How is it, asks the Moslem, that modern Christianity, with its philosophic ideals, cannot root out the evil of racial exclusiveness?

. . .

The key to the problem may perhaps be found in the saying of Jesus that he had come "to fulfil and not to destroy." Did he intend that his precepts were to be taken as supplementary to the Mosaic Law? If that was the meaning, it had become impossible, for the world had moved on and made difficult the observance of the old directions, even with the solvent of Christian doctrines.

[15]Matt. xii. 46–50

If his teachings constitute a new system, then it is permissible for the Moslem to think that the great Prophet left it incomplete, and that his holy work remained unfulfilled until another Master with a larger grasp of human needs and human limitations arose to convey afresh to mankind the message of God.

Moslems do not recognise that modern Christianity, overladen with Greek philosophy and Pauline mysticism, represents the religion Jesus in fact taught. They consider that Islâm represents true Christianity. They do not think that Jesus, who prayed in the wilderness and on the hillside, in the huts of the peasants, in the humble abodes of the fishermen, furnished any warrant for the gorgeousness of modern Christian worship, with all the accessories which beguile the mind, mystify the intellect, and thus divert the human heart from the worship of the great God towards a symbol and a type.

seyyed hossein nasr

Sufism and the Integration of Man

Seyyed Hossein Nasr (1933–   ) received his early education in Tehran, but came to the United States to study physics at the Massachusetts Institute of Technology and to earn a Ph.D. from Harvard. He has served as Aga Khan Professor of Islamic Studies at the American University of Beirut and Professor of the History of Science and Philosophy at Tehran University. Currently he is Dean of the Faculty of Arts and Letters at Tehran University. Among his books are *Three Muslim Sages, An Introduction to Islamic Cosmological Doctrines, Ideals and Realities of Islam, The Encounter of Man and Nature,* and *Sufi Essays.*

Islam is the religion of unity (*tawhîd*) and all veritable aspects of Islamic doctrine and practice reflect this central and cardinal principle. The *Sharî'ah** itself is a vast network of injunctions and regulations which relate the world of multiplicity inwardly to a single Centre which conversely is reflected in the multiplicity of the circumference. In the same way Islamic art seeks always to relate the multiplicity of forms, shapes and colours to the One, to the Centre and Origin, thereby reflecting *tawhîd* in its own way in the world of forms with which it is concerned.

Sufism, being the marrow of the bone or the inner dimension of the Islamic revelation, is the means *par excellence* whereby *tawhîd* is achieved. All Muslims believe in Unity as expressed in the most universal sense possible by the *Shahâdah, Lâ ilâha ill'Allâh.*† But it is only the Sufi, he who has realized the mysteries of *tawhîd,* who knows what this assertion means. It is only he who sees God everywhere.

In fact the whole programme of Sufism, of the spiritual way of *Târiqah,*‡ is to free man from the prison of multiplicity, to cure him from hypocrisy and to make him whole, for it is only in being whole that man can become holy. Men confess to one God but actually live and act as if there were many gods. They thus suffer from the cardinal sin of 'polytheism' or *shirk,* from a hypocrisy whereby on one level they profess one thing and on another act according to something else. Sufism seeks to bring this *shirk* into the open and thereby to

*The Divine Law, revealed by God.—R.E.
†The profession of faith, There is but one God.—R.E.
‡The Path.—R.E.

Seyyed Hossein Nasr, "Sufism and the Integration of Man." From Seyyed Hossein Nasr, *Sufi Essays* (1972). Reprinted by permission of the publishers, George Allen & Unwin, Ltd. Acknowledgment is also made to State University of New York Press.

cure the soul of this deadly malady. Its aim is to make man whole again as he was in the Edenic state. In other words the goal of Sufism is the integration of man in all the depth and breadth of his existence, in all the amplitude which is included in the nature of the universal man (al-insân al-kâmil).

Man, being the vice-regent of God on earth (khalîfah) and the theatre wherein the Divine Names and Qualities are reflected, can reach felicity only by remaining faithful to this nature or by being truly himself. And this in turn implies that he must become integrated. God is one and so man must become whole in order to become one. To be dissipated and compartmentalized, to be lost in the never-ending play of mental images and concepts, or psychic tensions and forces, is to be removed from that state of wholeness which our inner state demands of us. Many today would like to be sophisticated at all costs, even preferring to be sophisticated and enter hell rather than be simple and go to paradise; nevertheless, the state of simplicity is closer than that of sophistication to the innocence and purity which is the condition of celestial beatitude, for as Christ said we must be like children in order to enter heaven.

The end of Sufism is the attainment of this state of purity and wholeness, not through negation of intelligence, as is often the case in the kind of piety fostered by certain modern religious movements, but through the integration of each element of one's being into its own proper centre. Man is composed of body, mind and spirit and each needs to be integrated on its own level. Although the body is the most outward aspect of man, having its own objective existence and mode of action, it is not the greatest obstacle on the path of integration. The domain with which man identifies himself and in which he is most often caught up is the labyrinth of incongruent images and thoughts, or the intermediate mental plane including the psychological forces at play at this level. That is why Sufism turns first of all to the problems of this vast intermediate world that is so difficult to harness and bring under control.

Men are usually either of a contemplative or an active nature, or from another point of view they predominantly either think or make, but in modern times the balance has been tilted heavily in favour of action over contemplation, thus bringing about the disequilibrium which characterizes the modern world. Since it is meant for men of both types of spiritual capability, Sufism has provided the means whereby both groups of men can begin to integrate their mental activity. The person who is prone to thinking and learning and who wants to know the causes of things can only begin to follow a spiritual way if he is presented with a doctrine of the nature of reality, wherein different domains are interrelated and his need for causality is fulfilled. Sufi doctrine, which is precisely such a doctrine and which must be distinguished from philosophy as understood today, is not the fruit of an attempt by a particular mind to devise a closed system with which to embrace the whole of reality; it is not the objectivization of the limitations of a particular thinker as most philosophy has latterly become. In fact it is not so much the fruit of thinking as of being. It is the vision, *theoria* in its original sense and as still understood in Orthodox theology, of reality by one who has gained this vision through a new mode of existence.

Sufi doctrine is presented to the man with a bewildered mind as a theoretical knowledge of the structure of reality and of man's place in it. It is itself the fruit of the spiritual vision of seers and sages who, having achieved the state of wholeness, have been given a vision of the whole. And in turn it is the means whereby others can be led to wholeness. It thus stands at the beginning and at the end of the spiritual path. The role of doctrine in the integration of man can hardly be overemphasized, especially for modern man, who is over-cerebral, thinking too much and often wrongly. The maze of contradictory assertions, the ambiguities and intellectual snares that characterize modern thought, are the greatest obstacle to the integration of the mind and can only be cured through the purifying effect of Sufi metaphysical doctrine which washes away the dross of contingency and multiplicity. In traditional Islamic society doctrine is usually taught step by step along with practical methods to match the gradual advancement upon the path. Nor is there such an acute need for it at the beginning because the *Sharî'ah* and traditional teachings about the nature of things satisfy in most cases the needs of the mind for knowledge and of the imagination for images and forms. But in the confusion of the modern world Sufi doctrine is a *sine qua non* for the integration of man's mind and being, preparing the ground for the actual realization of the verities whose theoretical knowledge the doctrine conveys.

Sufi doctrine consists of metaphysics, cosmology, psychology and an eschatology that is often linked up with psychology and occasionally with metaphysics. The metaphysical aspect of the doctrine delineates firstly the nature of Reality, the Oneness of the Divine Essence which alone 'is' in the absolute sense and prior to which there is nothing; then the theophany of the Essence through the Divine Names and Qualities and through the determination of the different states of being; and finally the nature of man as the total theophany (*tajallî*) of the Names and Qualities. The doctrine of unity or *tawḥîd* forms the axis of all Sufi metaphysics and it is in fact the misunderstanding of this cardinal doctrine that has caused so many orientalists to accuse Sufism of pantheism. Sufi doctrine does not assert that God is the world but that the world to the degree that it is real cannot be completely other than God; were it to be so it would become a totally independent reality, a deity of its own, and would destroy the absoluteness and the Oneness that belong to God alone.

Sufi metaphysics, moreover, delineates the intermediate levels of existence between the corporeal world and God, levels of reality which Cartesian dualism removed from the world-view of modern European philosophy, leaving an impoverished picture of reality which remains to this day a formidable obstacle to the integration of contemporary man's mind and indeed of his being. The intermediate planes of existence are precisely those which relate the physical world to the purely transcendental archetypes and enable man to escape the puerile debate between idealism and realism, each of which has inherited a portion of reality as segmented and divided by the scissors of Descartes' *cogito ergo sum* and its consequent dualism.

As for cosmology, Sufi doctrine does not expound details of physics or chemistry but a total science of the cosmos through which man discovers where he is in the multiple structured cosmic reality and where he should be going. The goal of the spiritual man is to journey through the cosmos and ultimately beyond it. Sufi cosmology provides the plan with the aid of which man can get his bearings for this journey. It is a map of the Universe which he must possess if he is to pass through its dangerous pitfalls and precipices. Sufi cosmology thus deals, not with the quantitative aspects of things as is the case in modern science, but with their qualitative and symbolic aspects. It casts a light upon things so that they become worthy subjects of contemplation, lucid and transparent, losing their habitual opaqueness and darkness.

Sufism was able to integrate many medieval sciences such as Hermeticism into its perspective precisely because these sciences reflect the unicity of nature and the interrelatedness of things; inasmuch as they deal with the symbolic and qualitative nature of objects and phenomena they accord well with the perspective of Sufism. Moreover, since Sufism is based on experience (the one kind of experience which in fact modern man who boasts so much about his experimental outlook hardly ever attempts to undergo) it has found it possible to cultivate both natural and mathematical sciences in accordance with its own perspective. The history of Islamic science bears witness to many an outstanding Muslim scientist who was a Sufi. However, the primary function of Sufi cosmology and sciences of nature is to provide a prototype of the cosmos for the traveller upon the path (*sâlik*) and to demonstrate the interrelation between all things and that unicity of all cosmic existence which nature displays so vividly if only one were to take the necessary care to observe it.

As for psychology, it must be remembered that Sufism contains a complete method of curing the illnesses of the soul and in fact succeeds where so many modern psychiatric and psychoanalytical methods, with all their extravagant claims, fail. That is because only the higher can know the lower; only the spirit can know the psyche and illuminate its dark corners and crevasses. Only he whose soul has become integrated and illuminated has the right and the wherewithal to cure the souls of others. Anyone else who claims to have this right is either ignorant of the factors involved or, as is more usually the case, an imposter.

As for the doctrinal aspect of Sufi psychology, the human soul is there presented as a substance that possesses different faculties and modes of existence, separated yet united by a single axis that traverses all these modes and planes. There is, moreover, a close link between this psychology and cosmology so that man comes to realize the cosmic dimension of his being, not in a quantitative but in a qualitative and symbolic sense. Moreover, this cosmic correspondence objectivizes the inner structure of the psyche, thereby releasing the soul from its own knots, illuminating its darkest aspects, and displaying to the traveller of the spiritual path the manifold traps lying in his way, in the inner journey of the soul toward its own Centre. The descent to the 'inferno' is the means whereby the soul recovers its lost and hidden elements in dark and lethal depths before being able to make the ascent to 'Purgatory' and 'Paradise'. Sufi psychological doctrine lays this scheme before the adept, in both its microcosmic and macrocosmic aspects, before the actual journey is undertaken. But even this theoretical presentation has the effect of integrating the mental and psychic plane of the person who is able fully to comprehend it.

Eschatology likewise has both a macrocosmic and microcosmic aspect, the latter being what most immediately and directly concerns the adept. From this point of view the posthumous becoming of man is no more than a continuation of the journey on this earth to another level of existence, one which, moreover, can already be undertaken here and now by those who, following the advice of the Prophet, . . . 'die before you die', have already died to the life of the carnal soul (al-nafs al-ammârah) and been resurrected in the spiritual world. Sufi eschatological doctrines reveal to man the extension of his being beyond the empirical, earthly self with which most human beings identify themselves. These doctrines are therefore again a means whereby the wholeness of the human state in all its amplitude and depth is made known, preparing the ground for the actual realization of the total possibilities of the human condition, a realization which implies the complete integration of man.

The aspects of Sufi doctrine thus delineated address those whose intellectual needs demand such explanation and whose vocation is to think and to know. As for others whose function is to make and to do, in traditional Islamic society Sufism has succeeded in providing means of integration for this group by wedding its symbols to those of the arts and crafts. Through the process of making things the artisan has been able to achieve spiritual perfection and inner integration thanks to the bond created between the guilds (asnâf and futuwwât) and the Sufi orders. The transformations of colour, shape and other accidents that materials undergo in the hands of the artisan came to possess a symbolic significance connected with the transformation of the human soul. And in this same sphere alchemy, which is at once a symbolic science of material forms and a symbolic expression of the spiritual and psychological transformations of the soul, became the link between Sufism and art, and its language the means whereby the maker and the artisan has been given the possibility of integrating his outward and inward life, his work and his religious activity. In this way, as far as the question of the integration of the mind is concerned, the traditional crafts and the methods connected with them came to play a role for the craftsman analogous to that of Sufi doctrine for the contemplative and the thinker.

It may now be asked, what about the contemporary man who is neither metaphysically inclined to understand Sufi doctrine nor practises a traditional craft possessing a spiritual significance and efficacy? Or what about a man who lives in a society where the injunctions of the *Sharî'ah* are not applied and where the mind is therefore likely to be much more dissipated and dispersed? To such questions it must be answered that Sufism possesses the means of integrating man wherever he happens to be, provided man is willing to accept its teachings and discipline. In the cases cited above, methods of meditation are applied which in the absence of a coherent traditional ambience nevertheless enable the final and total integration of man, which includes not only his mind, but his whole being comprising also the body and the psychic and vital forces. Precisely because man is not a dismembered mind but a whole being whereof the mind is an element, doctrine, despite its extreme importance, is not enough: there must also be realization though the practice of a spiritual method. Between the theoretical understanding of the doctrine which integrates the mind and its realization in one's whole being there is a world of difference. In fact without an actual spiritual method too much study of Sufi metaphysics can only cause a further separation between the mind and the rest of one's nature and so make more difficult the final integration of man's total being. That is why doctrine and method are always combined together in all integral traditional spiritual paths like a pair of legs with which man must undertake his spiritual journey.

The role of spiritual method in the integration of man is an essential one, because it is only through the Divine Presence and the *barakah*§ contained in the methods of Sufism and going back to the origin of the Quranic revelation itself that all of the dispersed elements in man can be brought together. Ordinary man is forever moving away from the centre of his being towards the periphery, dispersing himself in the multiplicity of this world like waves that break up into a thousand drops against the rocks of the sea-shore. This outward-going tendency must be checked and reversed so that man may live inwardly, with his reactions and tendencies moving towards the centre rather than towards the rim; for at the centre resides the One, the Pure and ineffable Being which is the source of all beatitude and goodness, whereas at the periphery is non-existence, which only appears to be real because of man's illusory perception and lack of discrimination. To enter upon the Sufi path, to become initiated into the way or *Tarîqah,* is to be given this possibility of reversing the tendency of the soul from the outward to the inward, a change of direction which is possible only through Divine Succour (*tawfîq*) and

§Grace.—R.E.

affirmation (*ta'yîd*) as well as through the *barakah* contained in the methods of Sufism.

In order to bring this transformation about, to turn the attention of the soul from multiplicity to unity, the methods of Sufism base themselves first of all on the practices of the *Sharî'ah,* for Sufism is *Islamic* esotericism and not something else. To practise the *Sharî'ah* is already to gain a measure of integration as a necessary basis as well as by way of foretaste of the complete integration achieved in spiritual realization. Especially the daily prayers are a most powerful means of integrating man's psychic elements and harmonizing them with the corporeal aspect of his being.

The main method of Sufism, in fact, is to extend the prayers so that they become continuous, for as Hâfiz says: . . . 'How happy are those who are always praying.'

This extension is not quantitative, but qualitative and vertical; that is, Sufism uses the quintessential form of prayer, the *dhikr* or invocation, in which all otherness and separation from the Divine is removed and man achieves *tawhîd*. Though this process of transforming man's psyche appears gradual at first, the *dhikr* finishes by becoming man's real nature and the reality with which he identifies himself. With the help of the *dhikr,* as combined with appropriate forms of meditation or *fikr,* man first gains an integrated soul, pure and whole like gold, and then in the *dhikr* he offers this soul to God in the supreme form of sacrifice. Finally in annihilation (*fanâ'*) and subsistence (*baqâ'*) he realizes that he never was separated from God even from the outset.

The integrating power of the *dhikr* is reflected even in the body, whose very structure reflects symbolically man's inner being. Although at the beginning of man's awareness of the spiritual life he must separate himself from the body considered in its negative and passionate aspect, in the more advanced stages of the Path the aim is to keep oneself within the body and centred in the heart, that is, within the body considered in its positive aspect as the 'temple' (*haykal*) of the spirit. The mind is always wandering from one thought to another. To be able to keep it within the body means to be always totally present here and now, in the instant which connects the temporal with the eternal. When Rumî writes in his *Mathnawî* that the adept must invoke in the spiritual retreat (*khalwah*) until his toes begin to say 'Allâh', he means precisely this final integration which includes the body as well as the mind and the soul. In fact the Islamic and Christian doctrine of corporeal resurrection means above all the complete and total integration of man in the final phase of his becoming.

The man who has achieved integration possesses certain characteristics discernible only by those who are capable of observing them. But the integration of his inner being leaves its effect even upon his outward features, which of necessity reflect his inner states. Such a person is first of all cured of all the maladies of the soul, not by having all tensions and complexes removed in the manner of modern psychoanalysis so that he becomes like a plant quiescent but without an inner drive or attraction toward the Divine, but by having all those tensions which arise from man's profound urge and need for the transcendent realized and fulfilled. Moreover, such a man does not live a compartmentalized existence. His thoughts and actions all issue from a single centre and are based on a series of immutable principles. He has been cured of that hypocrisy in which most men live and therefore, since the veil of otherness which hides the inner light in the majority of men has been removed, like the sun he reflects his light wherever he happens to be. In him, the Islamic ideal of unifying the contemplative and active ways is realized. He does not *either* act *or* think; rather his contemplation and meditation is combined with the purest and most intense activity, And because by virtue of his becoming integrated he reflects Divine Unity and has become the total theophany of the Divine Names and Qualities, he acts and lives in such a manner that there is a spiritual fragrance and beauty about all he does and says. Somehow he is in touch with that *barakah* which runs through the arteries of the Universe.

Islam has always sought to bring about integration and unity, whether it be socially, politically and economically, or morally and intellectually. The integration achieved by Sufism is the essence of this Islamic ideal, realized in such a way that it has always been a supreme example for Islamic society. For the best way to integrate human society is first of all to be integrated oneself. One cannot do good unless one is good, an all too simple truth so often forgotten in the modern world. Nor can one save others unless one has first been saved oneself. Therefore the method of integration contained in Sufism concerns not only the individuals who are affected by it but also casts its light upon the whole of society and is the hidden source for the regeneration of Islamic ethics and the integration of the Islamic community.

The Sufi teaches this simple truth that the basis of all faith or *îmân* is unity, for as Shaykh Mahmûd Shabistarî writes in his *Gulshan-i-râz*: . . .

> See but One, say but One, know but One,
> In this are summed up the roots and branches of faith.[1]

The integration of man means the realization of the One and the transmutation of the many in the light of the One. It is therefore the full attainment of that faith or *îmân* which is the core and basis of Islam. He who has achieved this inner integration, in sacrificing his soul inwardly to God, also renders the greatest service to Islam and in fact to the truth in whatever form it might be found.

[1]*Mystic Rose Garden*, pp. 84–85.

further reading

Alfred Guillaume, *Islam* (2nd ed., 1956). A balanced introductory survey by a noted scholar who is also the translator of Ibn Ishaq's *Life of Muhammad* (Eng. trans., 1955), the earliest and standard biography of the Prophet.

Tor Andrae's *Mohammed: The Man and His Faith* (1932) is a scholarly, sympathetic study. The principles of the religion are summarized in Chapter III, "Mohammed's Religious Message."

W. Montgomery Watt's work on Muhammad originally appeared in two volumes, *Muhammad at Mecca* (1953) and *Muhammad at Medina* (1956), but these have been helpfully combined and abridged in *Muhammad: Prophet and Statesman* (1961).

Sufism: An Account of the Mystics of Islam (1950) is a brief history and study by A. J. Arberry, who has few peers in Islamic studies.

Margaret Smith (ed.), *Readings from the Mystics of Islam* (1950) and *The Sufi Path of Love: An Anthology of Sufism* (1954). Both of these volumes are outstanding collections of materials that are otherwise difficult to locate.

Robert Payne, *The Holy Sword: The Story of Islam from Muhammad to the Present* (1959). A popular history written in a colorful style quite appropriate to its subject matter.

The recent history of Islam has been concisely presented by H. A. R. Gibb in his *Modern Trends in Islam* (1947). The same subject is treated in greater detail by Wilfred Cantwell Smith in his *Islam in Modern History* (1957).

Frithjof Schuon, *Understanding Islam* (Penguin Books, 1972). Not an introductory work, but rather a profound, original study of the essential meaning of Islam in the light of the "Perennial Philosophy."

Among the outstanding modern translations of the Koran in English are Marmaduke Pickthall, *The Meaning of the Glorious Koran* (1930); N. J. Dawood, *The Koran* (rev. ed., 1974); and A. J. Arberry, *The Koran Interpreted* (1955), the preface to which is a very interesting discussion and comparison of the important English translations of the Koran.

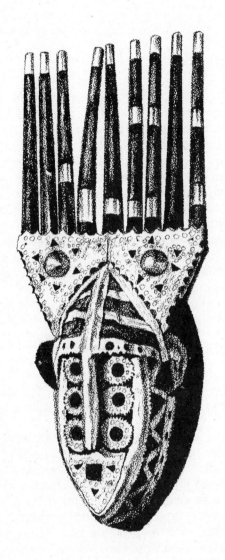

African Traditional Religions

_____ *god and life affirmed*

> Great Spirit . . . You are on high with the spirits
> of the great. You raise the grass-covered hills above
> the earth and you create the rivers. Gracious one.
>
> *Prayer of the Shona*

The term "African traditional religions" is now commonly used to denote that continent's indigenous religions, which today are generally to be found south of the Sahara in tropical Africa. There are a great number of traditional religions, and the significance of their differences ought not be minimized. Nevertheless, there is widespread agreement that the similarities that exist among the religions are sufficient to warrant their being discussed collectively, at least for introductory purposes. Just as is the case with the varieties of belief within Hinduism and Christianity, certain major themes and characteristics predominate.

The study of Africa's own religions is hampered, first, by the lack of a religious literature. The remarkable arts of African peoples did not include the art of writing, and thus there are no sacred scriptures, no personal accounts of religious experience, and no historical documents.

Religion in African societies is written not on paper but in people's hearts, minds, oral history, rituals and religious personages like the priests, rainmakers, officiating elders and even kings. Everybody is a religious carrier.

. . .

Where the individual is, there is his religion, for he is a religious being. It is this that makes Africans so religious: religion is their whole system of being.*

A second problem, which is discussed in the following pages by E. Bolaji Idowu, is that of the prejudicial attitudes and language that have been commonplace in materials written about Africans and African religions. The use of certain misleading terms is still widespread, and these terms entail disparaging misconceptions. All too frequently, to those who came to Africa and to those who wrote about that "Dark Continent," her peoples were "savages," "heathens," "natives," or "pagans." Their religions, moreover, were labeled "primitive"—a curious term indeed for very complex systems of belief held by peoples who are obviously our contemporaries.

The inappropriateness of the terms to which Idowu objects is further demonstrated by Geoffrey Parrinder's essay, "The Nature of God in African Belief." Belief in a Supreme Being is a basic feature of African religions, and

---

*John S. Mbiti, *African Religions and Philosophy* (New York: Doubleday, 1970), pp. 4, 5.

God's attributes are those typically ascribed to him in the theistic Western religions. Thus God is conceived to be all-powerful and all-knowing; he created the universe and sustains it. He is "mysterious and nobody can understand him, he creates and destroys, he gives and takes away. God is invisible, infinite and unchangeable." The good and bad acts of men result in rewards and punishments, either in this life or the next. Prayers are commonly addressed to God, who hears them because "his ears are long."

Marcel Griaule's "Ogotemmêli and the Dawn of All Things" is a report of the profound mythology and religion of the Dogon in the western Sudan. Griaule's long and close association with the Dogon resulted in his being permitted to hear their oral tradition; assigned to impart this knowledge to him was a blind old man named Ogotemmêli.

From the age of fifteen [Ogotemmêli] had been initiated in the mysteries of religion by his grandfather. After the latter's death his father continued the instruction. It seemed that the 'lessons' had gone on for more than twenty years, and that Ogotemmêli's family was not one that took these things lightly.

Ogotemmêli himself, no doubt, had from a very early age shown signs of an eager mind and considerable shrewdness. Until he lost his sight, he was a mighty hunter who, though one-eyed from childhood as a result of smallpox, would always come back from the chase with a full bag, while the others were still toiling in the gorges. His skill as a hunter was the fruit of his profound knowledge of nature, of animals, of men and of gods. After his accident he learnt still more. Thrown back on his own resources, on his altars and on whatever he was able to hear, he had become one of the most powerful minds on the cliffs.†

The final essay of the chapter, John S. Mbiti's "Divinities, Spirits, and the Living-Dead," illustrates the extent to which religion permeates the thinking and the lives of African peoples. Their spiritual world (that intermediate realm between God and man), Mbiti observes, "is very densely populated." Classification of the spirits is difficult, but they fall generally into three groups: (1) *divinities*, who are created as such by God; (2) *"common" spirits*, often believed to have once been men; and (3) the *living-dead*, men who have died not more than five generations ago.

---

†Marcel Griaule, *Conversations with Ogotemmêli* (London: Oxford University Press, 1965), pp. 14–15.

e. bolaji idowu _____

Errors of Terminology

E. Bolaji Idowu is the author of *Olódùmarè, God in Yoruba Belief,* and *African Traditional Religion,* from which the following selection is taken. He is concerned here with some of the derogatory terms often used to describe Africans and their religions. But it might be noted that these "errors of terminology" are only a part of a larger pattern of injustice. Africa, Idowu has written, "has been callously and frequently raped and despoiled by the strong ones of the world who are adepts in the art of benevolent exploitation and civilized savagery."*

Primitive. The Concise Oxford Dictionary defines this word as 'Early, ancient, old-fashioned, simple, rude; original, primary.' It should be obvious that in the light of some of the words in this definition, 'primitive' cannot be appropriate in certain contexts in which it is being currently applied. With reference to any people in the world today, 'early', 'ancient', 'original', or 'primary' does not apply. Primitive man, in the sense conveyed by the words quoted, disappeared from this world thousands of years ago. The peoples who are being so described today are contemporaries of, and as old or as recent in earthly lineage as, the races of those who are so describing them.[1]

The fashion that perpetuates the incongruous use of the word stems from the notion that anything that does not conform to a certain cultural pattern accepted as the norm by the Western investigator is regarded automatically as primitive; that is, that which belongs to the category of those things which have somehow been left behind in the race of cultural sophistication. 'Primitive' in this connection means, categorically, 'backward', 'rude', or 'uncouth'.

The anthropological or sociological use of the word 'primitive' has been defended on the ground that it only refers to that which is adjudged to be nearer in behaviour or pattern to the original with reference to the human race or culture. It is with this excuse that Western writers still persist in applying the word to Africa, and to African beliefs and practices. This follows also the slothful pattern that where a new, adequate term is not conveniently ready to

---

African Traditional Religion (London: SCM Press Ltd., 1973), p. 76.

[1] See E. S. Waterhouse, *The Dawn of Religion,* 1936, p. 13.

E. Bolaji Idowu, "Errors of Terminology." From E. Bolaji Idowu, *African Traditional Religion* (London: SCM Press Ltd., 1973). Reprinted by permission of SCM Press Ltd. and Orbis Books, Maryknoll, N.Y. Notes have been renumbered.

CHAPTER ELEVEN / *African Traditional Religions*

hand for any situation, an old one, however outmoded or unsuitable, is applied without any apology.

.   .   .

It is especially wrong to speak of the religion of any living people as 'primitive' simply on the ground of racial or ethnic prejudice. 'Primitive' in most Western writings is a derogatory term and therefore obnoxious. Therefore, it is not only inappropriate but also offensive to describe African traditional religion unreservedly as 'primitive'.

Savage. Here, in the use of the word 'savage', we meet again the inveterate streak in race-proud man.

.   .   .

'Savage' stands at the opposite end of the pole from 'civilized'. The terms are antithetic to each other. Too often, peoples or cultures and religious practices are described as savage through sheer prejudice, lack of sympathy, or understanding.

.   .   .

A few comparative illustrations will illuminate the subject for us. First, capital has been made out of the fact of human sacrifice in Africa. Human sacrifice, we trust, has become or is fast becoming a thing of the past throughout Africa. I have discussed the subject at some length in *Olódùmarè*.[2] The fundamental principle behind it is that 'it is expedient . . . that one man should die for the people, and that the whole nation should not perish'. This substitutionary principle has been put into practice from time immemorial, though, more often than not, its expression has been the perversion which has acquired the name of human sacrifice. What is both interesting and disappointing is that the Western world is putting on blinkers with regard to the perversion of this principle which is daily occurring in its midst. Political murders, euphemistically glorified as 'assassinations', negro lynching resulting in the death of countless numbers of people of African descent in America, the extermination of the aboriginal peoples in America, Australia and New Zealand in order that those who came to acquire their lands forcibly might possess the lands for themselves and for their posterity, the German gas-chambers which, like Moloch, devoured countless numbers of Jews, the wanton and wholesale murders of apartheid South Africa and Rhodesia: these perversions, in each case, are of the same character as ritual human sacrifice, although in these euphemistic instances, the case for it is very much weaker.

Secondly, I have never watched on the television the films on 'Wrestling from Canada' and 'Wrestling from Britain' without being filled with horror at what to me as an African is the sheer 'savagery' of the whole performance. In Yorubaland for instance, wrestling is an art implying artistic movements and

[2] E. B. Idowu, *Olódùmarè: God in Yoruba Belief,* 1962, pp. 120f.

beauty of strategy; and when once any part of a contestant's body (apart from the feet) has touched the ground, be it no more than the tip of a finger, that contestant has been defeated and the contest is over. There is nothing of the callous, cruel assault on the contestant, twistings of, or attempts to damage, any organs of the body, or sitting upon a person and buffeting him when he is down.

Thirdly, there are undoubtedly several parts of Africa where feuds are settled with hatchets and spears, dane guns or arson. The difference between this and such undertakings in the Western world is that weapons have been scientifically perfected—pistols, revolvers, bombs and nuclear appliances are civilized Western counterparts.

. . .

. . . No people should be called savages simply because they are technologically backward or because their own ways of reverting to the raw 'natural' state have not yet acquired scientific justification and technological polish.

Native. My wife and I were on a week's holiday, residing at a Quaker Guest House called 'The Blue Idol' somewhere in Sussex. There were other guests staying at the same time in the house. One evening, after supper, several of us sat round a table, playing a game of cards. It was my turn to shuffle the cards and I did it in a way which a British woman considered admirable: for she burst out, 'Oh, how wonderfully you do it! Do all natives do it the same way?' '*Natives* of where—England, Scotland, or Ireland?' I asked her. By the way she was taken aback and by the expression on the faces of the other Europeans in that room, it was patent that they were probably realizing for the first time that they themselves must have been *born* somewhere! The fact is that to her and, by and large, to the peoples of the Western world, the word 'native' has acquired a derogatory nuance and has become one that is reserved for the 'unfortunate', 'backward', non-Western peoples of the world. This is so, thanks to the anthropologists and missionaries, and the stay-at-home investigators who must always find terms of unmistakable distinction between themselves and 'those others'. 'Prayers for native Christians' are still being offered in churches of Europe and America; 'native Christians' being not Christians who are born and are living in Europe and America, but Christians of Africa and Asia and those other 'benighted climes'. This defines the Western mind on the issue beyond doubt:

It was about this time that Damu, quite unknown to himself, developed two minds, or rather his own mind split in two parts. One part was his civilized or white mind, the other his native mind which, gradually submerged by his life in England, had been reawakened by contact with his present surrounding. It was his native mind that trifled with the idea of rising against the people he hated, while his white mind laughed at the fantastic notions. Conversely, it was his white mind that made him curious about the

Leopard cult, for a native would have been terror-stricken at the very notion of probing into such mysteries.[3]

So also is this:

Oh yes. Abu bin Zaka is a pure European. Not a drop of native blood in him.[4]

. . .

Paganism. This is probably the oldest of the names adopted to describe the religion of the so-called primitive or 'uncivilized' peoples of the world. This word has a Latin origin—*paganus*—and means originally a village-dweller or a countryman, a person who lives away from the civilized community. Thus, originally, the word was a sociological term, a mark of distinction between the enlightened, the civilized and the sophisticated, on the one hand and the rustic, the unpolished, and the unsophisticated on the other.

The word must have travelled some curious distance in order to become a term with an exclusively religious connotation. In the world to which it originally belonged, what came under the term now was all the religion that there was. And yet, the *Pocket Oxford Dictionary* appears to be unaware of this when it defines 'pagan' as 'acknowledging neither Jehovah, Christ nor Allah; non-Christian'. The *Encyclopaedia of Religion and Ethics* in a passing reference links the term with 'primitive peoples'.[5]

. . .

With particular reference to African traditional religion, there is no doubt that the word 'paganism', whenever or wherever it is used, carries primarily a mark of racial and social discrimination. Even though the discrimination is now tinged with a religious overtone, the basic implication is sociological. . . .

. . .

Heathenism . . . is a word of Germanic root. The suffix -en has the same meaning as the -en in wood*en*; and the heath, originally, was the waste land removed from the outskirts of the town, where outlaws, vagabonds, and brigands had their abode; 'heathen' means a dweller on the heath. Thus, the 'heathen' is, primarily, one who belongs to, or has the habit of, or has the forbidding quality or characteristics of, heath-dwellers. 'Heathenism' means the habit or the characteristics, or the disposition, of heath-dwellers.

The Concise Oxford Dictionary, however, defines 'heathen' as (one who is) 'neither Christian, Jewish, nor Mohammedan; unenlightened persons'. Like the *Pocket Oxford Dictionary,* it makes 'pagan' and 'heathen' synonymous. . . .

[3]Webster, *Son of Abdan,* pp. 85f.
[4]P. C. Wren, *Sinbad the Soldier,* John Murray 1958, p. 148.
[5]On 'Abyssinia', *Encyclopaedia of Religion and Ethics* 1, pp. 55ff.

It is needless to say, after all that has been discussed so far, that with regard to African traditional religion, the name *heathenism* is most unsuitable and is, in fact, a very obnoxious misnomer. It has nothing to do with religion, basically. It is of all opprobrious labels the most opprobrious, and is culpably inexcusable.

geoffrey parrinder

The Nature of God in African Belief

Born in London in 1910, Geoffrey Parrinder received his B.A. and B.D. degrees from the University of London and his doctorates in philosophy and divinity from the University of Montpelier. Ordained a Methodist minister, he spent over twenty years teaching and traveling in Africa, and the religion of that continent has been the subject of his *Religion in Africa, African Traditional Religion, African Mythology, Religion in an African City, West African Religion,* and *Witchcraft.*

Since 1958 he has been Professor of the Comparative Study of Religions at King's College, the University of London, and he has also served as Wilde Lecturer in Natural and Comparative Religion at Oxford University. A member of the Royal Asiatic Society, he is the author of numerous volumes on the world's religions, including *Avatar and Incarnation; The Indestructible Soul; The Faiths of Mankind; Worship in the World's Religions;* and *Upanishads, Gita, and Bible.*

From the earlier view that African religion was crudely fetishistic, with an idea of God where it existed being an importation, informed opinion has now swung round to the conviction that most, if not all African peoples have had a belief in a Supreme Being as an integral part of their world view and practised religion. The symposium *African Ideas of God** did much to establish this finally, but it has been supported by countless books and articles. Missionaries have found, often to their surprise, that they did not need to argue for the existence of God, or faith in a life after death, for both these fundamentals of world religion are deeply rooted in Africa.

Some writers refer to 'the High God', but this term sounds derogatory to educated African ears, suggesting that God is merely distant or transcendent. Here we shall speak of the Supreme Being, or God, as in normal English usage. . . . African myths express many beliefs about God in graphic form. It is not necessary to accept the myths as true in detail; but they express a conviction in the spiritual direction of the universe. Modern science may express its theories in different ways, and in new symbols, but it is also making a religious search for truth and purpose in the universe. Myths speak about God in picture language, and other sources for an understanding of his character in African traditional religion are found in prayers, songs, proverbs, riddles, and some rituals.

*E. W. Smith (ed.), 1950.—R.E.

Geoffrey Parrinder, "The Nature of God in African Belief." From Geoffrey Parrinder, *Religion in Africa* (Penguin African Library, 1969), pp. 39–46. © Geoffrey Parrinder, 1969. By permission of Penguin Books, Ltd. Editor's title. Notes have been numbered.

The nature of God in African belief can be gathered from the qualities attributed to him. These correspond generally to many of the divine attributes postulated in other religions. That God is almighty is one of the most obvious assertions, since supremacy implies it. All-powerful is a common name for him and he receives many similar titles: creator, allotter, giver of rain and sunshine, the one who began the forest, the one 'who gives and rots', maker of souls, father of the placenta, the one who exists by himself. The omnipresence of God, less commonly expressed, is found in sayings such as 'the one who is met everywhere', and 'the great ocean whose head-dress is the horizon'. More clearly God is omniscient: the wise one, the all-seeing, the 'one who brings round the seasons'.[1]

These attributes imply the transcendence of God, and to some extent his immanence. God is always creator and ruler, the one beyond all thanks, the ancient of days who is from the first, the everlasting who has no limits, and he who alone is full of abundance. The Zulu particularly delighted in such titles: 'he who bends down even majesties', the irresistible, and 'he who roars so that all nations are struck with terror'. Then the nearness of God comes in such titles as 'the one you meet everywhere', 'the great pool contemporary of everything', and 'the one who fills everything'. In his immanence God may be conceived more physically or naturally. He may be found in big trees or thickets, on mountains or rocky places, and especially in rivers and streams. He may be spoken of as one but many, invisible at ordinary times but seen by a man about to die, and his voice may be heard when the bush is burnt or when a whirlwind blows.

It is clear that God exists by himself; he is not the creature of any other being but is the cause of everything else. His pre-eminence and his greatness go together. But since he is greater than any other spirit or man, God is mysterious and nobody can understand him, he creates and destroys, he gives and takes away. God is invisible, infinite and unchangeable. Although his wife or wives and children appear in myths, yet in himself God is one, and only rarely is the notion found of a twin deity. Heaven and earth, sun and moon, day and night, man and woman, are dual but God is the unity beyond all this. The duality is not discussed as it is in Hindu speculation, but the unity of God follows from his pre-eminence and sole creation. It has been said that God might have been banished from Greek thought without damaging its logical architecture, but this cannot be said of African thought, as God is both the creator and the principle of unity that holds everything together. He is the source and essence of force, Ntu, which inspires the whole vital organism.

The character of God appears not just in abstract attributes, but in more humane and moral qualities. Although he is supremely great, mysterious and irresistible, yet he is also kindly disposed towards men and his providence is

[1]See the Index of God-names in *African Ideas of God,* p. 305 f.

mentioned not infrequently. He is the God of destinies but also of comfort, the kindly-disposed and 'the providence which watches over all like the sun'; he can be angry but is also 'full of pity', the father of babies and the great friend. In the enigmatic Akan title he is 'the one on whom men lean and do not fall'.

The natural attributes of God come from his primary function as creator. Not only did he make the world, but he established the laws of society and the existence of justice depends upon obedience to him. Creation is not only in the past; the divine work is continued in sustaining the universe, and men turn to God if things go wrong today, complaining if they have been treated unjustly. God is the giver of destinies, and may appear harsh or inscrutable, but that does not make people fatalistic or console them if justice is perverted.

A well known Ila story tells of an old woman who came from a large family and had many troubles. God, Leza, 'the one who besets', smote all the family in turn. Her parents died and then other relatives. Although she married and had children, her husband died and then the children. Some had borne her grand-children but these also passed away. The crone was left and hoped to die, but strangely she grew young again (some would have said that she had eaten the soul-stuff of her relatives), and she decided to use her new powers to find out God and get an explanation of her troubles. First she tried to make a ladder to heaven out of forest trees, but as this Tower of Babel neared the sky the whole structure collapsed. So the woman resolved to travel to every country till she found the place where heaven touches earth and provides the road to God. In every land that she visited people asked why she was travelling and she replied that she had suffered so much at the hands of God that she was seeking him out. But her hearers said this was not strange, for such troubles come to all people and nobody can ever get free of them.

Although the ways of God are beyond man and can never be fully known, yet numerous titles speak of his sustaining and cherishing work. He gives rain and sun, health and fertility. He is also the deliverer and Saviour, moulder and providence. Disease and poverty, drought and famine, locusts and death come to plague man, but they are part of the mystery of nature. Although life is viewed, inevitably, from the human standpoint, yet man is not the centre of the universe in African thought, any more than in Christian theology. It is God who is supreme and the central moving force, and man submits to him as the great chief.

How far God is regarded in anthropomorphic fashion, as a big man projected into the heavens, or a glorified ancestor, has been debated. Human titles have been given to him: ruler, father, mother, and even more grandfather, the originator of the people. J. B. Danquah asserted that for the Akan God is the Great Ancestor, but other writers disagree. It seems rare for God to be thought of as linked to man in a family relationship. Rather man is his creation and God is the inscrutable maker. Other gods are spoken of but it is not normal to find the same generic term for 'a god' applied to the Supreme Being, who is in a class apart. And it has been noted that there are few, if any, sculptures of the great God.

Occasionally God may be spoken about in terms of either sex. Mawu-Lisa of the Fon is the supreme female-male, and Dr Aggrey, the Ghanaian educationalist, spoke of 'Father-mother God'. The southern Nuba, who have a system of matrilineal descent, refer to God as 'the Great Mother' and when praying beside a dying person they say, 'Our God, who has brought us into this world, may she take you.'[2] This is very unusual, and though most African languages have no sex in the pronoun, God is generally clearly personified as a great male ruler. In mythology God may have a wife and children, servants and messengers, and other gods act as his partners or agents in creation. God may be described with a body, head, eyes, ears, mouth, arms and legs. But both the Bible and the Koran speak of the divine body in this way, though theologians take such language as symbolical or, in a common Muslim phrase, assert the paradox that God has two eyes 'but without asking how'. Men have to use language, with its solid imagery, even when speaking of the invisible and indescribable God, and anything more than negatives is bound to involve metaphor.

Similarly God is related to heavenly objects, and at times apparently identified with them. His virtual identification with the sky, in myths of divine withdrawal, has been noted. In other stories God is closely linked with the sun, though this is not common. Some peoples may seem almost to identify God with the sun, but this appears to be metaphorical and due to the similarity of words used about God and the sun. The sun is sometimes personified in myths, or is regarded as a manifestation of God, but there are few clear indications that the sun is God or God is the sun. There is little ritual in connexion with the sun, such as that which was performed in ancient Europe or Japan to make the sun return from its winter journey to the south. In the tropics the sun is always overhead, and needs no encouragement to shine. However, as it is supreme in the heavens the sun may be an apt symbol for God, and stories are told of men visiting the sky and reaching the sun or God.

The Bakuta of the Congo speak of two supreme Gods: Nzambi above and Nzambi below. Often regarded as twins they act heroic roles in many stories, and have villages and families in heaven and earth. But in myths of creation it is Nzambi above who is supreme and his twin disappears, so that the function of Nzambi is creation. His first children were twins, the sun and moon, and death is attributed to his faulty messenger, here the goat. As in other myths it is said that Nzambi retired from the earth after a human offence and he has no regular worship. But he still has a concern for men and death is under his control. His name occurs in proverbs and exclamations: 'God sees him' is

---

[2] *African Ideas of God*, p. 215 f.

said about a man who escapes punishment from earthly courts, 'we have the grace of Nzambi' is uttered when people are spared by flashes of lightning, and 'Nzambi is with me' is said by a woman after childbirth. Some writers have identified this celestial Nzambi with the sun, but men prayed to him also at night, looking up to the sky, and when a thunderbolt falls at night it is his axe.

Any of the celestial bodies may be connected with God. The Akan of Ghana also say that thunderbolts are God's axes, though some other peoples have storm gods, inferior to the Supreme Being, who control the thunder. The rainbow is God's bow, and lightning is his weapon against evildoers. Different reasons are given for eclipses; they are due to the quarrel of sun and moon, or to clouds or storms devouring the moon, but ultimately God is responsible. An eclipse is viewed with alarm, since all nature goes quiet at this time, and drums are beaten to ensure the victory of good, but wise men know that the darkness never lasts long.

Earthly objects, and especially high mountains like Mount Kenya, are apt symbols for the dwelling or place of manifestation of a transcendent God, as in the Bible. They provide places where prayers and sacrifices can be made in time of need. Groves of trees are sacred, and the Gikuyu on important occasions pray to the Supreme Being there in the open. There are spirits of the earth, but unusual phenomena like earthquakes or floods may be ascribed to the direct action of God, and desolate places may be thought of as his special abodes, and precious metals in the ground as his gift. The regularity of nature is also ascribed to him, the succession of day and night, heat and cold, dry and rainy seasons. Although nature gods and ancestors are both objects of prayers for good harvests and plentiful rain, yet ultimately they are the concern of the supreme God.

WORSHIP OF GOD

The relationship of men with God is complex. Man is always the creature of the Most High, as mythology shows. The first man and woman are often called children of God, even though some stories say that they came from the earth instead of from heaven. Traffic between heaven and earth was easy in the olden days, according to the stories, but the separation came about by human fault, usually that of a woman. One result of the misunderstanding between God and man is that death has come, though a further reason is often given for this, and generally an animal is blamed.

Human life should be conducted according to principles which God gave to the founding fathers of the clan. Every clan has traditional history, some of it fact, some legend, but always important for revealing ideals and attitudes. The ancient heroes are often described as coming from God, or entrusted by him with ordering their lives and settling on their land. Morality is traditional, but it depends on the ultimate creation and the purpose of the world to maintain harmony and prosperity. Rewards and punishments for good or bad acts may be applied in this present life. Even notorious evildoers who manage to flourish like the green bay tree and avoid justice for a long time are believed, rather optimistically, to be due for punishment before death. Only rarely, it seems, is a judgement predicted for good and evil men after death. But the Yoruba say that all that is done on earth will be accounted for in heaven, and men will have to state their case kneeling before God. Then the final lot of the righteous will be a heaven of cool breezes, and for the wicked a heaven of potsherds, a sort of celestial rubbish-heap like the midden of every village where refuse and broken pots are thrown.

The above statements suggest that God is close to most African peoples and that he receives regular worship, as in Christianity or Islam. Therefore it is surprising to find that there is little ordered worship of God and few places where rituals are performed for him. That a Supreme Being is widely believed in, that he is the background of life, and is thought to be near to many people, is true, though there are exceptions. But regular worship is not usual.

The Dogon have group altars for Amma, at which the village chief usually officiates. Additional altars are made if some special object is found which is imbued with the divine presence, and there are special priests and priestesses who sacrifice here and at annual communal rites. Rattray provided invaluable photographs of temples of Nyame in Ashanti, with their priests, and of the small 'God's altars', forked sticks holding bowls for offerings which stood in front of houses. But the temples were relatively few even in the 1920s, and many of the forked altars have disappeared today, though the worship of God has increased through the Christian churches. The Gikuyu and Shona also worship God on occasion or at special and communal ceremonies, but few other African peoples have organized cults for him.

Generally there are no temples or priests for God, though there may be many temples for the nature gods, and there are always sacrifices and prayers made to the ancestors. Yet occasional worship of God, by libation or simple invocation, is quite common. Prayer is worship, and it can be made by any layman or woman, at any place or time. When the gods and ancestors fail, or when appeal is needed to the highest authority, then despite his greatness God can be appealed to directly, without any special formula or intermediary priest.

The lesser spirits are also important in this connexion. Although they may appear to receive most attention in sacrifices, it is often said that they receive the externals of the offering but the essence of it is taken by them to God. The gods are subordinates and may pray to God for men, and in prayers to them the Supreme Being is often mentioned first, in a recital of the spiritual powers that are being invoked. Even when God is thought to be far away and fearsome, he can be called upon in time of distress because 'his ears are long'.

The study of the idea of God in Africa has been weakened by theorists, some of whom think that there has been an inevitable evolution from fetishism, to animism, to polytheism, and finally to monotheism. Others consider that there was an original monotheism from which all Africans fell, in a kind of Fall of Adam. Looking at things as they are today there is a picture of a mixed religion, which is not mere animism, nor a democratic polytheism, nor a pure monotheism. E. B. Idowu calls it 'diffused monotheism'.†

Evans-Pritchard, in one of his thoughtful conclusions, says that 'a theistic religion need not be either monotheistic or polytheistic. It may be both. It is a question of the level, or situation, of thought rather than of exclusive types of thought. On one level Nuer religion may be regarded as monotheistic, at another level as polytheistic; and it can also be regarded at other levels as totemistic or fetishistic. These conceptions of spiritual activity are not incompatible. They are rather different ways of thinking of the numinous at different levels of experience. . . . At no level of thought and experience is Spirit thought of as something altogether different from God.'[3]

---

†He calls it a diffused monotheism "because here we have a monotheism in which there exist other powers which derive from Deity such being and authority that they can be treated, for practical purposes, almost as ends in themselves." *African Traditional Religion* (London: SCM Press Ltd., 1973), p. 135.—R.E.

[3]*Nuer Religion* (1956), p. 316.

marcel griaule _____

Ogotemmêli and the Dawn of All Things

Marcel Griaule directed and participated in field studies in Africa from 1928 until his death in 1956. Over the course of those years the Dogon came to hold Griaule in unusually high regard, and in 1947 the elders of the Dogon decided to give to him a full account of their religion and philosophy. Thus he met with Ogotemmêli:

. . . A head bent beneath the lintel of the door, and the man stood up to his full height, turning towards the stranger a face that no words can describe.

'Greetings!' he said, 'Greetings to those who are athirst!'

The thick lips spoke the purest Sanga language. So alive were they that one saw nothing else. All the other features seemed to be folded away, particularly as, after the first words, the head had been bent. The cheeks, the cheek-bones, the forehead and the eyelids seemed all to have suffered the same ravages; they were creased by a hundred wrinkles which had caused a painful contortion as a face exposed to too strong a light or battered by a hail of stones. The eyes were dead.

After their initial introduction, they met for thirty-two successive days, the first of which is described here.

_____

Ogotemmêli, seating himself on his threshold, scraped his stiff leather snuff-box, and put a pinch of yellow powder on his tongue.

'Tobacco,' he said, 'makes for right thinking.'

So saying, he set to work to analyse the world system, for it was essential to begin with the dawn of all things. He rejected as a detail of no interest the popular account of how the fourteen solar systems were formed from flat circular slabs of earth one on top of the other. He was only prepared to speak of the serviceable solar system; he agreed to consider the stars, though they only played a secondary part.

'It is quite true,' he said, 'that in course of time women took down the stars to give them to their children. The children put spindles through them and made them spin like fiery tops to show themselves how the world turned. But that was only a game.'

The stars came from pellets of earth flung out into space by the God Amma, the one God. He had created the sun and the moon by a more complicated

Marcel Griaule, "Ogotemmêli and the Dawn of All Things." From Marcel Griaule, *Conversations with Ogotemmêli* (London: Oxford University Press, 1965). Reprinted by permission of the International African Institute. Editor's title.

process, which was not the first known to man but is the first attested invention of God: the art of pottery. The sun is, in a sense, a pot raised once for all to white heat and surrounded by a spiral of red copper with eight turns. The moon is the same shape, but its copper is white. It was heated only one quarter at a time. Ogotemmêli said he would explain later the movements of these bodies. For the moment he was concerned only to indicate the main lines of the design, and from that to pass to its actors.

He was anxious, however, to give an idea of the size of the sun.

'Some,' he said, 'think it is as large as this encampment, which would mean thirty cubits. But it is really bigger. Its surface area is bigger than the whole of Sanga Canton.'

And after some hesitation he added:

'It is perhaps even bigger than that.'

He refused to linger over the dimensions of the moon, nor did he ever say anything about them. The moon's function was not important, and he would speak of it later. He said however that, while Africans were creatures of light emanating from the fullness of the sun, Europeans were creatures of the moonlight: hence their immature appearance.

He spat out his tobacco as he spoke. Ogotemmêli had nothing against Europeans. He was not even sorry for them. He left them to their destiny in the lands of the north.

The God Amma, it appeared, took a lump of clay, squeezed it in his hand and flung it from him, as he had done with the stars. The clay spread and fell on the north, which is the top, and from there stretched out to the south, which is the bottom, of the world, although the whole movement was horizontal. The earth lies flat, but the north is at the top. It extends east and west with separate members like a foetus in the womb. It is a body, that is to say, a thing with members branching out from a central mass. This body, lying flat, face upwards, in a line from north to south, is feminine. Its sexual organ is an anthill, and its clitoris a termite hill. Amma, being lonely and desirous of intercourse with this creature, approached it. That was the occasion of the first breach of the order of the universe.

Ogotemmêli ceased speaking. His hands crossed above his head, he sought to distinguish the different sounds coming from the courtyards and roofs. He had reached the point of the origin of troubles and of the primordial blunder of God.

'If they overheard me, I should be fined an ox!'

At God's approach the termite hill rose up, barring the passage and displaying its masculinity. It was as strong as the organ of the stranger, and intercourse could not take place. But God is all-powerful. He cut down the termite hill, and had intercourse with the excised earth. But the original incident was destined to affect the course of things for ever; from this defective union there was born, instead of the intended twins, a single being, the *Thos aureus* or jackal, symbol of the difficulties of God. Ogotemmêli's voice sank lower and lower. It was no longer a question of women's ears listening to what he was saying; other, non-material, ear-drums might vibrate to his important discourse. The European and his African assistant, Sergeant Koguem, were leaning towards the old man as if hatching plots of the most alarming nature.

But, when he came to the beneficent acts of God, Ogotemmêli's voice again assumed its normal tone.

God had further intercourse with his earth-wife, and this time without mishaps of any kind, the excision of the offending member having removed the cause of the former disorder. Water, which is the divine seed, was thus able to enter the womb of the earth and the normal reproductive cycle resulted in the birth of twins. Two beings were thus formed. God created them like water. They were green in colour, half human beings and half serpents. From the head to the loins they were human: below that they were serpents. Their red eyes were wide open like human eyes, and their tongues were forked like the tongues of reptiles. Their arms were flexible and without joints. Their bodies were green and sleek all over, shining like the surface of water, and covered with short green hairs, a presage of vegetation and germination.

These spirits, called Nummo, were thus two homogeneous products of God, of divine essence like himself, conceived without untoward incidents and developed normally in the womb of the earth. Their destiny took them to Heaven, where they received the instructions of their father. Not that God had to teach them speech, that indispensable necessity of all beings, as it is of the world-system; the Pair were born perfect and complete; they had eight members, and their number was eight, which is the symbol of speech.

They were also of the essence of God, since they were made of his seed, which is at once the ground, the form, and the substance of the life-force of the world, from which derives the motion and the persistence of created being. This force is water, and the Pair are present in all water: they *are* water, the water of the seas, of coasts, of torrents, of storms, and of the spoonfuls we drink.

Ogotemmêli used the terms 'Water' and 'Nummo' indiscriminately.

Without Nummo,' he said, 'it was not even possible to create the earth, for the earth was moulded clay and it is from water (that is, from Nummo) that its life is derived.'

'What life is there in the earth?' asked the European.

'The life-force of the earth is water. God moulded the earth with water. Blood too he made out of water. Even in a stone there is this force, for there is moisture in everything.

'But if Nummo is water, it also produces copper. When the sky is overcast, the sun's rays may be seen materializing on the misty horizon. These rays, excreted by the spirits, are of copper and are light. They are water too, because they uphold the earth's moisture as it rises. The Pair excrete light, because they are also light.'

While he was speaking, Ogotemmêli had been searching for something in the dust. He finally collected a number of small stones. With a rapid movement he flung them into the courtyard over the heads of his two interlocutors, who had no time to bend down. The stones fell just where the Hogon's cock had been crowing a few seconds before.

'That cock is a squalling nuisance. He makes all conversation impossible.'

The bird began to crow again on the other side of the wall, so Ogotemmêli sent Koguem to throw a bit of wood at him. When Koguem came back, he asked whether the cock was now outside the limits of the Tabda quarter.

'He is in the Hogon's field,' said Koguem. 'I have set four children to watch him.'

'Good!' said Ogotemmêli with a little laugh. 'Let him make the most of what remains to him of life! They tell me he is to be eaten at the next Feast of Twins.'

He returned to the subject of the Nummo spirits, or (as he more usually put it, in the singular) of Nummo, for this pair of twins, he explained, represented the perfect, the ideal unit.

The Nummo, looking down from Heaven, saw their mother, the earth, naked and speechless, as a consequence no doubt of the original incident in her relations with the God Amma. It was necessary to put an end to this state of disorder. The Nummo accordingly came down to earth, bringing with them fibres pulled from plants already created in the heavenly regions. They took ten bunches of these fibres, corresponding to the number of their ten fingers, and made two strands of them, one for the front and one for behind. To this day masked men still wear these appendages hanging down to their feet in thick tendrils.

But the purpose of this garment was not merely modesty. It manifested on earth the first act in the ordering of the universe and the revelation of the helicoid sign in the form of an undulating broken line.

For the fibres fell in coils, symbol of tornadoes, of the windings of torrents, of eddies and whirlwinds, of the undulating movement of reptiles. They recall also the eight-fold spirals of the sun, which sucks up moisture. They were themselves a channel of moisture, impregnated as they were with the freshness of the celestial plants. They were full of the essence of Nummo: they *were* Nummo in motion, as shown in the undulating line, which can be prolonged to infinity.

When Nummo speaks, what comes from his mouth is a warm vapour which conveys, and itself constitutes, speech. This vapour, like all water, has sound, dies away in a helicoid line. The coiled fringes of the skirt were therefore the chosen vehicle for the words which the Spirit desired to reveal to the earth. He endued his hands with magic power by raising them to his lips while he plaited the skirt, so that the moisture of his words was imparted to the damp plaits, and the spiritual revelation was embodied in the technical instruction.

In these fibres full of water and words, placed over his mother's genitalia, Nummo is thus always present.

Thus clothed, the earth had a language, the first language of this world and the most primitive of all time. Its syntax was elementary, its verbs few, and its vocabulary without elegance. The words were breathed sounds scarcely differentiated from one another, but nevertheless vehicles. Such as it was, this ill-defined speech sufficed for the great works of the beginning of all things.

In the middle of a word Ogotemmêli gave a loud cry in answer to the hunter's halloo which the discreet Akundyo, priest of women dying in child-birth and of stillborn children, had called through the gap in the wall.

Akundyo first spat to one side, his eye riveted on the group of men. He was wearing a red Phrygian cap which covered his ears, with a raised point like a uraeus on the bridge of the nose in the fashion known as 'the wind blows'. His cheek-bones were prominent, and his teeth shone. He uttered a formal salutation to which the old man at once replied and the exchange of courtesies became more and more fulsome.

'God's curse,' exclaimed Ogotemmêli, 'on any in Lower Ogol who love you not!'

With growing emotion Akundyo made shift to out-do the vigour of the imprecation.

'May God's curse rest on me,' said the blind man at last, 'if I love you not!'

The four men breathed again. They exchanged humorous comments on the meagreness of the game in the I valley. Eventually Akundyo took his leave of them, asserting in the slangy French of a native soldier that he was going to 'look for porcupine', an animal much esteemed by these people.

The conversation reverted to the subject of speech. Its function was or-ganization, and therefore it was good; nevertheless from the start it let loose disorder.

This was because the jackal, the deluded and deceitful son of God, desired to possess speech, and laid hands on the fibres in which language was em-bodied, that is to say, on his mother's skirt. His mother, the earth, resisted this incestuous action. She buried herself in her own womb, that is to say, in the anthill, disguised as an ant. But the jackal followed her. There was, it should be explained, no other woman in the world whom he could desire. The hole which the earth made in the anthill was never deep enough, and in the end she had to admit defeat. This prefigured the even-handed struggles between men and women, which, however, always end in the victory of the male.

The incestuous act was of great consequence. In the first place it endowed the jackal with the gift of speech so that ever afterwards he was able to reveal to diviners the designs of God.

It was also the cause of the flow of menstrual blood, which stained the fibres. The resulting defilement of the earth was incompatible with the reign of

God. God rejected that spouse, and decided to create living beings directly. Modelling a womb in damp clay, he placed it on the earth and covered it with a pellet flung out into space from heaven. He made a male organ in the same way and having put it on the ground, he flung out a sphere which stuck to it.

The two lumps forthwith took organic shape; their life began to develop. Members separated from the central core, bodies appeared, and a human pair arose out of the lumps of earth.

At this point the Nummo Pair appeared on the scene for the purpose of further action. The Nummo foresaw that the original rule of twin births was bound to disappear, and that errors might result comparable to those of the jackal, whose birth was single. For it was because of his solitary state that the first son of God acted as he did.

'The jackal was alone from birth,' said Ogotemmêli, 'and because of this he did more things than can be told.'

The Spirit drew two outlines on the ground, one on top of the other, one male and the other female. The man stretched himself out on these two shadows of himself, and took both of them for his own. The same thing was done for the woman. Thus it came about that each human being from the first was endowed with two souls of different sex, or rather with two principles corresponding to two distinct persons. In the man the female soul was located in the prepuce; in the woman the male soul was in the clitoris.

But the foreknowledge of the Nummo no doubt revealed to him the disadvantages of this makeshift. Man's life was not capable of supporting both beings: each person would have to merge himself in the sex for which he appeared to be best fitted.

The Nummo accordingly circumcised the man, thus removing from him all the femininity of his prepuce. The prepuce, however, changed itself into an animal which is 'neither a serpent nor an insect, but is classed with serpents'. This animal is called a *nay*. It is said to be a sort of lizard, black and white like the pall which covers the dead. Its name also means 'four', the female number, and 'Sun', which is a female being. The *nay* symbolized the pain of circumcision and the need for the man to suffer in his sex as the woman does.

The man then had intercourse with the woman, who later bore the first two children of a series of eight, who were to become the ancestors of the Dogon people. In the moment of birth the pain of parturition was concentrated in the woman's clitoris, which was excised by an invisible hand, detached itself and left her, and was changed into the form of a scorpion. The pouch and the sting symbolized the organ: the venom was the water and the blood of the pain.

The European, returning through the millet field, found himself wondering about the significance of all these actions and counteractions, all these sudden jerks in the thought of the myth.

Here, he reflected, is a Creator God spoiling his first creation; restoration is effected by the excision of the earth, and then by the birth of a pair of spirits, inventive beings who construct the world and bring to it the first spoken words; and incestuous act destroys the created order, and jeopardizes the principle of twin-births. Order is restored by the creation of a pair of human beings, and twin-births are replaced by dual souls. (But why, he asked himself, twin-births at all?)

The dual soul is a danger; a man should be male, and a woman female. Circumcision and excision are once again the remedy. (But why the *nay?* Why the scorpion?)

The answers to these questions were to come later, and to take their place in the massive structure of doctrine, which the blind old man was causing to emerge bit by bit from the mists of time.

Over the heads of the European and Koguem the dark millet clusters stood out against the leaden sky. They were passing through a field of heavy ears, stiffly erect and motionless in the breeze. When the crop is backward and thin, the ears are light and move with the slightest breath of wind. Thin crops are therefore full of sound. An abundant crop, on the other hand, is weighed down by the wind and bows itself in silence.

john s. mbiti _____

Divinities, Spirits, and the Living-Dead

Stressing the degree to which Africans are immersed in their religion, John S. Mbiti has noted that

Names of people have religious meanings in them; rocks and boulders are not just empty objects, but religious objects; the sound of the drum speaks a religious language; the eclipse of the sun or moon is not simply a silent phenomenon of nature, but one which speaks to the community that observes it. . . . For Africans, the whole of existence is a religious phenomenon; man is a deeply religious being living in a religious universe.*

Mbiti was born in 1931 in Kitui, Kenya. He received undergraduate degrees from both the University of East Africa, Uganda, and Barrington College, Rhode Island; his Ph.D. is from Cambridge University. Since 1964 he has been Lecturer in New Testament and African Religions and Philosophy at Makerere University College, the University of East Africa, and in 1966 –1967 he was a visiting lecturer at the University of Hamburg. Among his books are *Akamba Stories* (a collection of folktales), *Concepts of God in Africa,* and *African Religions and Philosophy.*

_____

The spiritual world of African peoples is very densely populated with spiritual beings, spirits and the living-dead. Their insight of spiritual realities, whether absolute or apparent, is extremely sharp. To understand their religious ethos and philosophical perception it is essential to consider their concepts of the spiritual world in addition to concepts of God. We have repeatedly emphasized that the spiritual universe is a unit with the physical, and that these two intermingle and dovetail into each other so much that it is not easy, or even necessary, at times to draw the distinction or separate them. . . .

The spirits in general belong to the ontological mode of existence between God and man. Broadly speaking, we can recognize two categories of spiritual beings: those which were created as such, and those which were once human beings. These can also be subdivided into divinities, associates of God,

African Religions and Philosophy (New York: Doubleday, 1970), p. 19.

ordinary spirits and the living-dead. Our time analysis* is here very useful in helping us to place the spiritual beings in their proper category, and to grasp the logic behind their recognition by African peoples. We can now take a closer look at these beings that populate the spiritual realm.

DIVINITIES AND GOD'S ASSOCIATES

I am using the word "divinity" to cover personifications of God's activities and manifestations, of natural phenomena and objects, the so-called "nature spirits," deified heroes and mythological figures. Sometimes it is difficult to know where to draw the line, especially since different writers loosely speak of "gods," "demigods," "divinities," "nature spirits," "ancestral spirits" and the like.

Divinities are on the whole thought to have been created by God, in the ontological category of the spirits. They are associated with Him, and often stand for His activities or manifestations either as personifications or as the spiritual beings in charge of these major objects or phenomena of nature. Some of them are national heroes who have been elevated and deified, but this is rare, and when it does happen the heroes become associated with some function or form of nature. Concrete examples will make these points clearer.

It is reported that the Ashanti have a pantheon of divinities through whom God manifests Himself. Thy are known as *abosom;* are said to "come from Him" and to act as His servants and intermediaries between Him and other creatures. They are increasing numerically; and people hold festivals for major tribal divinities. Minor divinities protect individual human beings; and it is believed that God purposely created the *abosom* to guard men.[1] Banyoro divinities are departmentalized according to people's activities, experiences and social-political structure. They include the divinities of war, of smallpox, of harvest, of health and healing, of the weather, of the lake, of cattle and minor ones of different clans. The same pattern of divinities is reported among Basoga, Edo and others.

The Yoruba have one thousand and seven hundred divinities (*orisa*), this being obviously the largest collection of divinities in a single African people. These divinities are associated with natural phenomena and objects, as well as with human activities and experiences. They are said to render to God "annual tributes of their substance in acknowledgment of His Lordship."

---

*In contrast to the Western linear concept of time, with its past, present, and future, the African concept of time is two-dimensional: there is a past (the Zamani period), a present (the Sasa period), but virtually no future. "Time has to be experienced in order . . . to become real." John S. Mbiti, *African Religions and Philosophy* (New York: Doubleday, 1970), pp. 19–36.—R.E.

[1] K. A. Busia in D. Forde, ed., *African Worlds* (Oxford, 1954), p. 191 f.; R. A. Lystad, *The Ashanti* (New Brunswick, 1958), p. 163 f.

Parallel to the Yoruba social-political structure, these divinities form a hierarchy. *Orisa-nla* is "the supreme divinity" in the country, and acts as God's earthly deputy in creative and executive functions. *Orunmila* is reputed to be an omnilinguist divinity who understands "every language spoken on earth," and who represents God's omniscience and knowledge. This divinity shows itself among men through the oracle of divination, and has the fame of being a great doctor. *Ogun* is the owner of all iron and steel, being originally a hunter who paved the way for other divinities to come to earth, for which reason they crowned him as "Chief among the divinities." He is ubiquitous, and is the divinity of war, hunting and activities or objects connected with iron. *Sango* represents the manifestation of God's wrath, though legend makes him a historical figure in the region of Oyo near Ibadan. He is the divinity of thunder and lightning, and there is a cult for him. These are but a few of the Yoruba divinities, an interesting study of which can be found in Idowu's book.[2]

There are many societies which have only one or two divinities of any major status. The Bambuti recognize *Tore* as the divinity in charge of death, to whom they refer as "the Gate of the Abyss" and "the Spirit of the dead."[3] Although the Dinka have several, three are most prominent. These are *Macardit* who is the final explanation of sufferings and misfortunes; *Garang* who is associated with men, and falling from heaven enters their bodies; and *Abuk* who is in charge of women's occupations.[4] The Vugusu blame their experiences of evil and suffering upon an evil divinity (*Wele gumali*) who is said to have servants.[5] The Walamo have one divinity connected with rain, said to dwell on a mountain where people take gifts in time of drought.

· · ·

SPIRITS

Myriads of spirits are reported from every African people, but they defy description almost as much as they defy the scientist's test tubes in the laboratory. Written sources are equally confusing. We have tried to include under the term "divinity," those spiritual beings of a relatively high status. If we pursue the hierarchical consideration, we can say that the spirits are the "common" spiritual beings beneath the status of divinities, and above the status of men. They are the "common populace" of spiritual beings.

As for the origin of spirits, there is no clear information what African peoples say or think about it. Some spirits are considered to have been created as a "race" by themselves. These, like other living creatures, have continued

[2]E. B. Idowu, *Olódùmarè: God in Yoruba Belief* (London / New York, 1962), pp. 55–106.
[3]P. Schebesta, *Revisiting My Pygmy Hosts* (E. T. London, 1936), p. 174 f.
[4]G. Lienhardt, *Divinity and Experience: The Religion of the Dinka* (Oxford, 1961), p. 81 f.
[5]G. Wagner *The Bantu of North Kavirondo* (Vol. I, Oxford 1949), p. 175 f.

to reproduce themselves and add to their numbers. Most peoples, however, seem to believe that the spirits are what remains of human beings when they die physically. This then becomes the ultimate status of men, the point of change or development beyond which men cannot go apart from a few national heroes who might become deified. Spirits are the destiny of man, and beyond them is God. Societies that recognize divinities regard them as a further group in the ontological hierarchy between spirits and God. Man does not, and need not, hope to become a spirit: he is inevitably to become one, just as a child will automatically grow to become an adult, under normal circumstances. A few societies have an additional source of the spirits, believing that animals also have spirits which continue to live in the spirit world together with human and other spirits.

Spirits are invisible, but may make themselves visible to human beings. In reality, however, they have sunk beyond the horizon of the Zamani period, so that human beings do not see them either physically or mentally. Memory of them has slipped off. They are "seen" in the corporate belief in their existence. Yet, people experience their activities, and many folk stories tell of spirits described in human form, activities and personalities, even if an element of exaggeration is an essential part of that description. Because they are invisible, they are thought to be ubiquitous, so that a person is never sure where they are or are not.

Since the spirits have sunk into the horizon of the Zamani, they are within the state of collective immortality, relative to man's position. They have no family or personal ties with human beings, and are no longer the living-dead. As such, people fear them, although intrinsically the spirits are neither evil nor good. They have lost their human names, as far as men are concerned —i.e. those that once were human beings. To men, therefore, the spirits are strangers, foreigners, outsiders, and in the category of "things." They are often referred to as "ITs." Viewed anthropocentrically, the ontological mode of the spirits is a depersonalization and not a completion or maturation of the individual. Therefore, death is a loss, and the spirit mode of existence means the withering of the individual, so that his personality evaporates, his name disappears and he becomes less and not more of a person: a thing, a spirit and not a man any more.

Spirits as a group have more power than men, just as in a physical sense the lions do. Yet, in some ways men are better off, and the right human specialists can manipulate or control the spirits as they wish. Men paradoxically may fear, or dread, the spirits and yet they can drive the same spirits away or use them to human advantage. In some societies only the major spirits (presumably in the category of divinities) are recognized, and often these are associated with natural phenomena or objects.

Although the spirits are ubiquitous, men designate different regions as their places of abode. Among some societies like the Abaluyia, Banyarwanda and

Igbo, it is thought that the spirits dwell in the underground, netherworld or the subterranean regions. The Banyarwanda say, for example, that this region is ruled by "the one with whom one is forgotten"; and the Igbo consider it to be ruled by a queen. The idea of the subterranean regions is suggested, obviously, by the fact that the bodies of the dead are buried and the ground points to, or symbolizes, the new homeland of the departed. A few societies like some Ewe, some Bushmen and the Mamvu-Mangutu, situate the land of the spirits above the earth, in the air, the sun, moon or stars.

The majority of peoples hold that the spirits dwell in the woods, bush, forest, rivers, mountains or just around the villages. Thus, the spirits are in the same geographical region as men. This is partly the result of human self-protection and partly because man may not want to imagine himself in an entirely strange environment when he becomes a spirit. There is a sense in which man is too anthropocentric to get away from himself and his natural, social, political and economic surroundings. This then makes the spirits men's contemporaries: they are ever with men, and man would feel uncomfortable if the ontological mode of the spirits were too distant from his own. This would mean upsetting the balance of existence, and if that balance is upset, then men make sacrifices, offerings and prayers, to try and restore it. In effect, men visualize their next ontological stage, in form of spirits, but geographically it is not another stage. The world of the spirits, wherever it might be situated, is very much like the carbon copy of the countries where they lived in this life. It has rivers, valleys, mountains, forests and deserts. Their activities of the spirits are similar to those of human life here, in addition to whatever other activities of which men may not know anything.

Yet, in certain aspects, the spirit world differs radically from the human world. It is invisible to the eyes of men: people only know or believe that it is there, but do not actually "see" it with their physical eyes. But more important, even if the spirits may be the depersonalized residue of individual human beings, they are ontologically "nearer" to God: not ethically, but in terms of communication with Him. It is believed that whereas men use or require intermediaries, the spirits do not, since they can communicate directly with God. We have already shown that in many African societies the spirits and the living-dead act as intermediaries who convey human sacrifices or prayers to God, and may relay His reply to men. We have also seen that in some societies it is believed that God has servants or agents whom He employs to carry out His intentions in the universe. The spirits fill up the ontological region of the Zamani between God and man's Sasa. The ontological transcendence of God is bridged by the spirit mode of existence. Man is forever a creature, but he does not remain forever man, and these are his two polarities of existence. Individual spirits may or may not remain for ever, but the class of the spirits is an essential and integral part of African ontology.

Becoming spirits is, in a sense, a social elevation. For this reason, African peoples show respect and high regard for their living-dead and for some of the important spirits. Spirits are "older" than men, when viewed against the Sasa and Zamani periods—they have moved completely into the Zamani period. Their age which is greater than that of human beings compels the latter to give them respect along the same pattern that younger people give respect to older men and women, whether or not they are immediately members of the same family. In relation to the spirits, men are the younger generation, and social etiquette requires that they respect those who have fully entered and settled in the Zamani period.

Spirits do not appear to human beings as often as do the living-dead, and where mention of their appearances is made it is generally in folk stories. They act in malicious ways, as well as in a benevolent manner. People fear them more because of their being "strangers" than because of what they actually are or do. They are said to have a shadowy form of body, though they may assume different shapes like human, animal, plant forms or inanimate objects. People report that they see the spirits in ponds, caves, groves, mountains or outside their villages, dancing, singing, herding cattle, working in their fields or nursing their children. Some spirits appear in people's dreams, especially to diviners, priests, medicine-men and rainmakers to impart some information. These personages may also consult the spirits as part of their normal training and practice. In many societies it is said and believed that spirits call people by name, but on turning round to see who called them there would be nobody. This sounds like a naughty game on the part of the spirits who probably derive a lot of fun from it. In folk stories it is told that the spirits sleep in the daytime and remain awake at night.

As the spirits are invisible, ubiquitous and unpredictable, the safest thing is to keep away from them. If they, or the living-dead, appear too frequently to human beings people feel disturbed. Then the spirits possess men, and are blamed for forms of illness like madness and epilepsy. Spirit possession occurs in one form or another in practically every African society. Yet, spirit possession is not always to be feared, and there are times when it is not only desirable but people induce it through special dancing and drumming until the person concerned experiences spirit possession during which he may even collapse. When the person is thus possessed, the spirit may speak through him, so that he now plays the role of a medium, and the messages he relays are received with expectation by those to whom they are addressed. But on the whole, spirit possessions, especially unsolicited ones, result in bad effects. They may cause severe torment in the possessed person; the spirit may drive him away from his home so that he lives in the forests; it may cause him to jump into the fire and get himself burnt, to torture his body with sharp instruments, or even to do harm to other people. During the height of spirit possession, the individual in effect loses his own personality and acts in the context of the "personality" of the spirit possessing him. The possessed person becomes restless, may fail to sleep properly, and if the possession lasts a long period it results in damage to health. Women are more prone to spirit possession than men. Exorcism is one of the major functions of the traditional doctors and diviners; and when spirits "endanger" a village, there are usually formal ceremonies to drive away the notorious spirits. In some societies family spirits have to be moved ceremoniously when the villagers move from one place to another. This insures that the family spirits and especially the living-dead, move with members of their human relatives and are not forsaken where there is nobody to "remember" them in their personal immortality.

Human relationships with the spirits vary from society to society. It is, however, a real, active and powerful relationship, especially with the spirits of those who have recently died—whom we have called the living-dead. Various rites are performed to keep this contact, involving the placing of food and other articles, or the pouring of libation of beer, milk, water and even tea or coffee (for the spirits who have been "modernized"). In some societies this is done daily, but most African peoples do it less often. Such offerings are given to the oldest member of the departed—who may still be a living-dead, or may be remembered only in genealogies. This is done with the understanding that he will share the food or beverage with the other spirits of the family group. Words may or may not accompany such offerings, in form of prayers, invocations or instructions to the departed. These words are the bridge of communion, the people's witness that they recognize the departed to be still alive. Failure to observe these acts means in effect that human beings have completely broken off their links with the departed, and have therefore forgotten the spirits. This is regarded as extremely dangerous and disturbing to the social and individual conscience. People are then likely to feel that any misfortune that befalls them is the logical result of their neglect of the spirits, if not caused by magic and witchcraft.

For spirits which are not associated with a particular family, offerings may be placed in spirit shrines where these exist. Such shrines belong to the community, and may be cared for by priests. Some of the spirits who are accorded this honour are venerated according to their functions, for example the spirits of the water may receive offerings when people want to fish or sail in the water; and the spirits of the forests may be consulted when people want to cut down the forest and make new fields. Here we merge with the category of the divinities, which we have already described above.

THE LIVING-DEAD

The departed of up to five generations are in a different category from that of ordinary spirits which we have been considering. They are still within the Sasa period, they are in the state of personal immortality, and their process of dying is not yet complete. We have called them the living-dead. They are the closest links that men have with the spirit world. Some of the things said about the spirits apply also to the living-dead. But the living-dead are bilingual: they speak the language of men, with whom they lived until "recently"; and they speak the language of the spirits and of God, to Whom they are drawing nearer ontologically. These are the "spirits" with which African peoples are most concerned: it is through the living-dead that the spirit world becomes personal to men. They are still part of their human families, and people have personal memories of them. The two groups are bound together by their common Sasa which for the living-dead is, however, fast disappearing into the Zamani. The living-dead are still "people," and have not yet become "things," "spirits" or "its." They return to their human families from time to time, and share meals with them, however symbolically. They know and have interest in what is going on in the family. When they appear, which is generally to the oldest members of the household, they are recognized by name as "so and so"; they enquire about family affairs, and may even warn of impending danger or rebuke those who have failed to follow their special instructions. They are the guardians of family affairs, traditions, ethics and activities. Offence in these matters is ultimately an offence against the forefathers who, in that capacity, act as the invisible police of the families and communities. Because they are still "people," the living-dead are therefore the best group of intermediaries between men and God: they know the needs of men, they have "recently" been here with men, and at the same time they have full access to the channels of communicating with God directly or, according to some societies, indirectly through their own forefathers. Therefore men approach them more often for minor needs of life than they approach God. Even if the living-dead may not do miracles or extraordinary things to remedy the need, men experience a sense of psychological relief when they pour out their hearts' troubles before their seniors who have a foot in both worlds.

All this does not mean that the relationship between men and the living-dead is exclusively paradisal. People know only too well that following physical death, a barrier has been erected between them and the living-dead. When the living-dead return and appear to their relatives, this experience is not received with great enthusiasm by men; and if it becomes too frequent, people resent it. Men do not say to the living-dead: "Please sit down and wait for food to be prepared!"; nor would they bid farewell with the words: "Great so-and-so in the spirit world!" And yet these are two extremely important aspects of social friendliness and hospitality among men in African communities. The food and libation given to the living-dead are paradoxically acts of hospitality and welcome, and yet of informing the living-dead to move away. The living-dead are wanted and yet not wanted. If they have been improperly buried or were offended before they died, it is feared by the relatives or the offenders that the living-dead would take revenge. This would be in the form of misfortune, especially illness, or disturbing frequent appearances of the living-dead. If people neglect to give food and libation where this is otherwise the normal practice, or if they fail to observe instructions that the living-dead may have given before dying, then misfortunes and sufferings would be interpreted as resulting from the anger of the living-dead. People are, therefore, careful to follow the proper practices and customs regarding the burial or other means of disposal of dead bodies, and make libation and food offerings as the case might be. In some societies, special care of the graves is taken, since the living-dead may be considered to dwell in the area of the graves, some of which are in the former houses of the departed. Attention is paid to the living-dead of up to four or five generations, by which time only a few, if any, immediate members of their families would still be alive. When the last person who knew a particular living-dead also dies, then in effect the process of death is now complete as far as that particular living-dead is concerned. He is now no longer remembered by name, no longer a "human being," but a spirit, a thing, an IT. He has now sunk beyond the visible horizon of the Zamani. It is no more necessary to pay close attention to him in the family obligation of making food offerings and libation, except, in some societies, within the context of genealogical remembrances or in the chain of the intermediaries. By that time also, additional living-dead have come into the picture and deserve or require more attention from the living. Those who have "moved on" to the stage of full spirits, merge into the company of spirits, and people lose both contact with and interest in them. They are no longer in the human period of the Sasa, even if they may continue to be men's contemporaries. Their plane of existence is other than that of men, they are ontologically spirits and spirits only. In some societies it is believed that some living-dead are "reborn." This is, however, only partial reincarnation since not the entire person is reborn as such, but only certain of his characteristics or physical distinctions.

further reading _____

Jerome Rothenberg (ed.), *Technicians of the Sacred: A Range of Poetries from Africa, America, Asia, and Oceania* (1968). Prayers, hymns, songs, and incantations, with very perceptive and helpful commentaries by the editor.

Max Gluckman, *Custom and Conflict in Africa* (1955). Note especially the chapter "The Logic of Witchcraft," in which that system of belief is held to be a theory of causation concerned with the singularity of misfortune. Thus witchcraft explains "why particular persons at particular times and places suffer particular misfortunes."

Basil Davidson is a recognized authority on the history of Africa. See his *Africa in History: Themes and Outlines* (1966; rev. ed., 1969) and *The African Genius: An Introduction to African Cultural and Social History* (1969). In the latter volume, Part Three deals with "Structures of Belief."

Peter J. M. McEwan and Robert B. Sutcliffe (eds.), *Modern Africa* (1965). A chapter on African "Value Systems" features Daryll Forde, "African Modes of Thinking," E. W. Smith, "African Ideas of God," Meyer Fortes and E. E. Evans-Pritchard, "Values in African Tribal Life," and other essays.

Other important anthologies are those by Daryll Forde (ed.), *African Worlds: Studies in the Cosmological Ideas and Social Values of African Peoples* (1954), a series of nine papers on a number of African peoples; Edwin W. Smith (ed.), *African Ideas of God* (1950); and M. Fortes and G. Dieterlen (eds.), *African Systems of Thought* (1965), which includes twenty-one essays ranging over such topics as indigenous systems of religious belief, ancestor worship, and Christianity and Islam in Africa.

John S. Mbiti, *Concepts of God in Africa* (1970). A most thorough study of the nature and attributes of God, the problem of evil, anthropomorphism, the creation of man, worship, ethics, death, and other topics.

Humanism

———————————————————————————*man is the measure*

introduction _____

> Man is the measure of all things,
> of those that are that they are,
> of those that are not that they are not.
>
> Protagoras

Humanism, as Julian Huxley has said, is a religion without revelation. Its source is man; its values and ideals are man-centered. Its hope is a good and rewarding life in *this* world. There are, then, no humanist "Scriptures." On the contrary, it is clear that this faith has evolved from human experience over the centuries, and it takes various forms with different individuals. It is expected, moreover, that humanist principles and goals will continue to evolve as the conditions of life are altered and human knowledge advances.

The term "humanism" was first used during the Renaissance; it referred to a renewed interest in man and his earthly affairs which was expressed in the arts, literature, and religion of that age. Sir Thomas More and Erasmus were Christian humanists, and in our own time Jacques Maritain has called for a theocentric (as opposed to anthropocentric) humanism. But the mainstream of contemporary humanism is naturalistic: it explicitly rejects all the supernatural elements in other religions.

The first reading selection in this chapter, Julian Huxley's "The Coming New Religion of Humanism," begins, indeed, with a harsh rejection of Christianity. That religion (and, it should be understood, any other whose claims cannot be scientifically verified) Huxley finds hopelessly contradicted by modern knowledge. Consequently, according to Huxley, Christianity is fading away, and moving into its place is the emerging religion of humanism.

In "The Good Life of the Self-Actualizing Person," Abraham Maslow finds that the self-actualizing person is one whose life incorporates "higher," self-transcending values. But such values are not of a realm different from the world in which we live. "The so-called spiritual, transcendent, or axiological life is clearly rooted in the biological nature of the species," Maslow states, and humanistic science should approach the eternal verities as " 'real' and natural, fact-based" phenomena.

The "Humanist Manifesto II," with which the chapter concludes, is a recent and well-received statement of the humanist position. A preface to the manifesto, however, emphasized that the manifesto was not "setting forth a binding credo." This, in short, is an open-ended religion.

julian huxley ―――――――――――――――――――――

The Coming New Religion of Humanism

Julian Huxley (1887–   ) is the brother of Aldous Huxley and the grandson of T. H. Huxley, who once said of the young Julian, "I like that chap. I like the way he looks you straight in the face and disobeys you."* Educated at Eton and Oxford, he became an eminent biologist and man of letters, and he more than held his own in the distinguished Huxley family. He lectured at universities in England and the United States, served as the first Director General of UNESCO, and was knighted in 1958. In addition to his scientific papers, he has written *The Uniqueness of Man, Darwin and His World, The Human Crisis, Evolution and Ethics, Religion without Revelation, On Living in a Revolution,* and *Essays of a Humanist.*

――――――――――――――――――――――――――――――――

It is certainly a fact that Christianity does not, and I would add cannot, satisfy an increasing number of people: and it does not and cannot do so because it is a particular brand of religion, which is no longer related or relevant to the facts of existence as revealed by the march of events or the growth of knowledge.

But first of all we must ask what we mean by a religion. A religion is an organ of man in society which helps him to cope with the problems of nature and his destiny—his place and role in the universe. It always involves the sense of sacredness or mystery and of participation in a continuing enterprise; it is always concerned with the problem of good and evil and with what transcends the individual self and the immediate and present facts of every day. A religion always has some framework of beliefs, some code of ethics, and some system of expression—what are usually called a theology, a morality, and a ritual. When we look closely we find that the beliefs largely determine both the nature of the moral code and the form of the ritual.

The theological framework on which Christianity is supported includes as its centre the basic belief of all theistic religions—the belief in the supernatural and the existence of a god or gods, supernatural beings endowed with properties of knowing, feeling, and willing akin to those of a human personality.

In Christian theology, god is a being who at a definite date—until recently specified as 4004 B.C.—created the world and man in essentially the same form they have today; a ruler capable of producing miracles and of influencing natural events, including events in human minds, and conversely of being influenced by man's prayers and responding to them.

*Quoted in Victor E. Amend and Leo T. Hendrick (eds.), *Ten Contemporary Thinkers* (New York: Free Press of Glencoe, 1964), p. 415.

Julian Huxley, "The Coming New Religion of Humanism." This article first appeared in *The Humanist* (January/February 1962) and is reprinted by permission.

THE CHRISTIAN BELIEF

Christianity believes in a last judgment by god at a definite but unspecified future date. It believes in an eternal life after death in a supernatural realm, and makes salvation through belief its central aim. It believes in the fall of man and original sin, that its code of morals has been commanded by god, and that all mankind is descended from one original couple. Christianity asserts a partial polytheism in the doctrine of the Trinity, and gives full rein to what the students of comparative religion call polydaemonism by its belief in angels, saints, and the Virgin and their power to grant human prayers. Officially it still believes in hell and the devil and other evil supernatural beings, though these beliefs are rapidly fading. It is based on a belief in divine revelation and in the historical reality of supernatural events such as the incarnation and resurrection of Jesus as the son of the first person of the Trinity. It claims or assumes that all other religions are false and that only Christianity (or only one brand of Christianity) is true. It assumes that the earth occupies a central position in the cosmic scheme, and that, though god is believed to be omnipotent, omniscient, and omnibenevolent, he has a special concern with man's salvation.

The Christian system of beliefs is quite unacceptable in the world of today. It is contradicted, as a whole and in detail, by our extended knowledge of the cosmos, of the solar system, of our own planet, of our own species, and of our individual selves.

Christianity is dogmatic, dualistic, and essentially geocentric. It is based on a vision of reality which sees the universe as static, short-lived, small, and ruled by a supernatural being. The vision we now possess, thanks to the patient and imaginative labours of thousands of physicists, chemists, biologists, psychologists, anthropologists, archeologists, historians, and humanists, is incommensurable with it. In the light of this new vision, our picture of reality becomes unitary, temporally and spatially of almost inconceivable vastness, dynamic, and constantly transforming itself through the operation of its own inherent properties. It is also scientific, in the sense of being based on established knowledge, and accordingly non-dogmatic, basically self-correcting, and itself evolving. Its keynote, the central concept to which all its details are related, is evolution.

THE NEW VISION

Let me try to outline this new vision as briefly as possible. On the basis of our present understanding, all reality is in a perfectly valid sense one universal process of evolution. The single process occurs in three phases—first, the inorganic or cosmic, operating by physical and to a limited extent chemical interaction, and leading to the production of such organizations of matter as nebulae, stars, and solar systems; in our galaxy this phase has been going on for at least six billion years.

In the rare places where matter has become self-reproducing, the inorganic has been succeeded by the organic or biological phase; this operates primarily by the ordering agency we call natural selection, and leads to the production of increasingly varied and increasingly higher organizations of matter, such as flowers, insects, cuttlefish, and vertebrates, and to the emergence of mind and increasingly higher organizations of awareness. On our planet this has been operating for rather under three billion years.

Finally, in what must be the extremely rare places (we only know for certain of one) where, to put it epigrammatically, mind has become self-reproducing through man's capacity to transmit experience and its products cumulatively, we have the human or psychosocial phase. This operates by the self-perpetuating but self-varying and (within limits) self-correcting process of cumulative learning and cumulative transmission, and leads to the evolution of increasingly varied and increasingly higher psychosocial products, such as religions, scientific concepts, labor-saving machinery, legal systems, and works of art.

Our prehuman ancestors arrived at the threshold of the critical step to this phase around a million years ago; but they became fully human, and psychosocial evolution began to work really effectively, only within the last few tens of thousands of years. During that short span of evolutionary time, man has not changed genetically in any significant way, and his evolution has been predominantly cultural, manifested in the evolution of his social systems, his ideas, and his technological and artistic creations.

The new vision enlarges our future as much as our past. Advance in biological evolution took place through a succession of so-called dominant types—in the last 400 million years, from jawless limbless vertebrates to fish, then through amphibians to reptiles, from reptiles to mammals, and finally to man. Each new dominant type is in some important way biologically more efficient than the last, so that when it breaks through to evolutionary success it multiplies and spreads at the expense of its predecessors.

Man is the latest dominant type to arise in the ecology of this earth. There is no possibility of his dominant position in evolution being challenged by an existing type of creature, whether rat or ape or insect. All that could happen to man (if he does not blow himself up with nuclear bombs or convert himself into a cancer of his planet by over-multiplication) is that he could transform himself as a whole species into something new. He has nearly three billion years of evolution behind him, from his first pre-cellular beginnings: barring accidents, he has at least as much time before him to pursue his evolutionary course.

Yeats implied, or indeed affirmed, that if the Christian God were rejected, a Savage God would take his place. This certainly could happen, but it need not happen, and we can be pretty sure that in the long run it will not happen.

The new framework of ideas on which any new dominant religion will be based is at once evolutionary and humanist. For evolutionary humanism, gods are creations of man, not vice versa. Gods begin as hypotheses serving to account for certain phenomena of outer nature and and inner experience: they develop into more unified theories, which purport to explain the phenomena and make them comprehensible; and they end up being hypostatized as supernatural personal beings capable of influencing the phenomena. As theology develops, the range of phenomena accounted for by the god-hypothesis is extended to cover the entire universe, and the gods become merged in God.

However, with the development of human science and learning, this universal or absolute God becomes removed further and further back from phenomena and any control of them. As interpreted by the more desperately "liberal" brands of Christianity today, he appears to the humanist as little more than the smile of a cosmic Cheshire Cat, but one which is irreversibly disappearing.

THE STUFF OF DIVINITY

But though I believe that gods and God in any meaningful non-Pickwickian sense are destined to disappear, the stuff of divinity out of which they have grown and developed remains, and will provide much of the raw material from which any new religions will be fashioned. This religious raw material consists in those aspects of nature and elements in experience which are usually described as divine. The term *divine* did not originally imply the existence of gods: on the contrary, gods were constructed to interpret man's experiences of this quality in phenomena.

Some events and some phenomena of outer nature transcend ordinary explanation and ordinary experience. They inspire awe and seem mysterious, explicable only in terms of something beyond or above ordinary nature—"super-natural" power, a super-human element at work in the universe.

Such magical, mysterious, awe-inspiring, divinity-suggesting facts have included wholly outer phenomena like volcanic eruptions, thunder, and hurricanes, biological phenomena such as sex and reproduction, birth, disease and death, and also phenomena of man's inner life such as intoxication, possession, speaking with tongues, inspiration, insanity, and mystic vision.

With the growth of knowledge most of these phenomena have ceased to be mysterious so far as rational or scientific inexplicability is concerned. But there remains the fundamental mystery of existence, and in particular the existence of mind. Our knowledge of physics and chemistry-neurology does not account for the basic fact of subjective experience, though they help us to understand its workings. The stark fact of mind sticks in the throat of pure rationalism and reductionist materialism.

However, it remains true that phenomena are charged with a magic quality of transcendent and even compulsive power, and introduce us to a realm beyond ordinary experience. Such events and such experiences merit a special designation. For want of a better, I use the term *divine,* though this quality of divinity is not truly supernatural but *transnatural*—it grows out of ordinary nature, but transcends it. The divine is what man finds worthy of adoration, that which compels his worship: and during history it evolves like everything else.

Much of every religion is aimed at the discovery and safeguarding of divinity, and seeks contact and communion with what is regarded as divine. A humanist-based religion must redefine divinity, strip the divine of the theistic qualities which man has anthropomorphically projected into it, search for its habitations in every aspect of existence, elicit it, and establish fruitful contact with its manifestations. Divinity is the chief raw material out of which gods have been fashioned. Today we must melt down the gods and refashion the material into new and effective agencies, enabling man to exist freely and fully on the spiritual level as well as on the material.

The character of all religions depends primarily on the pattern of its supporting framework of ideas, its theology in an extended sense; and this in its turn depends on the extent and organization of human knowledge at the time. I feel sure that the world will see the birth of a new religion based on what I have called evolutionary humanism. Just how it will develop and flower no one knows—but some of its underlying beliefs are beginning to emerge, and in any case it is clear that a humanism of this sort can provide powerful religious, moral and practical motivation for life.

EVOLUTIONARY HUMANISM

The beliefs of this religon of evolutionary humanism are not based on revelation in the supernatural sense, but on the revelations that science and learning have given us about man and the universe. A humanist believes with full assurance that man is not alien to nature, but a part of nature, albeit a unique one. He is made of the same matter and works by the same energy as the rest of the universe. He is not only a product of the universal process of evolution, but capable of affecting the process which has produced him, and of affecting it either for good or ill. His true destiny is to guide the future course of evolution on earth towards greater fulfilment, so as to realize more and higher potentialities. And this can only be done by intelligently co-operating with outer nature, not by senselessly exploiting and wasting its resources; and by intelligently guiding his own nature, not by senselessly succumbing to his conflicting instincts and moods—reproductive, acquisitive, despairing, idealistic, or aggressive.

Evolution is essentially creative. It is constantly generating improved, more varied, and higher types. During pre-human evolution from some pre-cellular submicroscopic speck to a dominant type of terrestial organism, the evolutionary process has realized almost inconceivable potentialities—of adaptability and power, knowledge and emotion, intelligence and love. During his own evolution, man has realized further and equally inconceivable potentialities. Some are good and have grandeur, in the shape of comprehensive scientific theories, soul-compelling religions, glorious buildings, fantastic machines, undying works of art, inspiring moral codes. But he has also realized equally inconceivable potentialities of horror and evil—torture by the Inquisition, Hitler's gas chambers for Jews, the ruthlessness of Genghis Khan, war after war after war, the horror of the atomic bomb, and the incredible stupidity of the nuclear deterrent stalemate.

A HUMANIST RELIGION

A humanist religion will have the task of redefining the categories of good and evil in terms of fulfilment and of desirable or undesirable realizations of potentiality, and setting up new targets for its morality to aim at.

In this process of transvaluation, to borrow Nietzsche's phrase, a humanist religion will certainly do something new—it will assign a high value to the increase of scientifically based knowledge; for it is on knowledge and its applications that anything which can properly be called human advance or progress depends. It will also assign a high value to the creative imagination and the works of art and beauty and significance which it produces; for it is they which are the highest expressions of the spirit of man.

As regards the individual, a humanist religion will, like the ancient Greeks, stress *excellence*. But as complementary to this, it will go further than the Greek principle of moderation: nothing too much—and will make psychological integration and total wholeness an essential aim, and in some sense the equivalent of the state of salvation in Christian terminology. Finally, it can give the individual much-needed protection against the tyrannies of society, much-needed support against the pressure of authoritarianism and conformism, by proclaiming the vital truth that in realising his own potentialities and in developing his own personality the individual is making his own unique contribution to the universal process of evolutionary fulfilment.

Integration implies the resolution of dichotomies and conflicts, through their incorporation in a unified, balanced dynamic pattern, well equipped with feedback mechanisms. In Marxism, the individual is presented in opposition to society. In humanism, the individual and society are seen as inevitably interrelated; integration here implies making the interrelation more profound and more harmonious. In the evolutionary humanist view, the dichotomy between heredity and environment can similarly disappear, by making heredity and environment support each other and act synergistically so as to secure a more complete development.

Humanism also differs from all supernaturalist religions in centering its long-term aims not on the next world but on this. One of its fundamental tenets is that this world and the life in it can be improved, and that it is our duty to try to improve it, socially, culturally, and politically. The humanist goal must therefore be, not Technocracy, nor Theocracy, not the omnipotent and authoritarian State, nor the Welfare State, nor the Consumption Economy, but the Fulfilment Society. By this I mean a society organized in such a way as to give the greatest number of people the fullest opportunities of realizing their potentialities—of achievement and enjoyment, morality and community. It will do so by providing opportunities for education, for adventure and achievement, for cooperating in worthwhile projects, for meditation and withdrawal, for self-development and unselfish action.

Above all, a humanist religion will uphold the ideal of quality, against the assaults of mere quantity, of richness and variety against drabness and monotony, and of active open and continuous development, personal, social, and evolutionary, as against static self-complacency or unreal millenary fanaticism.

abraham maslow _____

The Good Life of the Self-Actualizing Person

Abraham Maslow (1908–1970) was born in Brooklyn and received his A.B., M.A., and Ph.D. degrees from the University of Wisconsin. He taught at Brooklyn College and at Brandeis University, where he became chairman of the Psychology Department. An independent and innovative thinker, Maslow was known in his field as "Mr. Humanist," the prime mover of the humanist movement in psychology. Late in his life, following a serious heart attack, Maslow looked upon his being alive as "a kind of an extra, a bonus," and he called it his "post-mortem life": "One very important aspect of the post-mortem life is that everything gets doubly precious, gets piercingly important. You get stabbed by things, by flowers and by babies and by beautiful things—just the very act of living, of walking and breathing and eating and having friends."* But much of this attitude seemed always a part of Maslow's genius, and it was expressed in such his books as *Motivation and Personality, Toward a Psychology of Being, Eupsychian Management,* and *Religions, Values, and Peak Experiences.*

_____

Humanistic ethics have at times emphasized ''self-actualization'' as a desirable goal for man. This is an old idea in the history of thought. Plato and Aristotle were concerned with the concept. Recent psychological research has given support and a practical significance to the theory. Examining the characteristics of the ''self-actualizing'' person assists our continual quest for the good life.

Self-actualizing people are gratified in all their basic needs embracing affection, respect and self-esteem. They have a feeling of belongingness and rootedness. They are satisfied in their love needs, because they have friends, feel loved and loveworthy. They have status, place in life, and respect from other people, and they have a reasonable feeling of worth and self-respect.

Self-actualizing people do not for any length of time feel anxiety-ridden, insecure, unsafe; do not feel alone, ostracized, rootless, or isolated; do not feel unlovable, rejected or unwanted; do not feel despised and looked down upon; and do not feel unworthy nor do they have crippling feelings of inferiority or worthlessness.

Since the basic needs had been assumed to be the only motivations for human beings, it was possible, and in certain contexts useful, to say to

_____

*Quoted in *Psychology Today*, Vol. 4, No. 3 (August 1970), p. 16.

Abraham H. Maslow, "The Good Life of the Self-Actualizing Person." This article first appeared in *The Humanist* (July/August 1967) and is reprinted by permission.

self-actualizing people that they were "unmotivated." This aligned these people with the Eastern philosophical view of health as the transcendence of striving or desiring or wanting.

It is also possible to say and to describe self-actualizing people as expressing rather than coping. They are spontaneous, natural, and more easily themselves than other people.

What motivates the self-actualizing person? What are the psychodynamics in self-actualization? What makes him move and act and struggle? What drives or pulls such a person? What attracts him? For what does he hope? What makes him angry, or dedicated, or self-sacrificing? What does he feel loyal to? Devoted to? What does he aspire to and yearn for? What would he die or live for?

These questions ask for an answer to the question: What are the motivations of self-actualizing people? Clearly we must make an immediate distinction between the ordinary motives of those people who are below the level of self-actualization and motivated by the basic needs, and the motivations of people who are sufficiently gratified in all their basic needs and are no longer primarily motivated by them. For convenience, call these motives and needs of self-actualizing persons "metaneeds." This also differentiates the category of motivation from the category of "metamotivation."

Examining self-actualizing people. I find that they are dedicated people, devoted to some task outside themselves, some vocation, or duty, or job. Generally the devotion and dedication is so marked that one can correctly use the old words vocation, calling or mission to describe their passionate, selfless and profound feeling for their "work." We could even use the words destiny or fate in the sense of biological or temperamental or constitutional destiny or fate. Sometimes I have gone so far as to speak of oblation in the religious sense of dedicating oneself upon some altar for a particular task, some cause outside oneself and bigger than oneself, something not merely selfish, something impersonal. This is one way of putting into adequate words the feeling that one gets when one listens to self-actualizing people talking about their work or task. One gets the feeling of a beloved job, and further, of something for which the person is "a natural," that he is suited for, that is right for him, even something for which he was born.

In this kind of a situation, it is easy to sense something like a pre-established harmony or a good match like a perfect love affair in which it seems that people belong to each other and were meant for each other. In the best instances the person and his job fit together and belong together perfectly like a key and a lock, or resonate together like a sung note which sets into sympathetic resonance a particular string in the piano keyboard.

Often I get the feeling that I can tease apart two kinds of determinants from this fusion which has created a unity out of a duality, and that these two sets of determinants can, and sometimes do, vary independently. One can be spoken of as the responses to forces relatively within the person: e.g., "I love babies (or painting, or research, or political power) more than anything in the world." "It fascinates me." "I am inexorably drawn to . . ." "I need to . . ." This we may call "inner requiredness" and it is felt as a kind of self-indulgence rather than as a duty. It is different from and separable from "external requiredness," which is felt as a response to what the environment, the situation, the problem, or the external world, calls for and requires of the person. A fire "calls for" putting out, or a helpless baby demands that one take care of it, or some obvious injustice calls for righting. Here one feels more the element of duty, of obligation, of responsibility, of being compelled helplessly to respond no matter what one was planning to do, or wished to do. It is more "I must," "I have to," "I am compelled" than "I want to."

In the ideal instance, "I want to" coincides with "I must." There is a good matching of inner with outer requiredness. The observer is overawed by the degree of compellingness, of inexorability, or preordained destiny, necessity and harmony that he perceives. Furthermore, the observer, as well as the person involved, feels not only that "it has to be" but also that "it ought to be, it is right, it is suitable, appropriate, fitting and proper." I have often felt a gestalt-like quality about this kind of belonging together, the formation of a "one" out of "two." I hesitate to call this simply "purposefulness" because that may imply that it happens only out of will, purpose, decision or calculation; the word doesn't give enough weight to the subjective feeling of being swept along, of willing and eager surrender, or yielding to fate and happily embracing it at the same time. Ideally, one discovers one's fate; it is not made or constructed or decided upon. It is recognized as if one had been unwittingly waiting for it. Perhaps the better phrase would be "Spinozistic" or "Taoistic" choice or decision or purpose.

The best way to explain these feelings is to use the example of "falling in love." It is clearly different from doing one's duty, or doing what is sensible or logical. Also "will," if mentioned at all, is used in a very special sense. When two people fall in love with each other fully, each one knows what it feels like to be a magnet and what it feels like to be iron filings, and what it feels like to be both simultaneously. Very useful, also, is the parallel with the happy abandon of the ideal sexual situation. Here people resist and delay the inevitable climax, in a kind of fond self- and other-teasing, holding off as long as possible. Suddenly, in a single instant they can change to the opposite course of embracing eagerly and totally, the end which they were moments ago delaying, like the tides suddenly change from going north to going south.

This example also helps convey what is difficult to communicate in words; the lovers' sense of good fortune, of luck, of gratuitous grace, of gratitude, of awe that this miracle should have occurred, of wonder that they should have been chosen, and of the peculiar mixture of pride fused with humility, of arrogance shot through with the pity-for-the-less-fortunate that one finds in lovers.

It can be said of the self-actualizing person that he is being his own kind of person, or being himself, or actualizing his real self. Observation would lead one to understand that "This person is the best one in the whole world for this particular job, and this particular job is the best job in the whole world for this particular person and his talents, capacities and tastes. He was meant for it, and it was meant for him."

Accepting this premise, we move into another realm of discourse—the realm of being, of transcendence. Now we can speak meaningfully only in the language of being (the "B-language," communication at the mystical level which is detailed in my book *The Psychology of Being*). It is quite obvious with such people that the ordinary or conventional dichotomy between work and play is transcended totally. Such a person's work is his play and his play is his work. If a person loves his work and enjoys it more than any other activity in the whole world and is eager to get to it, to get back to it, after any interruption, then how can we speak about "labor" in the sense of something one is forced to do against one's wishes?

What sense, for instance, is left to the concept "vacation"? For such individuals it is often observed that during the periods in which they are totally free to choose whatever they wish to do and in which they have no external obligations to anyone else, they devote themselves happily and totally to their "work." What does it mean "to have some fun"? What is the meaning of the word "entertainment"? How does such a person "rest"? What are his "duties," responsibilities, obligations?

What sense does money or pay or salary make in such a situation? Obviously the most beautiful fate, the most wonderful good luck, the most marvelous good fortune that can happen to any human being is to be paid for doing that which he passionately loves to do. This is exactly the situation, or almost the situation, with many self-actualizing persons. Of course, money is welcome, and in certain amounts is even needed. It is certainly not the finality, the end, the goal, however. The check such a man gets is only a small part of his "pay." Self-actualizing work or B-work, being its own intrinsic reward, transforms the money or pay-check into a by-product, an epiphenomenon. This is different from the situation of less fortunate human beings who do something that they do not want to do in order to get money, which they then use to get what they really want. The role of money in the realm of being is certainly different from the role of money in the realm of deficiencies.

These are scientific questions, and can be investigated in scientific ways. They have been investigated in monkeys and apes to a degree. The most obvious example, of course, is the rich research literature on monkey curiosity and other precursors of the human yearning for and satisfaction with the truth. But it will be just as easy in principle to explore the esthetic choices of these and other animals under conditions of fear and of lack of fear, by healthy specimens or by unhealthy ones, under good choice conditions or bad ones, etc.

If one asks the fortunate, work-loving, self-actualizing person, "Who are you?" or "What are you?" he tends to answer in terms of his "call" . . . "I am a lawyer." "I am a mother." "I am a psychiatrist." "I am an artist." He tells you that he identifies his call with his identity, his Self. It is a label for the whole of him and it becomes a defining characteristic of the person.

If one confronts him with the question, "Supposing you were not a scientist (or a teacher, or a pilot), then what would you be?" or "Supposing you were not a psychologist, then what?" his response is apt to be one of puzzlement, thoughtfulness. He does not have a ready answer. Or the response can be one of amusement. It strikes him funny. In effect, the answer is, "If I were not a mother (lover, anthropologist, industrialist) then I wouldn't be *me*. I would be someone else, and I can't imagine being someone else."

A tentative conclusion is then, that in self-actualizing subjects, their beloved calling tends to be perceived as a defining characteristic of the self, to be identified with, incorporated, introjected. It becomes an inextricable aspect of one's Being.

When asked why they love their work, which are the moments of higher satisfaction in their work, which moments of reward make all the necessary chores worthwhile or acceptable, which are the peak-experiences, self-actualizing people give many specific and *ad hoc* answers which to them are intrinsic reinforcers.

As I classified these moments of reward, it became apparent that the best and most natural categories of classification were mostly or entirely values of an ultimate and irreducible kind! Call them "B-values": truth, beauty, newness, uniqueness, justice, compactness, simplicity, goodness, neatness, efficiency, love, honesty, innocence, improvement, orderliness, elegance, growth, cleanliness, authenticity, serenity, peacefulness.

For these people the profession seems to be not functionally autonomous, but to be a carrier of ultimate values. I could say, if I were not afraid of being misunderstood, that for example, the profession of law, is a means to the end of justice, and not a law to itself in which justice might get lost. For one man the law is loved because it is justice, while another man, the pure value-free technologist, might love the law simply as an intrinsically lovable set of rules, precedents, procedures without regard to the ends or products of their use.

B-values or metamotives are not only intrapsychic or organismic. They are equally inner and outer. The metaneeds, insofar as they are inner, and the requiredness of all that is outside the person are each stimulus and response to each other. And they move toward becoming indistinguishable, toward fusion.

This means that the distinction between self and not-self has broken down or has been transcended. There is less differentiation between the world and the person because he has incorporated into himself part of the world and defines himself thereby. He becomes an enlarged self. If justice or truth or lawfulness have now become so important to him that he identifies his self with them, then where are they? Inside his skin or outside his skin? This distinction comes close to being meaningless at this point because his self no longer has his skin as its boundary.

Certainly simple selfishness is transcended here and has to be defined at higher levels. For instance, we know that it is possible for a person to get more pleasure out of food through having his child eat it rather than through eating it with his own mouth. His self has enlarged enough to include his child. Hurt his child and you hurt him. Clearly the self can no longer be identified with the biological entity which is supplied with blood from his heart along his blood vessels. The psychological self can obviously be bigger than his own body.

Just as beloved people can be incorporated into the self, thereby becoming defining characteristics of it, so also can causes and values be similarly incorporated into a person's self. Many people are so passionately identified with trying to prevent war, racial injustices, slums, or poverty that they are quite willing to make great sacrifices, even to the point of risking death. Very clearly, they do not mean justice for their own biological bodies alone. They mean justice as a general value, justice for everyone, justice as a principle.

There are other important consequences of this incorporation of values into the self. For instance, you can love justice and truth in the world or in a person out there. You can be made happier as your friends move toward truth and justice, and sadder as they move away from it. That's easy to understand. However, suppose you see yourself moving successfully toward truth, justice, beauty and virtue? Then you may find that, in a peculiar kind of detachment and objectivity toward oneself, for which our culture has no place, you will be loving and admiring yourself in the kind of healthy self-love that Fromm has described. You can respect yourself, admire yourself, take tender care of yourself, reward yourself, feel virtuous, love-worthy, respect-worthy. You may then treat yourself with the responsibility and otherness that a pregnant woman does whose self now has to be defined to overlap with not-self. So may a person with a great talent protect it and himself as if he were a carrier of something which is simultaneously himself and not himself. He may become his own friend.

These people, although concretely working for, motivated by and loyal to some conventional category of work, are transparently motivated by the intrinsic or ultimate values or aspects of reality for which the profession is only a vehicle.

This is my impression from observing them, interviewing them, and asking them why they like doctoring, or just which are the most rewarding moments in running a home, or chairing a committee, or having a baby, or writing. They may meaningfully be said to be working for truth, for beauty, for goodness, for law and for order, for justice, for perfection, if I boil down to a dozen or so intrinsic values (or values of Being) all the hundreds of specific reports of what is yearned for, what gratifies, what is valued, what they work for from day to day, and why they work.

It is at this point in my theory that, quite fairly, both methodology and validity can be called into question. I have not deliberately worked with an *ad hoc* control group of non-self-actualizing people. I could say that most of humanity is a control group. I have a considerable fund of experience with the attitudes toward work of average people, immature people, neurotic and borderline people, psychopaths and others. There is no question that their attitudes cluster around money, basic-need gratification rather than B-values, sheer habit, stimulus-binding, convention and the inertia of the unexamined and non-questioned life, and from doing what other people expect or demand. However, this intuitive or naturalistic conclusion is susceptible to more careful and more controlled and predesigned examination.

Secondly, it is my strong impression that there is not a sharp line between my subjects chosen as self-actualizing and other people. I believe that each self-actualizing subject more or less fits the description I have given, but it seems also true that some percentage of other, less healthy people are metamotivated by the B-values also; especially individuals with special talents and people placed in especially fortunate circumstances. Perhaps all people are metamotivated to some degree.

The conventional categories of career, profession or work may serve as channels of many other kinds of motivations, not to mention sheer habit or convention or functional autonomy. They may satisfy or seek vainly to satisfy any or all of the basic needs as well as various neurotic needs. They may be a channel for "acting out" or for "defensive" activities rather than for real gratifications.

My guess, supported by both my "empirical" impressions and by general psychodynamic theory, is that we will find it ultimately most true and most useful to say that all these various habits, determinants, motives and metamotives are acting simultaneously in a very complex pattern which is centered more toward one kind of motivation or determinedness than the others.

If we can try to define the deepest, most authentic, most constitutionally based aspects of the real self, of the identity, or of the authentic person, we find that in order to be comprehensive, we must include not only the person's constitution and temperament, not only anatomy, physiology, neurology and endocrinology, not only his capacities, his biological style, not only his basic instinctoid needs, but also *the* B-values which are also *his* B-values. They are equally a part of his "nature," or definition, or essence, along with his "lower" needs. They must be included in any definition of the human being, or of full-humanness, or of a person. It is true that they are not fully evident or actualized in most people. Yet, so far as I can see at this time, they are not excluded as potentials in any human being born into the world.

Thus, a fully inclusive definition of a fully-developed self or person includes a value-system, by which he is metamotivated.

What all of this means is that the so-called spiritual or "higher" life is on the same continuum (is the same kind of quality or thing) with the life of the flesh, or of the body, i.e., the animal life, the "lower" life. The spiritual life is part of our biological life. It is the "highest" part of it, but yet part of it. The spiritual life is part of the human essence. It is a defining-characteristic of human nature, without which human nature is not full human nature. It is part of the real self, of one's identity, of one's inner core, of one's specieshood, of full-humanness.

To the extent that pure expressing of oneself, or pure spontaneity is possible, to that extent will the metaneeds be expressed. "Uncovering" or Taoistic therapeutic or "Ontogogic" techniques should uncover and strengthen the metaneeds as well as the basic needs. Depth-diagnostic and therapeutic techniques should ultimately also uncover these same metaneeds because, paradoxically, our highest nature is also our deepest nature. They are not in two separate realms as most religions and philosophies have assumed, and as classical science has also assumed. The spiritual life (the contemplative, "religious," philosophical, or value-life) is within the jurisdiction of human thought and is attainable in principle by man's own efforts. Even though it has been cast out of the realm of reality by the classical, value-free science which models itself upon physics, it is now being reclaimed as an object of study and technology by humanistic science. Such an expanded science will consider the eternal verities, the ultimate truths, the final values, to be "real" and natural, fact-based rather than wish-based, legitimate scientific problems calling for research.

The so-called spiritual, transcendent, or axiological life is clearly rooted in the biological nature of the species. It is a kind of "higher" animality whose precondition is a healthy "lower" animality and the two are hierarchically-integrated rather than mutually exclusive. However, the higher, spiritual "animality" is timid and weak. It is so easily lost, easily crushed by stronger cultural forces, that it can become widely actualized *only* in a culture which approves of human nature and, therefore, fosters its fullest growth.

paul kurtz _____

Humanist Manifesto II

Paul Kurtz, editor of the journal *The Humanist* and a professor of philosophy at the State University of New York, Buffalo, drafted the "Humanist Manifesto II," and it was signed by scores of distinguished thinkers. Published in 1973, it appeared forty years after the "Humanist Manifesto I," whose signers included John Dewey.* The rapid changes and momentous events of the intervening years had brought about the need for the new manifesto, as is explained in its preface: "Science has sometimes brought evil as well as good. Recent decades have shown that inhuman wars can be made in the name of peace. The beginnings of police states, even in democratic societies, widespread government espionage, and other abuses of power by military, political, and industrial elites, and the continuance of unyielding racism, all present a different and difficult social outlook. In various societies, the demands of women and minority groups for equal rights effectively challenge our generation."

The next century can be and should be the humanistic century. Dramatic scientific, technological, and ever-accelerating social and political changes crowd our awareness. We have virtually conquered the planet, explored the moon, overcome the natural limits of travel and communication; we stand at the dawn of a new age, ready to move farther into space and perhaps inhabit other planets. Using technology wisely, we can control our environment, conquer poverty, markedly reduce disease, extend our life-span, significantly modify our behavior, alter the course of human evolution and cultural development, unlock vast new powers, and provide humankind with unparalleled opportunity for achieving an abundant and meaningful life.

The future is, however, filled with dangers. In learning to apply the scientific method to nature and human life, we have opened the door to ecological damage, overpopulation, dehumanizing institutions, totalitarian repression, and nuclear and biochemical disaster. Faced with apocalyptic prophesies and doomsday scenarios, many flee in despair from reason and embrace irrational cults and theologies of withdrawal and retreat.

Traditional moral codes and newer irrational cults both fail to meet the pressing needs of today and tomorrow. False "theologies of hope" and

---

*"Humanist Manifesto I" first appeared in *The New Humanist,* Vol. VI, No. 3 (May/June 1933). Both manifestos have been reprinted in *Humanist Manifestos I and II* (Buffalo, N.Y.: Prometheus Books, 1973).

Paul Kurtz, "Humanist Manifesto II ." This article first appeared in *The Humanist* (September/October 1973) and is reprinted by permission.

CHAPTER TWELVE / *Humanism*

messianic ideologies, substituting new dogmas for old, cannot cope with existing world realities. They separate rather than unite peoples.

Humanity, to survive, requires bold and daring measures. We need to extend the uses of scientific method, not renounce them, to fuse reason with compassion in order to build constructive social and moral values. Confronted by many possible futures, we must decide which to pursue. The ultimate goal should be the fulfillment of the potential for growth in each human personality—not for the favored few, but for all of humankind. Only a shared world and global measures will suffice.

A humanist outlook will tap the creativity of each human being and provide the vision and courage for us to work together. This outlook emphasizes the role human beings can play in their own spheres of action. The decades ahead call for dedicated, clear-minded men and women able to marshal the will, intelligence, and cooperative skills for shaping a desirable future. Humanism can provide the purpose and inspiration that so many seek; it can give personal meaning and significance to human life.

Many kinds of humanism exist in the contemporary world. The varieties and emphases of naturalistic humanism include "scientific," "ethical," "democratic," "religious," and "Marxist" humanism. Free thought, atheism, agnosticism, skepticism, deism, rationalism, ethical culture, and liberal religion all claim to be heir to the humanist tradition. Humanism traces its roots from ancient China, classical Greece and Rome, through the Renaissance and the Enlightenment, to the scientific revolution of the modern world. But views that merely reject theism are not equivalent to humanism. They lack commitment to the positive belief in the possibilities of human progress and to the values central to it. Many within religious groups, believing in the future of humanism, now claim humanist credentials. Humanism is an ethical process through which we all can move, above and beyond the divisive particulars, heroic personalities, dogmatic creeds, and ritual customs of past religions or their mere negation.

We affirm a set of common principles that can serve as a basis for united action—positive principles relevant to the present human condition. They are a design for a secular society on a planetary scale.

For these reasons, we submit this new *Humanist Manifesto* for the future of humankind; for us, it is a vision of hope, a direction for satisfying survival.

RELIGION

First: In the best sense, religion may inspire dedication to the highest ethical ideals. The cultivation of moral devotion and creative imagination is an expression of genuine "spiritual" experience and aspiration.

We believe, however, that traditional dogmatic or authoritarian religions that place revelation, God, ritual, or creed above human needs and experience do a disservice to the human species. Any account of nature should pass the tests of scientific evidence; in our judgment, the dogmas and myths of traditional religions do not do so. Even at this late date in human history, certain elementary facts based upon the critical use of scientific reason have to be restated. We find insufficient evidence for belief in the existence of a supernatural; it is either meaningless or irrelevant to the question of the survival and fulfillment of the human race. As nontheists, we begin with humans not God, nature not deity. Nature may indeed be broader and deeper than we now know; any new discoveries, however, will but enlarge our knowledge of the natural.

Some humanists believe we should reinterpret traditional religions and reinvest them with meanings appropriate to the current situation. Such redefinitions, however, often perpetuate old dependencies and escapisms; they easily become obscurantist, impeding the free use of the intellect. We need, instead, radically new human purposes and goals.

We appreciate the need to preserve the best ethical teachings in the religious traditions of humankind, many of which we share in common. But we reject those features of traditional religious morality that deny humans a full appreciation of their own potentialities and responsibilities. Traditional religions often offer solace to humans, but, as often, they inhibit humans from helping themselves or experiencing their full potentialities. Such institutions, creeds, and rituals often impede the will to serve others. Too often traditional faiths encourage dependence rather than independence, obedience rather than affirmation, fear rather than courage. More recently they have generated concerned social action, with many signs of relevance appearing in the wake of the "God Is Dead" theologies. But we can discover no divine purpose or providence for the human species. While there is much that we do not know, humans are responsible for what we are or will become. No deity will save us; we must save ourselves.

Second: Promises of immortal salvation or fear of eternal damnation are both illusory and harmful. They distract humans from present concerns, from self-actualization, and from rectifying social injustices. Modern science discredits such historic concepts as the "ghost in the machine" and the "separable soul." Rather, science affirms that the human species is an emergence from natural evolutionary forces. As far as we know, the total personality is a function of the biological organism transacting in a social and cultural context. There is no credible evidence that life survives the death of the body. We continue to exist in our progeny and in the way that our lives have influenced others in our culture.

Traditional religions are surely not the only obstacles to human progress. Other ideologies also impede human advance. Some forms of political doctrine, for instance, function religiously, reflecting the worst features of orthodoxy and authoritarianism, especially when they sacrifice individuals on the altar of Utopian promises. Purely economic and political viewpoints, whether capitalist or communist, often function as religious and ideological dogma. Although humans undoubtedly need economic and political goals, they also need creative values by which to live.

ETHICS

Third: We affirm that moral values derive their source from human experience. Ethics is *autonomous* and *situational,* needing no theological or ideological sanction. Ethics stems from human need and interest. To deny this distorts the whole basis of life. Human life has meaning because we create and develop our futures. Happiness and the creative realization of human needs and desires, individually and in shared enjoyment, are continuous themes of humanism. We strive for the good life, here and now. The goal is to pursue life's enrichment despite debasing forces of vulgarization, commercialization, bureaucratization, and dehumanization.

Fourth: Reason and intelligence are the most effective instruments that humankind possesses. There is no substitute: neither faith nor passion suffices in itself. The controlled use of scientific methods, which have transformed the natural and social sciences since the Renaissance, must be extended further in the solution of human problems. But reason must be tempered by humility, since no group has a monopoly of wisdom or virtue. Nor is there any guarantee that all problems can be solved or all questions answered. Yet critical intelligence, infused by a sense of human caring, is the best method that humanity has for resolving problems. Reason should be balanced with compassion and empathy and the whole person fulfilled. Thus, we are not advocating the use of scientific intelligence independent of or in opposition to emotion, for we believe in the cultivation of feeling and love. As science pushes back the boundary of the known, man's sense of wonder is continually renewed, and art, poetry, and music find their places, along with religion and ethics.

THE INDIVIDUAL

Fifth: The preciousness and dignity of the individual person is a central humanist value. Individuals should be encouraged to realize their own creative talents and desires. We reject all religious, ideological, or moral codes that denigrate the individual, suppress freedom, dull intellect, dehumanize personality. We believe in maximum individual autonomy consonant with social responsibility. Although science can account for the causes of behavior, the possibilities of individual *freedom of choice* exist in human life and should be increased.

Sixth: In the area of sexuality, we believe that intolerant attitudes, often cultivated by orthodox religions and puritanical cultures, unduly repress sexual conduct. The right to birth control, abortion, and divorce should be recognized. While we do not approve of exploitive, denigrating forms of sexual expression, neither do we wish to prohibit, by law or social sanction, sexual behavior between consenting adults. The many varieties of sexual exploration should not in themselves be considered "evil." Without countenancing mindless permissiveness or unbridled promiscuity, a civilized society should be a *tolerant* one. Short of harming others or compelling them to do likewise, individuals should be permitted to express their sexual proclivities and pursue their life-styles as they desire. We wish to cultivate the development of a responsible attitude toward sexuality, in which humans are not exploited as sexual objects, and in which intimacy, sensitivity, respect, and honesty in interpersonal relations are encouraged. Moral education for children and adults is an important way of developing awareness and sexual maturity.

DEMOCRATIC SOCIETY

Seventh: To enhance freedom and dignity the individual must experience a full range of *civil liberties* in all societies. This includes freedom of speech and the press, political democracy, the legal right of opposition to governmental policies, fair judicial process, religious liberty, freedom of association, and artistic, scientific, and cultural freedom. It also includes a recognition of an individual's right to die with dignity, euthanasia, and the right to suicide. We oppose the increasing invasion of privacy, by whatever means, in both totalitarian and democratic societies. We would safeguard, extend, and implement the principles of human freedom evolved from the *Magna Carta* to the *Bill of Rights,* the *Rights of Man,* and the *Universal Declaration of Human Rights.*

Eighth: We are committed to an open and democratic society. We must extend *participatory democracy* in its true sense to the economy, the school, the family, the workplace, and voluntary associations. Decision-making must be decentralized to include widespread involvement of people at all levels —social, political, and economic. All persons should have a voice in developing the values and goals that determine their lives. Institutions should be responsive to expressed desires and needs. The conditions of work, education, devotion, and play should be humanized. Alienating forces should be modified or eradicated and bureaucratic structures should be held to a minimum. People are more important than decalogues, rules, proscriptions, or regulations.

Ninth: The separation of church and state and the separation of ideology and state are imperatives. The state should encourage maximum freedom for different moral, political, religious, and social values in society. It should not favor any particular religious bodies through the use of public monies, nor

CHAPTER TWELVE / *Humanism*

espouse a single ideology and function thereby as an instrument of propaganda or oppression, particularly against dissenters.

Tenth: Humane societies should evaluate economic systems not by rhetoric or ideology, but by whether or not they *increase economic well-being* for all individuals and groups, minimize poverty and hardship, increase the sum of human satisfaction, and enhance the quality of life. Hence the door is open to alternative economic systems. We need to democratize the economy and judge it by its responsiveness to human needs, testing results in terms of the common good.

Eleventh: The principle of moral equality must be furthered through elimination of all discrimination based upon race, religion, sex, age, or national origin. This means equality of opportunity and recognition of talent and merit. Individuals should be encouraged to contribute to their own betterment. If unable, then society should provide means to satisfy their basic economic, health, and cultural needs, including, wherever resources make possible, a minimum guaranteed annual income. We are concerned for the welfare of the aged, the infirm, the disadvantaged, and also for the outcasts—the mentally retarded, abandoned or abused children, the handicapped, prisoners, and addicts—for *all* who are neglected or ignored by society. Practicing humanists should make it their vocation to humanize personal relations.

We believe in the *right to universal education.* Everyone has a right to the cultural opportunity to fulfill his or her unique capacities and talents. The schools should foster satisfying and productive living. They should be open at all levels to any and all; the achievement of excellence should be encouraged. Innovative and experimental forms of education are to be welcomed. The energy and idealism of the young deserve to be appreciated and channeled to constructive purposes.

We deplore racial, religious, ethnic, or class antagonisms. Although we believe in cultural diversity and encourage racial and ethnic pride, we reject separations which promote alienation and set people and groups against each other; we envision an *integrated* community where people have a maximum opportunity for free and voluntary association.

We are *critical of sexism or sexual chauvinism*—male or female. We believe in equal rights for both women and men to fulfill their unique careers and potentialities as they see fit, free of invidious discrimination.

WORLD COMMUNITY

Twelfth: We deplore the division of humankind on nationalistic grounds. We have reached a turning point in human history where the best option is to *transcend the limits of national sovereignty* and to move toward the building of a world community in which all sectors of the human family can participate. Thus we look to the development of a system of world law and a world order based upon transnational federal government. This would appreciate cultural pluralism and diversity. It would not exclude pride in national origins and accomplishments nor the handling of regional problems on a regional basis. Human progress, however, can no longer be achieved by focusing on one section of the world, Western or Eastern, developed or underdeveloped. For the first time in human history, no part of humankind can be isolated from any other. Each person's future is in some way linked to all. We thus reaffirm a commitment to the building of world community, at the same time recognizing that this commits us to some hard choices.

Thirteenth: This world community must *renounce the resort to violence and force* as a method of solving international disputes. We believe in the peaceful adjudication of differences by international courts and by the development of the arts of negotiation and compromise. War is obsolete. So is the use of nuclear, biological, and chemical weapons. It is a planetary imperative to reduce the level of military expenditures and turn these savings to peaceful and people-oriented uses.

Fourteenth: The world community must engage in *cooperative planning* concerning the use of rapidly depleting resources. The planet earth must be considered a single *ecosystem*. Ecological damage, resource depletion, and excessive population growth must be checked by international concord. The cultivation and conservation of nature is a moral value; we should perceive ourselves as integral to the sources of our being in nature. We must free our world from needless pollution and waste, responsibly guarding and creating wealth, both natural and human. Exploitation of natural resources, uncurbed by social conscience, must end.

Fifteenth: The problems of *economic growth and development* can no longer be resolved by one nation alone; they are worldwide in scope. It is the moral obligation of the developed nations to provide—through an international authority that safeguards human rights—massive technical, agricultural, medical, and economic assistance, including birth control techniques, to the developing portions of the globe. World poverty must cease. Hence extreme disproportions in wealth, income, and economic growth should be reduced on a worldwide basis.

Sixteenth: Technology is a vital key to human progress and development. We deplore any neo-romantic efforts to condemn indiscriminately all technology and science or to counsel retreat from its further extension and use for the good of humankind. We would resist any moves to censor basic scientific research on moral, political, or social grounds. Technology must, however, be carefully judged by the consequences of its use; harmful and destructive changes should be avoided. We are particularly disturbed when technology and bureaucracy control, manipulate, or modify human beings without their consent. Technological feasibility does not imply social or cultural desirability.

Seventeenth: We must expand communication and transportation across frontiers. Travel restrictions must cease. The world must be open to diverse political, ideological, and moral viewpoints and evolve a worldwide system of television and radio for information and education. We thus call for full international cooperation in culture, science, the arts, and technology *across ideological borders.* We must learn to live openly together or we shall perish together.

HUMANITY AS A WHOLE

In closing: The world cannot wait for a reconciliation of competing political or economic systems to solve its problems. These are the times for men and women of good will to further the building of a peaceful and prosperous world. We urge that parochial loyalties and inflexible moral and religious ideologies be transcended. We urge recognition of the common humanity of all people. We further urge the use of reason and compassion to produce the kind of world we want—a world in which peace, prosperity, freedom, and happiness are widely shared. Let us not abandon that vision in despair or cowardice. We are responsible for what we are or will be. Let us work together for a humane world by means commensurate with humane ends. Destructive ideological differences among communism, capitalism, socialism, conservatism, liberalism, and radicalism should be overcome. Let us call for an end to terror and hatred. We will survive and prosper only in a world of shared humane values. We can initiate new directions for humankind; ancient rivalries can be superseded by broad-based cooperative efforts. The commitment to tolerance, understanding, and peaceful negotiation does not necessitate acquiescence to the status quo nor the damming up of dynamic and revolutionary forces. The true revolution is occurring and can continue in countless nonviolent adjustments. But this entails the willingness to step forward onto new and expanding plateaus. At the present juncture of history, commitment to all humankind is the highest commitment of which we are capable; it transcends the narrow allegiances of church, state, party, class, or race in moving toward a wider vision of human potentiality. What more daring a goal for humankind than for each person to become, in ideal as well as practice, a citizen of a world community. It is a classical vision; we can now give it new vitality. Humanism thus interpreted is a moral force that has time on its side. We believe that humankind has the potential intelligence, good will, and cooperative skill to implement this commitment in the decades ahead.

further reading

Erich Fromm's *Man for Himself* (1947) is a study of humanistic ethics. Fromm states that "man's aim is *to be himself* and that the condition for attaining this goal is that man be *for himself*."

John Dewey summarized his thoughts about religion and its essential meaning in *A Common Faith* (1934), and it amounted to an outline of his humanist ideals.

Long active in humanist organizations in England and the first Director of the British Humanist Association, H. J. Blackham writes with conviction and a sure grasp of his subject in his *Humanism* (1968).

Bertrand Russell, "A Free Man's Worship" (1903), reprinted in *Mysticism and Logic* (1918) and innumerable other anthologies. A classic statement by a renowned philosopher and Nobel Prize winning author.

Corliss Lamont, *The Philosophy of Humanism* (5th ed., 1965). A thorough review of the background and principles of humanism by one of its best-known and most active spokesmen. See also his *The Illusion of Immortality* (1959).

Paul Kurtz (ed.), *Moral Problems in Contemporary Society: Essays in Humanistic Ethics* (1969). An outstanding collection of essays by eighteen leading humanistic authors, including Carl R. Rogers, Sidney Hook, Abraham Edel, B. F. Skinner, and Kurt Baier.

Contemporaries

some older, some younger

introduction _____

Every religion is a
new religion every morning.

Wilfred Cantwell Smith

The contemporary scene in religion includes all the religions described on the preceding pages and, needless to say, a great many more than the additional sampling offered in this chapter. It is a scene so complex and variegated that even the most enormous generalizations about it tend to be half-truths.

By and large, however, it seems safe to say that the law of change holds sway in religion as elsewhere, and the pace of that change appears to be accelerating. There has been a rash of new movements (though it is indeed difficult to distinguish between what is new and what is old in religion) and a continuing proliferation of sects and schools of thought within the established religions. The movement and growth is in *all* directions. In the United States, for example, there is a noteworthy new appreciation among many, especially the young, of the teachings of the East; there is also the neofundamentalism of the Jesus movement. As the readings in this chapter will indicate, the American Indians and their religion have been "rediscovered," while astrologists like Dane Rudhyar look to the heavens, as it were, for guidance. Meher Baba is held to be the new avatar (Savior, Christ, Buddha, God); Joseph Smith is acclaimed as a latter-day American prophet. Jiddu Krishnamurti brings to his listeners questions whose answers require a radical transformation of one's habits of thinking and experiencing.

It is ironic that the much-maligned American Indian—the "primitive savage" of this land and of so many Hollywood movies—is now increasingly admired for his values. As described in the following pages by Joseph Epes Brown, the Indian of the plains felt that "the world of nature itself was his temple, and within this sanctuary he showed great respect to every form, function, and power." This reverence for nature and for life, Brown explains, was central to the Indian religion: man was seen as linking the heavens and the earth, and he had the responsibility of "guardianship over the world of nature." The Great Spirit, the Indian's concept of Divinity, was a Being both immanent and transcendent, and thus was the Indian's world pervaded and encompassed by a sense of the Sacred. All this, finally, was manifested in a life rich with religious ritual and symbol. The circular shape of his tipi, for example, had cosmic meaning, and the rite of smoking the sacred pipe is compared by Brown to the Christian rite of Holy Communion.

The ancient "celestial science" of astrology has had a long and checkered history (as has science itself). But in spite of that—and in spite also of its innumerable academic critics—astrology continues to thrive in both East and

West. Unquestionably, there is much to criticize in the world of astrology, and a very great deal that can be easily discredited. Dane Rudhyar is another matter. He is himself critical of those in astrology who continue to employ what he thinks are obsolete approaches to the subject. Rudhyar envisages an astrology wedded to modern physics and psychology. Scientifically speaking, "all living is a dynamic process of transformation," and he thinks that astrology ought to be the attempt to discern the principles of that process and of " the hidden order behind or within the confusion of the earthly jungle —physical or psychological, as the case may be."

Meher Baba, who is discussed in this chapter by Jacob Needleman, was born in India in 1894; he died in 1969. At the age of nineteen he had the first of a series of remarkable religious experiences which led to his conviction that he was the Incarnation of God. "There is no doubt of my being God personified," he has said. "I am the Christ . . . . I am the Divine Beloved who loves you more than you can ever love yourself." Disciples gathered about him, and a worldwide movement grew. Central to his teachings is the discipline of love; his followers strive to love Baba with selfless devotion and to accept his love for them. Immersed in divine love, one realizes his own Divine identity, and the illusion of the self is destroyed.

In 1820 Joseph Smith was fifteen years old; he lived with his family in the village of Manchester in New York State. Confused by the "great clash in religious sentiment" of different churches, according to his own account, he went one day to a grove and fervently prayed. Abruptly there came a vision of "two glorious personages . . . surrounded with a brilliant light which eclipsed the sun at noon day. They told me that all religious denominations were believing in incorrect doctrines . . . ." Thus were begun the revelations to a new prophet and what he and his followers have termed a "restoration" of the Gospel of Jesus Christ. The revelations continued even after Smith's death: each succeeding president of the church he founded is also a prophet of God.

Jiddu Krishnamurti is "not in any way concerned with organized religions, churches, dogmas, rituals, or the authority of saviours, representatives of God and all the rest." Religion, as Krishnamurti conceives it, is not a matter of belief at all, but rather "the quality that makes for a life in which there is no fragmentation whatsoever." That quality which is the key to wholeness is freedom: a freedom from fear and conflict, and even from method, effort, and thought itself. Such freedom—such *stillness*—results in an innocence of mind that can perceive the truth.

joseph epes brown _____

FROM *The Spiritual Legacy
of the American Indian*

After graduating from Haverford College in Pennsylvania, Joseph Epes Brown spent a number of years living and traveling with several of the Indian nations, particularly those of the prairies. He observed in the Indians "degrees of spirituality rarely found in the world today," and "in the rhythm of their society, and in the beauty of the forms of their ancient culture, those great qualities for want of which the modern world is becoming impoverished, in spite of its material wealth."* *The Sacred Pipe: Black Elk's Account of the Seven Rites of the Oglala Sioux,* which Brown recorded and edited, was the product of his having lived with Black Elk for eight months. Brown now teaches at the Valley Verde School in Arizona and continues to write about Indians.

One of the symbols that expresses most completely the Plains Indian concept of the relationship between man and the world of nature surrounding him is a cross inscribed within a circle. The symbol is painted on a number of ritual objects, and on the bodies and heads of men who participate in tribal ceremonies. Its form is reflected in the circular shape and central fire of the tipi, the Indian's home; its pattern is found in the Sun Dance and pūrification lodges and in many of the ritual movements. For example, in the *Hako* of the Pawnee, the priest draws a circle on the earth with his toe; the explanation given was that "the circle represents a nest, and is drawn by the toe, because the Eagle (symbol of the Great Spirit) builds its nest with its claws. Although we are imitating the bird making its nest, there is another meaning to the action; we are thinking of *Tirawa* making the world for the people to live in!"[1]

In complaining that the Indian must now live in a *square* log house, a form without power to the Indians, Black Elk once said:

"You have noticed that everything an Indian does is in a circle, and that is because the Power of the World always works in circles, and everything tries to be round. In the old days when we were a strong and happy people, all our power came to us from the

---

*The Sacred Pipe, recorded and edited by Joseph Epes Brown (Norman: University of Oklahoma Press, 1953), p. x.

[1]Alice C. Fletcher, *The Hako: A Pawnee Ceremony,* Annual Report of the Bureau of American Ethnology, XXII, ii, 1904.

CHAPTER THIRTEEN / *Contemporaries*

sacred hoop of the nation, and so long as the hoop was unbroken, the people flourished. The flowering tree was the living center of the hoop, and the circle of the four quarters nourished it. The east gave peace and light, the south gave warmth, the west gave rain, and the north with its cold and mighty wind gave strength and endurance. This knowledge came to us from the outer world with our religion. Everything the Power of the World does is done in a circle. The sky is round, and I have heard that the earth is round like a ball, and so are all the stars. The wind, in its greatest powers, whirls. Birds make their nests in circles, for theirs is the same religion as ours. The sun comes forth and goes down again in a circle. The moon does the same, and both are round. Even the seasons form a great circle in their changing, and always come back again to where they were. The life of a man is a circle from childhood to childhood, and so it is in everything where power moves. Our tepees were round like the nests of birds, and these were always set in a circle, the nation's hoop, a nest of many nests, where the Great Spirit meant for us to hatch our children."[2]

At the center of the circle, uniting within a point the cross of the four directions of space and all the other quaternaries of the Universe, is man. Without the awareness that he bears within himself this sacred center a man is in fact less than man. It is to recall the virtual reality of this center that the Indians have so many rites based on the cross within the circle.

One of the most precise ritual expressions of this "centrality" is found in one of the rites of the Arapaho Sun Dance, in which their Sacred Wheel is placed against each of the four sides of a man's body, starting from the feet and moving to the head, and is then turned four times sunwise, until finally it is lowered over the head, with the four attached eagle feathers hanging down over the man's breast, so that he is ritually at the center, a vertical axis to the horizontal wheel.

This concept of the vertical axis explains the sacredness of the number seven to the Indians, and it is interesting to note that their interpretation is identical to that which can be found in other major religions. In adding the vertical dimensions of sky and earth to the four horizontal ones of space, we have six dimensions, with the seventh as the point at the center where all the directions meet.

To realize this symbol in its fullness we must conceive of three horizontal circles inscribed with crosses, all three pierced by the vertical axis of man himself. For the Indians understand that man is intermediate between sky and earth, linking the two, with his feet on the ground and his head, or intellect, at the center of the firmament. The middle disc, like the vertical axis, also represents man himself, for in joining sky and earth, he is neither pure spirit nor gross matter, but a synthesis of both. This particular symbol may be found among the Crow in the three rings which they often paint around the sacred cottonwood tree at the center of their circular Sun Dance lodge. It was further

---

[2]*Black Elk Speaks,* pp. 198-200. [From *Black Elk Speaks* by Black Elk as told to John G. Neihardt. Copyright © 1961. Reprinted by permission of the John G. Neihardt Trust.]

explained to me by an old Crow priest or Medicine Man that these circles represent the three "worlds" which constitute man: body, soul, and spirit, or again; the gross, subtle, and pure.

Once this concept of man and his relationship to the Universe has been understood, one is able to understand the Indian's approach to the forms of virgin nature which surrounded him, and which he knew so intimately. In most of the great religious traditions of the world man built centers of worship in the form of cathedrals, churches, or temples, and in these centers and in the many symbolical forms which he introduced into them, he expressed his image of the Universe. It is certainly not difficult to sense this totality, or to feel that one is actually at the center of the world when one is inside the great medieval cathedrals of Europe. For the Indian, however, the world of nature itself was his temple, and within this sanctuary he showed great respect to every form, function, and power. That the Indian held as sacred all the natural forms surrounding him is not unique, for other traditions (Japanese Shinto, for example) respect created forms as manifestations of God's works. But what is almost unique in the Indian's attitude is the fact that his reverence for nature and for life is *central* to his religion: each form in the world around him bears such a host of precise values and meanings that taken all together they constitute what one could call his "doctrine."

In my first contacts with Black Elk almost all he said was phrased in terms involving animals and natural phenomena. I naively wished that he would begin to talk about religious matters, until I finally realized that he was, in fact, explaining his religion. The values which I sought were to be found precisely in his stories and accounts of the bison, eagle, trees, flowers, mountains, and winds.

Due to this intense preoccupation with the forms of nature the Indian has been described as being in his religion either pantheistic, idolatrous, or downright savage. To the two latter terms it is hardly necessary to reply, but the more subtle charge of pantheism, which involves equating God with his manifested forms, requires some clarification.

In the extremely beautiful creation myths of the Plains Indians, which are amazingly similar to the biblical Genesis, the animals were created before man, so that in this anteriority and divine origin they have a certain proximity to the Great Spirit (*Wakan-Tanka* in the language of the Sioux) which demands respect and veneration. In them the Indian sees actual reflections of the qualities of the Great Spirit Himself, which serve the same function as revealed scriptures in other religions. They are intermediators or links between man and God. This explains not only why religious devotions may be directed to the Deity *through* the animals, but also helps us to understand why contact with, or from, the Great Spirit comes to the Indian almost exclusively through visions involving animal or other natural forms. Black Elk, for example, received spiritual power (*wochangi*) from visions involving the eagle, the bison, Thunderbeings, and horses; and it is said that Crazy Horse, the great chief and holy man, received his power and invulnerability from the rock, and also from a vision of the shadow.

Although these natural forms may reflect aspects of the Great Spirit, and eventually can not be other than Him, they are nevertheless not identified with Him who is without "parts," and who in His transcendent unity is above all particular created forms. The Indian therefore can not be termed a pantheist, if we accept this term in the sense presented above. Black Elk has well well formulated this mystery in the following statements:

". . . we regard all created beings as sacred and important, for everything has a *wochangi*, or influence, which can be given to us, through which we may gain a little more understanding if we are attentive."

"We should understand well that all things are the works of the Great Spirit. We should know that He is within all things; the trees, the grasses, the rivers, the mountains and all the four-legged animals, and the winged peoples; and even more important, we should understand that He is also above all these things and peoples."[3]

To make these distinctions more precise, it should be noted that in the language of the Sioux (Lakota) the Great Spirit may be referred to as either Father (*Ate*), or Grandfather (*Tunkashila*). *Ate* refers to the Great Spirit as He is in relation to His creation, in other words, as Being, whereas *Tunkashila* is His non-manifest Essence, independent of the limitations of creation. These same distinctions have been enunciated by Christian theologians using the term God as distinct from Godhead, and in the Hindu doctrines which differentiate between *Brahma* (the masculine form) and *Brahman* (the neuter form).

In recalling the symbol of the circle, cross, and central axis, we can now see that although man was created last of all the creatures, he is also the "axis," and thus in a sense is the first. For if each animal reflects particular aspects of the Great Spirit, man, on the contrary, may include within himself all aspects. He is thus a totality, bearing the Universe within himself, and through his Intellect having the potential capacity to live in continual awareness of this reality.

". . . peace . . . comes within the souls of men when they realize their relationship, their oneness, with the universe and all its powers, and when they realize that the center of the Universe dwells *Wakan-Tanka*, and that this center is really everywhere, it is within each of us."[4]

The Indian believes that such knowledge can not be realized unless there be

---

[3]*The Sacred Pipe*, pp. 59, xx. [From *The Sacred Pipe: Black Elk's Account of the Seven Rites of the Oglala Sioux* by Joseph Epes Brown. Copyright 1953 by the University of Oklahoma Press. Reprinted by permission.]
[4]*The Sacred Pipe*, p. 115.

perfect humility, unless man humbles himself before the entire creation, before each smallest ant, realizing his own nothingness. Only in being nothing may man become everything, and only then does he realize his essential brotherhood with all forms of life. His center, or his Life, is the same center of Life of all that is.

Because of the true man's totality and centrality he has the almost divine function of guardianship over the world of nature. Once this role is ignored or misused he is in danger of being shown ultimately by nature who in reality is the conqueror and who the conquered. It could also be said, under another perspective, that in the past man had to protect himself from the forces of nature, whereas today it is nature which must be protected from man.

Nothing is more tragic or pitiful than the statements of Indians who have survived to see their sacred lands torn up and desecrated by a people of an alien culture who, driven largely by commercial interests, have lost the sense of protective guardianship over nature. Typical are the words of an old Omaha:

"When I was a youth, the country was very beautiful. Along the rivers were belts of timberland, where grew cottonwood, maple, elm, ash, hickory, and walnut trees, and many other shrubs. And under these grew many good herbs and beautiful flowering plants. In both the woodland and the prairies I could see the trails of many kinds of animals and could hear the cheerful songs of many kinds of birds. When I walked abroad I could see many forms of life, beautiful living creatures which *Wakanda* had placed here; and these were, after their manner, walking, flying, leaping, running, playing all about. But now the face of all the land is changed and sad. The living creatures are gone. I see the land desolate and I suffer an unspeakable sadness. Sometimes I wake in the night and I feel as though I should suffocate from the pressure of this awful feeling of loneliness."[5]

Too often statements such as this are passed off as nostalgic romanticism, but if we understand the full meaning of the world of nature for the Indian, we realize that we are involved witnesses to a great tragedy, whose final act is still to be seen.

.   .   .

As a thread binds together, and is central to, each bead of a necklace, so is the sacred pipe central to all the Plains Indians ceremonies. The pipe is a portable altar, and a means of grace, which every Indian once possessed. He would not undertake anything of importance unless he had first smoked, concentrating on all that the pipe represented, and thus absorbing a multitude of powers. It could in fact be said that if one could understand all the possible meanings and values to be found in the pipe and its accompanying ritual, then one would understand Plains Indian religion in its full depth.

The origin of the pipe is expressed in various myths of great beauty. In the

[5]Melvin R. Gilmore, *Prairie Smoke* (New York: Columbia University Press, 1929) p. 36.

Sioux myth a miraculous "Buffalo Cow Woman" brought the pipe to the people, with explanations concerning its meanings and use. Pipes used within historical times, and which are still used today, are made with a red, or sometimes a black, stone bowl, a stem made usually of ash, and, at least with the large ceremonial types, ribbon decorations representing the four directions of space, and parts taken from sacred animals or from nature. These pipes represent man in his totality, or the universe of which man is a reflection. The bowl is the heart, or sacred center, and each section of the pipe is usually identified with some part of man.

As the pipe is filled with the sacred tobacco, prayers are offered for all the powers of the universe, and for the myriad forms of creation, each of which is represented by a grain of tobacco. The filled pipe is thus "Totality," so that when the fire of the Great Spirit is added a divine sacrifice is enacted in which the universe and man are reabsorbed within the Principle, and become what in reality they are. In mingling his life-breath with the tobacco and fire through the straight stem of concentration, the man who smokes assists at the sacrifice of his own self, or ego, and is thus aided in realizing the Divine Presence at his own center. Indeed, in the liberation of the smoke man is further helped in realizing that not only is God's presence within him, but that he and the world are mysteriously plunged in God. The smoke that rises to the heavens is also, as it were, "visible prayer," at the sight and fragrance of which the entire creation rejoices. The mysteries of the peace pipe are so profound that it is not too much to say that the rite of smoking for the Indian is something very near the Holy Communion for Christians. It is therefore not without reason that it is commonly called a "Peace Pipe," and was always used in establishing a relationship, or peace, between friends and also enemies. For in smoking the pipe together each man is aided in remembering his own center, which is now understood to be the same center of every man, and of the Universe itself. It would be difficult to imagine a rite that could more aptly express the bond which exists between all forms of creation.

All true spiritual progress involves three stages which are not successfully experienced and left behind, but rather each in turn is realized, then integrated within the next stage, so that ultimately they are one in the individual who attains the ultimate goal. Different terms may be used for these stages, but essentially they constitute Purification, Perfection or Expansion, and Union.

If union with Truth (which is one of many possible names for God) is the ultimate goal of all spiritual disciplines, then it is evident that what is impure can not be united with that which is all purity. Hence the necessity for the first stage of purification. Expansion must follow, because only that which is perfect, total, or whole can be united with absolute perfection and holiness. Man must cease to be a part, an imperfect fragment; he must so realize what he really is that he expands to include the universe within himself. Only then, when these two conditions of purification and expansion are actualized, may man attain to the final stage of Union. All the great religions attest that there is no greater error to which man is subject than to believe that his real self is nothing more than his own body or mind. It is only through traditional disciplines, such as those which have been described for the Plains Indian, that man is able to dispel this greatest of all illusions.

The pattern of the three stages in spiritual development may be recognized in one form or another in the methods of all the great religions of the world. It is evident that the American Indian, or at least the Plains Indian, also possesses this same three-fold pattern of realization. If this spirituality has not as yet been fully recognized as existing among the Indians, it is due partly to a problem of communication, since their conceptions are often expressed through symbolical forms which are foreign to us. If we can understand, however, the truths which the Indian finds in his relationships to nature, and the profound values reflected by his many rites and symbols, then *we* may become enriched, our understanding will deepen, and we shall be able to give to the American Indian heritage its rightful place among the great spiritual traditions of mankind. Further, if the Indian himself can become more actively aware of this valuable heritage, then he may regain much of what has been lost, and will be able to face the world with the pride and dignity that should rightfully be his.

The Zodiac as a Dynamic Process

Dane Rudhyar (1895–   ) was born in Paris and studied at the Sorbonne and the Paris Conservatory. A composer, author, painter, and lecturer, he lives now in Southern California. He has long been interested in astrology and has written more than a dozen books on the subject, including *The Astrology of Personality, The Pulse of Life, The Practice of Astrology, The Planetarization of Consciousness,* and *The Astrological Houses.* Bemoaning the "fortune-telling" school of thought in astrology, he calls instead for a *humanistic* astrology that would be allied with humanistic psychology (hence, an "astro-psychology"). He believes that astrology should be *person*-oriented; it should help individuals to realize their potentialities as human beings.

These are days when all set entities and even the most material of objects are seen dissolving into the dynamic fluency of the new world summoned before our minds by the magic of scientific revelations. From the most common chair, on which we used to sit unaware of the electro-magnetic waves playing within its mass, up to the realm of the human personality, now intricately analyzed into drives and complexes, wherever our mind seeks to know reality it meets the modern emphasis upon rhythmic activity, wave-motion and electro-magnetic interplay of polar energies. Whereas our ancestors used to dwell in a comfortably static universe in which everything had a well defined and rationally reassuring name, a form and a permanent set of characteristics, today we find change enthroned everywhere. No moment is too small to be analyzed into component phases and events; no object too minute to escape fragmentation and resolution into mysterious somethings which turn out half the time to be electrical charges in a strange game of hide-and-seek.

Against the classical concepts of permanence and identity the realization that all living is a dynamic process of transformation from which no entity escapes now stands backed up by the whole edifice of scientific research and theory. On the ruins of the world of thought dogmatically extolled by nineteenth century minds we witness the reappearance of ancient concepts which were for millenia the foundations of human knowledge. The universe is once more to be understood as an ocean of energies in which two vast complementary tides can be distinguished. Everywhere a dynamic and electrical dualism appears as the foundation upon which all reality stands.

We are very close indeed to the ancient concepts of the ebb and flow of universal Life, of the in- and out-breathings of the universal Brahma. We are

Dane Rudhyar, "The Zodiac as a Dynamic Process." From Dane Rudhyar, *The Pulse of Life.* Reprinted by permission of Shambala Publications, Inc.

practically on the same ground as the Sages of China who described in their great "Book of Transformations," the *Yi King,** the cyclic waxing and waning of two universal forces of opposite polarities, *Yang* and *Yin*. Likewise modern thinking has come surprisingly near to some of the most fundamental concepts of ancient astrology; at least when these concepts are seen, not in the light of a classical European mentality, but in terms of a philosophy which is both a philosophy of dynamic change and a philosophy of human experience. It must be a philosophy of dynamic change if it is a philosophy of human experience, because all that man does experience is a sequence of transformations bounded by birth and by death.

It is because astrology can be seen as a most remarkable technique for the understanding of the life-process of change in so many realms—and theoretically in every field—that its renaissance during the last two decades in the Western world is particularly important as a sign of the times. But this importance is conditioned upon a grasp of astrology which is truly modern. Nineteenth century approaches and classical or medieval biases should be discarded in the light of the new twentieth century understanding of physics and above all of psychology, in astrology as in every realm of thought. The emphasis should once more be placed on human experience, and away from the transcendent categories and the mythological entities belonging to an ideology which today is, in the main, obsolete.

Astrology was born of the experience of order made manifest in the sky to primitive man immersed in the jungle and bewildered by the chaos of life on the prolific and wild surface of this planet. The search for order is one of the basic drives in man. At a later stage of evolution this search becomes intellectualized into science; but it has deep organic and instinctual roots.

Instinct is an adaptation to, and an expression of the periodical order of natural phenomena. It is based on unconscious expectability; and when the normal expectancy of life-circumstances is violently disturbed—as when a college psychologist conducts a certain kind of experiments with white mice or pigs—the animal becomes insane. He is unable to stand the pressure of external disorder upon the internal order of his biological functions, and the latter themselves become disordered.

The constant effort of civilization can be interpreted as an attempt to bring man's understanding of his sense-experiences to the point where the same basic quality of order which he feels in his own organism is seen operating effectively in what appears to him as the outer world. Such an attempt may be called an anthropomorphic illusion by the modern thinker, but why it should be so can never be proven or made convincing to any one realizing that man can never know anything save what man (collectively and individually) experiences.

*A variant spelling of *I Ching*.—R.E.

Man's experience is originally dual. He feels organic order within as such an absolute imperative that the slightest organic disturbance causes the most acute feeling of pain. Yet man also experiences what seems to him as chaos outside. All sorts of names have been given to this chaos, either to explain it away (as, for instance, Darwin's struggle for life, survival of the fittest, etc.), or to transfigure it into some kind of organic order (vitalistic philosophies), or to interpret it as one pole of a whole, the other pole of which is a noumenal world of archetypes, perfect Ideas and the like (as when the Hindus called it *maya*). Every philosophical system, every religion, every science, every act and every pattern of social organization is only one thing: an attempt to explain disorder and to reconcile it with man's inner organic order.

Astrology is one of these attempts, the most ancient perhaps, or at least the one which has kept its vitality intact for the longest time, because the dualism of celestial order and terrestrial disorder is a universal and essential fact of human experience everywhere. In the sky, all events are regular, periodical, expectable within very small margins of irregularity. On the earth-surface (be it the primordial jungle, the countryside of medieval eras or the modern metropolis) there is relative chaos, unpredictable emotions, irrational conflicts, unexpected crises, wars and pestilence. Astrology is a method by means of which the ordered pattern of light in the sky can be used to prove the existence of a hidden, but real, order in all matters of human experience on the earth-surface.

It not only proves order by relating types, categories and sequences of events to the periods of celestial bodies (as moving points of light—and nothing else). It shows how events can be predicted and how fore-knowledge may be applied in social and personal matters. Fore-knowledge is the power to build a civilization out of the apparent chaos of earthly phenomena. All science is based on predictability. Astrology is the mother of all sciences, the mother of civilization; for it has been the first and most universal attempt by man to *find the hidden order behind or within the confusion of the earthly jungle—physical or psychological, as the case may be.*

TWO APPROACHES TO LIFE

There are two essential ways in which the dualism of celestial order and earthly jungle can be interpreted in terms of meaning and purpose. The first—the simpler and still the most popular—is to consider the realm of the sky as that of positive, inherently ordered, energizing and eventually controlling Powers which exert a constant *influence* upon the passive, receptive, inert and inherently chaotic (separative) realm of earthly activities, impulses, desires and passions. The sky-realm becomes thus the "world of Ideas" or as medieval philosophers called it *Natura naturans:* active Nature, in contradistinction to *Natura naturata,* passive and earthly nature. "Human nature" in such a conception almost unavoidably acquires a pejorative meaning. It is seen as perverted by the "original sin" and requiring to be controlled by the will of celestial Powers and the reason of divine Intelligences, or to be redeemed by the sacrifice and compassion of a starry being—a "son of God."

Most religious and even classical philosophies have been based on such an interpretation featuring a quasi-absolute dualism of good and evil, spirit and matter, God and nature, reason and emotions, "higher" and "lower." The present catastrophic state of Western mankind is the result of such an interpretation which for centuries divided human experience in two parts fundamentally irreconcilable in spite of the efforts of human will and the sacrifice of divine love.

A different type of interpretation is possible, and at times has been attempted. Modern thinkers, from psychologists to physicists, are more than ever striving to build it on solid grounds; but as a more mature mentality is required to grasp its full implications, it is not yet popular, even among trained thinkers steeped in the old tradition of dualistic philosophy and in its transcendent escapes into idealism and absolute monism.

According to this "new" interpretation there is no opposition between the realm of celestial order and that of earthly chaos, because earthly chaos is merely an appearance or fiction. There is order everywhere, *but man is blind to it while he is passing from one type of order to the next and more inclusive type*. What he feels as chaos on the earth-surface is the result of his incomplete vision. When unable to apprehend the wholeness of a situation, man sees it as chaotic—as a jig-saw puzzle whose pieces are lumped into incoherent blocks. The picture cannot be seen while such a condition prevails. There can be only apparent chaos unless every piece is fitted to every other piece in the relationship which the "Image of the whole" determines and to which this Image alone gives meaning.

A human being, considered as a physiological organism, is an ordered whole. What we have called "internal order" is order within the closed sphere of the body—or of the generic nature; man, as a member of the genus, *homo sapiens*. This is the "lesser whole," the lesser sphere of being—and as long as it is not fundamentally disturbed by the pull toward identification with a "greater whole" or greater sphere of being, there is order and organic integration.

However, this state of lesser integration and narrow inclusiveness is never completely undisturbed. The "lesser whole" operates constantly *within* a "greater whole," and there is therefore a ceaseless interaction between the lesser and the greater. *This interaction appears to the "lesser whole" as disorder and is felt as pain. It is seen by the "greater whole" as creative cyclic activity and is felt as sacrifice.* What we call "life" is this constant interaction and interpenetration of "lesser wholes" and "greater whole." It is the substance of human experience; and human experience must necessarily be

CHAPTER THIRTEEN / *Contemporaries*

twofold or dualistic because human experience is always partly the experience of an individual and partly the experience of a collectivity.

The individual feels pain; but also as he tries to explain it, to himself or to some friend, he uses words. His feeling is individual; but his words (and the thinking which has conditioned their formation and their standardized use) are collective. Pain is individual as an immediate experience; but tragedy is social, because it involves a reference to collective values. In every phase of experience the individual and the collective factors interpenetrate each other. This "con-penetration" is life itself. It is reality.

Instead of two fundamentally separate realms of nature—one celestial, ordered and good; the other earthly, chaotic and dark with sin—we are now dealing with human experience as a whole and analyzing it into two phases. Man experiences what seems to him as jungle chaos and what seems to him as celestial order. In the first case we have human experiences conditioned by the pain felt by the "lesser whole" when relating itself in nearness and immediacy to other "lesser wholes," in the slow process of identifying its consciousness with that of the total being of the "greater whole"—the universe. In the second case, we have human experience when man is relating himself distantly, and through collective observations formulated into laws, with the "greater whole"—or with as much of it as he can encompass.

In both cases experience is one and fundamentally indivisible. We divide it *by establishing two frames of reference*; that is, by lumping together all painful, individual-centered, near experiences into one category—and all inspiring, remote, collectively integrated experiences into another category. We have thus two categories or classes. Each class refers to one *direction* of experience; yet both classes deal with human experience as a whole.

Every human experience is bi-polar. It is pulled by the attraction of the individual factor in experiencing, and also by that of the collective factor. These two pulls are of varied relative strengths. Education (a collective factor) gives more strength to the collective aspect of experience; thus an educated man may not go as wild under the stress of emotional disturbance as an un-educated person who will kill if jealousy possesses him. But the strongly individualized artist may lose his emotional balance faster than the business man who is steeped in social respectability. To the Romantic artist the world at large may appear thus as a grandiose tragedy; but the English gentleman will drink his tea while the Empire crumbles, unconcerned to the last moment with the impact of chaos.

From the point of view which has been described in the above paragraphs the substance and foundation of all is human experience. Every valuation is referred to it. All dualisms are *contained within it*. The sky is one aspect of human experience; the jungle, another. The Sage whose life is ordered and at peace, and whose love includes all forms of relationships possible to man (as today constituted), is a "lesser whole" who has reached a kind of integration sustained and measured by the organic order of the "greater whole." He is at peace with himself, because the peace of the "greater whole" is within him. He is at peace with other men, because his relationships to them are, in his consciousness, expressions of, and contained in his relationship to the "greater whole." They fit into a universal picture. Each piece of the jig-saw puzzle is where it belongs. The image of the whole is clear. There is no longer any question of the existence of chaos.

Chaos is the path to a greater wholeness of being and consciousness: a path, a transition, a process. The Sage is he who, first of all, understands this process, feels its rhythm, realizes the meaning of its polar attractions and repulsions. He is the man who sees all nature as a cyclic interplay of energies between "lesser wholes" and "greater wholes." Within him as without, he witnesses individual pain transforming itself into collective peace, and collective fulfillment sacrificing itself into the inspiration and guidance which those who are identified with the "greater whole" can bestow upon "lesser wholes" still struggling with the problems of their atomistic and painful relationships.

A cyclic interplay of polar energies: in this phrase can be found the key to an interpretation of human experience which does not produce irreconcilable dualities and the ever-present possibility of schizophrenia and nationalistic or class wars. Life is a cyclic interplay of polar energies. Every factor in experience is always present, but it manifests in an ever varying degree of intensity. The waning of the energy of one pole within the whole of experience is always associated with the waxing in strength of the other pole. Two forces are always active. Every conceivable mode of activity is always active within any organic whole, but some modes dominate, while others are so little active as to seem altogether inexistent. Yet non-existence is a fiction, from our point of view. It should be called instead *latency*. No characteristic trait in the whole universe is ever totally absent from the experience of any whole. It is only latent. And latency is still, in a sense, activity of a sort. It is a negative, introverted kind of activity.

Such a philosophical approach to the problem of experience gives to astrology a meaning and a value which few contemporary thinkers suspect it to contain. Astrology can be seen, in the light of this world-philosophy, as a remarkable tool for the understanding of human experience considered as the field for a cyclic interplay of polar energies or attitudes. Astrology is a means to see human experience as an organic whole, a technique of interpretation, an "algebra of life." It uses the ordered pageant of planets (and to a lesser extent, of the stars) as a symbol of what can happen to a man who sees life whole. Every event in the experience of that man is part of an ordered sequence, as every piece of the jig-saw puzzle is part of a complete picture —and because of this, it acquires *meaning*.

It is not that the planets "influence" directly any particular person by flashing a special kind of a ray which will make the person happy or cause him to break his leg. The cycles of the planets and their relationships represent to man reality in an ordered state and in reference to the "greater whole" which we know as the solar system. Men are "lesser wholes" within this "greater whole." Men can only find peace and lasting integration as they relate themselves in consciousness to the "greater whole," as they identify their own cycles of experience with cycles of activity of the "greater whole," as they refer their meetings with other men to the toal picture which only a perception of the "greater whole" can reveal. Every man is a whole—an individual. But to be an individual is meaningless except in reference to human society—or at the limit, to the universe. A man living on a desert island without any possibility of his ever being related to another man is not an individual, but only a solitary organism without meaning in terms of humanity. An individual is an individualized expression of collective (or generic) human nature. What he receives from the collective which existed before him, he must return to the collective which follows after him. No individual exists in a vacuum. There is no organic entity which is not contained within a "greater whole" and which does not contain "lesser wholes." To be an individual is a social status. Every man is in latency a universal—or, as the Chinese said, a "Celestial." To bring out the latent into actuality, to transfigure the sphere of earthly man with the light, the rhythms and the integrated harmony which is of the "greater whole" and which the movements of celestial bodies conveniently picture—this is the goal for man.

Astrology opens to us a book of universal pictures. Each picture is born of order and has meaning. Every astrological birth-chart is a signature of the cosmos—or of God. It is the image of the completed jig-saw puzzle. Man, by understanding such images can fulfill his experience, because he can thus see this experience *objectively and structurally as an organic whole*. He can see it as a whole, yet as integrated within the cyclic process of universal change which is revealed clearly in the stars and the planets, and confusedly in the nearness of his earthly contacts. Nothing is static, and no life is absolutely divided. Life is a process, and every process is cyclic—if we believe our experience, instead of imposing intellectual categories and ethical dualisms upon this experience. Astrology is a study of cyclic processes.

THE NATURE OF THE ZODIAC

All astrology is founded upon the Zodiac. Every factor used in astrology —Sun, Moon, planets, cusps of Houses, nodes, fixed stars, etc.—is referred to the Zodiac. But the Zodiac need not be considered as a thing mysterious, remote and occult. From the point of view above described, the Zodiac is simply the product of the realization by man that experience is a cyclic process; and first of all, that every manifestation of organic life obeys the law of rhythmic alternation—at one time impelled to activity by one directive principle, at another by its polar opposite.

Man acquires first this sense of rhythmic alternation by reflecting upon his daily experience which presents him with a regular sequence of day-time and of night-time, of light and darkness. But human life is too close to such a sequence, and human consciousness too involved in it, for it to appear as anything save a kind of fatality. It does so, because man normally does not keep conscious through the whole day-and-night cycle. He is confronted by a dualism which seems to him absolute, because it is not only a dualism of light and darkness but one which, from the point of view of consciousness, opposes being to non-being. Thus man is led to use this day-and-night cycle as a symbol to interpret the even greater mystery of life and death. The concept of reincarnation is nothing but a symbolic extension of the original experience common to all men of a regular alternation of days and nights; and so is the ancient Hindu idea of the "Days and Nights of Brahma," of cosmic periods of manifestation followed by periods of non-manifestation—*manvantaras* and *pralayas*.

The cycle of the year, particularly manifest in the seasonal condition of vegetation in temperate climates, offers to man's consideration an altogether different kind of regular sequence. There is no longer any question of one half of the cycle being associated with the idea of absolute non-existence. Man remains active, as an experiencer, through the entire cycle. Indeed the year can be interpreted as a "cycle of experience" because the experiencer is experiencing through the whole of it—whereas the day-and-night cycle is not normally susceptible of such an interpretation, because during a large portion of it man ceases to be an experiencer.

The Zodiac is the symbolization of the cycle of the year. It is so, essentially, in the temperate regions of the Northern hemisphere where astrology was born. Zodiacal symbolism is the product of the experience of human races living in such regions: experience of the seasons, of the activities of nature and of man through the changing panorama of vegetation—vegetation being the very foundation of animal and human life on earth. As such races have been, during the last millenia, the *active* factor in the evolution of human consciousness, their experience has come to acquire a universal validity in the determination of cosmic meaning and human purpose. Civilization, as we know it today, is therefore centered in a Northern-hemisphere and temperate-climate kind of consciousness. It may conceivably not remain so in the future, but for the time being it is; and our present astrology interprets thus accurately its cyclic evolution.

The Zodiac which is used in our astrology has very little, if anything at all, to do with distant stars as entities in themselves. It is an ancient record of the cyclic series of transformations actually experienced by man throughout the year; a record written in symbolic language using the stars as a merely

CHAPTER THIRTEEN / *Contemporaries*

convenient, graphic way of building up symbolic images appealing to the imagination of a humanity child-like enough to be more impressed by pictures than by abstract and generalized processes of thought. The essential thing about the Zodiac is not the hieroglyphs drawn upon celestial maps; it is not the symbolical stories built up around Greek mythological themes—significant as these may be. It is the human experience of change. And for a humanity which once lived very close to the earth, the series of nature's "moods" throughout the year was the strongest representation of change; for the inner emotional and biological changes of man's nature did correspond very closely indeed to the outer changes in vegetation.

Humanity, however, has been evolving since the early days of Chaldea and Egypt. Such an evolution has meant basically one thing and one thing only: the translation, or transference, of man's ability to experience life significantly *from the biological to the psycho-mental level*. At first, mankind drew all its symbols and the structure of its meanings from biological experience. Man, experiencing life and change essentially as a bodily organism, sought to express his consciousness of purpose and meaning in terms of bodily experience. These terms were the only available common denominator upon which civilizations could be built. Even so-called "spiritual" teachings (for instance, the early forms of Yoga or Tantra in India) stressed sexual, and in general "vitalistic," symbols—and corresponding practices.

Progressively, however, leaders among men have sought to center their experience and the experience of their followers around a new structure of human integration: the individual ego. Thus the need has arisen for translating all ancient techniques of integration and their symbols into the new language of the ego—an intellectual and psychological language. It is because of this need that astrology came into relative disfavor and was replaced by Greek science, logic and psychology as a commanding power in Western civilization. The language of the ego features rationalistic connections and analysis; and in his eagerness to develop the new function of "rigorous thinking" Western man has tried in every way to repudiate or undervalue all organic experiences and all techniques which had enabled his ancestors to give cyclic meaning to their life and to deal with life-situations as wholes of experience. Transcendent idealism broke man's experience in two and created the fallacious opposition of soul and body.

Yet an "occult" tradition kept alive throughout the cycle of European civilization. It tried to re-interpret the symbolism of astrology, and of similar techniques of human integration, at the psychological level. Alchemy and Rosicrucianism were outstanding examples of such an attempt, which had to be veiled in secrecy because of the opposition of the Church. A bio-psychological kind of astrology developed in obscure ways, in which four functions of the human psyche answered to the four seasons of the year and the symbolism of the Gospel became mixed with that of "pagan" lore. And all the while the old traditional forms of astrology, as codified by Ptolemy, kept in use, but mostly as a means to satisfy the curiosity of individuals and the ambition of princes or kings.

Today the remarkable rise to public attention of modern psychology offers to astrologers an opportunity for reformulating completely astrology and its symbols. Astrology can be made into a language, not of the individual ego, but of the total human personality. And, in a world rent with conflicts and made meaningless by the passion for analysis and differentiation at all costs, astrology can appear once more as a technique enabling man to grasp the meaning of his experience as a whole: physiological and psychological experience, body and psyche, collective and individual. Without fear of persecution—it is to be hoped—astrology can use the old vitalistic symbols of ancient astrology, the images derived from the serial changes in the yearly vegetation and from man's experiences with the powers latent in his generic and bodily nature.

These images are rich with the meaning of feelings and sensations common to all men since the dawn of civilization on earth. They are steeped in collective wisdom and organic instinct. They belong to the Root-nature of man, to "man's common humanity," the foundation upon which the later-date individual achievements of a rational and over-intellectualized humanity are built. Without the sustaining power of that Root-foundation man must ever collapse and disintegrate. And the very spectacle of such a collapse and disintegration is before our eyes in these dark days of mankind—days nevertheless pregnant with the seed of a new integration of human experience.

jacob needleman ───────────────────────────

Meher Baba

Jacob Needleman (1934–   ) holds a B.A. from Harvard and a Ph.D. from Yale. With a Fulbright scholarship he studied in Europe, and he has been a visiting scholar at Union Theological Seminary. Since 1962 he has been a professor of philosophy at San Francisco State University, in the environs of which he has witnessed the rebirth of the religious quest among the young. *The New Religions* (1970) is a study of the more prominent forms that quest has taken, and it is the source for the reading selection that follows. He is also General Editor of the Penguin Metaphysical Library, a series whose purpose, he writes, is to present "books from among the flood of estoeric, mystical and traditional material now available that can help us hear great ideas in a way that does not support our illusions about ourselves." It was in that same spirit that he edited *Religion for a New Generation* (1973). He is currently completing *Man in the Universal World,* a study of modern science and the new mysticism.

THE AGE OF THE AVATAR

How is one to place a man who says he is God, the Christ of this era, the avatar? This, and nothing short of it, is the claim made by Meher Baba and by thousands of men and women throughout the world who are his followers. "I am the Highest of the High," says Baba, "the Divine Beloved who loves you more than you love yourself."

There is no doubt of my being God personified . . . I am the Christ . . . I assert unequivocally that I am infinite consciousness; and I can make this assertion because I AM infinite consciousness. I am everything and I am beyond everything . . . Before me was Zoroaster, Krishna, Rama, Buddha, Jesus and Mohammed. . . . My present Avataric Form is the last Incarnation of this cycle of time, hence my Manifestation will be the greatest.[1]

His followers are not madmen. Among them are scientists, professors, psychologists, industrialists, businessmen, actors and even the very young.

"This is an avataric age," said one, "just look at the world." It is not only the Baba-lovers, as they call themselves, who hold to this thought. Almost everyone who is drawn to the new teachings accepts the Eastern idea of cosmic cycles of time in which the whole of creation progresses further and further away from divine unity until the last cycle, the darkest age, will see a

---

[1]Phrases in this quotation gathered from: Meher Baba, *Listen Humanity* (New York: Dodd, Mead & Co., 1967), and a pamphlet entitled *Meher Baba's Universal Message.*

complete dissolution and destruction of civilization and the immediate birth of another grand cycle, introducing a new golden age.

This idea is not unfamiliar to one who has read the apocalyptic chapters of our Western Bible. Though written in highly enciphered language, the books of Ezeikiel and The Revelation of St. John both agree with the Indian idea of an ultimate spiritual regeneration signaled by upheavals on a universal scale. Indeed, Eastern Orthodox Christianity still emphasizes the cosmic dimension of the human situation and its redemption through the suffering, death and resurrection of Jesus Christ.

Generally speaking, Western religion has lost this cosmic dimension. Both Christianity and Judaism have for long concerned themselves almost exclusively with man's moral and "legal" relationship to God. No doubt this abandonment of the cosmic dimension was to some extent based on the idea that God, if He is to be found at all, is to be found within each individual's mind and heart. But, we fail to realize what has been lost by turning over to science questions as to the nature of the universe, the structure of matter and the definition of life.

Psyche and Cosmos

The idea that God can be found within man was originally inseparable from the idea that the universe itself was in some way mirrored in man. Thus the discovery of God-in-man was impossible without the corresponding discovery and experience of cosmic law as well. As the cosmos became secularized under the banner of "scientific fact," the thought was fostered that one need only turn "directly" to God, while the study of the practical and experiential *laws* governing this turning were relegated to men with "a taste for the mystical."

The whole idea of the psychological effort of turning to God was set in terms of morality rather than cosmically determined psychodynamics. Man inappropriately estimated his resistance to this turning in terms of blameworthiness because he did not see this resistance as rooted in the laws governing the great scheme of nature.

In the religious disciplines of the East, this cosmic dimension of the human predicament and potential remains essential. And as new scientific developments such as the exploration of the moon, the discoveries of radio astronomy and microphysics, etc., once again bring Western man to a more emotional relationship to cosmic questions, it is that much more understandable that our young people have turned to the religions of the East.

The concept of the avatar is deeply rooted in this traditional Eastern sense of the universe. Within man is a finer quality of life which becomes obscured by the attractions of the isolated intellect and the concomitant force of individual desires. Relative to the ordinary "fallen-away" condition of the human being, this finer quality is divine. It is closer to, if not identical with, the quality of life by which creation itself is governed. Since it is finer than our ordinary mind, it may be said to be more intelligent, more conscious, as well as more loving and more powerful.

Moreover—and this is crucial—the universe *requires* that man in some measure come in touch with this finer quality of life. In so doing, of course, man himself profits in the coin of understanding, consciousness and life. But this is a fact which he can accept only when he actually does experience a moment of connection with this inner life.

In India the word "avatar" is often applied to any man who has realized this connection in a deep and persistent way. Understood in the above context, an avatar is quite literally God, or the highest quality of life, in the form and organism of man. All men are thus potential avatars, but the task of an actual avatar, in conformity with laws and requirements of the cosmos, is to help the rest of mankind toward the realization of its potential. "God needs man" is the way it is sometimes expressed in Western religious thought. The avatar is the Eastern embodiment of this need and, for man, of this opportunity. The appearance of the avatar is therefore a cosmic necessity when man has become lost to his own potential for intelligence, consciousness and power.

In the West, people who say they are God are almost by definition crazy. Probably, most of them are. And most of the rest are no doubt charlatans. But if we examine our own minds in this respect, it becomes clear that the standards we would apply to establish if someone is the God-man have to do mainly with his ability to satisfy our desires—by changing external conditions and providing us with various pleasures or allaying our fears. In other words, miracles.

THE INSTRUMENTALITY OF LOVE

But the question arises: is the performance of miracles a help toward awakening in man a need for inward freedom and an awareness of the illusions which govern his life? Are miracles a help in the work of obtaining that freedom?

This question in its relationship to the concept of the avatar may well be kept in mind when we attempt to understand something about Meher Baba and his followers. Otherwise, we shall find many reasons to be put off by the surfaces of this movement—unless, of course, we are one of those whose feelings immediately respond to what has been called "the immense and overpowering love that radiates from Baba and through his disciples."

If we are not one of these, we may well recoil at the "grandiose" statements of Meher Baba, some of which were quoted at the beginning of this chapter. He is God, he created the universe, his message supersedes all others, he is the Highest of the High, *the* avatar, the Master of Masters. Or we may shake our heads at the countless photographs which his followers tack to their walls, wear on their breasts, make into rings, etc.

Some of these photographs show an avuncular older man with warm, soft eyes, a wide and startlingly beaked nose descending over an enormous moustache that spreads out in an all-engulfing grin. Others are of a garlanded young "mystic" with flowing hair and an intense gaze. Still others are of a face in great concentration and suffering. The variety is endless, but they have one thing in common: the immediacy of the emotional.

We may smile indulgently at the sentimentality of the Baba-lovers who speak unabashedly of adoring their Master, whose prayers may say, "Oh, God, most Beloved Baba, may we show our gratitude for Your Supreme Gift of Yourself by receiving Your Love and giving Your Love and living Your message of Love in our lives." At their meetings they embrace each other, prop up each other's cushions as they sit on the floor, and warmly hold your arm as they shake your hand.

. . .

It is said that the avatar of the Kali Yuga, the dark or iron age which embraces our present span of history, shall reach mankind only by virtue of charity, the free giving of love, because man in the Kali Yuga is so far in delusion that nothing of his own efforts can be demanded of him save the effort to return God's love. One who has studied the history of Christianity will, however, acknowledge the mysterious fact that nothing is harder to give to man than love. And if the surface impressions of the Meher Baba movement lead us to think that Baba was nothing but "sweetness and light," a closer look will soon show how sharp is his demand upon his followers and how much they must struggle to come closer to him. The teaching of Meher Baba brings us directly in front of the problem of the laws of love, considered not only as a human feeling, but as a spiritual tool and a law of the universe.

THE LIFE AND WORK OF MEHER BABA

What follows is a sketch of the life of Meher Baba gathered from his own statements and those of his disciples.

He was born February 25, 1894, in Poona, India, of Persian parents and reared against the background of Sufism and the Zoroastrian religion. At the age of nineteen, after attending a Christian high school and while still in college, he sought out a certain Hazrat Babajan, an ancient Mohammedan woman, one of the five Perfect Masters of the age. (According to Meher Baba, five Perfect Masters or God-realized souls exist at all times for the spiritual governance of the world.) Upon seeing him, Babajan instantly kissed his forehead and, in so doing, "ripped away the veil which separated him from his consciousness as the avatar of the present era."

With just a kiss on the forehead, between the eyebrows, Babajan made me experience thrills of indescribable bliss which continued for about nine months. Then one night she made me realize in a flash the infinite bliss of self-realization (God-realization).[2]

For three days he lay like a dead man with wide vacant eyes.

(My mother) believed that I had gone mad. In her anguish she could not refrain from going once to Babajan and demanding to know what she had done to me. Babajan indicated to my mother that I was intended to shake the world into wakefulness, but that meant nothing to Shirinmai in her distress.[3]

There then followed a long, agonizing process of returning to normal consciousness while still retaining the ecstasy of being one with God, and the awareness of all levels of reality in the universe. In describing this process, Baba distinguishes the consciousness of the God-man from all other exalted states of mind in that it, and it alone, participates fully in the highest reality as well as in the world of illusion which is the object of ordinary consciousness. The Incarnation of God suffers to the last detail everything that ordinary man suffers, even as he continuously experiences the bliss of God. The reason that is given for this is that He comes to show the lowliest and poorest that they can live divinely without supernatural powers or magic.

Although the infinite bliss I experienced in my superconscious state remained continuous, as it is now, I suffered agonies in returning towards normal consciousness of illusion. Occasionally, to gain some sort of relief, I used to knock my head so furiously against walls and windows that some of them showed cracks. In reality there is no suffering as such—only infinite bliss. Although suffering is illusory, still, within the realm of illusion, it *is* suffering. In the midst of illusion, Babajan established my reality. My reality, although untouched by illusion, remained connected with illusion. That was why I suffered incalculable spiritual agonies.[4]

The disciples of Meher Baba assert that his entire life on earth involved this simultaneous participation in the highest and lowest states of human existence. Baba often reminded his followers of his dual nature, sometimes in small unexpected ways. For example, at a *sahvas* (a fixed period of time in which a number of disciples live in close physical proximity with the Master) Baba reproached a man who was suffering from a cold and who came up to be embraced: "While you are like this you would embrace Baba and give him a cold too?" In large and small, Baba's life is understood by his followers to have been a form of constant crucifixion.

The process of "coming down" continued for some nine months, during which time he sat, talked, walked purely by instinct, with no awareness of himself and his surroundings. He relates that for this entire period he neither ate nor slept. Finally, after he had regained some measure of normal awareness, he consulted another Perfect Master, Sai Baba.

[2][*Listen Humanity*], p. 245.
[3]Ibid., p. 247.
[4]Ibid., p. 248.

I intuitively prostrated myself before him on the road. When I arose, Sai Baba looked straight at me and exclaimed, 'Parvardigar' (God-Almighty-Sustainer).[5]

He then tells of how he was immediately impelled to walk to a certain nearby temple where a highly advanced disciple of this Sai Baba, a Hindu Perfect Master named Upasni Maharaj, had been staying for three years.

At that time Maharaj was reduced almost to a skeleton due to his fast on water. He was also naked and surrounded by filth. When I came near enough to him, Maharaj greeted me, so to speak, with a stone which he threw at me with great force. It struck me on my forehead exactly where Babajan had kissed me, hitting with such force that it drew blood. The mark of that injury is still on my forehead.[6]

With that stroke, Maharaj had begun the task of returning Meher Baba to full consciousness of the world of illusion, the world in which all men live. This final "descent" was not completed until seven years had passed under the guidance of this teacher.

At the end of this period Maharaj made me *know* fully what I am, just as Babajan made me *feel* in a flash what I am.[7]

Finally, on one occasion his teacher folded his hands before Baba and said "You are the avatar and I salute you."

.   .   .

In 1921 he drew together his first close disciples (called *mandali*) and soon established an ashram near Bombay. It was these disciples who gave him the name Meher Baba, which means "Compassionate Father."

After years of intensive training of his disciples, he organized a colony at Meherazad near Ahmednagar, some seventy miles northeast of Poona. It still exists today and remains the geographical and spiritual center of the world-wide movement. Externally, his work involved the caring for the sick, the establishment of various free hospitals and schools, and the organization of shelters for the poor. No distinction was ever made with respect to caste.

He moved from one thing to another, alternating long periods of seclusion with intense periods of physical service to the needy of India, including thousands of lepers.

Often my external activities and commitments are only the external expression of the internal work I am doing. In either case, my external activities and commitments may be continued indefinitely or I may end them promptly at the end of the inner work, depending upon the prevailing circumstances.[8]

A continuing element of his mission was his work with the deranged. Like

[5] Ibid., p. 249.
[6] Ibid., p. 249.
[7] Ibid., p. 250.
[8] Ibid., p. 254.

Plato, Baba distinguished between two fundamental types of madmen: those who were insane in the ordinary sense in that their mental functioning is impaired, and those who in transcending the limitations of the intellect are so God-intoxicated that they are unconscious of their bodies and surroundings. He cared for hundreds of the former by providing for their physical needs and indulging their innocent idiosyncrasies at what was called the Mad Ashram. As for the others, called *masts,* he spent a great period of his life and traveled thousands of miles throughout India and Ceylon searching them out in order to care for them and work with them. "The masts alone know how they love me and I alone know how I love them. I work for the masts, and knowingly or unknowingly they work for me."

Apparently, from what he has said about the masts, Meher Baba considered it possible for man to be spiritually advanced while lacking certain aspects of consciousness that even ordinary men possess. One of Baba's oldest American disciples told me there were often times when she just "blanked out." "In fact," she said, "all of us who have been with Baba do this from time to time. We couldn't tell you our own names sometimes—we don't know where we are, you see, so we're just *non compos mentis* for a few seconds."

THE SILENCE

The most well-known aspect of Baba's life was "the Silence." In 1925 he voluntarily ceased to speak. For the rest of his life he communicated by the use of an alphabet board with which he also dictated the many messages and discourses that have appeared under his name. Later, in 1956, he abandoned even the use of the board and reduced all communication to a uniquely expressive system of hand gestures.

What it must have involved to be Baba's interpreter and, as it were, his voice, we can only guess. Those who met Baba were astonished at the speed and fluidity with which his interpreters relayed their Master's words. In this respect these men surely served as a sort of paradigm of attention and surrender to the mind of their teacher. People very soon lost the sense of translation and felt they were being addressed directly by the Master.

Then, why the Silence? Was it that words are too tied to the intellect? Was this part of the Master's way of reaching directly toward the feelings? For there is very little about Meher Baba's way that is beamed to the mind alone. Was he silent in order to raise in the pupil the question "Who is speaking these words?"

In fact, the followers of Baba do not claim to know the reason for the Silence. "I don't think it was so much for its effect on people," said one. No, the Silence is much more important than that. It's the biggest mystery about Baba, and the mystery of it will be the main issue that will challenge everyone in the future, probably the main thing that will bug Baba-lovers and start all sorts of trouble.

He was very explicit: he kept Silence—yes, because they had had enough words and now it was time for action; and yes, because he wanted to encourage non-dependency on externals. But mainly, he kept the Silence so that he could break it. That's what he said once: I knew I had to break my Silence, so I had to start keeping it. He said that the only miracle he would perform was when he broke his Silence, that this would be the most significant event in the history of humanity. He never said when it would be . . . he'd kid people about it, give dates, and they would just go by. Some people even thought he was going to break the Silence in the Hollywood Bowl. And then Baba split for China and he laughed and laughed: Did they really think I was going to do it in the Hollywood Bowl?

Baba's own message on the subject is contained in the following statement:

I have come not to teach but to awaken. Understand therefore that I lay down no precepts. Throughout eternity I have laid down principles and precepts, but mankind has ignored them. Man's inability to live God's words makes the avatar's teaching a mockery. . . .

Because man has been deaf to the principles and precepts laid down by God in the past, in this present Avataric Form, I observe Silence. You have asked for and been given enough words—it is now time to live them. To get nearer and nearer to God you have to get further and further away from 'I,' 'my,' 'me' and 'mine.' You have not to renounce anything but your own self. It is as simple as that, though found to be almost impossible. It is possible for you to renounce your limited self by my Grace. I have come to release that Grace. I repeat, I lay down no precepts. When I release the tide of Truth which I have come to give, men's daily lives will be the living precept. The words I have not spoken will come to life in them. I veil myself from man by his own curtain of ignorance, and manifest my Glory to few. My present Avataric Form is the last Incarnation of this cycle of time, hence my manifestation will be the greatest. When I break my Silence, the impact of my Love will be universal and all life in creation will know, feel and receive of it. It will help every individual to break free from his own bondage in his own way. I am the Divine Beloved who loves you more than you can ever love yourself. The breaking of my Silence will help you to help yourself in knowing your real Self.[9]

Meher Baba "dropped the body" (the term Baba-lovers use instead of "death") January 31, 1969, at the age of seventy-four, after months of prolonged suffering from a variety of diseases which affected almost every system of his body, and which physicians were unable to diagnose. The predicted breaking of the Silence had not taken place, at least not in any obvious way.

"The controversy is already beginning about whether or not he broke the Silence," said one young man, a psychology professor in his late twenties. "There's already a school of thought that thinks he has." Another follower, a

[9]From *Meher Baba's Universal Message*.

lively, articulate woman of perhaps seventy, said "Some of the lovers say he broke his silence and no one is able to hear it, but I don't think so. The breaking of the Silence will come, and when it does it will be very interesting and very wonderful for everyone. There'll be no mistaking it."

Shortly before his death, his health long since failing, he broke a three-year period of tight seclusion to announce that he would receive his followers at a *darshan* starting in April of 1969. He allayed the anxiety of his close disciples, who feared for his health, by adding that he would give the darshan (a traditional Indian occasion for followers to enjoy the presence of their Master) "while reclining." After his death, the mandali cabled those in the West and told them they could still come to India and that darshan would still be given. Thus, for his last darshan, the body of Meher Baba was reclining in its tomb.

Thousands came, among them a great many young Americans who had never seen Baba. All claimed to have felt the overpowering, loving presence of the Master.

. . .

A SEARCH FOR THE EMOTIONS

What this extremely heterogeneous collection of Baba-lovers has in common is not simply the professed faith in Baba. More than even most other young people, they live by their feelings. Almost every story how they first came to Baba involves a sudden flash, a feeling, something in them that went against "common sense" or what their minds told them. I think this is very important to any understanding of Meher Baba's way. For it is quite clear to me that among the older followers of Baba, there is a strong reliance on what we might call *intuition*. And this direction toward the development of intuition is perhaps part of the discovery of something which we in the West do not even recognize: the emotions as a source of knowledge.

It is not really a question of whether or not the followers of Baba succeed in developing such intuition—I certainly cannot judge that. But the idea is ancient, that the "heart" of man is the center of real knowledge. And it would seem that a spiritual discipline based on love, which is surely Baba's way, could well begin with the fostering of trust in the feelings, even if these feelings are "confused" and "shallow" and "mixed," as they are in everyone, particularly the young. The seeming bathos and sentimentality of these young Baba-lovers may be existence on the fringe of intuition. "Love Baba" may well mean to them "revel in your feelings." Not one of them though, "revels" in his negative feelings: anger, envy or self-pity. This suggests some interesting questions as to the nature of our negative feelings, that perhaps they are not feelings at all, or that they are in some undiscovered way the result of the intrusion of the mind—that mind which so many Eastern teachings seek to control. Thus, what may appear on the surface as nothing more than a sort of saccharine mystagogy may be the beginning steps toward an ancient path like that first laid down for Western man through the "lovers" of Jesus Christ.

. . .

LOVE FROM THE POINT OF FAILURE

Listening to [some of the more experienced followers], I began to get a new perspective on the way Meher Baba worked with his disciples. "It was no bed of roses," [one] said, "far from it." Time and again, Baba would bring them into situations where they could not avoid seeing how they rejected his love, either through disobedience, mistrust or even betrayal. He had once said to his close followers:

It is easier for me to come as an avatar than for you to receive my grace . . . there is no end to the conditions which restrict your ability to receive my grace. Therefore, it is difficult for my grace to flow from me to you . . .

The sun is now shining brilliantly outside this hall, but the sunlight does not reach you here under the roof. The sun is doing its duty of giving light. You have also to do your duty in removing whatever comes between you and the sun. . . .

I am an ocean of grace, but I am also hard as flint when you try to draw that grace from me. The flow of my grace to you depends upon the intensity of your love, for it is love which attracts my grace to you.[10]

On the same occasion, Baba had related this story:

About thirty years ago, before I started observing my silence . . . a visitor came to surrender to me. He could not help weeping when I told him that what he intended was very, very difficult since surrender means obedience, and obedience has but one meaning, and that is to obey. He said he knew that, and was prepared to obey me implicitly. When I inquired if he would cut his own child to pieces if I asked him to do so, he even agreed to that. But when I asked him to remove his clothes and walk around naked in the streets of Ahmednagar he began to protest and ultimately went his way. I am not going to ask you to do that . . . I never expect anyone to do the impossible.[11]

This story was told to me by a man who had spent some time in India among the mandali:

I met a wonderful man in India named R. who is one of the outstanding Baba-lovers in his devotion. One time this man was visiting a hospital. He saw a little girl in great agony, suffering from I believe leukemia. In a fit of altruism, he wired Baba, saying, 'Let me take on the suffering of this little girl.' And, I was told by someone who was present at the time that when that was read out to Baba, that Baba reacted as if he had been stabbed in the back and he cried out aloud Uunh! Uunh! He sent a cable back to R. He said, 'How can you give your life away when you've given it to me? How dare

[10]*Listen Humanity,* pp. 50–51.
[11]Ibid., pp. 21–22.

you consider deciding how you will give your life. You have offered your life for my work, and you tell me where to relieve suffering?''

The way of love, then, is the way of obedience, surrender. What is to be surrendered? The answer that Baba gives is: oneself. But what is that? An answer to this question, as we have already glimpsed, can only appear to the individual in the instant when he *refuses* to surrender, when he fails to love. For once the "self" is surrendered—whether it be in the form of certain desires, or thoughts, or fears—it is no longer *my* self, at least at that moment. This is the exceptional moment, the experience of grace.

For, on the whole, failure is the rule. The *effort* is to love God from the point of failure. If put this way, one sees, I believe, how extraordinarily difficult for man is the way of love. Is it not true that human love, as we know it, is love from the point of *ability?* Ordinarily, "I love you" is a *promise* as well as a report. The "path of love" is nothing less than a brutal revelation to man that he cannot make his promise, that his feeling is founded on judgments of what is acceptable and what is not acceptable from another, judgments which come from the mind. Thus the mind screens man from the knowledge and experience of union by automatically setting up requirements for union. There is no *ability* here. It is the path of least resistance, following the desires. And since the desires each in their turn are only a fragment of a whole, man lives his life in pieces under the illusion, at each moment and in each fragment, that he is whole.

It is not therefore a question of whether Meher Baba is really God or just a fraud. The question is whether he acts among his followers in such a way as to help them toward the effort to love from the point of failure. As I see it, this effort means the attempt to accept for what they are the requirements that come from the mind—*in the instant that they are in force.* In this effort one might say that the *heart,* the emotions, may touch man—or, as it is sometimes put, man may enter a new state of consciousness.

For the purification of your heart, leave your thoughts alone, but maintain a constant vigil over your actions. When you have thoughts of anger, lust or greed, do not worry about them, and do not try to check them. Let all such thoughts come and go without putting them into action . . .

But it is not child's play to remember me constantly during your moments of excitement. If, in spite of being very angry, you refrain from expressing anger, it is indeed a great achievement. It means that when your mind becomes angry your heart does not know it, just as when your heart loves me your mind need not know it. In fact, your mind does not know that your heart loves when, prepared to give up life itself, you lead a life of day-to-day obedience and duty.[12]

One can find volumes and volumes of prose and poetry about love, but there are very, very few persons who have found love and experienced it. . . . Listen to love without

12 Ibid., pp. 44–45 and p. 17.

philosophizing about it. None present here loves me as I ought to be loved. If all of you had such love, none of you would be left before me. You would all have realized God and we would have become the *One* which we all are in reality and in eternity. . . .

Believe me, you and I remain divided by nothing but the veil of you, yourself. What does 'you, yourself' mean? When you feel hungry, you say 'I am hungry.' If unwell, you say, 'I am not well.' 'When you say, 'Baba, I slept well,' 'I am happy,' 'My son died,' 'They abused me,' 'I feel miserable,' 'Those things are mine,' it is this 'I,' 'me,' and 'mine' which is the veil.

It is only because of the veil of the false ego lying between us that you find yourself involved in so many difficulties, troubles and worries, all of which disappear automatically when touched by the reality of love. When the curtain of your limited 'I' is lifted—and it can only disappear through love, and love alone—you realize unity and find me as your real self, i.e., God. I say so because it is only I, everywhere. There is really nothing like you.[13]

Obviously, if a man believes in and trusts only the ordinary feelings (which, Baba says, come from the mind), he can never come in touch with the heart and its intelligence. This is one reason why life with Baba was, as his disciples report, "chaos." He changed plans "on a dime," he worked them "like coolies," he "disappointed" them in countless ways, he always "perplexed" them, and he never allowed them the security of knowing their *status* with him—except that he loved them and forgave them. In this way, it seems, their ordinary feelings were thwarted and confused, even as they continued as best they could the effort to love Baba.

At the same time, everyone, from the newest to the oldest of these disciples, tells of the love they felt radiating from the Master—as we have seen in the few reports we have quoted. In the midst of difficult situations—psychological or physical distress of various degrees, all they could hold onto was that love. The effort to turn to that love and look for it is, I think, what defined them as serious disciples.

Love, emotion, the heart in this extraordinary sense is understood as the divine in man. To accept Baba's love means to accept the chaos of the mind and in so doing to experience the fact that the self which one has spent one's life defending and preserving is an illusion. Thus the paradox that to love oneself is to know that there is no self. Here, presumably, the center of a man's identification shifts from the requirements of the mind to that which loves and to the act of loving. Thus man experiences himself as God. "To love God is to become God."

---

[13] Ibid., pp. 17–18.

The Faith of the Latter-Day Saints

The document that follows is known as the "Wentworth Letter," and it is greatly esteemed by members of the Church of Jesus Christ of Latter-Day Saints.* Its author is Joseph Smith, the prophet–founder of the church, and it contains both his own story of his life and an account of the early history of the church. The letter concludes, moreover, with a summary listing of beliefs which have since been entitled "The Articles of Faith."

The persecution mentioned in the letter was to continue: only two years after it was written, Joseph Smith and his brother Hyrum were murdered by a mob in Carthage, Illinois. The leadership of the church passed to Brigham Young,† and it was he who led the final migration to the valley of the Great Salt Lake.

March 1, 1842.—At the request of Mr. John Wentworth, Editor and Proprietor of the Chicago *Democrat,* I have written the following sketch of the rise, progress, persecution, and faith of the Latter-day Saints, of which I have the honor, under God, of being the founder. Mr. Wentworth says that he wishes to furnish Mr. Bastow, a friend of his, who is writing the history of New Hampshire, with this document. As Mr. Bastow has taken the proper steps to obtain correct information, all that I shall ask at his hands, is, that he publish the account entire, ungarnished, and without misrepresentation.

I was born in the town of Sharon, Windsor County, Vermont, on the 23rd of December, A.D. 1805. When ten years old, my parents removed to Palmyra, New York, where we resided about four years, and from thence we removed to the town of Manchester. My father was a farmer and taught me the art of husbandry. When about fourteen years of age, I began to reflect upon the importance of being prepared for a future state, and upon inquiring [about] the plan of salvation, I found that there was a great clash in religious sentiment; if I went to one society they referred me to one plan, and another to another;

---

*The members of the Church are popularly called "Mormons," a term derived from *The Book of Mormon.*

†The Reorganized Church of Jesus Christ of Latter-Day Saints, with headquarters in Independence, Missouri, grew from a group that disputed Young's leadership. And there are still other independent Mormon churches.

Joseph Smith, "The Faith of the Latter-Day Saints." From Joseph Smith, "Wentworth Letter," in Alma P. Burton, ed., *Doctrines of the Prophet Joseph Smith.* Reprinted by permission of Deseret Book Company. Editor's title.

each one pointing to his own particular creed as the *summum bonum* of perfection. Considering that all could not be right, and that God could not be the author of so much confusion, I determined to investigate the subject more fully, believing that if God had a Church it would not be split up into factions, and that if he taught one society to worship one way, and administer in one set of ordinances, he would not teach another, principles which were diametrically opposed.

Believing the word of God, I had confidence in the declaration of James—"If any of you lack wisdom, let him ask of God, that giveth to all men liberally, and upbraideth not; and it shall be given him." I retired to a secret place in a grove, and began to call upon the Lord; while fervently engaged in supplication, my mind was taken away from the heavenly vision, and saw two glorious personages, who exactly resembled each other in features and likeness, surrounded with a brilliant light which eclipsed the sun at noon day. They told me that all religious denominations were believing in incorrect doctrines, and that none of them was acknowledged of God as his Church and kingdom: and I was expressly commanded "to go not after them," at the same time receiving a promise that the fulness of the Gospel should at some future time be made known unto me.

On the evening of the 21st of September, A.D. 1823, while I was praying unto God, and endeavoring to exercise faith in the precious promises of scripture, on a sudden a light like that of day, only of a far purer and more glorious appearance and brightness, burst into the room, indeed the first sight as though the house was filled with consuming fire; the appearance produced a shock that affected the whole body; in a moment a personage stood before me surrounded with a glory yet greater than that with which I was already surrounded. This messenger proclaimed himself to be an angel of God, sent to bring the joyful tidings that the covenant which God made with ancient Israel was at hand to be fulfilled, that the preparatory work for the second coming of the Messiah was speedily to commence; that the time was at hand for the Gospel in all its fulness to be preached in power, unto all nations that a people might be prepared for the millennial reign. I was informed that I was chosen to be an instrument in the hands of God to bring about some of his purposes in this glorious dispensation.

I was also informed concerning the aboriginal inhabitants of this country and shown who they were, and from whence they came; a brief sketch of their origin, progress, civilization, laws, governments, of their righteousness and iniquity, and the blessings of God being finally withdrawn from them as a people, was made known unto me; I was also told where were deposited some plates on which were engraven an abridgment of the records of the ancient Prophets that had existed on this continent. The angel appeared to me three times the same night and unfolded the same things. After having received many visits from the angels of God unfolding the majesty and glory of the events that should transpire in the last days, on the morning of the 22nd of

September, A.D. 1827, the angel of the Lord delivered the records into my hands.

These records were engraven on plates which had the appearance of gold, each plate was six inches wide and eight inches long, and not quite so thick as common tin. They were filled with engravings, in Egyptian characters, and bound together in a volume as the leaves of a book, with three rings running through the whole. The volume was something near six inches in thickness, a part of which was sealed. The characters on the unsealed part were small, and beautifully engraved. The whole book exibited many marks of antiquity in its construction, and much skill in the art of engraving. With the records was found a curious instrument, which the ancients called "Urim and Thummim," which consisted of two transparent stones set in the rim of a bow fastened to a breast plate. Through the medium of the Urim and Thummim I translated the record by the gift and power of God.

In this important and interesting book the history of ancient America is unfolded, from its first settlement by a colony that came from the Tower of Babel, at the confusion of languages to the beginning of the fifth century of the Christian Era. We are informed by these records that America in ancient times has been inhabited by two distinct races of people. The first were called Jaredites, and came directly from the Tower of Babel. The second race came directly from the city of Jerusalem, about six hundred years before Christ. They were principally Israelities, of the descendants of Joseph. The Jaredites were destroyed about the time that the Israelites came from Jerusalem, who succeeded them in the inheritance of the country. The principal nation of the second race fell in battle towards the close of the fourth century. The remnants are the Indians that now inhabit this country. This book also tells us that our Savior made his appearance upon this continent after his resurrection; that he planted the Gospel here in all its fulness, and richness, and power, and blessing; that they had Apostles, Prophets, Pastors, Teachers, and Evangelists; the same order, the same priesthood, the same ordinances, gifts, powers, and blessing, as were enjoyed on the eastern continent, that the people were cut off in consequence of their transgressions, that the last of their prophets who existed among them was commanded to write an abridgment of their prophecies, history, etc., and to hide it up in the earth, and that it should come forth and be united with the Bible for the accomplishment of the purposes of God in the last days. For a more particular account I would refer to the Book of Mormon, which can be purchased at Nauvoo, or from any of our Traveling Elders.

As soon as the news of this discovery was made known, false reports, misrepresentation and slander flew, as on the wings of the wind, in every direction; the house was frequently beset by mobs and evil designing persons. Several times I was shot at, and very narrowly escaped, and every device was made use of to get the plates away from me; but the power and blessing of God attended me, and several began to believe my testimony.

On the 6th of April, 1830, the "Church of Jesus Christ of Latter-day Saints" was first organized in the town of Fayette, Seneca county, state of New York. Some few were called and ordained by the Spirit of revelation and prophecy, and began to preach as the Spirit gave them utterance, and though weak, yet were they strengthened by the power of God, and many were brought to repentance, were immersed in the water, and were filled with the Holy Ghost by the laying on of hands. They saw visions and prophesied, devils were cast out, and the sick healed by the laying on of hands. From that time the work rolled forth with astonishing rapidity, and churches were soon formed in the states of New York, Pennsylvania, Ohio, Indiana, Illinois, and Missouri; in the last named state a considerable settlement was formed in Jackson county: numbers joined the Church and we were increasing rapidly; we made large purchases of land, our farms teemed with plenty, and peace and happiness were enjoyed in our domestic circle, and throughout our neighborhood; but as we could not associate with our neighbors (who were, many of them, of the basest of men, and had fled from the face of civilized society, to the frontier country to escape the hand of justice,) in their midnight revels, their Sabbath breaking, horse racing and gambling; they commenced at first to ridicule, then to persecute, and finally an organized mob assembled and burned our houses, tarred and feathered and whipped many of our brethren, and finally, contrary to law, justice and humanity, drove them from their habitations; who, houseless and homeless, had to wander on the bleak prairies till the children left the tracks of their blood on the prairie. This took place in the month of November, and they had no other covering but the canopy of heaven, in this inclement season of the year; this proceeding was winked at by the government, and although we had warrantee deeds for our land, and had violated no law, we could obtain no redress.

There were many sick, who were thus inhumanly driven from their houses, and had to endure all this abuse and to seek homes where they could be found. The result was, that a great many of them being deprived of the comforts of life, and the necessary attendances, died; many children were left orphans, wives, widows and husbands, widowers; our farms were taken possession of by the mob, many thousands of cattle, sheep, horses and hogs were taken, and our household goods, store goods, and printing press and type were broken, taken, or otherwise destroyed.

Many of our brethren removed to Clay county, where they continued until 1836, three years; there was no violence offered, but there were threatenings of violence. But in the summer of 1836 these threatenings began to assume a more serious form, from threats, public meetings were called, resolutions were passed, vengeance and destruction were threatened, and affairs again assumed a fearful attitude, Jackson county was a sufficient precedent, and as the authorities in that county did not interfere they boasted that they would not in this; which on application to the authorities we found to be true, and

CHAPTER THIRTEEN / *Contemporaries*

after much privation and loss of property, we were again driven from our homes.

We next settled in Caldwell and Daviess counties, where we made large and extensive settlements, thinking to free ourselves from the power of oppression, by settling in new counties, with very few inhabitants in them; but here we were not allowed to live in peace, but in 1838 we were again attacked by mobs, an exterminating order was issued by Governor Boggs, and under the sanction of law, an organized banditti ranged through the country, robbed us of our cattle, sheep, hogs, etc., many of our people were murdered in cold blood, the chastity of our women was violated, and we were forced to sign away our property at the point of the sword; and after enduring every indignity that could be heaped upon us by an inhuman, ungodly band of marauders, from twelve to fifteen thousand souls, men, women, and children were driven from their own firesides, and from lands to which they had warantee deeds, houseless, friendless, and homeless (in the depths of winter) to wander as exiles on the earth or to seek asylum in more genial clime, and among a less barbarous people. Many sickened and died in consequence of the cold and hardships they had to endure; many wives were left widows, and children, orphans, and destitute. It would take more time than is allotted me here to describe the injustice, the wrongs, the murders, the bloodshed, the theft, misery and woe that have been caused by the barbarous, inhuman, and lawless proceedings of the state of Missouri.

In the situation before alluded to, we arrived in the state of Illinois in 1839, where we found a hospitable people and a friendly home: a people who were willing to be governed by the principles of law and humanity. We have commenced to build a city called "Nauvoo," in Hancock county. We number from six to eight thousand here, besides vast numbers in the county around, and in almost every county of the state. We have a city charter granted us, and charter for a Legion, the troops of which now number 1,500. We have also a charter for a University, for an Agricultural and Manufacturing Society, have our own laws and administrators, and possess all the privileges that other free and enlightened citizens enjoy.

Persecution has not stopped the progress of truth, but has only added fuel to the flame, it has spread with increasing rapidity. Proud of the cause which they have espoused, and conscious of our innocence, and of the truth of their system, amidst calumny and reproach, have (the Elders of this Church) gone forth, and planted the Gospel in almost every state of the Union; it has penetrated our cities, it has spread over our villages, and has caused thousands of our intelligent, noble, and patriotic citizens to obey its divine mandates, and be governed by its sacred truths. It has also spread into England, Ireland, Scotland, and Wales, where, in the year 1840, a few of our missionaries were sent, and over five thousand joined the Standard of Truth; there are numbers now joining in every land.

Our missionaries are going forth to different nations, and in Germany, Palestine, New Holland, Australia, the East Indies, and other places the Standard of Truth has been erected; no unhallowed hand can stop the work from progressing; persecutions may rage, mobs may combine, armies may assemble, calumny may defame, but the truth of God will go forth boldly, nobly, and independently till it has penetrated every continent, visited every clime, swept every country, and sounded in every ear, till the purposes of God shall be accomplished, and the Great Jehovah shall say the work is done.

We believe in God the eternal Father, and in his Son Jesus Christ, and in the Holy Ghost.

We believe that men will be punished for their own sins, and not for Adam's transgression.

We believe that through the atonement of Christ all mankind may be saved by obedience to the laws and ordinances of the Gospel.

We believe that the first principles and ordinances of the Gospel are: (1) Faith in the Lord Jesus Christ; (2) Repentance; (3) Baptism by immersion for the remission of sins; (4) Laying on of hands for the gift of the Holy Ghost.

We believe that a man must be called of God by prophecy and by the laying on of hands, by those who are in authority, to preach the Gospel and administer in the ordinances thereof.

We believe in the same organization that existed in the primitive Church, viz: apostles, prophets, pastors, teachers, evangelists, etc.

We believe in the gift of tongues, prophecy, revelation, visions, healing, interpretation of tongues, etc.

We believe the Bible to be the word of God, as far as it is translated correctly; we also believe the Book of Mormon to be the word of God.

We believe all that God has revealed, all that he does now reveal, and we believe that he will yet reveal many great and important things pertaining to the kingdom of God.

We believe in the literal gathering of Israel and in the restoration of the Ten Tribes: that Zion will be built upon this [the American continent;] that Christ will reign personally upon the earth; and that the earth will be renewed and receive its paradisiacal glory.

We claim the privilege of worshiping almighty God according to the dictates of our own conscience, and allow all men the same privilege, let them worship how, where, or what they may.

We believe in being subject to kings, presidents, rulers and magistrates, in obeying honoring and sustaining the law.

We believe in being honest, true, chaste, benevolent, virtuous, and in doing good to all men; indeed we may say that we follow the admonition of Paul, We believe all things, we hope all things, we have endured many things, and hope to be able to endure all things. If there is anything virtuous, lovely, or of good report or praiseworthy, we seek after these things.

CHAPTER THIRTEEN / *Contemporaries*

jiddu krishnamurti _____

Religion as a Life
without Fragmentation

Born in India in 1895, Jiddu Krishnamurti was only thirteen when he was "discovered" by Theosophists Annie Besant and Charles Leadbeater. He was introduced by them as the avatar of this age—an incarnation of Divinity who would be the new Buddha —and the Order of the Star in the East was organized with Krishnamurti as its spiritual head. But in 1929 he renounced his role as a religious leader on the grounds that no man can lead another to the Truth. And the order was also repudiated: "The important thing," he said, "is to free your mind of envy, hate and violence; and for that you don't need an organization, do you? So-called religious organizations never liberate the mind, they only make it conform to a certain creed or belief."* Thereafter Krishnamurti traveled throughout the world lecturing to (or, better, talking with) enormous numbers of people, and over his long lifetime he has won worldwide respect for his remarkable qualities of mind and spirit. He has also written voluminously: among his titles are *The Only Revolution, The Pool of Wisdom, The First and Last Freedom, Education and the Significance of Life, You Are the World,* and *The Impossible Question.*

_____

I think this morning we should talk over together the problem of religion. Many people do not like that word, they think it is rather old fashioned and has very little meaning in this modern world. And there are those who are religious at the week-end; they turn out well dressed on Sunday morning and do all the mischief they can during the week. But when we use the word 'religion' we are not in any way concerned with organised religions, churches, dogmas, rituals, or the authority of saviours, representatives of God and all the rest. We are talking about something quite different.

Human beings, in the past, as in the present, have always asked if there is something transcendental, much more real than the every-day existence with all its tiresome routine, its violence, despairs and sorrow. But not being able to find it, they have worshipped a symbol, giving it great significance.

To find out if there is something really true and sacred—I am using that word rather hesitantly—we must look for something not put together by desire and hope, by fear and longing; not dependent on environment, culture and education, but something that thought has never touched, something that is totally and incomprehensibly new. Perhaps this morning we can spend some time in enquiring into this, trying to find out whether there is a vastness, an ecstasy, a life that is unquenchable; without finding that, however virtuous, however orderly, however non-violent one is, life in itself has very little meaning. Religion—in the sense in which we are using that word, where there is no kind of fear or belief—is the quality that makes for a life in which there is no fragmentation whatsoever. If we are going to enquire into that, we must not only be free of all belief, but also we must be very clear about the distorting factor of all effort, direction and purpose. Do see the importance of this; if you are at all serious in this matter it is very important to understand how any form of effort distorts direct perception. And any form of suppression obviously also distorts, as does any form of direction born of choice, of established purpose, created by one's own desire; all these things make the mind utterly incapable of seeing things as they are.

When we are enquiring into this question of what truth is, whether there is such a thing as enlightenment, if there is something that is not of time at all, a reality that is not dependent on one's own demand, there must be freedom, and a certain quality of order. We generally associate order with discipline —discipline being conformity, imitation, adjustment, suppression and so on; forcing the mind to follow a certain course, a pattern that it considers to be moral. But order has nothing whatsoever to do with such discipline; order comes about naturally and inevitably when we understand all the disturbing factors, the disorders and conflicts going on both within ourselves and outwardly. When we are aware of this disorder, look at all the mischief, the hate, the pursuit of comparison—when we understand it then there comes order; which has nothing whatsoever to do with discipline. You must have order; after all, order is virtue (you may not like that word). Virtue is not something to be cultivated; if it is a thing of thought, of will, the result of suppression, it is no longer virtue. But if you understand the disorder of your life, the confusion, the utter meaninglessness of our existence, when you see all that very clearly, not merely intellectually and verbally, but not condemning it, not running away from it, but observing it in life, then out of that awareness and observation comes order, naturally—which is virtue. This virtue is entirely different from the virtue of society, with its respectability, the sanctions of the religions with their hypocrisy; it is entirely different from one's own self-imposed discipline.

Order must exist if we are to find out if there is—or is not—a reality that is not of time, something incorruptible, not depending on anything. If you are really serious about this, in the sense that it is a part of life as important as earning one's livelihood, as seeking pleasure, that it is something tremendously vital, then you will realize that it can only be found through meditation. The dictionary meaning of that word is to ponder over, to think over, to enquire; it means to have a mind that is capable of looking, that is intelligent, that is sane, not perverted or neurotic, not wishing for something from somewhere.

Is there any method, any system, any path which you can pursue and come to the understanding of what meditation, or the perception of reality, is? Unfortunately people come from the East with their systems, methods and so on; they say 'Do this' and 'Don't do that'. 'Practise Zen and you will find enlightenment.' Some of you may have gone to India or Japan and spent years studying, disciplining yourself, trying to become aware of your toe or your nose, practising endlessly. Or you may have repeated certain words in order to calm the mind, so that in that calmness there will be the perception of something beyond thought. These tricks can be practised by a very stupid, dull mind. I am using the word stupid in the sense of a mind that is stupefied. A stupefied mind can practise any of these tricks. You may not be interested in all this, but you have to find out. After you have listened very carefully you may go out into the world and teach people, that may be your vocation and I hope it is. You have to know the whole substance, the meaning, the fullness, the beauty, the ecstasy of all this.

A dull mind, a mind that has been stupefied by 'practising', cannot under any circumstances whatsoever understand what reality is. One must be completely, totally, free of thought. One needs a mind that is not distorted, that is very clear, that is not blunted, that is no longer pursuing a direction, a purpose. You will ask: 'Is it possible to have this state of mind in which there is no experiencing?' To 'experience' implies an entity who is experiencing; therefore, there is duality: the experiencer and the thing experienced, the observer and the thing observed. Most of us want some kind of deep, marvellous and mystical experience; our own daily experiences are so trivial, so banal, so superficial, we want something electrifying. In that bizarre thought of a marvellous experience, there is this duality of the experiencer and the experience. As long as this duality exists there must be distortion; because the experiencer is the accumulated past with all his knowledge, his memories. Being dissatisfied with that, he wants something much greater, therefore he projects it as idea, and finds that projection; in that there is still duality and distortion.

Truth is not something to be experienced. Truth is not something that you can seek out and find. It is beyond time. And thought, which is of time, cannot possibly search it out and grasp it. So one must understand very deeply this question of wanting experience. Do please see this tremendously important thing. Any form of effort, of wanting, of seeking out truth, demanding experience, is the observer wanting something transcendental and making effort; therefore the mind is not clear, pristine, non-mechanical. A mind seeking an experience, however marvellous, implies that the 'me' is seeking it—the 'me' which is the past, with all its frustrations, miseries and hopes.

Observe for yourself how the brain operates. It is the storehouse of memory, of the past. This memory is responding all the time, as like and dislike, justifying, condemning and so on; it is responding according to its conditioning, according to the culture, religion, education, which it has stored. That storehouse of memory, from which thought arises, guides most of our life. It is directing and shaping our lives every minute of every day, consciously or unconsciously; it is generating thought, the 'me', which is the very essence of thought and words. Can that brain, with its content of the old, be completely quiet—only wakened when it is necessary to operate, to function, to speak, to act, but the rest of the time completely sterile?

Meditation is to find out whether the brain, with all its activities, all its experiences, can be absolutely quiet. Not forced, because the moment you force, there again is duality, the entity that says, 'I would like to have marvellous experiences, therefore I must force my brain to be quiet'—you will never do it. But if you begin to enquire, watch, observe, listen to all the movements of thought, its conditioning, its pursuits, its fears, its pleasures, watch how the brain operates, then you will see that the brain becomes extraordinarily quiet; that quietness is not sleep but is tremendously active and therefore quiet. A big dynamo that is working perfectly, hardly makes a sound; it is only when there is friction that there is noise.

One has to find out whether one's body can sit or lie completely still, without any movement, not forced. Can the body and the brain be still?—for they are interrelated psychosomatically. There are various practices to make the body still, but again they imply suppression; the body wants to get up and walk, you insist that it must sit quietly, and the battle begins—wanting to go out and wanting to sit still.

The word 'yoga' means 'to join together'. The very words 'join together' are wrong, they imply duality. Probably yoga as a particular series of exercises and breathing was invented in India many thousands of years ago. Its intent is to keep the glands, the nerves and the whole system functioning healthily, without medicine, and highly sensitive. The body needs to be sensitive, otherwise you cannot have a clear brain. You can see the simple fact, the one needs to have a very healty, sensitive, alert body, and a brain that functions very clearly, non-emotionally, not personally; such a brain can be absolutely quiet. Now, how is this to be brought about? How can the brain, which is so tremendously active—not only during the day-time, but when you go to sleep—be so completely relaxed and completely quiet? Obviously no method will do it, a method implies mechanical repetition, which stupefies and makes the brain dull; and in that dullness you think you have marvellous experiences!

How can the brain, which is always chattering to itself, or with others, always judging, evaluating, liking and disliking, turning over all the time —how can that brain be completely still? Do you, for yourself, see the extraordinary importance that the brain should be completely quiet? For the

CHAPTER THIRTEEN / *Contemporaries*

moment it acts it is response of the past, in terms of thought. It is only a brain that is completely still that can observe a cloud, a tree, a flowing river. You can see the extraordinary light on those mountains, yet the brain can be completely still—you have noticed this, have you not? How has that happened? The mind, facing something of extraordinary magnitude, like very complex machinery, a marvellous computer, or a magnificent sunset, becomes completely quiet even if only for a split second. You have noticed when you give a child a toy, how the toy absorbs the child, the child is so concerned with it. In the same way, by their greatness, the mountains, the beauty of a tree, the flowing waters, absorb the mind and make it still. But in that case the brain is made still by something. Can the brain be quiet without an outside factor entering into it? Not 'finding a way'. People hope for the Grace of God, they pray, have faith, become absorbed in Jesus, in this or in that. We see that this absorption by something outside occurs to a dull, a stupefied mind. The brain is active from the moment you wake up until you go to sleep; and even then the activity of the brain is still going on. That activity in the form of dreams is the same movement of the day carried on during sleep. The brain has never a moment's rest, never does it say, 'I have finished'. It has carried over the problems which it accumulated during the day into sleep; when you wake up those problems still go on—it is a vicious circle. A brain that is to be quiet must have no dreams at all; when the brain is quiet during sleep there is a totally different quality entering into the mind. How does it happen that the brain which is so tremendously, enthusiastically active, can naturally, easily, be quiet without any effort or suppression? I will show it to you.

As we said, during the day it is endlessly active. You wake up, you look out of the window and say to yourself, 'Oh, awful rain', or 'It is a marvellous day, but too hot'—you have started! So at that moment, when you look out of the window, don't say a word; not suppressing words but simply realising that by saying, 'What a lovely morning', or 'A horrible day', the brain has started. But if you watch, looking out of the window and not saying a word to yourself—which does not mean you suppress the word—just observing without the activity of the brain rushing in, there you have the clue, there you have the key. When the old brain does not respond, there is a quality of the new brain coming into being. You can observe the mountains, the river, the valleys, the shadows, the lovely trees and the marvellous clouds full of light beyond the mountains—you can look without a word, without comparing.

But it becomes much more difficult when you look at another person; there already you have established images. But just to observe! You will see when you so observe, when you see clearly, that action becomes extraordinarily vital; it becomes a complete aciton which is not carried over to the next minute. You understand?

One has problems, deep or superficial, not sleeping well, quarrelling with one's wife, and one carries these problems on from day to day. Dreams are the repetition of these problems, the repetition of fear and pleasure over and over again. That obviously stupefies the mind and makes the brain dull. Now is it possible to end each problem as it arises?—not carrying it over. Take a problem: somebody has insulted me, told me I am a fool; at that moment the old brain responds instantly, saying 'So are you'. If, before the brain responds, I am completely aware of what has been said—something unpleasant—I have an interval, a gap, so that the brain does not immediately jump into the battle. So if you watch the movement of thought in action during the day, you realise that it is breeding problems, and that problems are things which are incomplete, which have to be carried over. But if you watch with a brain that is fairly quiet, then you will see that action becomes complete, instantaneous; there is no carrying over of a problem, no carrying over of the insult or the praise—it is finished. Then, during sleep, the brain is no longer carrying on the old activities of the day, it has complete rest. And as the brain is quiet in sleep, there takes place a rejuvenation of its whole structure. A quality of innocency comes into being—and the innocent mind can see what is true; not the complicated mind, not that of the philosopher, or the priest.

The innocent mind implies that whole in which are the body, the heart, the brain and the mind. This innocent mind which is never touched by thought, can see what truth is, what reality is, it can see if there is something beyond measure. That is meditation. To come upon this extraordinary beauty of truth, with its ecstasy, you must lay the foundations. The foundation is the understanding of thought, which breeds fear and sustains pleasure, and the understanding of order and therefore virtue; so that there is freedom from all conflict, aggression, brutality and violence. Once one has laid this foundation of freedom, there is a sensitivity which is supreme intelligence, and the whole of the life one leads becomes entirely different.

QUESTIONER I think that understanding you is very important to our understanding of what you say. I was surprised to hear what you said about Yoga, how you practise it regularly two hours a day. To me this sounds like a definite form of discipline. More important than that though, is the question of innocence—I am interested in the innocence of your mind.

KRISHNAMURTI To see the innocency of the mind, whether it is yours or mine, you must first be innocent. I am not turning the tables on you, Sir. To see the innocency of the mind you need to be free, you need to have no fear and a quality that comes with a brain that is functioning without any effort.

Is practising Yoga regularly every day for two hours, not a form of discipline? You know the body tells you when it is tired; the body says to you, 'Don't do it this morning'. When we have abused the body by driving it in all kinds of ways, spoiling its own intelligence—by wrong food, smoking, drink, all the rest of it—the body becomes insensitive. And thought says, 'I must force it'. Such driving of the body, forcing it, compelling it, becomes a discipline. Whereas, when you do these things regularly, easily, without any effort, the regularity of it depends on the sensitivity of the body. You do it one day and the next day the body may be tired and you say, 'All right, I won't do it'. It is not a mechanical regularity. All this requires a certain intelligence, not only of the mind, but of the body, and that intelligence will tell you what to do and what not to do.

QUESTIONER   We may want our minds to be quiet, but sometimes we have to take decisions; this makes for difficulty and causes problems.

KRISHNAMURTI   If the mind cannot decide clearly, then problems arise; the very decision is a problem. When you decide, you make a decision between this and that—which means choice. When there is choice there is conflict; from that arise problems. But when you see very clearly, there is no choice, therefore there is no decision. You know the way from here to where you happen to live very well; you follow the road which is very clear. You have been on that road a hundred times, therefore there is no choice, although you may find a short-cut which you may take next time. That is something mechanical, there is no problem. The brain wants the same thing to happen again so that it may function automatically, mechanically, so that problems do not arise. The brain demands that it operate mechanically. Therefore it says, 'I will discipline myself to function mechanically', 'I must have a belief, a purpose, a direction, so that I can set a path and follow it'; and it follows that groove. What happens? Life will not allow that, there are all kinds of things happening; so thought resists, builds a wall of belief and this very resistance creates problems.

When you have to decide between this and that, it means there is confusion: 'should I, or should I not do this?' I only put that question to myself when I do not see clearly what is to be done. We choose out of confusion, not out of clarity. The moment you are clear your action is complete.

QUESTIONER   But it cannot always be complete.

KRISHNAMURTI   Why not?

QUESTIONER   Often it is a complex choice and you have to take time, you have to look at it.

KRISHNAMURTI   Yes Sir, take time, have patience to look at it. You have to compare—compare what? Compare two materials, blue and white; you question whether you like this colour or that colour, whether you should go up this hill or that hill. You decide. 'I prefer to go up this hill today and tomorrow I'll go up the other'. The problem arises when one is dealing with the psyche, what to do within oneself. First watch what decision implies. To decide to do this or that, what is that decision based on? On choice, obviously. Should I do this, or should I do that? I realise that when there is choice there is confusion. So I see the truth of this, the fact, the 'what is', which is: where there is choice there must be confusion. Now why am I confused? Because I don't know, or because I prefer one thing as opposed to another which is more pleasant, it may produce better results, greater fortune, or whatever it is. So I choose that. But in following that, I realise there is also frustration in it, which is pain. So I am caught again between fear and pleasure. Seeing I am caught in this, I ask, 'Can I act without choice?' That means: I have to be aware of all the implications of confusion and all the implications of decision; for there is duality, the 'decider' and the thing decided upon. And therefore there is conflict and perpetuation of confusion.

You will say, to be aware of all the intricacies of this movement will take time. Will it take time? Or can it be seen instantly and therefore there is instant action? It only takes time when I am not aware of it. My brain, being conditioned, says, 'I must decide'—decide according to the past; that is its habit. 'I must decide what is right, what is wrong, what is duty, what is responsibility, what is love'. The decisions of the brain breed more conflict—which is what the politicians throughout the world are doing. Now, can that brain be quiet, so that it sees the problem of confusion instantly, and acts because it is clear? Then there is no decision at all.

QUESTIONER   Can we learn from experience?

KRISHNAMURTI   Certainly not. Learning implies freedom, curiosity, enquiry. When a child learns something, he is curious about it, he wants to know, it is a free momentum; not a momentum of having acquired and of moving from that acquisition. We have innumerable experiences; we have had five thousand years of wars. We have not learnt a thing from them except to invent more deadly machinery with which to kill each other. We have had many experiences with our friends, with our wives, with our husbands, with our nation—we have not learnt. Learning, in fact, can only take place when there is freedom from experience. When you discover something new, your mind must be free of the old, obviously. For this reason, meditation is the emptying of the mind of the known as experience; because truth is not something that you invent, it is something totally new, it is not in terms of the past 'known'. Its newness is not the opposite of the old; it is something incredibly new: a mind that comes to it with experience cannot see it.

further reading

Ira Friedlander (ed.), *Year One Catalog: A Spiritual Directory for the New Age* (1972). Brief descriptions of many contemporary gurus, ashrams, zendos, and retreats. Also included are notes on some sympathetic publications and bookstores.

Carlos Castaneda's *The Teachings of Don Juan* (1968), *A Separate Reality* (1971), *Journey to Ixtlan* (1972), and *Tales of Power* (1974) all portray the religious world of the Yaqui Indian don Juan, a "sorcerer, medicine man, curer," and spiritual guide.

Maharishi Mahesh Yogi, *The Science of Being and Art ot Living* (1963). The basic exposition of the principles and techniques of Transcendental Meditation.

In *A New Model of the Universe* (1931) and many other unique books, P. D. Ouspensky reflects the mysticism and wisdom of both East and West.

Richard Taylor, *With Heart and Mind* (1973). The beautifully expressed thoughts of a contemporary philosopher on life, love, and being.

Black Elk Speaks, as told to John G. Neihardt (1932). A vivid account of the life and remarkable religious experiences—the visions—of a Holy Man of the Oglala Sioux.

Jacob Needleman, A. K. Bierman, and James A. Gould (eds.), *Religion for a New Generation* (1973). Fifty-seven reading selections on topics ranging from the "Spiritual Revolution" to "The Struggle with Death."

Allie M. Frazier (ed.), *Issues in Religion* (1969). Literary and philosophical sources (including Dostoyevsky, Nietzsche, Tolstoy, Freud, Tillich, Kierkegaard, Sartre, and Altizer) on the major religious questions.

*epilogue*_____

> There is no religion above truth.
>
> Nikolai Berdyaev

A survey of religions, if undertaken honestly, inevitably raises troubling questions. Each religion is unique, and not infrequently the teachings of one religion may seem to be incompatible with those of another religion. Moreover, a number of religions whose essential doctrines are at variance, separately claim to possess the Absolute Truth. Not all these claims, it is evident, can be valid. Most of the religions do tend to agree in the area of morality, but the tendency is otherwise with respect to such beliefs as those regarding God (Brahman, Tao, Yahweh, Allah, and so on), revelation, immortality, reincarnation, the Law of Karma, the Last Judgment, liberation, salvation, Heaven, Hell, and Nirvana.

Who or what are we to believe? How do we choose among the many "Bibles"? Which of the claims of revelation or of mystical experience can be authenticated? What sort of verification ought we require? (Or is the request for verification irrelevant?) In the face of all the conflicting testimony, is skepticism warranted? (Or is skepticism just another system of belief, another "religion"?)

William K. Clifford, in the following essay, urges that belief be preceded by "patient inquiry," a search for all the pertinent facts. Doubts are not to be suppressed. Belief is justified only when it is supported by the requisite information. This approach is called *empiricism;* it is the method of scientific investigation. "It is wrong always, everywhere, and for anyone," states Clifford, "to believe anything upon insufficient evidence."

But is the method advocated by Clifford appropriate and adequate for *religious* questions? Will not much of what ordinarily goes under the name of religion be set aside on the grounds that is is not empirically verifiable? William James, in his essay "The Will to Believe," was very critical: "Objective evidence and certitude are doubtless very fine ideals to play with, but where on this moonlit and dream-visited planet are they found?"* Even what Clifford understands by "belief" is itself open to question. "It is not rational necessity, but vital anguish that impels us to believe in God," wrote Unamuno. "[To believe in God is] to feel a hunger for God, a hunger for divinity, to be sensible of His lack and absence, to wish that God may exist."†

Clifford's essay concludes this volume; it concludes nothing else.

---

*William James, *Essays in Pragmatism,* ed. by Alburey Castell (New York: Hafner Publishing Company, 1948), p. 97.

†Miguel de Unamuno, *The Tragic Sense of Life* (New York: Dover Publications, 1954), p. 184.

william k. clifford

The Ethics of Belief

William Kingdon Clifford (1845–1879) was born in England and educated at the University of Cambridge and the University of London. He was elected a Fellow of Trinity College, Cambridge, and was later a professor of mathematics at University College, London. Elected a Fellow of the Royal Academy, he was only thirty-four when death cut short his career.

THE DUTY OF INQUIRY

A shipowner was about to send to sea an emigrant-ship. He knew that she was old, and not over-well built at the first; that she had seen many seas and climes, and often had needed repairs. Doubts had been suggested to him that possibly she was not seaworthy. These doubts preyed upon his mind, and made him unhappy; he thought that perhaps he ought to have her thoroughly overhauled and refitted, even though this should put him to great expense. Before the ship sailed, however, he succeeded in overcoming these melancholy reflections. He said to himself that she had gone safely through so many voyages and weathered so many storms that it was idle to suppose she would not come safely home from this trip also. He would put his trust in Providence, which could hardly fail to protect all these unhappy families that were leaving their fatherland to seek for better times elsewhere. He would dismiss from his mind all ungenerous suspicions about the honesty of builders and contractors. In such ways he acquired a sincere and comfortable conviction that his vessel was thoroughly safe and seaworthy; he watched her departure with a light heart, and benevolent wishes for the success of the exiles in their strange new home that was to be; and he got his insurance-money when she went down in mid-ocean and told no tales.

What shall we say of him? Surely this, that he was verily guilty of the death of those men. It is admitted that he did sincerely believe in the soundness of his ship; but the sincerity of his conviction can in no wise help him, because *he had no right to believe on such evidence as was before him*. He had acquired his belief not by honestly earning it in patient investigation, but by stifling his doubts. And although in the end he may have felt so sure about it that he could not think otherwise, yet inasmuch as he had knowingly and willingly worked himself into that frame of mind, he must be held responsible for it.

Let us alter the case a little, and suppose that the ship was not unsound after

William K. Clifford, "The Ethics of Belief." Original publication in *Contemporary Review* (January, 1877); reprinted in *Lectures and Essays by the Late William Kingdon Clifford* (Vol. II, 1879).

all; that she made her voyage safely, and many others after it. Will that diminish the guilt of her owner? Not one jot. When an action is once done, it is right or wrong for ever; no accidental failure of its good or evil fruits can possibly alter that. The man would not have been innocent, he would only have been not found out. The question of right or wrong has to do with the origin of his belief, not the matter of it; not what it was, but how he got it; not whether it turned out to be true or false, but whether he had a right to believe on such evidence as was before him.

There was once an island in which some of the inhabitants professed a religion teaching neither the doctrine of original sin nor that of eternal punishment. A suspicion got abroad that the professors of this religion had made use of unfair means to get their doctrines taught to children. They were accused of wresting the laws of their country in such a way as to remove children from the care of their natural and legal guardians; and even of stealing them away and keeping them concealed from their friends and relations. A certain number of men formed themselves into a society for the purpose of agitating the public about this matter. They published grave accusations against individual citizens of the highest position and character, and did all in their power to injure these citizens in the exercise of their professions. So great was the noise they made, that a Commission was appointed to investigate the facts; but after the Commission had carefully inquired into all the evidence that could be got, it appeared that the accused were innocent. Not only had they been accused on insufficient evidence, but the evidence of their innocence was such as the agitators might easily have obtained, if they had attempted a fair inquiry. After these disclosures the inhabitants of that country looked upon the members of the agitating society, not only as persons whose judgment was to be distrusted, but also as no longer to be counted honourable men. For although they had sincerely and conscientiously believed in the charges they had made, yet *they had no right to believe on such evidence as was before them*. Their sincere convictions, instead of being honestly earned by patient inquiring, were stolen by listening to the voice of prejudice and passion.

Let us vary this case also, and suppose, other things remaining as before, that a still more accurate investigation proved the accused to have been really guilty. Would this make any difference in the guilt of the accusers? Clearly not; the question is not whether their belief was true or false, but whether they entertained it on wrong grounds. They would no doubt say, "Now you see that we were right after all; next time perhaps you will believe us." And they might be believed, but they would not thereby become honourable men. They would not be innocent, they would only be not found out. Every one of them, if he chose to examine himself *in foro conscientiae,* would know that he had acquired and nourished a belief, when he had no right to believe on such evidence as was before him; and therein he would know that he had done a wrong thing.

It may be said, however, that in both of these supposed cases it is not the belief which is judged to be wrong, but the action following upon it. The shipowner might say, "I am perfectly certain that my ship is sound, but still I feel it my duty to have her examined, before trusting the lives of so many people to her." And it might be said to the agitator, "However convinced you were of the justice of your cause and the truth of your convictions, you ought not to have made a public attack upon any man's character until you had examined the evidence on both sides with the utmost patience and care."

In the first place, let us admit that, so far as it goes, this view of the case is right and necessary; right, because even when a man's belief is so fixed that he cannot think otherwise, he still has a choice in regard to the action suggested by it, and so cannot escape the duty of investigating on the ground of the strength of his convictions; and necessary, because those who are not yet capable of controlling their feelings and thoughts must have a plain rule dealing with overt acts.

But this being premised as necessary, it becomes clear that it is not sufficient, and that our previous judgment is required to supplement it. For it is not possible so to sever the belief from the action it suggests as to condemn the one without condemning the other. No man holding a strong belief on one side of a question, or even wishing to hold a belief on one side, can investigate it with such fairness and completeness as if he were really in doubt and unbiased; so that the existence of a belief not founded on fair inquiry unfits a man for the performance of this necessary duty.

Nor is that truly a belief at all which has not some influence upon the actions of him who holds it. He who truly believes that which prompts him to an action has looked upon the action to lust after it, he has committed it already in his heart. If a belief is not realized immediately in open deeds, it is stored up for the guidance of the future. It goes to make a part of that aggregate of beliefs which is the link between sensation and action at every moment of all our lives, and which is so organized and compacted together that no part of it can be isolated from the rest, but every new addition modifies the structure of the whole. No real belief, however trifling and fragmentary it may seem, is ever truly insignificant; it prepares us to receive more of its like, confirms those which resembled it before, and weakens others; and so gradually it lays a stealthy train in our inmost thoughts, which may some day explode into overt action, and leave its stamp upon our character for ever.

And no one man's belief is in any case a private matter which concerns himself alone. Our lives are guided by that general conception of the course of things which has been created by society for social purposes. Our words, our phrases, our forms and processes and modes of thought, are common property, fashioned and perfected from age to age; an heirloom which every succeeding generation inherits as a precious deposit and a sacred trust to be handed on to the next one, not unchanged but enlarged and purified, with some clear marks of its proper handiwork. Into this, for good or ill, is woven every belief of every man who has speech of his fellows. An awful privilege, and an awful responsibility, that we should help to create the world in which posterity will live.

In the two supposed cases which have been considered, it has been judged wrong to believe on insufficient evidence, or to nourish belief by suppressing doubts and avoiding investigation. The reason of this judgment is not far to seek: it is that in both these cases the belief held by one man was of great importance to other men. But forasmuch as no belief held by one man, however seemingly trivial the belief, and however obscure the believer, is ever actually insignificant or without its effect on the fate of mankind, we have no choice but to extend our judgment to all cases of belief whatever. Belief, that sacred faculty which prompts the decisions of our will, and knits into harmonious working all the compacted energies of our being, is ours not for ourselves, but for humanity. It is rightly used on truths which have been established by long experience and waiting toil, and which have stood in the fierce light of free and fearless questioning. Then it helps to bind men together, and to strengthen and direct their common action. It is desecrated when given to unproved and unquestioned statements, for the solace and private pleasure of the believer; to add a tinsel splendour to the plain straight road of our life and display a bright mirage beyond it; or even to drown the common sorrows of our kind by a self-deception which allows them not only to cast down, but also to degrade us. Whoso would deserve well of his fellows in this matter will guard the purity of his belief with a very fanaticism of jealous care, lest at any time it should rest on an unworthy object, and catch a stain which can never be wiped away.

It is not only the leader of men, statesman, philosopher, or poet, that owes this bounden duty to mankind. Every rustic who delivers in the village alehouse his slow, infrequent sentences, may help to kill or keep alive the fatal superstitions which clog his race. Every hard-worked wife of an artisan may transmit to her children beliefs which shall knit society together, or rend it in pieces. No simplicity of mind, no obscurity of station, can escape the universal duty of questioning all that we believe.

It is true that this duty is a hard one, and the doubt which comes out of it is often a very bitter thing. It leaves us bare and powerless where we thought that we were safe and strong. To know all about anything is to know how to deal with it under all circumstances. We feel much happier and more secure when we think we know precisely what to do, no matter what happens, than when we have lost our way and do not know where to turn. And if we have supposed ourselves to know all about anything, and to be capable of doing what is fit in regard to it, we naturally do not like to find that we are really ignorant and powerless, that we have to begin again at the beginning, and try to learn what the thing is and how it is to be dealt with—if indeed anything can be learnt about it. It is the sense of power attached to a sense of knowledge that makes men desirous of believing, and afraid of doubting.

This sense of power is the highest and best of pleasures when the belief on which it is founded is a true belief, and has been fairly earned by investigation. For then we may justly feel that it is common property, and hold good for others as well as for ourselves. Then we may be glad, not that *I* have learned secrets by which I am safer and stronger, but that *we men* have got mastery over more of the world; and we shall be strong, not for ourselves, but in the name of Man and in his strength. But if the belief has been accepted on insufficient evidence, the pleasure is a stolen one. Not only does it deceive ourselves by giving us a sense of power which we do not really possess, but it is sinful, because it is stolen in defiance of our duty to mankind. That duty is to guard ourselves from such beliefs as from a pestilence, which may shortly master our own body and then spread to the rest of the town. What would be thought of one who, for the sake of a sweet fruit, should deliberately run the risk of bringing a plague upon his family and his neighbours?

And, as in other such cases, it is not the risk only which has to be considered; for a bad action is always bad at the time when it is done, no matter what happens afterwards. Every time we let ourselves believe for unworthy reasons, we weaken our powers of self-control, of doubting, of judicially and fairly weighing evidence. We all suffer severely enough from the maintenance and support of false beliefs and the fatally wrong actions which they lead to, and the evil born when one such belief is entertained is great and wide. But a greater and wider evil arises when the credulous character is maintained and supported, when a habit of believing for unworthy reasons is fostered and made permanent. If I steal money from any person, there may be no harm done by the mere transfer of possession; he may not feel the loss, or it may prevent him from using the money badly. But I cannot help doing this great wrong towards Man, that I make myself dishonest. What hurts society is not that it should lose its property, but that it should become a den of thieves; for then it must cease to be society. This is why we ought not to do evil that good may come; for at any rate this great evil has come, that we have done evil and are made wicked thereby. In like manner, if I let myself believe anything on insufficient evidence, there may be no great harm done by the mere belief; it may be true after all, or I may never have occasion to exhibit it in outward acts. But I cannot help doing this great wrong towards Man, that I make myself credulous. The danger to society is not merely that it should believe wrong things, though that is great enough; but that it should become credulous, and lose the habit of testing things and inquiring into them; for then it must sink back into savagery.

The harm which is done by credulity in a man is not confined to the fostering of a credulous character in others, and consequent support of false beliefs. Habitual want of care about what I believe leads to habitual want of care in others about the truth of what is told to me. Men speak the truth to one another when each reveres the truth in his own mind and in the other's mind; but how shall my friend revere the truth in my mind when I myself am careless about it, when I believe things because I want to believe them, and because they are comforting and pleasant? Will he not learn to cry, "Peace," to me, when there is no peace? By such a course I shall surround myself with a thick atmosphere of falsehood and fraud, and in that I must live. It may matter little to me, in my cloud-castle of sweet illusions and darling lies; but it matters much to Man that I have made my neighbours ready to deceive. The credulous man is father to the liar and the cheat; he lives in the bosom of this his family, and it is no marvel if he should become even as they are. So closely are our duties knit together, that whoso shall keep the whole law, and yet offend in one point, he is guilty of all.

To sum up: it is wrong always, everywhere, and for anyone, to believe anything upon insufficient evidence.

If a man, holding a belief which he was taught in childhood or persuaded of afterwards, keeps down and pushes away any doubts which arise about it in his mind, purposely avoids the reading of books and the company of men that call in question or discuss it, and regards as impious those questions which cannot easily be asked without disturbing it—the life of that man is one long sin against mankind.

If this judgment seems harsh when applied to those simple souls who have never known better, who have been brought up from the cradle with a horror of doubt, and taught that their eternal welfare depends on *what* they believe, then it leads to the very serious question, *Who hath made Israel to sin?*

It may be permitted me to fortify this judgment with the sentence of Milton[1]—

"A man may be a heretic in the truth; and if he believe things only because his pastor says so, or the assembly so determine, without knowing other reason, though his belief be true, yet the very truth he holds becomes his heresy."

And with this famous aphorism of Coleridge[2]—

"He who begins by loving Christianity better than Truth, will proceed by loving his own sect or Church better than Christianity, and end in loving himself better than all."

Inquiry into the evidence of a doctrine is not to be made once for all, and then taken as finally settled. It is never lawful to stifle a doubt; for either it can be honestly answered by means of the inquiry already made, or else it proves that the inquiry was not complete.

"But," says one, "I am a busy man; I have no time for the long course of study which would be necessary to make me in any degree a competent judge of certain questions, or even able to understand the nature of the arguments." Then he should have no time to believe.

[1] *Areopagitica.*
[2] *Aids to Reflection.*

further reading _____

The virtues of the scientific method are expounded everywhere in the Western world. An excellent philosophical treatment of the subject by one of its ablest representatives may be found in Bertrand Russell's *The Scientific Outlook* (1931).

William James, "The Will to Believe" (1896), reprinted in *The Will to Believe and Other Essays* (1897). Written, in part, as a response to Clifford's "The Ethics of Belief," James' famous essay is "a defence of our right to adopt a believing attitude in religious matters, in spite of the fact that our merely logical intellect may not have been coerced."

Norman O. Brown, "Apocalypse: The Place of Mystery in the Life of the Mind," *Harper's* (May, 1961). A brief but striking essay which criticizes the scientific method ("the attempt to substitute method for insight, mediocrity for genius, by setting a standard operating procedure") and urges us to seek the mysteries and magic and "holy madness" that have characterized poets and seers.

Theodore Roszak's *The Making of a Counter Culture* (1969) includes an impassioned critique of the method of scientific objectivity and the culture that rests upon it. See especially Chapter VII, "The Myth of Objective Consciousness," Chapter VIII, "Eyes of Flesh, Eyes of Fire," and the Appendix, "Objectivity Unlimited." Note also the annotated bibliography.

85 20 19 18 17 16 15 14 13 12 11